MW00636698

Princes of Cotton

The Publications of the Southern Texts Society

SERIES EDITOR

Michael O'Brien, University of Cambridge

EDITORIAL BOARD

Richard J. M. Blackett, Vanderbilt University

Susan V. Donaldson, College of William and Mary

Elizabeth Fox-Genovese, Emory University

Fred Hobson, University of North Carolina

Anne Goodwyn Jones, University of Florida

David Moltke-Hansen, Historical Society of Pennsylvania

David S. Shields, The Citadel

Steven M. Stowe, Indiana University

Princes of Cotton

Edited by Stephen Berry

The University of Georgia Press   *Athens and London*

FOUR DIARIES OF
YOUNG MEN
IN THE SOUTH,
1848–1860

Publication of this book was made possible in part by
a grant from the Watson-Brown Foundation.

© 2007 by the University of Georgia Press
Athens, Georgia 30602
www.ugapress.org
Introduction © 2007 by Stephen Berry
All rights reserved

Set in 10 on 14 Carter and Cone Galliard by BookComp
Printed digitally in the United States of America

Library of Congress Cataloging-in-Publication Data

Princes of cotton : four diaries of young men in the
South, 1848–1860 / edited by Stephen Berry.
    p.   cm. —
(The publications of the Southern Texts Society)
Includes bibliographical references and index.
ISBN-13: 978-0-8203-2884-3 (hardcover : alk. paper)
ISBN-10: 0-8203-2884-7 (hardcover : alk. paper)
1. Young men—Southern States—History—19th century.
2. Young men—Southern States—Psychology.
3. Sex role—Southern States—History—19th century.
I. Berry, Stephen William.
HQ1090.5.S68P74 2007
305.242'108621097509034—dc22   2006018990

British Library Cataloging-in-Publication Data available

CONTENTS

Gender history is at a crossroads. Either it will pursue men's history with all the rigor it has displayed in pursuing women's history or it will expire. Such an expiration is inevitable and not altogether a bad thing. Soon enough if not already gender will no longer be something a smaller group of scholars is focused on; it will be something the entire academy is attentive to. For now, though, an important question can have no answer: Is men's history where gender history goes to die or be reborn?

There are signs of the latter, but what is being born is as yet a rough beast. The field of masculinity studies seems at once a laudable extension of and a questionable reaction to the women's studies movement of the 1970s and 1980s. While problematized, not lauded, the American male again wrenches the spotlight toward himself. Heedless of intent, masculinity studies drifts along in the dominant culture's backlash against feminism and the prevailing sense that American manhood, under siege for two decades, is rightly going "over the top" again.

As Susan Faludi and others noted at the time, there was a pervasive sense of a masculine "crisis" in the 1990s. White American men had, since the Founding, been promised that they would always have a frontier to explore, an enemy to vanquish, a wife to adore, and a fraternity to join. That promise was broken after World War II. The final frontier was empty and cold; the "enemy" was massacred at Mylai; the wife had a new job, a new man, and a new attitude; and the white fraternity was downsizing, outsourcing, selling out their little brothers to the Mexicans and the Chinese. And no one felt sorry for them. They were sent on their way with a few prescriptions for being fat, bald, and flaccid—and they were not a little angry about it. The result, Faludi noted, was all over the news: Tailhook, the Citadel, the Spur Posse, gangstas, skinheads, abortion clinic bombers, schoolyard shooters, the right-wing militia, O. J. Simpson, Timothy McVeigh, David Koresh, the Unabomber, and the Angry White Male. Clearly, men needed to pull themselves together. And so they did, to the beat of Iron John's drum, in the menz movement, laddism, the Million Man March, the Promise Keepers, and the triumphant return of the Founding Fathers and other dear DWMs, back from the grave and ready to spread the gospel: America was and would always be a benevolent fraternity (now with a nuclear option). But all this chummy guy-guy action was suspiciously metrosexual (before metrosexual wasn't cool). Men's attitude had always been clear: Got an issue? Get a tissue. What men most wanted was to never have to apologize for being themselves. And so, inevitably, they fled South, in spirit if not in fact, to the land where the wellspring of masculinity still runs pure, to the land of army bases and NASCAR drivers, Jeff Foxworthy and his paeans to the redneck, Toby Keith and his love of American ass-kickin', President Clinton and President Bush, each in his own way behind the wheel of the Viagra car, burning rubber and spreading the gospel: the American male is back with a vengeance.[1]

And it's the vengeance part that's just a little disturbing. It's also the reason why the field of masculinity studies is so vital. For it's not just the American male's wounded pride that preoccupies our culture. There are a lot of angry men out there, and their misdirected rage is 9/11 deadly. For this, if for no other reason, the field is likely to *remain* vital. As the world continues to shrink and America comes into sustained contact with different gender systems, scholars will naturally seek better to understand how such systems work and have worked, change and have changed.[2]

In the field of the Old South masculinity studies appear slowly but regularly. Like any new field, knowledge proceeds in a way reminiscent of the old parable about the blind men and the elephant. Scholars may be talking about the same thing, but they are often talking about different parts whose connection to each other is unclear. Hunting, oratory, college curricula, courtship practices, eye gouging, and fraternal organizations are all part of the same animal, certainly, but how they are put together remains a mystery. No one has written a synthetic treatment. No one has laid out an agenda for the field.[3]

Broadly speaking, the agenda should be to understand (1) how precisely the Old South's masculine ideals were constructed and maintained; (2) how that process (and the ideals themselves) changed over time; (3) how males of different classes, races, ages, and regions resisted, modified, or flouted those ideals; (4) how the public expression and private experience of masculinity were different and yet related; and (5) to what degree and in what ways the Civil War created a seismic shift in Southern masculinity.

To each of these broad questions there are partial but suggestive answers. Before there was "masculinity studies," scholars studied the institutions and practices that "enacted" masculinity for the wider society. Beginning with analyses of dueling, scholars scanned the Old South's regional literature, religious life, political culture, and attitudes toward family, education, courtship, and recreation to better understand how the dominant culture defined what men should do and be. The leading conclusions are coded by the words "honor" and "mastery." Honor, as Bertram Wyatt-Brown has defined it best, was a "cluster of ethical . . . rules by which judgments of behavior [were] ratified by community consensus." Mastery, as Stephanie McCurry has defined it best, was the notion that manliness inhered not in the control of the self (though that was, to a lesser degree than in the North, important) but in the control of land, wives, children, and households. The two concepts are complementary. In the South men were the undisputed masters of their own bodies and their own households. Their right to rule these small worlds was scrupulously upheld by the courts, propounded from the pulpits, and flattered from the hustings. Any claims to mastery of a larger world, however, had to be set before the community to be adjudicated according to the dictates of honor.[4]

Masculinity studies is now engaged in the process of making these paradigms more supple, more subject to historical change, and more permissive of variation. What is taking shape might be called male worlds of love and ritual. New studies are providing a sense of how different subgroups of men related to each other (fraternity and competition), to women (love and misogyny), to themselves (dreams and doubts), and to their society (self-presentation and self-effacement).

To take but one example of the new suppleness, the work of John Mayfield in Southern humor provides a more richly human sense of how the rules of honor and mastery were observed in the breach. When Johnson Jones Hooper, a humorist and political hopeful, became exasperated with his region's political culture, he noted that if manliness, as defined, was all that his constituents valued, he had a Durham bull that would make a great candidate for Congress. His joke was the same one made today about males who drive Hummers — they must be compensating for something. Mayfield is undoubtedly right that the Old South was less rigid than its inhabitants, and occasionally its historians, would have us believe.[5]

With respect to the second agenda item, change over time, researchers are only beginning to understand how the country's deepening imperialism, romanticism, modernization, and sense of sectional crisis shaped the Old South's articulation of a peculiar masculine ideal. Differently from but with the rest of the country, the South became simultaneously enraptured by territorial expansion, nostalgic for republican simplicities, and preoccupied with the possibilities and perils of the market. How each of these changes, together and separately, affected Southern masculinity has yet to be fully determined. Certainly, scholars have the best sense of how masculinity was mobilized to meet the sectional crisis. In the 1850s, and with particular urgency after John Brown's raid, yeomen were invited to be the policemen of the racial regime and to enthusiastically accept the role that conflict with the North would bring them—defenders of white womanhood against "black" Republicans and their "Negro" allies.[6]

Only recently have scholars begun to look at the third agenda item, the various models for manhood that held sway in subcultures of the Old South. Masculinity was different in the low country than it was in the mountains, different among yeomen than among planters, different in the slave quarter than in the halls of Congress, and yet all were related. Historians are for the first time beginning to look at these variant masculinities and the linkages between them. To take but one example, scholars have shown that, despite the dominant culture's attempt to unman them, slave men found myriad ways to articulate their sexual distinctiveness. Not merely in their trickster tales, songs, and Christianity but in their "mastery" of private melon patches, pets, skills, and households, slave men accommodated and resisted the white culture's attempt to define their maleness, just as they accommodated and resisted enslavement itself. Thus, black masculinity remained a potent force that whites were aware of, even preoccupied by. The same could also be said of Indian maleness. To be sure, Native Americans got the worst of a conflict that decimated their population and then gutted their culture. But in important ways, Native Americans articulated a variant of masculinity that whites respected even as they tried to wipe it from the earth. Indianness, after all, had helped to make Americans American. In wresting the land from its aborigines English colonists had come to believe that they had earned it and that they had been altered in the process. Davy Crockett, a model for white masculinity, was himself full-blood white and half-Indian; somewhere in his battles he had eaten an Indian heart—and it was that heart that most defined him. Later, when Indian maleness had been all but vanquished, whites managed to be wistful about the "bold but wasting race" they'd slaughtered. The red man's doomed civilization became a symbol of everything Americans had lost in the process of growing up. Individualized, urbanized, commercialized, Americans couldn't help an occasional longing look back to a time when men had made common cause as a tribe, camping under an open sky and taking life as they found it. Thus, just as blacks had to resist not only slavery but whites' attempt to define blackness, so Native Americans had to resist not only eradication but whites' appropriation of Indianness to the purposes of self-congratulation and nostalgia.[7]

Much work remains to be done with respect to the fourth agenda item: how public and private constructions of masculinity created a sort of dialogue between selves and society. As Christopher Olsen has noted, the "new agenda" for gender studies must be topped by "works that discuss the conflicts, but also the linkages, between public expectations and private [successes and] disappointments, including the attendant psychological consequences." Increasingly, scholars will scan men's inner emotional lives to better understand the pleasures and pressures that attended their struggles to measure up as fathers, sons, husbands, workers, and citizens. Coupling inner experiences to outer behaviors promises a far richer sense of the private hopes and fears that grew out of and into a public culture. This is not to say that we need a *Patricide in the House Divided* for the South. Rather, we need a *Searching the Heart* for the South.[8]

Masculinity and the Civil War, the fifth agenda item, have received significant attention, of course. The Reconstruction of white manhood, overseen by Confederate widows and daughters, has been explicated well. What is less appreciated is the fact that Confederate defeat was only the last in a line of indignities suffered by the gray host. The Civil War was, like all wars, essentially ironic. Supposed to enforce, amplify, and clarify gender roles, it instead made them murky, distorted, and even inverted. Women had to protect their farms, attend to business, and provide for their families. Men had to cook, clean, and nurse each other like women; take orders and, in the case of imprisonment, wear shackles like slaves; have their time structured and endure punishment like children. Most important, their bodies were, in new ways, vulnerable to penetration. In dispensing death and punishment upon themselves en masse men created a kind of violence that did not regenerate but enervated white masculinity—and patriarchy with it. Thus, the war was simultaneously hypermasculine—a license to kill, gamble, drink, chew, curse, and fornicate—and infantilizing, enslaving, and emasculating. *During* the war, not after, many men felt helpless, dependent, and no longer in control of their destinies. Defeat and Reconstruction constituted a *second* crisis in Southern masculinity; the war experience itself constituted the first.[9]

The present study attempts with varying force to push forward on all fronts. The collected diaries suggest something about how masculinity was constructed, how it changed, how it was variously interpreted and internalized, and how it contributed to the Civil War. Most obviously, though, this book is animated by a belief that historiographical debates become stale unless scholars are regularly forced to meet the past on its own terms, in its own terms.

Following the model of Michael O'Brien's *An Evening When Alone*, this book collects four relatively short diaries under one cover and sets them off with an introduction and index.[10] It also seeks in essence to do what O'Brien's book did: petition that a relatively neglected group be equally included in the history of Southern gender. In O'Brien's case, of course, that group was single women. In this case it is single men. Considered as a whole, of course, most of Southern history has been written by men about men. Little of that work, however, considers masculinity, and almost none of it seeks to link public ideals of fatherhood, brotherhood, and manhood with men's inner experience of the attempt to fulfill such roles. In short, the revolution in women's studies has not been matched by a comparable advance in our understanding of men *as men*.

In editing this book I have accrued sizable debts. David Moltke-Hansen gave this project its initial impetus and encouragement. Archivists at the Southern Historical Collection, the South Caroliniana, and the Mississippi Department of Archives and History lent me their expertise along with their documents. My wife, Frances, toiled with me in the corn rows and cotton fields of Feasterville, and she is my boon companion.

I especially want to thank the Southern Texts Society and Michael O'Brien. *An Evening When Alone* had its tenth anniversary in 2003. The book launched the society, provided a model for its subsequent releases, and gave the world four distinctive voices to set beside Mary Chesnut and Sarah Morgan. I can think of no more fitting tribute than to give that book what it has always wanted—a brother.

INTRODUCTION

In the summer of 1860 Harry St. John Dixon was seventeen. His gamboling Mississippi boyhood was drawing to a close, and he knew it. In the fall he would leave for the University of Virginia and from there to manhood and all its burdens. The prospect was sobering, Harry admitted. Gone were the days when he and his friends had turned somersaults in the local creek. Gone were the giddy moments when he had skipped through the schottische with the local girls. At some point the girls had become women, and his friends had gone off to schools of their own. The forest paths of Deer Creek were quiet now, and Harry wandered them alone, overpowered by nostalgia. One evening Harry found the air unusually still and the moon unusually bright; from swimming hole to schoolhouse, each spot seemed a memento of bygone days. Thinking of the "happy moments which are gone and past forever," Harry began to sing "Home Sweet Home":

> I gaze on the moon
> As I tread the drear wild,
> And feel that my mother
> Now thinks of her child;
> As she looks on that moon
> From our own cottage door,
> Thro' the woodbine whose fragrance
> Shall cheer me no more.
> Home, home, sweet sweet home,
> There's no place like home,
> There's no place like home.

Harry was still singing the refrain when a black boy appeared on the forest path. They regarded each other for a moment before Harry sprang after him, meaning to scare him, hounding him all the way to the gate of the plantation. By then the nostalgia had passed, and, panting, Harry joyfully returned to the bosom of the Big House to record the incident in his diary.[1]

Moonlight, magnolias, and brutality—the Old South was replete with such scenes. Whatever hardship Harry might face in his life, he would always have

I

black boys to chase, just as he would always have turkeys to shoot at and "soft 'uns" to gawk at as they filed out of church. God had given Harry these things because Harry was a planter's son, destined for mastery and all its privileges. The vignette has another moral, however. The power Harry held (and abused) also weighed him down. With great privileges came great expectations, and so Harry shied from adulthood like an actor lingering offstage, preparing to take his mark, perhaps make his mark, but overwhelmed by the role he was called upon to play. Many of the boys who came of age with Harry felt the same way. "The time is approaching, when I must depend upon my own efforts for my daily bread," noted Alabamian Charles Hentz in 1845. "[I must] lay aside all childish things, and fit myself to launch out into the great theatre of this world's action, and play my little part." Unknown to them, of course, the parts scripted for this particular generation would play out on the fields of Shiloh, Antietam, and Gettysburg, where their gallantry would earn them early deaths and unmarked graves. Those who did survive would feel cheated. They would never inherit the mastery they had been promised when they emerged from their mud holes, sopping with boyhood, determined to become men.[2]

Few would feel sorry for them. Planters' sons had for years been objects of ridicule and resentment; their deaths were the only things they ever earned. "The young Southerner," Ralph Waldo Emerson explained in 1837, is

a spoiled child with graceful manners, excellent self-command, very good to be spoiled more, but good for nothing else, a mere parader. He has conversed so much with rifles, horses and dogs that he has become himself a rifle, a horse and a dog, and in civil, educated company, where anything human is going forward, he is dumb and unhappy, like an Indian in a church. Treat them with great deference, as we often do, and they accept it all as their due without misgiving . . . [but] the proper way of treating them is not deference, but to say . . . "Fiddle faddle," in answer to each solemn remark about "The South."[3]

Emerson's critique is one sided and unfair but not altogether wrong. Before the war Southern mothers and fathers said the same of their sons and more. "I am more and more convinced [that the South] is no place to rear a family of children," complained plantation mistress Anna King to her husband. "Bring[ing] up boys on a plantation makes them *tyrannical* as well as lazy." South Carolina planter James Henry Hammond discerned a similar failing in his sons. "They cannot work *with* any body for fear they may be working *for* them," he complained. "They growl, grumble, sulk and *do nothing* [except] shoot birds, buy fish, and gerrymander the county."[4]

Hammond's plantation held out another diversion to his boys, one discussed in the historical record (and only recently by historians). On a one occasion Hammond admitted that one of his slaves was pregnant, a culprit was his son—or perhaps himself. The Hammonds were not particularly exceptional in this regard. The slave population lightened considerably in the 1850s, from 7.7 percent mulatto in 1850 to 10.4 percent in 1860, an increase of 35 percent. We cannot know how much of that lightening occurred as a result of unions between slave women and planters' sons, but it was probably significant. An unidentified Southerner interviewed by Frederick Law Olmsted reluctantly admitted that only two lads in his small town in Alabama were not paying the "penalty of licentiousness" (venereal disease) for their conduct with slaves. We "might as well have [our sons] educated in a brothel at once, as in the way they [are] growing up," he concluded. Even if the vast majority of boys did not impose themselves on slave women, they witnessed repeated scenes of whips falling on sweaty, naked skin, brutalizing their tastes and impulses. For adolescents surging with hormones, the opportunity to take undue advantage must have been something they occasionally thought about, even if they did not act upon it.[5]

At the same time, the stereotype of Southern youth as hotheaded, hot-blooded, and steeped in sin must be approached with caution. Northern propaganda, especially on the eve of war, delighted in depicting the South as a backward region dominated by violent aristocrats and brutal urges, and these charges fell with particular severity on the delinquents and dandies of the planter class. An equal weight of evidence points to Southern sons as attendant to their honor, obedient to their parents, and desperate to do their duty. "Duty . . . is the sublimest word in our language," Robert E. Lee is supposed to have warned his son. "Do your duty in all things. You cannot do more. You should never wish to do less." For the Civil War generation manhood itself was a duty. A man owed a debt to his parents because they had given him life, a roof, an education, a name. He owed a debt to his sisters and sweethearts because they gave him their trust, their love, their lives. He owed a debt to the Founding Fathers because he breathed free air in a world everywhere else ruled by tyrants and kings. And he was desperate to discharge those debts and live up to that duty, even if it meant rushing headlong into a cannon's mouth, as many would go on to do.[6]

Planters' sons, then, were not delinquent but desperate—desperate to measure up to standards for manhood that became more richly brocaded with each passing generation. By the 1850s the country had doubled in size twice, once with the Louisiana Purchase and once more with the Mexican Cession. America was no longer a City on a Hill. She was an empire. She no longer posed herself as an example to the world. She imposed herself, sweeping across a continent, remaking the world in her image. Rising with the romantic tenor of the times, men's ambitions for themselves grew correspondingly more colossal. Boys dreamed not of becoming *President* Washington but *General* Washington. They admired the wills, if not always the deeds, of Napoleon and Caesar. "The bosom of generous youth throbs with the desire for fame and distinction—with a longing for immortality," Thomas Dew informed William and Mary's graduating class of 1837. "Each one of you, when he looks forward to the day when his body shall rest beneath the green sod of the valley, would wish that his deeds were entwined with his country's glory—that his name were embalmed on the page of her history, and repeated by millions, whose grateful hearts should join in paeans of praise to their country's benefactor." With such exaltations swimming in their heads, Southern boys dreamed of erecting a civilization that would stand as Rome had stood—expanding, agricultural, slaveholding, and magnificent. This rhetoric may seem to exaggerate the point, but these are exactly the terms in which Southern Americans understood the phenomenal—or, as they would say, providential—success of their country. America, noted one governor of South Carolina, would become greater than the "nations for which Alexander may have sighed, [stretching] over a greater number of degrees of latitude, and through a greater variety of climate, soil and surface than the sword of Caesar ever measured in his boasted conquest of the world."[7]

The problem, though, was that Southern boys who aspired to civilization building could not easily content themselves with the lives of clerking and pettifogging that met them as they left their colleges and academies. Their professors had plied them with stories of Napoleon and Washington, but living and realistic role models were in dwindling supply. The oddly coincident deaths of Henry Clay (1852), John Calhoun (1850), and Daniel Webster (1852) only cemented this sense of a rudderless generation, praying for fame, drifting toward disunion. This explains the tendency of the South's young men to oscillate between a bloated and a despairing sense of self. Aspiring to greatness, they tended, as by definition most men must, to mediocrity.[8]

The process by which men came of age in the Old South has yet to be fully explored. No one has ever asked the generation of boys who fought the war what they thought a man should do and be. This book opens up an avenue for that exploration, collecting the diaries of four young men who reached maturity in the 1840s and 1850s. Specifically, the diarists are Harry

St. John Dixon, a puckish planter's son who chafed at the indignities of boy-hood; Henry Hughes, a disturbed adolescent who believed he could domi-nate the world; John Coleman, a homespun farm boy who tried to content himself with agriculture; and Henry Craft, a depressive who could never mea-sure up to his own masculine standard. All of the diarists were from the Deep South (three from Mississippi, one from South Carolina). All of the diarists were young, between seventeen and twenty-five. And all of the diarists had a connection to cotton and slaves. Coleman's father was a planter; Dixon's father was a planter; Hughes's father was a cotton factor; and Craft's father was a merchant and surveyor to planters. All of them were slave owners, with holdings ranging from nine (Craft's father) to thirty-six (Dixon's father). Only Coleman and Dixon appear to have had direct, daily contact with slaves. Both mention individual slaves by name, and both punished slaves with their own hands. "The next negro that takes any thing out of my room," Dixon raged at one slave, "I'll try the virtue of that article upon his head!" Coleman was similarly accustomed to taking the upper hand with the family servants. "Was compelled by necessity to give Dave a thrashing," he noted of a runaway. Craft and Hughes were not as familiar with the physical aspects of mastery, but they each supported the institution. Craft's support was tempered and moderate: "[I] think that almost all slaveholders look upon the institution as an evil," he claimed, "a curse to the country & would gladly blot it out could any feasible plan be devised, but in complete destitution of any such plan [I] think that the evil is a necessary one & should be made as tolerable as possible." Hughes's support was more strident. "Let us . . . if expedient," he pronounced, "mark [slaves] like hogs and brand them like beeves; let us slit their nostrils[,] . . . pinch in their bleeding ears[,] . . . or, with hot and salted irons, fry on their brows and breasts lasting" badges of their race and status. Despite these dif-ferences in outlook and experience, however, all of the men were firm in their belief that the North had no business meddling in the South's peculiar affairs.[9]

Most obviously, all of the men were diarists. All endured night upon night of cramped hands and candle bugs because they wanted to write out their lives. As a genre the diary was changing in the period. Early in the century journals had tended to be chronicles—linear descriptions of what the self does, sees, and, to a lesser degree, thinks. By the 1840s journals were in the process of be-coming what we recognize as diaries, meandering discussions that use external events as moral mirrors to reveal what the self thinks, feels, and, to a high de-gree, is. Broad forces encouraged this transformation. Individualism, roman-ticism, and the secularization of evangelicalism all helped to create new pre-occupations with the interiority of the self. Gradually, diaries, like love letters, became sacred spaces dedicated to self-discovery and self-disclosure. To be sure, this process was in its infancy when these boys wrote, and each had internalized it to a different degree. Harry Dixon's diary was a private and secret space, if not yet a sacred one. When someone caused him to spill ink in his book he was enraged all out of proportion. John Coleman, by contrast, was amused when drunken friends made notations in his book, which he left out in the open as a sort of public novelty and conversation piece. Depending on their taste and tendency, then, these men confessed their hearts or chronicled their deeds or savaged their enemies—or made notations about the weather. Regardless, each man's book was his own, indelibly stamped with his own personality. Scholars have to be careful, of course. A diary is not a perfect reflection of the person who wrote it. Diaries conceal as much as they reveal; their writers record some things and not others. What these men constituted in their diaries were new personae altogether, related to but distinct from the others they created in their public and private lives. We can hope that these diarizing personae were more honest, more revealing, closer to the core of their selves, but we cannot know.[10]

This forces us to confront the tricky question of audience: to whom, for whom, does the diarist write? "No one ever kept a diary for just himself," claims Thomas Mallon in his history of diarizing. "In fact, I don't believe one can write to oneself for many words more than get used in a note tacked to the refrigerator, saying 'Buy Bread.'" Mallon is being flippant, of course. Diarists do not write expressly to be read. They write because it soothes them to write. They write because writing helps them to process emotion and order informa- tion. But Mallon is not altogether wrong either. Diarists are flirts. They long to be "read" in the same way that we all do—that is, they long to find some- one who understands and appreciates them. In the diarists' case, of course, the question is more literal: will I be read or won't I? And it is a question, always unresolved, that hovers over all they write. In this way their diaries retain their full potency. A secret, after all, has no power once it is told; it also has no power unless it *might* be told. And so it remains suspended yet unsaid, always threatening to burst its bindings and spend its power.[11]

In these pages four diaries burst their bindings and spend their power. Each diary has the pungency of youth; each smacks of adventures yet to be taken, pleasures yet to be tasted, limits yet to be accepted. Each man hopes he is doc- umenting some kind of progress, some kind of becoming. And yet each man worries, not once but often, that he is capturing only his own ordinariness. In their diaries, as in their lives, men rage against and thereby reconcile themselves to their own mediocrity, as anyone who has ever come of age must. Consider- ing, however, all the things these men had in common (age, era, region, caste), what is most compelling is the variety of their voices and distinctiveness of their styles.

THE DIARISTS

Harry St. John Dixon

Set in a rough-hewn planting community in the Mississippi Delta, Harry Dixon's journal is replete with the gritty realities of life in the land of cotton: wild hogs attack the unsuspecting, a tornado carries off the slave quarters, inebriates try to shoot each other's hats off and miss, relatives in New Orleans are poisoned by their servants, planter-patriarchs duck out of their libraries to play cards with their overseers, in their absence their sons raid their liquor cabinets and dream of deflowering virgins—and everyone goes to church on Sunday. The narrator of this Mississippi mélange is, like Tom or Huck, a self-admitted scamp and proud of it. When his mother told him it was her greatest hope to see her boys grow into good and righteous men, Harry replied that it was "the hardest task she could have imposed upon herself." "I am conscious that the sentiment she expressed was a most noble one, and as natural as could be," he admitted, "but at the same time I never had the least hope to be as she wished, 'good and righteous.'" Piety fit Harry like his Sunday clothes—too tight, too drab. His motto was *dum vivimus vivamus*, "while we live, let us live," and he filled his diary with the staples of a boy's life: swimming in mud holes, throwing dirt clods at friends, singing bawdy songs, and stealing the church organ to serenade the local girls. [12]

Harry was the oldest of eight siblings, seven of whom were boys. His mother, Julia Dixon, was a matriarch of the wilting type. In her defense she was probably exhausted. She had delivered eleven babies in sixteen years (losing three in infancy), and she was the sole caretaker of an overwhelmingly male household. Perpetually grieving something or someone, she hangs over Harry's diary like a mist—a dampening but insubstantial presence. Significantly more robust is Harry's father, Richard Dixon. Richard had left school at thirteen and home at seventeen. He had come to Mississippi without money or education and quickly amassed a large fortune in land and slaves. Typical of the self-made man of indifferent education, Richard had little countenance for fine art or fine feelings. He had made it by dint of hard work and clean living; the rest of the world could do the same. [13]

The Dixon family lived at Sycamores, a plantation on Deer Creek, twelve miles east of Greenville. For reasons that Harry's diary lays bare, the region

Harry St. John Dixon (Courtesy of the Southern Historical Collection)

has been called "the Mississippi of Mississippi," "the South of the South," "the heart and soul of the Delta," and "the most Southern place on earth." It was a region that would later spawn writers Shelby Foote, Walker Percy, and William Alexander Percy. When Harry was writing, however, Deer Creek was in its infancy. The alluvial plain had only recently been cleared for cotton. The forest paths had only recently been cleared of panthers and bears. The neighborhood families were wealthy, but the neighborhood buildings were clapboard, not brick. There was only one church and one school—and they were the same building. There was only one teacher and one pastor—and he was the same man.[14]

Harry began his diary just as he was beginning to outgrow that teacher's instruction and Deer Creek generally. Already better schooled than his father, he was quite possibly better schooled than his instructor, Mr. Herbert. He urgently wanted to go to the University of Virginia to become a lawyer, and he had read enough in books, magazines, and newspapers to fuel his dream of a world beyond Deer Creek. "I do not expect to live a fast life," he admitted, "but I do not intend to bury myself in such a place as [this]." The prospect of leaving, though, was a sobering one. Deer Creek was all he had ever known, and the wider world seemed foreign and unforgiving: "I [know] that I must in a short time launch myself into a world, cold and heartless, among strangers and men of corruption, men whose sins far out-balance those I have committed, and God knows they are many. . . . But I will not flinch; I do not dread it."[15]

But, quite naturally, Harry did dread it, which is one of the reasons he kept a diary. He intended in his journal to capture his fading boyhood, like a flower pressed in a book. Manhood might be a one-way door he longed to walk through, but Harry took comfort in the thought that at "some future day . . . in the winter of life" he would open his diary and return in memory to his "boyhood's cares and joys." This wistful sense of transition makes Harry's diary a true coming-of-age chronicle. In some entries he is a mere boy, rolling around in the leaf litter with his dog; in others he is a young man wrestling grimly with his future prospects.[16]

The other sure sign of Harry's transition to manhood is his intense preoc-cupation with sex. "A night or two ago," he confessed, "I dreamed of a perfect legion of women. . . . It seems as though my brain at night is wholly wrapped up in [them]." Of course, at that age, most young men's brains are wrapped up in them. What is unusual is that Harry documented his passions in some detail; he recorded his fantasies and wet dreams, his pornographic reading, the dirty jokes he shared with friends, and more. His peculiar preoccupation was the subject of virgins: "To these secret pages I will confess that to me they seem more like Gods," he wrote in his diary, "combining all good qualities" within humans. In another entry he gushed: "Send [me] a blushing maiden who knows no carnality; whose person is as God has made it, not as man has changed it! Give me the fair lily which knows not the wiltering sun of noontide, but whose soft folds have known only the gentle breezes of a vernal morn! This is what I look forward to: this is what [stimulates] me, what leads me into toil, this is the bright jewel I hope to fold to my bosom to protect, to cherish and to love, that it may shine for me, for me only." Having put women on such a pedestal, however, Harry had a difficult time bringing them down without feeling that he was also degrading them. Between his paeans to virginity and his indulgent visions of sexual excess, Harry reveals both a reverence for women's purity and a longing to defile it. In his dreams, especially, he was at war with urges, however natural, that seemed to him uncontrollable and even dangerous.[17]

If white virgins represented all that was pure and good in Harry's world, blacks represented all that was polluted and grotesque. Though surrounded by slaves who rubbed his feet and ran his errands, Harry found blacks physically repulsive. White beauty and black repugnance were integral to each other, of course, and Harry's descriptions of black ugliness are as richly brocaded as his descriptions of "fair lilies" tickled by the gentle breezes of a vernal morn. Mr. H's "boy" was "as ugly a negro as I ever saw," he noted in his diary after spending a night at Mr. Herbert's. "His mouth was unusually prominent and his lips were of a blackish blue, his high, projecting cheek-bones were like barricades almost to his rat-like eyes. His forehead retreated suddenly from his eyebrows and was very narrow and to complete his grotesque figure his . . . cranium was covered with black, notty tufts of wool, which seemed as much a stranger to combs as his scaly neck seemed to waters." Unsurprisingly, Harry Dixon did not question the essential probity of slavery, did not feel the slightest moral pang for its abuses; Negroes, he figured, were dirty and dumb, worthy of the work they were doing, beholden to the whites who allowed them to lead such simple, happy lives. If anything, Harry placed blacks actually below other mammals. "A little chicken's leg being broken," he wrote in his diary, "I assumed the duties of a surgeon and splintered and set it to the best of my ability in humanity as I could not see the thing suffer without attempting to ameliorate its pains all I could." And yet when his father disciplined a slave in front of him, beating the man with anything handy, including a hoe handle, Harry found it absolutely hilarious.[18]

More than the other diarists, Harry Dixon was deeply conscious that he would, on his maturity, inherit the mantle of the master class and the master race. Preoccupied with the respect accorded him by others, he was constantly alive to the slights and compliments by which he measured his emerging status. He took it personally, for instance, when a servant forgot to send up the cream for his strawberries and again when he left the room and returned to find another man reading his newspaper. On another occasion Harry's uncle and cousin rode by his window, as they often did, asking him to break into his father's liquor cabinet and pass out the whiskey. Harry could not contain his anger and replied facetiously, "Now it does look nice . . . that I must 'trapse' up and down a flight of stairs like a negro to wait on two great, lazy men that do nothing but drink liquor, sleep, and go to see women." "I considered it beneath my station to be *Mr. Anybody's butt*," Harry explained to his diary, and he would be damned if he would "gallop around [the] house drawing whiskey . . . for any one!"[19]

The beauty of white women, the repulsiveness of blacks, the preoccupation with respect—all were part of Harry's coming-of-age, part of a dawning awareness of the inheritance of mastery. Harry lived within a mutually reinforcing system of hierarchies (parent/child, man/woman, master/slave, white/black) whose legitimacy he did not question. Whites did not perform manual labor, because blacks did; men did not cook in the kitchen, because women did; children did not make decisions, because adults did; and so on. But the categories were partially fungible because at base they all coded for power: parent/man/master/white gave the orders, and child/woman/slave/black obeyed them. Raging at another perceived slight, Harry complained to his father that "Dr. Percy this evening took no more notice of me than if I had been a negro." And yet he could also tell his father: "I am nominally your slave until I am of age, but I glory in having you as my master and every day shows me how infinitely I am bound to love and obey you." Rhetorically, Harry could be a slave, because he was also a child. It is no wonder, then, that he was so obsessed with going to college. Until he did he could be neither fully an adult nor fully a man nor fully white.[20]

Henry Hughes

Like Dixon, Henry Hughes was a Mississippian. He was born in Port Gibson in 1829. His mother, Nancy Brashear Hughes, was descended from a relatively prominent Kentucky family. His father, Benjamin Hughes, was a cotton factor, local officeholder, and land speculator. When he died in 1842 Benjamin was deeply in debt. His surviving children—twenty-one-year-old Mary Ann, seventeen-year-old William, thirteen-year-old Henry, and ten-year-old Maria

Jane—were saved from poverty by a law that partially protected a widow from her husband's creditors. While Hughes seems to have admired his father, he rarely spoke of him, and it cannot have escaped his attention that he was the son of an insolvent merchant who died early and accomplished little. Certainly, the absence of paternal guidance affected him deeply. Hughes was bookish and intellectually gifted but also high strung and socially awkward. Without a father to guide him into the world he remained in the shadows, reading his books, dreaming of some dramatic emergence onto the world stage when he would claim for himself all that his father had been denied.[21]

In 1845 Hughes entered local Oakland College. Oakland had a four-year course of study, but he finished in two, first in his class of seven. Given his wealth of ambition and dearth of means, his choice of reading for the bar was logical. As a lawyer, he figured, he would find an entrée into the halls of power and a stage on which to demonstrate his brilliance. In late 1847 he moved to New Orleans to room with relatives and study law under Thomas Jefferson Durant, U.S. district attorney for Louisiana. It was here that he began making weekly entries in the journal he kept until 1853.[22]

The journal—every page of it—is dedicated to the cultivation and documentation of Hughes's coming greatness. It is no exaggeration to say that Hughes wanted to rule the earth or some large part of it, anyway; he wanted to winnow out *The Truth* and be recognized, even revered, for it in his lifetime. "The world is preparing for me," he claims in one entry. "Universal dominion is my aim—a consolidation of all the powers & principalities of earth into one happy, sublime Republic. I feel that the hand of destiny is on me. I am the Instrument of God."[23]

The first step in Hughes's plan for world domination was purely mental. He would read widely in economics, law, history, philosophy, religion, and the sciences, seeking to master each discipline and construct what he called the "Ultimum Organum," a revolutionary synthesis of all human knowledge. (In this he hoped to surpass Francis Bacon, whose *Novum Organum* was popularly regarded as having accomplished a total reformation of science.) The "Ultimum Organum" would then become Hughes's blueprint for the perfect society. He would put down the pen and pick up the sword, hosts and hordes would flock to his banner, and he would rule an empire that would stand as Rome had stood, but this time for all time.[24]

Hughes subordinated every aspect of his life to these ambitions. He studied oratory and gesticulation to develop techniques that could bend men to his will. He schemed at gaining affluence solely because it might bring political influence. He visited a prostitute because he believed it necessary to "feel every variety of woe and enjoyment in order to stimulate & control with certain and resistless power the emotions of the multitude." He wrote to women, sometimes even became engaged to them, to test his powers of persuasion. "These engagements," he admitted, "I contracted with a view to oratory, human nature, that is a knowledge of it, and composition." In short, all he did, read, or said was done with an eye to becoming "the greatest mortal man that ever was." "I will place myself upon a throne from which I can look down on Alexand[er], Caesar, Cicero, Bonaparte, Washington," boasted Hughes. "I [will] be . . . a despot. Almighty God let me be a despot."[25]

The life of the would-be despot was a lonely one. Hughes had no confidants, no conspirators, no close friends. The only one who might have understood him was God, and God wasn't talking. "God is my dearest, most familiar friend," Hughes admitted. "[I] pray without ceasing." "Can I not receive a sign, a proof [that] I am the darling of my heavenly Father?" But God did not answer, and Hughes occasionally resented him for it. "A thought fills me," he admitted, "to Shake off this mortal coil & boldly adventure among the Spirits of the universe, to invade Hell; to emulate, to—to dethrone the Almighty. Can I not expand my powers into infinity? Have I not a Will to war against Earth Hell Heaven? Have I yearned to reign the lone *One* in space, the unconquerable, Supreme Unsurpassable, Eternal Infinite. . . . What am I? Am I Jesus Christ or Satan?"[26]

Christ or Satan, Hughes had problems. In the absence of a father his adolescent ego operated without check; the principal figure in his Oedipal drama was the Almighty himself, from whom Hughes sought love and legitimacy or, failing these, a Nemesis or a Destroyer. Historians have hinted that Hughes had another problem exacerbating these: he was an unadmitted homosexual. Hughes was, to be sure, infatuated with his brother-in-law, Thomas Magruder. "He is one fitted to change the current of events," he gushed. "I so much—so much love [him]—for man can love man—& I will test socially the dear fact!" The phrase "test socially" is tantalizing but also obscure. Given Hughes's desperate need for paternal guidance, it seems safer to say that he looked up to Magruder and intended to love him unabashedly but not sexually.[27]

There is, moreover, strong evidence of Hughes's heterosexuality. He appears to have been in love with at least two women during the years covered by the diary. He yearned for women physically and romantically and dreamed of "embracing arms, kiss[ing] lips and pillowing bosoms." He even went so far as to wonder if he had "ever had a pleasure in which woman was not an element." Such quotations seem consistent with a heterosexual appetite. Hughes did use sexually indulgent language in other, oddly male contexts. "Oh, God!

Oh Father!" he exclaims in his diary. "Love me, my Papa. Hold me on your bosom. Let our hearts beat against each others'. Oh my love, let me be your pet. Am I not your darling? May I in Heaven, sit on your knee? Oh Jehovah, dandle me . . . ride me . . . kiss me, hug me; close, close." Here and throughout the diary Hughes's pent-up sexuality pours forth in ecstasies of belonging and becoming. Tangled in God's mighty limbs, Hughes writhes in erotic visions of fame, fatherly love, and a son's sweet revenge. He *may* have been aroused by men, but he was *certainly* aroused by Destiny. God and (to a lesser extent) Magruder were simply swept up in the excitement.[28]

In the five years covered by the diary Hughes made little progress toward that Destiny. While he passed the bar and practiced a little law in New Orleans, he soon returned to Port Gibson, where he remained materially dependent on his mother. He formed no new friendships and few romantic attachments, all of which dissolved. Most pathetically, his study of gesticulation, which he had hoped would help him command the hearts and minds of the multitude, had rather the opposite effect: "The rumor of my oratorical gestures, vocal and facial exercises with their accompaniments has suggested the question 'whether Young Hughes is not crazy?'" Was he? Hughes himself wasn't so sure. "I am not mad," he claimed; but it is a statement that tends to undermine itself. "Am I crazy?" he asked God in his diary. "Please help me. Push me on. I am half frightened. I am not. It is true. I must be the Greatest mortal man that can be; I must be the best mortal man that can be. I am God's Favorite. Earth, posterity, believe & obey."[29]

Such ramblings are typical of the diary. "Often when I attempt Composition," Hughes admitted, "my body, arm, and pen tremble. Then the golden Stylus is a conductor too feeble. The electric Spark of thought convulses my frame, or bursts forth in uttered words." The diary, then, was not meant for the "future biographer." Written in ecstatic surges, it was a place of catharsis for Hughes's overwrought, adolescent ambition. His entry for October 19, 1851, reads in toto: "Wherefore? Why? Speak! Open your lips: and tell—What?—Fool! child, babe, dreamer. Oh! Eye of God! Oh, Jesus'—bosom, Oh Holy Dove, coo in my ear. These fingers;—I clutch my hands; beat my bosom; tear my scalp;—swell veins & pop. There's blood; that: real. It is pain——That is in my mind; my mind is myself. Myself,—I, am—am: Planets, the blue deserts, wanderers of the camel's foot, & night-bird's eye: that man god of War & Glory. I am Glory's boy & Destiny's. Farewell: we will meet in——." Tearing at his heart, his mind, his imagination, Hughes daubs his brush in his wounds and paints his demented dreamscape. In the process he betrays the raging and too-long-bottled-up desires of a boy whose father died when he was thirteen—desires for recognition, legitimacy, and paternal love.[30]

Unlike the other diarists included in this volume, Henry Hughes went on to achieve a modicum of fame. While few sociologists know it, Hughes introduced the term *sociology* into the American lexicon, and he was the first man to designate himself a sociologist. Had his contribution to sociology been other than it was, he might be remembered as the father of the discipline. Because his *Treatise on Sociology* (1854) was a spirited defense of slavery, sociologists have preferred to see him not as their patriarch but as "something on the order of [a] bachelor uncle who died without heir." Hughes's importance as a proslavery theorist, however, has in some measure distracted scholars from his diary. Admittedly, it is an odd volume. But if its tone is recognizably adolescent, its terms ought to be recognizably antebellum. Hughes's martial romanticism and his sense that the world was consolidating and needed its Tamerlane were attributes shared by an unacknowledged number of Southern males. Here the diary is published for the first time and set in its proper context—young Southern manhood.[31]

John Albert Feaster Coleman

When a Southern family attains a certain size it becomes more than a family; it becomes its own community, even its own town. Such was the case for John Albert Feaster Coleman. When Coleman went fishing he took along "H.J., J.F., Dr., D.A., D.R. Sr., D.R., Jr., H.J. Jr., W.P.C., H. A. Colemans and T. D. & D. R. Feasters," all of whom lived in Feasterville, South Carolina.[32] The Feasters were originally Pfeisters, members of the Dunkard sect who came to America from Switzerland and settled in Lancaster County, Pennsylvania. After the Revolution members of the family migrated southward, first to Georgia, then to Fairfield County, South Carolina. The Colemans were also early arrivals in the county, and they too became Universalists. John Coleman, then, was born into a vast network of stable relations. Both wings of his family had lived on the same land for generations; both were large clans whose members ate large breakfasts and had little ambition for themselves outside of that. Though aristocratic in their status, they were fundamentally Jacksonian in their sensibilities.

Coleman was twenty years old when he began making nearly nightly entries in his journal. For the most part they consisted of brief, even curt notes on his daily activities: "Castrated six bulls," he wrote on May 22, 1851, "quite windy

John Albert Feaster Coleman (Courtesy of the South Caroliniana Library, University of South Carolina, Columbia)

all day. I gathered straw berrys enough for several pies and one for supper. Eat finely. Finished reading my book and went to bed." This was all Coleman felt compelled to mention about May 22, 1851. Admittedly, such entries do not make for gripping reading. Coleman's was an agricultural life, and his journal reflects it. There is little here of the other diarists' self-doubt or self-involvement. Here the primary characters are the cotton and the corn, withering in the heat, drowning in the rain. Here the crops are gathered and the plants are cut down, plowed under, and return in a rhythm that provides an easy backbeat to Coleman's own life. Coleman is in sync with these rhythms not merely because he is a farmer but because, as a farmer, he understands implicitly that he has a life cycle of his own, tied to the land his forefathers tilled before him. Indeed, he often underlines the point by jamming crop reports and wedding news together: "[This has been an] uncommon cold April," he notes, "having had snow and frost in an abundance with plenty of cold winds mixed in with it, &c. This has been a dry month in the marrying line, for I have not had the pleasure of recording any hymenial news. But I fancy May will have its share of doubleblessedness as reports would make us believe such if we were inclined to be superstitious."[33]

Coleman wanted very much to be married, but he does not put women on a pedestal, as do the other diarists in their different ways. "I have been thinking for several weeks of the manner in which the females (of supposed wealth) at the present time are educated," he noted in July 1849. "It appears as if their sole desire was to be admired for their external appearance, skin never warmed by the rays of that sun which is the life of all things." Such women, Coleman concluded, "are not fit to live, being no use to themselves nor to their fellowmen. They are fitted only to be waited on, being too lazzy to dress themselves or to make even their dresses." Coleman, then, wanted a farmwife and helpmate to share in the burdens and rewards of an agricultural life, and he measured women by a sort of agricultural morality. His own wifelessness, too, became a sort of moral failure; he was out of sync with nature, and it perturbed him. "I have felt different for the last week or two than ever I felt," he complained in November 1849, "not in boddy but seem dull and low in spirit. I fear love is the cause, and unreciprocated love at that. It is bad to love an object when your love is not returned." Introspection, however, was not in Coleman's nature, or, at least, self-revelation was not a part of his diary style. Two days after his lamentation on wifelessness he noted, "I feel better today. Worked pretty hard which is very good medicine to any love sick, low-spirited, no-account, good-for-nothing, trifling scamp. So now I pray you take the above perscription for maladies as used or possessed by myself."[34]

Coleman's world is mercilessly quotidian, and he knows it. His favorite literary device is "&c.," which he uses to mean "as one would expect" or "as usual." It signals a bit of information he hasn't the energy (or the need) to detail further: "a tremendious storm just at sundown, fences prostrated &c." or "[came] home and went to bed, had fine dreams, &c." It would never occur to him to detail his feelings about the storm, however "tremendious," or his dreams, however fantastic. He isn't that kind of diarist or that kind of man. He notes only the essential facts and leaves the rest to a well-turned "&c." Indeed, his use of this device is almost like a code. Something moderately dull or routine gets a single "&c.": "[Mrs. M.] had a miraculous escape [from poison] . . . because they doctored her so physically that she didn't die &c." Something truly dull gets multiple treatment: "bedded the sweetpotatoes, patched upp the garden, ginned a little [and] hauled some manure, &c., &c." The greatest string comes after a winter's evening cooped up with an acquaintance: "Very cold. Benjamin Revis came up in the evening &c., &c., &c., &c., &c." If Coleman isn't careful his diary will become nothing but "&c.," and on his tombstone they will carve simply, "He lived, &c."[35]

And this, of course, is his greatest fear. He is *literally* walking in his father's footsteps, down the same straight furrows through the same fields of corn. If he is curious where the footsteps lead, he can look farther down the row and see his grandfather, eighty-four and still hoeing, tracing out his son's and his grandson's future. Unlike Dixon or Hughes, Coleman bears the weight not of expectation but of inevitability. He will till the land until he's buried under it. Such a prospect gives him the blues occasionally, but it also gives him his sense of self. In a tradition as old as farming he sees his profession as somehow more noble, more moral than others. He is supported in this belief not only by all the men of Feasterville but by the almanacs he loves to quote in his diary: "A ploughman on his legs is higher than a gentleman on his knee," he quips. "The Plough. Its one share in the bank of earth is worth ten in the Bank of paper." For Coleman these are not homilies; they are truths. He inks them into his diary because he intends to live by them. Spun together they form a sort of philosophy: "the discontented man finds no easy chair," "men are as barrels, the emty ones making the most noise," "the man who lives with dogs may expect fleas for companions," "oil and truth will get uppermost at last," "pleasure is like cordial: a little is not injurious but too much destroys," "love thy neighbour as thyself—and thy sweetheart better than all," "far happier are the dead methinks than they / who look for death and fear it every day." The power of such platitudes has waned, of course; it was waning even as Coleman wrote them down. But from them he drew what he regarded as his most important lesson, the one he quoted more than all the rest: "Contentment is the greatest earthly blessing." Coleman, unlike Dixon or Craft, knew and accepted himself for what he was. He had been born into a vast familial undertaking, larger than any one man. Perhaps it did ensnare him like a net, but it also warmed him like a blanket. Ultimately, he remained in Feasterville because he wanted to, because he believed that contentment was his greatest earthly blessing.[36]

Henry Craft

Henry Craft was twenty-four when his fiancée, Lucy Hull, fell ill and died. The couple had postponed the wedding date twice, hoping Lucy would recover. Instead, her body was laid out in bridal attire, and Henry spent a last hour alone with her corpse. "It was the holiest hour of my life," he remembered. "Her countenance had resumed its natural appearance & was smiling & beautiful in death."[37]

Lucy's death triggered Henry's depression and his diary keeping, which were deeply related. His diary, he understood, was a memorial. It reads as if it were written by one of Edgar Allan Poe's bereaved narrators, lamenting his lost Lenore or Annabel Lee. Entry after entry, Henry faithfully recorded his anniversaries: the day he met Lucy, the day he admitted he loved her, the day they were supposed to be married, and so on. "Almost every hour, often every moment, I think of her," he admitted. "The train of recollections reaches from week to week till, should I live till then, the joys & disappointments & trials having passed one by one in review, it will end at that sacred spot where she sleeps the long quiet sleep of death." If it is torture to read such sadness, it must have been a kind of torture to write it as well. But Henry reveled in such tortures, as the grief stricken often do. At least in his melancholy he felt *something*. One day, he implicitly knew, he would think of Lucy's death and there would be no responsive pain. Until then, the least he could do for his beloved was to lash himself with her memory.[38]

Henry had been born in 1823 in Milledgeville, Georgia, where his father, Hugh, was a merchant. Henry's mother had died in 1826, when he was only three. His father had remarried shortly after, to Martha Cheney, but she too had died, and so he had married again, to Elizabeth Collier, who eventually bore him three sons and five daughters. Henry had grown up somewhat awkwardly in this swelling household as the child of his father's first marriage. He attended Oglethorpe College in Milledgeville and received his degree in 1839. In the same year his father relocated the family to Holly Springs, Mississippi, where he set up shop as an examiner for the American Land Company. Henry remembered his young adulthood on the Mississippi frontier as "the free roving of my woodsman days." He, like his father, became a land examiner. He had put some money away and had turned his mind to settling down when he met Lucy at a local soiree.[39]

It was not love at first sight. Lucy seemed to Henry just another typical belle—"brilliant, careless, gay & rather heartless." Gradually, though, he realized that she, like he, was "one of those who have a character to wear to the world." She wore a belle's costume, she played a belle's role—but only because that was what was expected of her. Beneath the "sham & parade" she had a tenderness Henry was proud to have discovered. He did not begrudge her her charade. He was a charade too and had always thought so. Uncomfortably playing the role of a man, he suspected he was something tragically less. "I have dreamed and drifted too long now to be a man," he admitted. "I feel and have always felt that I am not a man; and have no business with a man's affairs or responsibilities." Lucy, he hoped, was a kindred spirit. He wanted to remove not her clothes but her mask—and his own. And he believed he would feel better for such revelations. With her he might finally feel comfortable with himself.[40]

After Lucy's death Henry sank more deeply into depression. He had lived too long as an odd remainder in his father's new family. He had dreamed too long of a home of his own and a family that revolved around him. Unable to remain in Holly Springs amid so many reminders, he fled to Princeton Law School, where he hoped to find in the "emulation and competition of a class" some respite from mourning. Instead, he continued to sink. "The past is my only world," he wrote his sister. "For the future I have scarce a thought or a hope." Unable to concentrate on his studies, he purchased a diary and began his testament to grief. "When man has nothing left to love," he concluded, "he falls in love with his very sorrow."[41]

Henry had been at Princeton only a few months when his father wrote him to come home and read for the bar. Henry went willingly. He felt out of place at Princeton among all the young men striding stiffly to their destinies. Back in Holly Springs, though, his depression reached its lowest ebb. Studying for the bar seemed hopeless, pointless. Some part of him had died with Lucy, he believed, and without her he had no reason to exert himself. Other men, he knew, had suffered greater tragedies and yet risen to great heights. But Henry could not get over his loss, and he hated himself for it. "Self study & self analysis constantly increase my humiliation," he noted, "until loathing, utter contempt, are the only words to express what I feel for everything which I find to be part of my nature." Finally, it seemed to Henry that only death could release him from the humiliation of being himself. But, like Hamlet, he worried that death would offer not annihilation but a "terrible slumber in which dreams may come." Otherwise, he said, "I would leap joyfully to the embrace of Death." "My poor gewgaw of a heart," he lamented, "it is a hard rock of selfishness encrusted by a thin mould of sentimental sensibility in which mushroom feelings spring up & perish in a day." Lucy, he decided, had escaped the "wretched fate" of being his wife. "But had she lived," he wondered, "might I not have been different?"[42]

The intensity of Henry's melancholy could not be sustained, of course. By the anniversary of Lucy's death he found that "the eclipse of sorrow is passing or past." "This day brings with it no new sadness as I had supposed it would," he confessed. "My first waking thought was . . . 'One year ago she died.' But there is no new pain which memory can inflict, no new echo which can answer those words 'she died' in my heart." Henry gave his diary partial credit for the change. It was, after all, his and Lucy's story, however short, a narrative of their "love & . . . disappointment . . . right up to the closing scene." "I here dedicate" this journal, he wrote, "to the memory of the past year, here inscribe it as the tombstone which I raise over the grave of my former life. . . . [And so] let me take my farewell of [Lucy], bury the past & turn toward whatever may be my future." There had been, he admitted, a "sweet, sacred joy in communing with the dead," and he would miss it sorely. "In the busy hours of the day & the quiet midnight, in solitude & in crowds" Lucy had been always in his thoughts. But now he had to bury with her "the memory of what has been" and "summon up the energy & hope & strength for the new existence" that lay before him. "Farewell [Lucy]," he wrote, "the past, the bright, the dark, the joyful sorrowful past—farewell."[43]

THE DIARIES

The diaries that follow are arranged according to their keepers' ages when they started. Thus, Dixon, who began writing at seventeen, is followed by Hughes, who began at eighteen, Coleman, who began at twenty, and Craft, who began at twenty-five. In this way the diaries themselves comprise a coming-of-age story. The youngest diarist, Harry Dixon, opens with a tale of Mississippi boyhood. The second youngest, Henry Hughes, follows with vain imaginings of coming fame. The second oldest, John Coleman, follows upon Hughes with a somewhat successful struggle for contentment and resignation. And the oldest, Henry Craft, concludes with an older man's perspective on resignation and regret.

THE MANUSCRIPTS

Henry Craft's diaries are part of the Craft, Fort, and Thorne Family Papers at the Southern Historical Collection. Craft's Princeton journal (reproduced here) exists only in microform; the whereabouts of the original are unknown. The 181 pages measure 7½ inches by 9½ inches, though it is probable that the image was reduced or enlarged when the film was made. Nothing can be said about the binding and the cover either, as these were not filmed. The first page is titled in Craft's own hand, "My Journal," in large letters at the center of the page. In the top right corner he has written, "Henry Craft, Holly Springs, Mississippi, April 8th, 1848, Princeton, N.J." At the end of the diary Craft promised to write more: "I will continue this journal," he said, "in a large black book labeled 'Natural Philosophy.' " Whether he did or not is unknown. Craft did keep other diaries, however. A second volume for 1859–60 and a third for 1863–64 also survive in the collection.

Harry St. John Dixon's journals (labeled A through L) are at the Southern Historical Collection, University of North Carolina at Chapel Hill. The diary reproduced here (letter B) measures 8 inches by 13 inches and has a variegated cover (blue, yellow, red, and black) with a psychedelic pattern more reminiscent of the 1960s than the 1860s. The 288 handwritten pages are ruled, gray-blue in color, and have page numbers stamped in the top corners. Inside the front cover Dixon has inscribed: "A Journal of the weather and the most interesting events which take place during each day having been commenced Ja'n 1st A.D. 1860, by Harry J. Dixon, for *private use*. Deer Creek, Washington Co., Mississippi."

The journal of John Albert Feaster Coleman is part of the Coleman, Feaster, and Faucette Families Papers at the South Caroliniana Library, University of South Carolina. The volume is in pretty bad shape; the covers are gone, the binding has given out, the pages are brown and brittle, and the edges are dog-eared and frayed. The all-but-loose 121 handwritten sheets measure 7½ inches by 12 inches and are titled by a handwritten sheet, added later: "The Journal of John Albert Feaster Coleman, Feasterville, S.C., Fairfield County, South Carolina, 1848–1851."

Henry Hughes's diary is part of the Henry Hughes Papers at the Mississippi Department of Archives and History in Jackson. The volume contains 236 handwritten pages measuring 8¼ inches by 10½ inches. If Hughes kept other diaries, they have not survived.

EDITORIAL PRINCIPLES

My first editorial principle was to get the words right. Henry Craft and Harry Dixon were cooperative in this regard, both writing a very tidy hand. John Coleman was a different story. His penmanship (like his spelling) has a certain creative flourish. In general I erred on the side of caution. Where I was not sure of a single word it appears here as a [. . .]; where I was not sure of two or three words in a row they appear as a [. . . .]. Occasionally, a diarist has intentionally made something indecipherable, censoring his own work. In such cases < . . . > designates a single word that has been inked over or erased, and <. . . . > designates a series of words that have been so expunged. In those cases where I have been able to recover the self-censored material, the words are shown with strikethroughs over them. In Harry Dixon's diary, where material was sometimes encrypted, I have placed the coded words inside angle brackets. Where handwriting and context reveal an author other than the diarist, I have used curly brackets around the passage. All such instances occur in the Coleman journal. His diary, apparently, was an open book to his friends, who felt comfortable occasionally putting in their own two cents.

In the interests of chronological clarity I have standardized the format each diarist used in dating his entries. Thus something like "10th Nov." will appear here as "November 10, 1848." I have not, however, standardized the format *across* the diaries. Because Henry Craft and Harry Dixon thought it was important always to list the day of the week, I have included it ("Friday, November 10, 1848"). Henry Hughes didn't always include the day of the week but always noted where he was writing from. This information has an inherent interest, and, as it was his preference, I include it ("New Orleans, November 10, 1850"). John Coleman, again, was more irregular in his habits. Sometimes he included the day of the week, often he didn't, and sometimes he just started his entry with something like "Twentisixth." While I was tempted to use his format (eccentric spellings and all), I decided it would too greatly inhibit comprehensibility to leave out month or year for long stretches (hence "November 26, 1851").

In the interests of readability I have made a few silent changes to the text. Occasionally, I have buffed out a diarist's punctuation by either adding or deleting commas, periods, and the like. Henry Hughes, especially, was a splatter punctuator, lathering on the semicolons and the dashes with a flourish that sometimes overwhelmed his composition. Such a style reflects his personality, and I have for the most part let it stand, except where comprehensibility was threatened. Similarly, I have left Coleman's intriguing spelling alone and unaccompanied by [*sic*]s. Where an author has crossed out one phrase or one word in preference to another, I have silently deleted the misstep. These diaries, I concluded, are not the Constitution of the United States. There is no "original intent" to be ferreted out by the fact that a guy decided to go with "the" instead of "an." I have also silently supplied capitalization at the beginnings of sentences; deleted accidental repetitions of words or phrases; lowered all superscriptions (10th instead of 10th); supplied missing punctuation in the case of quotations or parenthetical statements the author has forgotten to close; and used indented paragraphs where the author has used line breaks or extended dashes. In addition to these silent changes I have made a few intrusions on the text. Where the diarist has underlined a word or passage it appears here in italics. Where an author clearly intended to write a word but accidentally rushed ahead to the next I have placed the intended word in square brackets.

I winced at every one of these changes, but ultimately I decided that it was folly to think that I could ever capture or approximate the original diaries anyway. A diary is not a mere series of words. Like a wizard's book of spells or Leonardo's codex, it has an untranslatable magic. There is a power in the object itself—the mustiness of the pages, the creakiness of the covers, the swoops and swells of the hand—that remains even after all the words have been extracted. That power comes in part, I think, from the fact that the book itself has survived so much. Like a message in a bottle that washes up onshore, it has made a journey of its own, one you will never really know. But the power of an old diary comes also, I think, from the fact that it has outlived its keeper. What you know perfectly well before you pick it up has the power of epiphany once it's in your hand—the person who loved this book and filled it with secrets, the person who endured icy winters and inky fingers to write out this story, the person whose blood, sweat, and tears literally color these pages, is dead and yet lives on in some small way in you. This emotional connection of past and present, made possible by the medium of a shared object, is not possible here. Nor can I footnote the smell of mortality—or the hedge against mortality— that is contained within the dusty old covers. Such things, and a host of others, are simply lost in transcription.

ANNOTATION

Annotation was a frequently rewarding and just as frequently frustrating aspect of editing these diaries. It's very easy to kill an entire afternoon trying to figure out exactly who "Mr. Morgan" was or where "Mc's store" might have been. Eschewing the ancillary and focusing on the principal, I tracked down many but by no means all of the people met, books read, plays seen, poems quoted, songs sung, and foods eaten in the 826 pages of these diaries. Where appropriate I have indicated my source of information.

Henry Hughes particularly and Harry Dixon to a lesser degree were voracious readers. Their diaries are replete with (partly accurate) titles for the books and articles they were currently digesting. In the notes I have given as full a citation as I can give with confidence. Some of the citations are precise. If a diarist is reading Wilkie Collins's *The Woman in White* in the spring of 1860, we can be perfectly sure he is reading it serially in *Harper's Weekly* because that's when and where it appeared. Sometimes, however, a more complete citation is impossible. Books like Sir William Blackstone's *Commentaries* and Edward Gibbon's *Decline and Fall of the Roman Empire* were often part of a general library and might just as easily be earlier editions as later. In these cases I have given the date of first publication. Such inconsistencies are regrettable, but the notes are intended merely as a point of departure for those interested in further investigation.

THE DIARIES

Harry St. John Dixon

We talked loud, laughed loud, danced loud and kept "racket" in most every form. Who will make old fogies of "Young Americans"? Go it while you are young for when you get old you can't go! . . . Is happiness a crime? Then let the fiends of hell reign in your sullen heaven.   —August 2, 1860

Sunday, January 1, 1860

Clear and cold—ground frozen all day. Attended church in the forenoon—read and wrote in the afternoon. Just before sundown I went down to Judge Rucks's[1] for a music book of Miss Ella Brown's,[2] and after she came into the parlor to get it for me, I found it extremely difficult to tear myself away from such a fair and interesting lady. She is undoubtedly one of the nicest ladies I ever knew.

Before going down I copied a piece of poetry called "Medora" but put the name "Ella" in its place and quietly put it on the keyboard before she came in and before I left asked her to play a certain piece for me at 11 o'clk tomorrow which she promised. At the close of the piece I wrote, "From one whose friendship is as pure as the sunbeams are clear that are now shining upon this page" and something more in hieroglyphics[3] and signed my name in them so that it might puzzle her.

Monday, January 2, 1860

No change in the weather. I repaired to the schoolhouse this morning with the determination to entirely stop visiting the ladies and to deny myself the pleasure of their company in toto and occupy myself exclusively with my books.

Tuesday, January 3, 1860

Weather the same. School. Yesterday Miss Ella and Miss Marian[4] stopped in a few minutes but did not get off. I took Miss Ella's book back yesterday evening about sundown. After coming from school I was just practising my music lesson when my dear old friend Hal[5] rode up to bid me goodby before he left for Oxford. Our parting was truly painful—at least it was to me. I cannot tell whether it was to him or not. Poor fellow! I can pity him. He leaves behind his love, his angel as he calls her, Miss <Mary Wingate>.[6]

Mrs. James Yerger[7] having come to see Ma about dark, I went home with her as an escort—we met Miss Dellie[8] and Miss Jenny.[9]

Wednesday, January 4, 1860

Cool and somewhat cloudy. School.

A boy came from Maj. Lee's[10] about dusk to invite me down there to tea. Pa[11] at first said not go, but Ma[12] having just returned from Greenville told me to go as there would be but few gentlemen. It is well I did for including myself there were but four and only four ladies. We first had a pleasant chat and then a little dance—supper—again a dance—and in about one hour and a half had wines, &c. after which we had a little chat and soon retired to our respective homesteads.

Thursday, January 5, 1860

Clear and cool. School. Read after coming from school. I omitted to say in my last entry that during a conversation I had with Miss Ella [I] asked her if her curiosity had lately been excited (referring to the poetry and hieroglyphics). She looked very knowing and said yes, and she believed I could gratify it by translating to her some hieroglyphical writing lately addressed to her in a very mischievous manner. She earnestly entreated me to give her an alphabet, which I of course refused, alleging as an excuse that my honor was pledged not to.

Friday, January 6, 1860

Cold, cloudy, and drizzly. School. Read after coming from school. My journal suffers woefully for some substance or something to feed on as Uncle Jack[13] would say.

Saturday, January 7, 1860

Clear and pleasant. Little or no fire needed. I took my music lesson late and was sitting in the parlor reading when Miss Ella and Miss Dellie rode up and Ma had welcomed them in before I saw them but met them at the door and exercised my conversational powers to entertain Miss Dellie.

They invited us all down to a private theatrical play at Judge Rucks's tonight. The young ladies were to be the actors. The evening occupied in making a sword for Miss Ella. I sent it down in the dark.

As they were about to depart they kissed Ma, and I remarked, "Miss Ella, do you believe a kiss is a sin?" She answered, "No." I said, "do you think it does any good?" "No." I then said, "then if it does no good it must do harm, so you will admit it is a slight iniquity." She reluctantly agreed with me, and I said, "as long, Miss Ella, as it is an iniquity and as long as a matter of course you believe in the Bible, it says that the iniquities of the parents shall be visited upon their children to the third and fourth generation and I think that this one at least should descend to the first—so Miss Ella, I am at your service." She blushed beautifully and with not a little embarrassment playfully struck me over the shoulders with her riding whip. I then helped her on her horse and she rode off.

I went down to see the play and liked it much better than I expected. It was the *Lady of Lyons*.[14] The hugging part was acted admirably. I wish I had been in either Miss Ella's place or Miss Marian's. After they got through we danced til 12 o'clk.

Sunday, January 8, 1860

Partially clear and pleasantly warm. Morning was occupied at church. I walked home with Miss Dellie and took a ride with her in the evening.

Monday, January 9, 1860

Cloudy and cool. Read and took a walk after coming to school.

Tuesday, January 10, 1860

Cloudy and rainy, ground perfectly saturated with water. School.

Wednesday, January 11, 1860

Cold, rainy and disagreeable all day. No school. Read and studied all day.

Thursday, January 12, 1860

Cold, rainy and wet. School.

Friday, January 13, 1860

Cold, cloudy, and rainy. School was dismissed earlier than usual on account of our speeches not being memorised.

Saturday, January 14, 1860

Weather the same. Staid in doors all day reading and studying.

Sunday, January 15, 1860

Clear and pleasant day. As usual I arose late this morning and in due course of time attended church for the last time to hear Miss Ella's sweet voice mingle in the Holy chanting.

Studied my lessons after dinner and then went down to Judge Rucks's about four o'clk to call on Miss Lou[15] and Miss Jenny. They being absent I pursued my original design of going to see Miss Dellie. I did so, and *she* was absent. It was then nearly dark. I started back when I met Mr. Hal Rucks[16] and stood talking in the road and while there I saw her (Miss Lou and Miss Jenny being with her) coming. I rode back and helped Miss Dellie out of the carriage and staid til after supper. Miss Jenny and Miss Lou did not get out. The principal topic of conversation was what I had said about having such a nice flirting with her when I went to Nashville. She most generously forgave me the foolish remark I had made.

As I came back I thought I would then call in and see Miss Jennie and Miss Lou. Miss Lou did not appear on account of a headache, but I found Miss Marian and Miss Jenny in the parlor with Andrew Carson.[17] They attacked me furiously about the poetry, and nothing I could say would do any good—they declared I did it. Miss Marian and myself had a private little quarrel about it while we were sitting on the sofa and while Andrew was talking to Miss Jenny. I told them if they could by any means prove that I did it then I would acknowledge it but not without. It had no signature to it and that of course favored me. I went home about 11 o'clk and got a scolding from the old folks for my late hours.

Monday, January 16, 1860

Clear and cool. School. I rode from school this evening.

Tuesday, January 17, 1860

Clear and cool. School. Read after coming from school this evening.

Wednesday, January 18, 1860

Clear and pleasantly cool. Left school at 12 to get ready to attend a party to be given at Mr. Bowen's out on Bl'k Bayou tonight. Uncle Jack, Bill Yerger, and George,[18] and myself got there about dark and in "little or no time had on our dudds" ready for the galls. The gayety commenced unusually early. I was among the first in the parlor and engaged to dance with every lady in the room except Miss Kate Lee[19] on account of a remark she made to me at a party at Maj. Lee's during Christmas week. I tore her dress accidentally and she turned very primly round and said something to this effect (as I was afterwards informed by Bill who was dancing with her: "Go to the place where it is hot." I did not hear it but thought it was some thing very harsh. If I had heard it I should have said, "If I do Miss Kate it is more than probable that I shall renew your acquaintance."

Oh I had such a splendid time! We danced til broad daylight. The fancy dances seemed to be more popular (as *Major Jones Courtship*[20] would say) than usual. I danced many times with Miss Ella (the fancy dances) as well as with the other ladies, but particularly with her. I was obliged to dance with Miss Lee—she asked me and I felt a delicacy in refusing so I put my paw around her and whirled away. She does not dance like Miss Ella—not near so good—she laid < . . . . >.[21] I do think Miss Ella waltzed nicer than any lady I ever had the pleasure of waltzing with!

We retired at daylight. The young ladies did not go to sleep but serenaded a set of "tight" gallants with their sweet voices. Bill and Valliant spoiled it all by calling up two drunken fiddlers with their crazy violins to return the compliment but only spoiled all my pleasure. I had come into the hall next to the ladies room in my stocking feet to listen to it and felt like knocking them down when they came up.

I did not start home till about 8 o'clk on account of my horse being loose. I saw them once more when I went to start and gave their sweet little hands a parting squeeze. John McCutchen rode with me as far as his house. I took breakfast with him about 10 o'clk on

Thursday, January 19, 1860

Which was as clear as a bell but as cold as an iceburg. I got home about 12 o'clk. By this time I suppose the young ladies are puffing down the "mighty river" at the rate of ten miles an hour.

Read some and went to Dr. Percy's[22] in the evening to carry some notes for Mr. Herbert and wrote a long letter to Nat[23] who is in Oxford with Hal.

Friday, January 20, 1860

Clear and cool. School. Times very dull. Read after coming from school.

Saturday, January 21, 1860

Clear and pleasant day. After taking my music lesson I dug some holes about in the yard for Ma so that she might plant some cedars. The old folks have taken up the idea that I don't take enough exercise and now won't let me read half an hour scarcely without either telling me about taking exercise or telling me to go and do something. Read and studied in the evening.

Sunday, January 22, 1860

I arose late this morning. A beautiful day. I attended church, the singing was not *near* so good as usual because Miss Ella's sweet voice was absent, but she seems to have civilized our singing a little. Studied, read, and exercised the balance of the day.

Monday, January 23, 1860

Clear and pleasantly cool. School. Worked in the garden after coming from school and took my usual walk.

Tuesday, January 24, 1860

Clear and cool. School. After coming from school (which but half an hour before sundown) I read and then took my walk.

Wednesday, January 25, 1860

Weather the same. School. Took my usual walk.

Thursday, January 26, 1860

Little cooler but clear. Went to school but came home about 10 o'clk on account of having a chill. Sick the balance of the day.

Friday, January 27, 1860

Clear and cool. School. Read and exercised after coming from school.

Saturday, January 28, 1860

Clear and pretty day. Indoors all day taking quinine and in spite of it had a chill.

Sunday, January 29, 1860

Pretty and cool day. Went to church in the morning and played ball in the evening. Much better today.

Monday, January 30, 1860

Weather the same. Layed in bed till 2 o'clk taking quinine and missed my chill. Balance of the day occupied in reading.

Tuesday, January 31, 1860

Cloudy and rainy in the morning and warm. Turned colder in the evening and at dusk the water in the edges of the gallery was frozen. School.

Wednesday, February 1, 1860

Clear and very cold. I did not attend school today on account of Ma's, Louly's and the little baby's leaving for New Orleans. May God bless them!

Thursday, February 2, 1860

Clear and cool. School. After coming from school practiced with my rifle.

Friday, February 3, 1860

Clear and cool. Just before school was dismissed John Byrne came in and after dismissal went home with me when I practiced my music lesson til 4 o'clk when we put on a clean shirt and went down to Maj. Lee's to see the young ladies.

We had not been there long, I mean I thought Harry Percy would ask us into the parlor, not dreaming that he supposed I came for any thing else, but we sat for some time before he asked us in the parlor. Probably half an hour before he said a word about going and after Maj. Lee had come in and gone out with Cab Green, an acquaintance. I thought at first that as Dr. Percy's family was there that the two waited to converse together privately but that Maj. Lee would invite me in after a while. I picked up a book and commenced reading and forgot all about it. I thought that we would go into the parlor after supper, but low and behold after a while here all the gentlemen (except Bill and Valliant who I afterwards found out were there) came into Nat's room picking their teeth. Maj. Lee remarked, "Why don't you come in to supper we blew horns and many bells." I did not hear them if they were and I did not like the way in which it was said. He then said, "John, won't you and Harry go in and take some supper?" I said, "No sir, I do not care about eating at all" in as ironical a tone as I could in the mean time putting on my overcoat, and then told John to order his horse which he did and as I went out of the door I said as politely as my emotions would allow me, "Good evening gentlemen" and went home. It was all I could do to keep my tongue in my mouth. I know my manner show'd my feelings. I must say candidly that it is the worst treatment I ever received from any person, and I don't intend to give an opportunity of its being repeated again soon. If my feelings are the same in the future that they are now I shall not go again til Nat comes home, and then only to see him. Not that I believe I am in any way annoying them, but that I believe it is my duty to myself. I believe I have been treated badly and I intend to let it be seen that I think so and am not such a fool as to think otherwise. I regret this thing exceedingly, more on Nat's account than on any other.

Saturday, February 4, 1860
Cloudy and drizzly—rain in the evening. Most of the morning occupied in practicing with my rifle. Mr. Wm. Percy[24] was here and we had a good deal of fun with Jimmy[25] and his shooting. He shoots very well. John Byrne left this morning. Read and studied all evening. I find that I am getting along very easy in Caesar now.

Sunday, February 5, 1860
Slightly cloudy. No church. Read and studied all day.

Monday, February 6, 1860
Clear and cool. School. Read and practised my music lesson after coming from school.

Tuesday, February 7, 1860
Clear and cool. School. My regular routine observed. My poor journal suffers again, but I suppose it will respirate more fully when I go to college.

Wednesday, February 8, 1860
Clear and pleasantly cool. School. I am making a satisfactory progress in my studies, i.e. to myself.

Thursday, February 9, 1860
Clear and pleasant. School. Nothing of any note has taken place today. I have written every entry for this month except the 1st and 2nd from memory.

Friday, February 10, 1860

I can say "ditto" for the weather. My composition not being acceptable, I translated a chapter from Caesar this evening at school. Pa was taken sick this evening.

Saturday, February 11, 1860

Clear and cool. Remained in the house all day waiting on Pa who is very unwell.

Sunday, February 12, 1860

Clouds floating. No church today. Read and studied a little. Had a chill.

Monday, February 13, 1860

Drizzly and disagreeable day. School.

Tuesday, February 14, 1860

Clear and cool. I staid in bed till 2 o'clk when I arose feeling very lightheaded having dieted on quinine. Pa and myself conversed on the subject of my education all evening as we both sat in his room, feeling I suppose as bad as we cared to.

Wednesday, February 15, 1860

Clear and pretty day. School. It has now been two weeks since Ma left and it seems to be an age.

Thursday, February 16, 1860

Pretty day. Read as usual and took my walk after returning from school.

Friday, February 17, 1860

Rainy, cold, and disagreeable day. School. Received a letter from Hal this evening as well as from little Willie (Uncle Moses's oldest son) and Lizzie. Hal sent me a *beautiful* valentine. The devil cannot be any uglier. I proceeded immediately to answer Hal's letter.

Saturday, February 18, 1860

A clear and pretty day overhead but very wet under foot. I studied all day. I am determined to be prepared for college by next September.

Sunday, February 19, 1860

Clear and pretty day. Read and studied all day.

Monday, February 20, 1860

Clear and cool. School. I forgot to say in yesterday's entry that Ma and the children returned.

Tuesday, February 21, 1860

Rained incessantly till about 4 o'clk when it partially cleared off. No school. The house in a continual uproar, the things having arrived last night.

Wednesday, February 22, 1860

Clear today. School. Nothing of any note has taken place today. I am reading a very humorous work called, *Maj. Jones's Courtship*. It will cure any one of the blues.

Thursday, February 23, 1860

Pretty and pleasant day. School. I finished Maj. J's C. this evening.

Friday, February 24, 1860

Weather same. School. My composition for this evening is a letter to Taylor.[26] I flatter him "powerfully." By the way, I got a letter from him last Mon. I answ'd it Thurs. or yesterday.

Saturday, February 25, 1860

A very pleasant day. I did not study any today but read the *Mysteries of Paris*[27] all day and have found it to be one of the best works I ever read.

Sunday, February 26, 1860

A beautiful day. Read until the time came for going to church, which I attended. Then I saw Miss Morgan of Ky. who I got acquainted with last November at Gen. McAllister's.[28] She is a blasted nice gall!

I was answering Lizzie's letter after dinner when Bug brought me a letter— it was from Hal and it brought bad news. It consisted of that gentle kind-hearted reproach which does not ruffle the feelings but makes them chaste and sorrowful. He dwelt tenderly upon my harsh letter to Nat on the 11th concerning my visit to his father's. I answered it this evening and enclosed a short letter to Nat, asking pardon for a *portion* of what I had said. I said that I should have asked for the young ladies, that I should not have been so harsh in my language towards him, that I was sorry it had occurred, but that what I had said in relation to not being asked in to supper I still said and firmly sustained my former sentiments. I really wish this embarrassing affair was over!

Fred came up and asked permission of Pa to be united to Diana by the "sacred ties of wedlock" tonight and was not refused but with these conditions: that she must be at her post as nurse at 10 o'clk every night and that on Saturday night she could repair to his "quarter," that if she did not conduct herself to suit him that she should go to the field and if she did not suit there that she would be sold. I think the thing is all a sham myself. Fred is one of the new negroes and heretofore has been a very good boy and is undoubtedly about four or five years younger than his intended.

Monday, February 27, 1860

The forenoon was clear but towards 3 o'clk clouds began to gather and at dusk while I was taking my walk it sprinkled rain. School. I still read at intervals at the M. of P. (i.e. every time I get a chance, which is only in the evening after coming from school). It gets more and more interesting. Pa went to town today. I sent for a blank book for my "Scrap Book" as I shall call it. I commenced three years ago to clip from the newspapers all witty and amusing pieces but in a short time relinquished it and only commenced it a few months back and have even now got a good little "file." By the time I am fifty years old (if I ever live that long) I will have an interesting book. I dreamed last night that I was <in a whorehouse>.[29]

Tuesday, February 28, 1860

Cool, raw, and rainy day—rained almost without ceasing til about four o'clk. No school. Remained in doors all day reading the *Mysteries of Paris*.

Wednesday, February 29, 1860

This day ends Feb. which has this year 29 days because this is leap year. I got two Valentines this month. One from a young man at Oxford Miss named Griffin and one from my dear old friend Hal Yerger. They are undoubtedly the greatest Valentines "you ever went a fishing with." This is a popular Oxford phrase.

Weather cool, cloudy and dark. School. We will take in at 8½ from tomorrow on. I got a letter from Hal this evening in answer to mine of the 17th inst. Nat, Hal, and myself carry on a double correspondence. The way it commenced was by their writing to me after having written once and shortly after receiving the first and answering it I receive their second and immediately answered it and they do the same thing. We agreed to answer each others letters as soon as we get them and by that means we keep up our (very pleasant to me at least) correspondence.

I received the shocking news of the death of Yerger Shall, a friend of mine and very intelligent one of between 14 and 15 years of age. He was attacked by congestion of the brain and inflammation of the spine and died in a stupor last Monday night. I sincerely pity his afflicted family! Other deaths have occurred lately in that unfortunate family.

Thursday, March 1, 1860
Beautiful and pleasant day. School. Read after coming from school.

Friday, March 2, 1860
Warm, clear, and pleasant day. School. I recited a speech of —— called Burr and Blennerhassett. Oh! I wish I could make a speech like that one.

Saturday, March 3, 1860
Pleasant and clear in the morning but towards night it got cloudier and cloudier and while I was taking my walk a little drizzle came up. I have been in doors all day reading that charming book, the "Mysteries of Paris." It is almost as charming as the ladies who are of all charming things the most charming. To these secret pages I will confess that to me they seem more like Gods than humans, combining all good qualities. So sweet, so gentle, so lovely in appearance, and as to purity of heart, they are unexceptionable. All virtue, purity, and chastity. But to this rule if so it may be called there are many exceptions, many exceptions, many, oh, very many! I said that to me they *seemed* to be Gods &c. Many things seem to be that in reality do not exist.

This a secret I confide to my beloved journal. This is an incident which took place in Virginia last summer. It was a beautiful, calm morning last August, an August morning peculiar to the mountains. It was at Uncle Findlay's, in the vicinity of Abingdon, Washington County, Va. in his place. < . . . . >[30] had that morning introduced me to a Miss <Cosby>, a daughter of Mr. <Cosby> a <Methodist preacher>.[31] We took a walk on the hill back of the house which was covered with forest trees. I, like all other boys at sixteen who are introduced to a pretty little damsel with long raven curls floating over her snowy neck, with a dimpled pair of downy cheeks who looked like they had stolen their color from the roses, with large dreamy eyes as black as they were sparkling and "to crown the enchantment" a pair of corral little lips, I, as a very pleasant as well as practical research commenced talking of love and unmercifully flattering the poor inexperienced girl. I never once thought she would believe the first word of it and continued (while my Cousin strolled on) to pour spontaneously into her ear as she leaned on my arm my protestations of devotion, love, and disinterestedness. Her beauty captivated me (but for the time only) that is exhilarating and animating me for it seemed that my tongue knew no bounds; my mouth was filled with flattery deceptions. We walked on; we approached further into the wood. I took within my own the hand that lay on my left arm and gently pressed it. Either from listlessness or wariness we seated ourselves upon an old log at the edge of the road. Still I kept up my avowals of devotion while I held the little dainty hand within my own. At last in my excitement and intoxication caused by her ravishing beauty and voluptuousness I pressed that hand to my beardless lips, next I put my arm around her waist. I imprinted on that downy cheek a kiss. She lent over on my bosom and our lips were sealed—kiss after kiss, as burning and as voluptuous and blissful followed each other. I became giddy with the intoxicating and alluring beauty of this sweet maiden. My sensations at that moment baffle description. As sudden as though I recovered myself, I listened to the soft whisperings of conscience—it said, "Will you dishonor this poor girl whom you have led on inch by inch to allow the liberties you are now taking? Will you condemn her to a life of misery, dishonor, and degradation, of shame and anguish for the gratification of a licentious and evil passion you yourself have aroused by improper liberties taken with this inexperienced and unsuspecting virgin whom you have beguiled by the machinations of your oily tongue and its base flatteries to allow them?" It acted like magic. I had her in my power but my conscience had me in its and after giving it a respectful audience I concluded for the sake of her honor and virtue and of my peace of mind and tranquility of conscience to obey its commands. I then very gently arose and as courteously offered her my arm and being joined soon after by my cousin, returned home with a much lighter heart and a much clearer conscience than if I had perpetrated the most detestable of crimes to which I was prompted by my evil genius.

Sunday, March 4, 1860

A warm and beautiful day. Mrs. Wm. Percy[32] stopped to see Ma (who has been sick since last night) and when the time arrived to attend church I proposed to accompany her as we both had to walk or at least choosed to walk. We had just emerged into the road when looking up the road we saw Miss Marian and Miss Dellie tripping along to "meeting" as the little sweet things can only trip. She insisted on my allowing her to go on while I awaited the "gahalls" and accompanied them to church (as I persist in calling it). At last I consented and took my seat on an old decayed stump before the gate and awaited their approach. When they came within a respectable distance, I arose, pulled off my right glove and having approached the little beauties warmly pressed their little hands which were to my regret—gloved. Miss Marian walked on before with Mrs. H. Rucks who accompanied them while Miss Dellie slackened her pace and as my old friend Taylor (Miss M's brother) would say "hung in" with her and had quite a pleasant time on the way to church.

They have just returned from Cuba whence they went on the 19th of last January after Mr. Bowen's party. They returned last Wednesday except Miss Ella Brown who is so charming, so fascinating, so accommodating and pleasant, who leapt on up the Mississippi Central R.R. Ah, she was a lady every inch of her!

After returning from church I read till dark.

Monday, March 5, 1860

Clear and pretty day. School. After coming from school I exerted myself to entertain Mrs. Carson and Estelle who came to see Pa on professional business.

After supper I walked back to the schoolhouse with Mr. Herbert who came to take supper with us. And oh what a delightful walk! The moon was shining so brightly that I for experiment took a scrap of paper from my pocket and tried to read which I did with little difficulty. It was all so calm, so tranquil, so reposing. The fresh breeze fanned my cheek gently, or rather my cheek was gently fanned by the quick walking. I observed. Not a murmur was heard; all was as silent as the tomb. After a while I walked slower, admiring wondrous nature. As I slowly and lonely sauntered along I thought of many happy incidents of my short life, of the giddy moments I had spent in the exciting dance, probably a Schottische when with my arm encircling the waist of some pretty girls, I went whirling and skipping so gayly around. I thought of Hal, Nat, and Taylor, and of many of our happy moments which are gone and past forever. I commenced singing "Home Sweet Home" when I got most home and seeing a negro boy coming along the road I ran after him to scare him and kept on to the gate and returned home and am now pleasantly engaged in writing in my journal but must go to my lessons for I have a long Ancient Geography to study for tomorrow.

Tuesday, March 6, 1860

A most beautiful day. Our [. . . .] begin to set in now and one of these has kept up a continual humming all day. School. Last month (the 17th) I wrote to the Presidents of the Universities of Virginia and North Carolina for a catalogue of their respective institutions and last night at 12 o'clk (I did not get

to bed till then) received one from Va. and am so much pleased with the arrangements &c. that as Pa seems to be of the same opinion I have not the least
doubt but that I shall attend it, probably next September. I know I shall if Pa
will consent. I wish I could have attended the military college at Nashville this
session and made myself proficient in drilling and tactics so that I might enter
the University of Va. next October or September and, it taking four years for
a thorough course, and I being then 17 years old would just graduate (in an
irregular course) when I am 21. I am going to do all in my power to get off
next Oct. Pa alleges as an excuse for my remaining at home another session
that it would be to my decided advantage for him to accompany me and see
me comfortably lodged and fixed and says that it will be very inconvenient
for him to leave the family there and that I can pursue the studies here that I
would pursue there. I contend that even if I should, I would not be able to avail
myself of the superior advantages at home that I would there and that knowing
that "time waits for no man" and as I have no great superfluency of it that the
sooner I am prepared and there, the better. Mr. Herbert (who being my teacher
and who ought to know if any one should) says that I am prepared *now*, and I
know that if that is the case I will be prepared by next October. And why waste
a year? Why should I remain at home when it is known that by next Oct. a
year, even by next Oct. Mr. H. will not be able to offer me the advantages held
out to me at an institution like the one of which I am speaking? Why compel
me to remain at college till I am 22 years old when, with the same ease, I can
graduate when 21 and thereby have one more year to devote to my profession?
Then why do this thing? Why make me throw a-way a year that might be much
more usefully occupied there than it can possibly be occupied here? I have to
put my shoulder to the wheel and why shrink from it? Why wait till the last
moment and then hurry and skimmer over the studies I would otherwise have
persued much more thoroughly? Am I not taught to believe that this is my
seed time? And if I waist this precious time for planting my crop and delay till
after a part of the season is gone and then plant hurriedly and lightly, will my
crop be as abundant, as rich, and as flourishing as the crop he who "takes time
by the forelock" and has all things done at the proper time and in the proper
order? No! I must have time, time—four years time to devote to the collegiate
course and without the four years I cannot come out with credit! And so long
as I will be prepared *thoroughly* next Oct I again ask, wherefore detain me?

Wednesday, March 7, 1860

Warm and clear day. School. After coming from school (which was at 5 o'clk)
I read in *Harper's Weekly* a novel published in it called *A Woman in White*,[33] a
very good thing.

Having practised my music lesson after supper I took a seat out on the porch (it being very pleasant) where Ma and Pa were, to converse on my anticipated departure for college. The stars being beautifully visible in the blue canopy and studies being the topic of conversation we touched deeply on Astronomy (not that we knew any thing about the science but about the advantages and disadvantages attending it if a man of business should study it). Pa contended that it was a useless expenditure of time for a man who intended studying law or any other profession. Ma contended that it was of considerable advantage as an accomplishment and as being a source of gratification to the person who studied it. For my part I have not the time to study it and will in consequence have to forego that pleasure. I do hope I will get off next September. Pa has voluntarily promised to let me take a trip (with him) to Richmond, Baltimore, and Washington when we go on (as he insists in seeing me comfortably lodged and fixed) for which I am very grateful. Oh! Have I not got a kind father? And he has promised to give me a watch when I go to college and that is one of the least of the inducements to incite me to study harder to be prepared sooner. He complains of my late hours, but I can't help it, I must have my lessons. I have a pretty tough time of it. Two music lessons a week. I do not get up as early as I ought, but this is my regular routine—at school at 9 o'clk, staying till 3¼ or 4. Read generally till dark when I take a walk, i.e. at sundown, return, eat supper, study my music an hour and study till 11 and 12, make an entry in this journal and go to bed.

Thursday, March 8, 1860

A day of varied weather, cloudy and warm in the morning, continued to get cooler and about 3 o'clk heavy, black clouds gathered in the north-west and from that direction came a cool, brisk wind, and before night it was raining hard. At 10 o'clk PM the "canopy of Heaven" was, with the exception of the stars, clear and blue, and the pale moon shone brightly and sparkled on the pools of water gathered in the yard.

School. On account of the stormy looking weather we were dismissed and did not say my Caesar or Grammar lesson. After coming home I read the *Mysteries of Paris* till dark.

Friday, March 9, 1860

According to my prediction before it stopped raining and when the wind was toward the north, we have had a clear and cool day—fires quite comfortable which have not been at all necessary for some time past. School. In accordance with my custom I took a walk this evening, starting just before sundown and returning at dusk. Going I (walking on this side of the creek) saw on the opposite side a lady also walking who I had not perceived till nearly opposite. I thought it was either Miss Marian or Miss Dellie but did not catch her eye though as I walked on rapidly I kept my eye on her even when I had gone so far as to have to partially look over my shoulder. She kept jumping over the little gullies on the edge of the bank (unintentionally showing a sweet pair of little feet and ancles). At last she came to me close to a stump by the edge of the bank, and just as she jumped it (I supposed wishing to know who I was) turned her face toward me, thinking my back turned. Our faces were perceived by each other, at least hers was perceived by me. She instantly turned around that pretty little head (I know it was pretty if it was either of the above named young ladies) and walked on briskly. I could not restrain my hilarity but burst out into a fit of boisterous laughter. It struck me forcibly that it was funny and of course if that was the case I laughed. It may not have appeared so to any other person, but it was done so nicely, she thinking, I suppose, that I was not looking and taking advantage of her body's being concealed by the stump, looked around—and was caught at it. I quickened my pace and walked on to my habitual point and quickly walked back to overtake her so that I could see if she went in at Judge Rucks's, which she did. At the time she entered the gate (I, being on this side of the Creek) she very naturally turned around in shutting it, with her face toward me. I, in a very military manner, touched with the back of my hand the rim of my hat, and immediately came home.

As soon as I arrived I presented to Pa my composition which was written on this subject: "Why is it I should not go to college?" It contained in sum and substance my entry of the 6th inst, expostulating warmly on the subject and winding up by supposing that they secretly retained an objection which was that they feared I should be led off "by bad examples and by the allurements of vice and debauchery." I added, "You shall never see me intoxicated, if it is the cup you fear. You may quiet then all your fears. I know too well the miseries of drunkenness and intemperance. I repeat it, you shall never see me intoxicated, no, never, never, never!" I came in after supper and asked their opinion of my composition for I had written it for the purpose of giving them an insight to my views of the case, though not in the least degree opposing anything they had said, but merely laid plainly before them what I thought of it. To my great joy I saw a sign greatly to my favor; it was that the only object they offered to throw in my way was their dislike to see me go alone, just as if I was as imbecile as a baby. They are too tender, too loving toward me! I cannot express my thanks, my feelings of gratitude for the love and tenderness! I think by a little persuading and reasoning (a great part of which I'll get Mr. Herbert to do for me) they will consent; and then, and then—I will go to college to return, a man!

Saturday, March 10, 1860

Pretty and pleasant day. In doors all day reading. Mr. Herbert took supper with us and the conversation drifted to my anticipated departure for College. Pa says I cannot go till I am perfectly proficient in English grammar (which I have never studied to any extent), Spelling, and Composition. I promised him that I would be ready in spite of every obstacle. Oh, there is no difficulty about my going.

Lately there has been a little feud between Maj. Percy, Amanda, and Louly of which I am very sorry indeed.

Sunday, March 11, 1860

A cool and pleasant breeze blew from the south all day—very clear and pleasant. There was quite a concourse at our little church today, which in attending I spent the morning. I read till about 4½ o'clk when I, with Ma and Uncle Jack, took a walk (Ma stopped at Dr. Percy's, we walked on) and coming back about halfway between here and Judge Rucks's bridge we met Miss Marian and Miss Dellie and at my suggestion we proposed accompanying them home—we did so. The honorable Judge (who is a model of kindness, justness, generosity, and hospitality, combining in one many most admirable qualities for which he is respected, esteemed, and loved by all who know him, as well as for his talents) met us at the door and courteously invited us in, which invitation we accepted thinking we would leave as soon as we had stayed a few minutes. When we arose to leave we were again asked to remain to supper, which also we did, I suppose being so happily situated in such exquisitely agreeable company and did not resist in the least when the old Judge said to us as he showed us into the library, "Gentlemen, you talk to the ladies while I go and smoke," (having asked us; of course, I refused).

We had a delightful time. Miss Marian asked me in her winning way to tell her a secret concerning Uncle Jack which I told her I would tell her. In reply I said if she would walk on the opposite side of the Creek (from this) that I would tell her from my side if she walked towards the Cunningham and in the evening. She did not seem to be satisfied and when I went to leave (when Uncle Jack had bid them "good night" and was out on the porch) she came into the passage and said playfully, "Tell it to me now"—Miss Dellie being in the room. I said, "Oh, Miss Marian, you don't want to know that secret." She said it so prettily that I was almost tempted to tell her the real secret as she lent over to me with her hand to her ear. I repeated my interrogation two or three times to gain time to invent something to tell her, fearing to tell her the real. She evidently seemed to believe that this was equivalent to a refusal and retreated into the room looking very reproachfully at me. I consoled her by telling her that the next time I saw her I would tell her. She seemd to be less displeased and as Uncle Jack has given me permission to tell I am going to take a ride with her before long and then tell her. I shall most certainly tell her for I love her so much—as a friend only for she is so kind and gentle, as generous as beautiful, as beautiful as intelligent! I shall tell her! I shall tell her!! I shall tell her!!!

Monday, March 12, 1860

A cloudy, cool, and comely day. School.

At Greenville a few days ago Mr. Byrne shot a young man named Jno. Chapman, formerly of Nashville and an acquaintance of Miss Ella's; the circumstances are these. B spoke to a gentleman walking through his store (having a pistol handy) saying, "Stop, let me shoot a hole through your hat." He refused, but C—— who was standing by said, "Shoot mine." Immediately B. raised the pistol and fired. C—— very good humouredly said, "You have shot me, sir." And raising his hat the blood trickled down his face. It is said that B. clasped him in his arms as if a brother. The ball struck near the roots of the hair on the forehead, glancing upward under the skin along the scull; though doing no serious harm, it was right dangerous. The ball was immediately extracted. Half an inch lower would have made him acquainted with some good company below in that warm region—as Caesar, Nero, Alexander, Domitian, Virgil, Cicero, etc. etc., Napoleon, Humboldt, Webster, Calhoun, Chatham, and many others. I suppose I will get acquainted with them some day.

I got a letter from both Hal and Nat this evening. Nat gives me quite a lecture on account of a very *plain* letter I wrote him on the 11th ult. and then forbids me to answer to that part of his letter. I told him at any rate that we would postpone the subject till we met and would confer upon it then as one is so liable to be misunderstood by writing. I answered this evening. I'm taking a walk this evening. I saw the "beauties" Miss Dellie and Miss Marian out riding. I have not been very well this evening. I would not be surprised if I had a little chill.

Tuesday, March 13, 1860

The wind keen from the north—clear. School. I contemplate in addition to my regular studies to take up English Grammar and one of the Readers which will greatly facilitate my reading, getting the lessons in the evening for at night I have my hands full till 10 o'clk when Ma makes me go to bed, to get a History (of Rome) or Classical geography lesson and a Latin Grammar lesson, with one hour devoted to my music which I wish (though I like it) that I had never commenced for I shall forget it all when I go to College, and it takes a good deal of time from my studies and reading.

In taking my walk this evening I met Miss Marian and Miss Dellie twice, going and coming. I also met Mrs. J. H. Yerger out walking. She is now in second mourning[34] for her departed and excellent husband. It is said that at the Montgomery White Sulphur Springs last summer that if she would have allowed she would have had many more beaux than Miss Marian. She is no ordinary woman either in intellect or looks. But it is a quarter past 10 o'clk now so off to bed.

Wednesday, March 14, 1860

Clear and pleasant day. School. Evening occupied in reading *Harper's Weekly*. Pa has decided to stop it on account of its abolition principles. I am very sorry for I think it is a most interesting paper.

I am sorry to record on these silent pages a fact, a lamentable fact. From injudicious treatment in my extreme youth toward my brother Jimmy has caused much, very much of the brotherly affection on his part to become extinguished. I regret it exceedingly but it is so. For the last four or five years, I have done everything in my power to bring about a complete reconciliation but to no effect. I do not think Jimmy has at all an amiable disposition. He is too contentious and disregardful of the feelings and opinions of others though he has a tender heart. Besides he is extremely negligent about most every thing—he has no order, no system about anything but *lies* everything down where he uses it. I think if we were separated from each other we would when we again met love as nature intended we should. This is one reason why I wish to go to College. Probably though much of this may be attributed to my faults, my eccentricities, and my love of order and system. Our natures are almost opposite in every respect. He is the star of the family—he surpasses the others as well as myself in fruit of mind. He can catch an idea quicker and forget it quicker than I can. Once I learn a thing it scarcely ever leaves me entirely. In conclusion, I sincerely hope that this coolness may soon be wholly obliterated from our memories.

Thursday, March 15, 1860

This is the season of the year when the atmosphere here is clogged with smoke from the innumerable logheaps burning in every field, and although the day may be clear the atmosphere assumes a bluish cast when there is not enough wind to carry it off. This has been a cool and cloudy day. The ground is being clothed in natural green robes and is casting off the dull colors of winter. Half of the day occupied at school. At 11 o'clk Mr. Herbert, having both the head and tooth ache, dismissed us and during the remainder of the day I was occupied in reading *Harper's Weekly*. Last night I got a letter from Hal and answered it immediately. I advised him to keep a journal. I told him of what incalculable advantage mine had been to me and is now, of the pleasure it might afford him (as I hope it will me) in some future day when in the winter of life he could read in its pages his boyhood's cares and joys. It is impossible for anyone to offer me an inducement to discontinue this one.

During my walk this evening I met again Miss Dellie and Miss Marian (I also met them yesterday evening) and this time they were walking. Yesterday I told them, or rather Miss Marian, as they rode horseback that I had gone down to tell her the secret but she was absent; but I was only taking a walk and said it to tease her. The first remark I made to her this evening (they were walking and as I told her that I had again gone down to tell her the secret for I met them just beyond the corner of the garden towards Judge Rucks's) was that I had again gone down to tell the secret ("ut super demonstravimus"[35]). She replied that I "always came at the wrong time." Then in a very excited manner with sparkling eyes, sparkling as her eyes only can sparkle, and in her excitement shook her little white finger at me said (when I refused to tell her there because Miss D. might hear it) "You have excited my curiosity and now you won't gratify it," and a host of smiles were on her lips, half reproachful, half-humorous, and her eyes sparkled with their usual brilliancy. I replied (for I had promised her more than once before to tell her the next time I met her), "There Miss Marian, you disbelieve me?" I do not recollect her reply. I added, "Miss Marian, I pledge you my word and honor that I shall soon call on you and will tell you then, I assure you." "Very well," she said, "I shall not let you forget it;" and seeing them "prepare to pucker" or more properly "to start," I made a most reverential bow and came on home laughing at the fun I had had out of one poor, little secret. I don't know why but it does me good "even down to my toe nails" to do them that way and see their impatience and their beautiful expecting eyes and smiling lips. Oh it is rich!

Friday, March 16, 1860

Smoky, windy, and cloudy day. Mr. H's indisposition continuing, we had no school, however I remained with him till after 11 o'clk. Balance of the day occupied with music and the interminable "Mysteries of Paris." It seems interminable to me for I have such a short time to devote to reading it. Soon after I was practicing, Mrs. Wm. Percy came in and by her exquisite performance on my piano lifted me into a land of sweet melodies and noises. She played many of the old and touching airs with the flowing variations—such as "Long, Long Weary Day," "The Last Rose of Summer," "Airs from the Child of the Regiment," "Airs from the Opera, Bride of Lammermoore" and others. The soft, flowing, swelling sound of the piano always throws me almost in a trance. Music has a most unaccountable power over me which is as enchanting as it is mysterious—particularly sweet, warbling singing (such as Miss Ella's).

At the supper table this evening the building of a Presbyterian Church out at Greenville was discussed, and Ma remarked that Mr. Wm. Percy had contributed to it. I said (probably I should not) that I believed that Churches did not make men do any better, that if they were going to be pious they would be so without Churches and Preachers. Ma vehemently condemned the idea, but I agree with pa. I believe that Preachers are no better than other men, that they ought to work like other men and not lay around all week and preach a sermon Sunday and get paid for their *Sabbath* labors while in those very sermons they condemn (and justly too) Sabbath labor. The sermons should be thrown in gratuitously, like Mr. Herbert's for instance; he preaches on Sunday and teaches school all week. And still they presume to come into a man's house and say what *must* and *must not* be done. They take their weekly rounds thus, and this is their employment during the week. I say d——n such employment! If I owned a house and any man was to invite himself to it (as is their custom) and grumble if I was not ready and down to prayers and to tell me what I must do and what I must not do I would show him the door, and if he did not avail himself of the invitation pretty quickly I should anchor my foot near the seat of his trousers and help him a little.

Saturday, March 17, 1860

Part of this warm day has been clear, part cloudy. Happily, I am nearly through the interminable "M. of P." I have read it all day.

About 11 o'clk, having promised myself that pleasure, I, as much for the purpose of fulfilling my promise as for making a most humiliating confession or rather apology to Miss Marian, sent a boy down with my card on which was written these words, "if it is agreeable to Miss Marian, Harry will call at 4 o'clk to ride." My answer was the following, "I am going up to Mrs. Yerger's Harry to spend the day, and I think it will be impossible for me to get back in time. I am *sorry* because I will miss both an agreeable ride and a secret.—M. Rucks." At once frank and passive, cool and decisive, lady-like and gentle. Still something stings—something tells me "she did not want to ride with you." But why? It is very probably that she wished to go to Mrs. Y's. And still I say something stings. Pretty late—11 o'clk and going to spend the day. I shall postpone, at least for a time, any proposals for riding.

Immediately on returning from my walk I was informed that I was invited down to a "storm" at Judge Rucks's. Accompanied by Uncle Jack, I went. Unfortunately, Miss Lee and Miss Wingate did not come and consequently two poor little women were overwhelmed with "beaux." We danced but two sets and I only one of these, acting as a lady. Pa, as I started, unexpectedly presented me with a bouquet to present to some of the "ga-halls." I gave it to Miss Marian as a secret recompence for her refusal to ride this evening. On account of the scarcity of ladies the thing was rather dull.

Sunday, March 18, 1860

Warm and cloudy day. Forenoon as usual occupied at our little "church." While the melodean sent forth its plaintive chants and I heard the familiar voices of those dear neighbors and friends who I had known all my life and who were associated with all the innocent pleasures of youth in extremis, I felt sad to think that in a few short months I would part with them almost forever, that I would be committed to a new life at College among strangers not knowing, not caring for me, and from that to the toils of perplexing business. But if these friends and neighbors were all, alas! they are not. My poor mother, my father! My beloved brothers and sister! Still it is a consolation to know that I will be missed and loved in my absence. True, my motto is "tum vivimis vivamus," but I do not mean but this that I shall lead a life of idle and selfish pleasures and prodigalities but that what I can afford consistently with my means I will not deny myself. But stop; I have more to say so enough now upon this score.

The balance of the day was occupied in reading *The Mysteries of Paris* which, with the exception of a few pages, I have finished. Ma, Uncle Jack, and myself took a walk up to Dr. Percy's and on account of coming with Louly I stayed till after supper. I was conversing with Dr. Leroy Percy[36] (a man of keen and solid intellect, well-cultivated by study and extensive reading) upon the mode of college life and &c. He informed me of a thing I had never thought of before, namely that when I first went boys who literally knew nothing would talk in my presence sumptuously of various sciences, using appellations and names which I knew nothing of and that after attending lectures for a short time and myself getting an insight to the affair could plainly see that they were only "gassing." He advised me to strike for the degree of AM. Would that I was prepared for that! But the time for such preparations is most unfortunately gone, never to return. It is with regret and pain that I look back upon the years of useless idleness spent and "frittered" away by not having school. I have never studied English Grammar. I can not analyze this sentence. But I am now determined to devote all my time in the evening to it instead of reading. I shall also scour my Spelling Book. The Catalogue of the University of Virginia says: *"As a due acquaintance with our own language is made indispensible to the attainment of even the inferior honors and degrees of the University, all candidates for degrees are subjected to an examination in order to test their qualifications in this respect."* I will here mention what I intend studying: French, Mathematics, a thorough course including Algebra, Geometry, Analytics and Descriptive, Chemistry, Surveying and Trigonometry, History (there is a school in which are given lectures on History as in every other class), Literature and Declamation and Composition (practices in the Literary Societies) and Law lectures from the commencement of the session in Oct. '63. My Latin will have one hour devoted to it each day and by this I will accomplish my object in studying it, viz. the derivation of the English.

Monday, March 19, 1860

Wind keen from the N. East—clear and cool. School. Mr. Herbert complains justly of my Grammatical deficiencies, but it cannot be helped without study, study which I have sorely neglected but which I am determined now to study diligently, both upon the Latin and English. It is the Latin he complains of. I have never studied the English but will devote all my spare time to it and Mathematics. I am now upon the eve of finishing the Arithmetic for the first time but will review thoroughly from the Rule of Three.

Last night after coming from Dr. Percy's I commenced a conference with Pa, lamenting that I was not prepared to take a Classical Course, but Pa says that it is much more useful to take a Scientific Course. I feel the want of early instruction exceedingly, but I must not repine; I must redouble my vigor and by diligent study make reparations. Pa knows best; he has experience. He thoroughly convinced me that Astronomy was of no use scarcely as an accomplishment by his hard common sense arguments; one of them was that with the exception of Professors that there was not one man out of 10,000 who really knew any thing about it. Nat is studying French, Greek, Latin, and Mathematics. Since January he has read through what is required in Caesar and is now in the second book on Virgil and has made way with arithmetic and is studying in the equations of the first degree Algebra. All I can say is that he has entirely outstripped me. I have not finished quite Caesar and am about to enter Algebra. In three months (give more than the real time) he has accomplished much more than it has taken me by pretty close study to accomplish in five. I believe it to be the most advantageous to make oneself perfect in what one does study than to take up many studies, skimmer over them and get the scurf and in reality know nothing—a mere smattering—no certainty—no solidity. We will see as I said to Pa last night who will *"come out of the big end of the horn,"* as the saying is.

A few minutes ago an Irishman who Pa has employed ditching kept me from devoting scarcely any of my time to my tomorrow's lessons. I had much fun with him—his dry chuckle—his pimply face and wincing eyes combined with his comical "brogue" made him quite amusing. He imagines he is splendidly educated, says he has studied Geometry, Trigonometry, Astronomy, &c. I asked him what was the large star that was in the west at this period of the year. He assumed a very contemplative mood, seeming to recall with assumed dignity Scientific facts. I seeing his perplexity substituted some Latin proper name and put it to him interrogatively, and he at once with great complacency said, "yes. Yes, that's it." In looking over my Sacred Geography lesson, I asked him if Syria was not one of the Apostles; he after meditating a moment very knowingly said yes. I was convulsed with laughter, having made some foolish remark for an excuse. He did not seem to suspect me. I asked him his opinion of several men (giving the names of cities and countries on the map before me) and to each one he with brazen complacency gave his opinion in varied terms. It was rich. I enjoy a good laugh, and he kept my sides literally shaking the whole time.

Tuesday, March 20, 1860

No alteration in the weather. School. After dismission this evening according to my promise to myself I took up the English Grammar and Arithmetic and studied till nearly sundown. I hope to commence Algebra by the 1st of April by studying in the evenings and Saturdays and Sundays.

Cousin Gus arrived here last night and in company with Uncle Jack went down to see Miss Marian immediately and they tell me they went again this evening and have made an engagement to go fishing with her tomorrow. Would it not be nice if she could make them keep the worms in their mouths? We three took a short walk this evening, and Uncle J. was carrying on in his usual dry way, keeping us laughing a good part of the time. He comically threw out his chest and said (we were talking of what a beautiful bride Miss Marian would make), "I would just 'squar' myself up long side in her and when the old Episcopal minister with his long white shirt on with the tail out of his pants hanging way down to his hoofs and asked me if I would have 'that thar 'oman' what had hole on her hand? I'd say 'yes, *sir*, me and thank yer too.'" He said it so quizzically that we had a hearty laugh over it. We got more serious after a while and talked soberly of marriage and married life. He (Uncle J.) remarked that for 16 or 18 months after one was married that he thought it a Paradise—that a young man who was in love with a woman imagined that it was all happiness to be where she was and to do nothing else but to "bask in her sunny smiles"—that he never thought of the responsibility resting upon a married man—that he never thought that in a short time he would have (as he phrased it) three or four snotty-nosed little brats around him—that all the charm and attraction would gradually wear off and that he would retire at her side at night with no sweet emotions. His words "ad hunc modum erant."[37] But on the contrary I should think that if two persons were joined together in the "sacred bonds of wedlock" ardently and devotedly loving each other, that the man instead of becoming indifferent to the charms of his wife would love her still as before, that instead of retiring at night at her side with cold "sang froid" he would fondly fold her to his throbbing bosom in rapturous ecstacies! That instead of thinking his children a burden and an annoyance, he would take pleasure in nursing, rearing, and guiding them in the way of the prudent, wise, and righteous, and that he would even still more love that wife because she was his, his, his only![38]

I have just heard through a note addressed to Pa by Mrs. Shall Yerger, who is uneasy about her little boy Campbell, who is unwell. The Judge is off on official business and is at home very little. Poor woman! She is sadly changed lately. Two sons whom she has watched over with a mother's love and tenderness have caused her to be cast down and dejected. I have seen them both under the influence of liquor. No doubt she has wept bitter tears for them—prayed for them with that fervor peculiar to mothers only. Her real hopes are in Hal who despised, happily, the taste of the demon. May she not be disappointed. Will *I* ever bring tears of shame and regret to *my* mother's eyes thus? *May my right arm perish when I raise the goblet to my lips and become intoxicated!* But Pa has just left, telling me to sleep in the room next to Ma's, and she has sent me word that it is bed time so I must go as it is about 11 o'clk.

Wednesday, March 21, 1860

It is near the "media diei," and I am writing here. I have just partly finished a letter for Sallie, one of Dr. Percy's servants. It seems that every negro in the county comes to me to write their letters, of love, of friendship, of matrimony, confiding to my care all secrets in relation to them.

Now I have invented or rather collected together an alphabet to write in my journal those things which, if that journal should ever be seen by others, that what I do write in them cannot be read without the key which I promise myself that no one shall ever have.[39]

My main motive <in writing> the <letter was> a <secret hope of scriggleing her soon. I hope to meet her walking tom. evening and appoint a rendezvous for the gratification of an evil passion—lust>.[40]

I am a scamp. I take advantage of the enthusiastic disposition of Mr. Morsheimer, my music teacher. When I do not know my lesson I will, just as I get through it, commence playing some lively air that pleases him, and, immediately I commence, he commences (in his love of music, he is almost a fanatic) to go tut-tut-tut with the time, and in that way I get him in a good humor. Then (I know his favorite musical authors) I commence an argument on the various disposition and habits, talents, compositions &c. of these authors and he will commence to a talk and will continue some time, forgetting or being in too good a humor to admonish me, and smilingly takes his departure.

I paste down here an interesting little tale:[41]

Can any thing be more humble and withal more strangely interesting than this little tail? To imagine one's self chained to the beloved one, the one who one so tenderly adores, to see her hanging, a "putrid mass, bruised, torn, mutilated, without a trace of humanity about it." And this terrible mass is the beloved one. No doubt that many occurrences of scarcely less brutality occurred during those days of tyranny and oppression. No tyrants here! May god bless my beloved country.[42]

As there was no school (on account of Mr. Herbert being unwell) I wish I had gone to the Bogue with Cousin Gus and Uncle Jack, who accompanied Miss Marian and Miss Dellie.

Uncle Jack and myself were this evening disputing whether Napoleon's personal courage and character was subject to reproach. I contended that it was to a considerable degree but at the same time acknowledging his genius. I consider the simple facts of his abandoning his freezing army in Russia, abdicating, and going to Elba, again equanimiously abandoning his devoted troops at Waterloo, his timorous and pusillanimous submission afterwards with 50,000 devoted troops at his back and his putting away Josephine. If he had either frozen with his soldiers in Russia, or died with them at Waterloo, his name would have been unsullied and untainted as a warrior. Why should he expect mercy from his most inveterate enemies? He was great in prosperity but small in adversity. I acknowledge his genius, his warlike qualities, but in point of moral courage, in point of personal character, of those generous and noble qualities, all that is admirable in man, he cannot compare with our Washington. No, he cannot, he falls as far short of ascending to that lofty pinnacle of poise, glory, as the earth falls short of Heaven!

Thursday, March 22, 1860

Warm, smoky, cloudy day. No school. Morning was occupied in practicing my music lesson, studying, and reading. I wrote some in my old journal A, 1858–9 this evening on the last two pages, concluding the party at Judge Rucks' on the 27th of December last where I courted Miss Dellie so quietly and boldly. The card on which the thing was written (for it was by writing on a card that I did it) I have stowed away in a recess of my dusty old trunk among a little collection of relics of a like nature, which I call "Relics of my boyhood's mirth, sorrow, and pleasure." Probably in my old age I shall look over these little boyish relics with as much pleasure as I contemplate by reading over these pages of my adored journal. Yes I have "taught my heart the way to prize," not my "home, sweet, home" but my—journal. I do not mean where I said I did not prize my home, that I really do not for it is quite contrary to my feelings. But I think that that sweet, touching, simple song Miss Ella used to sing, "The dearest spot to me on earth is home," which has these words:

> "The dearest spot on earth to me
> Is home, sweet home
> The fairy land I've longed to see
> Is home, sweet home."

Then my quotation:

> "I've taught my heart the way to prize
> My home, sweet home
> I've learned to look with lover's eyes
> On home, sweet home."

Not till one has heard combined with these lines Miss Ella's sweet, warbling voice, the piano's lingering, plaintive tones, sending forth a sad melancholy melody, can this simple piece of poetry be appreciated. And to "crown the enchantment of the scene" to see a beautiful woman singing it, to see her face saddened, to hear her voice tremble, to feel your heartstrings throb and vibrate with the gentle emotion awakened in one's bosom. It must be doubly touching to the homesick traveler far, far from home and friends to hear this melody, to feel these emotions.

But I have branched off. In compliance with a request of Cousin Gus's I accompanied him down to Judge Rucks's to ride with the young ladies. I had a pleasant ride with Miss Dellie. I do not know how Cousin G. enjoyed himself, but I do know that when we got back and were sitting in the parlor that my tongue went at the rate of 2.40.[43] Why I cannot tell, but it was so. I continued to talk and *laugh* most immoderately. I seemed to be in a perfect glee. Probably it was an intoxication from beholding two fair faces beaming with mature womanly purity. *Not polluted, not imbued in degradation, not stained by impious and vicious inchastity, but all purity, all virtue, fresh and blooming from the hands of God.* And to think, all these charms, all this unsullied virtue, all this blushing chastity 99 times out of 100 is sacrificed, all at the brutal altar of drunkenness and debauchery—that their tender arms must embrace this, that their luscious lips must kiss this, that their most gentle caresses are to be profusely lavished upon this, and in many cases, with what return? Indifference, brutal and vulgar epithets from a drunken husband who returns to her late at night from the houses of the drunken and pollution, who belches out volumes of oaths at her and who unmercifully brings upon her shame and humiliation. Poor woman. Varied are thy lots, varied are thy troubles!

Friday, March 23, 1860

I am, again, on account of there being no school seated in my old, dingy room half furnished and not yet cleaned up waiting here for what? We will see. I will commence by relating a little fragment of our rattling conversation in the parlor at Judge Rucks's last evening. Miss Marian was talking of my not telling her the secret. I went on at a terrible rate, saying that "I did not think you would do so, Miss M., after knowing that, not taking into consideration the pleasure I should enjoy in taking the ride with you. It was to accommodate you to have the honor of satisfying your curiosity, and to receive that cold, withering answer to my request." She looked puzzled and said, "But Harry I was engaged to dine at Judge Yerger's;[44] I could not help it. But you will tell me, won't you?" "I have not chance to tell you, Miss M.," I said, "if I should again offer to ride, I fear I should again be subjected to the humiliation of a refusal." Looking confused and slightly blushing, she said, with her head slightly inclined downward, she said, "You can make a chance." I laughed and answered, "Oh well! Then Miss M. suppose the chance is next Saturday evening. What time shall I call?" "Well, about 5 o'clk, I suppose." Yes, she said I *could* make a chance, and I at least *proposed* to make a chance. If it does not rain, I will at 5 o'clk tomorrow evening repair to the "old Judge's" and if she has not changed her mind and has not concluded to relinquish the "chance" of receiving the secret, or rather the *certainty* of receiving it, during the ride, I will both confide to her the secret and the humiliating apology of which "super demonstravumus."[45]

Last night I had two room-mates (as there was no other place for them to sleep)—two Irish-men who Pa had working for him about a year ago. The old one *seems* much pleased with me, and as Irishmen will complimented my face, growth, &c. very extravagantly. I laughed much at the old one, Matthew, an old comical-looking fellow. As they do most every thing, he took it as pleasantly. This morning before I had awakened he had gone into Ma's garden and coming back said many things in its favor while I was still lying in bed.

I see in the *Yazoo Democrat* an article headed, "Mystery of Kissing." I will select a few passages from it: "A kiss is a thing never to be forgotten." True. "It is as old as the creation and yet young and fresh as ever." I have one or more than one on *my* lips that feels as "fresh as ever" and as the writer of this article says, "It is a thing never to be forgotten." I agree with him; those that *I* have will never be forgotten. But again he says, truly (for I know from experience recorded in my third entry of this month, which I shall never forget): "But a kiss fairly electrifies you; it warms your blood and sets your heart to beating like a brass drum, and makes your eyes twinkle like stars on a frosty night." And still again: "The breeze as it passes kisses the rose," (I say then why not kiss the "buds" of womanhood as one passes?) "the pendant vine stoops down and hides with its tendrils its blushes as it kisses the limpid stream that waits in the eddy to meet it and raises its tiny waves like anxious lips to meet it." Once more: "There is the kiss of welcome, and of parting" (here I alter a little): "the downy, lingering, stolen, marital kiss of love, of joy, of sorrow; the seal of promise, the reception of fulfillment." Must not, then, this "reception of fulfillment" be of most exquisite and transcendent blissfulness?

A strange feeling has just passed over me. I can't tell why but I have a presentiment (which is as painful as repugnant) *that I will not go to the University of Virginia next September*. I am going immediately to studying.

Instead of studying as I had intended and as I should, I idled away the evening skimming over *The Arabian Nights*[46] and listening to a contrived discussion between Uncle Jack and Cousin Gus on the merits and demerits of the Episcopal and Methodist Churches. After supper all of us were sitting in the parlor and Ma announced the death of an old Grand Uncle of mine who is upward considerably of 80 and his wife is also over 80 and it is said that she does not look like a human.

We were talking of religion, and I remarked that we had no proof of the authenticity of the Bible, and we knew not but that it was an impious imposition, that it may have been changed by the Monks during the Dark Ages, that they might have transposed and added and subtracted from it as suited them, for it is known that the Roman Catholics rejected that part which did not serve to their doctrine. But this is a theory only—doubts of a wavering and fickle youth. But I cannot help thinking. Predestination is a question which has often caused conflicts in my mind. And again, I cannot help thinking that if the Almighty really wishes to save us, if he can see into all futurity, if he knows that we are going headlong to ruin, why does he not save us? We are to believe he can, and if he wants to save us, I say why does he allow so many temptations to be thrown in our way; when still he knows our depravity and weakness, I repeat it, why don't he save us?

And another thing. What am I taught that God is? A man like us? A spirit? Or what? Does not the book say that Moses "saw his hinder parts"? that (substantially) no man shall see his *face*? that if he does that he shall surely die? Does it not say that the Savior was God, that they were one and the same? Does he not speak of seeing the *face* of his "father in heaven?" Do we not pray to God for the sake of the Son? And while the Son is the Father and the Father the Son, and while they [are] both God, one, and one, why pray to one God for the sake of another? We pray to the "father, Son, and Holy Ghost." Do these three constitute the Deity? Thus, why pray to one God to appease the Anger of another? If they are one only, pray to one. Does the book not say that we must "swear not at all but by heaven (I believe it is this: I only give the substance of my citations of those passages that bear upon my point) for it is the Lord's throne, not by the earth, for it is his *foot*stool.

It is a mysterious thing. I believe that every one should examine the thing themselves, for it concerns themselves *directly*. I sometimes think that it is best to be ignorant in toto, for it is said that he who knows little, little shall be demanded. It seems to be an impenetrable, fathomless mystery—that we are in an awful darkness, surrounded on all sides by immense cliffs, from the top glimmers a faint ray of light and the higher we ascend the sheer cliffs, the deeper seems the darkness and ignorance by which we are surrounded.

Saturday, March 24, 1860

Last evening (I forgot to mention the weather in my excitement—I am easily excited) was cloudy and rainy, as well as cool, morning cloudy and warm. There was no school. According to my prediction we have had a clear, cool, bright morning. I took my music lesson first and while Jimmy and Louly were taking theirs wrote a very incoherent letter to Hal, stating the outlines of my "Miss Marian Affair," and of the storm at Judge Rucks's. I could have said much about a "fuss" at Oxford where a boy, or rather young gentleman, was expelled on the testimony of a Negro rejecting what *he* said. I think that it will offer me a broad field for indicting Hal and Nat to accompany me in my projected and prolonged visit to the University of Virginia. I would see the University of this State (which is at Oxford, and where the young man was expelled) sink so low in that place (where if you take one of its occupants out and place him in a "fiery furnace" heated seven times hotter than it could be heated, he would freeze to death in a second, that if a pigeon were to fly in that direction at the rate of 140 miles an hour, he would not reach it in a month) before I would now attend it, because I would be liable to be treated in the same manner.

Here is the copy of a quotation from the *Woman in White* which I copied on a card last Jan., when I could with sincerity have repeated it with a full consciousness that it was my sentiments. "I loved her. Ah! How well do I know all the sadness and all the mockery that is contained in these three words. I can sigh over this mournful confession with the tenderest hearted woman who reads it and pities me. I can laugh at it as bitterly as the hardest man who tosses it aside in contempt. I loved her! Feel for me or despise me. I confess it with the same resolution to own the truth."

"Lulled by the siren song that my own heart sings to me, with eyes shut to all sight, and ears closed to all sounds of danger, I drifted nearer and nearer to the fatal rocks."

In this one passage there is something at once simple, plaintive, and melancholy that touches my heart, for even now that passage words my feelings. I can now, without the least hypocrisy, repeat those lines. They make me sad because I have loved as a boy of sixteen can love only—without foresight, without anything but love. They look not at station, neither at gold, but solely at the woman—her beauty, her charms, her fascinations, are all they see, all they love. It engages their being. With a blind confidence reposing in the balmy influence of the subject of their love, listening to the "siren song that their own hearts sing to them" they smilingly glide on, revelling in the "sunny smiles" of this love, quietly sipping the sweet and voluptuous ecstacies of this love, while the azure canopy of heaven, as it were, glitters with many brilliant stars of hope until the pitchy clouds of reality sweep over the enchanting scene and the dreaming youth is awakened from his trance.

Bill called about 3 o'clk, just as Miss Marian and Miss Dellie left. *They* came while we were eating dinner and when they were announced Cousin Gus laid down every thing and "struck a B" line for the parlor. I did not leave the table so precipitately, but, as a good dinner is no usual thing to a schoolboy, I chose rather to finish my repast first. I went in and jabbered at them, or rather Miss Marian, till they departed. Cousin Gus was talking to Miss Marian too, but for some unaccountable reason suddenly jumped up as is often his custom and went over where Uncle Jack and Miss Dellie were. Miss Marian blushed and tried to talk on but looked a little confused. As they were about to get into the carriage, having passed through the door out on the gallery, I walked down the steps to open the door of the carriage, let down the steps to help them in, which I did. All three of us went into the parlor. Uncle J. threw himself back in a rocking chair and seemed to contemplate something very assiduously. Cousin Gus asked him what he was thinking about so hard, and he replyed that he was just thinking "how Harry done about helping the ladies into the carriage—he went right down *before* me." I was so mad it was all I could do to hold in by choking the words down. I was full—I felt my blood boil. I was not particularly pleased with Uncle J. and the tone and manner in which he said it made me, as it would any one else, mad. For a moment I only looked at him as contemptuously as I could and said, "The steps were not down sir, the door was not open, and I saw no impropriety in helping the ladies into the carriage. So far as helping them in is concerned, I cared nothing about it further than to observe due respect to their sex."

What exasperated me more was that he had been to Dr. Percy's and was to a certain degree intoxicated. At a future time I will say more upon this subject.

In compliance with my engagement with Miss Marian to ride this evening, I went at 4 o'clk. As they rode off I asked if it was too cool to ride. She said, "no" and that I "must come up earlier than usual," which I did. I did not wait long before she made her appearance. While standing in the Hall waiting for her horse to come to the steps she asked me (no, it was in the Library that she did it, before I came out) if I had any objection to going down toward Maj. Lee's and stopping in. I felt a little confused but complied and so we went. We had on the way a good laugh at my dog Sam (who goes with me every where I go, to parties, fish fries, dances, church, school, to see the "golls" and best of all, hunting). He had a Cackle Bur in his hind foot and ran along and kicked up very ludicrously.

As I went in Miss Kate appeared at the door. I very coolly said with much formality, "Good evening, Miss Lee" and walked in.

During our return I told Miss M. the secret. And bringing a remark she made to me last spring to her memory which was that she "did not like the attentions of boys." She frankly acknowledged it and as frankly said that she preferred that of grown gentlemen—but still liked to have the boys to pay her attentions. Though she would not slight a boy for a grown man, she did not like their attentions to such a degree that they would become tiresome. It was a little piquant, but I in plain terms told her that I very much admired the independence she displayed.

Before we got back I made the humiliating confession of which I have before spoken. I told her simply my motive for writing the poetry in the first place, that when attacked by all three—her, A.C., and Miss Junie on the 15th Jan.—that I did *not* deny it but only evaded it to them but when *she* asked me I told a black falsehood at the time, intending to undeceive her at the shortest period and hoped that after having had my conscience to reproach me for such a long time, that after being subjected to taunts of self-reproach that she would forgive me. Like an angel she did not only forgive me but said she could "see clearly the embarrassing position in which I was placed." I felt so happy, so much lighter at heart, that I believe I should have kissed her hand if I had been sitting by her, but as it was there was no chance. As we rode in at the gate, I again spoke of my gratitude, and she said that she thought that my "humiliating apology" as I called it was made with considerable credit to myself. Our arrival stopped further remarks upon the subject. Being invited to take tea I did so—what occurred before I retired I will tell in my next entry.

Sunday, March 25, 1860

Pretty and cool day. Uncle Jack and myself went up to the schoolhouse but there being no church we returned. Read some during the balance of the day and played marbles. In the latter part of the evening while walking among five of the lady neighbors was Miss Marian and Miss Dellie. I mended a whip Miss Marian broke yesterday evening and told her that she would have to answer for that sin. After coming from the garden I commenced my walk but meeting Uncle Jack and Bill who had called on the ladies at Maj. Lee's got into the buggy and rode back.

Now for what occurred after tea at the old Judge's last night. I had expected Uncle Jack and Cousin Gus down and told the young ladies and when they walked into the parlor after supper I, having stopped and talked with Mrs. Yerger in the library about music, went in, intending to stay only till they came. Their arrival soon took place and after chatting awhile (one of our most [. . .] subjects was this—it was stated by Uncle J. in his usual droll way that he had heard of a doctor near Philadelphia who was able to raise 1200 lbs. of stone and who could catch himself by the coat collar and hold himself out at arm's length) when the cards were brought into acquisition. I, not wishing to play, amused myself looking at them awhile, and then went into the Judge's room and he gave me some wholesome advise, advise that I shall never forget.

Monday, March 26, 1860

Cool, clear day. No school, and am *very sorry* of it. Very little reading or studying done today, at least till now, 4 o'clk. I must put on a clean shirt (a fellow is dressed when he has on a clean shirt) and on my way walking take in the whip to Miss Marian.

I called in to give the whip to a servant at the door and rapped lightly three different times—waited a few minutes—no one came. A deathly silence pervaded the premises. Three more times did I knock and wait 5 or 7 minutes—no one came. I heard a servant walk across the hall and just as he entered the Library I again knocked, hoping to arrest his course, but failed. Waited a few more minutes thinking that I would have to lay the whip (and a book, the *Georgia Scenes*[47] which I brought down for Miss M. to read as it was amusing) on a chair and depart but concluded to try a fourth time, which I did and at last succeed in being invited in. I said to the girl who "opened unto me" that to "give these to Miss Marian" and turning on my heel stalked out and over the bridge on my walk as proudly as a millionaire. I think that on this occasion I persued the advise of the old addage, "try, try again." Not more than 400 yards beyond the bridge I met the carriage in which I saw Mrs. Yerger and if I am not mistaken two other ladies which I supposed to be the young ladies for I do not see who else would be riding out with her. This accounts for the inattention and silence of the house. Just above the gin at the Judge's part of a drift was on fire in the Creek and looked beautifully as I returned while it was dark. I read the *History of the United States*[48] part of the evening.

Tuesday, March 27, 1860

It is now morning—and through my devotion to this book I am writing in it instead of improving myself by reading or *preparing* myself for studying; and before I proceed to do either I will at least record a short and most pleasant dream (*would to God that it had been real*) that I dreamed this morning. I had awakened I think about day-dawn and again fell to sleep. All at once, I cannot tell why (I suppose it must be attributed to the impenetrable mystery of dreams) I ascended a narrow and winding staircase and suddenly entered a room as I thought neatly but plainly furnished. Strange. I thought that there I met some *cousin* and that Ma also was there, that there were a good many children in the room. After saluting them all I lastly turned my eyes to a setter near the door I had entered and there saw Miss Ella Brown—saw *children* on her knee which she was caressing and with whom she was playing. I caught her hand as soon as I saw her and pressed it softly. She smiled. Yes, she smiled the same old sunny smile of yore, and the same wavy brown locks were gracefully laid across that noble brow, the same sparkling brilliancy glittered in her eyes as fascinatingly as ever, but those lips had lost their nectarine softness and are no longer rosy and moist, those once pink and dimpled cheeks! They are now sallow and emaciated; no longer do they look plump and downy. It is gone. A hollowness seemed to have supplanted the dimpled plumpness, and that sallowness was appalling. Nothing remained of former days but the hair and eyes. She smiled but it was not the smile of old, only the [. . . .].[49] I tried to speak. I could not. Something seemed to oppress me. I was suddenly awakened to consciousness by a vigorous shaking from the hands of a negro boy. I *was* awakened from a dream—one which was strangely mingled with pleasure for the *meeting*, with sorrow for the *changing*. It was *so* real. My little brother was, in company with the little negro, laughing and playing with my faithful dog Sam who had slept at the head of my bed in a blanket which I had spread there for him. Notwithstanding the keenness of the air, I raised myself in bed, rubbing my eyes, but soon fell back upon my pillow with strange thoughts. In a few minutes I arose, thinking: while adjusting my apparel I was still thinking and when having finished I raised my feet up to the mantle, still thinking; and only dispelled my wild conjectures by perusing Cooper's *Spy*[50] till breakfast.

Practised, read, and "done nothing generally" in the morning. Read some in the evening and had got ready to visit Mr. Herbert who is sick at Dr. Taylor's, i.e. at the time I started. Seeing a vehicle at the schoolhouse stopped and found Mr. Mosby with him there; and little before sundown went back home and ate supper, after which I walked back accompanied by Sam to remain all night with him. I brought my journal and a *Harper* to while away the lonely hours. The old man now seems a little better though he is right sick. He has piles, inflammation of the bladder, and rheumatism. I compel myself, assisted by a negro boy of his, to attend him with servile assiduity.

Now it is near midnight. Sam is crouched at my feet—the negro boy sits by the jam of the fireplace with his head hung down, and except the crackling of the wood fire and occasional moans from Mr. Herbert, all is still and dismal. My thoughts are as dismal as the silence because this evening I received appalling news. I was out in the yard playing and romping, as though I was again twelve, with Sam, and hearing that Pa had returned from town and thinking there was a letter for me I laughingly ran to him to be disappointed. Would that this was all. Pa informed us that at Mr. Lemley's in New Orleans an Uncle of mine by marriage, a complimentary dinner party was given to a young gentleman of his acquaintance. From what I can hear there are two negroes implicated with having injected Arsenic into a certain dish of which all the company ate except one young lady and consequently all were poisoned. The names of the two negroes are Harry and Ann. The latter for some time previous had been impertinent and unruly. Her son was to be sold on account of his vagrant habits and this was supposed to be a cause of the crime. She also had been chastised and had made the remark that "This will be the dearest whipping you ever gave." It was. The boy was seen stirring the dish that had the poison in it by Mrs. McKee. He denies having had any thing to do with it. They are both in custody. The way it was ascertained that it was in a certain dish was that the dish which the boy was seen stirring was sent over to Mrs. McKee, who was not at the table, and she was not expected to live. She made a dying statement. It is reported that the whole family are grievously sick, and that both little Emma and Willie, two of the only three children of my widowed Aunt Lousie, are dead and the other is very sick as well as herself. Poor woman! Her grief must be insupportable. And she loved them so devotedly. But I believe that for *them*, it is best that they should have gone for they have no more troubles. They were of Loulie's and Pet's sizes. Yes, their troubles are over. One of Mr. Lemley's daughters is expected to die. I do not know which — Lou or Julie. When it was announced Ma seemed to be thunderstruck. For some time she only stared at Pa with dry and hard eyes, not saying a word. Then she commenced shedding them and with her the children. All sobbing and crying. I sorely felt for the grown people but thought it was well for the children.

Having made the preceding entry at about midnight or earlier, I composed myself as well as possible in an old straight-backed rocking-chair and fell into a disturbed sleep, at irregular intervals being awakened by Mr. H. or his boy, as ugly a negro as I ever saw. His mouth was unusually prominent and his lips were of a blackish blue, his high, projecting cheek-bones were like barricades almost to his rat-like eyes. His forehead retreated suddenly from his eyebrows and was very narrow and to complete his grotesque figure his [. . .]-like cranium was covered with black, notty tufts of wool, which seemed as much a stranger to combs as his scaly neck seemed to waters. Such was my companion for the night.

At 3 o'clk this morning I was aroused by Mr. H's moving from the bed to the fireplace. Not feeling inclined to sleep, I procured a piece of paper and wrote to Lizzie. When I finished the day was breaking, and at 4 I took my departure through the cold, keen air. Sam, my dog, having stayed with me through the night, accompanied me home. Read till breakfast and took my music lesson soon after when I went into Ma's room to find both her and Mrs. Walker Percy[51] in tears — for the misfortunes of others. Notwithstanding Ma's usual fortitude she seems to have given away under grief. I believe that the sooner such things are forgotten the better for grief cannot remedy them but only depresses the spirit and emaciates the body.

While I write it is 11 o'clk AM and I have just heard that Mr. H. is worse and have seen Dr. Mears go by to the schoolhouse. I shall go up to see him after dinner; God speed his recovery!

Jimmy has just told me that Ma has determined to send either Uncle Jack or myself down to N.O. after her. I wish she would send me. Oh, I do!

FAMILY HISTORY

My great-grandfather, John Dixon, emigrated from England some time before the Revolution and having settled on the —— River in —— County Virginia was enrolled as one of the defenders of his country's rights. His residence was upon an island in this river. A Captain John Dixon is spoken of as being in Gen. Green's army during his command in the South in the history of his life by Simms.[52] I am not certain whether the name "John" is mentioned or not. Would that I had the proofs to this conjecture. If I mistake not a Capt. Dixon is mentioned in Graham's life of Morgan[53] as well as in Irving's life of Washington.[54] I have the proofs that he was fighting for his country, a soldier or officer, he fought. That makes my heart leap with pride. The circumstances attending his death are not known to me.

During his absence from home while in the army, he left his large estate to the care of an old and infirm Uncle who took care of the children. Whether his wife was dead or whether she was living at the time and was on the place is not known.

This offspring was three sons; the second of them was my Grandfather, Henry St. John Dixon. One of the two remaining died heirless and the other moved to Richmond, Virginia where his decedents now reside. Henry St. John, having made himself a lawyer, removed to Abingdon, Washington County, Virginia, where he married a woman of a pure "old English" descent, Miss Bodicia White, who was among the first families of the place which is noted for its high toned customs and manners. She was of a wealthy family, her father was a man of capricious disposition and gave her nothing. The young and independent lawyer lived a happy life with his beloved wife, and both reached a "good old age." They were blessed with three sons, Henry Oswald, Richard Laurence, and Leonidas Virginus. But I anticipate. Let me carry myself back to the time of the Revolution.

My Great grandfather, John Dixon, had at the place of his residence on the —— River in the —— County large landed estates and many cattle and was considered and recognized as being one of the first men in his community. While absent at war with the enemies of his country's freedom "ut super demonstravimus," he left an old Uncle in charge of the place. While this old Uncle was on the place, a body of British foragers stopped and supplyed themselves with every necessary quality of provisions and offered pay to the old gentleman but was refused with indignation. He pressed them to take their *booty* and leave immediately, and notwithstanding they threw the gold upon the floor as true men should do and departed. A short while afterward a marauding band of Tories came and sacked the whole place. Not willing to wait till the doors and drawers were opened, they busted them open marking their cause by havoc among the furniture. They relieved the stables of its burdens of grain and its horses, such as suited their convenience, and having slaughtered the cattle and packed their train with the flesh and provisions, they drove the remainder into a small lot and fired in upon them, wounding and killing the poor brutes horribly for mere destruction. They either ran off or carried with them every negro and proceeded to burn the house and the torch was being applied to the building when the old gentleman (the Uncle) recognized in the leader of the band an old schoolmate and asked proudly even in misfortune for the words tell me so, no doubt with the most bitter irony, "Do I deserve this from an old schoolmate?" No doubt the vagabond felt humiliated for he immediately ordered the flames to be extinguished and fled with his booty and plunder, leaving the place a scene of desolation and ruin. Words are incapable of expressing my abhorance of such malicious and wanton depravity of heart, such blackness, such perfidy.

But to return to my grandfather who had, at the time I left him in this little history of family events, three sons. The second, Richard Laurence, is my beloved father. The eldest married and moved to Jackson, Miss, and there settled as well as the two younger. Richard Laurence, on the 20th day of April, AD 1837, then being in his 21st year, married Julia Rebecca Phillips of Jackson Miss., daughter of Judge James and Sarah Phillips. My Grandfather, when my father was 13 years of age, was compelled to take him from school on account of his embarrassments, pecuniarily, thus leaving him with an imperfect education except in Latin Classics. Having, by hard labor, accumulated the sum of $75 in Abingdon, Va., my father in addition to this had only a horse and therewith started by land to this country. So close was he compelled to be with his small sum that he only ate Ginger-bread and drank water from any spring which happened to be at hand, having his horse bet regularly. He was then 17 years old. He arrived at Jackson with only $20 in his pocket and worked in a law office merely to procure a reputation of being attentive to business and to learn the profession of being clerk. For some time his wages were only his expenses, but his employer seeing him studious and attentive to his occupation began to remunerate and at the end of a year he became clerk of the Chancery Court. He remained in this occupation till 1847 when he moved up to this place on which he now lives.

I was born 2nd day of August at 8½ AM, 1843. Before myself two others were born but were either delivered dead or died soon after, receiving no names. Since then the family has increased to eight now living, one only being a girl. In 1855 my mother gave birth to twins—a boy and a girl—the girl named for my grandmother Phillips was called Sarah but died 8 days after birth.

My grandfather Dixon was married in 1804, having been born in 1773, soon after the dispute commenced with the mother country. He, having been oppressed still more by his pecuniary embarrassments, sold his place near Abingdon, and removed to Jackson and took up his abode at my father's house at Jackson with his wife, now both old and gray. Still he was erect as though but 25. In 1846 on the 15th day of November he died at my father's residence, after a couple of years of the most agonizing tortures from a cancer on his ear; during his illness he suffered death many times. Death was a remission of his sufferings—it was a blessing to him. He survived his wife but a short time, she having died on the 15th day of September, 1844, also at my father's.

Leonidus Virginius practiced law in Jackson till December 1857 when he removed to Memphis Tenn., where he now practices law and has seven girls and one boy. Henry Oswald is heirless—his wife is barren. From my mother's "side of the house" I inherit my Scotch-Irish blood and my temper, while from my father's I get my love of system, order, and regularity.

Her grandfather, my great-grandfather, resided near Savannah in Georgia during the Revolution and was a staunch Whig. Being too old to take the field, he did all in his power with his tongue. The country was overrun and devastated by Tories. He was known far through the country for his Whig principals and was consequently watched by them. His wife was much younger or it might have been his daughter, my mother's mother, who attended the old man. During the summer months he was accustommed to take a blanket and repose on it in the shade near a spring in the woods near by, every day. The Tories found it out and were on their way on a certain occasion to murder him while asleep when they were met by this young woman, either his wife or daughter, his daughter I am inclined to think*,[55] seeing them persuing the direction to the house, begged them to spare him. She was on her way to mill. They promised to do so. On returning she found his lifeless corpse covered with gore on his blanket near the spring in its usual place, having been riddled with bullets.

My grand-mother Phillips did not long survive her faithful consort. He dying on the 11th August, 1838, she, 30th November, 1843.

This is the plain history of my progenitors as far back as I have any light, and I am the oldest male child having the name of Dixon, i.e. of the descendants of the three sons of Harry St. John Dixon, my grandfather, and consequently inherit the Coat of Arms of my family. I am in favor of keeping up these old customs. If it does no good it certainly does no harm. It is a Lion standing on his haunches holding a ball in one paw, and of the African species. When I get the money I will have me a seal made and in it carved this emblem of ancient customs. It can be ascertained at Richmond what the motto is. I shall do it when I go on with Pa in '61. Read some and went down to see Mr. Herbert this evening.

Thursday, March 29, 1860

Warm, windy day. This day two years ago I commenced my Journal, though its birth is dated from the 1st of the preceding January. As to what I did from that time up to the 29th Mch '58, I was unable to record and till 1st July the same year, I thought only to make a *School* Journal of it and in consequence only made entries for the school days, but in July commenced my entries on Sat. and Sun. It was kept up without intermission until the first part of July '59 when I went to Virginia and becoming negligent from travelling about in the country from place to place, I lost my little book in which I made my entries, and then totally abandoned it till I got home here last October. During the Christmas holidays it was neglected on account of there being frequent parties and dances and Hal being on the Creek (having come back from Oxford) as well as half a doz. young ladies, but taking a new start of the 1st of last January I have faithfully attended to it since and resolve to neglect it no more.

In my old Journal I commenced copying an article from *Harper's Weekly*, headed the "Last Arctic Expedition"[56] and will resume it and paste a fac similie of a document found by one of the last explorers on one of the last pages of my old Journal.

Quotation from the "Last Arctic Expedition," resumed:

In 1853 four expeditions were dispatched to the same region: 1. Mr. Grinnell and other Americans sent Dr. Kane in the *Advance*. He struck out a new path for himself; instead of turning into Lancaster Sound he sailed due north as far as he could, then, abandoning his ship, pushed on with sledges and on foot as far as 82° 27' N. lat., by far the most northerly point ever reached. He is believed to have discovered the "open Polar Sea" with which Kane's name will ever be connected. His party endured hardships barely describable. The thermometer during part of their journey was 99° below zero, but they found no traces of Franklin. 2. Lady Franklin dispatched the *Rattlesnake* and *Isabel* by Behring's Strait. Their effort was mainly to rescue Capt. McClure, about whose fate grave apprehension was felt. They achieved nothing. 3. The *Lady Franklin* and *Phoenix* were sent by the British Government to support Sir. E. Belcher, who, when he abandoned his own vessels, returned in them. 4. Dr. Rae set out by land once more to re-explore Boothia. Of all the expeditions this was the only one which yielded fruit. He reached the southern termination of Prince Regent's Inlet and there met Esquimaux, who stated that in the year 1850 they had seen forty white men on King William's Land dragging a boat southward. They appeared to be starving; they were led by a stout officer who had a telescope slung around his neck; they had guns and ammunition but appeared to be very weak. The same Esquimaux stated that they had seen thirty corpses on the continent and some graves. Dr. Rae discovered among the Esquimaux watches, guns, telescopes, silver, etc., in considerable quantities.

"The return of Dr. Rae with this report was generally considered to have settled the fate of the Franklin Expedition, especially as some of the relics which he had brought with him were identified as belonging to the unfortunate explorers. To make matters sure, Mr. Anderson, another Hudson's Bay's Company explorer, was dispatched to Montreal Island at the mouth of the Black River in 1855. He also met with Esquimaux, who had in their possession furniture belonging to an English boat. This they declared they had obtained from a boat which had been abandoned by its owners, who had perished of hunger. They stated that five men, belonging to the same party as the owners of the boat, had perished on Montreal Island. On that Island Mr. Anderson found rope, chain, and other relics of civilized men; but the only article which could be distinctly identified was the piece of wood bearing the name of Mr. Stanley, the surgeon of the *Terror*.

"This final exploration settled the question that Sir John Franklin and his expedition had perished partly on King Williams' Land, and partly on the way from thence to Black River. The British Government, we believe, paid the $100,000 and announced that no more expeditions would be sent to the Arctic regions. The Government of the United States, which had sent an expedition to the rescue of Dr. Kane, was in no mind to adventure more men in ships in so perilous a locality. All were content to accept the prevailing theory with regard to the fate of the gallant crews of the *Erebus* and *Terror*."

Pa having given me a scolding in his usual kind way about my taking such a little quantity of exercise, I concluded to go fishing, which I did and met with tolerable good success. While I was thus occupied between here and Dr. Percy's, Mrs. Wm. Percy called to me from the top of the bank and told me that she saw in a newspaper that Aunt Lucinda was not at the time of the printing of the paper expected to live and that Emmy had recovered so as to

are the following, obtained from the Boothian Esquimaux, near the magnetic pole:

"Seven knives made by the natives out of materials obtained from the last expedition; one knife without a handle; one spearhead and one staff (the latter has broken off); two files; a large spoon or scoop, the handle of pine or bone, the bowl of musk ox horn; six silver spoons and forks, the property of Sir John Franklin, Lieutenants H. D. Vescomte and Fairbolme, A. McDonald, assistant-surgeon, and Lieutenant E. Couch (supposed from the initial letter T and crest of lion's head); a small portion of a gold watch chain; a broken piece of ornamental work, apparently silver gilt; a few small naval and other metal buttons; a silver medal obtained by Mr. McDonald as a prize for superior attainments at a medical examination in Edinburgh, April 1838; some bows and arrows, in which wood, iron or copper has been used in construction—of no other interest."

Saturday, March 31, 1860

A day of tears and mourning and calamity, not to me but to my poor mother. Mr. Morsheimer brought a letter from Uncle Rice this morning announcing Aunt Lucinda's death, as well as the hopeless state of Lou and Emm. Ma has been in bed all day, and three of the children have been sick. I read some this morning and pasted a fac simile of the record found in King William's Land by Lieutenant Hobson in my old Journal. In the evening I studied till 5½ o'clk, when Ma sent me to Mrs. Yerger's for a paper that had some news relating to our poor poisoned relations in N.O. The weather had been threatening rain during the whole day and then sprinkled rain. When I returned at dusk it was raining large heavy drops, and I had not been in the house long, reading the papers to Ma, when hail began to fall. Soon after I heard a [. . .] roar. Ma asked what it was, and I answered that it was the whind, which, at the time I came in, was blowing very hard. Not long afterward Pa went out on the gallery and in five minutes I followed him. Instead of the roaring be[ing] merely the wind, it was a terrific whirlwind. It had passed. It's course was from the back part of our field easterly to Dr. Percy's quarters, which it utterly annihilated, sweeping in its devastating course everything. The negroes were in the houses. Presently we heard shrieks of distress, and I ran down to our quarter and ordered Pero to take all the men with their axes and go immediately to assistance and soon after having caught me a horse, I went down myself. The appearance of the whirlwind was of a pitchy blackness, a huge pillar of darkness, from which proceeded the growling. Having come in the range of hog-heaps &c. burning back of the field it carried sparks of fire with it. Its rapidity was incredible. A cool wind now fanned my cheek as I hurried to the scene of ruin.

Half of the blue firmament was clear and the pale moon peeped from behind a cloud as if to view the devastation so recently perpetrated—and the stars too twinkled as if with satisfaction at what had occurred. Quarters to the length of two hundred yards were laid to the ground, and the moanings and bewailings of the women met my ear, the flickering fire still in the shattered fireplace formed a sad contrast to the cold rays of the moon. A cold painful shiver ran through my frame. I approached a group of ashy negroes and in their midst lay a mutilated corpse covered and clotted with blood, stretched upon a few rough planks covered even to slipperyness with gore. The flickering rays of the moon shone on his ghastly brow. The hips were parted and the eyes partly closed. His arms lay open and in his breast there was a cavity*[59] caused by the forcible thrust of a beam large enough to admit my fist. I stooped over him and as closely as possible examined his person. The wound was horrible—it gaped and the torn fragments of flesh hung around the edges and his whole breast was covered with crimson blood. From what I could learn, he was the only one killed or injured. It seems that the houses were thrown over with such force that most of the timber fell beyond the inside of the building or many would have perished. I soon returned and related my news.

This morning I got a letter from Hal and according to our agreement sat immediately down and answered it on 8 pages of paper nearly as large as Fool's Cap. In my letter to him on the 14th inst. I urgently advised him to keep a Journal, assigning many reasons, and he tells me now that he will and that he will let me read it next summer. My letter is still here and I will have to wait for some time probably before I can send it out, as I did not get through writing it till Mr. M. had left Dr. P's and Judge Rucks's.

Sunday, April 1, 1860

Clear, beautiful day. Soon after breakfast Uncle Jack and myself went through our field to the place where the tornado first made its exit from the swamp and from there to the quarters of the unfortunate Dr. It had opened a channel through the woods, tearing and twisting the largest trees most astonishingly. It is a mere miracle that 20 or 30 were not killed; but I suppose it must be attributed to the houses falling forward and over them. About 12 o'clock we returned. But I will say here a little upon the authority of Dr. Percy. Nine bales of cotton under a shed 20 feet from the creek bank were carried to the other bank of the creek—three two-horse sweeps were conveyed with such force across the creek as to be buried almost entirely in the bank on the opposite side. A negro was sitting against the wall of his house, towards the wind and the log on which his head rested, as he says, was suddenly whirled forward, rather pushing than knocking him at full length on the floor, the others passing over him. A little child was found so completely hemmed in as to be unable to even turn over. An old man seeing it coming tried to get in his house and said that he was carried back very fast and was struck on the head by something (I suppose as he was going with the thing that struck him it could not hurt him much) and went through the fence that was in front of the quarter down the creek bank (I suppose the bank protected him from the pieces of timber which were undoubtedly in the wind) and trying to go up was struck in the leg again and was brought to the ground. By this time it was over.

Bill came up to see Uncle Jack in the evening, and they both laughed at me about my long letter to Hal of yesterday (10 pages as large as this one taking off about 10 lines and a little broader). I am going to tell him in my next candidly to tell me if he would rather they would be shorter for I do it not for my pleasure but for his—if it is a pleasure for him to read my letters. Most assuredly it is no pleasure to write them. I at least do it with a good intention.

I went up to see Mr. Herbert this evening and found that for the time he was easy, the Dr. having with an instrument drawn off the accumulated urine. Before I left I was in Ma's room. She has been in bed nearly all day. I found her weeping with both the Mrs. Percys with her. Mrs. Wm. P. was not crying outright but her large eyes were moist with tears and Mrs. Walker P. felt, I know, if she did not shed tears. They are both most admirable women— indeed, I do believe that the world might be searched and a more brotherly and sisterly neighborhood could not be found. Every person has sent hands to Dr. P. to help put up his quarters and when any accident befalls one the others aid him. If one of the ladies get out of any article of household provisions she has only to send to anyone of them and it is immediately sent and when she gets her supply it is repaid. When our house was burned down, April 17th 1857, ladies 20 miles distant, knowing Ma's number of children and the difficulty attending her getting clothes made for them, sent for work; and those in the immediate neighborhood came after it and did a great deal toward aiding her. Judge Rucks, God bless him, sent for us to come, and even came and pressingly invited us to his house till ours should be rebuilt. Our whole family staid there, living on his bounty from that time till the 22nd of June '57, when we went to Va. and returning the following Oct stayed till the middle of Nov. the same year. We dared not offer the least remuneration lest we should loose his friendship. Such is this blessed neighborhood.

Monday, April 2, 1860
Morning clear and pleasant but toward night it became cloudy and warm. In company with Bay, I went to the Bogue soon after breakfast and staid until 4½ o'clk when I got home. I met with pretty good luck, but in putting on a

fish the string on which the others were on broke and I lost a good many that I had caught. I caught one Trout that would weigh about 3½ lbs.

The Tornado crossed the road about half way between the Creek and Bogue and was at least 300 yds. wide, presenting a more forcible specimen of its fury. I got through it with some difficulty and seeing a more open way and knowing that the young ladies both from Maj. Lee's and Judge Rucks's would be along shortly, I took the trouble to pick and clear a path for them by this more open way by cutting the twigs, vines, &c. out of the way so as to have as few obstacles as possible. I had just attained the road on the side first approached by the road when they arrived, Bill and Miss Kate Lee being in the front, the others arriving in a very short time. I told Miss K. and Bill that they would not be able to get through by going straight forward but that by going to the right the way I had picked and prepared I thought they could get through with a little difficulty. They did not seem to give much credit to my words, and I felt the devil rising in me. They pushed forward, saying that they thought they could get through. The others came up pretty soon, and I told them the same thing but they followed suit. I went back and rode off in a trot most of the way, having to get down once to cut a vine, having deviated from the cut path. They, as I knew, did not go more than 75 yds. before they came to a dead halt. I was by that time about opposite them, about 100 yds to the right going in a trot as the way there was open compared with theirs. I heard a call, I thought, probably to me—I only laughed one of my habitual loud laughs and went on, leaving them entangled. I suppose they will listen to what a *boy* says the next time they want to get through the track of a Tornado. I was piqued, and I did not care whether they got to the Bogue or not; they did not. I afterwards heard that Miss Dellie was knocked off of her horse by a limb. I was sorry to hear it.

Tuesday, April 3, 1860

Sky cloudy—atmosphere warm—wind strong from the S.W. Morning was occupied in trying to get a mess of fish from the Creek but did not succeed. When I returned I read *Mental Philosophy*[60] till dinner and found it to be quite interesting. In the evening I occupied my time in reading the same book, studying English Grammar, and making the two last entries, having neglected to do so at the proper time. As soon as I finished I went into the garden and having pulled a few flowers (the only pretty one was a Tulip) and proceeded to take my walk, stopping at Judge Rucks's for the *Georgia Scenes* that I left there a few evenings ago. All the occupants were absent, and I could not get it. I will have to call again for it.

At the supper table from some cause I do not recollect what, Preacher's religion &c. came to be our topic of conversation. I, as moderately as I could, expressed my opinion of the world and religion generally, which was to this effect: that the world was "a hollow thing"; that in religion especially, there were many hypocrites; that many preachers under the cover of piety were as big rascals as any one, and that I thought that the forms &c. that are gone through in inniciating ministers or at least the ceremony (I do not know what it is called) was all unnecessary, and I believed every man, wicked or righteous, had a right to preach, provided he could get a congregation. Ma in particular seemed to be quite opposite in her more matured views of the thing and said to this effect: "You are too young to express any opinion on the subject; you do not know the world, and I have always expected to make a good man of you. My greatest hope has always been to see my sons good, righteous men." I told her it was the hardest task she could have imposed upon herself. I am conscious that the sentiment she expressed was a most noble one, and as natural as could be, but at the same time I never had the least hope to be as she wished, "good and righteous."

Wednesday, April 4, 1860

A lovely day of sunshine and pleasant breezes. The trees have now just become entirely coated in fresh green; the flowers that I love so much are just blooming; all nature seems to have been awakened and seems fresh, smiling and bouyant.

Before I arose this morning I lay lolling in my bed, the light breeze fanned my cheek; I was happy; I was loosened from the chains of boyish love; I had just awakened from a thrilling dream of a charming lady—Miss Ella Brown. She has not been mentioned for some time in these pages, but I love to mention her because with her, around her, cling some of the dearest associations of days gone by. Dearest I say because with those associations mirth and happiness are mingled. But to my dream. With that unaccountable, dramatic unaccountability I imagined myself most happily seated at her side talking to her. This dream is short, but oh! How sweet, how blissful was even the dream! All at once I thought she caught me around my neck. I could feel, seemingly, her soft, plump, downy arms gently press my rough sinewy neck; I felt that little rosy, blushing cheek against mine. It was warm. Our lips met, my arms clasped convulsively that symmetrical waist. Did I say our lips met? They did. And oh what lips! So soft, so red, so delicate. Oh! Of such transcendent lusciousness. I kissed, rapidly, nervously. I trembled, every nerve quivered under overwhelming bliss. Her cheek waxed brighter and warmer. I clasped her tighter to my bosom. I could feel her warm sweet breath. I sucked it. I drunk it. My soul was awakened. All was so vivid, so heavenly. Cruelly it ceased, reality supplanted the scene of my excited fancy. I was awakened not to find myself in a splendidly furnished room in a rosewood bed with crimson curtains but in my old half furnished room in my dingy walnut bed.

The baby, Laurence, a few minutes ago, my trunk being open, went into the tray where all my letters are and where there was a box of steel pens and did it cunningly for he knew it was my "sanctorum." He got the box and wasted the pens into the tray. When I saw him I jumped up and ran to him bellowing at the top of my voice, "You baby!" It frightened the little fellow and he commenced to cry outright saying, "Me put em in" with his little lisping tongue. The little fellow fell nervously to put them back and when he had finished I gave him the box to play with—he was quite satisfied. Not long since he was repeating the little piece of poetry, "Twinkle, twinkle, little star" &c. after one of the children. His nurse had been cleaning off the yard all day and kept him picking up chips when he got to the place "twinkle, twinkle, all the night" and had just finished the line he asked, "pick up chips all day" very pertly.

A gentleman on the River was whipping a little boy, a negro, and he kept hollering, "Oh pray master, oh pray master!" The old fellow said, "Don't tell me to pray, pray yourself." He let him go for the purpose and told him to pray quick. The little smutty knelt down in a very sanctimonious manner said, "Oh Lord bless us all and let us be dismissed" in his African way. It was so artlessly done in such "dead earnest" that it convulsed the bystanders with laughter. The boy *was* dismissed and got no more of the lash.

During the morning, I read Philosophy and fixed me a kind of a swing about 6 inches higher from the floor (of my gallery) than myself to pull up by and exercise my arms. My chest has pained me a little for a day or two and I am fearful. After dinner I occupied the time principally in studying English Grammar and reading Philosophy.

Pa will start to N.O. tomorrow to nurse our unfortunate kindred. He called me up this evening and gave me instructions concerning the course I am to pursue with regard to the sick and in taking care of the house, &c. He flattered me by calling on me while there was a man in the house just twice my age and myself being a *boy*. He gave me a lecture about my free way of expressing myself about religion, the world, &c., mentioned in my preceding entry, and showed me plainly that I was wrong and doing myself an injury.

After practising my music lesson after supper, I went into Ma's room to see Pa a little while and a few moments after I got in she commenced shedding tears. Poor Mother! I am sorry for her.

Thursday, April 5, 1860

Can I record any thing worthy of note concerning myself today? Little. Most of my time was occupied through this almost summer day in reading, studying, and exercising on my gymnasium, as I shall call it.

This morning Pa and Jimmy left for N.O. I can say again with sincerity the last sentence in my entry for the 1st Feb.—"God bless them!"

Mrs. Yerger (J.S.)[61] came up to see Ma today, bringing the *N.O. Picayune* containing some account of our poisoned relatives but left it in the carriage, only showing her the *Eagle* giving a description of the intended funeral of Willie (which was postponed on account of hearing of Emmy's death). The only grievous part of the news was that Mr. Lemley was in convulsions and was not expected to live and that the situation of the others was quite precarious— sometimes better, sometimes worse—keeping their friends in dreadful suspense. I took the papers from the carriage with her permission, and to keep a piece or two of humorous articles as well as the news of our relations and to keep Ma from seeing them locked them up in my trunk. Uncle Jack saw them at the time I did. A short while after supper I was seated in my room reading them over when, unexpectedly, Ma entered. There was no retreat. She saw the paper, or piece of it, in my hand. Fortunately the leaf had nothing of any consequence in it but some on the bed at my side had the news above mentioned. She questioned me closely as to where I got the paper from and examined it minutely. I found it quite difficult to evade her, and once she hemmed me in so closely that I came very near telling her. At last she espied the papers on the bed and took one of them up and went out with it. I was exasperated because Uncle J. had told her and because I knew it would make her feel much worse. I was nervous and excited. I soon went up to her room and saw that I had not been deceived. Soon I returned and commenced writing this entry but was called up by her to read her two Chapters in the Bible—I did so.

I went up to see Mr. Herbert this evening and found him to be some better. About sundown our carriage came along and availing myself of the opportunity I came back home. The boy brought a letter for me from Hal—an April fool letter—and I found it to be quite amusing. In my answer I shall tell him that I knew that fool always wrote April fool letters. He will be pretty certain to give me a pretty good "cussin" in his next if I do. I shall not answer it till I hear from him again.

This is a lovely night. The moon gives every thing such a strange, pale color. I sit at my open window writing—it is now 10 o'clk PM—the cool refreshing breeze breathes its exhilarating breath in my face. But I must to bed as soon as I have seen to the fire!

Friday, April 6, 1860

Most of this cloudy, warm day was spent at the Bogue fishing. I did not return till about 4½ or 5 o'clk. The balance of the time I practised my music lesson.

I was very hungry—supper was late and badly cooked—the fish (of which there were 50 as fine as I ever saw) were half done and half scaled and to "crown the enchantment of the scene" (yes for it was enchantment, shure enough) Laurence, the baby, was squalling at the top of his voice. I was mad at first because supper was late. Every thing went wrong. I was *so* mad. I wanted to take the little scamp and give him a good whaling. I wanted to order the cook to receive fifty lashes and to knock down things generally. What made me worse was that I could not. Speaking of the baby, I will here note a genuine piece of originality of his. Before I started to the Bogue, he got hold of my bait box which had in it very large worms, nearly as large or quite as large as a pen holder. They were covered with slime. As soon as he saw them he said, "Lordy! Yook at de Maccayrny!" I held my side for it nearly split.

At the supper table last Wednesday evening the subject arose how Jimmy and myself came to be called "James," which is my middle name. I said I did not like it, that it looked bad that two in the same family should have the same name. Pa suggested that I should take my grandfather's name in full, Harry *St. John* in the place of Harry *James*, that then I would have his father's name and Jimmy Ma's father's. I agreed to it and now my name is Harry St. John Dixon.

Yesterday evening a boy came from Maj. Lee's, inviting Uncle Jack and myself down to a dance there. Miss Marian and Miss Dellie went up to Bolivar in the morning and of course would not be there. I thought that there would be no dancing—only two women, three or four men—that I would not greatly contribute to the gayety of the young belles and beaux—that it would be better for me to abstain from the alluring charms of beauty, wit, and pleasantry—that finally I would learn more by studying at home.

Saturday, April 7, 1860

Light winds and sunbeams compose this delightful April day. Have I accomplished much as to my studies? Sorry to say that the portion is diminutive. Most of the morning was occupied in reading *trash* not *substance*. Can trash be instructive? To a certain degree it can. At any rate I read some of the United States' History.

As I returned from dinner I saw on the mantlepiece Cooper's *Prairie*[62] and opening it read a pleasing scene—one in which one of that once haughty race, the Indians, played an active part. It recalled early recollections, recollections that were once the continual daydreams of my youth in extremis. Once my only ambition was to be a man, to have my camp, my dog, my rifle, and my pony. To be far on the border of the praries towards the setting of the sun. To live among the fallen red men and be their friend, to fight their battles against my race. With them to chase the red deer and hunt the wild buffalo. In my fantastic camp I wished to have a wife, an Indian princess, possessing that peculiar beauty of nature, pure unblemished nature, radiant with its fascinating simplicity, all so rustic, so charming. To educate her and in that same domicile to have my choice little library. Even now these same notions animate me in my more advanced youth. Still that life seems to have its charms. But enough of this. I write too much. I must off to study for it is 2 o'clock PM.

I had intended to study. Did I do so? No; I was prevented by Bill's coming to see Uncle Jack and myself and of course I was obliged to consume my time in attempting to entertain him but do not flatter myself that I have any of that flowery language, pleasing anecdotes to tell, neither any exciting incidents to relate of my life. But sometimes when in company with a pretty woman my sluggish soul becomes exhilirated and my tongue rattles considerably. I cannot say as to its sound and substance and subject being interesting. Speaking of tongue rattling I will tell (to myself when I grow older) an occurrence that Bill related of himself in substance as follows: on one occasion he was travelling in a stage coach and having been introduced to a pretty "gall" and her brother who was accompanying her to school he took a seat by her and of course commenced "rattling" on and courted her. She looked puzzled, twirling her handkerchief around her fingers and biting it. He thought he had her sure. When he finished, having talked to her for three hours without intermission, she turned to him in a most languid and exhausted manner and said, "Have you finished?" The words were nothing compared with the manner he says. He immediately got out on top. I pity the girl for having gotten such a "bour-ing" and Bill for having gotten such a decided "cutting." A just reward for flirting.

Sunday, April 8, 1860
Strong breeze from SE all day—fleecy clouds floating about. Various trifling things occupied the morning, but among them was one that was not trifling, that of attending a little sick negro in the quarter.

In the evening I read newspapers mostly and wrote some in a "tribute to the victims" as I called it, intending if it was accomplished to suit me that I would send it down to Vicksburg and request (incognito) its publication. Ma got a letter from Pa today bringing favorable news.

I am now sitting up with the little "nig" to give it medicine and before I came up I was seated on my gallery, my feet were cocked up against a post and I was whistling some old familiar airs while gazing on the bright stars twinkling in the blue canopy. I thought of Hal, Nat, Taylor, Miss Ella Brown, Miss Ella Scott and a host of other acquaintances and wondered what they were doing. My thoughts were dispelled for they were all conjecture as to their respective occupations.

A night or two ago (I can't help it) I dreamed of a perfect legion of women. I imagined that I was going along the Creek bank by our garden and saw Miss Ella Scott and nearly all of my recent lady acquaintances with an almost innumerable number of others on the opposite bank, some fishing, some gathered in groups conversing, while others reclined gracefully upon the grass. It seems as though my brain at night is wholly wrapped up in women.

Mr. Herbert called and ate supper with us this evening and announced the most welcome news I have heard for some time—he will teach school in the morning.

For some time I have been promising myself to write a eulogy here on the appearance and character of some of my most intimate friends—ladies. I will commence with a Deer Creek "gall," Miss Marian.

A gentle ecstacy pervades her whole being when animated in conversation while the pure brightness of her eyes and the soft articulation of a pleasant voice, slightly lisping, add greatly to her personal beauty. Her nose is aquiline, arched, smoothe eyebrows and an expansive forehead. An ample suit of black hair covers her head. A small waist—of middling height with small well-formed hands and feet. Her bust would admit of a little more fulness, but it cannot be complained of. She is a belle and is admired by every one for her sweet disposition, candidness, and impartiality. This impartiality is so strict that it is impossible to tell who she likes and who she does not. Kind and affable towards every one. Still there is an unaccountable, impenetrable mystery that surrounds her movements in society.

Miss Ella Scott next: A lady little over the medium height with a form void of fault as well as her disposition. She is not pretty but when one has become acquainted with her he utterly forgets all the allurements of beauty and only sees her mental charms. Her only pretty feature is her eyes. They are melancholy, dreamy, blue eyes that interest me so much, and their languid lustre surpasses her exceeding amiability.

Next will come Miss Kate Lee: Of medium size—slight form. Intelligent and witty, possessing smiling dark-blue eyes, but not exactly a pretty mouth.

Rather coquetish and capricious and inclined to practice petty tyranny but whose real disposition I believe to be unblemished.

Who comes next? Miss Mary Wingate. Deep auburn hair and a pure transparent skin enclosing a fairy form of a size under medium. Pretty cheeks blush under a pair of pretty blue eyes. A nice little nose projects gracefully over a well-chiseled mouth, rosy and full. Her hands and feet are extremely dainty. Her disposition though void of serious exception has at times presented itself to me as slightly inbued in sarcasm and imperiousness.

Miss Jennie Hunter is one of the most agreeable ladies I ever knew. Though not *beautiful* she nevertheless is very entertaining. Over the medium she is not in the *least* awkward in her movements. She has laughing eyes that laugh on all and seem to frown on none. An amiable disposition is hers, and she commands the respect of all who know her.

Miss Dellie Nichol is next in order. Plump and "put up from the ground" is this little, entertaining woman. Her full little "chis" is unexceptionable. It is exceedingly well-formed. She has pretty feet and soft little hands. The shape of her face is a dainty oval. Her little blue eyes and pouting lips are a match to her form. She has capriciousness but with it she is quite lenient and forgiving— though quick to get offended. She is what is called a "nice gall."

I must not forget Miss Louise Yerger, my dancing school companion as well as an old friend as we have attained our respective ages in friendly intimacy. She is of quite a different style of beauty. A brunette skin, raven locks, and most beautiful black eyes. Intelligent and entertaining. She too has a very pretty little foot and hand. Pretty popular among the young men and has a gentle disposition.

While the pale moon pursues its course through the spangled heavens and the wind moans through the forest trees in the yard, I will close this entry by making a few observations of Miss Ella Brown.

Imagine a lady of the medium size, plump, yet slender enough, whose small and symmetrical waist formed a beautiful contrast with her exquisitely-formed bust, undulating with a gentle, billowy motion. Arms that would have made Cupid stare, so tapering and graceful were they. Her feet were most lovely, as well as her ancles. Her complexion was blonde and her cheeks sweetly dimpled and often their delicate pink tinge could be supplanted by an enchanting blush by making a certain remark. The soft, rosy colour of her lips was transcendently sweet even to behold! Eyes that were far more sparkling, a sparkling that was much more charming than even the vivid flush of a diamond. They were of a pure chestnut. Her eyebrows were very singular—they were curly, like little *wavy* tresses! Her hair was brown as were her eyebrows and were like them, wavy. Her beauty sinks into insignificance when compared with her affability, disposition, talent, mental, towering mental powers glittering with transcendent splendor, diffusing its brilliancy among a legion of admirers. Her education, accomplishments, and disposition combined with her beauty and fascinating manners render her exceedingly sought after.

Monday, April 9, 1860

Windy, cloudy day—warm. Attended school today. According to a resolution formed some time ago, I took up *English Grammar* and a *Natural Philosophy* that were at the schoolhouse and studied them until almost 5 o'clk. It is my custom after school to take my spelling book and look out in a Dictionary all the words in my lesson that I do not understand. By this time I had expected to be in Algebra but loosing the last two weeks has prevented me. In two weeks I expect to enter it.

Tuesday, April 10, 1860

Part of the day partially clear but towards night clouds gathered and by dark silent, glimmering lightning gave warning of rain, though I did not think we would have much for part of the sky was the whole time clear. Before I went to bed in a N.N.E. direction to the eye there appeared a space the colour of a bright red, seemingly about 50 yds. in diameter, while the rest of the sky was in total darkness—it looked very singular. We had but little rain and much wind.

School. This evening I went in baithing the first time this year and neglected my voluntary studies (as I shall call them) for it. I enjoyed it very much.

It seems as though the negroes waited till Pa went away to get sick. The little child is much better. I feel the responsibility exceedingly. Does Pa rely more on my youthful judgement than that of either Ma or Uncle Jack?

Wednesday, April 11, 1860

As I expected the sun arose clear and the sky was cloudless this morning as it was all day, though the atmosphere has been much cooler though but little rain fell. Little wind today. After taking my usual evening studies after school I returned home and to my gratification found the two Mrs. Percys and Mrs. J.H. Yerger here. Ma seems to have regained to a considerable extent her spirits.

More negroes come in, but so far as my knowledge of the ordinary diseases of the country extends I can see nothing serious and applied the usual remedies. Pa is expected tonight and I hope he may come.

This evening I take up the more elaborate Grammar of Latin. I did not know till lately that Pa intended me to take a degree in that study and now must make up for lost time and as it is now time for that night study—to it!

Thursday, April 12, 1860

Grievous news has accompanied this pretty day. It seems as though three deaths are not enough—the fourth must come. Pa arrived this morning and brought the news of Uncle Hadley's death. My poor mother—one brother and one sister and a nephew and niece. "We know not what the morrow bring forth." "The iniquities of the father are visited upon the children, even to the third and fourth generation."

I did not know it till I returned home at 1 o'clk (Mr. Herbert letting out at 12) when on entering Ma's room saw her lying on a couch, exceedingly distressed, Pa rubbing her hands and Mammy (my negro nurse) rubbing her feet. Naturally I asked what was the matter; my answer from Pa was, "distress my son," and I saw that what he had said was too true.

Rest of the evening was occupied in exercising and study.

Friday, April 13, 1860

Pretty, pleasant day. After school I went in swimming and studied till nearly sundown.

Mr. Herbert and myself were conversing about the seduction of women. We coincided exactly, viz, that there was nothing on earth that a man could do so base and perfidious as that of depriving an innocent girl of her honor, virtue, and happiness, and plunging and steeping her in the dark chasms of perfidy, wretchedness, and degradation, casting from her brow the bright wreath of chaste maidenhood and placing in its place an iron band weighing her youthful head to shame and misery. Not only for the selfish gratification of an unholy passion does he consign her to a life of utter isolation from society and all its alluring fascinations, but he envelopes her innocent family in darkness and shame.

To take advantage of nature's inclinations, to entice her on with black lies, to convince her that it will never be known, that pregnancy will not follow. Carried on by the impetuosity of her passions, her fears quieted by, probably, the promise of a speedy marriage, she submits and before really she is awakened to consciousness, while wrapped in the blissful intoxication and voluptuous sweets of sensuality, she sees her virginity, honor, virtue, afar off—they mock her and reproach her for her wickedness. Then her life of wretchedness and misery begins, to end in death only. Abandoned by her faithless seducer, for long, long years she is to suffer the stinging, keen, pangs of conscience. Can there be mercy in heaven for such a wretch? Can the Just Judge forgive such a man? If a relation of mine were thus ruined, sooner would I thrust my right arm into the scorching flames than lay down my arms till my hand was imbued in the monster's heart's blood. Never would I cease to hunt him, no, never, never, never.

Saturday, April 14, 1860

Sluggish, cloudy day. Soon after taking my music lesson in company with Uncle Jack, Jimmy, and Bay I went to the Bogue, after digging bate, and had splendid luck. The Perch, Brim, Goggle-Eyes, &c. bit elegantly—as fast as the hook could be thrown in. We caught 113 fine ones. While there Uncle J. stooped down to put a fish on the string, snakes were seen every minute they being numerous, and his spur stuck into the higher extremity of his thigh, or his inexpressible, and he uttered a loud "bawl." All were startled and had a good laugh when the joke was known. He thought a snake had bit him. I had a nice "mess" of fish for supper which I relished and riding a carriage horse that could trot "all day under the shade of a tree," throwing me six inches from the saddle 24 times per minute and catching me at each descent. They were so large that I sent a mess down to Dr. Percy's and Judge Rucks's but as negroes will do— stupid fools as they are—the boy took all to Dr. P's and Judge R. got none. I intend to go again next Saturday and then I will see that he gets some, provided I catch any. All the game we have I think ought to be sent there instead of Dr. P's as it is generally for there is no one there except the old Judge to hunt and fish and he is too old while at Dr. P's there are three men in the prime of life and I think they should be able to furnish the table with such things. But enough upon this score.

Thursday evening I got a letter from Hal. Part of his letter puzzled me. I did not know what to think of it, but considering our warm friendship and his repeated avowals of his being my "best friend," that probably it was done to tease me, or was a piece of thoughtlessness. I will only cite those parts bearing upon the point, viz. "I can hardly believe that such a thing as a tornado should cut up so much dog down there when times are so hard. . . . Tell me whether it is a fact or not because I thought perhaps you were trying to fool me." "Cut up dog" is a school boy phrase. Truly it puzzled me. In my answer I asked if I had given him any cause to disbelieve me, if I had ever told him a liar, and if not why should he doubt my word, &c., &c., that if I thought he really meant harm and if were not such friends that it should not drop here, that it would end seriously and what I had stated was received from unimpeachable sources, concluding by asking him to explain to me his motives &c. and that I would wait in suspense till I heard from him, hoping for the best.

He has, as I see from his letter, got into a similar scrape to mine—the Miss Kate Mitchell affair. I gave him advise about how to get a *kiss* and I had by a like process obtained that luxury from "my gall." All I can now do for him is to wish him success in obtaining that luscious prize. I know it is luscious from experience; may he know it from the same cause!

Sunday, April 15, 1860

Little of consequence can be recorded that has transpired during this warm, cloudy, April day. There being no church, part of the morning was occupied in study. Having ascertained that there would be no school tomorrow (very much to my chagrin) Uncle J. and the boys in company with myself concluded to go to the Bogue in the morning and with that object in view I consumed most of the evening in digging bait, which I found to be difficult as they were deep in the ground on account of its dryness.

Mr. Herbert took tea with us this evening and the question arose, how was assifoetida was spelled. I said *asafetida* and was ridiculed. Uncle J. then tried it *asafoetida* and Ma *asafoetida* also. It went around in various forms and was discussed considerably. Mr. H. did not spell and neither Pa (he was not at table). When we had finished I got Worcester's *Dictionary*[63] (which Pa presented me with) and found he spelled it *assafetoeida* and on looking at Webster's saw that he spelled it *asafetida*, as I did precisely and the laugh was reverted for none had spelled it according to either book except myself. It was quite a triumph for me on account of their exultations at first. Ma at first thought I was joking, and when it was seen that I was in earnest the laugh went around at my expense.

Monday, April 16, 1860

Part of this day has been cloudy and part clear. At the Bogue the greater part of the day fishing, though with less success than Saturday. Jimmy was the only one that stayed with me the whole time, the others going home about 11½ AM. As we started home large drops of rain fell and a strong wind came from the South. I feared a storm and being on an old mule went through the wood but slowly. Balance of the day nothing was done worth note.

Near dark I was out toward the garden playing in my usual way with Sam and was walking to the house when I saw Mrs. J. H. Yerger standing at the steps talking to Ma and Pa who were up on the gallery. She was standing with her side to me. In coming up I walked behind, in politeness, and spoke to May who was with her, loud enough for her to hear me. I thought, that she

(Mrs. Y.) did not seem conscious of my presence. I walked by her up the steps and took a seat on one of them, watching an opportunity to speak, seeing that she was engaged in conversation. Still no demonstrations of the least regard of my being present, which I felt assured she then knew, if from no other cause, the noise I made in ascending the steps. I sat a few minutes before I felt it, attributing her "sang froid" to other motives than any intention to slight me. I *always* speak *first* to a lady and with that purpose watched my opportunity but none was afforded for several minutes when I caught her eye and instantly looked away, avoiding my salute. I then arose and left. Whether she intended it or not, I cannot say, but I had too much independence to speak after waiting unnoticed for such a length of time. Probably this independence is an injury to me. I cannot say that Mrs. Yerger would treat *any* one thus intentionally, and I cannot say whether accidental or not such a thing is without its sting.

Tuesday, April 17, 1860

Having slept on two benches at the schoolhouse with Mr. Herbert last night—he being sick—I awoke this morning to see the sky still overcast and in a few moments rain began to fall, so welcome to planters. It did not last long and a drizzle followed it that is now pattering on the roof (it is 11 o'clk) and from prospects it seems as though we will have more. I came home before breakfast and but little of consequence has been done thus far, but as soon as I pack away some old clothes in my room, I shall lock the door and study.

In accordance with my resolution I studied some during the balance of the day and read a good deal of History. Little or no time spent out of doors. Here is a really *good* piece taken from a newspaper. I think it so good that I will quote it verbatim et literatim.

"It is an old and true saying that a man should not marry unless he can support a wife, and from some examples we have seen we are beginning to doubt seriously whether a woman can prudently marry unless she can support a husband."

The point is, "unless she can *support* a husband." And with regard to their future beauty, I agree with Mons. Editor but know from examples in this very neighborhood that they cannot "prudently marry" until they "can *support* a husband." Let me illustrate in my usual rough way what I mean. Suppose there was a tempest to arise, fierce and ravishing, and that there stood side by side one tree matured and developed, one tender and soft. They are both alike beautiful. When the storm has passed we see the former still beautiful, though it may have been divested of many of its charms, while behold the other. Maimed, shivered, and drooping—fading and withering away from its shock. The storm is time and man's passions; they thus represent women married *maturely* and *immaturely.*

Wednesday, April 18, 1860

A day of clouds and warmth. Mr. H. came up (or rather down—I always get it wrong) yesterday evening to remain with us till his illness has subsided and is better today.

Most of the day has been occupied in reading Goldsmith's English History,[64] which I find very interesting. I finished with interest Henry the Eighth's reign and was surprised to find that he was such a monstrous tyrant. I knew that he had had the boldness to oppose the papasy because it would not consent to divource him from his first wife. The motive I condemn, but the independence I admire. I did not know that he was so fond of blood. Mr. G. has corrected another of my erroneous suppositions, that of Elizabeth's looks. I formerly thought her to be a beautiful woman.

Some pity Mary Queen of Scots, but I cannot find such spacious grounds for this pity. It seems that she was privy to the murder of her second husband, Darneley. She, though a woman (and doing what I think no woman was intended to do) at the head of different armies, fought the interests of Elizabeth and ended by conspiring against her life, though possessing the most holy religion. Her prolonged confinement may be an excuse for this, but I do not think that it is the place of women to lead armies, govern kingdoms, or in any wise wield power. The first one was given to man as a supplement, and I believe that they were made solely for the domicile, for diffusing cheerfulness around the toils of man. She was first taken *from* man—cut even the largest limb from a tree, will it be as powerful as the trunk?

Thursday, April 19, 1860

Quite a similarity with regard to the weather. Most of the day occupied in study, partly Grammar and partly of History (of England). Again I corrected an erroneous idea of English History, that there was never a commonwealth.

9 o'clk PM. Having taken my seat a few minutes ago to make this entry, I had to stop and pay attention to Mr. Herbert's recital of one of his previous adventures. He told it in his usual deliberate, strictly grammatical style. The old fellow is quite fond of recitals, somewhat to the weariness of his hearers (at least it is the case with myself, though I feel not the least displeased but rather feel sorry for the defect, knowing that probably I may possess the same). In the beginning of his conversation he spoke of condensing, that he formerly was told that in preaching that the want of that most admirable art caused his

sermons to be much less acceptable. If ever I speak in public, will I have to correct such a defect?

I am perplexed with relation to Nat. I have not heard from him since the first part of March and cannot imagine what is the reason. Have I offended him? I hope not, for if I have surely I did not intend it. Probably the sting caused by my "plain" letter of the 11th of Feb. has not subsided. That letter he, in a later letter of his, acknowledges he did not answer because I, as he said, slandered his father. I suppose the slander of which he speaks is contained in these lines— "Then I would have seen your father or any other man, even my dearest friend, in the lowest pitts of Hell before I would have eaten a morsel." He said in this letter that mine of the 11th was "not worthy of his answering." I bore it on account of my warm and friendly regards for Nat, complying with his request, saying nothing more about it further than that he had misunderstood me and that on a suitable occasion next summer while Hal was with us, we would discuss the subject, and if possible bring things to an amicable close, dissolving all animosity in blessed friendship.

Friday, April 20, 1860

Mostly clear with fleecy clouds floating in a pleasant breeze. Until 12 o'clk I was at the Bogue with Uncle Jack, Jimmy, Bay, Pa, and Willie. We had most admirable luck and that luck gave us an admirable dinner. Balance of the day occupied in reading English History.

At dusk according to my custom I went to the Piano to practice, Dr. Mc-Clung and Dr. Leroy Percy being out on the gallery, and Pa called out to me to play a certain piece, which I did, and at the close Jimmy came in to play some tunes we had learned together for them. Before he got his fiddle in tune Dr. McClung came in (I have never [been] introduced to him) and in consideration of civility, at my own house, I accosted him: "Good evening, sir," seeing that he was not inclined to speak, taking little notice of me. He was soon followed by Dr. Percy and Pa. Dr. Percy stood within three feet of me and paid no more attention to me than if I had been a servant. I did not press matters but held my place. Presently the violin was tuned and we played two or three tunes and Dr. McClung in particular seemed much pleased with them and said, "It is nice [. . .]." (Then speaking of Jimmy), "He will make an excellent player," "Remarkable for one so young," &c., &c. and as he went out (neither of them noticed me in the least) he said, "Both of them will make good players." Yes! Probably their consciences told them to say *"both"* —yes, it is *both!!* I abominate this vile flattery. Why was he not candid? Why could he not have finished and gave it all to Jimmy? For *he* deserved it, because I only played an accompaniment. But this is not the thing. It is this d——d slight; this way people lately have got of utterly overlooking me. Have I offended them? Or have I committed some monstrous misdemeanor? Is it because I am a *boy*? Because I have no hair on my chin and have not been to College? If this be the cause, if this be the reason why within one week I am subjected to this humiliating indignity, I consider them too far below me, too much of lick-spittles to even deserve my contempt. But what exasperates me is, why they should do so? At the supper table I mentioned it. I felt my eyes swell and a knot in my throat, as is always the case when I am very angry. I commenced by saying: "People these days don't seem to think it worth while to speak to me. Dr. Percy this evening took no more notice of me than if I had been a negro." Pa attempted to justify him in saying that some people spoke to boys and some did not, that I ought not to be so sensitive, that he knew Dr. P. would not do such a thing with the intention of slighting me. I tried to answer and stammered out a few words about "being treated with contempt" but that knot was in my throat. I could say no more. I was too mad. No more was said about it, but there will be something more said about it on the first occasion I have of seeing Pa when no one is present. I could not study my music lesson for thinking of it. I've been thinking of it ever since, and still thinking of it, and this won't be the last time I will think of it. But enough now—more of this anon.

Saturday, April 21, 1860

Weather various—a couple of sprinkles, and from the aspect of the clouds at 10½ o'clk rain seemed inevitable, but toward night, sky clear. Morning consumed in fishing in the Bogue though with less success than usual. On my return accompanied by Bay in coming through the track of the Tornado I got a little puzzled but found the way out pretty soon.

Perplexities seem to have attacked me lately or I have lost some of my hardly-gained control over my rebellious temper. I was angry at the dinner table because a trifling old woman who attends to the milk never sends up cream to eat with the strawberries but always "blue John."[65] After bending over a bed picking them for some time it makes me mad to have to eat them without cream. Having taken a *Harper* and having seated myself for a good read, I was called off by Pa to help carry a log in the garden and this put me again in a "stew" (very much to my discredit for I ought not to have allowed myself to do so) and layed my paper down. Getting back I found Mr. Herbert reading it and of course had to wait till he got through. This made me worse (again to my discredit) I hung on to it the balance of the evening when I did get hold of it.

Between sundown and dusk Mr. H. read Milton's *Paradise Lost* to me and for the first time I was interested in it. He says that "Milton was the greatest literary genius that the world ever produced." He is a perfect enthusiast.

Sunday, April 22, 1860

Capricious weather, sun shining in the morning at 10 o'clk while at dinner a gusting puff of wind came up and with it a pretty good rain and during the evening, cloudy and clouds red in the west about the time the sun was to set.

Nothing of any note has transpired today, i.e. similar to what occurred Friday. I have done neither any reading or studying worth notice. Most of the morning, after rising late, was passed upstairs reading some letters of Grand Pa Dixon addressed to father before he died—some of them while at the Infirmary near Memphis during the time that he had the cancer on his ear which affected me sincerely. He always spoke of me in the most tender terms, so much so that I felt sad. Let me, not to flatter myself but show the heavenly disposition he possessed, quote one or two of his benedictions, "Ten thousand kisses to my dear little boy—you now call him 'Harry' and he is no longer the baby. God bless him. I wish I could hug him to my heart." This was while he was near Memphis suffering numerous deaths each day as he describes it, being a man who did not make mountains out of gnat heels—"I have never felt a cessation of pain for an hour together—no words can convey to you the torments I have suffered and am now suffering." Again, when speaking of the operation performed on his ear, one among many that he endured—"But upon removing the plaster it was found that it contained a large quantity of clotted blood, the inflammation and swelling much worse, and if possible more painful. He (speaking of the Dr.) uses caustic which produces such agony I have had recourse to Elixeter and Opium." Among all these tortures, these agonies, he remembered me in all his letters in the same tender, touching manner, and to say he wanted to "hug me to his heart." Would to God I could even hug his knees! My recollection of him is quite distinct, though only three years old at the time. He is the only one of my Grand parents that I recollect at all. I remember his being confined to his room and eating eggs for breakfast and leaving me some in the shell. Also his corpse as it lay in his bed after his death is still and ever will be vivid in my mind. I recollect my nurse took me into his room before any one was stirring in the house in the morning and pointed him out to me saying, "Look, your Grand Pa is dead" or something to that effect. I wanted to see his face, but I was not allowed to raise the green vail thrown over it. Part of the evening has been passed as the morning was, perusing his letters, and my mind has been

gloomy with sad reflections about him. Shall my course through
such as to make him smile on me from his home in Heaven?

Monday, April 23, 1860

Strong weather. Went to the Bogue and found a number of p
our luck was only tolerable. The evening was occupied mostly in reading. Mr.
Herbert expects to teach tomorrow to my great delight.

Tuesday, April 24, 1860

This pretty though unusually cool day for this period of the year, commenced in due season with school. I studied as usual my English Grammar
and Natural Philosophy after school which I did not get through with till late.

At the supper table Pa and Mr. Herbert had quite a warm discourse about
education, school books, &c., and it was carried on very vehemently upon Pa's
part. Pa denounces the supremacy of Latin and Greek; Mr. Herbert advocates
it. In my humble opinion I differed with Pa when he said "that teaching was a
hang-dog life" (Mr. H. having made the remark that Latin and Greek would be
a resource in that respect) "and that none of his sons should with his consent
lead it." Mr. H. spoke of merchandising being another resort, and Pa said that
"that employment would do for women but men should lead an outdoor life."
Again I differ for it would be a grievous thing if they were to be exposed to
as many insults as I know they would. In his plain downright way he spoke of
his contempt for a man who gave himself up to idleness and that he expected
me to be a thorough mathematician, a surveyor, and civil engineer. The old
parson was stung for I could see it.

This evening I got a letter from both Nat and Hal. Hal spoke very frankly
of the doubts he expressed in the last one and said in warm terms that he was
only joking and now to my gratification the thing is mended. I got enclosed
in Nat's letter a short epistle from a Mr. Griffin, a particular friend of Hal and
Nat. I have never seen him, but he writes to me in these pleas—I quote the
language—"having so often heard of you" &c. "and my friends Lee and Yerger
speak of you so often, I do now through the medium of the pen" &c., &c. "I
have heard so much of your kind heart and noble character that it has induced
me to pen these few lines," &c. Unless it is a "catch," which I would scarcely
believe, I feel highly honoured and will answer his letter soon.

At dusk Cousin Gus, Uncle Jack and myself were about to enter the gate on
the return from a short walk (down toward Miss Marian's region, of course)
and saw Pa's buggy coming from the opposite direction and went to meet

.im, he having gone to town. Messrs. Percy and Valliant were in with him. He got out and left them in, and just as they were starting away Mrs. Wm. Percy came running to the gate calling to them to stop and let her get in. Mr. V. was so gallant that he got out to help her in but she made him get back and Pa helped her in between the two gentlemen in the seat which was pretty narrow for them and from appearances the three were pretty well "jammed." In a jolly manner her husband put his arm 'round her waist and Mr. V. made a similar motion, and as the vehicle moved off she said in her peculiar, girlish way, "Stop squeezing my hand, Mr. Valliant!" and there was a laugh both in and out of the buggy. All I have to say of it is that I wish I could sit as close to the young ladies as those two gentlemen sat to her.

Wednesday, April 25, 1860

No change in the weather. School, and this day has been passed in assiduous study—before breakfast, during school hours, at recess, and in the evening after school, as well as at night.

After finishing my studies last night, I wrote an answer to Nat's letter and put it on my mantelpiece and when I sent to get it for Mr. M. to take to town, it was gone. Whether a two legged rat or the common rats who inhabit a closet adjoining and who have a doorway through the wall to the mantelpiece*[66] took it off into their abode as they did Uncle Jack's watch, I cannot say, but it was gone and I have not seen it since. It could not be found.

Thursday, April 26, 1860

Still no change in the weather. School. Having been invited to a dance at Dr. Meare's this morning for tonight, I studied my lessons for tomorrow in the evening, in order to go, which I did in company with Uncle Jack and Cousin Gus. We were among the first there and were soon followed by many, some strangers intermingled. As most of the things came off after 12 o'clk I will speak of it in my next entry.

Friday, April 27, 1860

Weather the same still. School, and I found study to be a little tiresome after the last night's dissipation. I will here insert a few remarks concerning it.

Having the soft hum of female voices in the parlor and occasionally having a lively laugh, I went in in company with the rest. After speaking to the ladies near the door I seated myself at a respectful distance from Miss Mary Wingate and fired away at her on general customary topics—weather, recent occupations, reading &c., and soon after in company with the rest led her to the room alloted to dancing, she leaning gracefully on my arm. That set was a lively one, after which I floated around poking my bill in here and there, making engagements, and prompting the whole time, during the balance of the evening. Chattering, dancing, and feasting was carried on during the whole time, and I partook considerably. Pretty eyes rivaled the brilliancy of diamonds, and smiles and witticisms were copious. Vivacity prevailed among both sexes and the nimble little "footsy-tootsys" of the "fair ones" tripped through the dance as prettily as of old (when poor Hal and Nat were here) and their hands were as soft as ever. While dancing the fourth set with Miss Dellie her shoe string came untied and at her request I knelt as gracefully as my gangling proportions would let me and tied it. The ribbon laced over the instep and around the ankle. One thing is certain, I had a nice squeeze at that little, little dainty and prolonged my kneeling position for that purpose. She has a plump little hand and at every opportunity during the evening while dancing I gave it a gentle squeeze. As I expressed it in a letter to Nat (a duplicate of the one written Tuesday) this evening, I was "almost thrown into ecstacies" by waltzing with her. She waltzes elegantly and more for the hug than the dance. I solicited the opportunity which I obtained of throwing myself into ecstacies almost by clasping her slender waist. It is enough to make a boy of sixteen feel curious to have his arm around a pretty woman's waist, her left hand on his shoulder and her right in his left (and in some cases, their bosom on his) and in the later instance to feel the gentle undulations of it. My arm does not go half way or touch them lightly, but goes as far around as it can and holds them close and firm while my left as I have before said squeezes their right. Isn't it a blessing to be a boy? It is, it is! To feel ankles, squeeze hands, and clasp waists! I accompanied Miss Mary to the carriage and asked her what I should say to Nat for her, and she told me to give him her love. In a low tone I said with my mouth inclined toward her ear, as she tripped along at my side and said, "Is there no one else at Oxford to whom you wish to send a message?" and in answer she said: "Yes, I'll leave that for you to do," which told me to send *something* to Hal, I don't know what, but it was a message and let me hope, for his sake, it was one strongly tinctured with pure love, as pure as the noble love he bears for her. In my letter of this evening to Nat I gave him as glowing an account as I could of the party and particularly of the supper, saying that I thought of him, probably "delving over a hard lesson at the very time that I was luxuriously seated at a pretty woman's side, chattering and feasting while he was in the position aforesaid with his intestines crammed with dishwater and tater-peelins,"* [67] &c. + [68] I also laid before him my future views and plans and attempted to induce him to go to the University of Virginia with me. He says he has an idea of going there. I wish he would. I pray that nothing may keep me from going.

Saturday, April 28, 1860

The greater part of this fine day has been spent, I am sorry to say, to little effect. Most of the time having been occupied in exercising. Today I was invited to a dance as I understood at Judge Rucks' tonight (it was yesterday I was invited) but Mrs. Yerger rode up this morning saying it would be put off till next Mon. evening and I found out at the same [time] that it would not be a dance but only a supper party—as great drags as ever came into vogue. I shall not go. When I want to talk to a woman I shall put on my beaver and hunt one.

Sunday, April 29, 1860

A portion of this sunny day has been occupied in assiduous study—the evening. Church occupied the morning. I done my studying in the parlor and was about to write my Composition when in stepped Mrs's. Percy and Miller and Miss Alexander (the lady Mrs. P. invited me to call on) and found me in blue cottenade pants, an old grey coat, and without my vest or suspenders. There was no retreat—my clothes were clean if they were common, and my "brass" served me. Mrs. M. spoke and I "gabbed" her "cornstealer" and having spoken to Mrs. Percy was introduced to Miss Alexander—"Mr. Harry Dixon, Miss Alexander." I made my bow muttering, "Miss Alexander" and took my seat at the other end of the room while Mrs. M. played some hymns knowing it was no use to attempt to say any thing where the "old folks" were and when they were so close to her. I contented myself by contemplating a plump, little beauty, similar in form to Miss Dellie, and possessing a face something like Miss Kate Foster's. Her face has a sweet expression, and as Mrs. P. said, she is a perfect blonde, and I must confess that I should answer as the fellow did when the young lady asked him to clasp her cloak—"I'll clasp the charming contents, too." She looked like she would make a soft, sweet little arm full! Soon after, they left for a walk in the garden, and I resumed my pen and having taken a walk near nightfall, ate supper, and soon afterwards went for Louly at Dr. Percy's and will bring this entry to a close, hoping to encircle her waist with my arm in a waltz at a party I hear that is to be given there next Wednesday night.

Monday, April 30, 1860

My Latin Grammar has just been layed aside after delving lustily at it for two hours and after a day of hard study. As to the weather, it has been favorable to planters—today we had a good rain in the morning and a clear, pretty evening.

Uncle Jack and Cousin Gus are down at Judge Rucks' to the tea party, but that old misty, brain-racking Grammar there on the mantelpiece has been my tea party tonight. I cannot say that it was a very interesting tea party, but such things should be accomplished and I intend to do so.

It is late and my eyes feel dull from having studied 12 hours today and Pa has called me or rather told me that "it is bed time, my son," and I will now on my little bed partake of "nature's balmy restorer—sleep."

Tuesday, May 1, 1860

The moon's pale face was in the clear heavens before the bright rays of the sun had disappeared. Another day of study has fled by and again having finished my Grammar lesson I am seated to make another entry—a short one. This evening I got my Grammar lesson for Thursday and nearly finished my History lesson so as to be able to attend the dance at Dr. Percy's tomorrow night, to take a last waltz with Miss Dellie—she will go home Friday. When the sun was nearly setting I left the schoolhouse and on my way home stopped to study my History lesson, having told Mr. H. before I started that I believed I would stop studying and take a little exercise, as I had studied the whole day. While I was seated there, he came along on his way to our house and in a humorous way said, "That's taking exercise, isn't it?" I forget what reply I made, but I got up and came on to the house.

Wednesday, May 2, 1860

Warm, pleasant day. With studying after school I have got my lesson for to-morrow and am now (it is nearly sundown) making my entry, though the day has not entirely passed. As I was about to leave the schoolhouse this evening, Mr. Herbert asked me if I was going to Dr. Percy's tonight; in answer I said, "I may go." "Oh, don't use the Potential Mood but the Indicative future tense, for you know you are going." I laughed and came on home, where I had not been long before Miss Marian and Miss Dellie came to call on who, I do not know, but I thought I would help Ma out so off I put and having adjusted myself in a loose linen coat, went into the parlor and hammered away at them till they left. As they went down the steps Miss D. asked me if I would be at the party and answering I said "yes, Miss Dellie I must go to take one more waltz, a last farewell waltz! Oh! Is it not doleful to think of?"

Thursday, May 3, 1860

A long, long weary day has slowly glided by, as slowly as it was sunny. But for the party. To be brief, all was loveliness and beauty. The ladies seemed to be prettier than I ever saw them before and one particular little "lady bird" floated through the dance like a little, snowy fairy—long raven curls hung in all their natural grace, casting a beautiful contrast with a soft (looking) delicate neck, undulating, oh! so voluptuously. A pert little mouth, rosy and well-formed, was enough to tempt a saint to wish for one thrilling kiss. To complete my heavenly picture, she had two meek, maidenly black eyes, radiant in their downcastedness. She seemed all innocence; all this is combined in—Miss Mary Alexander. I would forfeit part of my life to have her stay for two or three months and for me to have nothing to do but carry on a pleasant amour with her. Before the dancing commenced, I made my way to her and presenting myself solicited the honor of the first set she had unengaged, which was the second. Beauty emulates me; my heart was joyous and my tongue was free; and I found that her beauty scarcely exceeded her mind. I took occasion during the evening (before supper) to ask: "Miss Alexander, will you allow me to have the honor of attending you to supper, provided you have no previous engagement?" The queenly head bowed and the coral lips said, "Certainly, sir," and making a profound bow, I retired. I fulfilled my engagement and went into supper with her and had anticipated having a "good time" of it but a very annoying circumstance withered all my expected pleasure. Two old married women sat within three feet of us and it was utterly impossible for me to say a thing on that topic that young folks when together always talk of. I "wadded" her though with what I could talk about and she having touched on a subject, as I thought, reflecting on my youth. I came down with all my might on the superficial education young ladies generally receive, contending that I could not see "why nature should lavish her gifs so profusely on the females and proscribe such a regimen for males &c., &c." She made but little reply, probably knowing the truth of what I said too well. We closed merrily with this toast, which I proposed, "Let friendship be our bark, Truth our anchor, and Love our guiding star." Having said something to her about the recent state of my heart, it's susceptibilities, etc. I, with her slender arm in mine, went into the parlor.

I took a farewell schottische with Miss Dellie to some elegant music on the Piano, Violin, and Flute by Dr. Percy, Mrs. Wm. Percy, and Mr. McCluny. While they were playing a waltz, what I wanted to dance with her, I went over to ask her but before I did so Miss Kate, who was sitting at her side, asked *me* and instead of the one I waltzed with the other. It was after three when we broke up and before we got in bed it was not far from daylight. But I must not close this entry till I relate (to myself) this: George, Miss Kate and myself were conversing together about the happiest period of one's life. I said (and sincerely) that I believed this period to be the happiest time that I ever saw or expected to see. She said that I ought to have said that this very moment was the happiest. My answer was, "Miss Kate, you would not have me say what I do not mean!" She saw the hypocritical smile on my face (I know it was) and immediately hit me some hard lick about my tender years. I took it very composedly and know from looks that, if a triumph it may be called, it was very diminutive.

In Nat's last letter he spoke of a "thing" he sent to Miss Dellie, and she says she never received it, but now wants me to find out its name and write it on a card and transmit it to her, which I will do if I can.

Friday, May 4, 1860

Warmer than any day this year. School. Today I finished reviewing the Arithmetic and have made some notes on the most difficult and practical rules and intend to make notes on the whole course and believe that in future they will aid me. Monday I shall commence Algebra.

This evening after school I wrote Hal a long letter, giving him a description of the party. One clause was, after elaborately informing him of Miss Alexander's beauty, of my being "struck" with her—it was: "A young man's life is but a bright pilgrimage from one sweet woman's bosom to another, till he reaches that one in which he shall find—happiness and bliss."

A few minutes since I received the appalling news that Dr. Dunn is lying sick and is not expected to live. Pa will go up in the morning.

Saturday, May 5, 1860

Pretty, warm day. Spent my morning in lazyly lolling on a sofa in the parlor reading a couple of *Harper's* Mr. Morsheimer brought this morning and the evening in nursing cousin Gus, reading the *History of England*, and walking. Cousin G. came home from a fishing excursion with a high fever on and with our nursing is free of it tonight. Pa went up to see Dr. D. today and says that he is poisoned, having got some of the poisonous fluid that is in all human bodies*[69] into a wound on his hand while dissecting one and is very dangerously sick. I am sorry to write as he has been a particular friend of the family since before my birth.

My temper most probably contributes as well as my love of order to make me impatient under little annoyances that I am continually subjected to. My beloved father has taught me to love order and system and to have "a place for everything and every thing in its place," and everything that I can put beyond the reach of Uncle Jack, Ma, the children, and the servants is always in perfect order even to the place where I keep my pencil at the schoolhouse, and I can go to my trunk and get any letter or any article whatever at any time and in the darkest night with no light. I am the only one that Pa will allow to go in the little drawers and it is because he knows the things will be put back where they were found. Now for instance before I commenced this entry I had to go for my inkstand. Ma had told one of the servants to get one, and she knowing that I always kept mine on my mantelpiece, in one particular place on it, came straight for it and gave it to her, leaving it up stairs. The consequence was as "super demonstravimus."[70] I had to look it up, as mad as a hornet. I went up stairs to Ma's room and as placidly as possible (I know my tone was kind) asked Ma if she had sent for it and received a negative answer. I then turned to the negro who had brought it and in a voice trembling with rage said: "The next negro that takes any thing out of my room that belongs to me, I'll try the virtue of that article upon his head!" These little things occur so often it is almost insupportable.

I had some idea of calling upon the little "lady bird" this evening but taking into consideration my youth and short acquaintance concluded to postpone it until I shall stop in my journey (or rather journeys) to Charlottesville and back, at Knoxville (where she lives) and see if she is as pretty and looks as sweet and as lucious as she does now, with those dreamy black eyes that arouse sensasions in my soul as tumultuous as her curls are. Oh! to look at these fair creatures does it seem possible that any one of their sex is capable of dark deeds of crime?

Sunday, May 6, 1860

A most beautiful day—a calm, still evening, and the "twinkling stars" are shining brightly. At church this morning I took a tender farewell look at Miss Alexander till I have the pleasure of seeing her in Knoxville next September when I go on to College. Oh! she looked as fresh as a budding pink, upon the verge of maturity, still containing the engaging qualities of a girl and all the nobleness of a woman. Her charming eyes made my heart flutter. I wish I did not possess this weakness about the pretty ones, but I am such an ardent admirer of them. I admire beauty so much and especially such thrilling beauty as she possesses! This is no foolish, boyish passion but a pure admiration of beauty. It makes me feel sad to think she leaves tomorrow and I will at least be deprived of knowing that she is in the neighborhood. In fact I have been sad this evening (after dark). Something seemed to make me reflect on the future and see all its trials and vicissitudes. After supper I took my seat out on the gallery after walking back and forth for some time and looking on the stars thought over some of the little scenes recorded in this book and wished to see them again. I heard my little brother's rich voice in the room adjoining prattling merrily while the loved voice of my mother was mingled with it and I felt lonesome and downcast because I knew that in four short months I was to leave all, all these rural pleasures, these home ties for the stern course of College discipline, from that to a Law office, and whence, I knew not. I knew that this green yard and spacious garden was to be my home no more, that I must in a short time launch myself into a world, cold and heartless, among strangers and men of corruption, men whose sins far out-balance those I have committed, and God knows they are many. It is not because I dread the toil and privation I must subject myself to but because of my parting with the spot that has been the scene of my younger days, when even this period as early as it is was looked forward to as being a time when I should be happier, but I find that every period of my short life has been embittered more or less by childish troubles. Yes! because I must tear myself from all these endearments and stem the current. But I will not flinch; I do not dread it; it is my duty to myself, to my country, and my God that I improve and put in practice the few faculties I have. But enough of this. A boy with as much before him as myself and who, nevertheless, has a kind father to help him to make the beginning, ought not to look gloomily upon those things that his care and affection will make less iniquitous for him.

Cousin Gus, Uncle Jack, and myself took a walk this evening and on the way back I killed an owl with a brick-bat. This, studying, and writing a letter to Lizzie, which I shall have to write over again, consumed the evening.

Monday, May 7, 1860

A nice day has flown by fastly because it has been occupied in study. My first lesson in Algebra was got today. I am trying to improve my reading by reading aloud to myself and hope to profit by it.

The little "lady bird" was here this evening, but I did not indulge myself— only so far as to take a sly little look at her and cannot but think every time I see her: "ut pulchritudine eximia femina est."[71]

Mrs. Wm. Percy played some of Miss Ella's old tunes that revived very pleasant feelings and thrilled me entirely. Oh! I love music so much. If ever I live to be able to marry (and I never will till I can support one) my wife shall understand music well. Will this day ever come? Or will I depart first? There! what melody! I have just come back to my Journal after finishing the line at the foot of the last page when the soft notes of a flute floated in at my door, even at this late hour. I went out toward the garden, leant on a tree, and listened to some familiar airs—"Coral Schottische," "Willie we have missed you," &c., &c. I enjoyed it very much.

Tuesday, May 8, 1860

Unexpectedly we had a very desirable rain to visit us about 3 o'clk. School. Mr. Herbert is pleased with the manner in which I get my Algebra lessons and also likes my progress in Latin Grammar. Not long since he paid me a compliment (sincerely, for he would not tell a lie) saying that he would venture his word that my knowledge of Latin was more perfect than that of either of the boys that left last fall and June. I hope I shall please the professors at the University as well as I do him.

Wednesday, May 9, 1860

Notwithstanding a little shower that fell a little after dark, this day has been clear. School. I got my morning lesson after coming from school and took a walk, once for some time, and saw the little fairy out reading, and saw Bill was, I suppose he is now, talking to her as he told me he intended to call on her. Uncle Jack and Cousin Gus are at Judge Rucks's paying a visit to Miss Marian, so it seems that most every one is taking a "squint" at the gulls tonight. Before they started they wanted a drink and called on me for it. I went up and got the bottle and sent the tumblers, sugar, &c. down by a boy. Very little was in the bottle, and they wanted me to go after more, up to a closet in the garret. I am willing to do every thing that is right and my duty, but I do not think it was my place to perform the part of a valet and run up stairs to get whiskey for any man (my father excepted) to drink. I may be in the wrong, but I did what I thought was right. I told them so in this manner as far as I can recollect my words leaving out some imprecations*[72] that would be as superfluous as they were ungentlemanly: "Now it does look nice Cousin Gus that I must 'trapse' up and down a flight of stairs like a negro to wait on two great, lazy men that do nothing but drink liquor, sleep, and go to see women." I said let a negro do it. "But a negro can't go into the closet," they say. Independence said, "it's servile," pride, "it's low." I obeyed their whisperings and firmly refused to comply with their repeated solicitations because I thought it would be casting away from me the respect that is my due. Cousin Gus laughed and Uncle Jack looked sullen. All I said was in such a manner not to convey the idea that I was indignant but that I considered it beneath my station to be *Mr. Anybody's butt*. As I have before said this independence may be to my disadvantage, but I will sternly reject all such proposals. Here are the identical gentlemen! Cousin Gus came in first and in speaking of the thing, I put the question to him at the same time saying that I would do any thing that was right to accommodate him "if he would like to gallop around a house drawing whiskey &c. &c. for anyone!" His answer perfectly justified my course.

Pa returned from Dr. Dunn's this evening and brings grievous news. He says that he was sinking rapidly and that there was not the least hope for his life, news that has thrown a gloom around the family that is painful. He was a man of such correct principles and honesty, such an excellent physician as well as citizen that he will be sorely lamented by his community.

Thursday, May 10, 1860

Much cooler than is usual at this period of the year; fires being comfortable to dress by. Every day I see the great necessity of my leaving home for schooling myself somewhere else — not in any of my studies but Algebra. Mr. Herbert does not understand it at all compared to the way a teacher should be conversant with a branch to be able to give that instruction and give it in such a manner as to make all obscurities clear and plain. He has to study along before me and a student cannot properly instruct a student. If for nothing else, I should leave next fall.

Friday, May 11, 1860

Warm and sunny day. 5 o'clk PM. Pa and Ma got to the house of affliction in time yesterday morning only to see a dear friend depart to the land of spirits after incredible sufferings for 8 days. His body was in a horrible state from mortification even before his death. I never saw Pa lament any one's death so in my life. In company with Uncle J., Jimmy and Bay (Pa going with Mr. A. Rucks) I went up to his funeral. The ride was long and dreary as was the time till the procession commenced. A Mr. Preston of Abingdon recognized me and spoke first (I did not know him), he having been introduced to me last summer. He is the brother of Miss Amelia Preston of that place who is as pretty a woman as ever I saw. But none of this here. I was astonished to see the gaudiness of dresses and the indifference paid by the large concourse of people who came to see the ceremony to the recollection of the deceased. They laughed, talked of crops, roads, and every thing they would have talked of if it was a gathering for festivity. The procession to the place of interment was long and the ceremony was imposing, being first performed by Messrs. Hines and Herbert, the first reading the funeral sermon, "dust to dust," which was very interesting, and Mr. Herbert delivering an eloquent prayer in behalf of the stricken family and their loss. Then came the first part of the Masonic ceremonies while purple bibles, badges and regalias were pompously displayed. The casket was carried first between two little blue pinions crossed, having been conducted between two lines of Masons. One with a sword in his hand led the way and in double file the rest of the masons followed, the corpse close behind. [. . .] on foot came next, followed by a long train of carriages. I walked close to the coffin. Occasionally the little pinions were crossed and the Masonic part of the procession passed under it and they then took their stations or rather their places near the front. (Pa has just come down to send me up to Judge Yerger's on an errand and suspecting the tenor of this entry lent over the table and read what I had written and then turned to the beginning of the entry and read to the foot of the last page. Casting his eye on page 126 and turning over read the whole of the entry and in my asking him his opinion of my course, his answer led me to believe that he agreed with me so his assent confirms all doubts. I was happy to see that I could interest him.)

9 o'clk. I have been to Judge Y's and have eaten supper and now will finish my entry. The coffin being placed over the grave and the near connections and chief mourners (some of the family including the lady were sick and could not attend) being stationed properly, silence reigned while Dr. Finlay[73] read the burial ceremony of the Masons that was beautifully composed as well as read. It was then lowered into the grave and the forms having been gone through with (the clapping of hands) they slowly moved around the grave, each one taking a piece of Arbor Vita from his button hole and throwing it upon the coffin. As Dr. F. commenced reading the service, Mrs. Gregory, the sister of the deceased, gave a stifled sob, and this combined with the touching manner that the piece was read and the solemn occasion made a cold shiver run through my frame. As the service proceeded I could not suppress the tears from coming to my eyes, honorable tears for which I do not blush and hope that I shall never be so base to be ashamed of tears shed for a man like him! I was not the only one in tears. Pa's eyes were moist and his face betoken[ed] more grief than tears can express. The last office being finished toward the dead, we went back to the house and I shortly took my departure for home. Probably there is not a man in the country whose death would be so universally lamented as his. Truly he was "vir exempli recti."[74] But I will not eulogize upon his virtues here but will close this entry as well as my eyes this night sincerely hoping that his soul is at peace! Sincerely hoping that his stricken family may have the remembrance of this bereavement wiped gently from their memories—not entirely either, but that time may soften the accuteness of their affliction and that they may look up to Him, He who is the sustainer of the widow and the father of the fatherless and say with sweet resignation, "he whom the Lord loveth, he chasteneth. Blessed be the name of the Lord."

Saturday, May 12, 1860

Only a half of this lovely day has passed in an advantageous manner. I read English History till 12 o'clk and lazyly lolled upon my bed in my room reading fiction till nearly sundown when Uncle Jack and myself walked up to the gin where nearly all the family were fishing. I returned about 25 minutes before dusk and walked down toward the bridge with Mrs. J. H. Yerger. Every time I converse with this admirable woman my opinion of her is increased. Her sentiments seem so solid and well-grounded. She expresses herself so well and all in such a becoming, womanly manner that any one of taste cannot fail admiring her. We spoke of education and her observations were masterly—so much so that they showed me the great abyss between me and the attainment of my education. I returned home thoughtful and pensive, feeling gloomily, and with my thoughts wandering vaguely.

Sunday, May 13, 1860

2½ o'clk. I am writing here in my journal because my mind is not at ease. Having arisen late, I went to church. Then, before the service commenced, I sat and had a most delightful little conversation with Miss Mary Alexander, all the while enjoying the gentle luster of her pure black eyes and the beauty of her pert little mouth. I do think she is one of the prettiest little beings I ever saw! I must not, however, eulogize upon her fascinations here; probably I have done so too much already in previous pages. But let me bring myself down to the present time. After this engrossing conversation, I listened to a very good sermon (read) by Mr. Herbert—so good as to bring tears into the eyes of the two Mrs. Percys and who else I know not. On my way home I felt a restless desire to see this little "lady bird" again, and it has clung to me until now and taking into consideration my desire to take a last "squint" and to satiate this inclination to be in her presence again, I came to the conclusion that at all events I would try to obtain her company in a ride this evening, and accordingly just before I commenced this entry I dispatched a boy with a card on which was written the request, penned as advantageously as was in my power. Because I am liable to a refusal is the reason why my mind is "not at ease," and to kill time until an answer shall reach me, I write here to "kill time." Until it comes I will read—I am very impatient—will she say no? I hope not.

Night in its sable folds has enveloped the rural scenery around my happy, tranquil home since the time I transmitted the request, "ut super demonstravimus" to ride this evening. The answer at last came. I tore rather than opened the delicate envelope and read an equally delicate refusal to my proposition. Strange to say I was rather amused than otherwise. I could not suppress a smile that I felt to stretch my clumsy mouth (just beginning to be white with "fuss"). Of course she "regretted," she being an "inexperienced equestrian" &c. I do not think I shall again ask to ride through the medium of pen, ink and paper, this being the second time I have been refused, though each time with good excuses. So I shall only "nod my cranium" to her as she passes tomorrow on her way to Greenville and from there home. Sweet girl, may thy path be bright with flowers and thy innocence be always gay and happy!

Monday, May 14, 1860[75]

Silvery clouds floating about. I did not return from the schoolhouse till after sundown. As I advance further in Algebra I find that Mr. H. gets more and more disqualified to teach me. Examples that I cannot master and take to him he if he shows me takes a considerable length of time that if I was shown expeditiously could apply to further study. I do wish he understood it as well as he does Latin.

Tuesday, May 15, 1860

Weather during the morning cloudy and now (9½ o'clk PM.) it is raining, having commenced at dusk. About 11½ AM. I had occasion to go to the Creek and saw, or rather heard and saw, a very strange thing. Off in a W. direction pure white clouds, intermingled with others of various coulors—I heard a distant roaring as that of a wind. There was very little air stirring on the surface. I was very curious; probably it was a hard wind in the upper elements. School. On my return from school I found a letter from Nat and answered it "sine [. . .]" and did not get through till dusk.

Wednesday, May 16, 1860

All clear and bright. I did not get back from school till nearly dusk and found that Pa brought a letter for me from Hal. It contained exactly the news I have looked for for months passed, viz—that his boyish passion (like mine) has gradually given away to the effects of time and that now his engagement with Miss Wingate, as well as the trouble of keeping up the appearance of love to her, is bouring (like my Va. engagement was). In answer I offered my services and at the same time telling him that I thought he had better, if he intended to break it off, to give me her address and that I would adjust the matter to the best of my power.

Thursday, May 17, 1860

A warm clear day has passed in study. At the supper table I received another letter from Hal, almost contradicting what he said in the letter yesterday, saying that he still loved her as ever and never expected to love any other but would not marry. He made a suggestion that if it could be accomplished it would suit me exactly, that we would live together. I really think that he had better break it off by allowing me to address the young lady on the subject, as it would be an awkward thing for him to do, placed as he is.

Friday, May 18, 1860

Warm and sunny. When I had finished my lessons I went to the old swimming place in front of Mr. Yerger's quarters and went in swimming with the boys. These pleasures bring back sweet memories—each spot is as a memento of some boyish festivity and in particular an old sycamore log extending into the water from the opposite bank makes me remember the gay times when Nat, Taylor, and Hal and myself would sit dabbling in the water off of which we would plunge and glide down to a large flat beam off of which we would dive and turn somersets. I cannot but be melancholy when I know that we are virtually separated and our bright days of boyhood have passed for we are separated probably to meet but a few more times and then each shall remember the other as a schoolmate, then each shall be cast into a different land to toil and wrestle with adversity.

Mr. Herbert found that the introductory lessons were as much of a puzzle to himself as to me and put me at the beginning of the Algebra proper, where I got more by 1½ pages than he had looked over and consequently he did not hear it. I spoke of this deficiency to the old man, to Pa, the other morning and was surprised to see that he not only agreed with me as to his inability to instruct me as I should be but spoke rather reproachfully to me on account of my having told him of my prediction or rather my presentiment set forth in my entry of M'ch 23d; he seemed to regard it as frivolous and spoke of my going as a firmly settled fact.

Saturday, May 19, 1860

Taking off a little walk up to the schoolhouse (where I was bored by Mr. H. about his little "ailments," &c.) and some little "jobs" done for Ma in the morning, I have read Grecian History, in which I am delighted, the balance of this pretty day.

The sun is now about to set, and I have just come down from getting liquor out for Bill and Sam Starke. This thing is contemptible to me and each time I am placed so that I cannot avoid it. They come, I have to go up, and the next thing I hear is Uncle Jack calls me off and says: "These boys want a drink, can't you get it?"—knowing all the time that all is locked up except what Pa had in his drawer for his private use—"can't you get his bottle out of his drawer? I don't like to go into it." I could not help myself; I had it to do. Could I say there was none? I will go right up and tell Uncle Jack that under no circumstances will I again do this thing and that he only will subject himself to a refusal, flat and positive, by asking. I went "straightway" and in the plainest tone told him of my determination. Either from a conviction of the justice of my cause or from contempt he made no reply. I cared very little which he thought for I was confident I was right. I spoke warmly and I got still more vexed than before and went off passionately walking down the road. Going I met Miss Kate Lee and coming Miss Medora Cook (I knew her from reputation only) whose locks (wavy as I took them to be) were flying to the breeze and Miss Marian; three gentlemen were along. I "snatched" my cranium at them as they passed. Before I got back my vexations had disappeared, and I was as "happy as a lark."

Sunday, May 20, 1860

The morning of this warm though windy day was spent at church where there was quite a collection of people to hear Bishop Green preach. I cannot say I either liked the sermon or the service. I do not like ceremony about religion but instead of written prayers and answers to questions laid down, the pompous display of satin and muslin on the minister. I love the good old-fashioned Methodist way, where the minister goes up and shows, without ceremony show or parade, the true and open faith for the sinner to go and to pray and prayer from the heart not from the book; one though extemporaneously delivered is as the spontaneous outbursting of a fountain, pure, serene, and unsullied. These forms are abominable to me; even more so is the ceremony of christening children, for in it I see in the part of the ministry as grasping after power which has been the case from the earliest period. This bishop I believe to be a good old man doing what he thinks right, but bigotry blinds him and this same bigotry despaired me of earlier study than I have had—but I forgive him.

Studied during the evening and took a walk.

Monday, May 21, 1860

No study of consequence has been performed this warm and sunny morning, firstly because the seats and desks were turned "topsy-turvy" at the schoolhouse for the bishops sermon and secondly because Laurence was christened this morning, Ma desiring us to remain and see the ceremony, which I did solely because she wanted it, it being all "fal-lal" in my estimation. It is 12 M. and the company has retired. About 11 AM the bishop not having come, Ma sent me down to Judge Rucks's after him, *me*, because he was bishop. Again this indomitable independence; it will present itself and my disposition will receive it hospitably. It seemed as though I had to go, paying him this homage (however small, still repugnant in the extreme) simply because he is a man holding a high position in the Episcopal Church. The repugnance did not arise from any disinclination to obey Ma, no, far from that, but it was placing me in the position of a servant, a courier to him, that made me shrink from it, as I would if he had been supplanted by *any* man. Fortunately I was saved by the mortification of delivering my message by meeting him with Judge Rucks. Let people scorn or ridicule it, but I do homage to no man! For causes above stated there being no school, I read Grecian History all evening, taking off a walk and some time devoted to my music. It is late. I had a dream of Miss Alexander last night but am too drowsy to record it here now, so Good night old Journal!

Tuesday, May 22, 1860

During this sunny May day nothing of consequence has transpired within the narrow limits of my little sphere. My life is quite monotonous. I know each day what I shall do the next, the next, and the next. I think often of Hal and his "scrapes" and wonder if he will trust its conduct to me—will he?

Wednesday, May 23, 1860

The sun of a warm day has sunken to rest before I quit the schoolhouse, though an hour was devoted to swimming after school *proper* was finished, which hour I enjoyed pretty well, not having a companion of my size and age. No studying done tonight on account of Mr. Cook being here and Jimmy and myself having to play for him. It is nearly eleven o'clk and he has gone and again I am unable to record the dream, but it shall be recorded at the earliest opportunity.

Thursday, May 24, 1860

Warm and sunny day. I recruited myself this evening by a protracted bathe in my native Creek, paddling most of the time about with an old door that was on the bank, but not having recited my Latin lesson I called, or rather stayed, at the schoolhouse on my way back home and recited it and studied my Ancient Geography lesson. This morning before I went to school a servant came to me telling me that Ma wanted me. I proceeded to her apartment where she was sewing on a shirt for me and she wanted me to show her where to put the button-holes in the sleeves for my sleeve buttons. I had on a little plain gold pair that she had given (last July) and after I had shown her, she said, "Here, take these," handing me a large and very pretty gold pair, "and give me those," looking as mothers only can look—kind and sympathizing. I took them and was much pleased.

On returning from school, I found a letter from Nat for me, directed "Col," a "nickname" given me in '54 and my friends often call me by it now. He beats me, oh! a long way; he is about entering Geometry and Trigonometry and is reading Cicero. I would like to swap heads with him. I would rather build a cottage on a rock than a castle in a "sunny place." I read it while walking and walked about 100 yards behind Miss M. & Miss M. Cook—behind because I was a *boy!*

Friday, May 25, 1860

Half past five o'clk PM. Having occupied the greater part of the time intervening between supper and bed-time in answering Nat's letter (in which he said he had a difficulty with his tutor), I done little studying. This morning before school "took in" I told Mr. H. of his surprising progress, and he effectually said that with what he (as well as Hal) knew where they left him, without almost superhuman exertions they could not have traversed such a space so as to thoroughly understand it. I agreed with him. School only was held till 12, Mr. H. being sick, and the balance of the evening has been passed in reading Grecian History in which I am very much interested and am storing my mind with useful knowledge, thereby filling up blank places therein. I will now go down to see the old gentleman, who not withstanding his peculiarities, I really love. Dusk had come before I got back from the schoolhouse.

Saturday, May 26, 1860

Very warm day but a pleasant breeze from the South tolerated the heat to a considerable degree. No activity today; most of my time having been occupied in reading Grecian History and was astonished to see as I penetrate into it the striking similitude between the character of the Greeks and Romans—fickle and enthusiastic, comprising great genius and depravity and always being led by a master spirit, sometimes patriotic, as Pericles, sometimes wily, as Alcibiades, and again courteous, as Niceas.

Before sundown I took a bathe in the creek and after, a little walk. At the dinner table there was quite a catechising on Geography (modern) and without boasting and telling the plain truth, I was not "blunted" in but one question about Lyons being a sea port. A thing very uncommon for him, Pa paid me a compliment—that I understood Hist. and Geog. very well—an ample remuneration for long study!

Sunday, May 27, 1860

Weather without change. There being no church, the morning I passed in reading Grecian History and cannot but fear, seeing that to almost every nation that has been a republic that eventually the liberties of the people are usurped, that this my beloved native land will yet have its rippling brooks and green fields stained with the life-blood of its dwellers—my people, my countrymen, when I shall have passed into eternity many, many years. I love my country and therefore I lament even this liability of her woes that may come.

My mind has by no means been in repose or at ease during the evening, Pa having told me at dinner table that I would not leave for the University till Nov. instead of Sep. because he fears for my health, much to my regret; but more of this hereafter. Took a ride with Uncle J. and got my lessons in the evening. It seems as though I can't get a chance to put that dream in here!

Monday, May 28, 1860

All this warm day has been passed in study. I study my Grammar lesson at recess, my morning lesson for the following day in the evening after dismission my spelling lesson and look out the meaning of all the words in the spelling lesson I say before dismission, pondering over a few so as to remember them. This generally occupies me till sundown, having taken off an hour for bathing. When I get home, a little walk, and then as soon as supper is over, to my music for an hour and the balance of the time till bed-time I study Grammar.

Tuesday, May 29, 1860

School through a day as warm as yesterday. I found a letter from Hal at sundown when I returned from school. A lucky fellow! has got a "gal" so much in his power as to get as many kisses and squeezes as he wants—charming—and calls him "sugar." Bright life that. I'll lead it one of these days. I told him to kiss her once for me even if she could not reach that bright pinacle of beauty that Miss Alexander held so modestly. I want to see him very much and as the time approaches to vacation the wish appears oftener. During my walk my mind was in a very troubled state. I cannot but feel despondently when I think that 5 long months must go slowly by before time comes for me to go.

Wednesday, May 30, 1860

Two showers fell this morning, but the balance of the day was clear and before I got back from my walk the beautiful moon that I love to look at so much was out. I was standing in my gallery looking at it when I saw a star shoot that looked strange and incomprehensible. The sun was about to set when I left the schoolhouse; after recess which lasts till 1 o'clk I go in and unless I go to swim I never leave till 6 or after. My first lesson in Cicero today and am much pleased with him, though he is a little harder than Caesar, which I left yesterday. Would that I could arise and extemporaneously say all just as he commenced his memorable oration against Cataline, "Quousque tandem abuten, Catalina, patientia nostra."*[76]

Thursday, May 31, 1860

Beautiful and warm day. In Algebra I have gone to the division of polynomials and with the exception of the fractioning of them I have as yet found no difficulty. That I did not satisfactorally understand as Mr. H. was not able to give me that light on it that I needed. Sometime since I dropped my book keeping, the time I had to devote to it being too little to enable me to carry it on with advantage. I went in swimming this evening after school. Returning, I recited my Cicero and having talked with Mr. H. about the genius and forcible eloquence, writings, &c. of the man, I came home and soon after went down to Judge Rucks' for a *Harper*, Pa having stopped it on account of its abolition proclivities, it then being nearly dark. The sun was nearly setting as I left the schoolhouse. I forgot to say while speaking of my studies that this morning I finished Ancient Geography. But to my little trip to Judge R's. I found Miss Marian pacing (gracefully of course) up and down the gallery. She looked very sweetly and stepped up, I accosted her with the usual salutation. I soon made known my object and soon received it at her fair hands but found it rather difficult to depart, being much interested; it is not worth the while or space to state even the outline of our conversation. Suffice it to say, to me at least, it was engaging. Within 15 minutes I did depart notwithstanding and returned hence with a heart as light as the pretty moonlight in which I walked.

I will "out" with that dream which was short and too sweet for me to think of. It was on the night of the 20th inst. We cannot account for dreams. I cannot say why it was so, but I seemed to be in a very lonely place with that little "bonny bird," water before us to be crossed and no way to do it but for us to wade. She wade? I'll die first, I thought. I lifted the darling burden in my arms, oh, I have no words to express how I felt then—her arms were around my neck. I commenced my crossing. I looked in that sweet face, could I help it? I kissed those nectrine lips. I pressed her still closer to my throbbing heart—my cup of bliss was filled to overflowing![77]

Friday, June 1, 1860

Hot and clear. The division of polynomials made me study pretty hard today. I read the speech I will recite on the 24th inst this evening, the translation of the 1st chapter of Cicero's 1st oration against Cataline. Went in swimming after school and had not been reading a sketch of Cicero's life long on my return to the schoolhouse before Bill came up and stopped. During the conversation he asked me what was the matter with my eyes. Uncle J. has asked me the same question lately and says that at times I look a little crosseyed. Mr. H. who was talking with us said he also had marked something peculiar about my eyes. One of my eyebrows are nearly white and likewise the underlash—they are almost entirely white, a decided grey. My eyes are of a grey, sneaking of course, and if they are crossed I will be a perfect monkey with the freckles on my face. "But the wealth of the mind is the only true wealth." Take off my feet and from my waste down (with one other exception) I am made very much like a woman (so all say who ever saw me "nudus membra"). Lately at times my eyes would pain me, though slightly, and when I would arise a dizziness would come over me. Howbeit I hope all this is an illusion. I came home a little before sundown and took a very pleasant walk, thinking a good deal about my long looked for departure for Va.

Saturday, June 2, 1860

Through a long hot day I have lazily kept myself in doors dividing the time indiscriminantly lounging, reading, and my music. I took for my lesson today Saracuse Polka and think it right pretty. Ma gave us some Ice-cream and cake this evening, and I for exercise more than anything else took hold of the freezer and turned for some time and had a relish for it. Mr. H. ate supper with us and among us there were some "big" tornado stories told.

I have just seen a thing of common occurrence here; the negroes, i.e. a good many of them, have assembled on my gallery, one plays on the Banjo, some pat while others dance. The songs are rattling in my ears now.

During a walk Uncle J. and myself took this evening we recalled some scenes of mirth we partook of last summer at Grayson Spr's in Va. and I had quite a hearty laugh. This evening he ridiculed my hair or rather laughed at it. He said some was light, some dark, some brown, and a number of colors. I took it very good naturedly. My hope is that I have a reasonable quantity of brains under it, for if that is the case I shall be popular (with the ladies too) and if I am handsome and senseless I shall most assuredly be unpopular with both.

Sunday, June 3, 1860

Some have complained of the heat today, but I have not been troubled with it much. At the usual time I went to church and there saw Deer Creek arrayed in all her glory. Mrs. Medcalf was there, once a pretty woman but for me now spoiled by corpulency. Nihil est femina formosius.[78] But this rule only applies to those like Miss Alexander. A modest pretty woman is in my eyes a luxury ever to behold—a maiden pure and chaste; Oh! What word will express the luxury of ——? For them I study and toil; to them (such only as have above spoken of) I have dedicated my life—they are my God!

My evening has been past partly in bathing and partly in translating the first chapter of Cicero's first oration against Cataline, which I expect to declaim on the 27th. I took a walk this evening. Pa and myself talked over his plan of detaining me till Nov., and though I hate to wait five long months and loose all of October, I cheerfully coincided with him, hoping to be able to commence with the class I would enter by applying myself through the vacation.

Monday, June 4, 1860

After a day hot and breezy I sit perspiring while I scribble here. I must be brief and soon to bed. No lesson in Chronology said this morning, the time being taken by a meeting of the trustees which was characterized by the peculiarities of this neighborhood. I am not yet through the division of polynomials but hope to enter fractions by Wednesday. There will be no school tomorrow; most of the boys will leave for a little munkey show in town. I found it rather hard to study this evening, suffering from dysentery. Until this morning I did not know that Nat was dismissed from school. John tells me that he has been dismissed twice—once for brickbatting the academy and again for getting "tight." I am sorry for him; I can't help it; if a boy of Nat's age chooses to do these things, he can only expect to abide by the consequences. For sometime before I commenced this entry, I was codgitating over the subject on which I will write my composition. I fear they will expect too much. I can only do my best. They must be content with that, and I can ask them in the simple and forcible words of that little poem so favored by boys:

> "Don't view me with a critic's eye
> But pass my imperfections by."[79]

I think that it will be written mostly from historical scenes. I at least expect not to disgrace myself.

Tuesday, June 5, 1860

I have suffered from the heat today much more than I have before this year. I made an attempt to write a composition after breakfast, studied at it for a long time, and finally, disgusted with myself, I threw down my pen and left. Very little of the remainder of the day was spent to advantage. I practiced my music, hunted cool places and read some. I drove the buggy down to Judge

Rucks's bridge for Pa who was over to see the old gentleman and had to wait about three quarters of an hour for him, which did cheerfully, knowing that I am incapable of repaying them for what they have done for me. I have intended to go up to see John McCutchen this morning, but Pa (always with that same tenderness) said to me: "My son I would not go now but I would wait till evening. It will be very hot coming back and you are not used to the sun, it might make you sick." Because he wanted it and on account of his reasons that I had not thought of before, I did not go and did not feel like doing so in the evening.

Wednesday, June 6, 1860

Last evening we had a little shower and up to this time (12 o'clk) the atmosphere has been more pleasant. No school again today. I wish [. . .] shows and weddings (Mr. H. went up to Hale's to marry a couple (Hale's sister, I believe)) would suspend proceedings till after this month. They break into my arrangements woefully. My music lesson this morning was "Ever of Thee,"[80] one of Miss Ella's pretty songs (her name on these pages again?) but I have only the air. I wanted the words and thinking that maybe Miss Marian had them, I sent a boy down with a note (polite as possible, of course) requesting her to lend them to me to copy. To my discomfiture he returned (there now! a fly was in my inkstand. I, in getting some ink, picked him up on my pen and in bringing it over to write, he fell on the page and made that ugly splotch). But to what I was saying: He returned bearing a note from Mrs. Yerger saying that Miss Marian was from home and that she, reading my note, took it upon herself to answer it, and that the music was Miss Dellie's and that she had taken it away with her. What did you do that for Miss Dellie? It makes me think of that woman that interested me so last winter all the time I am playing it. I remember these fragments. Oh! she used to sing them so sweetly and if Miss Mary could hear me say now that

"Morn, noon, and night
Where ere I may be,
Fondly I am dreaming
Ever of Thee"

and one more little sweet line

"Every kind thought like a bird flies to Thee"

I think of taking a ride with Miss Marian this evening, i.e. if she does not think within herself, "oh, he's a boy" and say "no." I think I shall try her at all hazards. Not long after taking my music lesson I was in Ma's room talking with her about education, parents' cares about their children, and how she had got along with her privations for her children. When she spoke of how disheartened a mother feels to see a son, after expecting her whole life making it full of cares and vicissitudes for him to turn out a vagabond and a drunkard, how illy repaid they were, she shed tears. She need shed none for me. She shall never sigh for my conduct. She said that out of the number of boys she had that she feared greatly that some one would turn out badly and repeated to me a verse that she memorized years since. It ran thus:

"Ah! brandy, brandy, bane of life
Spring of tumult, source of strife
Could I but half thy curses tell
The wise would wish thee safe in hell."

Night has come and instead of riding with Miss Marian I have unequally divided my time between my piano and my Grecian History because of the boisterous weather.

Thursday, June 7, 1860

While I lay in bed this morning, I saw heavy clouds, pitchy black, in the west through my window and from it came much rain and such a quantity of wind as to lay the corn over. The rest of the day was of various weather.

Mr. H. ate breakfast with us, and he and myself got to the schoolhouse just in time to escape a heavy shower. I was the only scholar at school and got along with my studies very placidly, getting my first lesson in Algebraic fractions. I wish I could study the same way every day.

This morning Mr. Herbert gave me the poetry of "Gentle Annie"[81] and I copied it. It is a beautiful song and there are two lines of it that are peculiarly adapted to my own experience (*and particularly to recent experience*).

"Thou art gone, alas! like the many
That have bloomed in the summer of my heart."

What if Miss Mary could hear me say those two pathetic lines? Hear me say them mournfully to myself as I walk home from school, a poor school boy, the monotony of whose life is not even broken by some boy associate. Perfectly isolated from every pretty face and every gayety, buried in myriads of book, oppressed about his forthcoming entrance into College, with a thousand annoying vicissitudes to harrass him incessantly and to complete his woes he must not even so much as see a lady. Oh! that would be an egregious transgression upon his attention to his books. But I will, I will see one sometimes! I get away from my little thread. I commenced by asking this old Journal (Will it ever answer my questions?) if Miss Mary Alexander saw all this whether or not she would with those fascinating eyes that such a short time since shot such fire into the very core of my heart which has so often been lascerated by love's cruel lashes, whether they would say in a mute language peculiar to them, "I pity you"? Oh! woman, truly "thou was't the last" and best gift of God to man. Thou, who like the clinging Ivy clings to the ruddy oak, nestle in his bosom, and who, when the cold blasts of adversity do assail him, shelters him from its pelting fury in his decline like the verdant branches of that Ivy protects its once strong supporter from the vigorous weather. Thou art his ministering angel, his heaven on earth.

Friday, June 8, 1860

Time rolls on but slowly; every time I measure the time that is to pass away slowly or wearily it seems to grow longer. Will the time never come for me to leave? None of us knew our declamations this evening as we should. I know mine not at all having changed my mind as to the one I would get. It is now an old Revolution speech by James Otis, firey and deep. I am going to labor at it. My good old teacher has no one to whom he can pour out his troubles except for me and not without reason no doubt he looks upon me as the nearest one to him with regard to friendship and hence I become the harbinger of his troubles, at least of many of them. Though it is by no means pleasant to me, I fear it on account of my regard for him. He poured out some upon me this evening, about the peculiar circumstances by which he is surrounded &c. keeping me from coming home (after I had gone in swimming) until sundown.

Saturday, June 9, 1860

Well it seems that I was determined to make some pretty mistakes in writing Saturday. My memory has been divided between books and music. I was much amused at Pa and an old negro, Edmund, with whom he had a misunderstanding. He wanted to give the old fellow an order, and he refused to hear it, breaking in whenever Pa commenced. Pa told him to hush, and he would not do it but persisted in interrupting him until Pa threw a chair at him. That made him worse. Pa became exasperated and when he advanced upon him, he retreated. Pa then told him to leave and said, "if you put your foot outside of that gate you shall never enter it again, go sir!" The old fellow stopped and continued his retorts. Pa picked up a brickbat and advancing told him if he ran he would knock him down and catching him by the collar jerked him about and, pushing him on before him, made him go to the quarter. Edmund shied off wanting to run off still. Pa was angry. He made him come on over the stile, and then he made another attempt to run, but Pa, picking a hoe handle, told him if he would not stop he would try the hoe on him. He stopped and on the driver's coming up, he was whipped and then went about his business very peacibly. He's an old negro that Pa found a cripple and has nursed the last 12 years; still he won't do anything but what suits him—so much for negro gratitude. While it was being transacted all of us stood in the gallery (it was in the front yard) and because I laughed the children would say, "Brother Harry, haven't you got any feelings; I don't see anything to laugh at." Nevertheless it was funny to me.

Part of the evening was passed in memorizing my Declamation. I got more than half of it practiced and read most of the remainder of the evening. I had scarcely got seated comfortably on the west gallery after my walk while I watched the timid lightning bugs one by one as they made their egress from their woody homes among the forest trees in the yard and sparkled prettily through the twilight like so many "twinkling stars" (a scene peculiar to my adored South) when (after leaving the cheerful spectacle and had seated myself at my Piano) Pa called me to walk home with that interesting little lady Mrs. Lou Yerger. Our conversation turned upon the origin of the Episcopal Church. I touched delicately and made few assertions, drawing forth her views and knowledge on the subject by interrogations and found that she was pretty conversant with English History of the period that the Church of England appeared. Her view was quite different from the one I had formed of the matter. Knowing that many of her nearest relatives are members of that church, I forbore to express my sentiments but will speak them to these pages. Briefly, they are: that the Episcopal church is only the church of England; that the church of England is simply a reform church of the Roman Catholic church, formed and embodied by Henry VIII to carry out his vicious designs, viz. to be divorced from his wife, which on the Pope refusing to do, we immediately see the Dissenting church (now called the Church of England) rise up with the prostitute monarch at its head. And while he is the originator, while he broke it off from the Catholic church because that church would not accomplish his insidious designs, where on earth except through that church can the Episcopaleans claim Apostolic succession? I can substantiate what I say by authority of Dr. Goldsmith. For under the auspices and administration of Henry VIII the Episcopal church sprung up, still with a bulldog pertinacity it claims Apostolic succession.

I pointedly object to the service on the ground that it is folly for one to go to church, take his book of prayers (in which all supplications to the deity are laid down by the ministry) opens it and with his eye reads over the prayer the minister from the pulpit reads that prayer—is mechanical, not from the heart. The minister in his flowing robes goes on to read questions under which (in the churchman's book) there are answers proscribed and laid down for them to read out aloud in answer because it is the service not because they feel it, not because their hearts dictate to them these answers. I look on it as a perfect mockery of religion which I reverence as much as any one. These prayers and answers are utterly superficial—reverence done to God with the lips. I condemn it because it is absurd and foolish. It would be superfluous to say, I desist.

I am sorry to see that a reconciliation between Jimmy and myself will never take place. I have tried by every art, every kindness and regard for his return of affection for me, but without effect. He is inexorable. He takes every opportunity of opposing my wishes however much I may give away to him. I never advance an opinion but he asserts exactly the opposite; I can mark not the least approach to play with him, but he takes it as a desire on my part to dominate over him and strikes me; his every look and action betoken a desire to oppose me and a grievous rivalry has from my earliest recollection existed between us that has arrested every motive of affection in my past toward him. And I must say that his studied desire to wound my feelings and his continued avowel by epithets as stinging as he can invent—his actual dislike to every thing that I do or say and his repeated refusal to believe my word, have I must confess dampened my feelings as a brother toward him to a great degree. I can say nothing to him but that I am mortified by an abusive answer and a brotherly word has not passed between us for many a day. Can it be expected that under all these abuses that I can always act the part of the lamb? Though I have my high temper under excellent control, it has its bounds. Patience and endurance alike have an end with myself as well as other people. I regret this thing for Pa's and Ma's sake as much as ours, but I have strove, regretted and lamented in vain. This very night to my grief Pa was called in by him to settle a feud between us. Oh! will this hostility never cease?

Sunday, June 10, 1860

We were disappointed in seeing Miss Marian at church this morning because Mr. H. was sick. Little or no reading was done before I went or till after dinner when I studied my speech, wrote nearly the whole of my composition, read some and studied my Chronology lesson. About 5 o'clk I went down to ride with Miss Marian, but her horse being absent I was at first denyed that pleasure. While I sat in the parlor (knowing nothing of the wanting vacative) she stepped in from a side door looking very "entisin" announcing the bad news. I concluded to sit and chat a little with her at any rate and I expected to have a nice time of it—disappointment awaited me. An irrepressible embarrassment overcame me and seemed to banish all levity and vivacity, dampening to no small degree the pleasure on my part at least of our interview. When I had arisen to depart, her horse came back and at her proposal we took a short ride for the sinking sun would not, even if both parties had wished it, have allowed it. I had hoped that the embarrassment would cease, but it did not and a constraint existed the whole evening. I did a very fooling thing while riding which I know has lowered me in her estimation considerably. I told her of my having heard of her being addressed by a young gentleman not long since. I saw plainly that it was so—her confusion and answer confirmed my suspicions. Her answer to the untimed interogatory was: "it is impossible that you should have heard such a thing" in a mild, lady-like tone. I was cut, not on account of anything she said, but for the blunder I had made. I did not accept her invitation to take tea with her and came home a chastened boy, thinking that "he whom the Lord loveth, he chasteneth."

Monday, June 11, 1860

When I had recited my Chronology lesson and was about to take up my Algebra, Mr. H. requested me to suspend the latter for a while as he needed "brightening up." I disliked to do it but assented to the old gentleman's request with all my diminuitive stock of grace and studied English Grammar in the time allotted to Algebra. The old fellow got wrathy today and brought down the hickory upon Harry Percy sharply. From some unknown cause I felt as though I could, if he attempted it on me, notwithstanding my regards for the old man, break my milk bottle over his head for his flailing me in Dec. '58; a rankling in my bosom to have vengence—the devil was in my neck.

I had an exhilarating bathe after school and in the evening of a warm day. The Creek was swollen by recent rains and was deeper, more rapid, and of a nature to support one as he glides through its waves.

While sitting on the gallery with Ma and Pa (Uncle J and Cousin Gus being at Judge Rucks') we talked a long while about what I should do at College, what I should study, what rules I should make for my conduct, et cetera. Pa's counsel was deep and wholesome, advise that I shall never forget because it was so sound. To it I listened almost in silence. He told me of my pride; the way it made me act, pointed out my errors arising from it when in the presence of others, showing me many little peculiarities which stung me but I knew their value too well to allow the least rebellion. May I never forget the advise I received this night!

Tuesday, June 12, 1860

Few hours of this long hot day was passed in study. When I had got my English Grammar I took up my Algebra to see whether I could solve some of the difficulties Mr. H. had requested me to suspend that study for and found no difficulty whatever except the last example under the rule (to subtract algebraic fractions) but in studying it a little solved it. I showed him the sum and explained it to him as he could not do it. Does this not look a little like the pupil teaching the tutor? I did not say a Latin lesson this evening but studied over my composition very hard, but did not finish it till near sundown having resumed it after school was dismissed. Its subject was "Napoleon and Washington" but I went into very few incidents of W's life as it would not interest my hearers on account of their familiarity with it and cited only some of Napoleon's, making the whole composition with few exceptions a continued invective on his character &c. I hope that after bestowing so much labor on it (I always have to labor hard to obtain an object) that it will "pass muster." Even if it was excellent there is a great uncertainty about any one being there, i.e. many persons. I took a walk feeling exhausted and worn out. I met Mrs. Yerger going and coming and saw Nat (he got back Sunday) who was riding out with his sister. Judge Rucks came up to see Pa and Jimmy and myself had to play for the old gentleman. All the praise was Jimmy's, probably justly his. I could but deplore my "shortcoming." I am slow to make friends and by no means prepossessing in my personal appearance. I am of a rather tall figure, large muscular legs, well-made arms and chest, a small waist, large feet and hands, rather a small head covered with hair that turns colour as the light varies, pouting lips, a long face covered with freckles, gray eyes and a white eye brow and eyelash (i.e. it is almost white—much lighter than the other—it is the right one) completes my uncouth personage. All my hopes lay in the cultivation of the few brains I have! Jimmy is quicker than I am and can learn faster and forgets faster than myself so that if it is not so easy for me to learn it is "thar" when I have learned it.

Wednesday, June 13, 1860

My first attempt in pedagogism today. Mr. H. being sick, I at his request taught the boys in the evening but saw that they did not like to look upon me as their preceptor. I got along very easily to myself. I continued my Algebra and progress (as Mr. H. says) with repitity.

Thursday, June 14, 1860

This like the preceeding and many other days has been warm. Entered Equations of the First degree today. A little blustering wind came up about 2 o'clk and at the earnest solicitations of the boys Mr. H. dismissed them, but I remained and "stood it out." Mr. H. lately has often expressed his belief that as to general information and of mathematics particularly I know much more than either of the boys that left him last fall and further said that I had improved myself very much. My composition which I wrote to read on the 29, he says is written in the best style — but three slight mistakes in spelling and no grammatical errors. Truly from him (because he would not tell an untruth and because his praises at least are sincere — I wish all I received were merited and as sincere as his) I deemed it as a soothing recompense for two years of toil at my books. No one would judge so if they could see my incoherent scribblings in here and with my permission few shall ever see any of these pages. I returned home late and found some books Mr. Herbert had sent for which were directed to Pa and were wet from a shower that came while the wind blew. Among them was for me as my prize the life of Franklin and from Ma a Classical Dictionary. Not long ago Pa gave me a Worcester's English Dictionary which I like as well as I do anything of the kind I have ever seen.

Friday, June 15, 1860

The rewriting and reciting of our Compositions and Declamations occupied the whole of a warm evening. (Is there not ambiguity in that sentence? Truly no one but myself could even understand it and that is only because I wrote it.) As I advance I am more and more captivated by the technical reasoning in my Algebra; if this absorbs me, what will I do when I study Chemistry, Geometry, Trigonometry, &c.? I am going to exert every nerve to get the medal for mathematics at the University. May that Providence against which I have so long rebelled still assist me in its mercy as it has heretofore done and enable me to pluck this bright honor. I know my deep culpability and can only cast myself on its mercy hoping that in this line at least it will enable me to be at the head of my competitors.

I was upon the point of taking my usual walk when John Byrne came up and he not accepting my invitation to alight took a glass of water and went along down the road with me, I walking and he riding. I went across Judge Rucks' bridge and soon after we had gone beyond his gin, John alighted and we walked together to the old Cunningham bridge where I again crossed the creek and walked briskly home. Before I crossed while walking along we came within

4 feet of a very large moccasin snake lying across the road. One of us would certainly have been bitten had I not seen it at the very moment I did. I grasped John by the breast and threw him back, arresting very suddenly his progress, for one step more would have placed him in the reach of the venomous reptile. It would have been certain death if he had have bit. My first step was to strike it with a piece of rail about 3 feet long and next took a whole one up from the road side and mashed its head to jelly. He was an ugly, nasty looking thing. John was so excited that he did nothing toward helping me (though I need none). I was perfectly cool having done the like oftentimes.

Saturday, June 16, 1860

For the first time in six months I made a regular visit today, not having had any intercourse with a person of my age in that time. That visit was made to Nat, on which I set out soon after taking my music lesson. It was a hot ride of 3 miles. He met me very cordially and through the whole time I stayed (till 3 o'clk PM) he made no allusion to the affair of Feb. 3d or to the cause of his expulsion, and I having no particular curiosity to know his views of either circumstance kept silent on both subjects. I was first led into a porch where sat Maj. and Mrs. Lee and Miss Kate. I said "good morning" to each and bowed stiffly. The first mentioned transaction was not absent from my mind, but I still believe that Mrs. Lee was not privy to that contemptible treatment I received on that night. I have always liked her and to repeat my language in a letter to Hal written Wednesday night and judging from her openhanded and cordial conduct toward me ever since I have known her (from Dec. '57) "she is one of the few that do not hold me in contempt." If all women acted toward persons as she has toward me, they would be loved much more than they are. I was amused at Nat trying to turn a samoset from the bank over the water as I did, and at each attempt turned just far enough to run his head into the mud under the water. I had a good laugh at him. He could beat me jumping on land but it seems that I beat him jumping *over* water. I walked and made my entries from Wednesday to this one.

Here is a specimen of Uncle Jack's gratitude for my nightly rubbing him when he first came here, crippled up with rheumatism. I have often rubbed him until my wrists and arms ached. In fact for a long time I did it every night, not allowing a negro to do it because I sensed that he might be hurt. Most of this evening I have had a twitching pain through my right shoulder and a smaller one in my right foot, each being very painful when I moved. Before I went to bed I wished to have it (my shoulder) rubbed with some linament and as I could not reach it and none of the servants being about, I asked him to rub it for me and his answer was a peevish disgusting refusal half spoken and filled up with proposals though short and without turning his head to me. I do not recollect my answer but know that it expressed an indifference and my old nurse going past my room door soon after I called her in and *she* did it for me. This is the return I get from the man who my father has supported for two years and who he has furnished all the comforts of home—horse, room, water, clothing, and *every* thing, while he sets an example before his children of abject sloth, indolence, and drunkenness. His expenses far exceed mine and he consumes the substance due to me and deprives me of many things that otherwise I might have had. Still I have treated him with all the respect due him as my Uncle, not because it was due him as a man for no *man* will fold his hands in idleness and compel another to support him. I will go no further; it is painful to me to write this in these pages.

Sunday, June 17, 1860

A warm sun shown down upon us as our little congregation assembled at our little church. My evening was pleasantly passed in study mostly on a composition about "ladies and their dresses." I gave them particular "goss" for tight dressing. I write while candle bugs fly in my face, on my paper, crawl up my bare legs, bothering me nightly while a little negro rubs my rheumatic foot.

Monday, June 18, 1860

Hot day. Stopped in my algebra again because Mr. Herbert could not give me information. To me his excuses were paltry. In fact, I know as much about the study as he does. I wish by Jupiter I had a competent teacher. It is enough to vex a boy that wants to learn to be stopped continually, to be detained by a teacher who, when he asks for the elucidation of an example, reads the rule even two or three times, turns back and reads the preceding ones, hums and haws, bewilders the student and if he tells him at all takes half an hour to do it and two weeks in succession brings the study to a full stop. He thinks of quitting next Oct, and if this does take place it will bear considerably towards getting me off to Va. before that time. I wish heartily that these perplexities which touch such a vital place for me were over, that I was away where I could learn, and in the stead of an impediment being thrown in my way, a friendly, aiding hand was offered to aid me up the steep path to scientific excellency. For my future welfare, though it would separate me from all that I love and hold dear, my home and my kindred, I long to hear the dull [. . .] of the boat which will convey me from all these endearments.

Tuesday, June 19, 1860

Hereafter I shall not make it a rule to state the exact state of the weather but will only notice it when it is connected with the little incidents that I record here or when something unusual happens, as today we had a very hard wind and rain. I returned home from school about 12½ o'clk to drive back the calves that had got out and was going back when I had put on dry clothes, but Pa said not, that I could study here which I have done faithfully, spending a very pleasant evening over my Grecian History. My plan in all reading is this, and especially in my regular reading: I take my map of the countries in which the scenes take place and have it open ready for reference if I should feel any doubt as to the locality of any feature mentioned, my English Dictionary in my lap to which I refer whenever I am at a loss for the definition of a word, and my Classical Dictionary, which Father (I will call him this henceforth) gave me and read the sketches on the lives of every noted individual that is mentioned in the history. This practice of looking out words has lately contributed much to my little stock. What Franklin advises I feel confident in doing.

I finished Alexander's glorious career and though some may censure his character, I find nothing so very egregious. True his murdering or I might more properly say slaying his companion Cleitus was and still is a blot upon his otherwise generous course, but though he is much to be blamed for being intoxicated, it must be considered that he did labor under the influence of wine, that the action was aggravated by epithets and taunts from Cleitus, and his inordinate grief afterward, all shows that if he had been himself it would never have been done. His clemency to the vanquished throughout (and I only mention some of the principal that recur to my mind now): his pity for Darius, his treatment of that unfortunate man's family and his leniency toward Pourus; not leniency but nobleness. I could mention more. I do not in this trusty diary even stop to eulogize on those I have mentioned.

In my C. Dict'y I read an interesting sketch of the great philosopher's life, Aristotle. Oh! I wish I was able to be such a man. I also read, was interested by a sketch of the god, Apollo. I will check myself; if I would let go my pen it would scribble off pages here about my admiration of literature, the fine arts and the sciences till pages would be consumed and would derive more pleasure and probably more benefit from it than from the delineations of my puerile trials, but if I keep a journal I must keep it faithfully. As I said to mother this evening, my only real pleasure is in study. Hence these puerile trials, as I have called them, which nevertheless are acute, when my favorite study is compelled to be dropped for the want of a preceptor. Mother told me a while ago that I had stopped all my boyish ways and acted like a settled person much older than myself; when this is the case and not only this but the perpetual anxiety which attend me concerning my going to College it is not to be wondered that I should grow serious. I am serious; I feel serious and I know of no way to drown my despondency but with my books.

Wednesday, June 20, 1860

It would seem superfluous to say more about Mr. H's total inability to teach me algebra. Every morning it is the same whine about his not "satisfactorily seeing into the principle &c. &c" which makes me mad to think of without having to be bored by hearing it. It is at times only that I do not feel dispirited, those times only when I have some company or am reading, and as soon as I am left to my own thoughts I feel an oppression and seriousness which is by no means pleasant. Formally[82] when I was left to myself I had a light heart, whistled all the time and built castles in the air, i.e. when I was not reading for I would much rather read history than do anything else. Such boyish pleasantries and daydreaming I fear have vanished and that sterner things impend over my youthful head. I know that many trials and temptations await me and I trust that I shall still have that firmness which thus far has enabled me to withstand at least *many* of them. I stop this strain.

Pa (or father) last night said that I would be missed much when I left about helping him with the sick, weighing and administering medicine, and helping him about here in every way. He said Jimmy was too careless, and he could not trust him as he has me. Mother also said that I had been of help to her about the keys &c. It made my heart glad to hear them thus tell me frankly that my endeavors to please and obey them were not altogether in vain. I am sitting up now (10½ PM) to give medicine to a sick one who lays cracking ice on my floor, and I will not go to bed till 12¼ and while I sit cramped up I will make a sketch of my life up to this time, or very near it. Before I begin let me state what occupied my evening after school—it was in sewing and reading. In my olden days when I shall have hoary locks, I must not condemn too hastily the blots on these pages for bugs of every description are flying all around me in my face, on my paper, and every where else, and this should be an excuse alike for my hasty penning of this sketch. The blots were made by thumping at them when on they came and [. . .] the ink.

I was born to parents of the highest standing in society in Jackson, the capital of this state, on the 2nd day of August 1843, the third child to which my mother gave birth, both either being dead or dying soon after birth. I resided in or near Jackson with my father and mother, being an exceedingly handsome but delicate child, until the spring of 1848 when my father removed to this place, I having lost many of my "buty spots," for instance my auburn curls have trimmed into straight brown hair like I have now. In the thick swamp (for all this open, rich country was then newly opened places) I remained under the supervision of my father and mother in innocent childhood till 1850 when all the family went on a visit to Jackson in the summer. After our return I remained at home till the winter of 1852 when for about two months I was sent to school to Mr. Cokey at Greenville having learned to read and spell in the primer imperfectly. There I took my first lessons in reading and spelling, boarding from Mon. until Fri. when I came home at Dr. Finlay's nearby the schoolhouse. From some cause I do not know what, I was stopped and taken home and idled until December 1854 when I was sent to Mr. Mathews at Maj. Lee's, three miles down the creek where I boarded as I did at Dr. F's. I had lost nearly all I had ever known. Mr. M—— started me in the first rudiments of arithmetic, in reading, spelling, writing, and primary geography, in all of which I progressed as young schoolboys will, sometimes getting whailed and at others knowing my lessons. It is not to be supposed that I should get along without any boyish dissensions with Nat, Henry Percy, John and Jimmy (part of our stay at Mr. Lee's Bill, Taylor and Hal came also) in which all of the partialities, intrigues, &c. were practiced. I recollect I had a fight with Nat and the schoolteacher had a fight with us both. Nat was always my rival in every thing and is to this day. About April 1855 Mr. M. began to teach in the Cunningham house about 1¼ miles down the creek on Judge Rucks' land. Here I began to declaim first and progressed on in my studies (about to reduction of denumericate numbers in arithmetic and the third reader). The ladies and gentlemen of the neighborhood often came to hear us declaim. I continued at school here till July of the same year when vacation commenced which lasted until 1st October when it again commenced at the same place: Modern Geography, English Grammar, and Arithmetic in which I progressed with credit until the Christmas holidays when Mr. M. left the school destitute of a tutor. During this time we had in the school Jim[83] and Will Yerger,[84] Lucian Gay, besides those already mentioned.

In November of that year I went camp hunting with some gentlemen in Bogue swamp. About Christmas the family took a trip to Jackson and Yazoo City. At the latter place I enjoyed myself very much. On one occasion I was invited to a public hall and notwithstanding my age was formally introduced to the ladies by Uncle Moses and was much of a "pet" with them. I need not say that I enjoyed myself. I omitted to state that while in Jackson in the summer of 1854 that I took dancing lessons for two weeks and my teacher told every one that I was his best scholar. I have yet a good reputation among my friends for my dancing. Whether I deserve it or not Miss Dellie told me many times (whether she did it to flatter me or not I can't tell) that I waltzed better than anyone she had ever waltzed with.

While at dancing school I fell desperately in love with a beautiful little black-eyed brunette, a kind curly-headed little damsel with whom I had a standing engagement to dance with just when I pleased. Many parties were given to the scholars all of which I attended and "splugged" around considerably. I have finished this item and will return.

Some time during January 1856 we came home and went to school to a lazy scoundrel named Philson, until July and rather lost than learned. The boys said lessons when they chose, played when they chose and in short did exactly as they pleased, learning not the least thing. In June I had another fight with Nat, each of us being foolish enough to be incited to it by tales carried between us by other boys. It was a draw fight, the boys parting us to which both agreed and made friends on the ground. My face had very little skin on it, and his eyes were red and blue for the next week. School again commenced in October and the teacher having been appraised of the non-progress of the boys and accordingly went into the other extreme. He gave me a grammar lesson to get; I did not know how to get it, he never having shown me and would not show me at the time, and because I did not know it, whipped me severely with an unusually large switch. At recess I came home. Father would have taken summary vengeance on him but was dissuaded by Judge Rucks. That same day he whipped both Nat and Taylor. My attendance was discontinued and I studied (such as it was—it could scarcely be called study) at home through the year and how far into the next I don't know, but I do know that I did not love my books.

On the 17th April 1857 our house was burned down. At the cordial solic-itations of Judge Rucks we all aboded at his house (I in idleness) until the 22nd June when all went to Virginia. I was delighted with seeing the coun-try where my Grandfathers had lived and especially the house. While at the Holsten Springs in July and Aug. I was again quite a "pet" with the young ladies and fell (as I thought) desperately in love with one about my age. Kisses were superfluous and the luxury of laying my head in their laps was of com-mon occurrence. We visited a natural tunnel and a cave in Scott Co. In Oct. we returned, and he again requesting it, we entered Judge Rucks' hospitable door and remained under his roof till the 22nd November following when we moved into two cabins Father had built here and I was all the time in idleness.

On the 18th January 1858 I commenced school under Mr. Herbert, know-ing only how to read, write (a very little spelling) and the four first rules of

Arithmetic. I was injudiciously allowed to take up Latin instead of my English Grammar and hence I have it to study now. About March I became enamored with my books and taking off Latin during May and June '59 I have kept up my regards for them.

My little tale is finished, my old Journal will give an account of me up to Jan '60 when this one commenced. I close my book with many little incidents which I have not written down here in my mind and can see many faults and many ludicrous things. I close it hoping that some day far in the future that this delineation of my early youth may interest me when my memory shall have lost them; I close it with a deep consciousness that all I know I have learned since Jan. '58, and that I am under many obligations to Mr. H., Ma and Pa, and not a few to my perseverence for it.

Thursday, June 21, 1860

Augustus a boy of few mental power but of a good disposition asked me to aid him with his composition (for he could not make an approach at one) which I did because I felt sorry for him. He is a dull boy, and I pity any one who is dull. Little time was left after he had gone not having finished it. While taking my walk I recited to myself my declamation, returning at dusk.

Friday, June 22, 1860

My school of perch in the creek grow every day. They are beautiful pets. I love so much to see them dart up to the top of the water for the bread, and the water looks alive with them. Three or four catfish come in occasionally, and they take it much more actively than any of the others. The boys complemented my composition on the ladies and their tight dresses very much. I wish I could write one which could merit praise. A very pleasant swim. Helped Augustus to finish his composition at recess, consuming it all.

Saturday, June 23, 1860

Mr. Herbert had requested me to aid him about computing the merits of the boys, and I had intended to do so but while Ma was cutting off my hair I was talking to her about the dissatisfaction demonstrated by Mrs. Yerger last year on account of the Dixons beating both times and Pa coming up I said I thought it prudent not to handle them in my way this year, and he in strong terms affirmed my proposal. I soon after addressed a very polite note to Mr. H. telling him that for reasons inexplainible I found it impossible to assist him. Grecian History was read during most of the morning. I am almost through it. Mr. H. ate dinner with us and argued the honesty and fairness by which we obtained possession of these lands, that it was intended by the Creator that this world was intended for others than savages, that they were as happy now as they ever were and that it was right for them to be treated as they are and were. Having Dr. Franklin's advise in mind, I persued it and put questions to him, arguing my point by them instead of absolution assertions. I asked him, were they happy before we came? Are they happy now? Were these lands theirs? Are they theirs now? How did we come in possession of them? Did we not hunt them down like wild beasts, slaughter and murder them, burn their villages, cut down their hunting grounds, wrest from their feebler grasp all they had? Did they not in many instances extend to us the hand of hospitality? Did we pay them with friendship and gratitude, or did we not rather pay their confidence and brotherhood by fraud, deceit, and butchery? When we bought from them did we not give them a string of beeds, a blanket, or a musket for acres of fertile valleys and productive hills? Was this honest? Was this right? Does not God tell us not to imbue our hands in the blood of our fellow man, and do you say that he intended that this dispossession, this brutal murder, should be practiced? Did the Author of us all put them here that we might glut our cold remorseless eyes in the gore of this benighted race, that their extirpation might be accomplished by our bullets and our "firewater"? Why impugn their mode of warfare when it seems so plainly that they are so justifiable in using any means to clear their homes of such persons? If a man was to step in your door and tell you, "I am whiter than you. I know more than you and god has not intended these blessings for you and does not intend that they should be desecrated by you. Take your departure, leave!" would you not "resist even unto death?" Many more which I do not recollect were put to him, and those I have placed here I have not in the order they were given, but what are laid down is the principal part of my interrogations. By his candid answers I gained my victory, one of which I am proud because I exerted my little knowledge in a noble cause.

Sunday, June 24, 1860

Of consequence today I have had nothing to transpire worth recording be-yond what I do every Sunday viz. loll around till I go to church, eat dinner, read and study after I return, look at our enlightened little congregation lean their heads on their hands instead of kneeling while Mr. H. prays; listen at the usual gab before I go in, and feast my eyes on Miss Marian's beauty, inflaming my imagination by indulging my fancies (*naughty ones*) probably too far. My good mother is exempted from what I said about kneeling for she does—so do some others occasionally, and I love to see church-folks kneel.

Monday, June 25, 1860

So far as I remember this is the third day I have taken from my school willfully since I commenced in '55, and I took it today that I might accompany Father to Greenville, which I did and by no means enjoyed the "trip," it being a long hot ride there and a tedious stay after arriving. Things looked as usual, old John in his habitual mood. Uncle Jack drove the carriage and coming back evidently he was three sheets in the wind and judging from appearances he did not enjoy his situation. Mr. Wm. Percy came back with us and I (sitting in the front seat) unwittingly heard Pa tell him of my showing Mr. Herbert the example in Algebra and much more said of him on both sides which it would be idle to write here. The moon was out when we got back.

Tuesday, June 26, 1860

At school promptly but had no Geography lesson and got but little Algebra as Mr. H. could not explain to me. My lesson in Cicero this evening was pretty tough—however I got through with it. In studying my Classical Geography this evening after I came home I had a very pleasant time in reading the lives of those persons mentioned. Among them was that of Leander, the gallant fellow who swam the Hellespont nightly to visit his mistress Hero. Taking off his end and granting that Hero was like some women I have seen, I would like to be placed in his shoes if possible. I can applaud his purpose, his motives. I can conscientiously say, "go it Leander"; this, at its best, is but a transitory life which has few pleasures, of which I consider *love* as the greatest—and you seem to have been of the same opinion and being actuated by its sacred influence you wallowed in her most voluptuous sweets. You must have had my motto, Dum vivimus, vivamus.

Wednesday, June 27, 1860

I studied English Grammar mostly this morning and recited neither my Cicero or Spelling lesson in the evening, Mr. H. having given us leave to come home, the rain at that time holding up (for little of the day has passed with rain falling). Read nothing substantial after I got home but accounts of brutal prize fights. I will not take my time or space up in writing upon this subject but will say only that although I love to see every muscle of a man fully developed, I look upon it as disgusting to see men mashing each other up as they do, abusing and crippling the noble power nature has given them.

The entries for Sun., Mon., and Tues. were made this evening, and I forgot to say in the first mention that I took a walk in the evening and having heard that Judge Rucks was sick I stopped in to see how he was. I found him in the gallery (much to my astonishment) looking pretty well with Miss Marian leaning very gracefully on his breast and his arm around her waist (at this I was not astonished as the old gentleman makes it a practice to hug every young lady he sees). My Jupiter I wanted to change places with *him!* He soon left us and I had quite a nice "tete-a-tete" with the smiling virgin of my native soil. Not love but literature was what we talked about—the merits and demerits of Burns, Byron, Young and Thomson were discussed. The result was that Miss Marian loved Burns and I Thomson. I referred her to the place where that luxurious poet depicts the maiden bathing in his ode on "Summer."[85] Most truly there is a peculiar fascination about *maidens* that exists in no other women. The associations connected with them, the consciousness of their chaste purity, unpolluted by man's vile touch, all serve to concentrate my regard for them. When I look in one's eyes it seems that I see something that I do not find in other women's. It is something which makes my heart bow in reverence, a bright holiness seems to be there which I have no words to convey an idea of, something insoluble and inexplicable!

Thursday, June 28, 1860

A rainy morning was passed partly with my Arithmetic and a Universal History which I brought home this evening hoping to find time to read it through in the coming vacation as it is an abridged work. I was much pleased with a Chronological Chart I found in it as well as another chronological arrangement called the "Temple of Time." Rehearsed my declamation and read my composition mostly this evening that I might deport myself with credit.

My hopes in a certain point important to me are revived to a good degree. I am sitting up with Bay to give him medicine as he is sick, and I may write on. Let me resume where I left off. Augustus and myself went in swimming alone after school. Bill overtook me on my way back and he stopping at the schoolhouse we sat under the shed and had a very pleasant little "chat." We talked over some scenes of our last winter and grateful memories were revived. Mr. H. joined us after a while and we discussed law and afterward medicine. Subsequently our topic was women, giving childbirth, and on this question Bill and I agreed that they paid right dearly "for the whistle."

Pa at the supper table said to me that he had come to a definite conclusion as to what I should study, viz., that I should attend the Mathematical Professor, the Professor of History, and General Literature, a tutor in Latin and the French Professor for the first year; and I suppose as I advance and become proficient in these at least I know I shall take up Chemistry and if I can Natural Philosophy. I think this my best course, and I like it. If I make myself a thorough Mathematician, a good Latin scholar, and also a good French scholar, a no. 1 Chemist and am thoroughly acquainted with the English Classics I shall be ready to put my bill advantageously into the Law. Father also said that he was not settled as to keeping me at home until Nov. but that he had not determined. This was the good news; this was what made me feel glad and as though I had 20 lbs. taken off my shoulders. From the aspect of things now I think that when my dear old father looks at the various disadvantages that (as he often calls me) "my boy" and "my son" will labor under if he detains him, he will "cave in," yield the point, and send me on, a light-hearted boy in Sep. I hope, I trust he will let me go; I can but look at the bright side of the picture.

Friday, June 29, 1860

After some vexation I arrived at the schoolhouse prepared to undergo my "exhibition" as Mr. H. terms it, expecting to see no one besides the boys and was not disappointed in my expectation. As Mr. A. Rucks was very sick, it was not to be expected that any of his family would come. I suppose pro causa the others remained. It was 12 before I had returned home and the prizes had been distributed. Augustus beat in his class, Bay in his, Full in his, and Amanda and myself were in classes by ourselves. On the fly-leaf of mine was written, "Harry St. J. Dixon's book, reward of merit for gentlemanly deportment and diligent attention to study. Deer Creek Select School, June 29th, 1860."

I had not been at my reading long in the evening when Father in his usual affectionate manner that touches me so told me that he wanted me to go and see how Mr. Rucks was. I started about 5 o'clk and to my astonishment met Hal (my good old friend) and Will Yerger just above the schoolhouse. It was a cordial meeting. Friendly smiles were exchanged and hearty shakes of the hands. Talking was profuse and lively. They turned and rode back to the mouth of the lane where we separated, I going to Mr. R's and they back to Judge Yerger's. I must be growing very fast: Mr. H. often speaks of it; Ma, Bill spoke of it yesterday, and this evening Will exclaimed as soon as we had exchanged salutations, "why H——y! I never saw any one grow as you do!"

I found Mr. Rucks in a very critical condition, three Drs. around him, he looking almost like a dead man, his stomach blistered, his breast was being scarified and cupped, spitting up tough phlegm, with his whole throat raw, violent pains through his stomach and breast and worst of all his lungs were congested. With regard to the pains and congestion I was informed by the Drs., the other I saw; I saw him spit up phlegm constantly tinged with blood. I did not see his throat; I was told of that. The spectacle that he presented was a piteable one. He looked then like a dying man. He knew me and spoke to me.

From appearances I thought there was little chance of his recovery. His father and other connections were with him. I met Mrs. James Yerger at the schoolhouse and her looks betokened serious apprehensions. The sun had sunken when I left, and I had not gone far from the door when Mr. Y. stopped me and told me to tell his wife and Mrs. Yerger that Mr. Rucks was a good deal easier.

It was dusk when I got to Judge Rucks'. I shall never forget the grief I saw. Mrs. Ja's[86] and Alex Yerger,[87] sisters of Mr. Rucks, were sitting on the steps crying. I approached and delivered my message. Mrs. Ja's Yerger in a most piteous manner buried her face in her hands and moaned aloud as women only can moan. Mrs. Alex Yerger seemed able to control her feelings a little better but acted as if the good news was too much to give credence to and asked repeatedly in a bewildered, anxious manner, "Did you say he was better? Better Harry? Did you say he was better?" She then burst into tears and turning round said, "Where's Marian? I'll go and tell her." Their grief seemed so pure and still so overwhelming that my sympathies were deeply touched. Such grief is to me sacred and inviolable; I can feel for a man who has cause to grieve but I can produce no words to tell my pity for a tender, impulsive woman who is afflicted. Man is of a coarser nature and can sustain trials, but woman was not made to be exposed to the troubles of this world: man was made to shield them. I soon left the painful scene and came home apprehending as much as they.

Saturday, June 30, 1860

Read *Harpers Weekly* all the morning after taking my music lesson. Mr. Morsheimer told me he would not come next Wednesday as it was the 4th. He said that wherever he was, in Europe, Asia or anywhere else, he would on the fourth of July make merry, employ a band of music if possible, hoist the American flag and enjoy himself. In that I saw that foreigners cared more for our nation's anniversary than we do.

Not late in the evening, Hal dropped in as I was playing on my piano and stayed until dusk. We had a good old fashioned talk while walking in the garden and he in his usual exaggerated style related many of his personal adventures, which of course interested me. Obstinate as he always is when he takes a notion (like myself) and would not stay to supper.

Pa brought home the news of Mr. Rucks' death this morning. It is a calamity which could not be averted and we can only sympathize with his family and deplore his loss. It seems that though only six months of the year has passed they have been as remarkable for grievous occurrences in the annals of our little sphere of acquaintances, friends, and relations as it has in the history of my country.

Sunday, July 1, 1860

The manner in which I have been accustomed to put down the dates of my entries I have concluded to change and place only the date of the first entry for each month in the old manner, with all the rest at the beginning of the lines. I arose with a headache and felt badly all the morning, walking about to see if exercise would not dispell the feeling. I felt no [better] at 11 o'clk when I started to Mr. R's funeral and when I got there I was so sick I vomited and feeling a little better took a seat but soon found myself in a hot fever. Jimmy drove me home, I took the usual remedies, salt water and mustard, to vomit, calomel and ipecac in broken doses, and any quantity of crushed ice. About dusk my fever subsided entirely and the quinine (24 grs.) was commenced.

Monday, July 2, 1860

Kept my bed until 12½ o'clk, my head roaring with the quinine. The only one who ever does come to see me when I am sick came this morning to (as he said) see whether I was dead or alive, and brightened up my spirits and in all respects making me feel much better with his anecdotes and fun—the identical man was Hal Yerger. Taylor used to come occasionally to see me on such occasions. It is worth a good dose of medicine to me to receive such a visit at such a time. I have always made it my rule to go and see any of my friends when they are sick for I look upon it as a duty. I felt weak and of course did little of consequence through the evening.

Tuesday, July 3, 1860

Again I had to lay in bed weltering in perspiration until after 12 o'clk. I gritted my teeth and swallowed the bitter quinine. No ministering Hal today. Indoors all evening, strolling languidly about and reading some. Took a faint little walk near nightfall and left a little fatigued from its effects. I do not feel like the same person and when I look in the glass it is evident that I don't look like the same.

Wednesday, July 4, 1860

This is the third time I have made an entry for our jubilee day which cannot be called by that name properly in this immediate vicinity. Formally there was a barbecue, a dance, and general "tight-getting" here, but those sort of things have been forgotten and the fourth is passed now unheeded. *Sic transit gloria mundi.*[88] I could expatiate lengthily on this subject, throw out many bitter invectives against the diminutive spark of patriotism, this gradual dying out of the old enthusiasm shown for this day of all days, shown so palpably by the citizens of Washington County. If anything I could do or say would amend the matter I would labor lustily and cheerfully at my tasks, but nothing I can say here will remedy the thing so I will close this subject by saying I have not celebrated this day externally (I have internally).

Still felt rather weak today and read indoors nearly the whole time. Dr. Lee Percy[89] left for Europe this morning, a place I one day expect to spend one or two years in. Evidently that day is far in the future; it may not come till I am 35, but if I am able to spare 3 or 4000$ and am of the same opinion concerning the matter that I am now, these grey eyes will yet see Rome, Athens, Sparta, Thebes, Thymophylae, Cyrene, Alexandrea, Carthage, Jerusalem, and Babylon, or at least their relics.

Thursday, July 5, 1860

Wanting exercise and wanting more a cool drink of ice water (ours has defrosted) I walked down to Dr. Percy's and sat a while that I might enjoy a little of that necessary beverage. On my way back I met that same old jocular friend Hal. He dismounted and we took our seats in the shade on the creek back and there conferred for some length of time—say an hour. When we came back he stopped in to get a drink of water (Ma had got some ice in my absence) and with his usual obstinacy refused to get down so I had to remain under a china tree and converse with him there in the absence of a better place. Before he went away though I made a "nigger" bring me a chair and we chatted till after 11 o'clk. From that time until this (20 min. to 4 PM) I have done little else but read news-papers, eat dinner, and make my entries from Sun. up to this very line on which I am now writing and must soon be at my music if I would elude a scolding from Mr. M. and Ma about it in the morning, and if I wish to fulfill a promise I made Hal this morning to make him a visit this evening. I have today concluded to answer the letter Hal's friend wrote me last spring, he having set at rest all suspishions as to the "satch," and I will proceed instanter to carry out my conclusions.

Friday, July 6, 1860

Having finished my more urgent duties for the evening, yesterday about 5½ o'clk I proceeded to get ready for my promised visit to Hal and at dusk found myself sitting patiently on his porch awaiting his return from a ride. He soon came in, but three other minor persons were around and so far as seeing him was concerned it was not much of a "see," nor did it become much of a one until late that night as Bill, Nat, and Will came before supper. I met them with light words, but I can't say I welcomed them. Will went on in his usual contemptible braggadocio way, all vaingloriness and making himself ridiculous to me. I do not know how he appeared in the eyes of others. It was kept up. At the supper table a thing was done (I am heartily glad to say Hal had no hand in it and in justice neither did Nat or any one except Bill and Will) which I looked on and still look on as a thing a little below a gentleman's dignity. I do not know what to call it if not a vulgarity. It was directed at me, though in a manner that forbade its being resented except by words. I was eating my supper, not being engaged in a continuous conversation with any one but putting in where there was occasion as Nat and Hal were closely going over their freaks at Oxford while the rest at the table were engaged in the same conversation in which I figured so faintly. At my expense there was a laugh at what is called in college slang my being "chawed" which they supposed but which in reality was untrue. It was an *invented* remark a young lady made about me. But I am wandering from my point—it comes now. I saw Bill lean over and whisper something in Will's ear. From what had just passed I at once conjectured what was coming. Will immediately said to me (I forego to write *one* of his words), "Harry, they tell us your p—— is harder than your head. Is it so?" Evidently it was done to plague me, and it was just as evident that it was thought very smart. A loud laugh went around at the vulgarism. My brass served me splendidly and having smiled at them (I might almost say laughed), I said very quaintly, "Do you judge others by yourself?" The laugh was turned. He answered "they tell me this, I speak from hearsay." "Oh! Well" I said in the same strain "what they tell you may be true—it is possible," and by thus acquiescing defeated their expected fun.

These sort of things gradually wore off after supper and some of the ruffianism wore away, and we had Nat to play the fiddle while we danced. I had not had a good waltz with Hal since last Christmas. This lasted for some time. Then we had a terrible fit of singing in which "all hands" joined. Such singing, such singing! It is said that a "multitude of discords make a harmony," but I know from this experience that it don't. Getting tired of this Hal and I undertook to dance longer than Nat and a negro could fiddle. We "pitched in" on the "double shuffle" style and did worry them out. But was it not tough work! Our shirts were perfectly wet. George came home from a visit and arousing up one of the "minor chaps" renewed the singing, but Hal and myself being tired and sleepy and warm as possible went up to bed where we lay for an hour talking placidly about things that concerned us, as our educations (I halfway persuaded him to go to Va! God!) and women mostly. I advised him (as he asked me and seemed concerned) to resume his connections with Miss Mary, and I think he will do it. I enjoyed that talk for it was uninterrupted by any unpleasantries. About the time we were ready to leave this world, in one sense of the word, Will and Nat came up and with their incessant talking kept me awake until about 3 o'clock this morning. It was 1 when Hal and I went up, and I know we talked an hour or more. I felt pretty drowsy this morning and from the effects of my revel (could it be called a midnight one?) and have done but little reading in Universal History. (I finished Greece day before yesterday.) After taking my music lesson Mrs. Percy gave me some *music*, music worth hearing. Had a right pleasant ride in the evening.

Saturday, July 7, 1860

The heat has been more intense today than yet. In the cool of the beautiful morning I arose and took my old pony and notwithstanding his laziness had a very pleasant ride. Pa declares that if I do not arise earlier that he will not allow me to go to College and this is a spur to me. Knowing that it is to my interest in every way, I shall continue it. Nearly the whole day I was lost in the meanderings of my histories. I adore history and love to read it. Though it is not as exciting as fictions, I find much pleasure in reading it. Who can cast an indifferent eye on Hannibal's career, Caesar's victories, Sylla's and Marius' struggles, the patriotism of the Gracchi, Cicero, Brutus, Pericles, Socrates, Epaminendas, Lycrugus, and Demosthenes? Who can see without interest Athens demolished, Sparta humbled, Mithradates braving Rome, Carthage smoking in ruins, Rome itself enthrawled in mistery and degeneration under its long line of profligate emporers and Alexander scouring victoriously the eastern world? It would take pages even to name the engrossing events and scenes which arise in myriads before me, even not viewing modern history. Because I love history, it is by no means to the exclusion of other literature. No one can love a pretty poem and good novel more than I can.

Sunday, July 8, 1860

I had squared myself back in a rocking-chair in the parlor with my history in my lap while a pleasant breeze blew in through the open blinds, expecting a day of placid study. My time and attention was however destined to be occupied far differently. I was just loosing sight of the external world when John Byrne was announced and my day has been passed very pleasantly with him. We strolled about until 2½ or thereabouts when at his proposal we mounted our horses and took a ride. The first part of our ride was pretty hot. As we expected to ride in the woods, I did not take a coat. We concluded to go down to Maj. Lee's quarters and call for Nat there and not to enter the house, which after many windings in the woods back of Dr. Percy's field and ours, we did. I went in swimming with Nat and the boys (some black) and on my exit from the water saw it was time to be moving home. J. said to avoid the circuitous route by which we came, that he would take off his coat and ride through the yard and cross the bridge that we might go on the opposite side. I agreed. On the bridge we encountered Maj. and Mrs. Lee. I apologized for our uncouth appearance to the lady and while J. was confering with Maj. on business I had a merry little talk with the Maj.'s wife. She as usual was affability and graciousness itself. John having finished we came home at sundown and took a short walk overtaking Mrs. Wm. Percy, returned at dusk, and having finished these entries I will soon retire.

Monday, July 9, 1860

Another day of running about and of no study. Was it my fault? Could I waive courtesy? I could not. My guest was entitled to my time and attention, and I cheerfully gave it to him. At our arising from the breakfast table we mounted our horses and rode up to Judge Yerger's. We went in at the overseer's house and Hal and Will soon came up. We sat a while, and I inviting them and Hal having some business at my house we all rode down. I rode with Hal and of course enjoyed it. They sat about an hour when nothing would do them but to return and to take me with them. I yielded and went. It was fully 11 o'clk when we got there. I had a good time before dinner, looking at a pretty stereoscope. Little was done after dinner but welter in the excessive heat. I think this has been the hottest day I ever felt.

While upstairs lolling in a rocking chair I picked up a volume of Byron (that profligate genius) and Bill pointing me to it I read that pretty piece of his generally known as "Byron's Dream"[90] and liked it very much. Late in the evening the boys accompanied me back on their way to Maj. Lee's for a fish on the Bogue tomorrow and stopping in for something *pressingly* invited me to go with them, but I declined thinking "duty before pleasure." Judge Rucks came in to see Pa who had gone riding and I fanned the old man the whole time as if he had been my father.

Tuesday, July 10, 1860

True I had talked of her to Hal yesterday as I had of many other ladies, but did I expect this? Why has she appeared to me the third time, and why two of the three in an inauspicious light? Did I think last night when I laid myself down to rest that ere I arose that such a dream would disturb my equanimity so? Do dreams come as preludes of events to come long years hence? I cannot tell; but I can tell that things do transpire (even yesterday one did) that seem to have been enacted before of which I had a vague, misty recollection and which excites me to recall the remembrance of. The ancients were warned and admonished in dreams, and why should such things cease now? May I never in reality do what I did in my dream. The latter was the part which affects. The lady of whom I spoke in the beginning was one who has commanded attention in these pages, who did not figure in the first part of my dream—that lady was Ella Brown.

I will begin at the beginning. I was in the town of Abingdon, lechery had propelled me to devise means to entrap a little, pale woman but those hellish designs failed after many manuevers and I came very near being exposed. The Mitchell girls seemed to rise up against me, but I escaped uninjured. Now comes that part which through my ride before breakfast haunted me and as it were made me commune with the subject of this malicious dream in which all the malice rested on me. I proceed and my hand trembles as I write. Miss Ella was at my side and looked as blooming as she ever did. We were walking seemingly in a lane while others straggled in the distance. Twilight surrounded us and we were not near any one, and I was yet happy in my innocence. Her soft, plump arm was far in mine and our shoulders touched. I had her hand in mine. Like electricity the touch of that shoulder and the pressure of that hand shook the deepest foundations of my soul. We walked on. How long I retained in that position I know not, a mist rises before my eyes. I am going over the dream, but still through it all I see the dread end. What comes next? Could I shake off that terrible excitement even if I had tried? Its grasp was like iron. I went on. She yielded. Still we glided on our way. Strange, strange how this has come. Her surpassing beauty made me mad; all reason was gone. I saw nothing but her, her sparkling eyes turned to me in which was fear and apprehension, saw a snowy bosom panting, cheeks and lips that no mortal could resist. I had her in my arms, in arms which pressed her convulsively, frantically to my bosom. Did I kiss? If I did I do not remember it now. I lifted her from the ground and her head lay upon my shoulder. One arm passed around her shoulders, one under her lower extremeties. Jupiter what a heavenly form I embraced! What a gentle pressure her sweet arms placed around my neck! I knew but one thing. I in my madness had but one object. I knew I possessed her charms, that object was fiendish beyond thought. My soul was on fire, my brain was dizzy with excitement. I was strangely enthralled, and my feelings defy words. <My vile hand felt its way to the sacred grotto of love. Then my arm should have been severed from my body. It was unendurable—nature's pent up substance flowed from me as I stood. I thought, "it is over," but it was not. As the flood was subsiding, I found myself lying almost senseless be-

tween her downy thighs, wallowing in a deluge of illicit love. We awoke from our intoxicating bliss to view our shame, awoke from reposing on the bosom of a woman whose beauty is indescribable! She still in my arms, I kept on my journey, but ere long I became faint under my beauteous burden and despite all my efforts, despite my ardent wishes to keep her in my tender embraces, I was forced to disentwine her arms from around my neck, to release her symmetrical legs from my wearied but reluctant arm. > [91]

"A change came o'er the spirit of my dream." [92]

< I was pursued by my mother. We still travelled on foot, and she spoke of our iniquity lamentably. I tried to console her, showing her the impossibility of pregnancy, but still with downcast eyes and with tears she bewailed the departure of her virginity. My heart sickened and sunk within me. > [93]

Again "a change come o'er the spirit of my dream."

She was gone. Where was she? I searched. At last I found her in an uncouth place, found her weeping and could scarcely get her to proceed to our destination (I knew it not). We had commenced. Her face still looked sad. I was gazing upon its beauty when consciousness suddenly burst upon me. But that dream was too life-like, too vivid. So real did it seem that every particular stood forth in my heated fancy, and many times it has recurred to me this day. I leave the subject. I have dwelt too long on it already.

About 10 o'clock when I had got about half through my hieroglyphics John came in and consequently the remainder of the day was devoted to him. After the excessive heat had subsided a little in the evening late, I took a ride in the buggy. The thermometer for the last two days has averaged 94.

Wednesday, July 11, 1860

The heat today has nearly equalled that of yesterday and for the first time since 9 o'clk I have been cool and hope to stay cool the balance of the evening (it is 3½ PM). My music lesson was by no means good this morning but from some cause I escaped an admonition. Read a little, transferred my book from my trunk to the bookcase and brought some books from the schoolhouse before 12. Read a little more before dinner and looked at Miss Alexander's name which I cut in a tree on the creek bank yesterday as I had walked down there. Since dinner I have finished the preceeding entry and will most probably do little else than read the rest of this evening.

I did so; I read till late in the evening when Hal rode in and said he would come back and remain all night if I would ride up home and let him get another shirt, which I did, it being dark when I, or rather we, got to Judge Yerger's. Supper was over when we got back, but mother set a little for us. On the way he got into one of his frivolous ways, laughing immoderately and whipping my horse. I was "thar" though I did not feel much like it. I swore I would not go any farther if we didn't get any supper and humorously supplied myself with a good sized clod, and he then kept his distance. We galloped along very quietly after that, but I did not drop my clod.

Thursday, July 12, 1860

We at 12 last night retired after a great romp and a quiet talk on the gallery about Miss Alexander mostly, he depreciating and I eulogizing her (and justly too). He left after breakfast and from 9½ to 5 PM I studied without intermission. Till 1 I stuck at my Modern Geography as I wish to review it, and my English Grammar getting as far as Conjugation, and read my history all evening. I was just about to stop when old "dad" came out in the gallery (I was out in the yard under a tree) and said to me, "Stop, my son, you have studied enough today." Little else was done afterwards.

Friday, July 13, 1860

The haze which has hung over our heads on every side seeming to cut off all that is cool. However all is bright this morning as to the weather and I might with equal veracity say as to my homestead for while sitting here in the hall writing on the opposite page Judge Rucks and Miss Marian came. She is the cause of my homestead being bright. I have just returned from a medical visit to the quarter. It is after 9. They are gone as well as my parents. Howbeit I will at any rate relate for myself what transpired while they did stay. I must be quick—I have to study. As I said I was here writing when they came in at the door at my back. I had on my hat, but when I saw Miss Marian it did not stay on, I casting it to the floor as I made my obeisance to the Deer Creek belle and shook the old gent's hand warmly. I took my seat and tried to write, but I found that it required an effort as the pretty smiling face of the young lady was turned toward me not 20 feet distant, and I soon saw that my eyes were on her as much as my page. Pa called me off and told me about the *visit*, and as I came back in the hall I found him and the Judge praising this old diary, Pa turning over the leaves and saying, "he has written all this since Feb." The J. said something to its enhancement, and Miss M. smiled. Laughingly I said to Pa, "that is a private affair." He made some apology. I then seated myself opposite Miss M. and talked of the good it did me to write here, mentioning my dream and hinting about who it was and telling her it must be a secret. She knew who it was. She said, "that shows how much you think about her." "I study all day," I answered, "and never think of her and can't tell why she visits me in my dreams so often." "But you do think of her," she said, "or you would not dream of her." "I may do it unconsciously, Miss M.," I said, and we talked of something else, and they walking down the steps I assisted her to get into the buggy, catching hold of a soft arm and at the same time seeing a sweet little foot peep from under the muslin as she ascended. She remarked that she always tore something when she got into a buggy. "Did you tear any thing then, Miss M.?" I enquired. She answered in the negative. As the J. ascended he said, "that was because you helped her in so well, H." Miss M. bowed and smiled, the J. bid me good morning and they were gone. Dr. Mears and Mrs. Holmes have just departed, and I have been just detained this much longer; I will go at it immediately. It will be 10½ when I get settled, so I must leave my journal for tonight.

Dusk came to find me seated on the steps after a studious evening listlessly reading in my classical dictionary about Lucifer and others when Ma called Miss M. in to get something she had left in the morning, thereby again exposing her son to the dangerous presence of a pretty woman—dangerous because such things as I looked at have caused many a boy to foresake his interest and seek their faces until his time had gone. "Time and tide wait for no man." I listen not to the siren song of such beauteous little things, but Miss M. is no siren but a fair, virtuous woman whom my eyes love to behold. I am compelled at present to shut my eyes to such allurements or I may come out at the wrong door to enter upon my legal career with credit.

Saturday, July 14, 1860

I arose before the sun this morning and mounting my old pony rode 8 miles before breakfast, meeting Mr. Morshiemer and coming back with him. The air was fresh and cool and my ride was enjoyed. I did not study any in this morning, Bill coming and my time being taken up in talking with him and Uncle Jack on trifling subjects; one though was substantial, viz. whether a man's success in life depended on chance or his own management, abilities, and exertion. I contended the latter, he the former, and I know reason was on my side. I know father takes the same view that I do. I don't care who would be arbiter if he possessed a sane mind I would stake a little on my triumph. I read of chivalry, Charlemagnes's empire and crusades today. I ardently laud knight errantry and admire their motto, "God and the ladies" and especially the latter part. Long live the ladies and downy be their couches! If I were omnipotent no woman would ever shed a tear. *Pro patria et feminis semper!*[94]

I walked up to eat a water-melon with Bledsoe but he was absent. A grunting host of swine attacked me on my way. Sam, my dog, barked at one and she attacked him and he ran to me for assistance, which I gave him. She retreated and on Sam's following she again persued him, grunting fast and shortly. Two or three more were with her and she was much bolder and made a "pass" at me, which I barely eluded by springing aside. Many had now collected and formidably assaulted me, and I found it necessary petere salutem in fuga,[95] and gathering a chunk made a log my fort, they making hot pursuit. As I steadied myself on my log I gave one a blow with it and was perfectly defenseless. About 55 were in reach of me, evidently swayed by the fiercest pathos. They presented a formidable appearance, and I would have sustained serious damage if they had got me among them. I wished for a long pole. I called off the dogs and in 15 minutes they had quieted so that I descended unmolested, but before I walked 50 yds. was menaced again, and keeping quiet got off. A fellow would stand a poor chance with 50 infuriated hogs hold of him.

Sunday, July 15, 1860

Darkness reigns; few sounds disturb my ear while I detail the simple facts of this pleasant day. This was not as bright a morning as the preceding, nor was I up quite so early. There was some books belonging to Judge Rucks here, I thought I would walk down with them and take breakfast but meeting Mrs. Yerger at the door in her riding habit and seeing that breakfast was over did not accept her invitation to seat myself. I noticed that her eyes looked as though they had recently emitted tears and this evening found out the cause. That cause was that Miss Marian had left this morning for Kentucky. I felt sorry for expecting her to remain until next Sun. I had intended to see her as it is probable I shall never see her again while she is still in the sacred bonds of celibacy which always makes a woman so much more acceptable. But the nonexistence of a woman's virginity cannot be made an objection if she is immutable as to virtue. Still, for me, send a blushing maiden who knows no carnality; whose person is as God has made it, not as man has changed it! Give me the fair lily which knows not the wiltering sun of noontide, but whose soft folds have known only the gentle breezes of a vernal morn! This is what I look forward to: this is what emulates me, what leads me into toil, this is the bright jewel I hope to fold to my bosom to protect, to cherish and to love, that it may shine for me, for me only. I wander from my path. I resume and drop to an humbler subject.

I returned and ate my breakfast but my studies were light through the day being interrupted. However I have a few more historical facts laid up for use when an occasion offers.

Jimmy had a box and $7.70 stolen from him by one of the negroes and two about the house being implicated and getting Pa's leave asked me to accompany them in a search which I did going through every quarter without effect keeping me out of bed till 11 o'clk. I took no hand in it but knew that they would fail from the course they took. Each one had a long harangue to give of his probity tried and respected by his former master, if a million laid before him years he would not take 5 cts. It was amusing.

Monday, July 16, 1860

I was awakened sometime before day by loud claps of thunder. The first time Jupiter's bellowing has been able to disturb my slumbers, but this was enough to awake one of the "seven sleepers." The vivid flashes were almost continuous and the crashing was deafening, seeming to shake the very earth with its vehemence and the rain fell in torrents. After being awake sometime, I fell asleep and did not get up early. My regular studies today—English Grammar, Spelling, Modern Geography, and History, which kept me until about the usual time, though I did not study as regularly as customary, the younger Percy and wife spending the day with us.

The pilfering affair has come to light and the "prisoner at the bar" plead guilty of the charge made against him by plaintiff, and the condemned will tomorrow receive as many stripes as his honor Judge Dixon shall deem as a sufficient chastisement for the aforesaid crime.

Tuesday, July 17, 1860

The katy-dids sing for me and I shall not keep them long. I shall not have much to say and that said briefly. I commence by saying that I have conceived the idea of devoting the whole morning to Grammar and take my Hist. Geog. and Spelling after 12. I did so today and find it more convenient and more to my advancement in the study of all others I am anxious to be familiar in by next fall. All I ask for is health and the little I do not know concerning it I shall certainly know. My music lesson was not touched till after dinner, but I took hold of it to the exclusion of my His. and knocked "duck fits" out of it, however I got my other lessons. I keep a sheet of paper before me while studying and any word I come across that I fancy or look upon as one of utility, I write it down with the definition. This sheet I keep near me most of the time, and the most striking words I ponder over and fix in my memory. I look out in my Dictionary every word I do not understand while reading or studying and especially when studying my Spell. lesson. By this means I accumulate my little stock of words diurnally. I have just got far enough to see how little I know, to see how utterly I have been in the dark. Oh, the goal seems so far off!

Today Pa said to me, "my boy, go and get me the catalogue" (meaning that of the U. of Va.). Last night I mentioned that I was anxious to hear how matters stood, and he as usual delivered to me adamantine advise about how I should act at college, saying among the rest of his remarks that there must be no gallanting. I suggested that I would like for him to make arrangements with the president to get me in a room with some steady young man. What was his answer to this? Affectionate, kind, and considerate, in these words: "my son, I suppose I will put you in a room to yourself," but I said I would rather have some young man of sobriety a little older and advanced than myself to room with me as my companion. He agreed that it would be better. To go to the trouble and additional expense of giving me a room, private from all intrusions! I wanted to kiss him. Since I see every day what faithful guardianship he exercises over me, how long he has done it (and my loved mother has shared fully his task) and how little I am able to return for it though I exert every nerve and stretch every muscle. When these tender cares and loving attentions present themselves to me every day, my love increases its huge dimensions, increases to overflowing. No, loved mother and kind father, it is beyond my feeble abilities to repay my ponderous debt to you. All I can do is as the widows write—no, no, no, I can never repay you, neither can I tell my gratitude.

Wednesday, July 18, 1860

At the usual hour and usual place under a clump of verdant Elder trees near the fence at the north-west corner of the yard, where the shade reigns nearly during the whole day, where, if there is a breeze, I get it—but my studies in the evening were disturbed by an "old blow" who overseed for us in '57 and who seemed all delight at seeing me. I can't say I relished the meeting as we, about the time of his exodus (in Nov. '57) "fell out" as the vulgar expression goes about a trivial thing in which he took many rude and unfair advantages of my youth, which were indicative of his "low-flung" character. Of course I had "grown amazingly" and was right in studying "my son," knew I was "going to make a man" of myself, "looked like a student" &c., &c. with highly flattering encomiums heaped upon Pa's head which of course boared me, and I thought I could get along sine oratio blanda.[96] He relieved me in the course of 15 or 20 minutes, when I perused my studies till night.

Thursday, July 19, 1860

Ten o'clk had scarcely found me in my quiet and pleasant retreat, my natural studio, till I was again visited by the auger which this time did its boaring in the parlor where I invited him to seat himself and where he stuffed me with politics (the only thing interesting [to] me was his account of the bone of contention from which arose the late Mexican war) but most of all lauded his two daughters so much—"Pussy could read Shakespeare better than any one he ever saw," possessed "such capacities and so little application," "Ella was such a student," that I felt sick. At last Pa supplanted my place as a host; I was released to do but little studying, having read *Harper* all the evening except when I wrote a little here (in my entry for Tues) sitting in my "studio," when Mrs. Percy first came by and remarked cheerfully to me that I had a nice place to study in and next Miss Kate stopped and desiring a little conversation she asked me to come and see Nat, he being sick, which of course I promised to do. Dark soon came on and I left my retreat for my noisy home.

Friday, July 20, 1860

Old Clay was pacing toward Maj. Lee's soon after breakfast with me. I killed time on the way by memorizing some fragments I had written in my little blank book from pretty pieces of poetry I had read. Here is one:

> "To greet,
> Among these lovely forms the well-known face
> Of one in past years loved; to live again
> The fast-flown days of busy memory o'er
> To weep o'er ever-vanished joys, and look
> Still nearer on the mystic future world
> From this divided by a strait so small."

I will cease these diversions. I will proceed. Nat was up and looked tolerable. I had a very nice day and returned about 4 to practise my music lesson but did not do so. Nat has got his appointment to the Va. Military Institute, pocket money not to exceed $2.00 per mo., and my opinion is that Nat won't stay long—still I hope he will. He is very anxious for me to go with him, but I prefer the U'ty after West Point. A little headache this evening. Mr. Trigg and John Dunn came in about dusk when uncle Jack and myself were gathering pears. J. kept me up till 12 o'clk PM carrying on a conversation by no means interesting. I was so sleepy! I talked of every thing I could think of. He was too green to appreciate literature and I thought, "How long, O Lord, how long!"

Saturday, July 21, 1860

My verdant friend did not depart till evening when I wrote a letter to Lizzie which I scarcely will send as it contains many errors and blots. Few things of any note done this evening. I got hold of a very good lady author or authoress, the best woman writer I ever saw. Her book is called *Characteristics of Women*[97] and treats mostly on Shakespeare's characters, among which I read of Cleopatra, that beautiful, educated, refined but horribly profligate woman who could allure two of Rome's greatest soldiers from war's glories and vicissitudes, and Portia, Pompey's wife. I have conceived the idea of completing a book composed of the prettiest gems of both prose and poetry of our great writers, though with no idea of ever publishing it, but that I may have a little volume in which is displayed the bright jewels of my language. This is not all; I have in view another compilation (for I am too conscious of my feebleness and am too fearful to venture any thing of my own composition for even a friend to behold) one of a humorous nature, embracing all the wit I may stagger against in my career of the next four or five years. My first prospective book will mostly be taken from the reading of these master works at college, for that will embrace one branch of my studies Pa marked, "History and Literature."

Sunday, July 22, 1860

Arose feeling badly—a dull headache and feeling that my system was deranged. It soon developed itself in a chill followed by a fever which though not in its most active form was formidable enough to keep me in bed from about 10 till night. But didn't I sink the lemonades when the fever was on me! I never had anything to taste better in my life, so cold and such a flavor. They were to my burning lips like welcome rain to the parched earth. Neither did I spare the crushed ice, but what can make sickness sufferable?

Monday, July 23, 1860

By no means a pleasant day. Is it possible to lay in bed this sort of weather with your head ringing almost to bursting with quinine and in every way feeling disagreeable? I've had many chills but I've the first pleasant one to find yet.

My straight-forward old friend Taylor came to see me this morning and stayed for some. Of course his visit revived my drooping spirits, but after he left they relaxed and I drooped about the house the balance of the day, feeling badly though I had missed my chill. I am afraid I will have these infernal chills all summer and have my faculties so emaciated by the time I hope to leave that I will not be so vigorous at my studies as I would otherwise be. And I moreover think that all of this ill-health goes to bear upon the point of my not leaving this coming September. I feel doubly confident that it would have been to my incalculable advantage to have left as soon as I arose from my bed in the first part of the month as I wished to do. Pa and Ma objected to it so I dropped it. I do wish I could take all the love they have for me and box it up for the next 2 mo's. Suppose I were to die, would my good parents not feel some remorse? Uncle J. and Ma reproached me for sighing, but I was sick and dispirited and was heartily sick of this unhealthy country. Though it is worth million on millions, if Deer Creek, from its head to its mouth was offered gratuitously to me with the sole condition of my making it my residence, I would hoot at it contemptuously. What is money without health? Bury me in all earth's luxuries and make me sick from time to time, keep me in suspense of a spell of sickness and how much of it could I enjoy? Give me health! I will go where I can have it even if I make little, even if I am all my life to be a poor man. What does gold bring with it but care and trouble? Verily on every side I daily see it seducing men from true happiness. It is a yellow devil, a vile deceiver of mankind! Excess in nothing is desirable; in beauty it brings vanity as in excessive mental powers, in birth arrogance, in prosperity unthankfulness, and lastly in money care, trouble, and contention as I have before said. Every one should strike for a mediocrity, for with it in the majority of things comes happiness in its true sense; few, few, very few are the instances where excess has made a favorable end.

Tuesday, July 24, 1860

Laid in bed again until 12 o'clk when I arose feeling top light and under the effects of quinine. However towards evening it wore off and I felt much better. John and Harry Percy were here and called and sat a while with me. In coming from a stroll in the garden this evening I pulled some nice pares and sent them by John to that good lady—one whom I esteem—Mrs. Lee.

Read mostly trash or my Classical Dictionary—accounts of Antigone the old tragic heroine, Domitius, the distinguished general whom the Hellish Nero ordered to be executed, who, when he disembarked at Corinth and was informed of the emperor's orders said as he plunged his sword into his bosom, "Well deserved!" and of Coriolanus, the unjustly banished patriot whose patriotic feelings were reversed by exile. It is touching to read of the manner in which, before the gates of dismayed Rome, he received the last and only availing embassy from his countrymen—his family—his mother and the matrons of his former country; when his babes were held up to the stern warrior, when his aged mother quietly reproached him and moans and sobs were heard around, when he saw kneeling at his feet Rome's fairest daughters, the heart of that stone warrior melted and flying to his aged mother's arms he exclaimed, "O my mother, thou has saved Rome but lost thy son." Such sense of humor, such a man! such a man!

Wednesday, July 25, 1860

Wrote Lizzie a lengthy letter which absorbed my morning together with my listening to Judge Wm. Yerger[98] panegyrizing the University of Virginia. Judge Rucks invited me down to talk to Taylor about going there. Knocked around till after dinner when I seated myself comfortably on the gallery, sipping from the sweets of that fluent poet Thomson, where I remained for some time enjoying them. My literary pleasures were broken off by Ma's getting me to fix a tree for her out in the yard which however I failed to do. I again had taken up Thomson (at nearly dusk) when Nat rode up in a little shower. So again my reading was stopped. He and Jimmy played very prettily on their violins together, at which they stayed till after supper some time. At my instigation they practised over some tunes and about 10½ went down and serenaded "old Ruck," who, though all others were asleep, was prowling around. We gave them (for Will was with him) a few tunes and they then accompanied us on our way back nearly half way, to a large gum tree where we halted and had a good time of it, singing, dancing, laughing, and talking. Our songs were not of the most refined quality, such as boys of our age generally like best (but I do not)—those who are of a *loose* tinge. It was 12½ when Nat and myself got in bed. Then he informed me of the admirable resolution he had made of never again taking a drop of liquor. May you keep it my friend.

Thursday, July 26, 1860

The effects of our late hours and revels were felt this morning, but rise we did and rode down to see "old Ruck," where I stayed till after dinner. Had a right nice morning. At the dinner table the Judge spoke of my departure to college and the subject was kept up during which I remarked that in the early part of the spring I had sent for a Catalog of the Universities of this state, Virginia and N.C. and liked that of Va. the best and that Pa also liked best. Mrs. Yerger, I suppose with the intention of piqueing me, answered something which went to show that *my* liking that institution the best was of little avail if Pa chose a different one. It was palpably a stroke at what she supposed arrogance in me. If she really intended to sting, she did not accomplish her purpose. I was what is vulgarly called "slightly chawed." I at once justified myself by saying that I by no means looked upon my choice of my own as being in opposition to what Pa should wish or choose but that if I should fancy another that I believed he would let me attend that and that any thing I could or would say on the subject was altogether a minor affair. I flatter myself it was satisfactory.

Last night Nat and myself got to debating about when we should be put to the study of Latin Grammar. He argued that it should be commenced as soon as the boy was able to study any thing, that it learned him his own language and grammar, and was in every way the most propitious. I contended for the exact opposite. That no one was a scholar or educated thoroughly without a knowledge of his own language and grammar, that a man might be given all the Latin in Christendom and if he did not know how to speak, read and write his own tongue properly that at every step in life he would make a blunder, that his life would be in a great degree a complete failure. I grew warm, probably too warm, as I did at Judge R's this morning when all three were abusing the University of Va. Nat turned off his arguments last night by going into foolishness showing that he was convicted of the reasons I advocated. One might as well build a house in reeds and expect it to stand as to expect an education to be of feasibility and utility sine scientia.

Friday, July 27, 1860

The old man shelled out $250 this morning for our music lessons to our teacher who came unbeknown to me as I looked for him tomorrow morning. This is the last lesson he will give til Oct. he taking vacation. I hope I will be gone when he gets back.

All day Thomson lead me through his flowery labarynths while at many ambrosial springs I met on my way I drank sweet draughts which made my soul and heart feel light and untrammeled from all external things. Verily he is a goodly poet, particularly in nature. I am not reading him regularly. I first read "Summer" in which I found sweet strains but I did not make notes on them. In "The Castle of Indolence" there are some places tiresome but toward the end of the second Canto his flights in two or three places are, in my estimation, purely classical poetry. I shall have to look it over and make notes as I neglected to do so when I read it as I also shall have to do in the "Summer." Toward evening I entered "Spring" and there made notes of some passages which I believe is of the purest "metal." Every day my love of poetry increases, but it shall never disturb study in solid reading.

Company for supper or at supper more grammatically. Judge Yerger was as redundant as ever in his pleasing humor. I love to see such old fogies as he and Pa get together. Politics noisily reigned after supper and seemingly more when Mrs. Percy sat herself down in growing infancy to give us some sweet music. I would, if I had been able, have choked all three of the gentlemen who were so noisy at the other side of the room. Music must be a sister to poetry, yes! They are the two sisters which absorb my very soul when they are represented in their original, native, spontaneous outburstings of sheer beauty as of the mighty volcano who sends forth his bright volumes of fire. This is beauty, this is nobility, this what lifts me from this dire world into the Elysian fields of these sisters' habitations.

Saturday, July 28, 1860

Nine o'clk found me seated in Judge Yerger's parlor on a visit to Hal who is suffering from a large boil on his neck. We did not remain alone long before Bill came in and we (B. and myself) got into a noisy discussion about colleges in general and especially the University of Va., the worth and worthlessness of young men from college, and the probability of my being seduced from study. We agreed that the U. of Va. was as good as the globe saw but differed as to a young man's liability to become dissolute there more than any where else. I said he was not, he that he was. He said that I would attend a lecture and study for 6 mos. after I entered but afterward would dissipate. I said in strong terms I would not. Let's see if I will.

The fat, good-humored master of the house gave us a good laugh while at dinner, though he ate in the hall. Nearly every one combined to tease me or as it is oftener termed, "plague me" but as usual I used my brass and acceded to every proposition so they made a "poor out" of it. Will was as usual forward and unreserved, not adding to my pleasure for one. I can't see why some people will make such geese of themselves. It is strange to me how they can expect people to like them when they persue such a course as he does.

Thomson showed me the close of his "Spring" this evening after I came back (which was about 5 o'clk PM) and some pretty things he showed me. Huzza for Thomson!

Sunday, July 29, 1860

With the above named poet's entertaining volume of poems in my hand, I seated myself at Pa's side on the gallery expecting to do little else today but hold converse with the scenes that book would place before me. Those expectations were not accomplished. Poets, poesy and their results became the theme of a long conversation (Pa did all) redundant in invectives on Pa's side against all three of the points; showing that they were nearly always poor wretches who wrote, as he said, "while they were starving." One of his objections was that their writings seduced one from the substance of life, answered no good end, and that they were utter trash. He said, "show him a poet and he would show you a worthless man, useless to himself and every one else." True, Homer, Virgil, Horace, Milton, Young, Byron and Thomson were men whose lives were to a great degree more or less worthless and unhappy. Pa is too much of a utilitarian to admire poetry, hence he condemns it as trash to amuse people of leisure and an unfit thing for a boy like me to read. The old practical gent, my dad, got warm though I did nothing to aggravate. I saw plainly the feasibility of what he said and justly excused myself to him by saying that since Christmas I had read nothing but history except one novel and that I only took this up for a little recreation but when he wound up by expressing his fears on account of my "romantic disposition," "being impressed easily," that I "would be led off by boys at college" I was a little touched. I said something about being sorry I did not deserve more confidence, and there being a calm I went up stairs and laid away poor Tom, read a sketch on Young's life, and afterwards His. till walking time. I could not suppress a laugh when I read of Y's absentmindedness, e.g. his forgetting whether he had dined or not. You'll catch me forgetting that, won't you?

Monday, July 30, 1860

In the calm heavens the meek god of night reigns; the distant chirping of insects, lonely and dismal, form a contrast with the reel Jimmy plays up stairs. I have just come from there, displeased and chagrined but the influence of the soft beams that illuminary sends to rule the night dispelled my disagreeable feelings. Jimmy, my intractable brother, caused them as he often does, and this time among the multitude, it was in paying no attention at all to repeated requests to come and play a tune with me we have recently learned. I asked kindly and am not answered yet, but he has come even now and ruffled my feelings again, maliciously and without provocation. When I got my journal from my drawer I found an egg there where he had put it, a little negro having found it this evening, and having had it cooked was about to eat it when he came in and commenced quarreling at me about it, I answering good-naturedly, and he wound up by snatching it from the saucer and crushing it in his fist. My patience gave way; I was angry and I acted angrily, much against my will and without violence made him behave. Though I have done all I could to arrest this for years past, it has always been thus between us and I have no hope of its ever being otherwise. But my consolation is that these virulent contacts will soon cease, virtually for the balance of my life. I have with him borne and still bear much for Ma's and Pa's sake. I do not deny it, he has embittered much of my brotherly feeling for him.

I will leave this. I will soon close. Studied English Grammar till 12, but read hist. in the evening, a hard rain coming up and keeping me from my usual place of study. I do not go to bed with a light heart.

Tuesday, July 31, 1860

Odd jobs for Pa engrossed most of my morning and in fact I read and studied little till after dinner (at 2 PM). I gathered some nice pears in the evening and laid them in the grass to take some decayed ones to the house and supposing them to be safe did not go back for them till late when to my astonishment something had eaten them. Served rightly—ought to have had more discretion!

I do love the moonlight; I love to look on the prettiest of luminaries, and I always think of, and,

"Live in one short hour,
O'er vanished years, too bright to last."

Wednesday, August 1, 1860

Late in the morning Taylor dropped in at my "studio" and we had a lively talk for some time. John Byrne and Nat came along soon and took him away, leaving me as I declined to dine with Taylor where they were going. I found F. like other boys who go to school from home, he had diverse adventures to relate. Until about 5½ I read history on returning to the house after they had left, whence I apparelled myself very modestly because it was compulsory and rode down to Maj. Lee's to see Nat, stopping at Dr. Mears' for him to proscribe for a subtile and annoying disease I've had for a year called scurvy or scaldhead—like dandruff except if it is let alone it will turn into sores. But I will follow myself on. . . . On my arrival at Maj. Lee's I found Will seated comfortably in the gallery talking to Miss Kate, whom I had seen out riding with him. I seated myself and gradually got myself into the conversation, which as all that young folks carry on was composed of *all* trash, and as my tongue felt free and I was in a good humor I "clattered" away as I could see to Will's detriment for he "hung on" with one who when he chooses and is in the right humor doesn't stand back for any one. Miss Kate excused herself from the supper table on the plea of fearing a bat while Nat and myself ate on. Will went out with her and sat in the port gallery, so when N. and myself finished, at my proposal, as I was not being consumed with anxiety to talk any more nonsense, we took our seats elsewhere, and I enjoyed some of his music. Mrs. L. being sick wanted me to play for her which I did and my compliments I fear were undeserved.

Nat, H. Percy, John and myself played first "Euchre" and then "Smut" till late. I felt restless and could not sleep till some time after I had gone to bed—a thing *very* unusual with me.

Thursday, August 2, 1860

The Maj., Miss K. and myself talked politics for some time after a late break-fast (before which I arose 1½ hrs., read, and took a walk) and then rode up to Judge Rucks' intending only to stay a short time, but in finding Will and Hal there and they soliciting it, I stayed until about 4 o'clock, playing Euchre most of the time. Nevertheless we did not lay aside much of our more boistrous inclinations. We talked loud, laughed loud, danced loud and kept "racket" in most every form. Who will make old fogies of "Young Americans"? Go it while you are young for when you get old you can't go! If it is not vicious—"Is happiness a crime?" Then let the fiends of hell reign in your sullen heaven. I returned home about the time mentioned, thinking how fleetly these guileless days of happy boy-hood would pass away when I would have to struggle with a frigid world—to lose such thoughts in reading *Harper's Weekly* the rest of the evening.

This is the third time my birthday has rolled around since I commenced journalizing two years ago and this is the seventeenth time it has come since I have been in the "land of the living." How many times will I write an entry on this day? I do not know. This I will close by saying I was plagued at the dinner table by the only person who can plague me, Mrs. Yerger, about the "poetry affair" of last Jan.

This[99] my loved mother gave me to show that she loved me as the mother there loved her child, and I have pasted it here because I think so much of it and that I may have it where I can see it often and read it. It overbalances in my estimation the gold and silver trinkets mothers usually give. Verily it does.

Friday, August 3, 1860

By no means satisfied with my course today, hist. being the only thing I studied because probably my habits have been broken into of late. Let us see if this is again repeated. I threw away part of my evening in cutting citron for Ma, some with the names of some of my lady acquaintances on them and some with caricatures. One had on it the Latin which is on the 191st page.[100] Late in the evening I took a walk up to our now desolate schoolhouse. All is still and the cricket in my chimney seems to be calling me to bed, whether or not I shall soon land there.

Saturday, August 4, 1860

During a long hot day I have killed time, very little to my advantage, skip-ping from one thing to another, and with the exception of some history I have impressed upon my inferior memory, very little, as I said, has been done for my good; cutting citron, strolling about and eating watermelons, with a little reading and a nap I took in the afternoon, having taken up my time. At dusk I started a walk but meeting a boy at the gate with some papers turned back with them and read in one a pretty little tale called *The Phantom Bride*[101] which I will clip and put in a little collection of short and interesting pieces which some day I may have bound and have it to while away some dull winter evening in my prospective *bachelor* life.

I measured myself today and found that I was, in stocking feet, 5½ feet in height, circumference of chest, 31 inches, do. of thighs 20½ inches, do. of legs 13⅛ inches, and breadth of shoulders 17½ inches. From this time '58 I have gained in height 6 inches and in breadth of shoulders 3½.

Sunday, August 5, 1860

Took a ride with Ma after breakfast during which we talked of the course a young man should persue in this life, and I was pleased to see that my sober, matter of fact view of the case met her approbation, as is the case with Pa. Anyone who should hear my views would think I was an old fogy. I do not expect to live a fast life, but I do not intend to bury myself in such a place as Deer Creek.

Pa and myself both disapproving of Willard's *Universal History*[102] on account of its arrangement and excessive brevity (as the history of the world cannot be contained in one volume, not even a synopsis) I took up on my return the life of one of the most noble men the world has ever seen, whose just praise no tongue can speak or language express and who stands among the first of the long line of heroes history lays before us—the Marquis de Lafayette. For him I shall ever base in my heart the same love, admiration, and homage that I bear for the great heroes who shed their blood with him on the same fields and plains. The magnitude of my adoration is stupendous. Oh! I love them "past man's thoughts!"

Till about 5 PM I with almost enthusiasm traced the eventful course of his life up to the time of Arnold's nefarious treason. Mr. Wm. Percy & Lady then coming (in the evening I was under the Creek bank) I came to the house, put on a clean shirt, ate a melon with them and listened to a conversation which made me firmer in my resolve never to marry if I reach blessed maturity.

Monday, August 6, 1860

My intention was to have Ma to trim my hair (according to Dr. M's directions) but after she had ridden, after I had become interested in Lafayette and had waited her motions the morning had gone by without my having studied my grammar at all. Mr. Carvell coming as also did a *Harper* soon after dinner, I found that between entertaining him and reading my H. no hair was cut or grammar studied in the evening. The most important thing that has happened to me today was the arrival of Pro. Maupin's[103] letter in answer to Pa's of the last month. It occupied my thoughts mostly during the evening.

Tuesday, August 7, 1860

It is 10 o'clk and yet nothing is done. A stroll in the garden, a prolonged talk with Mr. C. about colleges and a second perusal of Mr. M's plain, straightforward letter has thus far been all I have done. About that letter, now is as good a time as any. I said it was plain and straightforward, explicit and unreserved, as I love to see a man act. It was perceptible that Pa had been equally as open in his epistle, stating as I conjectured that I was poorly prepared for college. Let that be. Listen at what he says after stating the minimum age of admission: "If your son is sufficiently mature in years to have acquired habits of self-reliance, industry and perseverence, he might no doubt enter the University next session and persue with advantage the course indicated in your letter. But if he is very young, say 16 or 17, it would be hazardous to send him with the slender preparation I infer from your letter he possesses." Under the last-mentioned inference he suggests a preparation at one of the preparatory schools in the vicinity, stating the advantages accruing from such a course and under that head concludes thus: "He could then" (referring to my preparation) "enter the institution under much more favorable auspices than he could do next session." Then stating the time of commencement he says, "Should you conclude to send your son to us, it will be *greatly to his interest to be here at the very beginning.*" However cloudy may appear this part of his letter, he frankly states in a prior part that if I am of the requisite age (16), I can be admitted into the schools of Mathematics, French, and History & General Literature in the institution.

Thus things stand; I am perplexed and Pa is perplexed. I shall leave it all to him. I shall to the best of my ability pursue the course he marks out for me. I rely upon him. I shall abide by the consequences that may attend that course, disregarding their nature and recollection "temeritus est florentes statis precedentia senectutis."[104]

I attempted to study but was foiled by the children who would keep Satan from studying or doing anything and having eaten a watermelon with others of the family. The remainder of the day was passed in reading Lafayette, where I still find cause for nothing but plaudits, all nobility and honor.

Mr. Carvell when we all had collected in my room (U. Jack, Jimmy, and myself) told us an interesting tale of his shipwreck at Whitehaven, he having been a sailor and having travelled much. He's a clever fellow if he is not of the first notch, though he has a liberal education.

Wednesday, August 8, 1860

English Grammar claimed my attention till 12 o'clk except an intermission that a call from John Burne, Taylor, and Nat made about 10½, during which we ate watermelons, played the fiddle and had a rather mirthful time. I followed Lafayette through his heroic course from the fanatic mobs of Paris to his horrid imprisonment at Olmutz. When I read of his privations and cruelties I foamed with indignation and desire to revenge his wrongs. I could have enlisted in his cause with the same enthusiasm that he espoused ours 50 years ago and could have and still could see the last drop of his enemy's life blood flow with pleasure.

Having set up late talking to Mr. C. and U.J. and being awakened in the morning late, Pa gave me a severe admonition, saying that he was sorry to see that I was led off by the first temptation here at home and had serious fears that I would give way when from under his care and much more. I felt hurt, mortified, and chagrined, but as it was just, though it was the first time I had failed since I commenced to get up early, I made no excuse, only stating the facts. He exercised his usual rigidity and straight forward austerity.

Thursday, August 9, 1860

Again visitors interrupted my studies in the prior part of the day, they were Hal, John, and Joe Percy. To the latter I was introduced by J. We had a vociferous arguing about a *Methodist Preacher* who, it seems, has been inciting the slaves to an insurrection and attacking in strong terms the virtue of the ladies on the Creek down about 12 miles, which was suspected from some cause and in examining his papers found virulent libel, proofs of his guilt. Some persons, it is said, have gone down to *lynch him*, success to them. But my argument; all were for shooting, hanging and burning. I for the law, tar and feathers. Their ground showed me how far boys and even all people, will allow their passions to carry them. It was resolved by Pa that I should go down to the "scene of action" this evening but afterwards countermanded.

After they left I continued my Grammar till 12 when I took up Lafayette and stayed with him till night, finishing his most eventful life. When I saw depicted, by language and picture, his mournful visit to Washington's tomb, it was all I could do to restrain my tears. My sympathies and feelings were aroused. On the flyleaf, I wrote a few lines expressive of my admiration for him—"How little, how little, is worth and glory valued here!"

At supper, I, having broached the subject of Lafayette, and they (for all were against me—I'm always in the minority) had a trump at my expense—I having forgotten that [he] made us a visit in 1784. On this they trumped.

Friday, August 10, 1860

Some of the earlier part of my morning was passed in little jobs, the principal of which was emptying my room of a good deal, in fact all of its already confused furniture for Mr. C. to paper it. Then, as usual, my English Grammar till 12 and historical reading till in the evening. I seldom break my habits of study. May I never intercept them. *A Visit to the Camp Before Sevastopol*[105] was my book, with which I am not as well pleased as I expected the author relating too much about his *visit* (true to his title) and not enough about the war, its causes, movements, etc. Howbeit, it is interesting, but not as *solid* a style of writing as I feel it to be my interest to read. Pure, unbiased history is what I want and what I will soon have in the annals of my country as I am more than half through the "visit," it being a medium-sized volume. Two more things before I close; I will commence, where? with a ride I took this evening after I stopped reading on "old Clay" *without a saddle or bridle* a mile meeting only Nat and H. Percy and will end by saying that Mrs. Percy, who, with her consort, ate supper with us, gave us some of her music such as I have before said that soothed my spirits and for the time made me another boy. Will I ever marry unless the object of my choice understands music so that she can enliven a home, which without I will never marry, by the exercise of this inestimable, *mingled* science and art? If I do my views will be changed vastly from what they are now. I am done for this night—the same old answer to all these interrogatories (and it is as good as any)—time will show, it will show if I ever marry—if I ever get the consent of myself to immolate the liberties of a batchelor's life at Hymen's altar!

Saturday, August 11, 1860

Having taken quinine to prevent the return of chills, I found study disagreeable and took up my Sevastopol. I finished it a short time after dinner and then read till sundown in the "Heroes of the American Revolution" a sketch on the life of Washington, an *extremely* cursory affair and a part of Green's life. The style is about the same as that of Sevastopol—pleasing by nothing extraordinary. My reading for the day finished, I walked down to the bridge memorizing on the way the words I entered in an old blank book, the meanings of which I did not understand when I read them in the books before mentioned. Returning I met Miss Kate and Joe (ought I not to say Mr.?) and to my surprise they stopped. The young damsel commenced a lively conversation with me in which I bore a part not at all easy as I was unexpectedly drawn into it. After mutual regrets that I could not accompany her to Norfolk in the 1st part of Sep. (Nat is going) she commenced an apology for some poems *of her own* which she sent in for me to read the other evening (and one was necessary even if the next morning I did compliment them profusely) and promised to write one about *me* (?). Of course, I was much flattered that "I was not conscious I was capable of inspiring poetry, etc. etc." "begged leave to see it" and thought "if I did cause her to write a piece of poetry I was entitled to [the] privilege of seeing it &c." to which she smiled and to her smile, I bowed and scraped terribly. Sic mundus et.[106] She then requested me to come down and to use her words, she wanted "me to come with old pill-box. She wanted to give me one more ride; she wanted to kill me." I politely agreed to come soon, not meaning the first word of what I said, not any more than she meant what she said about the poetry. We soon parted and on my way home could not refrain from laughing at the hollowness and foolishness of the interview and to see what course she chose to let Joe know she wrote poetry. Really it was amusing. Now, I wonder if she'll get me to ride?

Sunday, August 12, 1860

Being under the disagreeable effects of quinine all the morning (I did not get up until late for fear of a chill) I could not bring myself to study but read *The Heroes*[107] and even did not find that congenial to my feelings, however not from the subject matter but from morbidness. *Harper* and myself communed most of the evening until Nat came in (to my displeasure setting on his horse — not time to alight) and I threw away the time that he stayed because I was not interested particularly. He was not in a mood to please or engage me. He wanted me to accompany him to the Bogue with some other boys in the morning, but I declined as I thought it "wouldn't pay."

Wishing to show my attachment to my candid and loved old friend Judge Rucks, who is almost a foster father toward me as he is toward all, I selected from my private library (it is small and I love all my books) one, *Party Leaders*,[108] a book of political history and biography of eminent political men. I resolved to make it the medium through which to express that attachment and conflicted with myself sometime how I should inscribe it, but at last fixed upon this modest form: "To Judge James Rucks as a token of regard from Harry" and the date. I think I will call on Taylor tomorrow evening and then I will present it.

Monday, August 13, 1860

Father having notified me, I was ready and took my seat with him in the buggy destined to town, having a cool pleasant ride, starting after breakfast. I can but infer from what he said on the road about my leaving and for where that his (or rather mine) views are in accordance with his. Indeed he said, he would rather I could go to the University than to one of the schools and that the only obstacle was that I could not attend to my English so well then, which I can easily obviate and think I removed much from his mind by what I said. He seemed to accept it, and this ain't all—he told me to call on a young man who attends the U. from Bolivar and *see when he was going*. Good! From the position of things I expect to start from here to Charlottesville about the 20th of next month. The old fellow talked to me much about the future (especially that short at hand). I think all things come right. He also said he would send down to N.O. for a watch soon—a thing I've needed and wanted for some time.

After a dull stay I rode part of the way back by myself, Pa riding with Mr. Percy. Howbeit, I whistled and sung my way through. A little stay on the road, and a ride home at dark or very little sooner and forthwith a walk down to the old Judge's to tea and afterwards a jolly chat with Taylor, a dark walk home. During that jolly talk I nearly made him split his sides laughing at my description of me courting my "Virginia gal."

Tuesday, August 14, 1860

Wishing to do all my visiting today and end these hours of idleness I have been rather inclined to indulge in for a short time past, I mounted my horse and put off for Maj. Lee's, stopping at Judge R's to leave the *Party Leaders* and get Taylor to go down with me, but he was out so I left a note and went on. N. was not at home but Mrs. L. and Miss K. entertained me better than he can because they were women. Music (good) and chat was plenty. I had started home when I met Nat and turned back and stayed till after dinner, returned home, but did little or nothing besides clipping some pieces for my scrap book, entertaining John and then Hal, eating a watermelon and knocking around generally. I may mention that I read a sketch on Jerome Bonaparte's life,[109] the timorous old sensualist. I may also mention here a little piece of deception I am in the habit of practicing at the Maj.'s in the form of petting the baby (who I only like as I do other babies) to gain the favor of his mother. I take him on my knee, talk to him, give him my pencil, compliment him and make myself agreeable generally, mostly because I know it pleases his mother and because I wish to do rather what pleases than what displeases her. Still I may, as I expect often to do, say, as in a former entry, *sic mundus et.* It is policy—policy is wisdom.

Wednesday, August 15, 1860

Reluctantly have I allowed myself to pass this day as I have—in pleasure, though it was not of an exciting nature. I generally fulfill any engagements I make (but will I keep the one made last Sat. evening?) and in conformance with that habit rode up to see Hal after breakfast and at his request rode on up to call on John McCutchen and we did not get back to his house till after 12, where I ate dinner and again came back home about 4 PM, he accompanying me. Before I go any farther, I have very little to say. I may state a compliment John payed me while at his house which was as he expressed it, "Harry, you ought to study Law for you have the gift of gab." There are different kinds of gab—sensible and nonsensical, too much of either being injurious, especially if a man was arguing before a dull jury, which I expect to do often times. I have found that if even a little is said with earnestness, force, and point, it outweighs much said in a different manner. Yes, it was gratifying to know that he thought I was fit for *the* profession.

I may now say I read *some* only after coming home, most of my time being taken up in assisting Pa about his cotton sacks and other things. Two of the most touching incidents I have ever read in history: I mean the executions of those patriots Hayne and Hale by the ruthless, bloodthirsty Britons, presented themselves to me. The manliness, the disinterested devotion to their country, the heroic valor and undaunted intrepidity of these men challenge antiquities fiction in brilliance. Why should we depart from our country for heroism, for beautiful actions that chain admiration captive, for patriotic words whose pure lucidness would seem to rival the "gems in the diadems of the Caesars"? Strange how people bow to what is antique, to what is foreign. We can hear spoutings in abundance in praise of Pericles, Lycurgus, and Solon, Cicero, Seneca, and Scipio but few, very few, words can we hear lauding *our* heroes! Who raises his voice with the same enthusiasm for our Ciceros, for our Demostheneses as he does for those of the Greeks and Romans? Who raises his voice with equal force to praise *our* Lycurguses, our Pericleses, and our Cipios? Are our orators—Henry, Hayne, Webster, and Clay—so far beneath these men (whose justly earned fame I will not diminish) that they deserve thus to be cast into the background? Are our warriors, or saviors, so far inferior to

Pompey, Caesar, and Scipio that they deserve the same fate? Can any man conscientiously detract the first iota from the glory of our Washingtons, Greens, Sullivants, Putnams, Marions, and Schuylers by saying that they deserve less renown than the ancient generals above mentioned? Whom did Caesar fight in Gaul but raw barbarians who after a few blows laid down their arms? Whom did Scipio fight but an enervated set of voluptuous men in the shape of the Carthaginians? And Pompey conquered in the East a like band or bands of undisciplined men. Their fame easily gained is to be contrasted with that of our lion-hearted forefathers who achieved the greatest end the human mind has ever arrived at—glorious liberty—without any army, without money, without arms, provisions, clothing, ammunition—literally without anything that could be called a means of defense, and nothing to sustain them but a watchful Providence who nerved and strengthened their naked arms to deal death to their villainous enemies, an enemy whose thirst for blood seemed insatiable, who was looked upon as invincible, no timorous barbarians or effeminate townsmen but whom those same starved, naked men drove from the bright shores of America, then to plant as the last rippling wave from the retreating bardges of that implacable enemy dashed upon the pebbly beach, the great standard of liberty which let us hope shall stand through all eternity!

Thursday, August 16, 1860

Although I have not left home, I can not say that I am satisfied exactly with my Grammar, most of my morning having flown by while being busied in little unavoidable jobs—but I read a good deal in the evening. Coming to the sketch on Lafayette's life, I fancied from the length I was going to have an interesting summary of his life but was disappointed to find that so little was said of his life up to his visit in '24, taking up only four or five pages while much space was wasted on unnecessary description of his visit to N.Y.

I did a thing this morning (one of the "jobs") which my cautious father has often told me not to do, viz. the cutting of the fuzzy germs of (let me hope) pretty whiskers. He had gone out electioneering for the office of probate Judge and I took from his drawer his shaving "couterments" and perpetrated the deed. By Jupiter, I could just hear the scrape!

I sat up last night till 12½ to give Louly medicine, and my time was principally occupied in writing the long entry for yesterday. I am now sitting up for the same purpose. A negro boy who cut his foot with an ax yesterday comes to me tonight, waiting til Pa has gone for me to fix it after getting it in an ugly plight. I had cause to get mad and did so. Thanks to my experience in these plantation worries. It really was a long and a very dirty task to handle the stinking, nasty foot of a rough negro. However, after giving him a genteel raking down in the shape of a ———, I accomplished my work.

I had finished half of this entry when Dr. Mears was announced, who called on Jimmy who is sick. The conversation turned upon his rupture, and upon that desease I gained much light, I am proud to say, from him. Something he could not say before Ma he told me as I stood on the steps with him (he being about to leave) treating me in a manner I did not expect—with decided deference, and all voluntarily for I had forgot the subject. Probably it was because he saw I wished to know that he took the pains to tell me. I make it a rule if an opportunity offers to draw forth by interrogations the views or knowledge any one may have on any subject who is conversing with me, though I am careful not to be too abundant in my inquiries. By these means, as I did tonight, I gather a little here and there without committing myself (if in argument) and which in course of time will count up like throwing a pea into a bucket occasionally—it will be full after a while.

Friday, August 17, 1860

To the neglect of my Grammar I took a volume of poems Nat's mother and her sister composed, "the two sisters of the west," and passed my entire morning in copying off the "Wife Seen" to put in my Gems of Poetry (shall I call it thus?). Would my matter-of-fact father agree to this? *I* thought it would do no harm, so I did it, being interrupted once during my work, no, twice, for after dinner as I was finishing it Taylor came up and *he* even admired the piece, as old-fogyish as he is.

Read history the balance of the day. From dusk till midnight was not so tranquil. A negro boy whom Pa left sick sent for me at dusk. I found him too sick for me to tamper with as he was always inclined to congestion of the stomach and then had a light fever, with purging and vomiting. I put on a coat and walked down to Dr. Percy's supposing the boy needed immediate attention. He had not come from the road, a horse was caught for me to go and meet him and stop him at our house, but before the horse came around he had come. I laid the case plainly before him stating our alarm, Pa being from home, and telling him we heard that Dr. Mears would not come at night. He "humed and hawed" and said he was very tired and would go if Dr. M. would not. I said no more but got on the horse after bidding them good evening and rode down and got Dr. Mears to come. I think that situated as we were it was as little as he could do to come after telling Pa he would do so if any thing of the kind occurred, which was a voluntary promise. I know if Mrs. Percy had been placed as we were Pa would have arisen from his bed and gone into any sort of weather to gratify her, not consulting his comfort. This is the difference between the two men; one does and the other does not look to personal convenience when he can assist a neighbor. The question is now, did the Dr. keep his promise? Still, Dr. Percy is a man much esteemed and liked, but I do not make him an exception to the general rule *that man will have self-interest under all his actions.* If he makes himself agreeable, it is to be popular; if he give to the poor, it is to be praised, and in all the notice I have taken of these sort of things, self-interest is nearly invariably under all. Very few men can be found who will give their money when they know he will get no credit for it, and I do not exempt from this rule that (so-looked upon) immutable class of men—the Preachers. It is not only in pecuniary matters this much favored sect is immutable. I believe it to be all fudge when they tell me a young man (say 15 years of age) can commence the study of Divinity and wait till he is 35 or 40 before he is married *underhandedly* if not openly. I believe it, and history confirms my belief, that men have and reports are coming to us daily that they do make religion for which [. . .] I am a vile sinner. I have a sincere reverence, a cloke to hide sensuality and crimes that a man who even has the most trivial pretentions to respectability would hoot at! I have expatiated too much already so I will hurry over the balance; then forward! To my astonishment, the fever had left the boy when we got here, and the Dr.'s prescription having been carried out, and I having missed my supper at both places, I pitched first into Ma's crackers, pickles, preserves and poundcake and then into bed. Before I finish this entry I may say that the Dr. and myself were quite talkative during our ride upon the professions of Law and Medicine, study, education, and life generally.

Saturday, August 18, 1860

Frequent interruptions which I anticipated prevented me from studying but my morning was passed pleasantly as my evening. A volume of poems and a *Harper* I got from Judge R's composed my companions most of the time and the rest, the Constitution of the United States, that sage article. In H——r I read of the arrival of "His Royal Highness, the Prince of Wales." Now the young "Prince" may be a very clever chap for aught I know, but we have been raised (thus far) in different countries under different auspices, and it is very natural that we should have different views. I do not suppose the chap cares much—neither do I. I know the young "intended," but it is highly probable he knows extremely little of me and cares less. He is only 2 years older than I am and we both have a life before us. How different our ways! He is to be surrounded by wealth, opulence, the beauty and glitter of a court, regal pomp and regal toils and tribulations. I am to be surrounded by modest competence, a quiet way and instead of *regal* I shall have *legal* trials and tribulations. I am not opposed to aristocracy as it is in Europe, and I will not say I do not envy the prince his position; I do not say if a dukedom was offered to me (?) I would refuse it; I do not say I would oppose the introduction of nobility upon the same footing it now stands on in England into this country, for I now believe it would be to the advantage of the country and society for the simple reason that the number of blacklegs to be found in the highest circles of society here could then be excluded. But I am not going to make a fool of myself because I am not a Marquis of a court. I am going along through the world unostentatiously, enjoying those pleasures which a kind Providence may place in my reach and not repining for those that are *not* in my reach. I commenced this subject however to say this: that the people with their accustomed foolishness are going to make a great blow over "our hero" (is he one yet?) and plainly show the world their want of common sense. He's the son of Queen Victoria! and he comes to travel through our country as a private gentleman. Let him travel then as such. Why kick up a great hullabaloo about him? His "Royal Highness" when he enters this blessed union is no more than the weak little boy who is now writing about him, and I ask, "why not treat him accordingly?" No! they will have balls, hops, banquets, and processions. I prognosticate this; let's watch the papers and see it verified.

Sunday, August 19, 1860

Two auspicious omens have fallen from Pa's lips today, auspicious to my departure. The first at the supper table when something was said of cream, Ma sending some of that article around to me, he remarked *"yes, eat it now for you won't have long to eat it."* The second was while we were all sitting on the gallery after supper. I said something to Ma about some linen I needed and he spoke to Ma saying *"you had better finish them soon for he has not got but five weeks to stay."* Does this not look promising? Oh! he will come to after a while. His contumacy is gradually lessening.

I wrote my last entry after a late breakfast and a long letter to Mr. Herbert. I would have done so some time ago but did not know his P.O. till Pa got a letter from him this morning which was characteristic of the old fellow. In mentioning the news concerning our friend, the preacher Early, I gave preachers as a sect particular Jerusalem. I came down on that highly esteemed gentleman's movements with all my might.

I had scarcely finished the last word in my last sentence when Jimmy who, notwithstanding my expostulations would wash his gun on my hearth before which sat my table where I was writing, in his absentmindedness and inatten-tiveness put the muzzle on the table and turned the other end of the barrel up, pouring out over the table and (as may be seen) my good old diary, a flood of black dirty water. I was very ireful and evinced it in my words and actions. I arose passionately and severely reproved him for what he done—probably more harshly than I should, but I have no patience with such inexcusable con-duct.

Twenty-four hours has passed since it occurred; I write this part of this entry afterwards as I at once did all I could in the way of using blotting paper and pressing my book between dictionaries to relieve it. I will finish this entry by stating that my evening was spent to little literary advantage as I divided most of my time between listening to the interesting words of Judge R. and skim-ming around. I have one more word to say: in my walk I met Mr. & Mrs. Wm. Percy and he said to me, "Why Harry you are getting as fat as you can roll." I know it and hate it very much. I detest corpulency. I do not think however that it is as bad as the casual observer would imagine. My pants by no means fit me. U.J. says that I am big enough from my waist down for a person much larger than I am. I do hope it will not grow upon me. College will diminish me.

Monday, August 20, 1860

My indulgent father must have "my boy" to fix his cotton slate for him this morning which with its little worries made me in substance loose all of that part of the day I had hoped to devote to study. Then a mother who has much confidence in her oldest son's taste must have him waste one more hour and a half cutting citron for her. When I finished these things dinner was on the table, and after doing the entries justice I by no means neglected the peaches and cream. I enjoyed them because I know these things won't be with me long. Arising from this necessitous though pleasant occupation I passed my whole evening in rummaging over my old letters, assorting them out, sealing them to lay away in a box with my books when I leave, looking over my scraps of humor, making additions to my little stock of "Tales" as well as to my "scraps" and stirring my old trunk up powerfully, spending my time very pleasantly.

I did a little thing during my walk this evening which I will not overlook as it is clearly indicative of my inordinate and ungovernable I don't know what towards the soft sex. I had gone about 300 yards below Judge R's bridge and was returning when I happened to look back and saw a couple of ladies— one in mourning, whom, at the distance, I did not know. My curiosity was immediately kindled, and to quench the flame of that curiosity, in turning a little bend and being out of their sight (they coming on toward me) I slipped down the bank and stood observing but not observed. I laid close while they were close but came out when they had passed on about 50 yds beyond, having previously recognized them although it was growing dusk. They were Mrs. James and Susan Yerger. I will do anything to get a peep at a woman. Who won't?

Tuesday, August 21, 1860

It was not my fault that I did no studying today but the fault of the same things that prevented it yesterday morning. When these things were finished the morning was so far gone that I took up two or three old *Harper's* and cut some wit from their columns for my "scraps." I found them in an obscure drawer in my bureau, where also I found one of the most useful books I ever saw, one which Pa has often tried to purchase another copy of—the Dictionary of Quotations from Latin, Greek, Italian, French, and Spanish. I shall appropriate it to myself as I believe I need it more than Pa does.

The beginning at least of the patriot philosopher's life is not near so interesting as the dullest part of Lafayette's for the reason that one was a man of peace, the other of strife. Part of my evening went by slowly with this book in my hand and the other part in strolling around the grounds. Miss Kate first and Will and Hal next came by while I sat on the roof of a new building in the lot driving a few nails. I wondered what they thought. Didn't care much. Labor disgraces no man, but a man's conduct *can*. I went to the Creek and washed all over about dusk intending to walk down to Judge R's after supper as I wished to see a book T. has, but not having a very neat pair of shoes (?) and hearing of the good news—the arrival of Judge Wm. Yerger's two daughters—I concluded to wait till I was better prepared so that I might kill two birds with one stone.

Wednesday, August 22, 1860

True to my resolution the morning found me hard at my studies where I staid till about 11 when I bethought myself of a thing I have for some months meditated, viz. the drawing of my schoolhouse and of this. My 1st attempt at this house was abortive, and I concluded to try Mr. Schoolhouse. Putting off, merrily whistling "Even of Thee" &c. I soon brought myself by fast walking to my destination, and pencil in hand I took my sketching paper and likewise a seat and succeeded in executing the outlines by 12½ when I went home. Returning after dinner, I accomplished my work much more to my satisfaction than I had anticipated, if I could not draw the boys playing marbles as I wished. I never took a lesson in my life and would do so now but Pa says I have not got the time. I have a lively taste for the art and ever since I can recollect I drew whenever I got a chance. I have not even seen a person sketch so what I know (and it is little) I have learned from observation of pictures and of nature. I think I will start a "march" on the old man and procure a stock of blanks and draw once a week—Sundays while I am at college. By these means I hope to obtain proficiency in the admirable art. Hal and Will came by and looked at my picture. I knew *they* were not able to appreciate a *good* picture let alone my crazy scratchings. A thundercloud disturbed me and drove me hence, but I had so nearly finished that I ended it at home, i.e. all but the boys. From that time (about 5 o'clock) till night I read newspapers and strolled around a while. But for want of time I will mention in my next entry an occurrence which took place this morning. Would that I did not have it to enter on these pages, but I have said it—if I keep a Journal I will keep it faithfully.

Thursday, August 23, 1860

At Pa's request I mounted his horse to ride up and see if I could get some workmen to come down from Capt. French's to do some work. Before I got to his bridge I stumbled on John McCutchen and got him to accompany me. We took a road (as I found out on our arrival) different from the one the men whom I was hunting had taken to come down to our house. Thus 20 miles were ridden to no purpose. We sat and ate dinner with Mr. Johnson, a very clever man but who was not an exception to the contaminations of his class of men. He was talkative and not unentertaining though the want of mental culture was palpable. A rain came up as I neared Dr. Taylor's (J's home) and kept on notwithstanding his invitations to stop. I got in at Judge F's just in time to miss the shower, which being over I came home to "roll" around till dark.

At Judge F's I was amused at some of his anecdotes, especially at one concerning the *private* whereabouts of a bill he had to open on a negro woman. His manner was amusing almost as much as the subject. Will, who with the others was on the gallery where we sat, indulged in a remark as I rode off which its manner more than itself made it look rather *little*. It was, "Harry, where did that horse learn to pace." I ought to have answered "from you" but I did not. The horse did pace badly.

I will now state the occurrence. It was briefly this: Jimmy, with his usual pertinacity at thwarting everything I undertook and in opposing my every wish, wished to take my dog Sam hunting with him whether I wanted it or not—by main force. My reasons for not lending Sam to him were that he told me that he shot or attempted to shoot in among a flock of turkeys where he was and said he wished he had killed him. I did not want my dog killed, therefore I opposed his going. Pa and Ma took his side in an altercation which ensued. I was angry. I looked Ma in the face and said, "he will regret it if he takes my dog," turned upon my heel and walked down nearly to Judge R's bridge madder than I have been for a long time. J. overtook me and said, "take your dog. I don't want him!" but would not drive him back because he *did* want him and knew as long as he had a gun the dog would follow him. It was some time before I reversed my temperature. This morning it was still worse. I do Pa the justice to say he was in neither one, but as I heard yesterday morning reproved Jimmy for his conduct. I took the dog by a series of maneuvers. I give him the credit of executing masterly by the aid of circumstances to a great extent. He got the dog away despite all I could do. He has kept much, very much, happiness from my home; he has been the cause of nearly all my trouble, and I rejoice I have not to bear with him much longer. He won't let me treat him as a brother. This very morning I rose in my bed and asked him in as kind and tender tone as I could not to take my dog. My answer was, "shut up, I don't want to talk to you." This is always the case. He tries to force me into doing what suits him and if I, to avoid a breach or fuss, give way he taunts and hoots at me for it. He abuses me at all times and all places. Scorn and reproach are on his lips always. He never is at all civil unless he wants me to do something for him. I stand much for Ma's and Pa's sake—much that they never know of. I have taken so much that it seems as though my cup of bitterness will never be filled. It has become intolerable. I can not and will not suffer it any longer. I do not say I am clear of blame; no one is, but I say I have done my duty, more than my duty. Neither Ma nor Pa can say I have not been a dutiful son. This I claim because I know it is nothing but justice. There is an end to all things—there is an end to my endurance and my patience. I have said it, though it pains me, though it may pain Ma and Pa, he shall suffer directly or indirectly as he has for years made me suffer. Mark it. I mean what I say.

Friday, August 24, 1860

That innocent dog again was J's chosen medium through which to aggravate me. Suffice it to say this time his manuevers were foiled and that I had my mother's dark countenance turned upon me. On her asking me some question in anything but a good humor, I spoke apertly and passionately to her for I was not yet pleased and laid the thing in very few words before her—but she seemed determined to judge me as I have nearly always been judged—wrongfully. I know she thinks she is doing justly. Pa too seems to favor J. It always has been thus. Let it be so still. I will not detract the first iota from my mislead brother's estimation in my parent's eyes. Although he took the dog this evening surreptitiously, my better feelings as usual begin to become paramount. Occasionally it seems as though I can't find it in my heart to retaliate.

My usual time for study was taken up by my Grammar today. I find the life of Franklin to be much more interesting than it was at the commencement. At sundown I finished his memoir, finding but one fault in him—he was for the emancipation of the slaves, *an abolitionist*. I ran my pencil through this, but his other transcendent virtues counterbalance this erratum. The course taken by the scurrilous ministry to attack him politically at the mock trial for the transmission of some important letters to the Mass assembly, the purpose of which was not a *trial* for the got-up offence but a stealthy occasion they took of making the facile dog Wedderburn their tool to spout out at the patriot, the philosopher, the sage, America's Aristotle, their base vituperation and ribaldry, which was too low to elicit a reply from the unoffending victim, proud in his contemptuous silence, too pusillanimous to appear in print without being revised. His sententious letter to Madam Helvetius is demonstration of his tact, wit, and humor—an ingenious apologue. From the description given by Mrs. Adams of that lady and this quotation from one of his letters (I would not positively state it as my opinion) I would not be surprised if he indulged a passion (which he in his autobiography confesses to have indulged in his youth) towards this Madam H. Here is the quotation: "I stretch my arms towards you in spite of the intensity of the ocean that separates us and wait that celestial kiss I hope one day to give you." Had he given her one that was *not* celestial? But I will cast into oblivion such unworthy ideas of such a man, a man who has had few superiors. I will not allow myself to discant on this venerable and discrete diplomatist. I may say more about him before I am through with his life, if my words do avail nothing.

Saturday, August 25, 1860

Arising from the breakfast table I walked down to Judge R's though when I started I had no idea of stopping but was merely taking a walk. My object was to obtain a *Harper* and to take a memorandum of some books, the names of which were in a book of Taylor's, *Anecdotes of Love*,[110] *Dictionary of Love*,[111] and Byron's works. Having found F. and Will in bed and having obtained the object of my "stop" I came towards but not entirely home until I had read the greater part of my H——r while sitting on an old log coolly under the bank enjoying my silent retreat. Nor was I disappointed in not finding in the columns of this paper something about the distinguished (as Ma will have it) person spoken of in my entry a week ago. My prophecy has been more than verified. They must even enumerate the number of sets he danced at a ball given him, how he was dressed, even to the color of his gloves, rode out, got drenched, looks when he entered the ballroom &c., &c., &c. This great hullabaloo is not all; municipal meetings were held in N.Y. by the merchants, a committee formed of the most respectable men—of which Aster and Scott were members—to invite his "royal highness" to visit New York and participate in a banquet which will be prepared for the *private gentleman*," who is to pass through our country. Everything that is foreign must have attention—musicians, singers, etc. Where will this subserviency to these things end? Now it does look pusillanimous that because queen Victoria's son visits us in the above named capacity, giving us a hint it would seem to refrain from our customary folly that all this blow and fuss must be made. If our *President* were to make a tour in England, unless he went in the name of the nation, would not be slobbered over in this manner— no banquets would be shoved under his nose; no conventions of merchants would be called; no one would go into such minute descriptions of his dress, actions, and appearance, but he would be allowed to pass along as though he was traversing the country of men who were not lickspittles, men who had a little regard for national and self-respect.

But to return: It was about 11½ when I got home, and I then read Franklin till dinner. A pain by no means dull slightly attacked me before breakfast and by dinner time my left leg (where it was) from the knee down was in much misery. To alleviate it I walked down (or up) to the gin where the workmen were and found by propping it up against something I experienced a little alleviation of the pain—in fact a cessation. I then came home soon to be visited by Taylor and Hal while enjoying a newly arrived newspaper, to have quite a saturnian time waltzing while the other whistled having no fiddle "ready for action." We were very boisterous and did not act towards each other (especially Hal and myself) as knights of the 16th century would. He once struck me back of the head with his open hand while I was off my guard and I returned the compliment by bearly missing his head with a dictionary. They left at nearly sundown when I read my paper on till dusk and limped out on my walk if I did waltz with my "game leg," it hurting me.

I see Humboldt's reputation as a man and philosopher is being impugned by the French papers in consequence of the publication of his correspondence,[112] in which he is accused of having exhibited some of Sir Walpole's[113] "gossiping cynicism." I know the man only by reputation, and if I am to judge from the philosophical reputation of his *Cosmos*,[114] that single work would confute the last attack.

Sunday, August 26, 1860

Reading has been neglected for drawing today of which I am too fond for my more substantial good. However, after a walk soon after breakfast, I read some in Franklin. I then looked over most every book I could find to discover a picture from which I could learn to make a bird flying on my picture of the 22nd. Failing, I took the original and transferred it on another and larger sheet with, I fancy, many improvements. Such things, especially in one as utterly inexperienced as myself, take time to be finished, and from about 10 o'clk till sundown my attention was devoted exclusively to my new picture. Nevertheless, I yet have some more touches of importance to make. Uncle J. and myself walked up to the schoolhouse (my subject) to see how to place some trees &c. As we neared the quarter-gate we espied Taylor, Miss Lou, and Miss Bettie[115] about fifty yds ahead coming toward us. I being in my shirt sleeves got over the fence where Pa was and set my mouth to speak to them but lo and behold! *they pass us with as little concern as if we had been so many pigs.* I spoke, but the "gals" did not turn their heads. Oh! you little heart-stealers, did you think you could "cross grain" ye Uncle Fuller? Den dar's jus whar ye was in a shortcummin, ye old unkle didn't [want] to speak to ye so conswaggedly no how, ye little dilsies!

Monday, August 27, 1860

Being annoyed by the disappearance of my drawing from my drawer where I had laid it, I hunted and searched every corner until late in the morning before I found it away behind all the drawers in my bureau between there and the back. So much of my studying hours being passed in this vexatious search and two walks to the gin, I concluded to finish as far as possible my picture and by little after dinner (about 2½ PM) I finished all except a group of boys I wish to put in front playing marbles. I shall have to take it to Judge Y's to do this as I have no picture to draw it from.

Dr. Franklin and myself were not in communion more than 1½ hours before John Byrne with my accomodating little friend Johnny Lee[116] came in and a little while after, Hal. A short time having elapsed after Hal's arrival our stock of more sober conversation having been exhausted, I set out on a more frivolous strain, ludicrously telling of how the young ladies "plaid off" on me yesterday evening in a manner more nonsensical than even my description in my last entry. My headache (a slight one) did not impede me and I had the pleasure to make them laugh almost incessantly. They only left me half an hour to resume my reading in between their departure and the time to take my walk. As I "piped" out of our gate whistling vehemently a lively reel (I will whistle when I am alone if not studying in some way) I was astonished when I discovered

Mr. Yerger and Miss Bettie Yerger leaning on the pailings, looking into our garden (I know on weeds). They turned and seeing me started on down the road and as I observed each *looked back two or three times*. Was it because they did not know me? Not feeling inclined to do so, I chose to stroll along behind them rather than join them.

Coming back I met Jimmy who said to me, "did you know that what you said the other day at the dinner table has made Joe Percy mad at you?" What I said was a rather indiscriminate though jocular attack upon the really unfeeling practice some persons have of shooting game during the months when they have young, mentioning him among others (as he had told me he would shoot an old dove or partridge off her nest) when I said if "I had the power I would give every one who killed any game while they were increasing 100 lashes." What I would say about the best friend I had. May, who was at the table, conveyed to him this. I told Jimmy I was not very particular about the circumstance and walking on before I was out of ear shot met Mr. Percy in our buggy from Greenville. He invited me to take a seat and wished me to bring it back, which I did. Just before we entered the gate (Jimmy being in with us) one of these painful singing gnats got into my eye and Mr. Percy asked me in, offering to get it out for me. I was willing enough to agree. In passing in I was in so much pain that I only cursorily said "good evening" to the family and Mr. and Mrs. Yerger who were on the porch in front of the door. Having been relieved of the pest I came out to leave. Joe sat immediately in the door and without thinking or caring I very cordially offered him my hand, at the time standing a little in his rear as he sat. He turned away very contemptuously—I suppose to show me and the company his indignation. This might have disconcerted some people, but it did not disconcert me—however I felt a little piqued. I very coolly reached over my hand to Judge Yerger who sat just beyond him who took it at the same time remarking to Joe that "he did not notice," to which I very sternly answered "yes sir, he saw me" so loud that all heard, and he himself immediately confirmed what I said by a dogged answer. I then bowed politely to the company as I walked down the low steps to the buggy being asked some questions about Ma and Pa by Mrs. Dr. Percy which I answered without any indication of emotion. The affair was contemptuous in my eyes toward him, though amusing when I saw how, because he was just getting old enough to be noticed by adults, he must stand on etiquette as if he was 25. I could not suppress frequent outbursts of laughter as I rode home. We are both boys and for that reason I am not going to humor his caprice by letting him at one time play the gentleman and at another the lad. He has probably got hold of a harder nut than he can crack. I don't believe I've done anything to apologize for and only one thing will elicit one, and that is to prevent any hard feelings between our families and not for the sake of a reconciliation between *us*. Master Joe, I shall treat your little puerility in "silent contempt." If an apology is made I judge you will make it if you are very desirous for one, for I having no such desire shall certainly wait your convenience.

Tuesday, August 28, 1860

I wished to study this morning but becoming interested in Franklin's autobiography I forgot my grammar until most of the morning was gone. To please the children I made a little futter in the gutter, rain falling nearly all day keeping me from my walk. About 11½ o'clk I took my pen and scribbled off a protest against our "fuss" about "his royal highness," ending by exhorting or rather reproaching men for expending their money in such entertainments, intending to send it to the Ed. of the *Vicksburg Sun* under the name "Nazianzus";[117] though through the day I have almost given out the project on more than one occasion. Here is the part named: —— "but if they are so anxious to show respect to some one, let them (speaking of the men making this hellabaloo) cast off the character of the courtier and dedicate their means to putting tombstones over the graves of men who *do* deserve their notice, whose whole lives have been devoted to their welfare and their freedom — our Jeffersons, our Franklins, our Greens, and our Schuylers. Commemorate Hale and Hayne. It is an old song, but I am proud of it. The nobility and purity of it makes it dear to every American who feels in his bosom the blessed emotions of patriotism and gratitude, who can unblushingly raise his voice for those so inexpressibly deserving, so shamefully forgotten. Let them expunge with their money the blackest stain on the character of our country, let them seek out the neglected and mossgrown tombs of our heroic ancestors and erect there fair monuments to their fame, their honor, their glory, and permit this puerile prince to persue his journey unnoticed and as he has chosen to designate himself, a 'private gentleman.' "

"The man who said 'republics are ungrateful' knew not the prophetic verity contained in his words." I wrote as if I were grown; it speaks for itself.

I read Franklin all the evening and find his style quaint and at the same time unassailable.

One of the workmen we have is a dry, amusing man, prolific in yarns which he tells in a manner most diverting, a quick mischievous eye that twinkles while he relates. Here are some too good to pass: "A methodist preacher was travelling through N.C. and being very fond of tea carried it in his saddle bags to have it prepared if it was not at the house in which he stopped. On one occasion stopping at rather a rickety house he enquired of the lady who was not by-the-by a very polished woman, such a thing being unknown in that out-of-the-way place, if she had any tea and was answered in the negative. Upon this he produced his bundle of tea and gave it to the lady. Sitting down to supper the old fellow waited very patiently for his tea, though he had observed a flaxen-haired girl bring in something in a tin pan. After some time he enquired if his tea was ready and the old woman pointing at the pan said, 'why thar hit is, and hit has tuck all the lard in the house to *fry* it!' Our hero melted." I can write no more tonight, all are abed; but I will give the others tomorrow evening.

Wednesday, August 29, 1860

Agreeable to my promise to myself, after a warm walk in a warm sunshine, I took up my grammar and studied for some time when my writing project coming across my mind I took my pen and gave it my attention till dinner time, making many alterations but choosing to be on the shure side I took all and put them in the fire, thereby ending the affair. I then read the remainder of Dr. Franklin's autobiography. A little chicken's leg being broken I assumed the duties of a surgeon and splintered and set it to the best of my ability in humanity as I could not see the thing suffer without attempting to ameliorate its pains all I could. Near sundown my reading was again disturbed by my becoming a brickmason in plastering a little duck pond for Ma, from which I was called by a visit from Taylor and Hal who stayed till dusk. Being embarrassed by the presence of the "old folk" I found it rather difficult to entertain them, of which I am not altogether certain though I hope I have.

Jimmy told me my captious friend I've had told him "he was ready to meet me any where" &c. which I laughed to see how ridiculous it was for him to propose etiquette duelling. He is the first person who has ever refused to speak to me, and I hope he will be the last; and I also hope he may not be the cause of making Miss Ella and Miss Dellie dislike me which is not improbable as he is their cousin. If he did I should feel much inclined to give him a good drubbing for it and choke out some of his town nonsense.

The old man told me today to remind him of writing to N.O. for a watch for me this evening which I did not forget. He has just finished the letter as he says sending for "a neat, lever, serviceable gold watch." Upon asking if he had sent after a chain he suggested one made of Ma's hair saying he had not sent and that he looked upon one of hair as the neatest. I said, "yes sir," reluctantly willing to comply as I look upon them as horrible things. The probability is that I shall not wear it long. Here is another of Spencer's "yarns":

"Two gentlemen were travelling in Arkansas and one evening stopped at a log house of ill appearance and perfectly characteristic of that 'hard' country and staid all night. At the supper table the crusty old lady at the head of the rickety table asked one of them if he would have *long* or *short* sweetening in that scarce article—coffee. He took 'long.' She thereupon reached over and picking up a dingy, mashed tin cup poured out a stream of *molasses* for the individual to his utter amazement. The other in hope of bettering his case took 'short' and was disgusted to observe her gather from out an old dirty rag a piece of mutilated maple sugar, bite off a piece and drop it in his coffee. These gentlemen were of the opinion they were among a tough set." The last tomorrow.

Thursday, August 30, 1860

In spite of the interruptions from Ma and pa, I made satisfactory progress in my grammar, which was laid aside about 11½ to participate in the pleasure of eating a fine watermelon. Weighing medicine, giving it to negroes, going to Judge R.'s for Pa and attending to other things for him detracted much, indeed almost all, my attention from reading in the evening. I came from my errand to Judge R's in our wagon and in a hot sun. What did the Miss Yergers think? If they think less of me because I work I care very little. People who think less of one on account of labor are not of the stripe to suit me. If I lose the friendship of any one on that ground I know I lose very little.

Near sundown I had to walk down again and found the urbane old Judge at the mill with the lumber sawed. I was not in a very tidy attire and coming back as I got to the bridge I saw the above mentioned gals with Mrs. Swan Yerger on the opposite bank and a lady and gentleman about to come out from the gate to cross. I scarcely knew what to do but determined to cross and go down the creek which I did and was glad to see the gals on the other side walk up. Thus, I got away, but concluding to walk on behind the little clump I turned and was obliged to resort to subterfuge to avoid encountering them for they turning to come back sooner than I expected I got a large tree between us and fairly flew down the bank where I stayed till they passed. The other evening I took to the bank to see a woman and this to avoid seeing one.

Here's the anecdote: "Dr. Johnson and a companion was travelling in Scotland and night coming on they put up at a dilapidated stone house which formally contained one large room only but there was a scanty partition put up which had many holes and cracks in it so that one sitting near it could see into the kitchen. The Drs. companion had the opportunity and observed the boy who was tending the steak scratch his head and saw also something fall from that orb into the steak. Immediately he resolved to eat the pudding for supper and leave the steak for the Dr. When supper was announced the Dr.

was observed to eat heartily of the steak and his companion of the pudding. Through ludicrous malice he told the Dr. of what he had seen which much exasperated that gentleman, and he called up the boy and angrily asked him why he did not keep the cap on which he saw him wearing on his arrival. The scamp looked pitifully into the Dr.'s face and said in a whining tone, 'mammy tuck it to bile de puddin' in, zir.' Their suppers were left."

I tell the substance in my own language. That fellow can just keep steadily on and tell one after another all day I do believe, for it is nearly all he talks about. He tells some I cannot write here on account of their *smut* which does not detract from their worth at all in verbally telling them, but I will not blot my pages with such. Wit is always founded on vulgarity. He will say, "and that puts me in mind of &c., &c." and goes on.

I was reading an article concerning the old "hellcat" John Brown from an old paper to Ma who said there was not a negro in our quarter who did not know all about him, if he (the negro) was grown. Thinking it a good chance to get a gold watch chain, I said, "Ma will you bet me a gold watch chain and let me choose it in Memphis when we go through if I find one who knows nothing about him?" and she consenting, at night I went down and enquired of the most intelligent (if I may so express myself) men but not one thing did they know about him. Some wanted to know whether he was white or black. My watch chain was got easily. One piece of good luck!

Friday, August 31, 1860
Being virtually through syntax in my grammar I read Franklin most of the day—in the morning until about 10½ and nearly all the evening. Nat came around from a tramp in Sunflower with Andrew Carso, the deputy sheriff, taking the census of the negroes about 10½ (as named), which I gave him, Pa being absent on a canvass (in his independent way) in the lower part of the county, having started yesterday morning. Though I had some fun over the transaction, I did not treat Nat as a man treated a young gentleman who was assisting A——w. He came up to the house and introducing himself proposed the business and was refused. He told the man he would be put in jail and after many unpleasant words they commenced. The young man would ask him whether the named negro was black or mulatto. After studying some time and looking very serious, he would ask, "is a pumpkin yellow?" "is tar black?" &c. A——w came at suppertime to take the white ones and after some embarrassment, he, ma, and I got through with it.

My reading was a second time interrupted by Mrs. Wm. Percy's coming (the Dr., Mr. W.P., May, and Joe, my friend, have gone to Tenn.) and to avoid seeing her (for I was not of suitable appearance) I came on the back gallery, but Ma brought her out and I did not run after she had seen me. Before she went away, my drawing must be seen and the compliments she paid it I confess abashed me. She said it looked "very natural" and "you ought to take lessons in drawing, Harry" &c., &c.

Saturday, September 1, 1860

These two months are gone swiftly, and I cannot say unpleasantly for my books have been and I am confident always will be a pleasure to me. Three more weeks, at the outside, and I am gone; I will go to lay my eyes on this home no more for two years and never again as my *home* in its literal sense! My industrious mother is preparing little comforts in the shape of linen, etc., and at the dinner table I thought her eyes looked as if she had been weeping. Let me hope not on my account. Everything bears favorably.

Boistrous weather has kept me indoors, excepting a walk up to the gin. I sent for a *Harper* and did little else but read it till dinner. I do not like *Capt. Brand*[118] much, *A Ride for a Day*[119] is too dull, but I am still engrossed by the *Woman in White*, which of all the novels I ever read is written in a most singular style, the incidents are brought about more singularly and all is carried on in a more usual manner than anything of the kind I ever saw. I like it as well as I did *Trumps*.[120] Franklin's Philosophical papers occupied my evening. I like very much his ideas about the "art of swimming" and so far as I am able to appreciate it, his "theory of the earth," but regard such things as too hypothetical and as Pa says, "they do to speculate on but not to rely on." I look upon his "memoir" as a thin affair, too thin for such a man, but I am much interested in this part of his "Select Works" and relish much of his acute reasoning. Mr. F——n, venerable old sire, we part for tonight.

Sunday, September 2, 1860

Various things of various natures have filled up the programe of this day which has been quite the opposite of yesterday—bright, warm, and cheerful. But little reading has been done and no studying, and that little reading was done immediately after breakfast and after a vexation caused by the stupid behavior of a sick negro. Ma called me from it to look over her letter and correct it, and it was no ordinary letter, in some places even touching. I found only one letter omitted, i's to be dotted (which I always forget to do when writing) and a few punctuation mistakes. I cannot see why mothers look with such dread to the departures of their sons from home. Is it because they fear for them lest they should fall into dissipations? If not this, I do not know. Hear what she, *my* mother, says in this letter to her sister: "I have not allowed myself to look forward to Harry's leaving home until now, and it makes my heart ache when I think of it." Ah! my mother you need not fear for me. If no unforeseen and unexpected change takes place you shall see me come out of college the same sort of a man as I am now a boy. You need not fear the "bane of life." I repudiate that totally and strenuously. But this little verse would seem to controvert this:

"Oh, how many happy hearts
May shout today in gladness
That e're tomorrow's sun may rise
May weep in tears and sadness."

I took a box and putting paper in it packed my books away with my little trumperies or was doing so when the dinner bell rang. When I stepped into the dining room there sat two strangers, Pa's Sunflower friends. Some embarrassment was occasioned in introducing Spencer and Goodrich to them as there was in I myself being introduced to them. Neither was very interesting. They boured me after dinner till 2½ when they left and also left a headach for me to bear up under. I soon alleviated the pain by having cold water poured over my head. Nothing is more tiresome to me than to even attempt to entertain persons whom I do not know (a pretty woman excepted of course). The rest of the evening was passed in hurriedly finishing the packing of my books. I have some flowers Ma gave me which are from the immortal Washington's tomb, one of which I took, tied around it a pink bow, and fixed it in the first part (fly-leaves) of the first volume of that most noble man's life, with this written under it: "this flower is from the tomb of the illustrious Washington—made sacred by being on that tomb. He could say, 'Amor patria vincit omnia,'"[121] the date and my signature.

I am sorry to state that a little negro died last night which for months has been suffering from the gross neglect of its unmotherly mother, and I am glad *not under my hands.*

Pa came back tonight much tired. He, in his old fogyism, did not like a pair of boots made for me which had high heels contrary to his orders, but as they fit everywhere else and as I want them to accompany Nat in accordance with promise to Judge Rucks to see the young ladies tomorrow night, he said "take them." I wonder if it will be a surprise after my waiting so long?

Monday, September 3, 1860
Nine o'clk has come, and I must soon be at my studies; however, I will scribble a little upon a subject I have thought much upon and which I have

intended to write upon for some time. That subject is polygamy and luxury in the East and West.

We will first ask, did the patriarch fathers have more than one wife? Did not Jacob marry two sisters, Leah and Rachel (Gen. XXIX)? Besides Sarah, his wife, did not Abraham take Hagar his maidservant to wife when even Sarah was his half-sister? Did not David have a plurality of wives? Here is proof: "and I will take thy wives before thine eyes" &c. (Sam. XII) "and I gave thee thy master's house and thy master's wives into thy bosom" &c. How many did Solomon have? One thousand virtually, 300 lawful and 700 unlawful. Those were times when the Lord communed face to face with men and in all my reading of the Bible I have yet to see the passage forbidding this thing. And why forbid it? If a man chooses to take upon himself the care of 500 or even more wives, if he feels it would conduce to his pleasures and enjoyments of this short life, if he feels that he can support them as women should be supported, and if the Supreme One does not intervene his hand, who has a right to dispute this right, who has a right to controvert the enjoyment of these pleasures? What harm can it do? Whom does he harm? What iniquity is there in it? If there is any suffering, who bears it but he himself? If he chooses, forbid him not. No one answers but himself for his misdoings. By what prerogative has one man to peep into another's private affairs? No one is concerned but himself. He takes all the responsibility of it. The men who have (David, e.g.) committed adultery and caused murder, who have, like Solomon, practiced this thing to such an extent are held up as examples to us. I blame D——d but not Solomon. I would do the same if I were as he was. I am done.

Night. Eleven o'clk had come this morning when I got through with my searches in the Good Book and my writing from them on the opposite page. The balance I read Franklin and was much taken by some, I should have said a great many, of the sayings in "Poor Richard's Almanac."

I could not keep from looking forward to my visit to the Judge's. Nat did not fulfill his engagement and I was not disappointed. After supper I concluded to go down alone and having ensconced myself in my "dod-burns" I soon found myself an intruder behind the curtain of a tableau. I thought I would not disturb the scene so I stood in the door. Jim immediately conducted me to the company and audience where I found all the "old folks." They were well performed. Capt. Smith, Selim, Hamlet, Turkish groups &c. composed the scenes. The old folks from some cause objected to a dance and some foolish, childish plays were started which were by no means interesting. I must play on the piano, though I protested. I did all I could (of course I disgusted them) on a miserable instrument. Nat then on being asked made himself disagreeable by scratching, hesitating, and piddling until every one was entirely out of patience, and when he was let alone he played. Miss Bettie gave me some music at which I was surprised. Miss Lou, dressed as Pocahontas, showing a pretty foot and ankle and a prettier bust, a flood of glossy "raven wing" streaming down between two brunette shoulders, sparkling large black eyes with a crown over her brow made of artificial flowers, made her seem almost a rival to Miss Alexander. I did not have an opportunity to talk with her more than 10 minutes and will soon make up for lost time. Nat came home with me and since I have commenced this page has often interrupted me with a laugh and foolishness. It is 11½ PM. To bed!

Tuesday, September 4, 1860

At this moment I had expected to be talking (what?) to Miss Lou instead of doing my duty to myself by writing here in my diary. But even into a short day of futurity it is impossible to see. Ma got sick so the folks at Judge Rucks' were not invited to tea this evening. Will they according to expectation be here this time 24 hours hence?

But this won't do. I must to the necessary part. Nat and myself did not keep quiet by any means after we went to bed, although I wished and tried to be so. Pa with his usual rigidity admonished me this morning but not severely as I told him I could not keep N. quiet and (when he said he feared I could not say "no" when I ought to and something about not having the moral firmness to do so) I felt a little sting and said with some warmth, "I assure you, sir, I do not care so much about popularity as to buy it at the cost of my interest. When I am away from home and am under no obligation to a boy, I should plainly tell him to leave my room, that I wished to study." Ma (who was in bed sick) too said that a boy at one's house and one away from home made the case quite different. He did not like it and tacitly "caved in." I don't blame him. I know he meant well if he did wrong me.

I got on my horse and rode down to Maj. Lee's with N. after breakfast and had a "middling" time, coming back about 4 o'clk PM. Maj. Lee was not at the house or at dinner *but at the overseers house playing cards, with whom I do not know. He sent for the deck and jug.* Methinks if I were a man and had such a wife as Mrs. Lee (to all I can see she seems to fill my "ideal" in that respect) that I could not leave her to go off and play cards and drink liquor with any man. What woman of sensibility and who loves her husband can be indifferent to this sort of treatment, who does not feel neglected and slighted? I have said it before in these pages that many, many women are, and will always be, linked to men who are unworthy of them, who are not capable of appreciating them, who are capable of wounding willfully their feelings and disregard the love which is extended to them in all its unblemished purity. To leave this and court such occupations and company—and all to the confiding woman who has left mother, father, sister and all the tender endearment of childhood's love and childhood's home, who has placed in his hands all she has and all she expects to have, who has unhesitatingly given up all for him? Truley it is doleful. Hear what Hume says of such creatures, such as Mr. Lee appears in my eyes: "There is something of immaculate purity, something of the very divinity of virtue, in the countenance and deportment of a woman of chaste desires, elevated moral sentiments, and cultivated intellectual powers, that represses the low-born suggestions of lust and depravity and awes all the vicious passions into submission to the dignity of female perfection." Sentiments long cherished are at last found in those words—sentiments of sincerity and truth. I cannot believe but that

"Woman alone was formed to bless
The life of man and share his care
To soothe his breast where keen distress
Hath planted a poison'd arrow there"

and to be treated with nothing but kindness and affection for they, such as are above cited, were in my eyes intended to be the mistresses of Alhambras. Sterne[122] says this of *woman's* love:

"No tint of words can spot its snowy mantle, nor cynic power turn its ceptre into iron; with *love* to smile upon him as he eats his crust, the swain is happier than the monarch from whose court it has been banished."

On my way home I narrowly escaped getting my left leg broken. Old Clay in going over a little bridge in the Judge's field by which ran a large ditch, stepped on a plank which being rotten gave way, throwing him forward into the ditch with much violence. The ditch I think saved me, for in falling I instinctively propelled myself as far forward as I could and being further down into the ditch than the horse was enabled from his struggles to arise and my position to extricate my leg *sine injuria*. Arrived safely at home, I read Franklin to Ma till sundown. I can say no more now but will state something more of this entry (or rather day) in the next.

Wednesday, September 5, 1860
One of the principal things I was, for want of time, compelled to postpone, spoken of in the last entry, was my forgetting to execute an order Pa gave me, which was to go down to Sousdale's and see a workman for him before I went

into the house. This I forgot as I came to the bridge though I thought and spoke of it a few moments before. I did it, I suppose, because I was engaged in conversation with Nat. It never occurred to me until I was ready to return, when on going there, to my exceeding vexation at myself, he had gone. I felt very badly about it, more so because I knew Pa would not make any allowance for me. The other thing was the absurd idea John Byrne and all the Lee boys have taken up and tried to convince me that there was *science* in the *art* of boxing, and I thought hard-riding made a horse better. I worried them mightily by turning into a ridicule in a laughing way all the ridiculous arguments they brought up, such as, "suppose den, John, det aunt Harriet was to git some greese and bile a pot of soap, would there be science in that?" etc. I knew that they never would even listen to anything I said so that was the way I did, having a good deal of fun.

Feeling badly still, and fearing that Pa would ask me about the workmen as soon as I could get through with my breakfast and some pills Pa wanted me to make out for him, I rode down in the hot sun to see the man. He had not returned. I repented my forgetfulness and my only consolation was that he was obliged to return to finish some work. Pa coming up, I soon left, not feeling much better. I read Franklin till dusk after my return, when Mrs. Percy wanting some one to walk home with her, I notwithstanding my dirty dress, at her request accompanied her as Jimmy and Bay were absent. She is a pleasing woman, though not by any means handsome, and whose only recommendation lies in her mental cultivation, which, like most women's, is only of the light entertaining sort. She, as all women will, tried to hide from me her "growing infancy" and I should judge she felt its effects as during the incessant conversation we kept up, she seemed once and a while to get out of breath. The Percy family and ours are on the most intimate terms, and she spoke to me about my future course more like a relation than a neighbor, though not looking down on me on account of my age and her advice was both entertaining and instructive. When I told her of my resolution not to drink, how the bottle was "poked" at me last summer and in what seductive forms, she told me I did right, exhorting me to persue the same course, just as if she had been an elderly sister, and seemed to think that people who were acquainted with me did not think I was a wild boy (as I told her). As I turned to leave (after being invited in) she thanked me for "she would have been really frightened if it were not for my presence" to which I playfully added something about a "boy" not being able to protect one. In good humor I came on home, knowing and valuing her acceptable advice, and believing (from what she said on the way) that she was a good wife and a woman of warm and kind feelings. At all events I have (with one little exception) to see yet anything to the opposite.

Four men whose names I did not know and of whom I knew nothing but that they were of uncultivated minds as well as manners showing their awkwardness and ill-ease, were at supper (and will remain all night) who, on account of not knowing their names, subjected me to some embarrassment in waiting on them from the foot of the table, where I have for two years had the misfortune to sit. They, though, are the stamp of men who form the bone and sinew of the nation—plain, unpolished yeomen who in many cases far surpass men in higher grades of society in goodness of heart and moral rectitude. I only pity their ignorance; I do not hoot at them and would rebuke a fool who did because they had been thus misfortunate. No, I would not do this.

Thursday, September 6, 1860

Embarrassment was absent at the breakfast table, but I can't say I felt as free as if we were alone. One of the number from Texas, a red-faced, red-bearded, sharp-featured, bullet-eyed fellow much amused me with his singing voice and that openness so proverbial among most of his class. He was quite loquacious speaking of what he had, where he had been, where from, what he had done, and what doing, where he was, etc. etc. etc. He was hunting land and I gave him an old map of this state which I had, and he seemed as thankful for it as all of them were for there being no charge made for fare, it not being the custom here.

I took my horse after breakfast and rode up to see Hal, and he being absent I employed myself, as indeed I did most of the time I stayed, with a late *Harper* until he came. John McCutchen[123] came in before he did and Taylor after. I found I must say more entertainment in my *Harper* than I did in them. I never enjoy much the company of two or three boys at a time and always find it in a good paper. I went to have a good old talk with Hal, but it was prevented. Taylor having left before dinner, after that meal we other three rode (stopping at our house and twice on the way for me to fix a worsted old girth from which circumstances I had much fun with them by being slow and keeping them in the hot sun) rode—after the lengthy parenthesis—down to Rucks' (Taylor's) but he was not at home so they determining to go on down to see Nat I accompanied them a little ways, but it being late and wishing to get home and prepare for the ladies tonight (alas! it is to be put off till Sat. night!) I turned back. Seeing T's horse I rode in and had a short chat with him when I returned home to walk down to Dr. Percy's with the baby as nothing else would do him, Ma having gone down. I did not take much of a part in the conversation as they were "old folks" and as I always in respect to them curb any desire to be free with my tongue, and when saying anything I use the Socratic method so as to extract their knowledge on the point discussed, to escape entrapments and if I see a chance, to trap them in the same respectful way as Dr. Franklin did his printing master, shunning resentment or more properly speaking ill-feeling which direct contradiction produces and giving your adversary (provided he is not a headstrong unreasonable science-boxer) a higher opinion of you for your reasonings and non-exultation.

While there I ate some fine figs, the first I have eaten for three years. I came home for supper. Mrs. P. offered me a glass of wine (a cordial), the cake and decanter being sat out, but I remarked to her, "can you offer me wine after what you said to me yesterday evening?" in a laughing, playful way, whereupon she told Ma how she talked to me and of her telling her "old man" about it last night, ending her remarks by saying I "had enough sense if I would use it," which, though I knew it probably to be idle flattery, hit my vanity (a quality Franklin approves of) just as it would any other boy's.

Friday, September 7, 1860

A phenomenon of which so much has been said and written, which I never before witnessed, appeared to me between 9 and 10 o'clk last night (Thurs. 6th). I never in my life saw such an interesting, sublime, and splendid sight. In the direct north, seeming to the naked eye to extend along the horizon about 300 yards and perpendicularly about 100 in the center, tapering gradually in a circle to the extremities. The color was a bright and rather deep transparent pink. Two long, pale spars shot upwards from the bottom to the top. A few stars could be seen dimly though accurately through it. I do not doubt but that it is the far-famed *Aurora Borealis*. Let it be what it may, it was transcendently grand and brilliant! Such things I believe to be beyond all the boasted philosophy and reason of us humans, too deep and profound for weak mortals to fathom. They may say, *"O vitae Philosophia dux!"* [124] but their leader deserts them when such difficult pathes are to be persued. But I need not discuss this here.

Ma wanted me to drive her up the road and then down to Judge Rucks' as soon as she could dress after breakfast, which I did as I expected to accommodate her and see Miss Lou. In the first I succeeded, in latter I only *saw* her, old-folks preventing any intercourse. It was rather a dull visit for me as T——r was gone. I found my way into his room where I found Jim and the time was not so dully past as we talked of education, a subject of engrossment to me.

Our views coincided except that he thought History of no practical use and that a regular course was the best. He said divide the time (and I had before fixed upon it exactly) into 8 hrs. for study and recitation, 8 for sleep, 2½ for exercise, and the remaining 6½ for meals, reading of any kind, for pleasure or knowledge, and for mixing with my fellow students. These are my main heads, and I will arrange them to suit recitation hours after my arrival.

This subject is finished. I have good news! Better, far better, than I dared hope. Pa, after all his determinations, *has at last not only concluded to send me in time to be there at the beginning of the session but has concluded to send me next Tues. or Wed. week!!* What man knows today what he will do one or two months hence, one week, or even one day? Whose eyes can see into the future? Verily no one can tell what he will do tomorrow.

I am near finishing Franklin but only read his correspondence because it is in the book not because it is interesting, though there are places where one can be engaged. I think his biographer committed a great error in giving place for his correspondence to the exclusion of a more elaborate memoir.

Uncle Jack and myself took a walk this evening and saw my little friend John Lee and my other little female friend Miss Fanny Yerger out riding. Neither, I suppose, is over thirteen. I thought Hal, Taylor, Nat and myself came out soon enough when we were in our 16s and 17s, but I see the young 'uns advance with the age. Thirty years ago they waited till they were 20 and upwards. Where will it stop?

Saturday, September 8, 1860

With no idea of it when I seated myself at the breakfast table, when I arose with me rose a whim for hunting, the first thing of the kind for many a day. Under this inclination I seazed a little bird gun, filled my pockets with ammunition, and started on foot, first to the schoolhouse and then around to the Cunningham house in the hot sun. I roused only twice or it was three times. My shot being of the very small kind called mustard seed I missed two [. . .] and once at a partridge flying, which was too far. It was the little gun I learned to shoot with, and I was surprised at the distance and accuracy with which it threw the shot and as much surprised at my dog's performance of his part as I had woefully neglected him. But wasn't it hot in the sun! Under my arms my whole shirt and most every part of my clothing was wet with perspiration, and to make my long, hot trapse of four miles worse, I was destitute of good water. My mouth was parched. Stopping at Judge R's, I was disappointed in getting a glass of ice water. And as the little we had was to be used at the supper given to Mr. Y's family, I had to do without it at home. I feared lest I would be sun struck. My head was so hot and throbbed so as I knew my inclination to get warm and very warm by a little exercise. It was 12. If I had had half a mile further to walk I think I should have suffered, although I frequently raised my hat to let my head strike the air. By dipping my head in a bowl of fresh water I soon cooled off.

After playing "Tetotal" before and reading F——n after dinner till about 4, at Ma's request I got on a horse and again went in search of game at the same place, killing one dove, making in all (that I killed) 3 doves, one partridge, and one owl and snipe. Returned at sundown, dressed, and went in the parlor after candle light where I found those two excellent fellows, my good old friends, Hal and Taylor. I did not sit more than five minutes before some of the old folks (this being the night set at last for us to entertain Mr. Y's family) and that little "gal" spoken of in last Monday's entry as dressed in the character of Pochahontas came. This time she was bundled up in the present clumsy fashion of the ladies. I lost no time in seating myself by her side on a sofa and doing what a fellow is obliged to do with the pretty little things—talk all sorts of trash to them as it would make a woman disgusted with one if he talked common sense to them. One must be all frivolity and levity. That I might not be reflected on, when Miss Bettie came I made it convenient to "lead" her awhile and found her not uninteresting, though not as pleasing as Miss Lou. Until they left I took all occasions of talking with Miss L. but only got one more good "set" at her as those same games were played though with more interest than they were the other night. Though I have no room to regret it upon the score of not being entertained by them, I made a gross oversight in not taking a vacant seat at the supper table by Miss B. and in taking one by H. and T. and was forced to make an apology for it which was happily received by the "gal." In helping Miss L. into the carriage I missed her hand and caught hold of a soft wrist. The thing being all over and all having left, I tumbled into bed.

Sunday, September 9, 1860

Taylor and Hal told me last night that they would start this evening for Oxford this state, there to prepare themselves for the sophomore class in our University. True to a promise I had made to them and myself I rode up to Judge Yerger's first to tell H. goodby. I met him in the yard and we walked on down to the quarter together, talking regretingly about our separation and of our not going to the same place. I trust that what he said was as sincere as what I said. We advised, told each other the course we would pursue, and all in a tone and manner subdued and regretful. Can I help it? I have said and done all I could with propriety to get him to go with me. I am sorry that we must part. We soon came back from the quarter and on our arrival at the house our simple unostentacious parting took place where no idle words of flattery and unfelt sorrow was expressed, but we parted as friends should part. Clasping hands we simultaneously uttered the true feeling old words, "good-by." But we know not the ways of a mysterious Providence; we may yet be brought together and still, despite the years that may intervene before our duties as students will allow us to meet, we may yet be joined in a friendship the same as we bear for each other now. I leave this subject.

About 11½ I went on down to fulfill the same office to Taylor, but he was out so I came back immediately without having had that pleasure. These two boys I claim as my best friends. Truly they are good and rare fellows!

I did not get much of a chance to read after my return during the evening as I took a walk with Uncle J. and a ride with him before dark.

Ma has commenced giving me messages for our kin at Abingdon, little bundles of seed, &c.

Monday, September 10, 1860

Franklin was finished this morning, although I spent some time in hunting for my trunk keys to get at some blank books I had in my trunk to make (as I may have before mentioned) mathematical notes in, writing down observations, &c. This search took up much of my time. I did not succeed in finding them but near dinner time succeeded in getting it open and from that time till about 4 when I commenced dressing to ride with Miss Lou whom I had engaged for that purpose last Sat. eve, I made my notes. Our plain friend of plentiful anecdotes, Spenser, was kind enough to lend me his mare instead of my old worn-out horse. I had not been sitting in the parlor after my arrival more than three minutes when in came my smiling, little lady-friend all neatly caparisoned for a ride—whip, plumed hat, etc. I commenced to eulogize her punctuality immediately, congratulating myself on being remembered by her to such a degree as to view her now "all right" and without any tedious waiting. But what was my astonishment when she told me she had understood me as engaging *Tuesday* evening and that she was then waiting for Bill to come and take her up to Judge Yerger's! Was my comb not cut? The matter was palliated by her saying I could ride up with them and proposing that I should come some other evening. Bill soon came and before we reached the door Miss Kate sent in word if Miss Lou would ride with her? "Certainly," was the answer, so off we went. I remembered too well the last ride I took with Miss Kate to wish that honor again. I will look at my old Journal. Well! after a long search I have found it. It was Sat. 30 April '59. That ride (though I did not then mention it as I was not in the habit then as I am now of writing my feelings and impressions) was much sprinkled with vexation and any thing but pleasure. I then promised myself never to ride with her again. I said all I could to get Bill to ride with her this time, but to no use "he couldn't go home with her" so as I had to go further for my horse than he did he had the "choice of positions" and facing no alternative I fell in with her; nor can I say my ride was unpleasant though it would have been more so if Miss Lou had been my partner. Stopping in at Judge Y.'s for a glass of water, as we came out I said to her in a half-joking, half-serious way, "I'll be hanged Miss K. if we have any more hard riding this evening," giving her to understand she would do it all by herself. She took me at my word, and we did *not* ride fast. I concluded to stay all night with Nat and left word at the gate with U.J. to that effect. Before I go further I will say Miss Lou and myself came to terms before we parted, viz. that I should be at Judge Y.'s at 5 o'clk on the following evening, to which time I swore (or I mean solemnly affirmed) strictest punctuality.

I believe Miss K. is almost crazy on the subject of horses. She adores hers. I told her I did not think she would ever marry. She wished to know why. "Because," I said, "I don't believe you will ever love a man as hard as you love that horse." She wer kinder tuck under. Notwithstanding the flattering proposals from Miss L. I was not in a very good humor so I took occasion to abuse her horse for every imaginable defect because she said Mr. Sammy McFatten, my adored brute, was ugly. She wer under agin. On our way home, however, we got on better terms and my tongue went without restraint on every subject brought up, the Prince of Wales (abusing with all my warmth and force our conduct to him, declaring I would respect her less if she moved from Norfolk, where she will go about the time I go on, to see him when he came) and various others—this being decidedly the most interesting part of the evening, but not on account of conversational powers or any strikingly interesting point in her character.

Arrived and supper over, she seemed quite urbane, *taking me into her room* (would Miss Marian have done it?) where she showed me pictures, drawings, &c., and I must in justice say while writing here in my quiet room with my quiet uncle reading on the opposite side of the table, that she showed taste and tidiness.

I have no peculiar fancy for Miss K. though I really have not hatred or anything of the kind for her, but her manner toward me on some occasions, unladylike behavior in others, possessing few accomplishments and not of pleasing conversation, vain, supercilious, and not being at all pretty alienates me from her. One thing I will state, which I did not do on my entry the 3rd May last and which occurred at Dr. Percy's party. I was the last one who left the parlor. Miss Alexander was in there with her, and I was about to leave but was addressing some farewell words to them, when saying something about what I don't know, she leant on Miss A. and actually *put her foot up on my thigh—almost touching my waistcoat!* The occurrence of Nov. 9th last is another specimen of her conduct about which, as she mentioned it, I gave her particular Jerusalem in my own way so that she could not get me into any mesh. I would not let her apologize. No doubt Miss K. thinks I am a "hard one"; it's true I'm as candid as Cato. I rather pity than censure Miss Kate, mostly because she suffered a great calamity early in life—she lost her mother whose place no one can fill. I readily forgive all she has done to me, but I cannot like her as I could one who was more modest. The ways of this world are various, mysterious, and many. I stop. She may even now be censuring me as I have her! Again, I forgive all.

Tuesday, September 11, 1860

Every day I see more and more into the depths of the human character. I need not, however, decant upon my observations here, further than to notice one among those I hold most in detest. That one is amply imbued in the tastes and character of one whom I would otherwise esteem and regard as I do Hal and Taylor. The fault is the little narrow-mindedness of placing one's whole attention on dress. Nat has that fault. He thinks more of the cut of a shirt, the figures on a cravat, the color of a coat, the shape of a boot, and the set of a collar than he does of the only lasting embellishment with which we can decorate ourselves—the cultivation of the mental faculties. His mind seems to run on this pitiable subject altogether. He, as well as Harry Percy, is bowingly inquisitive about one's apparel; talking as though such noticeable things were of the last importance. It is supremely disgusting to me. When we were about to retire, regarding my boots he (Nat) exclaimed, "Harry, I've got the finest pair of boots here you ever saw!" Gets them out—I must try them on—he must try mine on—many and diverse speculations and remarks must be made for each, *pro et con.* "Don't you think this a pretty cravat Harry?" and here it comes again. And "Ain't this a beautiful watch chain?" and all such contemptible stuff. His mind is more completely carried away by this insignificant thing than I ever saw any one's before. Why should people make such fools of themselves? Take your greatest fop and put him before a man of education and science dressed in blue jeans and your little fool will in five minutes look worse than a feather in the wind. Take such a man as Jno. C. Calhoun, put the plainest possible clothing on him, put him in the Senate Hall and is he not the same giant headed man, the same invincible Jn. C. Calhoun? Does it make the man? Does it make him more acceptable? I do not object to fine clothes for those who can afford them, but I do object to any one's playing the goose and imbecile by giving their whole attention to it. Every one should wear at all times decent clothes, but no one should make it the sole leading idea of their time and pleasure. Broadclothes and Satins are not objectionable except when they become the causes of such consummate folly. Really this vice is too low, too mean!

My conduct for the day must not be forgotten. Rising before the family I started on a walk but was stopped by the dew. When returning I found most of them up. Much literary conversation took place at the breakfast table in which I was not silent though doing nothing too forward or at all intruding. Bulwer, poetry &c. &c. were discussed in which Nat remarked something about Byron but seemed a blank on history and some novels his father asked him to describe as he had read them. Asking the character of the hero of one, he answered in a shamful embarrassed way, "he was a gentleman and a . . . a . . . a . . . a . . . and a good fellow" etc. showing that he was ashamed of his ignorance even of the books he himself mentioned as having read. I defended the practice of putting the finest pieces from all authors in our Grammar as against Miss F. My amiable friend Mrs. Lee took my side, and she had to give way though reluctantly. One who might read this probably would think I am rude in ladies company, but I could not be more polite and I have that reputation. What I say is always in such a manner (when I am arguing or keeping them from making an apology) that they cannot reach me. A word said in one tone to a person and the second the same word said in another tone and manner would give offence to the same person. This subject was commenced principally to mention that Nat is an example of one who has neglected that all-important object for dress. Nat is a very clever fellow with this exception, and I regard him as a friend. I will say in concluding this subject that Mrs. Lee kindly offered *Pencillings By the Way*[125] upon the promise of returning them speedily as they were not hers.

We sat together on the porch after our morning meal, where the whole family conversed pleasantly at least I know I did with Mrs. Lee, confining myself more to her as she was the most interesting. Our tastes coincide exactly (except in poetry) and hence I suppose our friendship.

Nat was coming home with me and I waited some time for him and then, his father opposing it, I came home (part of the way) with Jimmy whom Pa had sent up. As is always the case, we must dispute in sour and unbrotherly terms. At last I told him rather than do so we would be entirely mum. The cause this time arose from some serious faults and indiscretions he is always guilty of towards larger boys than myself and my telling him how he had treated me. I cannot say how much this thing hurts me.

Nat proposed a visit to Miss Lou this evening, but I said as I had an engagement to ride with her this evening that I did not know that it would be right. Sending back for the books Mrs. Lee loaned me I took occasion in a note to him to say that "after cooler consideration I did not know that it was in conformance with decorum but to use his discretion. I was agreeable to his pleasure," or something to that effect.

Busied myself in transcribing mathematical observations in my blank book till time to dress for my ride. This time I found her as punctual as when she did *not* intend to ride with me. Was I not flattered? Horse and all ready and waiting—for me! The parlor was full of ladies. We soon were off on a pleasant and agreeable ride, though I was not as talkative or as well-pleased with myself as I was yesterday evening—however no embarrassing silences occurred. We talked of days gone by, love, woman, Cuba (where she went last Feb.), and all sorts of trash. She was very communicative about her trip to Cuba, explaining and telling much of use and interest. Up to the time she stopped at Judge Rucks' (where she stayed) I know I had a nice time. Their riding habits are so becoming, their little plumed hats look so tidy and neat, and in this case a blooming, girlish cheek, dark sparkling eyes, and a trim little form in which a well-formed, plump little bust set off to such advantage by the closely fitting body of her habit, contributed not a little to the pleasures of the evening. But for her nose she would be "one of 'em." I know she'll make some man a splendid wife—intelligent, industrious, and pretty—no one could make an objection. I have as yet seen no bad point in her disposition and am confident she possesses amiability and good feeling, if I am to judge from long and intimate intercourse with her. From my regard for Miss Lou, I hope she will take her excellent young aunt Miss Marian as her example and moreover that she may when the right time comes marry a man worthy of her.

Wednesday, September 12, 1860

Fall is coming. The leaves are dropping from the trees, the grass seems worn out, and the weather wears an autumnal aspect. This day has from its coolness been like one of Nov., and fires would have, and were, comfortable in the morning.

The transcriptions of my notes on Mathematics kept me busy until $1\frac{1}{2}$ together with the greater part of the last entry. Feeling an oppression about the chest which was annoying, I left my visiting and took up the book Mrs. Lee loaned me called *Pensillings by the Way* by one who travelled in Europe. I was much pleased with his description of Herculanium and Pompei but more so by that of a pretty Italian girl who waited on him at a luncheon taken among their ruins. *Pro feminis semper!* I read him most of the evening.

Just before dinner a long and interesting letter was handed me from my eccentric old teacher Mr. Herbert. After laying aside my book I answered it, not finishing till time to take a walk. In one place he says, "your letter afforded me, I assure you, unfeigned gratification as a promising specimen of the proficiency of a pupil of mine in composition and penmanship." To look at these scribblings would anyone believe either compliment even if one of such a character were to assert it? But he frankly agrees with me in my censure of Early for indeed I wrote of little else. Again he says, "your remarks touching the conduct of ministers might by some be considered *bold* for a youth. . . . I understand you as expressing yourself to *me* with that freedom and familiarity" &c. Again [. . .] "amid the many gloomy misgivings in relation to the integrity of the ministers of the M.E. church, that is, I will not judge all by one."* [126] He gives me a splendid piece of advice which I shall always remember, "I tell you that the acquisition of truth in all subjects is the result of labor and care, and if a man will not be at the pains of exercising patient enquiry and even some forbearance, why, he cannot arrive at truth and be at last the dupe of deception to his ruin and endless regret." About my *boldness* here is what I said, "In regard to the almost only subject of my letter, you misunderstood me if you for a moment thought that I was directly or indirectly guilty of the least vituperation toward the Methodist E. Church. Though always surrounded by the members of the Episcopacy, I sincerely believe there is more religion in its true sense in your church than in any of the others. At this time, you know my sentiments of religion too well to mistake any thing I might say as *sacrilege. I venerate religion as much as any one!* But I say this, that there is sensuality, murder, incendiarism, and crimes of fiendish atrocity committed by detestable hypocrites in *all*. Such I believe to be few from the known fact that man's temerity is scarcely so preeminent as to make him lose all awe for the Deity in this manner. Virtue, piety, and benevolence reigns in the churches where they shine now as brightly and as purely as they did in St. Paul's time. I believe Religion to be the great foundation of all nations, a stay to the wild passions of man, a beneficent mistress whose sway is gentle and whose punishments are just, whose rewards are many and whose course is guided by her motto 'Iustitia virtutum regina.'" [127]

Thursday, September 13, 1860

I love my dog, and to please him I took a tramp to the "Cunningham" but did not have any "luck." The atmosphere was clear and cool up to 10 or half past. I walked in the old Cunningham grove for the last time probably for two long years to come. I love places connected with pleasant association and I, on this account, felt melancholy when I would think that I was so soon to leave it as well as other spots dear to me for the same cause. I have many kind feelings for Deer Creek if I do wish to live elsewhere.

I returned a little tired at 12 PM and commenced a transcription of my letter to Mr. H. or rather I deducted in some places and added in others. When down about half way the first page Pa called me and gave me instructions about sending me to town to get a lever like one he had broken belonging to his press. My dinner down, I mounted Mr. S's mare and set off not in a pleasantly warm sun as it was slightly too warm. My ride to town was pleasant with the exception of loneliness, but my inclination to fall into reveries helped me much as it always does in such places. The sun had approached near the horizon when I entered the dull little village of Greenville. "Business before pleasure" is one of my rules. I did not forget it on this occasion. This over, the sun had gone and all that remained was a gay trot in the West where he disappeared. Agreeable to Pa's wish and my inclinations, I went out to stay with Mr. McAlister, my pleasant old friend, during the night.

As I came through town I got my present from Pa, the "neat, lever, serviceable gold watch," which I liked very much as it filled the description given above. For long years back, when I used to cut the lead from around Pa's chimneys to make mock ones up with chains of the same pliable metal, I had looked forward to the time I should get my gold watch. I thought of it with many boastful feelings and speculations, how I would strut etc. and now I have it and I feel as matter of fact as I did before I had it. "The wealth of the mind is the only true wealth."

Before I retired I finished Mr. H's letter and modified some and much changed it better to suit myself. The place from which the quotation in the other entry was taken I polished a little, leaving out "murder" and spreading the remainder so as to keep the blister from burning too much in one place. The part about "man's temerity" I much improved.

The old gentleman was tolerably entertaining, but I think I can see the effects of time in his conversation as he jumps from one subject to another very abruptly.

Friday, September 14, 1860

The General's family returned from Ky. before breakfast and when they got to the door I retreated to my room as I thought I ought not to be present at the meeting. At the breakfast table I was introduced to a Miss Somebody—I forget her name—who was not at all pretty and not at all charming. I left soon after breakfast and on my arrival in town (2 miles distant) I was annoyed and vexed at the stupid negro whom Pa had ordered to get the lever I came for but who had remained in town all night contrary to orders—Pa wanting the lever immediately. I gave him a few "damns" and sent him on after (with a negro's help) putting the heavy piece of iron in the wagon. I never saw but one or two negroes who had a grain of discretion. I had a very pleasant chat with Bud Joyes who was at the P.O. I sitting on my horse and he standing on the portico being in close proximity he leaning on my horses neck. He is a right good fellow, said to be all pluck, but I think he is too much inclined to libel people. *He may libel me.* How can I tell? A ride of the same nature as the one I took yesterday to town brought me back home at 12 PM. I had expected a censure from Pa, but when he heard how punctiliously I had done my duty in spite of his punctuality in frowning upon neglect in everyone and most especially in *me*, he said not a word to me but promised the negro a whaling for his fault.

My watch of course was a subject for inspection and speculation to the whole family from Pa to Willie. It was "pretty," "neat," and "worked well" &c., &c.

A disagreeable task was performed after dinner, viz. the marking of all my clothes, which, with the repacking of my books (Ma wanted the other box) occupied my attention till 5½ when I read *Pencillings* till time to walk when I took a *short* stroll as I felt tired from the day's activity.

Louly is making me a pincushion and Ma is fixing divers little things for me, which looks much like going. Sometimes I see Ma looking sad. No doubt it is for me, but I say again my mother "you need not fear for me." Pa and myself will leave here next Tuesday and will take the Victoria Wed. morning. I hope nothing disagreeable will turn up and that Nat, Miss Kate and myself may go on together.

Saturday, September 15, 1860

Contemplating a quiet morning devoted to reading, I took up *Pencillings* but did not enjoy it's entertaining descriptions—St. Peter's, the delapidated mausoleum of Virgil, the villas of Cicero, Sallust, Hortensius, Versuens, Campo Santo, and lake Avernus (Virgil's Tartarus), the disintered cities of Herculaneum and Pompeii, the "Palaces of the Caesars" and many other things too many to mention have appeared to me in plain, though sometimes impassioned language which gives one a little room to exercise one's imagination. I liked his description of Beatrice Cenci's picture—here it is: "There are engravings and copies of the picture all over the world but none that I have seen give any idea of the excessive gentleness and serenity of the countenance. The eyes retain traces of weeping, but the childlike mouth, the soft girlish lines of the features that look as if they had never worn more than the one expression of youthfulness and affection, are all in repose, and the head is turned over the shoulder with as simple a sweetness as if she had but looked back to say a good night before going to her chamber to sleep. She little looks like what she was, one of the firmest and boldest spirits whose history has been recorded. After murdering her father for his fiendish attempts upon her virtue, she endured every torture rather than disgrace her family by confession and was only moved from her constancy at last by the agonies of her younger brother on the rack." Who would read capabilities like these in these heavenly and child-like features? I think she was a noble girl whose dire fate is to be pitied. She did rightly when she sank a dagger in the unnatural bosom of her hell-inspired father. Yes! to strike him to the ground!

I have deviated. I commenced to say that I was called off from these scenes that seemed to unfold to my eyes as I advanced, that make me almost imagine myself among the ruins of Nero's "Golden Palace"—I was called off from my chief pleasure to play the part of the host to Nat and John about 9½ til 12. I had a note lying on the table addressed to Miss Lou requesting the "honor" of a ride this evening if Miss Lou's time "was not otherwise engaged." Nat saw it and wished immediately to follow my example and ride tomorrow at the same time but wished to read my note which I refused. However, we examined each other's when he had finished. He soon exclaimed in a manner intended to pique, "why H——y, don't you know how to spell?" I requested him with a smile to show me my mistake. He kept up his self-important, ridiculing air and pointing at the word (Miss Lou's name) in the possessive case, making all sorts of remarks to its disparagement. The words were "Miss Lou's time." "Look here! he has spelled her name Luss!" "He has dotted the u." I told him to take care he would sell himself but this made him worse. No explanation could be received. He would hear to none but kept on laughing and ridiculing because he did not know that what I had written was true grammar from his shere ignorance. Uncle Jack came in and I refered it to him and he said I was right but still Nat kept up his noisy crowing about a supposed mistake which he clung to like a "sick kitten to a hot brick" as the saying goes. By this time I was excited and finding he would listen to no reason, I said to him what I would not have said if cool, "That's the possessive case of the proper noun Lou you d——d fool, you don't know your own language!" He did not seem to take it to heart but soon stopped as I walked out of the door on the gallery where John was, pitying his ignorance. This is what his love of dress gets him and what sort of

English he learns by studying the Latin Grammar and from that only drawing his English. The reason why he was so quick to cavil at what he thought was an error in me was because he knows and in company where it can be appreciated feels his inferiority to me in mental acquirements and knowledge. He loves to be well thought of but is too lazy to work for it. We always were rivals and in the two or three years past he has felt much his being beneath me in this manner and is always on the watch to catch at the least thing to assail me through, but my knack for argumentation, which is augmented by constant and close reading, enables me almost invariably to defeat him. I can see although we are on the familiarest terms there is the same old rivalship which made us fight in '55 & '56, which breaks off the tender branches of friendship and makes us both feel that there is something between us. He went away in a splendid humor, but I will voluntarily apologize for my harsh and ungentlemanly expression used toward him.

I sent the card which caused this dispute. My answer was written in the margin of a *Harper* which was sent but which the little negro Glenn had thumbed so that I could only conjecture from the commencement and end of the note (from Mrs. Jas. Yerger) that (as it is expressed) "Louise is at brother Hal's" (motley spots, all letters gone) "will ride with you with pleasure." I suppose something to the effect that she (Mrs. Y.) supposed Miss Lou would ride. Sprinkling rain and clouds kept me from going over and trying as I had intended. The balance of the evening was passed in reading my *Harper* in which ended that singular tale *The Woman in White*, some in my *Pencillings* and in doing many little jobs and tinkerings for Ma and Pa and among others one for myself—the marking of half a dozen wine bottles in which Ma will seal some wine made by herself and Pa that I promise not to drink until after I am 21 and probably not until I am married. Won't it be old and mellow if I wait till the latter time? It was marked "Muscadine Wine. Harry St. J. Dixon, September 15th, 1860." I have made a long entry and will go up and tumble in with the children as a brickmason Pa has here has without leave or excuse occupied my bed. Let him sleep. I hope, as he has it, that he may have a good nights rest as I do *not* expect to have.

Sunday, September 16, 1860

What I anticipated yesterday morning has during most of this day been pleasantly realized. I cannot say more than that too many charming scenes were presented to me which entirely engrossed me—Rome, Elba, Vienna— the opulence of the Pope, ruined palaces at Palermo, ravishing pictures of nude nymphs, and all that can charm the fancy. Talk to me about staying buried here in one little spot secluded from all the beauties of a world given to us to be enjoyed. The day is yet coming when I shall be able to look on these wonders of taste and art with my own eyes. I sometimes wish I did not have such a keen taste for these beauties lest it might lead me from what might be called my more sober interest.

Just before I went in to dinner Spenser returned from a trip up the Creek and stepping into my room turned his eyes around and said, "step this way, Harry." What did he want? What did he have? Four colored cuts on leaves torn from a book, very fair women "nudus membra," more tempting and beautiful than decent. I acknowledge it; who will blame me and point out a single youth of 17 who would not gaze at them as I did?

John and Nat called in this evening about 5 and staid till after 6. I can't stand a joke and N. kept up a continual tease all the time (to J. but a pleasure to me) which much exasperated John. I could not keep my countenance when Nat was going on in his clownish ways, but when I saw that John was mad I felt sorry that any thing of the kind should occur under my father's roof and did all I could to conciliate J. Nat still kept up his laughing and a few "damns" and "fools" were exchanged together with some rough words. I was glad to see them leave peacably, i.e. without any blows but still in a bad humor though Nat kept it up as long as I could hear him as he left.

I had scarcely taken up my book again when Ma requested me to drive her out which I did, it then being sundown. She told me this had been one of the saddest days she had spent for a long time and that she had not till very lately realized that I was in reality to go. The peculiar embarrassment always attending such a topic between those closely connected attacked me this evening. I tried and was lively but still there was that same inexpressible embarrassment for some time. I feel sorrier to leave Ma than any because I think she loves me more and will miss me more sincerely than others of the family. As the time has approached my ardor has diminished. I do not feel a reluctance to go, but I cannot leave all that I have been raised with, without pain.

It is 20 min. to 9. I will go up and sit till bedtime with them instead of reading. I expect a lecture and advice such as mothers and fathers only can give.

Monday, September 17, 1860
Midnight is near at hand; I must hasten. Time waits for no man (or boy). I commence.

I was not disappointed. Pa, in our conversation turning upon my wish to travel in Europe convinced me of the folly of such an attempt by his stern arguing. He treated me not as he would a son, but seemed to place himself on the same level and treated me as if I was 25. He said in substance, "no man can gain two things at the same time; he cannot look at a dozen things and try to get each, for while he is looking at one, some man snatches the one next to it, and finally he gets none. Who goes to Europe? Idlers who have nothing else to do. Where do they get their money? Their fathers gave it to them. This does very well for such men, but when a young man starts out in life expecting to work for himself, he must let nothing turn him aside from his business; he must turn neither to the right or left, but must keep straight on to his object. Suppose you go to Europe? When you come back, if you like it, you'll say, 'well, I like that very much. I've just seen enough now to give me a taste for it, I want to go again.' Suppose he don't want to go again? Is he fit for hard work and business? No. Then if it makes you unfit for work, makes you dissatisfied with what you have, if you have not the means to do it as rich people do, why go? If I had jumped from one thing to another and for pleasure had neglected my business, you would not now go to the University of Va. but would have had to content yourself with what a common school could give you. This steadiness about my business accounts for my success. If what I will leave you out of my estate would take you there and back, I would rather see you turn it into paper money and lay it on these coals (pointing to the fireplace) than to use it thus. You may remember it long years hence when you are of my age and I am in my grave, no man will succeed who jumps from one to another." This is a compendium of what he said. It was not angrily or harshly said, but in a firm manly tone, cute conception and good argumentation, irresistable reason and hard common sense. It gained its intended purpose. It showed me plainly I was in duty to myself bound to relinquish my long cherished and anticipated visit to the other continent. While he spoke I leant against the mantlepiece and when he had finished I was frank enough to acknowledge that "I must forego my trip to Europe until I have got enough money to retire on." All the ivy vines, charming women and pictures, guilded churches, Italian moonlights and marble halls of the Caesars vanished. The lamented reality that I must work long, long years before even I have a chance to go pried itself upon me and despite an occasional desire to laugh (how strange) I retired feeling sad.

Time wears apace—the last night for years perhaps which remains for me to spend on the spot where so much happiness and fun of boy's joyous sort has been seen, is nearly half gone—it is 25 min. to 12. All is slumber but the crickets which chirp in the crevices. Move on pen! Much work lays before you. Let not the stillness of this last night lead you into paths leading away from your main track. Commence this day's occupations.

Fifteen minutes besides meal times has been my only recess, yet I am not wearied—not wearied of looking on the stillness, the solitude and silence of this night—not wearied of the slick little loon which has been sitting at my feet, licking my hand when a chance offered, nor am I wearied of my woolly pet, my dog who lies asleep at my feet under the table while I write. Poor fellow! He will have no master now, no one to feed and pet him and love him as I have done. The affectionate thing seems to know I am going to leave. He had staid closer to me the last two or three days than ever before. My foot is now his pillow. He has licked my hands and seemed more loving of late than before and I must say, I hate to leave him. Is it strange? Is it uncommon? Astray again!

Packing my books, unpacking them and putting them up stairs consumed the morning except the part rather dully passed in Miss Lou's company who came to see Ma this morning because "old folk" were present. My picture was the cause of my being there. Of course it was complemented. Was it deserved? Was it sincere? I was busy all evening with packing my trunk, unpacking it (won't I *unpack*?) as Pa told me to put my clothes in the smallest one up stairs. I did so as I thought exactly to his order. This threw to the winds an engagement I was sorry I could not fulfill, to ride with Miss Lou this evening. I got off at sundown to go around (to Maj. Lee's, Dr. P's, and Judge R's) according to my intention this morning though later. Mrs. Wm. Percy said she would *come up and tell me goodbye in the morning*. Mrs. Lee was there. She said she would see me at home where I would not have gone but that I had some book for that place. Met Nat and turned back. Miss Kate not very interesting. Very foolish ideas offered at the table of a late supper. *No Mrs. Lee*. What's that? For the Judge! We must see Miss Lou once more. After some trouble in getting Nat's horse after a wait beyond the bridge for him and after he had been pulled from his horse by a clothes line, we started for our destination in as pretty starlight night as I ever saw. At a sharp trot we soon arrived and stumbled through the new building into the parlor where Miss Lou *without Miss Bettie* (though we asked for the "young ladies") came in. Her father who was in the parlor wisely went out but her little sister did not and this was the only thing amiss during as pleasant an evening as I ever spent. Nat's envy put him under the weather. *"He who spits against the wind spits in his own face."* Then Nat spit in his face this evening. What is good for a fellow? Fine clothes? No. What? A little knowledge. He came at me at the wrong one. My reading gave me advantage. He became confused. I was like a cucumber. He from his fear Miss Lou's opinion of him would be lowered if he did not try to "cut" me got his "foot" in so far that in Miss Lou's eyes I could see she pitied him. Here's a fair specimen. We were speaking of what "nuts" Washington County boys were considered abroad. He said something about you must always play draw poker or freeze out with them and take a drink or so and then you can make friends. I asked him if he would advise such a means of making friends. He commenced immediately to tut her how I would jump into a drinking saloon when I got to Memphis &c. I put on a cool aggravating grin and looking him quisically in the face said in a low mocking tone, "Nat, do you make your friends that way?" All laughed and N. withered. The pique was in his being dismissed for drunkenness. He is so vain I like to do him so. Although he said he enjoyed himself I don't think he did much from the frequency of these things. I had a good quiet talk with Miss Lou, "short and sweet," about woman and man, and I of course exalted the former to the skies and the latter I put very low. Have I not said in these pages that a sparkling eye and a pretty cheek inspired me? My same loquacious mood which occasionally comes over me visited me tonight and I am glad to say two three times silenced N. Was he not mortified? I took occasion to say to Miss L. that some hard licks had been exchanged between us, and she said I ought not to have done him so. I also said that I [. . .] which way she was leaning this evening (before Nat) and what did she answer? That she thought she had rather leaned toward *me*. Ah! Is that so?

She invited me the other evening to come and stay at their house when I came to Jackson and pay a good visit to her. As we were about to leave (nearly so) I said to her in a joyless (affected) tone "Miss Lou, you remember what you told me? That promise shall be a bright star through all the glooms of my college life to which I will look." With a smile and a pressure of her extended hand, we parted. One only knows for how long. I went in and told the "old folks" goodbye. The old Judge said as he extended his hand and grasped mine firmly (he was in bed), "Good luck to you boy! Good luck to you!" It was a hearty cheer.

Vexation awaited me at home. I had to unpack and repack trunks again having got the wrong one. I have made this long and capricious entry. I will creep up among the children to spend the balance of my last night I hope in dreams of a woman such as a boy's active imagination only can picture. It is Tues.; it is 10 min. to 12.

Tuesday, September 18, 1860

Most of the day up to the time I left home was passed in company with Ma. I cheered her up and tried to dispell a sadness which has shrouded her for the last few days, and I am happy to know that I succeeded to a degree I did not venture to hope. She gave me some motherly advice. Packing and sending off my trunk (I had to get another) occupied part of the morning. The time at last came. All was ready and the dreaded parting took place. The first tears ever shed for *me* came from the eyes of my mother today. She wept. I restrained my emotions till I had left the house. Looking back I saw all the family standing in the gallery watching the buggy as Pa drove along the road. I could not force the tears back. They would come! I left my home, I left all—a loving mother. It was my duty; I did not shrink from it. I shed tears, but Pa did not see me.

At dusk we drove into town. I still felt sad. Supper eaten, Miss K. and Nat arrived. I changed my clothes and went according to a promise made to N. and myself after some waiting to Dr. Finlay to see Miss Helen and Miss Annie. I got out of patience and went on without him about 9 o'clk. Some one had beet me. Carson and Penny were there. Some one else too! Miss Ellen Smith sat on a sofa opposite to the door. As I entered I squoze Miss Helen's hand (as I had not seen her for some time), and she immediately said, Miss Ellen Smith, Mr. Dixon. I sat myself down by Miss H. and she and I carried on a lively talk, Mr. F. not seeming inclined to "take a hand." I found her more interesting than I had expected. She is a member of the Methodist Church and consequently opposed dancing for which doctrine I upbraided her, but she still clung to her opinion as I knew she would. Nat came creeping in about 10 o'clk. While Miss H. played on her piano, decidedly the finest instrument I ever heard or touched, I sat on a sofa with Miss Ellen and after five minutes conversation with her we were as good friends as if we had known each other for years. Miss Helen played some beautiful tunes and among others some schotisches and I tried with all my might to get Miss Ellen to dance with me but to no effect. *We were at a Methodist's house.* I silently damned them all for such a preposterous doctrine. Bah! What folly! I was in one of my loquacious moods. My tongue rolled while my eye was engaged by the pleasing countenance of my lady. Not by any means an unpleasant voice and a pretty flashing eye served not a little to make her company pleasant. I pleaded my youth and all other things but to no avail. The ball would not roll. I was much pleased however with Miss E. I never enjoyed myself more. Her laugh and my pleasure now are before me. Pleasure thus enjoyed cannot find words in my vocabulary. After attempting it for half an hour we left at 11½ waiting very imprudently until the *old folks* had sent in for "Miss Helen." We would shake hands and start out but someone of one party or the other would say something and thereupon all would commence talking. Again we would shake hands and again for many times the same thing was repeated until this girl came in and then we left. I felt reluctant to leave such an entertaining scene—really I did. I gave Miss E's hand a convulsive squeeze which was returned as we finally separated, I throwing kisses to her through the door as I stood on the gallery. She paid me many (I mean a *few*) compliments which I scarcely know whether to believe or not, but one I will believe—that I knew how to talk because this was a fact within my own knowledge. She promised to meet me if possible at the Montgomery White Sulpher. Will she do it? Can I expect it? Will next summer be more gay than this? Bed awaited me. It did not wait long.

Wednesday, September 19, 1860

Although "media nox" had come before I entered bed the sun beat me up but a short time this morning. I was not entirely dressed when the boat was announced to be in sight. I had some little thing to attend to so I hurried and when I finished the *Victoria*, the boat we came out to take and in whose cabin I now sit and write, was at the bank. The Lee's as usual were behind. Pa and myself got an accommodating officer to wait a few moments for them. The day has been passed as it is usual on steamboats. Nat introduced me to a Mr. Cringle so Mr. C., Mrs. Lancaster (a friend), Nat and myself had a game of Euchre. Loafing around and talking with Miss Kate some whiled away the morning. Miss Kate introduced N. and myself to a Miss Kate Batchelor, a childish, light-headed thing of only 13 summers, not pretty or interesting; but the wife of a Mr. Furley, a talkative, goodnatured fellow, is an interesting woman—good looking though not beautiful. There is about her an inexplicable something which makes one like her. Miss Katy was the "bone of contention" between Nat and myself in which I participated only to let folks know I was not to be run over. Nat's better looks made him her preference. I did not care. It looked foolish to be "pupping" around such a scrap.

All of the little party (the Trulies, Mrs. B, the two Miss Kates, N. and myself) went up in the pilot house in the evening, and Miss Kate Lee and myself did not come down till supper. Hal's affair with Miss Mary was our principal subject. I was disgusted with her conduct before a goodlooking young pilot who stood up before us at the wheel. She did not decry she was a flirt, and she ought to learn how to behave herself. She thinks she's some "pumkins in the bar fight." The young man laughed. No wonder. Hal loved Miss M. and Miss M. loved Hal is the fact. Miss K. played a double hand in the affair, writing letters which were copied, &c.

Thursday, September 20, 1860

Last night Nat brought a poor devil of a gentleman on board, an Oxford student who was drunk though I found him a very clever fellow as I may presume from his conduct toward me to day. Nat and myself still kept our attention to

Miss Katy. I like Mrs. T's company far better. Miss Katy's mother has taken an exceeding liking for me and Mrs. Truly seems to like me, and I am certain she does not "play off" on me. There was quite a funny affair about Miss Katy and Nat exchanging hair. I playfully snatched Nat's from her and kept it for some time having a good laugh about it. I got hers from Miss Kate who was fixing it for Nat, and it is now in a dirty vest pocket in my trunk.

The pilot house was our resort again this evening as well as Euchre. About 9 o'clk PM we touched the wharf and Memphis while our party (except Nat) were playing at cards in the cabin. Pa was going up town and for salutary reasons wished me to go with him. The Truly company were to leave at 6 tomorrow morning so I got up and bid them goodby. I have made them laugh at me very much by making jocular remarks about my own homely looks and by "cutting" Nat some, though this time I checked my sarcasm. By these means I have got on quite familiar terms with all. The grown ones palpably do not like Nat as well as they do me, but Miss Katy does—better. Boohoo! I made them stop calling me "Mr." Mrs. Truly said at our parting I must be certain to come to Fayette to practice law, and all was smiling as I left for quarters at the Worsham House where I slept soon after my arrival, often before I slumbered thinking of home and my dog.

Friday, September 21, 1860

I arose a little after 5 this morning and to see my steamboat friends off went down to the wharf. Such a search through fog and Irishmen I at last found the *Victoria* but none were up. Waiting till nearly the time for the cars to leave which they would take I went up to my hotel and took breakfast. All the forenoon passed in purchasing clothing and going around town. Knowing that my friends had gone to the Gayoso House about 3 o'clk, after I had finished all business and had had Pa's and my own ambrotype taken (his for me and mine for ma) I went down to their hotel and saw them. Seemingly they were very glad to see me. I had to walk down to the boat with Mrs. Batchelor (or her daughter) to the boat on which they were to leave. On my return to the hotel and after sitting a while (till they left for their train) with many regrets for the event, Mrs. Truly and myself as well as her jocular husband parted at the omnibus in front of the door to which place I escorted Mrs. T. Her last words were "you must be certain to write, Harry." And Harry promised to do so whether he does or not. My good father would pack my trunk before it went to the boat and I did not have any surplus time after walking back to the Worsham House and getting all ready. Less advice was given me than I had expected—only a little about how I was to do on the cars. Dusk was closing in when I left Memphis and my loved father—for a long year. We parted with firm hearts, as a father and son should part! God bless you my father as well as all the others of my kindred at home.

Pa said to me as we drove out to the depot that he would either send me a nice gold chain or bring it out with him next summer so the good thing I won from Ma did not come.

I found Memphis to be a thriving pleasant town, its streets crowded with the people of every stamp and grade. I wish I could remain in it for a week.

Saturday, September 22, 1860

If we had had anything but an exceedingly good-natured conductor in the sleeping cars where Miss Kate, Nat and myself "put up." Nat and myself (more than he) cut up what school boys call "dog." Laughed, said all the foolish things we could think of and made ourselves out what is called wild fellows. The little conductor evidently thought I was intoxicated, and I do not blame him for I acted as badly as if I had been. One thing was an almost continuous repetition, till very late, of this amusing anecdote in a laughable tone of voice: I went into the St. Char-les Hotel and feeling in my pocket I found that I had *twenty-five cents* in cash, in American coin and all in one piece, and says I to my friend "will ye imbibe?" and he says to me "I will" and *immediately* 17 others stepped up and remarked *"they'd take sugar in them."* I riz my hand and found I hadn't "a pair" so I "passed out with my usual dignity." I dropped this.

The whole day passed in the cars which went at their usual speed through a country of not unpleasant scenery. Miss K. getting acquainted with Miss Penny of N.Y. city she introduced Nat and myself who had (I did I know) a passable chat with her after eating a supper at one of the stations which reminded me of home's comforts.

Just before we got to Knoxville (where the "lady bird" lives) the member of Congress from that district made a short political speech to a motley crowd while standing on the platform of the cars. I also saw the celebrated Parson Brownlow[128] to whom I spoke. We for a few moments talked of his acquaintance with my grand father and relations about Abingdon. He is a hard "crusty" looking old fellow.

Sunday, September 23, 1860

Eight o'clk found me in old Abingdon dirty "accordin" and feeling less fatigued than I had expected. The morning was cool and bright. At Bristol where we changed cars I was vexed by having to wait for the train which we were to leave in and which could not come up to the platform for an engine which had run off the track a little way up the road. I paced back and forth on the platform to keep warm as it was then but a little after sunrise and pretty cool. Soon however we were off. Uncle Robert Beatie and Cousin Bettie McConnell were at the depot and Cousin Bettie made me promise to come out and dine with her. Not exactly made me but asked me and I promised. Waving a farewell with my hand to Miss Kate, I got into an omnibus and up town went not very pleasantly. The same old Abingdon of last summer was before me; the same men stood at the same corners and all things looked as if I had only left them yesterday.

In a cold room at the Washington House (how many hotels have this name?) I put on a clean shirt and my new Memphis suit of "dodburns" to gallant some gal to church. Miss Amelia Preston was of all my acquaintances my choice, so I addressed a note to her out of my most select words requesting that honor most respectfully. My answer was "Miss Amelia Preston begs Mr. Dixon will excuse her this morning." Is it because you are going to the Female College here Miss Amelia that you will not allow me to accompany you to church or because you do not wish to go with me? Let me hope at any rate that it is the former cause.

Miss Lizzie Jones was not at Mr. Alex. Findlay's so after walking around a little I sent my card to the young ladies at Mrs. Mitchell's, the gals I was so familiar with last summer. I saw Miss Rachel and Miss Docia but not Miss Kate, the youngest and the one to whom I was engaged last summer! Ha ha! I went to church with Miss Rachel and then a *mighty* pretty gal from the female college, a Miss Worth. The generality of them were not at all pretty. I sat nearby this pretty one and two or three times caught her eyes whose color and meekness reminded me of Miss Alexander's.

Uncle Hickman (I call him uncle though he is no relation but from congeniality of tastes and association) was very glad to see me, so much so that being in his dotage poor old fellow he whimpered almost like a child, his hand on my knee and looking in my face for sometime made many expressions of gladness at my coming. It took him by surprise; he did not expect me. He is a good old man and is much attached to me. We had many a long talk last summer while I staid in town and at his beautiful residence—one of the most lovely and complete places I ever saw. Visits occupied the whole day. I cannot enumerate them all. I found Uncle Leonidas' family out at Grand Pa's—Uncle Sarah being in bed. Notwithstanding the alienation existing between the two families (Pa's and his) or rather between Ma and Uncle S., all seemed glad to see me. Granny, an old negro of 100 years of age who was the nurse of my grandmother Dixon, was so glad to see me that when I had got close to her before she saw me and had spoken she caught my hand and squeezing it harder than I thought she could actually kissed it. The kisses did not end here. Cousin Anna Eliza (Uncle Hickman's daughter, a kinsman for the same cause he is), a lovely woman not only in looks but in disposition, gave me a sweet soft kiss in our meeting. Ah! how I can now imagine it over again! Another yet. When Miss Docia Mitchell walked into the room this morning, as I shook hands with her, I said unmeaningly "give me a kiss!" and lo and behold! she did give me one scarcely less acceptible than the one Cousin Anna Eliza gave me.

Monday, September 24, 1860

Grand Ma would have me to come back from Uncle Hickman's where I promised him I would take supper last night and stay with her all night, which I did. I had expected to recommence my journey at 8 o'clk this morning but finding that I had more time and that there was to be some speaking in town today I concluded to await till this evening. Hence to be at that speaking Uncle Leonidas and some of his little girls walked to town. The town band though by no means good made me cut short a letter I was writing to Ma and follow it on to a rusty hall called "Temperance Hall," where I heard Preston and Goggin speak. Neither gesticulated elegantly. They stooped too much. After coming from here about 3 PM being invited to dine at Mr. Henritze's I found it impossible to get off this evening so I visited around till 9½ after eating a good dinner there and having a dull talk with my sweetheart of '57, Miss Linn. Miss Kate, on my visit to Mrs. Mitchell's, refused to see me because as Miss D. told me in the hall as I was leaving *"I had told too many tales on her."* I like the other two very well—they are clever good ladies, but she has before now made a fool of herself. It hurt her sisters more than it did me. Miss D. on my saying "I was sorry I could not tell Miss K. goodby" followed me into the hall and tried to smooth it over but "I never get offended at any thing a lady said or done, never said any thing injurious to any lady" &c. and would allow no apology at all. I never said the first injurious thing about her to any one except Hal, and I am persuaded *he* would not divulge any thing of the kind. I'd thought I would write either her or her sister a note on the subject but on deliberation concluded to let the thing stand.

I sat too long with Cousin Anna Eliza and Uncle Hickman after coming from Mrs. Mitchell's and having promised Grand Ma to be out there to sleep tonight I found after a walk out to that place in the moonlight that I was too late. Every one had retired. A vicious dog prevented me from going in and it being about 10½ and finding no one awake and no lights in the house, I made a virtue of necessity and after trying to write in this journal (which I had brought with me) by the moon I fell into a box of straw in the stable near by ensconced in my heavy overcoat and soon after fell into a comfortable sleep from which I only awoke once until the morning of

Tuesday, September 25, 1860

Uncle Findlay was as much astounded at finding me there as all the rest of the family were when I told them of it. They all wanted to know why I did not holler and awake someone etc. I had but little time to spare if I was to take the 8 o'clk train for Lynchburg so I had my little cousins awaked and told them goodby with those of the family who were up (all except Uncle Leonidas and Aunt Sarah). I've rode this little pony along by my side while I walked into town at no slow gate. I had no time to loose. I found them just up at Uncle Hickman's where I had told him I would eat breakfast as he promised to have an early one for me. No doubt it was a nice breakfast, but I did not eat it. I went over to my room at the hotel and had scarcely time to strap my trunk, go over and tell them goodby. Cousin A.E. would have me to drink a cup of her good coffee, expressing regrets that I could not stay to breakfast, all the while hurrying the servants and putting up something for me to take in my hands. In the words of a comic speech I read not long since, I can sincerely say *"Wummun, she is a good egg!"* At least I know Cousin A.E. is a good "wummun." She has a heart as big as all one side of a meeting house. Well, but my theme. The coffee was so hot that it almost scalded my tongue but down she went. Emerging with two apples and my bundle of bisquet and butter in my hands and my overcoat over my arm, I gave or rather took another of those delectable kisses from Cousin A.E. and in all conceivable haste and bristle started up the street in a run for the omnibus which was to take me to the depot—but it was not where I had left it! A few more leaps showed it to me up the street a little way. I ran to it and jumped in with all expedition, behind time for the first time and in my confusion and breathlessness experienced its admonition.

The cars came soon after we got to the depot and I experienced some inconvenience in getting on as the freight train was on a track between the passenger train and the platform. I did not wait for the former to move as young White did who got on the same train, but I got over between the boxes and took my seat in them. White is a young man from this county (Washington) who is attending the University. I knew him in '57. He invited me to partake of some excellent grapes his sister had put up for him. "Wummun" again! I thus had company to Lynchburg where he chose to remain till Wed. morning. The most beautiful mountain scenery presented itself to me in Roanoak County as indeed in many places between Abingdon and Lynchburg. Their blue hazy peaks seeming to rest on the bluer horizon were greeting to the eye. We would some times be nearing along the side of a mountain through pitchy tunnels and well cultivated valleys. My taste enabled me to enjoy these scenes which some people can pass by unnoticed.

We arrived at Lynchburg soon after dark where I was perplexed and beset by a dozen porters' "This way, master," "I'll take your trunk," "Which way you going," &c. After rambling around in a bad humor I at last got it over but could not get my trunk checked. A canal boat carried me about ¾ of a mile to the cars where the road was not finished and having no security for my trunk I did not feel comfortable. When "Charlottesville" was announced I could not help feeling relieved and joyed. I had arrived at my destination! at the place where I had longed to be so long! I was relieved by seeing my much cared for trunk put on the little omnibus of the "Farish House" whose porters attacked me as others did at Lynchburg. We went whirling around corners and up streets to the hotel where I took a room, wrote some of the preceeding entries and retired. Misery! I could not tell anything of the country (50 miles or more) which I traversed as it was night and 11½ or thereabouts when I got to C——e.

These 288 pages are written. Who would have believed it? I expected this book, at first, to last until Jan. '62, then till Jan. '61, and now it has not lasted me through the year in which it was commenced. I find myself at the time-honored University to commence a new Journal ere this one has grown old! Who knows what a day may bring forth?

Henry Hughes

I never had many to love me. From my childhood [I] have been esteemed, honored, flattered, admired, yet there were no spirits with whom I could feel a sympathy. I found at length a soul which could mingle with my own. A year since then has passed. After a protracted absence I have met her again. I love—she tells me that she loves me—Here while the pale sorrowing stars look down upon me for a little while & sink into darkness, while one by one pleasure after pleasure has receded, I renounce the pure joys which sacred marriage would bestow until the jealous Glory which I woo shall give her Consent. I love, but I tear down the idol from the alter where a sublimer divinity is placed. My Father in heaven be Thou my witness, Search me, Assist me, O my God I have now no other support but Thee.   —March 19, 1848

New Orleans, January 1, 1848
   This record is dedicated to my soul and to Fame, wherever I may be during the present year, a portion of my time shall be unfailingly devoted on the sacred night of every week, to the purposes of recording my meditations, emotions, aims, and circumstances. Scanning these pages, the future biographer will read my thoughts, & learn my history.

In this as in all other things may my God my Destiny grant me that assistance which He has promised.

My Father was Benjamin Hughes, born in Kentucky. He died, while my life was in its Spring, at Grand Gulf Mississippi. Nancy Hughes, formerly Nancy Brashear, is my Mother. I have two Sisters and a brother.[1] Providence has been kind in making me the Son of such parents, the brother of such sisters and of such a brother. I commenced & read Blackstone's *Commentaries*[2] with J. B. Thrasher[3] at Port Gibson Mi about the first of August 1847. Under Thomas J. Durant,[4] U.S. District Attorney for the District of Louisiana, Hallam's *View of the Middle Ages*[5] was the first work which I perused. I next begun Hallam's *Constitutional History of England.*[6] I read thirty pages a day. At night, I ponder over it and infix it in my memory. What time I have not otherwise occupied, I consume in studying Logic in the Edinburgh Encyclopedia.[7] To this, I was induced by observing the importance attached to it in the office, and by my desire of Knowledge. I neither drink, chew, Smoke or play cards. May it ever be thus. Between the hours of 11 & 12 PM I study Gibbons *History of the Decline & Fall of Rome.*[8] This sagacious & fascinating work, I commenced in December 1847.

I now reside with Dr. Wm B. Lindsay. He married my Maternal Aunt Ruth.[9] To them both I am indebted for affectionate and unremitted Kindnesses.

I graduated at Oakland College[10] in Claiborne County Mississippi. Received the first honors in a class of Seven. Of this class James Alexander and myself were the only two members of The Adelphic Institute. At College, Smith C. Daniell, Wm. Thomas Magruder[11] & Peter Alexander were my esteemed & intimate friends.

During my Collegiate time, Oratory occupied an inferior Share of my attention.

During the Summer of 1847, I joined a Division of the Sons of Temperance, in order to gain the honor of addressing them. I accomplished my aim in two or three months subsequently. The Speech was published in the Port Gibson *Herald*. For a similar purpose, I united myself to the Young Men's Magnolia Division of New Orleans. It is my custom on every Sabbath Morning to hear Mr. Clapp preach,[12] on Sabbath evenings, to hear Mr. Nicholson. It is my rule to retire to bed at 12 o'clock, & to rise at about 7½ or 8 o'clock in the morning. I would prefer to repose earlier and rise sooner. Domestic circumstances render it inconvenient. Would that I might Sleep less. A feeble frame already admonishes me that my slumbers even now are perhaps too much abridged.

My God bestow thy blessing.

New Orleans, January 2, 1848

Tomorrow, My Little Sister, who has been Spending a few brief weeks with me, departs for home. Her departure Saddens me. None of those who guided & gladdened my young life will then be near me. I will return to my books, and forget my sadness to learn knowledge from them.

Unhallowed desires have filled & delighted my mind. This is a day sacred to elevated refined pleasures. My thoughts seek diversion and imagine forbidden things. Deeds may hereafter realize them. For I esteem it necessary that I should stir up even the sediment of pleasure and taste the dregs of every cup. Will it not be required that I shall feel every variety of woe and of enjoyment in order to stimulate & control with certain and resistless power the emotions of the multitude. Thus Byron. But let this desire of experiencing pleasure never cause a heart to ache, a tear to flow. Tomorrow, I return to studies—repress every carnal thought, and devote myself unreservedly to ambition—to knowledge & fame.

May nothing interrupt the continuity or diminish the amount of my acquisitions. May I be for the allotted period of sole, pure, powerful intellect, turning every thing I touch into imperishable treasure. And when the coming Sabbath sets free my soul, may my Guardian select for it such sensual gratifications as will best adapt it to the task of the orator—the animation and government of human passions.

Today, I have been happy, my happiness has been as unalloyed as is usually permitted. But a shadowy fear, a mournful assurance that in the unceasing mutations of existence, prosperity will harbinger adversity, joy usher in grief, success precede failure; this prescient dread mingles with my fullest delights.

The past is happy—the present is happy, the future, alas—the future——

New Orleans, January 9, 1848

The past week has been fraught with invaluable experience. I have learned the vanity of sensual & forbidden enjoyments, from experiments purposely tried. From my most trivial acts, I have extracted wisdom. My observation has not been so habitual, penetrating and comprehensive, as must be. Unhallowed thoughts have possessed my mind, they have distracted its attention.

My Study of Hallam's *Constitutional History* has been prosecuted with customary energy. It is my custom to study, write, or mediate until twelve o'clock. I rise a[t] half past seven o'clock AM. My eyesight is, I think, becoming worse. Many days of the week have been purely happy, days which I would live over. But this happiness has been chiefly derived from myself and my studies & moral experiments. I care but little for life, and as I become more careless, it presents to me brighter prospects, and wooes me with present joys and well-founded hopes of future Success. I feel that if I now should die, death would be a noble excuse for the non-acquisition of the fame, the power which I would lose. Day after day, I become more firmly convinced that there is a Destiny which shapes my ends. I believe in the Christian Religion. From this day, with the help of my Destiny, I will devote myself, unreservedly, conscientiously with all my heart & with all my strength, to the attainment of that greatness, glory, power, which no mortal man has ever possessed. I will place myself upon a throne from which I can look down on Alexand[er], Caesar, Cicero, Bonaparte, Washington. May my God help me. Thomas S. H. McCay was for a time, a classmate of mine.

New Orleans, January 16, 1848

I commenced studying French with Mr. Cezanne on Monday ult. the 10th. This week has been one of happiness, occasionally mingled with feelings of indifference, & regret. I have again reaped a little of the whirlwind of experience, have fully tested the insufficiency of carnal enjoyments. Though as systematically industrious as usual, I have this week acquired but little knowledge, such has been the nature of my books. The prospect before me is as bright & alluring as previously. If I could only believe that there was a God, how happy I should be. I should then be unreservedly confident in my fortunes.

New Orleans, January 23, 1848

My knowledge & experience have increased. My pleasures have been almost entirely independent of others. During the past week, I purchased Cicero's Essay on the character of an Orator.[13] I will study it. My ambition is unabated, my hopes increased. Fear not, the result of boldness can be but death. My God, My Destiny love me.

New Orleans, January 30, 1848

Let me return thanks to the powerful Divinity upon whose bosom I breathe my nightly prayers. He has advanced me on my sublime career, promoted me nearer to the blest zenith. The seductions of sense and attractions of the world are yielding to my will. The praises & expectations of friends, jealousy even of the name of schoolmates who perhaps may attempt to rival me; the mention of great living men, and of great ancient, contempt of the world, the flesh and the devil, all force me on. In the silence of this night, while my Destiny looks down on me from heaven, I swear that my unceasing ambition shall be to become the greatest mortal man that ever was or will be.

Hear heavens, and give ear O Earth.

I have purchased Cicero *De Oratore*, and Demosthenes' Orations, I already have Cicero's Orations. These works are translated. They will be the objects of my future study. I have procured Whately's *Logic*.[14] I will master the science as far as it may be useful. I delivered an address before the Crystal Fount Division of the Sons of Temperance on the 24th ult. It was received in a manner so flattering as to give me high encouragement. It created a gratifying sensation. It will be published. What is life without unbounded glory, that I should love it. If death should come it will relieve me from the infinite toil before me, and afford my soul an excuse for not achieving its purposes.

New Orleans, February 6, 1848

Success has crowned my efforts. My knowledge of men & things has increased. During the past week, I commenced Studying Bancroft's *History of the United States*.[15] This is at the advice of Mr. Durant my legal preceptor. He has pursued a wise course in thus conducting me through history to law. Thoughts and plans of wealth have occupied my mind. They do not interfere with graver meditation. Wealth is necessary to my destiny. That which I accumulate, I intend to devote to the purposes of glory and fraternal & filial piety.

From nine to ten o'clock at night I compose upon themes connected with eloquence. From ten until eleven, I study works connected with oratory—at present Cicero *De Oratore* translated and every third night Whately's *Logic*. From eleven to twelve I read Gibbons *History of the Decline & Fall of the Roman Empire*. Other hours are devoted to Law and Nature.

May my God never forsake me. Would that he would Speak to me and assure me of my unparalleled greatness, hereafter.

I[n] my scrap-book will be found a copy of an Address delivered before the Crystal Fount Division of the Sons of Temperance. I belong to the Crystal Temple of Honor.

New Orleans, February 13, 1848

Of the past week, many of the days have been days of Vanity—nothingness. A slight but obstinate Sickness has impaired my concentration, diminished my impetuosity of spirit, and decreased the periodical increase of my knowledge. I have felt the weakness of flesh and am frightened. If blindness should darken my eyes, the example of Homer, Ossian, and Milton would repel despair. I feel that my God would inspire me with a Song such as the world and heaven with all their inhabitants, would wonder at. But when sickness comes, the clay clogs me. I still cherish my ambition, but my energy is enfeebled, and my thoughts do not grasp with their customary rapidity, force, & constancy the things Set before me. My Destiny protect me from Sickness, Remove the obscurities from my eyes and pain from my brow & breast. Yesterday I visited the Municipal

Library of the City. The vastness of knowledge which I yet must accumulate does not appal me.

Tomorrow, I will complete the purchase of two lots of ground in the City of Lafayette, which I am buying for my elder Sister.

My Destiny never let my ambition Sleep; let me be courageously, profitably, and incessantly industrious. Renew within me a right Spirit. Let me be the greatest mortal man that ever was or will be.

New Orleans, February 20, 1848

During the past week, ill health has enfeebled my energies. I have increased my knowledge regularly but not vigorously. I am not afraid of diseases; they may afflict, but cannot kill me. Yet I would not be timorously loth to yield up this burden of life, before the evil days come. However I may seem animated in society by the forced enthusiasm of the moment, however my face may be wreathed with smiles; yet I still have but little pleas[ure] in the ordinary conviviality of company. My nature is social. If I had founded my continued gratification in the society of the world, I could be as happy as is usually permitted. Amidst festive recreations, the memory of my ambition will rise, and interrupt the flow of soul. In the throng of pleasure, I often feel a bitter contempt for the frivo[li]ties of the world, and gladly turn to the lettered manuscript, open page, & Solitary lamp.

May my faith in my Destiny never be lessened. During the last week I was emancipated from minority.

New Orleans, February 27, 1848

Would that the flesh had no weakness. Disease has been preying upon me. It has come not in the undisguised form which openly attacks its victim, and tortures until its power is confessed. Beneath its noiseless influence I feel my nerves relax, strength decrease, energy slacken. But my ambition is as unwearied as ever. It knows no change of health, no secret fever, feeble pulse or throbbing brow. I have not gathered knowledge during the past week so rapidly as I would wish. My eyes do not improve, Yet I grieve not. All things tend to my glory. But what I most lament is a disposition which is so naturally convivial that in the gentle but unguarded excitement of a Society in which are many gay female friends, I descend from the grave seriousness which should characterize my demeanor and participate in their levities. May Age remedy this fault. I begin to revolve Schemes of amassing the wealth necessary to support my designs. Yet I love not money, But I love to be liberal.

My Father, guide me.

New Orleans, March 5, 1848

During the week, my physical vigor has been impaired by a vague, prostrating disease. It has clogged my energy of application, and occasionally my ambition has perhaps sickened. But sick or well, it has never failed me. If disease should permanently fasten itself upon me, if languor, pain, & weakness of sight should be my heritage, would I continue to drag out for a few troubled, vain days, a life worthless, unknown, contemned. Nor fear of death nor love of life binds me here. Glory holds me to an earth hated, to the company of men for whom I have no sympathy or reverence. God give me eyes, strength, body, to work out my unparalleled destiny.

I have seen the great tragedian Forrest[16] play King Lear. It is my aim to be perfect in gesticulation.

New Orleans, March 12, 1848

My health has been & is bad. Last Monday I consulted the oculist. He directs to read for the time of two weeks, only two or three hours a day. My only resource is in meditation—the nerves of my eyes appear to be affected. My eyes are too convex for perfect vision.

My Father, thy will be done.

New Orleans, March 19, 1848

My soul is rising above the seductions of humbler pleasures. I never had many to love me. From my childhood [I] have been esteemed, honored, flattered, admired, yet there were no spirits with whom I could feel a sympathy. I found at length a soul which could mingle with my own. A year since then has passed. After a protracted absence I have met her again. I love—she tells me that she loves me—Here while the pale sorrowing stars look down upon me for a little while & sink into darkness, while one by one pleasure after pleasure has receded, I renounce the pure joys which sacred marriage would bestow until the jealous Glory which I woo shall give her Consent. I love, but I tear down the idol from the alter where a sublimer divinity is placed. My Father in heaven be Thou my witness, Search me, Assist me, O my God I have now no other support but Thee.

New Orleans, March 26, 1848

Tomorrow, I expect to depart for Port Gibson Miss. I do this in obedience to the advice of the oculist. I leave with a sigh the fascinating studies in which I forgot wretchedness & found hope of glory. Tonight I have heard the Rev. J. N. Maffit[17] preach. His style & success have instructed & encouraged me. I begin to turn my thoughts to the practical business of life. [If] I were not a lawyer, I would like to be a banker. My sister Mrs. Mary A. Morehead is here. I thank my heavenly Father that he has blessed me with such a sister. She has greatly assisted in the formation of my character. She is, with one dear other, almost the only one who appreciates my spirit & sympathizes with my desires. There is, there was another. O love, O fame. Come not to me lovely vision. It is only in heaven, when the loathed turmoil of life is over, when earthly tired ambition has run its race, when unsurpassable glory has rewarded my exertions, that I can hope to meet with thee. Wo is me. But I make the sacrifice. Farewell.

My Father, to thee only, I can now look for the little pleasure which will be granted me on earth.

Port Gibson, April 2, 1848

On last Monday evening, I left New Orleans, I went to Vicksburg; I came to Port Gibson. I left the city in pursuance of the advice of the oculist. O weak flesh, O cursed body.

Port Gibson, April 10, 1848

Last night, I forgot to continue this faint record. Let it be so no more. The disease which besets me begins to assume shape. My eyes do not improve. How long, O Lord, shall I suffer this tantalizing thralldom; when shall my soul be free—free from the load of clay which oppresses it, free to rush into the vast apartments of the universe, free to sport with the powers of humanity? My present days are miserable. I am a sword hung up to rust. The poor scabbard is day after day dropping from my spirit. The small pitiless dew & sickening damp rest upon & corrode my soul. O God, how long shall it be thus? O My Father in thee I trust. Snatch me up to thy bosom, breathe into my tired heart thy blessed love.

Port Gibson, April 16, 1848

Tonight I have come from the country to Port Gibson in order to continue this record. My eyes seem not to recover strength. My physical system is still weak. Is God thus restraining me from books in order to develope my powers of observation? Daily I grow more familiar with the principles which govern & motives which urge men. But my soul still pants for increased knowledge, still loves to commune with the great departed. Inactivity is making me miserable. Tomorrow is my birth-day. The thought exasperates my wretchedness. The world is preparing for me. France is a Republic. Universal dominion is my aim—a consolidation of all the powers & principalities of earth into one happy, sublime Republic. I feel that the hand of destiny is on me. I am the Instrument of God.

Port Gibson, April 23, 1848

I have been requested to deliver an address to the occasion of the presentation of a Bible to the Claiborne Division of the Sons of Temperance. I accept the solicitation. The ceremony takes [place] in Port Gibson on next Wednesday. The week has passed bringing no vivid pleasures but many bitter pinings for a more active and unrestricted pursuit of glory. I watch Europe with keen yet confident anxiety. The World is making ready for me. I feel my mind growing within me. It seems big, bursting with something yet unexplained, with pantings for knowledge, with the swelling strange consciousness of its divine, its peerless energies. Since my compelled cessation from study my powers of Observation have been wonderfully developed. They are yet in the embryo. I will nourish them into a giant slave. I long to search the mysteries of Association—suggestion, and of space, time, words and relations. It is to the human mind that I will direct my chiefest meditations. I improve doubtfully in my body. My eyes are I think but little benefited.

(Expenses to 27th April $60.00.)

New Orleans, April 30, 1848

I left Port Gibson on last Friday morning at about half past four o'clock and arrived in New Orleans on Saturday morning at about half past ten. My eyes and health are but little improved. I expect to rise at about half past four o'clock in the morning and to retire at ten at night, to exercise more freely to think and observe more constantly. God help me. The condition of Europe arouses and encourages me. I will be the President of America and Europe. The Republics of earth shall all be joined in one Government. I will be their ruler. I feel that for some such destiny as this, God has marked me out.

O My Father, My Destiny still hold me in thy arms.

John Quincy Adams kept a Journal. This co-incidence pleases me.

(Expenses of the past week were $9.00.)

New Orleans, May 7, 1848

My eyes seem not to improve. I do not read at night; I rise early.

The sources of knowledge are reading, observation and thought. I have always endeavored to discipline intellect and refine fancy by reflection. Am I thus debarred the pleasures & profits of unrestrained reading, in order to quicken & develop my observation?

My Father, be it So. It is hard but I deny myself. The time will come when I shall Satiate my wild soul-heaving aspiration after the power of knowledge by familiar communings with thee; when I shall repose on your bosom and feel your spirit infusing itself through my disenthralled soul; when your lips will inform me of the mysteries of space & causation. My pleasures have not been vivid during the last week. If my political opinions are not those of my highsouled earthly father, let it not be ascribed to the influence of any with whom I have intercourse.

Since leaving Port Gibson and my parental home, this second time, I have felt an indefinable sense of loneliness. My heart has hung heavy within me, and my blood has oftentimes flowed chill sickening and creeping. Was my destiny affected at Port Gibson? Was still another destiny intertwined with mine?

My Father, remember the oath.

New Orleans, May 14, 1848

My health is bad. My eyes exhibit a tendency to inflammation. By its mysterious connexion with my nerveless flesh, my mind seems to lose its pure, quick spirituality, my thoughts wander from the learned page, and yet, when uncontrolled they revel on the Soft couches of the pleasurable emotions, or willingly rise and walk the narrow but ornate passages of reason. I crave for time to think. Is there to be no Sabbath for my mind, when I can freely meditate, reason, combine, apply, when these failing sickly senses and organs will suffer me for the meet time to devote my uninterrupted days & nights to intense absorbing Study? I watch my actions, & from even the most insignificant deduce general rules of conduct. Principles which I have already adopted or established, I daily illustrate. On earth, of all whom I have ever known, my eldest Sister, Mary Ann Morehead had the most powerful influence on me. Her soul is the sister of mine. She and one dear other seem alone to have *fully*, sympathetically appreciated me. Others lavish their compliments upon me, but for these two loved ones only have I felt a kindred, a unison of mind. God protect & love my sister, God—

My Father love me.

(Expenses $1.35 cts.)

New Orleans, May 21, 1848

Are my days to be vanity? Are my strong yearnings after glory to be powerless? Am I to agonize with the pantings for power and feel a mortifying sense of my Impotence? When Shall I accomplish Something which will confer visible tangible fame? When will consummate unsurpassable eloquence reward my studies, the revealed mysteries of primal truths, my midnight analyses. When shall a knowledge of the supreme universal original principles of law enable me to meet fearlessly and vanquish every erring opponent? Am I impatient? Am I too young? Are my aspirations beyond my years? Cannot summer produce the fruits of autumn? Can I await while slow-paced Destiny brings her successes? O my Faith waver not. There must be a God, else whence this holy confidence, this contempt of death, this consent to live. Can I not receive a sign, a proof? Cannot spirit convince spirit of its existence by other than spiritual means? I must believe, or I will die. My faith is interwoven with my ambition. I will rise above doubt, dread, Sense, Sin. I will be the greatest mortal man that ever was. I am the darling of my heavenly Father. I still Shall stand upon the pinnacle of Fame and look down on Washington & Napoleon. O God clasp me to to thy breast, press thy lips to mine.

(Expenses .50 cts.)

New Orleans, May 28, 1848

Time steals from me. It now leaves but slight traces of its passing. No vivid emotions now stir me, save when impressible agitating pantings for power & glory convulse my soul & make my heart swell & sink almost to bursting. Glory is my being's aim. I must be the greatest mortal man that ever was. Failing sight & feeble body are but slight impediments. Are they not advantages? O My Father let not my divine desires satisfy themselves with words; let them not evaporate in vain declarations to my friends & prayers to thee. Let me be the perfect orator, reasoner, statesman, philosopher, warrior, philanthropist; which shall show me worthy of thy familiar love, worthy of being thy bosom darling?

(Expenses of the Week .50 cts.)

New Orleans, June 4, 1848

My eyes are very weak, My constitution seems to struggle to support itself. My Father help me.

I have been reading Eliot's *Debates on the Constitution*[18] for the last two or three weeks. A portion of my daily time is appropriated to unassisted investigations into the Art of logic and the nature of truth. I have Whately's *Logic*; I do not wish to study it until my own unguided examination of its principles is more thorough. I sometime since read upon Logic an article in the Edinburgh Encyclopedia. From it I gained many ideas in regard to language.

My Destiny, shall disease or blindness terminate these studies?

(Expenses of the past week—20 cts.)

Steamer "Natchez," Mississippi River, June 11, 1848

I am on my way to Port Gibson in Mississippi. It is my native place. I expect to Spend the Summer there. I left New Orleans yesterday evening about five o'clock. It is for the benefit of my eyes & health that I pursue this course. I had hoped to remain longer in the city. Eyes irritated by use & by the dust & glare of Streets & houses; a breast made painful by regular confinement—have banished me to shadier walks & purer air.

My Father still prompt me.

(Expenses of the week, $7.60.)

Port Gibson, June 18, 1848

Let it be remembered that on the 22nd of November 1847; I commenced studying law in New Orleans, with Thomas J. Durant, United States District Attorney for the District of Louisiana. I was borne on the 17th of April 1829 at Port Gibson in the State of Mississippi. Bad eyes & health interrupt the regularity of my reading. My chief resort for improvement is now in observation & thought. My observation to a certain extent includes the other source of knowledge—conversation. I observe the conversation of others in preference to participation.

My present plan is to rise early, walk before breakfast, ride for a while after, then exercise, then practice with my voice & in gesticulation, then study the principles at present of logic, then read. My unoccupied time I at present devote to the investigation of the human will.

Bless me God.

(Expenses of the week 15 cts)

Port Gibson, June 27, 1848

I still continue my investigations of the human mind. Resemblance, contrast, contiguity in time & space & quantity strangely stir my attention. I desire to study the nature of scientific classifications. Indeed I have already remarked some of the principles of generalization.

May not the Baconian Method of acquiring knowledge be imperfect—false? I continue my examination of the human will.

In my exercises in gesticulation & oration, I profitably consume much time in the mornings.

For happiness I depend almost entirely upon my internal resources. My eyes have become so bad that it is at length highly imprudent for me to read. The tranquilities of home often diffuse a full quiet delight through my heart. These cannot long be mine. I feel them but to forego them & remember. Let me free myself from the Seductions & frailties of earth. Let me stand among men, with no sympathy but philanthropy, no aim but unsurpassable glory. Let me make myself the mere instrument of reason & will. God banish [me] from irrelevant thoughts, liberate me from the senses. What will be the result of my Metaphysical studies? My Father, let [me] surpass Bacon. Let it not be at the expense of that peerless political greatness at which I aim.

(Expenses 40 cts)

Port Gibson, July 2, 1848

I still continue my exercises in oratorical Action. My improvement is gratifying & inspiring. My lessons in "Expression of the Human Face" are to me gravely interesting. The third of my daily lessons is the "Improvement of Voice." In this branch of my practical oratory, I am again successful.

Look down on me Demosthenes. If thy Shade is not jealous of the Aspirant after perfection; inspire my limbs with the action & with all the graces which my celestial Studies have developed.

My investigation of the Mind is prosecuted with unabating vigor.

I do not despair of revolutionizing art & Science.

O My God was it for this that you ordained my eyes to fail? Wild & awful ideas rush like devils across my mind. My Ambition & Will enlarge until they become boundless. They are not satiated with aiming at unsurpassable earthly glory. They rush with me beyond the confines of the grave, walk with defiance through the valley of the Shadow of Death & scorn the grim sentinels who line its mountain Sides. A thought fills me to Shake off this mortal coil & boldly adventure among the Spirits of the universe, to invade Hell; to emulate, to — to dethrone the Almighty. Can I not expand my powers into infinity? Have I not a Will to war against Earth Hell Heaven? Have I yearned to reign the lone *One* in space, the unconquerable, Supreme Unsurpassable, Eternal Infinite? O God if there be a God, suppress my agonizing desires, Communicate with my Spirit; let me know Thee. What am I? Am I Jesus Christ or Satan? Is there no God, and am I the embryo of a God? Come to me spirits, I fear nothing.

My Father press to my lips, love me thy Pet, thy Darling.

(Expenses of the week, .00)

Port Gibson, July 9, 1848

The past week has conferred but little knowledge. Friends & acquaintances have consumed much of my time. My customary exercises have been suspended. Let it be so no more. I am dissatisfied. My eyes are still very bad. For the last few days I have been attacked with a slight deafness.

O my Father, let me waste no moment.

(Expenses of the week 10 cts)

Port Gibson, July 16, 1848

This has been a week of indifference. My joys have been languid. Health & eyes are very bad. My hebdomadal increase in knowledge has been Slight. O, Vanity of Vanities, I am not satisfied.

My attention has been stimulated in regard to the discussion & proof of political doctrines. The tide is rapidly approaching. So it leads to Glory. I care not over what rocks & quicksands it bears me.

God guide me.

(Expenses of the week 10 cts)

Port Gibson, July 23, 1848

Without much excitement or profound inquiry, the week has passed pleasantly. On Sunday, I am accustomed to meditate upon Death. I do not shrink from death—therefore nothing can appal me. For personal pain & inconvenience, for anything that irritates the Senses, I cherish contempt. Let me be the Slave of Will, let me know no desire which is not Slavishly obedient to the master Passion. Let not impatience or rebellious hopes, let not sword pestilence or famine seduce me from my servility to Will.

I examined Locke.[19] We both arrived at our idea of a God in a similar manner. I confess disappointment. Be it so. I study mental philosophy. I do not despair of surpassing Lord Bacon. The hope is not presumptious, My God, is it? Into the Science of Metaphysics, I enter reluctantly. A latent fear haunts me that I might be allured from the fame of Power.

My eyes are still bad, chest still disturbed with an occasional pang.

In regard to Politics, I am fully aroused. The orations of Demosthenes[20] will be my study. In the possession of these orations, I bless God for my advantage over Demosthenes. When I shall, by a Study of these speeches, have made myself equal to the Athenian orator, my own powers & opportunities will enable me to excel any orator that ever was.

But the future, curse the future. When in heaven, I will control the future & prevent any Aspirant from making use of my productions & surpassing me.

I continue my vocal, facial & gesticulatory exercises. I congratulate myself with manifest improvement; the prospect still opens. Let me soon possess all that it embraces.

During the present Presidential canvass, the temptations to enter the political arena are almost resistless. The tide is approaching; I stand ready with my bark.

(Ex—35c)

Port Gibson, July 31, 1848

This pleasing duty again escaped me. I have studied the principles of this incident, as I usually do those of the most ordinary occurrence. I hope my memory will not again fail me. From this failure I have extracted much instruction. Would that my mind was so meditative, so vigilant as to confer insurance against all neglect. At such a mental condition, I do not despair of arriving. Alas, why can I not be perfect?

Mr. John Locke & myself agreed most flatteringly in our views of the origin of the idea of a God. I confess my disappointment; I indulged the hope that I was exploring an untrodden field. Lock has anticipated me, & I consent. May the results of my next investigations be such as will not dread to confront the past. I still continue my Study of mind—spirit. When my duties are uninterruptedly performed, when difficulty after difficulty is boldly encountered & finally Subdued, when my thoughts are wholly bent upon Study, I often feel a delicious enthusiasm. This enthusiasm, So vivid, So continuous, often animates me into pure happiness. Then I feel the love of Glory, the contempt of the Senses, the aspirations after the Infinite. Of my pleasures, this emotion is the chief.

My eyes are still very [bad]—chest weak. Can it be that these failing organs & members are to control my actions, can I not free myself from them & commune with Nature & spirits undisturbed by the pangs of flesh?

Today, I commence the Study of the Association of ideas with Gesture, In the Mechanical part of Action. I have attained Some skill. My muscles do not yet exhibit that grace & docility at which I aim. The improvement in my voice affords me heart-felt gratification.

Let me be of good cheer. Fame shall be won, though the Heavens fall.

.15 c.

Port Gibson, August 7, 1848

My eyes are still bad, chest still aches. I prosecute my study of Oratory & Mind. My only Sources of improvement are thought & observation & conversation. My sisters are however accustomed to read to me. I am investigating the principles of Generalization in connection with knowledge & Oratory.

My Destiny, God, guide me.

(oo.oo.)

Port Gibson, August 13, 1848

During the past week, I have made but slight increments to my knowledge. My eyes do not Seem to improve. What cloudy darkness rests upon the future. Let some ray of light beam upon me, even though it be the inauspicious lightnings angry flash.

God aid me.

(ex. 25 c)

Lake Concordia, August 20, 1848

From Mississippi, I have come with my friend & College-mate, Peter Alexander to spend a few days. My wisdom increases. When shall it be perfect? My eyes & health improve but slowly. I entertain the idea of visiting Europe.

My Father help me.

3.30

Port Gibson, August 27, 1848

I still abstain from reading. I continue my accustomed investigation of Mind. I pant for omniscience & omnipotence. If souls are immortal and there is no God, I will, I feel that I will be the sovereign of the spirits of the departed. I yearn to be separated from my fellows, to inhabit Some lone spot where I may hold convers with the quick spirit of the Universe, pore over the revelations of the Sages, & Search the deep treasures of Self. O God, let me be perfect. If thou art, I will worship Thee. Yet I feel that I would give my soul for the unprofitable world.

At present, I have reduced the principles of Mind to "Space, Time, Resemblance, Quantity, Association, Habit, Desire, & perhaps Beauty." I expect to reduce this classification to fewer elements. Desire associated connected attached, to what I include under the word "Space" will perhaps account for what are termed by the distinguished & profound Dr. Thomas Brown[21] of Edinburgh—the Prospective Emotions.

I indulge a Slight, perhaps irrational hope of establishing a method, by which, a priori, all our ideas may be enumerated & combined. It would be by means of the classification which I have just developed, in part. Contrast, I have I think, identified with Quantity. This I have written without much premeditation. In all things O My Father help me.

4.25.

Port Gibson, September 3, 1848

I have progressed in knowledge. The themes of my meditations are Mind, Extemporary Oratory, Schemes of myself, & Classification. I am rapidly developing the principles of Extemporary Oratory. A chronic irritation of the throat, resulting from an elongation of the palate, has deterred me from using my voice as freely as I would desire. This disease now is almost overcome.

Fate, God, I am thine.

00.00.

Port Gibson, September 10, 1848

I continue my investigations of Mind, & of extemporary oratory, & of Classification. A chronic palatal irritation denies me the use of my voice at present.

I think myself secure in being the orator that I am to be.

00.00

Port Gibson, September 17, 1848

This has been a week of but little profit. Business of a pecuniary character has demanded my attention. Across my mind, there sometimes flits a temptation to abandon the high career which God and myself have marked out for me and seek happiness in the amassment of wealth & possession of wedded beatitude. My contempt for these enjoyments soon urges me with keener desire to power & glory. I am recovering from the disease of my throat, produced by elongation of the palate.

I trust in God & myself.

2.00

Port Gibson, September 25, 1848

Yesterday I was in the country. Of this record I had taken a page with me. My memory again was faithless, & I did not write this at the allotted time. May it be so no more. The knowledge which I amassed during the past week has been large & valuable. I have not yet reached the primal principles of mind; I still cherish divine hopes. God illumine my soul. Will less than omnipotence & omniscience satisfy me? I feel that every bow is becoming too light for me. I may though find my strength taxed in governing the embodied spirits of men now & their disembodied spirits hereafter. But when this is done, what satisfaction will there be? Vanity of Vanities, Power & knowledge are the only things which will satiate me.

Port Gibson, October 1, 1848

The intellectual principles, which I have developed, I wish now to apply practically. My eyes prevent anything more than an occasional glance at the page, the treatment prescribed for my throat renders imprudent any protracted exercise of my voice. I trust in Destiny and await my time. My Constitution imperiously exacts frequent physical exertion. This loss of time I regret. I yearn to be pure spirit, unclogged, untiring, & undecaying. If I could retain the uses of the senses, I would be willing to resign their pleasures rather than be encumbered with their dull pangs & unavoidable inconveniences.

I have commenced to investigate the principles of Electioneering and the art of Popularity.

I confide in Providence & myself.

Port Gibson, October 8, 1848

If we fear neither death, carnal pain or eternal punishment, o[u]r conduct will be influenced by duty and desire only. The opinions of others do not necessarily control our actions. To me, their opinions are more to be desired than death & eternal punishment are to be feared.

If there is a Destiny, let it lead me on.

(1.60)

Port Gibson, October 15, 1848

The past week has brought the customary increase of knowledge. I have felt some emotions of a nature almost too strong to suffer frequent repetition. My eyes seem to improve in strength.

I am accustomed to classify one set of synonymes & remark a resemblance — a comparison, observe & memorize a generalization — every day. This I usually do when I walk before breakfast. I rise early, am now in good health, except an occasional aching in the chest. This however is very slight. Every night except Sunday night, I exercise in gesture. This has been my custom for several months.

I daily become satisfied with existence. To me annihilation is not terrible. The pleasures of a God would afford me but little dignified complacency. I feel mournfully assured that the joys of heaven — the desires expanded, refined, and gratified, would upon a calm reflection bring me not much for which I would love to continue existence. To me, power & fame are almost the only things which invite me from a yearning after annihilation. But when omnipotence is attained, how insufficient the possession.

II.60.

Port Gibson, October 22, 1848

Like the sea-bird which rides upon the storm & is pleased at the roar of the angry ocean, I feel a fierce delight in whatever excites. Even the remembrance of a stirring incident makes my spirit glow.

A latent consciousness that excitement is essential to a consummate orator sometimes steals upon me and extenuates any excess of noble pleasure. Let my follies be attributed to the love of excitement.

.10.

Port Gibson, October 29, 1848

A committee of Claiborne Division No 23 of the Sons of Temperance have invited me to deliver an address on the occasion of the celebration of their anniversary of the division, on the 19th of November next. I accepted the invitation last monday, and have been assiduously engaged in preparing the address. May God aid me. I have already begun to apply the principles of my philosophy to composition. My eyes are bad.

$25.80

Port Gibson, November 5, 1848

A slight illness yesterday, directed my thoughts towards death & heaven. Would I exchange my soul for the World? Can I prove the existence of the Deity, or the immortality of the soul? Do I fear death? Since it cannot be averted, it is unwise to fear. If I become a Christian, will I not have to abandon the earthly destiny which I have appointed for myself?

.10

Port Gibson, November 12, 1848

I still burn with the passion for power-glory. Is this desire becoming unquenchable? Can it be allayed on earth? Or does it proclaim my spirits immortality, and animate me to walk boldly through the valley of the shadow of death, and gratify it among angels and demons? Alas can the world satisfy me? When I have possessed all which here on earth can be obtained will not my aims still fly higher & wider? When my soul has winged her way to the Mountain-tops, will she not then pine for the thunders home, the ether, the void, the stars?

On next saturday I deliver an address before Claiborne Division of the Sons of Temperance. My God, My Father, My Destiny let me not fail. This is the only address in which my mind has displayed any of the ability which it possesses, in which I have felt my mastery over my powers, in which the production has to any full extent answered to the will—I may not succeed. At all events my mind is too firm-set to despond or be disappointed. If I succeed, let not success impair my energy.

It has passed through my mind to write a work on Mental Philosophy.

Port Gibson, November 16, 1848

It has this evening occurred to me that the chief aim of my life shall be to unite the great powers of the earth in one Republic, to abolish slavery, and to reform the system of human laws and human philosophy.

God the Father, God the Holy Ghost, God the Son, aid me.

At my Mother's house, Thursday.

Port Gibson, November 19, 1848

My emotions have been agonizing and Sublime. I have marked out the out-lines of what will probably be my future course. I *will not* doubt of success. My soul enlarges; I grow melancholy, fearless and charitable. In my unseen medi-tations, tears flow freely to my eyes. If there is a God, I trust in him and feel that he dwells within my soul and incites me to my destiny. If there is not a God, my proud mind trusts to its own power here and hereafter. If I die young and my soul is as I believe immortal, it will be but a change of the stage on which & actors with whom I am to play an unparalleled part. I do not desire life, nor fear death. I live prepared for every emergency—for I fear neither death nor all the eternal punishments which my Father will inflict on me, his child, his instrument.

New Orleans, November 26, 1848

I left Port Gibson last Wednesday. I remained a short time in Grand Gulf. On Saturday the 25th ult. I arrived in New Orleans. The anniversary address before the Sons of Temperance, which I was to have delivered on Saturday, the 18th ult. was postponed until the Succeeding Tuesday.

The address was then delivered. It will form an epoch in my oratorical life. The principles of Delivery and to a certain extent of composition, which during the Summer I had developed, I then endeavored to exhibit. Tears, I was told, flowed freely from the Audience. The result of the Effort was encouraging. But let not success abate my vigor in the prosecution of my high aims. The Address will by request of the Division be published. I have continued my study of Cicero on the character of the Orator and concluded the reading of Milman's tragedy *Fazio*.[22] I expect to commence the study of Reasoning & Wit. I will first take up the consideration of Reasoning. I commenced last Spring,

I think, Whately's *Logic*. I discontinued it that my mind might be free from prejudice and that I myself might originate a Logic. The past Summer has, to me, been one of inconceivable benefit. The suspension of my reading, on account of my eyes, gave me leisure to meditate. I studied oratory, mind, men — refined my observation, improved my conversational talent, and deduced rules for thought and reading.

God help me.

9.30

New Orleans, December 3, 1848

This has been a week of severe but pleasant toil. By the advice of Mr. Durant, I am glancing cursorily over the "Madison Papers."[23] In the mornings, I study alternately Cicero on the Character of an Orator, and Gibbons Rome. My reading has constant reference [to] the objects of life. Whately's *Logic*, the reading of which I suspended because I desired to make some previous investigations, I have again begun to study. This study is a portion of my nocturnal labor. I daily study without a teacher a short lesson in the French language. These daily studies are I think not too numerous to distract my mind or consume Time otherwise than profitably. That part of a mental philosophy which relates to the emotions & moral feeling contains the chief impediments to my progress in my investigations of mind.

3.60.

New Orleans, December 10, 1848

During the past week, I progressed steadily in my studies. My eyes have not been much affected since I commenced the perusal of the Madison Papers. Day by day, I become more discontented with life. Would I be satisfied with heaven? I fear that I am displeased with the powers of the human soul. If its moral & intellectual attributes were expanded into perfection and possessed with omnipotence & eternity would I be willing to support life?

God help me.

.60

New Orleans, December 17, 1848

I finished the "Madison Papers," and on last Thursday commenced the study of Story, *On the Constitution*.[24] I have finished the perusal of Cicero on the Character of an Orator. I have commenced Whately's *Rhetoric*.[25] In Gibbon's Rome, I progress slowly. I progress slowly but profitably. Siddons on Gesture,[26] & Rush on the Voice,[27] which I have at hand, I expect to read. After

Whately's, my next work upon Rhetoric will, I think, be Campbell's. My investigations of Mind, will I hope, be ere long, perfected. I regret that I have no suitable place in which to exercise my voice.

I confide in God.

4.57

New Orleans, December 24, 1848

On last Thursday week, I commenced Story's *Commentaries on the Constitution.* Yesterday I had a slight attack of Asiatic Cholera. I am now recovered. What influence is this terrible pestilence to have on my destiny? O Glory, O Love, O Death!

The nature of the organization of Society is attracting my attention.

Why am I averse to being a practical lawyer? It is said that if all would labor in production, four hours in every day, the remaining portion of the day could be spent as desire prompted. I have a longing to cultivate with my own hands a "few paternal acres" for this little part of the day, and then be free.

I trust in God.

.20

New Orleans, December 31, 1848

This is the last night of the year. I need not now review. It has been a year the most important of my life. In it, I have fixed schemes, which will be the labor of my earthly existence, and which can never be changed except to be magnified; I have been thrilled with emotions, wild, grand, melting, sweet, humiliating, and terrible; I have explored the principles of the Philosophy of mind; added to my knowledge, classified and improved it. I have prosecuted my study of human nature, and from practice, developed general principles; I have acquired a confidence in my soul which exalts me above fear, pleasure or agony, and makes me reckless of the dangers of hell or felicities of Paradise; I have confirmed my belief in a God who is to make me the greatest mortal man that ever was.

In regard to the coming year, I expect to prosecute my study of the Law, with the view of obtaining a license to practice on my arriving at my Majority; I expect to go on to perfection in the study of Oratory; I expect to investigate the principles of Society, and of mind.

O God Omnipotent and Omnipresent, who hast inspired the great and Wise of every Nation, who for inscrutable purposes, enlarged the souls of Alexander, Caesar, and Bonaparte, Demosthenes & Cicero, of Washington, of Aristotle and Bacon, display in me a wisdom, power, and goodness, which shall surpass all their divine qualities; Concentrate your ever-present omnipotence into my soul, and let Us beatify Mankind; when death carries to your bosom your *slave* child, let me then—O my soul perish, for what has Life, Infinity, Eternity, Deity, worthy of existence?

.50

New Orleans, January 7, 1849

This year has begun in happiness. I still burn with the same passion, which has made my life a labor and a pleasure.

Under the direction of Thomas J. Durant, I continue my law studies. I board and lodge at the house of my Uncle—Doctor Wm B. Lindsay.

Before proceeding to the office, I study, alternately Gibbon's Rome, and Whately's *Logic*. After returning, I study for a few minutes before dining, Shakespeare; after dining, a little French—the law or logic. At night, I continue my investigations of mind, study, and write. Before retiring, I practice an exercise in Gesticulation, after retiring I pray, and then resign myself to thought. My nightly Prayer is, "Let me be the greatest mortal man that ever was,"—mortal, because I esteem Jesus Christ the Son of God. I rise about Sunrise. My health is now good; my eyes are, I think, stronger, but still admonish me to be a[s] temperate [as] possible in Study. The coming year will I think be one of preparation, rather than Action. If there is a Providence, I feel that it will lead me to Glory.

New Orleans, January 14, 1849

During the past week, I have seen Hackett[28] perform Falstaff in "The Merry Wives of Windsor" & Booth,[29] Richard the third. More & more deeply am I impressed with the power of Action, voice, and expression.

I pine for something to try the powers of my soul. But I see little worthy of grasping, nothing of sufficient magnitude to demand my exertion. I am dissatisfied with the impotence of the Universe. Within me stir powers which seem omnipotent. Are they? But what can omnipotence conceive, at the conception of which my mind does not grow weary? Oh, Oh! Let me not be compelled to live forever. Let me forever sleep and dream not.

New Orleans, January 21, 1849

I have finished the reading of Story's *Commentaries* & Whately's *Logic*. I concluded the perusal of the *Logic* on the 17th last. I expect to continue the Study of it.

I am now studying Whately's *Rhetoric*. My Oratorical Classification, I have nearly accomplished. In my Scrap-book will be found a copy of the Address which I delivered at Port Gibson, Mississippi on the occasion of the celebration of the first Anniversary of Claiborn Division No 23 of the Sons of Temperance. It was published by the Division.

My contempt for human knowledge is daily increasing. I think I discover a necessity for a Reformation in [the] existing system of acquiring Truth. Bacon reformed the System of Aristotle; is Bacon perfect?

In the connexion between words and ideas, I think I discover an explanation of Habit & Logic.

Sublimity depends upon Quantity; Beauty perhaps upon Resemblance.

Let this be always borne in mind that all knowledge is mental.

Are not four of the Senses, Modifications of the Sense of Touch? Are not the eye, ear, nostril, tongue, nerves of Touch adapted to Light, Atmosphere, Odorous and Sapid particles?

My eyes now are not as weak as they have been. Next week, I expect [to] commence the Analysis of Cicero's Oration for Milo.

New Orleans, January 28, 1849

I grow wearied with hopes, memories & imaginings, weary of existence. My weariness changes to impatience, impatience to ambition, till my frame quivers with passions which find no vent. I fear to yield to the pursuit of knowledge all my powers. My frame would soon sink beneath the labor, and eyes go out in blindness or death. Why do I not resign to the fascinations of the Alluring Enchantress and follow her wherever the Almighty Mind mingles with matter? I feel the impotence of a Clay-clad soul. Let me shuffle off this mortal coil and burst forth into the unpenetrated regions of Space where God dwells in solitude, and rush around the Circuit Infinety. Am I a man, an angel, God, Devil. Is there a God, or a Devil? Why then do I not fear & shrink from, O, I feel like I could drive Satan from Hell. Down, down, thoughts, I am weary, O God let me die.

On the 27th last, I finished Whately's *Rhetoric*. On the next day, I began, Henry Siddons on *Gesture*. I am now reading Blackstones *Commentaries*.

New Orleans, February 4, 1849

I have finished the reading of H. Siddon's Work on *Gesture*, and commenced Doctor Rush on the *Human Voice*. I am reviewing Logic & Cicero on the Orator. I study King Lear & the oration for Milo.

I have commenced my exercises in Composition. I will probably write upon the Retrospective, Immediate, & Prospective Emotions, the Intellectual States

& Senses, as laid down by Doctor Thomas Brown in his Mental Philosophy.

I read Dyers "Grongar Hill."[30] Life grows weary. I would find Something immense enough to expand my soul. Since turning in upon myself & Studying Mind, I can find no theories which I could not have invented, no beauties of Speech which I could not have created, or discovered, no truths which I could not have developed. And this, this wearies me. My only hope of life is in Action; else must I explore that undiscovered country from which no traveler returns.

New Orleans, February 11, 1849

On last Tuesday, I commenced Kent's *Commentaries*.[31] When I have leisure, I am in the evening accustomed to compose.

Life—thought is to me become a confinement. All combinations of reasoning, all emotions, regrets, wonders, and desires have been tried, but bring no newness. Would that I could be amazed. The elemental principles of the human Soul are too few. When they are known, their combinations are known; thenceforth, alas, all is weary, Stale & flat. I am cabined, cribbed, confined. O let me be annihilated if Save pain & pleasure, nothing but Space, Time, Resemblance & Quantity are to Surround my intellect. Can I not dash down these bars? Is there not in the boundlessness of the Spiritual realm, Some undiscovered continent to which I can Sail? O God, O God, I pine for the apathy of obstruction.

My Soul is drowned in the current of thought.

New Orleans, February 18, 1849

If death is sleep, then I am sleepy.

During the week, I have seen the tragedian, Macready[32] perform. I have finished the reading of Cicero's Oration for Milo.[33]

New Orleans, February 25, 1849

O God, O God, I grow childish with passion. O Ambition, O Frenzy, My hand clenches, my brow knits, I groan in Spirit. The name of a great man, an allusion to glory, makes my heart Sink and blood flow back until I almost faint. Would I were a Shepherd boy, Remote from the busy haunts of men. I would walk beside Still Waters, or look tearfully on the landscape. O burst my heart, or cease to swell, I am choked. But there is no loved breast on which I can resign myself. The last hope is gone. Heroes' Souls, if you can Sympathize with the agony of the Aspirant, I beseech you—Away, Curse you, I will beseech none; I will suffer, suffer, aspire, Succeed or die.

New Orleans, March 4, 1849

This is the day of the month on which it is customary to inaugurate the President of the United States. When shall I be President?

I was invited to deliver an Address before the Sons of Temperance. The address was to have occurred last Friday at an open Meeting in Lafayette. A disappointment in regard to obtaining the church for the meeting postponed it, I suppose indefinitely.

I have thought of the delights of heaven, the energy which I might display in hell, & the mutations of human existence from desire on to realization; nothing seems to me so grateful as annihilation, or a dreamless sleep to wake—to wake—to wake and sleep again. I am homesick for the grave. Is this unhealthy phantasy, distempered imagination? Ah, no, no. I am a young, feeble, weary being. I am not, I am a power, a passion, a God. I can fight against Hell and all its devils. Woe is me, Woe is me.

New Orleans, March 11, 1849

On Thursday, I finished Kent's *Commentaries*. On Friday the 9th ult. I began Vattel's *Law of Nations*.[34] Daily I read from 125 to 180 pages of *Law*.

I have witnessed Mr. Macready's performances.

My hopes are becoming confirmed into confidence—certainty.

I converse but little; This from necessity, for at the office, I read; here, I read or think. I prefer female conversation, except when men can give me valued knowledge. From all, it is my rule to gain knowledge.

Let me take care that looks do not become more interesting than thought.

Weary, Weary, O Death where is thy sting?[35]

The Literature of the Scriptures, whenever I Study it, appears more noble.

New Orleans, March 18, 1849

I finished Vattels['] *Law of Nations* last week. On Thursday, I commenced Justinians Institutes. I have commenced *Hudibras*.[36] I wish to study Anatomy.

My faith in God—Destiny is confirmed. Yet I am impatient. The birth-day of my twentieth year approaches.

What Shall be done to heighten my fame during the coming year.

I think I could demonstrate the unity of the Senses by reducing them to touch or rather what Doctor Thomas Brown terms muscular feeling—the nerves. Shall I publish? Are not the eyes, ears, Seat of taste & smell, contrivances for exposing to the action of light, air, sapid & odorous particles, the nerves? Are not all the nerves—optic, auditory, olfactory, divisions of the nervous System, not differing from each other save in sensibility, if in that?

I regret that there is no place where I can exercise my voice. This exercise will I suppose be reserved for Port Gibson's Arpinum. Oh for the Attic Sea-shore and cave.

I converse but little.

When a limb of a body is Severed the remainder grows Stronger—larger; what other passion, what tender leaves of hope shall I strip from me?

During a few, brief days, a "change has come o'er the Spirit of my dream;"[37] I have lived sorrowing, bowed down, have felt that I am a man. No more, no more will the fresh feelings of childhood, even of youth fall on my soul; the desert feels not the dew. Before my time I am old; On my spirit are gray locks. But it needs no staff; would that its foot were in the grave. Towards the pilgrim years o'er which I must travel, I look wearily. Fain would I lay off my burden and lay me down here on the Wayside. Here could I sweetly sleep nor wish to wake or dream.

New Orleans, March 25, 1849

Read Alphonse De Lamartine's *Raphael*.[38] Finished Justinian's Institutes; commenced Pothier on *Obligations;*[39] finished the *Lady of the Lake;*[40] continued reading *Hudibras*.

On the 22nd of March 1849, I commenced my oratorical notebook. It is intended to consist of Several large volumes, to embrace all literature, Science & Arts. I wish to classify and note according to the system of my own mental philosophy. What philosophy can suggest all thoughts. But my project will, from necessity, be, at present, circumscribed. O Death, O God.

My father died when I was young. My brother-in-law Doctor B. W. Morehead soon after died. They are each buried in the Cemetery at Port Gibson Claiborne County Mississippi.

I fear. Why do I fear? My heart is heavy. I am become exhausted. A zepher would move me. Temper the wind—I have lived long enough. O break this paining Stillness of existence. Alas can it be. To the Sea-Sailor, the river waves are calmness. I, who am a mariner, am infinitude, can find no "exulting Sense, no pulse's maddening play"[41] upon the bounded ocean of this worldly existence.

New Orleans, April 1, 1849

During the last few days, I have been confined to bed. Where Sickness is not accompanied with active pain, it Seems to me a pleasure. The reading of *Hudibras* I have continued, and commenced that of *Romeo & Juliet*. When will the battle open? Weary, Weary, I grow weary of this long preparation. Is this life to be a prelude, proem, exoridum, prologue; let the play, poem hasten then to the "last Syllable." But I fear that this world will always appear to me as a vestibule. Where can I find a temple?

New Orleans, April 8, 1849

I have read Pothier on *Obligations*.

Linus Parker,[42] who under the direction of C. W. Hornor[43] (I believe), studied law in our office, has abandoned law and Commenced Theology. He studied law but a short time. For him, I predict a high career.

Although I have not commenced the Study of Social organization, it attracts my observation. Mr. Durant has, I think, adopted opinions favorable to Social reformation. Let it not be Supposed that he can, or any one, influence my opinions. Whenever truth is offered, I accept it. In every thing, *I* judge. It matters not who propounds.

Will ever any action be great enough to wake all my Soul. Alas what will drive away this languor? In knowledge was once my hope, now nothing seems new, original. I have lost—am dead to the emotion of novelty. I pine; for what, I know not. No woman has ever frowned on me. I am successful to weariness. Mour[n]ing and disappointment may have power to make me feel. If they cannot, then welcome the neve[r]-opening grave. Better non-entity, than mere entity; better the sunken wreck than endless calm. Am I walled by Resemblance, Quantity, Space and Time? Are there no new combinations of which I know not? O I am a prisoner for eternity. God look down on me. Why does the Shriek burst from me? Why do I stretch forth my hands to you? Do you, day by day, infinity after infinity thus endure, confined in the universe? Do you know, or Since the labor of knowing is irksome, are you able to know all combinations of matter? Can you know all combinations of ideas? Must we ever feed on the Same food, See the Same prospects, hear the Same elemental Sounds, Scent the same elemental odors. Where is the Cherub who can fly with me from this intellectual Confinement? You who for your first apostles Shook open the prison, I am yours.

Port Gibson, April 15, 1849

Last Thursday, I left New Orleans. Today I arrived at my native place—the residence of my Mother, brother, and sisters, Port Gibson, Mississippi. Why do the kind Gods make me So happy. I could bear any Wretchedness, but it is kept far from me. Are the evil days coming. The past and memory are unchanging. I Sought not happiness, and it came. I will not beg it to remain. Yet for what you have given; my Father, I thank you. Love my Mother, Sisters and brother.

If affliction must come, let me alone meet it. To them be kind, for the Sake of your child.

Port Gibson, April 22, 1849

Last Tuesday was my birthday. The Rubicon is past. I am a man. In another brief, brief year, I will have attained my majority. O how my Shuddering Soul draws back. O Time, O Death, O Glory, O Tears, O God. And I could die—die, smilingly and tearfully. I am weary weary, oppressed. Of the tree of knowledge, I have eaten too much fatal fruit; have I? It must not be. Alas why this pining for obstruction's apathy?

I commenced, last week, Greenleaf on *Evidence*[44] continued Page's *Geology*[45] and Dryden's *Eneid*.[46]

The Physician has told my brother that two years will terminate my life if I do not change my habits of Study. I am happy.

My brother is now a Merchant here. A few weeks ago, he purchased the store, chiefly dry goods of a firm of Port Gibson.

Port Gibson, April 29, 1849

My eyes are bad; health imperfect. I have commenced the improvement of my voice, daily exercising it. Since my birthday the 17th ult. I have nightly memorized passages of Shakespeare, and Spoken extemporaneously upon Subjects usually selected from the Bible. These, I expect to continue.

The *Eneid* & *Geology*, I have not neglected.

After my main meal, I am accustomed to compose for about three quarters of an hour. After this I read law, & take notes. I rise early, indulging from Six to Seven hours parsimonious Slumber.

O Glory. "How long O Lord, how long."[47]

I have not finished my investigations of music and mathematics. But I think I will be enabled to discover in each, the principles of "Resemblance and Quantity."

In my study of the philosophy of the human mind, I am prosperously progressing. An "Ultimum Organum."

I will perhaps publish when about twenty-five years old, April 29th 1848. Port Gibson Mississippi, U.S.A.

Port Gibson, May 6, 1849

On next Saturday, I am to deliver an Address before the Sons of Temperance, at Rocky Springs in this—Claiborne County. I received the invitation but last friday. I continue to memorize Shakspeare. The Speech I have written, concluding today. This however is but the first writing. I am accustomed to re-write until the eleventh hour.

During the past week, I have been Suffering a depression of the chest, which may terminate in a disease of the heart. Since my return to Port Gibson, I think, I have not during any day been perfectly well. In New Orleans, I hardly know how long the Promethean Spark would have burned. The physician limited my life to two years, without a partial abandonment of Study. But in Destiny my faith is too implicit. Nothing can snatch me from the great career.

Port Gibson, May 13, 1849

Yesterday, I delivered an address before the Sons of Temperance at Rocky Springs in this, Claiborne County. My health has not been good during the week. I was unwell when I began Speaking and omitted that part of the Speech which required the most energetic action.

Port Gibson, May 20, 1849

Health Still bad. Read no law during the past week; been Social from necessity; filled with pinings, filled with passions. I am tantalized. Before me; within the grasp of my pining Soul wave fruits of knowledge, the[y] touch my lips; I almost taste. But this hunger must not be appeased, Still must I wait, wherefore; wherefore, What ignorant Sin have I committed; what purpose fulfilled by that I thus must be punished? O God, O God; to die; to live, obstruction — Hell — angels — glory.

The address delivered at Rocky Springs characterized in the report of the editor, as "eloquent but brief."

Port Gibson, May 27, 1849

Days of vanity — days of disease. Alas that the precious links in the chain of my existence should be so corroded, when they should be transformed — transmuted into gold. But my Soul must leave the laboratory of knowledge where it made the hours golden. Alas, dull, leaden existence. Farewell the neighing Steed and the shrill trump. To me there is a truce, My God, My Mars — let the battle of life begin. For me too long the temple of Janus has been shut. Welcome this war, Come and with you bring, the "banner, and all quality, pride, pomp and circumstance,"[48] Or come Stern and simple as the contest of patriotic poverty against opulent despotism. Come, for I can be, will be more constant than Washington, more dazzling than Napoleon. But I would not be a valetudinary. Would there were some armor which the arrows of disease could not penetrate.

For the last few weeks, my reading has been irregular. I have not been well—an affection of the throat. Power—God.

Port Gibson, June 3, 1849

I fear to ask the day of the month. I groan when I remember it. Health not perfect, Eyes weak. I walk about seven miles before breakfast. Diet Spare.

Port Gibson, June 10, 1849

When I visited my dear friend Peter Alexander at his residence on Lake Concordia Louisiana, we happened to engage as we were often wont in a philosophical discussion. Between the adjacent cotton fields and the lake, there is a shady grove. Within this, upon a fallen tree, before the morning dews were fled, we Sat. In the neighborhood, a physician he said, had told him, that the Sense of taste was affirmed to identical with that of smell. This proposition disturbed me. I endeavored to confute it, But to myself my arguments were unsatisfactory. By resemblance, I applied the principle to the other Senses. Are they not all the same, adapted to light, air, unatomic contact?—I have finished Greenleaf on *Evidence*, and taken up Story on *Promissory Notes*.[49] When eyes & health permit, I read a hundred pages of law daily.

Port Gibson, June 18, 1849

This duty last night escaped my memory. Memory to me is more humiliating than death. But I must not Submit to its mortality, uncertainty. Can I not So contrive that remembrance Shall not fail? Otherwise I am less than the angels. Otherwise clay pervades this "distinguished link in beings endless chain."[50] On Friday, I concluded Story on *Promissory Notes*. I began on Saturday Chitty on *Bills*.[51] My health I promote by fast at dinner on Wednesday and rigidly Spare diet throughout the remainder of the week.

My life passes in the passionate quietude of Studious Preparation.

For about thirty days my throat has been So Sore as to interrupt materially extemporization and vocal exercise. God & our Glory—his—mine—! give me pause!

Port Gibson, June 23, 1849

The thought that in my, our, wills purposes, the Christian religion is to be preached by me has come from Heaven to my mind. It came as a conviction. I was returning from my vesper walk; I was gazing at the Sky; I was communing with *my* (O more than that)—my God. South of Port Gibson there is a little Stream. Between that and the town came the thought. On the road which crosses that Stream, and where it becomes a street, my mother lives.

Port Gibson, June 24, 1849

Finished Cowper's *Task*;[52] commenced Anatomy. I wish books, but am at present pecuniarily unable to procure them. When the necessity for them is absolute—consummated; then I will have them. Such is my faith in God, with other things, thus. Health, especially of eyes, precarious. Last night, I was for the first time appointed Secretary of a public meeting, and on a Committee of three to prepare toasts for the 4th July inst.

Port Gibson, July 1, 1849

Began on Tuesday evening last Story on *Partnership*;[53] finished it yesterday; glanced at Mineralogy; continued Geology; rose early, exercised, but not enough.

The reformation of Law I can effect by classification. The classifications would be founded on my *principles* of Mental philosophy. They would embrace in order to perfection every case & contingency which could occur. This would though vast & elaborate be clear. Read the life of Lord Bacon in the Edinburgh Encyclopedia.

P.S. This Scheme of Reformation of the Law has for some months been conceived.

Port Gibson, July 8, 1849

Commenced Smith's *Leading Cases*.[54] Commit Cowper on each Successive night, except the third. On the third Shakspeare, Meditate applying my philosophy of —— to Bills of Exchange.

In my childhood I think I was converted by the Holy Ghost. I may deceive my Soul, but this evening there came over it a clear firm recollection of Something which at the time of its occurrence, and at present, I think was the operation of Spirit of God. Often it was forgotten, often I Committed what Seemed Sin; Often like a magnet my Soul was compeled from its divine attraction. But it always trembled to its North again. Of the mind many are the emotions. He who would control must know the— The most I have known There are others—passions and gratifications, which I must experience. Some may Strictly call them Sinful; I feel that God will approve—not for their Sake but for thine and mine O Lord.

Port Gibson, July 15, 1849

On yesterday, finished Smith's *Leading Cases*. Tomorrow, I expect to begin *American Leading Cases*.[55]

I have commenced investigating the problem of Longitude. The conception occurred to me last night. Health not good & failing. Rise at little after four o'clock AM. But little exercise; will be compeled, I think to reform.

Port Gibson, July 22, 1849

On Friday last, I received from New Orleans, Bacon's Works. In the mornings, I read law. In the evenings, I read now Robertson's *Charles the 5th.*[56] I have finished Geology, and have sent for Davies' *Shades*[57]—and a Mineralogy. To Gibbon's *Rome* I will perhaps devote a week. Anatomy, I will perhaps continue after finishing "Charles 5th." Health good; eyes improved—Continued Longitude; directed my attention to the cause of animal heat. I think I discovered a resemblance between *chemical* & *mechanical* agency.

Motion is motion to me, the most inexplicable of phenomena. Its nature would perhaps explain to me the causes of all changes. The doctrine of atoms in connexion with motion occupies my attention. On these two, I think hang all the laws of nature. To me, there seems no necessity for chemical power. But I keep my [. . .] in unfeeling suspense.

P.S. I have left church, to record that my letters are, many of them in haste, and late in the watches of the night, when duties performed have permitted. Let this excuse their unrevised faults.

Port Gibson, July 29, 1849

On the 26th last, I read in the Edinburgh Encyclopedia, the life of Immanuel Kant.[58] I was filled with pride and wretchedness. I was proud that the philosophy of that divine mind was So like that System the result of my own young reflections which I vainly flattered myself to have been alone in developing. I was bitterly wretched to think that my Glory would be in part deprived of the praise of novelty.

By God, I will not despair. He will wrench asunder the bars which confine my Soul & liberate it, liberate it to wander far & wide and dwell on all things.

Port Gibson, August 5, 1849

Received Trimmer's *Geology & Mineralogy,*[59] & Davies' *Shades, Shadows and Linear Perspective.* Commenced *Shades & Shadows* & Macaulay's *History of England.*[60] Finished Robertson's *Charles 5th.* Continued my meditations on mind, Longitude, animal heat Heat, Light, & Gravitation. Does light proceed from the Sun? Is it not dependent upon a gaseous or other medium, as the atmosphere? Will not the passage of electricity as in lightning & Leyden jars; the explosion of a gun, the experiment of the air pump-gun, and flame illustrate this? Will not phosphorescent lights, the experiment of the diamond, admit such an explanation? The nature of flame occupies my attention. Is it not an atmospheric compression of the particles whose passage produces light? If thus, may it not be made a measure of atmospheric pressure, and the momentum and weight etc of atoms or compound atoms? Does gravitation as an independent force have an existence? Might it not be reduced to chemical or mechanical force? Is not chemical force identical with mechanical, or is there another which comprehends both?

Of knowledge, the Statistics of Science I feel my need. But present debility forbids application, Smother your longing Soul. I now read law in the evening only; in the morning literature, Arts, & Science.

P.S. Are not Light & Smell, as hearing, atmospheric? Are they chemical or mechanical or both in their affection of the Senses, or dependent on form?

Port Gibson, August 12, 1849

If I can secure the pecuniary means, I propose visiting during the next Summer Great Britain and the Continent of Europe.

Before arriving at my majority I cannot be admitted to the bar of New Orleans. On the 17th of April, I will be twenty-one years of age. Then I expect to pass my legal examination and about the 1st of May, to embark. My return, I have located about the 1st of the following year.

Will my Father direct this?

Wrong Small tubes or wire-gauze, flame will not pass. Flame is the atmospheric compression of certain particles? The greater the compression the greater the *density* of the flame. Finally it becomes so dense—which—viscid, as to make it impermeable through tubes. This, a reflection, but not thorough. I am doubting skeptical on Gravitation.

Finished *American Leading Cases*. Yesterday, I began Phillips on *Insurance*.[61] Eyes I think Stronger. Health worse. Obtaining some knowledge of Zoology from the Edinburg Encyclopedia. Still my throat is bad.

Port Gibson, August 19, 1849

Continued Anatomy, & Insurance, Commenced Exercises in Composition, on the Annexation of Canada to the U. States. In connexion with this, Study the invention and application of arguments. But on me, my thoughts rush so overpoweringly that the tardy pen becomes a weary medium of retaining them. Often when I attempt Composition, my body, arm, and pen tremble. Then the golden Stylus is a conductor too feeble. The electric Spark of thought convulses my frame, or bursts forth in uttered words. Then at the reflection of the limited nature of man's material means, I grow almost hopeless. Read in the

July number of the *Eclectic Magazine*[62] another article on the Organization of Labor. It contained an explanation of the Schemes of Fourier[63] & St. Simon.[64] Health unsettled. Throat still Sore & resisting remedies. This has restrained my vocal & gesticulatory exercises. Passions crush me. If I continue Study as I have, death is threatened me. If I intermit—Alas, Alas, death is welcome.

Port Gibson, August 26, 1849

"Days Steal on us, and steal from us."[65] I grow alarmed. The time of action approaches, O, why heaves my heart? The prelude is finishing; the Strain—the theme of life commences. I will not tremble. Boldly, freely, calmly I will pray; the world Shall listen and be pleased. But now I am unstrung—Disease makes discord.

Upon the nature of atoms—motion, mechanical & chemical action; my reflections become graver & more comprehensive. Does chemical differ from mechanical action? What, if not, are the consequences? Will not motion and the forms of atoms & their combinations produce all material phenomena? What is motion? Does it depend on Resemblance?

Port Gibson, September 2, 1849

Finished Phillips on *Insurance*. Yesterday commenced Abbot on *Shipping*.[66] At present, I read during the day, fifty pages of law. This in the morning. The remainder to Mineralogy chiefly. About Sunrise I bathe, and walk until breakfast. After breakfast compose; then law; then about an hour of reading on miscellaneous—general information. This occupies the morning. Having finished anatomy, I now study in the evening until five o'clock Trimmer's *Mineralogy & geology*. This done allows me leisure before night to ride out to the Mineral Springs adjoining Port Gibson. Night is allotted to reflection. But before retiring, commit to memory something from the poets, and something from the works of Belles-Lettres or physics.

Health bad; new diseases, eyes no better.

Port Gibson, September 9, 1849

Today, I finished an obituary of Miss Caroline Campbell. It is to be published in the next number of the Port Gibson *Herald and Correspondent*. On Monday commenced Stephen's *Pleading*.[67] Health bad.

Port Gibson, September 16, 1849

Finished Abbot on *Shipping*, & Stephen's *Pleading*. Commenced Conkling's *Treatise*[68] and the review, with notes of Greenleaf's *Evidence* & Story on *Promis-*

sory notes. Finished *Cadenus & Vanessa*,[69] and Mathew Green's *Spleen*.[70] Delighted. Finished *Paradise Regained*; *Paradise Lost*, I read at College—Oakland. Continued Macaulay's *Hist of Eng*. Meditate devoting two weeks to Gibbon's *Decline & Fall of Rom. Empire*. When I have concluded that, Rollin,[71] Bancroft's expected Continuation of *Hist of U. States*, & Hallam's *Hist of Literature*,[72] my historical course will be nearly completed. Eyes & health for a few weeks have Sustained. But every day, I say "I am ready to die." The annexation of Cuba & Canada attract my attention. My fancies now dwell more on war. I believe that I am the darling of Earth, of God.

Port Gibson, September 23, 1849

Finished Conkling's *Treatise*. Began the *Civil Code of Louisiana*. I have thought that I would direct chiefly towards Criminal Cases, my early practice.

A Sea-voyage has been recommended by my physician Dr. Robt. W. Harper. Mr Durant, my preceptor, is his Son-in-law. His character is such that when I have been Sceptical & soul-sick at human dishonesty & unfaithfulness, it almost alone, preserved me from despairing of my species. For I could not know his esoteric history and believe all men villains. Commenced a poem entitled "Cider" by Phillips. A[t] night I memorize alternately from Shakspeare, Cowper & now *Eloisa to Abelard*[73] and after this, a principle or two in *Logic* by Whately. I wish my body was brass, for my powers of body bear no proportion to my schemes of study. But I trust in God. He will consummate all.

The obituary, I suppressed.

Port Gibson, September 30, 1849

Began Bullard & Curry's *Digest*.[74]

Port Gibson, October 7, 1849

Received Carpenter's *Physiology*.[75] If it will conduce to my philosophical schemes, I will, If I have leisure, take a full course of medicine. It would give pleasure, but one of my chief teachings is to disregard pleasure. I hope it will consist with my glory-duty, nosology & pathology. I will perhaps endeavor to understand.

Daily, momentarily, I am in communion with God. I have trained to flattering acuteness, my observation. In my series of thoughts, when it discovers a prejudice, I immediately refer it, with tacit prayer that he will remove it, to God. Thus, I, in a manner, pray without ceasing. This Summer, I first remarked in myself a Strong love of children—infants. The sight of a beautiful babe opened this sealed fountain. I fondle it in my arms, press, kiss, Sigh over it. Such is the nature of the passion—the intercourse between myself & God.

Port Gibson, October 14, 1849

Twenty-one years from eighty leave 59 years. Three-hundred-&-sixty-five & one-fourth days multiplied by 59 produces, 21,549¾ days. The eightieth year, I fix as the limit of my life, because aims cannot, I think, be until then fulfilled. Long before, they *may be* realized. Already I am grown weary of earthly existence. Finished. Finished *Civil Code of Louisiana, Code of Practice* and Bullard & Curry's *Digest*. With the exception of *Decisions of La Sup Court*, this completes the list of law-books which Mr Durant sketched for my summer reading. These decisions are not in our Libraries. Until I depart for N Orleans I shall continue my scientific & historical & poetic reading, with law notes and composition. Yesterday commenced an essay or exercise in which I am to reduce the dynamical department of music to melody. Commenced in Carpenter's *Physiology*, the Chapter on the senses with a view to reduce to touch all the five senses. Reading Gibbon's & Macaulay's Histories. Finished Swift on *Poetry*.[76] Memorizing at night before retiring; from the Minstrel, Shakespeare, & the Task.

Port Gibson, October 21, 1849

Finished the first two extant volumes of Macauley's *Hist of England*, Continued Gibbon's *Rome* & Exercises in Composition, Commenced Somerville's *Chase*.[77] I have not yet attained the health of my throat. This during the Summer has interrupted my exercises in vocalization, extemporization & gesticulation. But what thus, I have lost, has been repaid in metaphysical discoveries & habits. Nightly however, I continue before retiring the oratorical gestures & the exercise of my chest. Previously to this I memorize from poetry & Science. The notes on Greenleaf's *Evidence*, I have nearly completed. Now, I am accustomed to observe every State of my mind; & generally to refer to its cause, effect, & resemblance. During each of the weekdays, I analyze something, compose something, define something, form synonyms; frame or remember a miscellaneous & law classification; produce & witticism; & discover resemblances. All this, I usually accomplish in my morning walk. I propose to make the whole circuit of human knowledge.

Port Gibson, October 29, 1849

Last night, I forgot this accustomed Oct 29th 1849 duty. It reminds me of the feebleness of human minds. Commenced the 2nd volume of the *Decline*

& Fall of the Roman Empire. Commenced Pollock's *Course of Time.*[78] Finished notes of Evidence. Analyzed some of the elemental principles of mechanics. This, with a view to the nature of motion. Began the chapter in Carpenter's *Physiology* on the Senses. This with a view to reducing the number of Senses. I now Suppose that touch or contact is the only sense. The organs, the nerves may or may not be different from each other. If different, the difference probably is their adaptation to the various molecules whether of light, odor, or atmosphere which affect them. Health bad. Suspended the readings at night, in which for some time I have indulged.

Port Gibson, November 4, 1849

Commenced the *Course of Time*, Trivia, & Young's *Night Thoughts.*[79] Finished on Friday the 2nd volume of *History of Rome*, & the *Chase* by Somerville.

Health, precarious. I expect to arrive, on Sunday next in New Orleans, & am to have a week's vacation.

New Orleans, November 13, 1849

Memory again postponed this until this morning. Left Port Gibson on Friday last; arrived in New Orleans yesterday. Under Mr. T. J. Durant, I am to continue my law Studies. Again I am domesticated with my Aunt & Uncle Doctor Wm B Lindsay.

The past Summer has been one of importance. The disease of my throat restrained me in oratory from consuming in practical exercise, much time. That time which was allotted to this duty was occupied in thought & the accumulation was Systematic & large, but painfully limited by ill-health. In mental philosophy, I have made liberal progress. This Science is the basis of all my improvement. During the winter, I hope to develope its primary principles. In politics, my principles have gradually assumed shape. But are still not as definite as they should be. Of *Socialism*, I have obtained a knowledge, but no means perfect.

New Orleans, November 18, 1849

Finished Story on *Agency*[80] on Saturday morning. On Wednesday, I began it. Commenced Barton's *Suit in Chancery*,[81] the *Endymion*[82] of Keats. Finished Isaiah, Commenced Reese's *Vegetable Physiology.*[83]

Before breakfast, I compose; after breakfast, study a little in *Vegetable Physiology*. Then to the office. There I study law. This from 9 o'clock AM. to 2 PM. Returning home, I glance into a French book; then until dinner, which in about a quarter of an hour, occurs, read Shakspeare. After dinner, read Young's *Night*

Thoughts, and Carpenter's *Human Physiology*. At candle-light, review law. Before retiring, memorized a classification in Law & Political Economy; from Logic, & my Law Note Book, learn something; memorize a passage from the poets and exercise in oratorical gesticulation. While walking, I anal[y]ze, classify, combine, & study the principles of conversation, discover a rhetorical resemblance & synonyms. At a disengaged interval, exercise in facial expression. Thoughts of writing a tragedy—"The Aspirant." Thoughts of improving the process of setting (or composing?) type.

New Orleans, November 25, 1849

Finished Young's *Night Thoughts*. Began Keat's *Endymion* Continued *Vegetable Physiology*, & 3rd volume of Gibbon's *Rome*. All sensation results from touch. I will probably endeavor to prove that there is no motion without contact; that there is no gravitation; that the gravitating universe is filled with atoms throughout; that whatever power communicated to the planets, motion, is the power or motion which causes every succeeding material change; that light and heat are atoms in rapid motion; that electricity and kindred substances are also atoms in rapid motion; that atoms are indivisible, and perhaps of regular shapes; that these shapes are discoverable & all their combinations; that quantity is the same with Resemblance; that Resemblance, Coexistence & the principle involved in the notion of motion are the fundamental principles of mind; that in society that system which produces most abundantly & distributes most justly should be adopted at the proper time; that a republican government is more philanthropic when it covers the unit of territory; that this unit depends on locomotion.

New Orleans, December 2, 1849

Finished Jeremy's *Law of Carriers*, Story on *Bailments*, Keats' *Endymion*, *Hyperion*, *Eve of St Agnes*, Shelley's *Queen Mab*, & *Adonais*, & *Vegetable Physiology*, & *Midsummer Nights Dream*, Bulwer's *Money*, & Commenced Story on *Bills of Exchange*, Shakspeare's *Henry Eighth*, & *Pilgrim's Progress*.[84]

Want money to purchase books. Throat still diseased; eyes weaker. Thoughts of life, death & immortality, Unbidden sighs for annihilation. "I 'gin to grow aweary of the sun."[85]

I am developing; consummating my system of mental philosophy. Its distinguishing feature will, I think, be the method of conducting induction. Another feature will perhaps be its refutation of the system which refers ideas to sensation as one source. Another, the mode of generating all ideas & their combinations; establishing plain principles by which all science, inventions &

discoveries may be educed, & style be reduced to mechanical science; The perfection of the process of classification & its application to Law will be another feature.

New Orleans, December 9, 1849

Finished Story on *Bills of Exchange*. Commenced Story on *The Conflict of Laws*.[86] Finished *Vivian Grey*.[87] Through this, I in two nights & evenings, glanced, Commenced Shakspeare's *Henry Eighth*, & Shelley's *Prometheus*, Brougham's Review of Cuvier's Researches. "I 'gin to grow aweary of the Sun." I wish to shake off a weight, to—to is it?—to disembody. No! no! to sleep, and, and; Oh, weary, weary. "Much study is a weariness of the flesh." Without books; and yet, without books, I the drunkard of knowledge would succumb. The cup of knowledge has given me its *mania a potu*.[88] Would that I could quaff, quaff and quaffing, die. How many are the suicides whom the world does not know? I feel the tempting.

New Orleans, December 16, 1849

Finished Story's *Conflict of Laws*, the *Dunciad*,[89] & Brougham on Cuvier's *Researches on Fossil Osteology*. Began Curtis's *Rights & Duties of Merchant Seamen*,[90] Brougham on *Instinct*,[91] & the *Odyssey*, & *Troilus & Cressida*. After licensing in April next, I wish to return to my Mother's roof in Mississippi. There in the study of literature and science chiefly, and law incidentally; in investigating & practising the principles of composition & eloquence, above all of mental philosophy; I wish to consume the Summer & a portion of the Fall. Of the importance of time, earthly time, I am aware; but it seems to me that prudence, a liberal view of the brief, temporal prospect allotted me, would sanction such a use of a half-year, of his life who will have few half-years to pass. "I 'gin to be aweary of the Sun." Particularly studied the principles of invention. Perfection in this will be one of the noblest rewards of my metaphysical investigations.

New Orleans, December 23, 1849

Read about 113 pages of Kant's *Critic of Pure Reason*, translated, & glanced into Analysis of it by the translator. Commenced Angell & Ames on *Corporations*.[92] Life has no novelty.

Sep. 24th 1849

"Does not this cool weather revive you? Another winter is approaching and I am not permitted to indulge the hope of seeing you. I hear I have no claims to your love now, does one of your ——— acquaintances inform rightly when he says you have forgotten me? We promised to be very incredulous about *some things* we might hear, and I have been true to my word, for I have ever been true to my ~~word~~,—some who do not excuse your ———e and are not willing to disbelieve unpleasant reports."

Dec 23rd 1849.

April 23rd 1847.
  "C— Henry you promised to send me your *speech*. I have been expecting it every mail. I would like to read it very much. I thought of you a great deal the 1st of April. I pretended to study, but my lessons were not very perfect; but, I have been a very good girl lately. I am bad *sometimes*, yet I *will* promise to *behave* very well, if you will promise to come to—see me ——— and when far away think of her who loves you."[93]

New Orleans, December 30, 1849
  Time, Death, Eternity, God—O God, stay the rolling year. Hold fast this planet. What gives it thus to so quickly bring us to the terminus? Is it affrighted? Are the coursers of the heavens' azure prairie flying in some wild stampede? Alas the once lazy pacing earth, the slow jade that bore its worthless burden, had joined the crowded race. Like Sacs and Pawness the days chase them. How they lift their heads; how toss their manes. Now their swift feet cleave the wind, Towards the abyss of eternity they rush. The chasm yawns, the relentless drivers press. Earth will leap from the crumbling verge of Time, or hurl from its back, us its miserable riders. Another year *short*, hurried space is past. We will leave it behind. From our sight, other objects intervening will hide it. Its scenes at which we glanced in passing begin to lessen. We see but their tops. Into a new *and* unknown country we have burst. O Mazeppa, you were never bound to such a steed as hurries me onward.[94] Finished Angell & Ames on *Corporations*, & Curtis' *R. & Duties of Merch. Seamen*.

New Orleans, January 6, 1850
  Began with notes, the review of Pothier on *Obligations* & the *Code of Practice of Louisiana*.[95] From 1st Jan to April, when I am to be examined for licensing; I am exclusively to study law. But before dining, during a few minutes I read Shakespeare; and before breakfasting I compose. Before retiring, I as usual, execute a series of gestures, and for the strengthening of my chest a dumb-bell motion. In connexion with these, I glance in Logic, Horace, Zoology, vege-

table Physiology, Political Economy, Ethics, and Blackstone's *Commentaries*, at some classification or passage from the poets. These are my Secular nocturnal duties. On Sunday, I read, or the Bible, several pages, think of Death, & God, and rest.

My cousin, William Preston Hughes, attends in this City, the Lectures of the Medical School. He possesses powers of which he is ignorant. Began an investigation of curves. While nothing differs from something; there can be no squaring of curves, nor conceivable curves.

New Orleans, January 13, 1850

With notes on Pothier on *Obligations*, continued the Law-review. Attended Professor Mitchell's Lyceum lectures on Astronomy. Managed to glance into Lord Brougham's Sketches of Eminent men.[96] To read the lives of great men agonizes me.

O Life, O Love, O Glory, knowledge, Death, God, Eternity.

To me, hope prophesies fancy dreams, faith enchants, my Soul! "to your prophets and diviners, your dreamers enchanters & Sorcerers;" shall I "hearken" (Jeremiah). To the whispers of fancy, I have listened with credulity. And I *will* listen. I will—will I—O, vain boasting. Let not words, flighty purposes escape and the deed does not accompany.

Commenced reforming the present System of Law. I have dated my Analyses and Propositions.

New Orleans, January 20, 1850

I can, I think reduce to one principle, the notions of time & motion.

My first amatory engagement is dissolved. "T'was bright, t'was heavenly, but tis past."[97] I dissolved it. There now remains one avowed engagement, and two tacit ones. Since previous by a few months to my eighteenth birthday, I have never been disengaged. But I have conscientiously acted. These engagements, that is, the latter ones, I contracted with a view of oratory, human nature, that is a knowledge of it, and composition. Of my life, blot out any other portion, but not that, not that, no—no—not that. It has been my liquor, cards, Otherwise I never gambled, never drank. For me, there was some excuse, some palliation to be pleaded. I never trifled, was never rejected. Woman, dear, dearest woman, if the exertions of the loving Aspirant can accomplish it, you shall be advanced towards, shall attain your deserved dignity. "How weary, stale, flat & unprofitable, seem to me all the uses of this world."[98] Purchased Locke's Essays, preliminarily to the Summers study.

New Orleans, January 20, 1850

The review, I continued. On saturday evening, ambition—the passions of the aspirant so overcome me that I could not read. I laid on my bed, and agonized.

On Sunday, I read several pages of the Holy Bible, and think of God and death. In the art of conversation and popularity, steadily progressing. My throat is, I think much improved; eyes perhaps growing more short-sighted. Some thoughts of writing a comedy in connexion with my study of wit. This study, I daily (Sunday excepted) prosecute.

I have, I think, this week arrived at the long-sought identity of time and motion. Time is the principle of succession—I think of no better word, applied to ideas; the other or motion is the same principle applied to matter, (or space?), one is "internal," the other, "external." This according to Doctor Thomas Brown's classification. To study gesture. Saw Murdock[99] perform.

New Orleans, February 3, 1850

Continued the Law-review, with notes. Mediocre fame is not worthy the labor. I have lately reflected—painfully revolved the nature of Glory. "Great actions having excited a temporary admiration often pass away and are forgotten," because they leave no lasting results behind. My soul, I call on you & all that is within me. To my help, impassioned Fancy come. In your wildness with "eye quick glancing from heaven to earth,"[100] you I envoke. What is the most daring, wise, beneficient godlike—no, no, that is not enough.

How can I be the greatest mortal man that can be? What Scheme can you point out? I would I were a Soldier; but no, a statesman, for he commands, the Soldier obeys. A Statesman: He commands, but never executes. Then the flighty purpose would be ne'er o'ertook. I would be statesman & soldier, master & servant: a despot. Almighty God let me be a despot. A kind one; I would be a kind one. None should be slaves. Earth, we would republicanize & unite in one government. O let me die, Loose; From this torture loose me.

New Orleans, February 10, 1850

Continued the Law-review.

My ambition has become an agitation, my brow frowns, lips quiver, bosom heaves. Trifles suggest my nothingness, & others greatness. But I do not envy. What brings in others envy; brings in me more passionate exertion and severer criticism. She who watches me, believes beloved & rejected. I never where I set my amorous hopes was unsuccessful. But I love Glory, Power, Fame, Energy.

What is her name? She is my Soul's idol. To her, I, with a lover's hot devotion, kneel. She is my sweet. Romeo never more truly loved. I am her Antony. In her soft arms, on her fair bosom, beneath her warm eyes and balmy breath, I forget all joys & pains. To me, she is Cleopatra. But for her, I will not lose but gain a world. Come Caesar, Come Lepidus. Glory is mine, or death. Whose bosom, is the softer, I do not care. For soon or late, I will repose me there. I *would* the time was come, for I—.

New Orleans, February 17, 1850

On Monday, began Domat's *Civil Law.*[101] Days of passion, thoughts of God, Death, & vanity. Why over me, do they thus throng? Are others thus? If all are, then let us die. For if the Soul's conflicts are so outrageous; What when myriad others' souls are its enemies?

How delicious is calm! When the lake is unruffled is it ever more beautiful. If "there is no breath of air to stir the wave," the sea grows lovely. But the oer-wrought mind is never thus beautiful. Its unfathomable gulfs are ever beneath some moon & sun. Towards some equator or pole, its warm or cold streams are ceaselessly rushing. To it, the Eolian cave is forever opened, and zephyrs and tornados amble out or madly curvet & career.

New Orleans, February 24, 1850

Continued Domat's *Civil Law.* Saw the actress Miss Charlotte Cushman;[102] *was* benefited. When we subtract from life, which is but a series of thoughts & emotions, the time expended in necessary but valueless sensations; how short seems the remaining leisure, the intellectual states and feelings. Of this tene-ment of clay, I am weary. My Soul, my Minerva would leave its Parthenon, and adopt the universe.

The Consecration & Oath of Henry Hughes.

New Orleans, February 25, 1850

At night, between the hours of Seven and Eight.

Now my Father I consecrate myself to Glory. By our long loves; by your omnipotence, and omniscience; I swear it.

New Orleans, March 3, 1850

Yesterday, finished Domat's *Civil Law.* Last week, began Curtis' *Admiralty Digest.*[103]

My legal examination approximates. That I shall successfully pass it, I cherish a solemn faith. But no faith is absolute. If I should fail?—but I will not think of it. Yet if—if I should fail, Great God, my Father, help me. O furies. Let me first die. Let me—

Where are my books?

New Orleans, March 10, 1850

Began Betts *Admiralty Practice*[104] & in Russel on *Crimes*[105] finished the book on Evidence. My examination approaches; I am not afraid to die. If in that, I should fail: O do not blame me; of life, I am weary. Where the shady grove waves, the turtle coos, and violet breathes, how sweet would be repose, the gentle hillock fresh grass—and—and the offered flowers, the tear from Mother's eye. Alas it must not be. Off, seducing thoughts, or lead me through glory to the grave.

Saw Miss Cushman (Charlotte). From her, I learned.

New Orleans, March 17, 1850

Finished Curtis' *Admiralty Digest*, Reviewing *Louisiana Code* (Civil). Throat, still sore.

Am I heart-broken?

New Orleans, March 24, 1850

The force exerted by the magnetism of the Earth varies in different places. (See Olmsted's Natural Philosophy, Magnetism.) This force, arranges itself about the earth in isodynamic curves. These curves bear towards certain points of the Earth, a certain relation. By this relation these points are made magnetic Poles. These poles do not, with the extremities of the axis of the Earth or its geographical poles, coincide. If the magnetic & geographical poles are determinable & also the comparative magnetic intensity in different places, *Longitude* is determinable.

Throat still diseased. Continuing the Law-review. Sometimes sad; love; my eyes not "unused to the melting mood."[106]

New Orleans, March 31, 1850

Placed on the list of the Supreme Court of Louisiana, my name, as a candidate for admission to the Bar.

In the practice of the law, Mr Durant and Mr C. W. Hornor have, for some months been partners. In Washington City, Mr Durant has, during the whole of my instant residence here, that is since November, last, been detained. But in office, I was with Mr Hornor. To me, he has ever been kind, Who ever, otherwise. I know no one who has towards me a hostile feeling. Hereafter, hereafter, will it thus be? I *love* God, and care not.

That exhaustion, that debility, that nerveless want of energy, with which prating Age & frowning Pathology love to menace the intense Student; I—alas I never believed them—begin to suffer.

After the Summer's study & exercises, I would wish to visit Europe. From tomes, I would turn to "the books in the running brooks." Let, for me, the "tongues in trees" now prattle to garrul[it]y. The "sermons in stones,"[107] I would sit beneath the droppings of their sanctuary. To me they should be as Sherlock or Chalmers.

At the Law-Examination, if I should not succeed; down hideous, damned, execrable, treble-damned thought. But I will not be, God so tells me.

New Orleans, April 7, 1850

Successfully passed the Examining Committee of the Supreme Court of the State. On Friday last, the examination took place. Present Messrs Seghers, Grima, Elmore, Hennen, [. . .] and T. H. Clarke.—Messrs Roselius & Judge Watts, though I personally solicited them, were not in attendance.[108] Some questions, I missed. Tomorrow perhaps, I apply to the Supreme Court. Alas, for how long have I been in expectancy, College—faculties, committees. I am almost a freedman—libertinus. My emotions? let Fancy whose cheek is yet Hebe-smooth, imagine when her locks are silver-gray, what they were; are. Over them, let Age, "recubans sub tegmine fagi,"[109] rejuvenate. Over the 2nd volume of the *Caxtons*[110] I am now ambling. Throat still sore. Today, heard Mr Clapp preach. Flushed by the sermon, were flying thoughts that I would never do ought which I would after death & in Heaven desire undone. Electro-biology is exciting attention. It is offered as a curative agent. What the operator does to others sick, for instance, I have thought they might do to themselves—might direct to any portion of *their* bodies, this animal electricity. Thus they might cure themselves.

(Copy)

Mississippi River Steamer "Natchez No. 2," April 14, 1850

Yesterday, Saturday-evening, left New Orleans on the way to Port Gibson, Mississippi. There, I am, until Fall, to sojourn, in order to perfect myself in oratory, philosophy, politics, sciences & various learning. With me are my two sisters and—God.

Port Gibson, April 17, 1850

On this the 17th day of April 1850, I complete my twenty-first year. Through the Past, I have thus far, marshaled my forces. The Rhone, Forests and Alps are past. In the battle of my life, this day is the Rubicon. [I am] on its banks now. Now Ambition! Striding, the vigor of my Soul, a "courser of ethereal race," solemnly careers. Behind, are the provinces, where preparation has, I hope, made veteran my young sword. Before is [the] Rome of my Hopes. O Day, O Rubicon. I see Pharsalia; Earth—Pompey; hail. Caesar, my soul? your Genius, savour God now fills you. To conquer is given you. Death—how sweet—Alas, tears now; am I not more than Caesar!—death—is withheld.

On this "bank and shoal of Time"[111] let me review. And after, let all our troops on.

The omens are now my allies. "The blue sky is so cloudless, clear, and purely beautiful"; that Jove "alone is to be seen in heaven," the mocking-bird—dear Jenny Lind[112]—mingles with the black-bird's manlier note, her delicious throat.

As to Mental Philosophy, I have reduced to two classes its phenomena. The first class embraces to a certain extent the consideration according to the old system, of things in *space*. This would include rest as *part* of *abstraction*. The other class comprehends the principles of motion, analysis, contiguity, cause and effect, reasoning, judgment, memory, resemblance, quantity, contrast, change, invention & association. All notions are in the mind or are the mind—with the consequences. I have at present under consideration, the innateness of notions. Thus far I am disposed to think that *matter* is a part of the mind. A part of the mind. For my psychology, the eminent feature is that the simple mind may originate all thoughts, notions, conceptions, & their combinations. This proposition is to be the ground-work of one of my aims of life, to be entitled, the Ultimum Organum. Of another aim—the reformation of the system of law, it is also to be the basis. This reformation will consist among other things in *perfect* codification. There are few sciences with whose general principles, I am not now conversant. This Summer I shall perhaps complete the jeweled Circle.

Since graduating at Oakland College (Mississippi), I composed. For perhaps the last year, this has been almost diurnally though briefly regular. For the last year or thereabout, I have practiced gesture.

Before the judges & Committee of the Supreme Court of Louisiana, I successfully passed my examinations. For me, the Judges kindly suspended their rule & I was examined eight or ten days before my majority. I was about to leave the City. But they refused to let me be sworn in before attaining the full age. That I am a member of the invisible church, I—believe.

The Father and his Child; let their oaths be unbroken; the Creator & his Creature.

April 17, 1850

Evening In physics, I shall endeavor to demonstrate that all material changes can be produced by motion applied to atoms and their combinations, independently of chemical affinity, gravitation or any other force except "mechanical." This supposes matter to be impenetrable & to have form.

Light & heat do not *both* come from the sun; one is a meteoric consequence of the other.

My philosophy of the mind could now furnish all the Canons of proceeding to ascertain methods or a method of finding longitude.

Port Gibson, April 21, 1850

On the 17th, began *Elements of Zoology*, Story's *Equity*,[113] Getty's *Oratory*;[114] continued Gibbon's *History of Rome*. Began Rush on the voice. With it pleased, for by it I can illustrate the principles of my infant philosophy. On the 17th, began investigations—*philosophical*—into Rhetoric. These will be extended into Logic. Compose at night. On the 17th of this April, I ceased [to] be zoophagous. P. B. Shelley, the poet, suggested this.[115] An experiment, thus far highly satisfactory. Now it gives but little pleasure to eat. I abandoned meat to spiritualize.

About half past four o'clock AM I rise; shower—bathe; walk a distance to be fixed at about four miles; return to a frugal, & chiefly, farinaceous breakfast. During the matin, walk, discover first resemblances for figures; then, form synonymes; notice mnemonically a law-classification; analyze; compose; define; study conversation. After morning tea walk a short distance; studying wit and conversation—oratory. The[n] a period is to be devoted to thought, playing for a little while the flute. Read the *Decline & Fall* until the midday repast. In the evening, about twenty pages of zoology; but previously thought diversified with music. After zoology, history; then about ten pages of Law, then the free, the happy vesper walk. In it I expatiate at large, but usually over matters of [. . .] & address. Tea. Thought, with music usually. My younger sister Maria dearly beloved, is a sweet pianist. My brother William plays the flute. Mother & sister & guests without whom our hospitable & popular though unostentatious roof rarely is: listen. Then Getty's *Oratory*, or Rush on the voice. Study then and generally write down principles of oratory including Composition.

Afterwards, compose, then practice pronunciation, then extemporize; then the gesticulation systematic; ultimately and penultimately, concluding with dorsal, thoracic, respiratory, and from literature, science, art, mnemonic exercises. Reposing, I pray. This is my prayer: "My Father in Heaven? let me be the greatest mortal man that can be." After Supplication; think in mental philosophy; afterwards the luxury of tender or miscellanyeous thought. Sabbath suspends generally these rules. Then I think for awhile usually brief; of death and God. Every day I mentally exclaim: "give me will; in energy let me be a god; I am ready to die." Since my majority on 17th of this April 1850, I remark the passage of each day. Throat still sore.

Port Gibson, April 28, 1850

Finished 3rd volume of Gibbon's *History of Rome*; Commenced the last volume, Continued Getty's *Oratory* & Rush on the Voice. The week has been one of progress. Daily conscious of the lapse of time. An important change: instead of night, I will, after this, take for oratory, the mornings. At night, read.

In conversation, improving. Of my conversation, the character is, I think, with the men, more humor than wit. With women, ladies, those whom I love or study; it is all, often all my eloquence. Indeed, with them, I study oratory. If it may be said that I have [been] cruelly successful; let it thus be explained. For if Parrhasius racked a slave; But I regard woman more than man, as individuals.

Port Gibson, May 5, 1850

Through the week daily wore & spurred myself with the thought of times' flight. Time progresses; do I. This week, am to give the whole of my mornings to thought and oratory. Now God of Philosophy—inspire.

The rumor of my oratorical gestures, vocal and facial exercises with their accompaniments has suggested the question "whether Young Hughes is not crazy?" With the customary—"They say he acts very strangely! Mrs. —— told me that he ——; and I heard besides that ——." Ha, Ha. O God, God, father of my embryo—my—my unborn soul! I am yet in the womb, earth is my womb, and I am an overgrown child! Draw near, I will recognize your voice & presence, make my little stir; then await gestation into the Divine, Infinite & Enduring. O Mother Earth, let some surgeon—cherub by a Caesarean stroke cut me from your bosom. . . . O shell burst, & fling me out, or on your outer crust, its loftiest ridges, let me stand . . . O mountains of years, let me be transalpine—ultramontane . . . O ocean of time, let me be; quick; transatlantic.

Alas passion! my life is become an interrogation & an exclamation; "where-fore" and "Oh."

Still phytophagous; commence tomorrow, and for six days a dietetic mor-tification. With me Young is a "favorite poet." Alternately from him & Shak-speare, I every night memorize. Walter Scott who caught your mantle; here the romance of my heart is not written. Walter Scott? Bah, to myself shall I be a *vain* egotist. Of our fates, the threads, for a little while, were interwoven, then torn asunder. "O never more for me"—"Had we never loved so kindly Had we never loved so blindly;"[116] But my heart *is not* broken. What though, my sister did I not subdue the agony.

In socialism, should man do anything except from choice; & are oaths binding, and obligations, except from choice and except from choice should obligations—oaths, contracts—have legal compulsions, or depend on the will of obligation?

May 5, 1850

Should obligations be enforced? If it is for the good of the obligor, he will do it; if it is not, ought he?

Port Gibson, May 12, 1850

Commenced, today, Horne's *Compendious Introduction.*[117] (Bible) This work will have on me an important bearing.

O Days, passing away; passing away. Through the "seven ages," I have passed & am scarcely a man.

Winged Cupid! Thursday night was engaged to —— "Fie on't, O fie."

Port Gibson, May 16, 1850

When, of mercury two or more drops are brought into a certain contiguity, the[y] run together. I propound that this does not result from any gravita-tion, (there is no gravitation), but from the effects among others of atmo-spheric pressure & the nature of the aggregation of the mercurial & atmo-spheric atoms. Without contact, motion is impossible. Let this be developed. But from this phenomenon of the drops of mercury, could not a principle of motion—a "motive power" be obtained?

Port Gibson, May 19, 1850

In conversation, improving. With ladies, more agreeable than with men. I am with the ladies more.

Want time for, O, for every thing. Now, read but little; chiefly in investigation engaged.

Phytophagous regimen, admirable fitting my health. Eat sparely; occasionally transgress.

Pantheistic ideas dimly irradiating or obscuring my metaphysics. Nothing definite, O Time.

I fear nothing. When necessary, I will always be under perfect self-control; these things, God has given me. Now—first, this month—I pray to be "the best mortal man that can be." "Let me be the best mortal man that can be." To the other prayer of my soul, this is additional.

Port Gibson, May 26, 1850

Days of passion; days of pleasure; passions for knowledge, power, fame & loving souls, and beautiful. In psychology, composition, gesture, vocalization, politics & conversation: steadily investigated & advanced. From woman I have & am gathering a large & opulent experience. My principles in oratory, I illustrate in Love. In my old note-book, which, I at College used, I have written many thoughts—the results of my various investigations. Had thoughts of joining the proposed expedition to conquer Cuba.

Port Gibson, June 1, 1850

My thoughts have been turned towards insanity. What is it? The power of discovering resemblances; how easily is it prevented? Knowledge consists in the resemblance of the state of mind to that of the external mind or matter which is the object of the knowledge. Of this knowledge, some or all may be approximately conceived—that is before it is ascertained, or may not be. If it is beforehand conceived, the conception either perfectly resembles, or in part, or is totally? different, if things can totally differ.

Of the mind one of the prejudices is to mistake things which in part resemble for those which perfectly resemble. Thus a child having a notion of the devil, having in her mind the image—may when seeing something black or moving mistake it for the notion in her mind, or if she "sees a bush think it a bear." Analysis preceeds comparison; the analysis must be complete. Otherwise the resemblance or truth is as to the part not analyzed & compared uncertain. Resemblance is the source of *all* pleasure sensual or emotional. This explains beauty. What is too various or too uniform do not afford the greatest amount of resemblance. Finished *Zoology*, began "Varley," Mineralogy. Almost painfully clear-headed.

Port Gibson, June 9, 1850

Time, Time! stay your wings, Shorten their plumes. Falcon come, on my arm, perch. I will stroke your glossy foliage, feed you & adorn. Your beak shall with yellow diamond-dust be gilded. Venus' cestus—the gods—she—for she is love—shall clasp your throat, Glass-bells with silver tongues shall be your pendents. Their sound shall be concord, and tinkling clearness. I am sure it will charm you. Orpheus' harp shall not be more enchanting, nor Homer's or mist-covered Ossians. And I—I—I will be so good. If you are herbivorous, I will father for you the most esculent flowers of poesy. These, I could with the mature fruits of history, diversify. Off off, off. You are a loathsome bird. Your wings are black and tireless as hungry vultures. Your beak is a harpy's so are your claws. At all my meals you flap down. I can not eat, nor drink, choice Falernian casks to me are brackish water. O! O! Be a vulture, and eat me.

Finished Mineralogy, Civil Engineering next—perhaps—Eyes menacing.

Port Gibson, June 16, 1850

Commenced Civil Engineering; pleased. Among the emotions during the week, ambition has predominated.

During the day: study 1 before breakfast—Gibbon's *Rome*—nearly finished, 2 and then extemporize; 3 after breakfast, Study or rather investigate the nature of composition—perfection being the end—4 psychology—the noblest and best-beloved of my investigations—the supporter of all—5 vocalize 6 gesture & principles & practice, 7 compose study Milton's & Getty's *Oratory*; dine; 8 of Civil Engineering, read ten pages, 9 investigate the nature of law, with a view to a perfect system; 10 read aloud; 11 study—investigate politics; 12 study Demosthenes translated—a little; 13 Study words—synonyms chiefly—writing them; 14 read of law ten pages, walk;—sup; 15 read of Civil Engineering ten pages; 16 miscellaneous reflection; 16 before retiring memorize from Young or Shakspeare alternately, & for principles or classifications, look into law, zoology, ethics; extemporize, jesticulate; 17 retire, pray, thoughts of psychology, miscellaneous thoughts. After dinner read a few lines in French & Horace; & during usually my morning walk, discover a resemblance, synonyms & classifications. In Composition, I am practically illustrating tropes & figures; Getty's *Oratory* is my text; began to illustrate 1st figures for exciting the passions, Commenced a more fundamental analysis of the Tariff; this on account of some new suggestions of a friend. In my mind, I every day, say to God: let me be the greatest mortal man that can be; let me be the best mortal man that can be, and additionally—"give me will; in energy, let me be a God! I am ready to die;

let me be the most daring man that can be; let me be the most fearless man that can be; let me be the firmest man that can be."

My moral principle is so to act that when in Heaven, I will not be ashamed of my remembrances. Am I now so acting?

O God, I am thine.

Port Gibson, June 23, 1850

Commenced Hallams Introduction to Literature, & Civil Engineering. Read on the tariff, some papers on Carey. Received from Mr. Durant a first letter. For some months he has been in Washington City. Read Walter Scott's *Woodstock*.[118]

Port Gibson, June 30, 1850

For some days, reading has on account of my eyes, been suspended. To-night, they are improved.

In the investigation of the principles of politics & law, steadily & some-what satisfactorily progressed.

My happy days have been more than fourteen. Yet of my life, the aim has not been happiness.

Port Gibson, July 7, 1850

During the week, eyes are disabled from reading, me. In politics & system of law, steadily but not very rapidly progressed; gleaned, of labor, wealth, capital & value, more exact & working notions. In mental philosophy; advanced; & in the practice & principles of ethics.

Lopez invasion of Cuba failed.[119] As it might have on my scheme of an Universal Republic, an influence; I watched with interest, it. Some new improvements in Grammar, have occurred to me.

Tonight, eyes are better; still weak, & health unconfirmed.

Port Gibson, July 14, 1850

During the week my eyes have intermittently been very much inflamed. Reading almost entirely suspended. Exercised more vigorously.

Of the decease of Mr. S. S. Prentiss[120] who I thought was to have been my Hortensius,[121] heard; & of that of President Taylor.

Chiefly on account of my eyes, system, not accurately pursued. Thought that perhaps I might deliver on Taylor an eulogy.

Mississippi River Steamer Chancellor Capt. Bacon, July 22, 1850

On Friday 19th ultimo decided to go in place of my Mother to Kentucky. Left on Saturday, Port Gibson, Mi. Left today (Monday) Grand Gulf. My Mother's proposed visit was one directly of business—aid to her brother; and indirectly of filial piety. Cholera in Kentucky gave me a pretext to go as her substitute.

A spirit—devil or divinity—will not let me rest. Eyes & health bad.

Ohio River Steamer, July 28, 1850

Eyes & health improved. Listen to the conversations of men; Sometimes suggested it; always improved.

Still, God's glory darling. Action, health & action, I want.

Began to study burlesque, satire, humor, ridicule, imitation & the cognates; daily increasing a list of subjects.

Mouth of Salt River, August 4, 1850

Eyes much improved & general health. But through D'Israelis *Young Duke*[122] & *Contarini Fleming*[123] ricocheted; pleased, instructed, & animated. Using no artificial stimulus; it has, with me, been a question, how hereafter I, as an orator, may obtain excitement. One source shall be reflection; another woman perhaps novels & poetry. Additionally, will be emulation & envy.

Today resolved to thoroughly devote to self-improvement my constant time. During the week; progressed.

Niagara Falls, August 11, 1850

Through the kindness of Mr. Charles Shreve & his wife—my second cousin,[124] my tour is to be prolonged from Kentucky to New York & Washington Cities. Mr Shreve advances for me, the money. This is kind. Mankind have to me been very good.

Eyes still inflamed & quite weak.

Yesterday, resolved to abandon those daily trains of thought which I have so long—so happily—and I may add successfully pursued. But this temporarily only. My mind lies fallow, yet it is for future fruits & flowers.

Went under the Central Fall of Niagara. To me, it was glee; I lived. The view of the Falls, was, to me, not astounding; I might say not astounding I think it is because I have with combinations of masses philosophically familiarized myself; I preconceived them. Action! I want action. Nibbled the kernel of D'Israelis' *Venitia*.[125]

Near Mouth of Salt River Kentucky, August 18, 1850

After I, at Niagara Falls, had a few days remained, I received from Mr. Shreve whom on account of the sickness of his wife, my cousin I at Buffalo left: a letter. It stated the illness of Corinna. I hurried back. Within a brief time, after my arrival, she died. We returned to Kentucky. She was here buried. Eyes improved, and health. By rubbing my eye-balls, I am endeavoring to meliorate, by lessening the convexity, my sight. Began August, eleventh, last.

Louisville, August 25, 1850

Having successfully I hope, arranged the business on which I came to Kentucky, and after several days, delightfully lingering with my Uncle Robert Brashear,[126] I for Louisville on my way home, departed. Eyes again worse, Health improved. This travel of a few weeks has to me been of inestimable value. I feel myself a man. Before I did not. Purchased to—monday through forgetfulness some *Latter Day Pamphlets*.[127]

Mississippi River, September 1, 1850

On Monday last, left Louisville. Grand Gulf, my landing is now near. Began Alison on *Taste*.[128] Read of Carlyle's *Latter Day Pamphlets*, the 3rd, 4th, 5th & 6th Parliaments. They more fully developed in me the principle of perfect execution.

Port Gibson, September 8, 1850

On Monday last, arrived. How my mother loves me. Nearly finished the obituary of my cousin Corinna. Through Scott's *Monastery*[129] & *Abbot*,[130] skipped. My love of knowledge is becoming almost frantic. Its fields before me, expand. I see their hills, dales, and rolling streams, the lilies of the valley and roses of the cliff, I inhale their fragrance. I am withheld, I am at sea; those fields are my soul's home. It suffers a calenture. I would wish to some flowery-kirtled cottage to retire. No human face should view, But there should be books, the living oracles of the inspired & mighty Dead.

Port Gibson, September 15, 1850

Commenced—again—Davies *Descriptive Geometry*.[131] Finished Locke's *Essay on the Conduct of the Understanding*.[132] Took a few mouthfuls of Turnbull's *Genius of Scotland*,[133] & of the reviewer Wilson.

Thought on suicide, often have the wish, but something seems to detain me. But little binds to earth, me.

Finished the obituary of "Corinna H. Brashear wife of Charles Shreve." It was, in the Port Gibson *Herald & Correspondent*, published. My style, the arrangement of periods, & their members, as well as the ornament, is a type of my future composition.

Tomorrow I again to my system of thought, action and speech, expect to return.

If I, in Mississippi, lived, I could, I think, enter Congress, immediately after my twenty-fifth year. Tomorrow, I lash down to hard preparation, my mind. God is my God.

Port Gibson, September 22, 1850

Through Bulwer's *Last Days of Pompeii*,[134] skipped. Commenced Locke's *Essay on the Understanding*, & Mill's *Political Economy*.[135] Acquainted with the most general principles of *Descriptive Geometry*, & Shades, Shadows, & Linear Perspective, Continued Hallam's *History of Literature*, & extemporizations, composition, and investigations, especially of law.

The obituary has excited from ordinary readers, much criticism. "The sentences are too short," — rather a good objection; "too high-flown," "has, I think, injured himself;" "wrote better three years ago." This all will teach me how hereafter to adapt to the reader my composition. The most natural observation was that the periods seemed written hind part before. If I can establish by philosophy, the truth of my plan, these comments shall not influence me.

Wrote to Mr. Durant a second letter. Mesmerism & the Cognate sciences are attracting my glance. Voice & gesture improved. Eyes, well: I think.

Port Gibson, September 29, 1850

Through the first volume of Carlyle's *Letters & Speeches of Cromwell*,[136] of two hundred & fifty pages about. Yesterday, read. Delighted & instructed. I finished *Clinton Bradshaw*.[137] It enforced several principles not, to me, new, yet not enough familiar. A revolution, an advance has in my mind, onward & upward wheeled. I have hitherto nursed for my profession a regard of which its utility was the cold sire. But a new, warm and ruby-cheeked affection leaps, like a father's prattler to my arms. It is the child of my soul's own bosom. I recognize, I welcome it. Young & rose-lipped cherub: you shall be dandled. I will give you nectar. It shall be sweet as that of Emma's breast.[138] And when I grow older, and need your hand & heart, you will help me. You tell how to labor & gain. Gain what? The desires of my Father — God.

How I love God. I love him like He was my sweetheart.

I have been in my mind, developing of logic, Evidence, Civil & Criminal

Practice & General Law, the leading doctrines, the physiology, the causes. I still, to my design of wooing Criminal Practice, adhere. Its bar is more a rostrum. I will wed, to it, my young eloquence. Apollo shall marry Hecate. The fullfledged eaglet & aged phoenix' unburnt grizzliness shall mate. In systematic conversation, improving. Expending on the art but a sincere one, of popularity, & the expression & decoration of argument, an earnest attention.

God, as I for you live, love me. I have added to my daily prayers—Sunday's excepted—one to "restrain to health, my appetites & pleasures."

Port Gibson, October 6, 1850

Last Sunday night, attacked with the fever called "Dengue." Convalescing. This sickness has had on me an important bearing.

Port Gibson, October 13, 1850

On the Sunday-night of my last sickness, occurred to me the conception of republicanizing the world and other reforms, by means originally of a Secret order of devotees. Enthusiasm shall be of achieving the divine aims for which I am set apart, one of the means.

Read of Whewell's *Elements of Morality*,[139] about the first two chapters. This, with a view to oratory & philosophy.

On account of my approaching return to the City, returned to meat diet. My experience and appetites approve phytophagous subsistence.

The *Natchez Courier* copied with some remarks, the obituary. "As a specimen of transcendentalism, it is a unique production"; regretted to see "so vicious a style" applied [to] an obituary. If I remember this was, of its remarks, the pith. It was headed—unjustly—"Carlylism on the rise."

Port Gibson, October 20, 1850

I would—I know not what. Why am I vexed?: why despondent? These wounds without a cause! I will bleed to death. Woe is me: woe, woe, woe, woe.—It shall not be. I will—my mighty soul, the God within me shall—O, no, no, no. O cursed wretch, why was I born? Mother—when I think of you I calm, dearest mother, I wish I labored with my hands. I wish a little cottage, with honeysuckles around it, was mine. The yellow Tiber—of Time, grows for me, too strong: Help, Help me Cassius or I sink.

I commenced on the 19th of October 1850—last night—the Ultimum Organum. I was in my mother's room, sitting. The fire burned. My mother by me, sat. I am the child of Destiny & Favorite of God.

Port Gibson, October 27, 1850

Began Ruschenberger's *Conchology*.[140]

Health, good. Now I eat heartily. My appetites are—all strong—impetuous. I would without cogitant self-control be libertine, glutton and drunkard. There is in some an antipathy to the Sensual. It disgusts them. They fear it. Yet they are to the luxury of it, acutely sensible. While enjoyment is thus rolled under the tongue it is with self-rebuke made intensely bitter; this sometimes is also an after-taste. Sensual pleasures are to them of this aloe-dust never rid. It, if they are not stupefying, disgusts from more than fitful indulgence. Great men may be drunkards; they never are gluttons or excessive libertines. Their effulgence scatters before they can reach a large size, these sin-fat clouds. I have of animal gratifications, this dread & disgust, yet with these, almost ungovernable appetites. Prayer is my chief means of controlling them; for in resolve I place there no trust.

I am unfolding with some satisfaction, a logical system. The present one, that by Whately, recommended: is imperfect. It is neither completely intellectual nor completely material, metaphysical or physical. It is a mixed system. Truth is Resemblance. This is of my theory, the basis.

I think that I am destined to be the greatest Warrior of Earth.

Port Gibson, November 3, 1850

Finished of Horace's Odes, Anthon's Edition,[141] the first book. Began the second. I expect to read throughout my life, every day, a portion of the classics. This for philosophy—the structure of language—and for oratory.

I expect to, on Tuesday next, depart for New Orleans. I will be Caesar; it shall be my Pharsalia. In God, my faith that I shall be the greatest mortal man that can be, & the best mortal man: is supreme & indestructible. Such is, if there is a God, my destiny; if there is not; I care not what it is.

I go to New Orleans. Between this present time & then, my faith is that by the help of God I shall nobly distinguish myself & that my fame shall arrive at Port Gibson. My Elysian home; on the ocean of life, I will suffer calenture; you & the best beings who beneath her flower-feathered wings, nestle: will haunt the feverish orbs of the tempest beaten & onward Sailor.

New Orleans, November 10, 1850

On last Thursday the 7th of November, I arrived in New Orleans. Here, earnest life begins. I occupy the office of Mr. Thomas J. Durant, my preceptor. At my Uncle's Doctor Lindsay's I board & lodge.

I am in no mood to moralize. Before me, the prospect is fair. But it will extort time in earthly labor wasted. Celestial thoughts farewell! Farewell fields where joy forever dwells, Hail horrors! hail, infernal World! I care not much to live—live or die. My health makes precarious, either, why, here, am I? O Earth, Hell, God, Mystery, Heaven, Thought—

My first law case thrown by Providence into my hands is a "Capital" one. It is the defence of a Negro-boy charged with "striking, wounding & shedding the blood" of a white girl. In God my faith is an entity.

New Orleans, November 16, 1850

With a friend, called on some strange ladies; cheerful. Had another law case; made an argument; my first real one; I triumphed. In art of popularity, improving.

New Orleans, November 24, 1850

Have now on my docket five law cases. They are the gift of the office, four of them & small. I will, by the power & love of God, never lose a just law-suit. Rest, rest, I yearn for rest. For I lack vigor.

Before breakfast, I read, alternate mornings, *Conchology* & *Elements of Drawing*.[142] After breakfast, French & an Ode or less of Horace. Then to the Office. At night, compose; gesticulate; reflect; memorize from the poets.

New Orleans, December 1, 1850

Began *Festus*![143] I want rest. I am sinning. Such sins will be through eternity remembered. Yet what care I? It is to me no sin. It does not stain my soul. For while God still loves me—O my Soul, O God—I wish I was beneath grave-yard arbor-vitae, buried; wash me & I shall be whiter than snow, purge me with lyesoap & I shall be clean. Is there any water, in the undulations of the sea; or fallen from Summer clouds; or in rivers or fountains: can clean me?

New Orleans, December 8, 1850

A protracted spell, a convulsion of melancholy. Alas, has it yet passed?

I directed a friend to inquire whether any editorial chair of two of the leading City Newspapers were vacant.

I have felt an intolerable deficiency of physical & intellectual energy. I wish to lie down, & Sleep, O forever Sleep.

Eyes! still, bad? I have endeavored to repose my mind.

New Orleans, December 15, 1850

Finished *Festus*. Had thoughts of a disquisition on a New System of Taxation. Should not taxes be proportioned to the ability of the proprietor? Let no man who owns less than a given amount of means be taxed. Let it not, as it now does, bear an equal proportion to Capital. Let the proportion be greater than an equal proportion. If he who possess $1000 pay one cent per centum; Let him who possesses $100,000, one hundred-thousand dollars, pay five or six percent.

New Orleans, December 22, 1850

I have thought to pray God to inspire me: that I might be his Slave to reform and, Oh! God help me! to perfect human thoughts, words & deeds.

Shall I be a worldly man or a heavenly one? My Father! I, on your bosom, rest! There, I sleep. Prompt my dreams, Then wake me to do them. The year closes. It leaves me a poor ploughman to till a continent. I am but a single architect. Yet I helpless, would build a castle, so tremendous fair & undecaying — & in the little night of my lifetime, that Genii shall envy and the noblest desire it.

New Orleans, December 29, 1850

Began an investigation of Taxation & one of Logic. These are although they may separately [be] published, parts of the Ultimum Organum.

Sipped an occasional teaspoonful of *Genevieve*[144] of Lamartine & *David Copperfield*[145] of Dickens.

Meditated my existence & its aims. Read the Hero as Divinity, as Prophet & as Poet.[146]

New Orleans, January 1, 1851

My Father: I renew my oath and consecration. Now my Father, I consecrate to Glory, myself. By our long loves; by your omnipotence, and omniscience: I swear it.[147]

I could now assassinate, or on an adversaries' dagger, plunge. I could now rip open grassgrown graves and tear to pieces their blackening tenants. I could lie on my mother's bosom and remember the shaded and fallen trunk on which, while memory went a-maying over childhood's lawn, I dreamily shut to the future, my eyes & sprawled my length. Pah! Why this? My soul, and all that is within me: awake! Sleep no more! Murder sleep! or let it be eternal. I never shall till my earthly work is done; till then O let me never rest.

Of an effect in human affairs: the antecedents are desire, conception, and means. The desire and the conception of an effect, being in nations, generated, the means of the effect are sure. I am by God set apart; O, I know that I am — for my fellow-being's happiness. I am to be the Greatest Mortal Man that can be; & the best Mortal Man. God loves me. I am not raving! I am not mad, I pray.

I am God's implement to reveal the philosophy of the Human Mind & to illustrate it, to reform legislation, to reveal perfect politics; these, of thoughts and words; of deeds, to be the leader, and beloved of the World.

I am set apart to be the greatest Orator that can be; one whose power of Language is the greatest that can be. The orator now, begins. I will this year, speak to my fellowmen, and win their ear. God, love me.

New Orleans, January 5, 1851

Law business, improved; but few cases, yet tried. I talk with my fellow-men so little that my speech now is, until I grow animated, awkward.

My work—literary—is yet crude. The propagation of some of my doctrines, truths—and the wooing—the winning of the public ear: are two of its aims.

In the purposes of my existence, my earnestness becomes greater; my self-ambition, less. I feel more—more, my heroism; thus Carlyle terms it. I feel as if I could dignify Jove's throne; hold the chain which holds the world; hurl thunderbolt, and shake the poles.

I, I could, could! A boaster; braggart, fool. Am I a man? a god? a fiend? I could lie down; forget, weep, shriek; lose all my thoughts.

I am, but what? How? why? I wish that I could crack the nectary of that secret, and suck its honey! I wish I could saw open that shell and gulp its juice. But I have no tools, nor beaver's tooth, insect's gimlet, or bird's beak.

"Give me will; in energy, let me be a god; let me be fearless; let me restrain to health, my appetites; let me work." Thus, I daily pray.

New Orleans, January 12, 1851

More practice of the Law. I feel the deficiencies of inexperience in cross-questioning witnesses and recollecting—so as to apply—testimony. I was, during the most important suits, listless. I think it is over-exertion of the nervous system. This from constant thought or study. I have therefore tried again the experiment of repose. I have suspended all save my necessary exercises of mind.

The most Successful lawyers have, I observe, but brief opportunities of extraprofessional reflection. I would rather be a basketmaker and think, than the most opulent counselor, and attorney at law.

I think God has not condemned me to the perishable and indifferent acts of lawpractitioners; I am to be a jurisprudent; a maker, not a fitter. But I neither wish, nor fear, what God offers me; I try, I hope, to achieve. "I wish my heart was calm & still, To beams, that fleet; and blasts that chill."

New Orleans, January 19, 1851

Rest is the mother of energy. Indolence is powerful. My repose of systematic exercise of intellect has restored sensibility and concentrativeness, I learn. To apply knowledge becomes daily less difficult.

I now must collect, and hurl, on all which employs me, my forces.

Law-business not, I think, decreased. I have in addressing the Court, preferred in style, the Serene. I study my cases. I build on each one, a hope of glory. I for that pray, in each suit, I am a man. It now neither grieves or glads me. Yet—alas, why yet? I yet wish that I were a chaser of butterflies; a gatherer of wild roses in the valley; and shells on the shore. I wish that I now were on the hillside, a rover; under the dreamy beech, a listless loller; or in the shadowy wood, a forester. Are there on the continents of Eternity, butterflies, wild roses, white and dimpled shells, forests and rivers swimming to the sea.

New Orleans, January 26, 1851

Of the "Ana of an Aspirant," a speech shall be upon Taxation perhaps; one, on the Right of Secession—perhaps.

Is there a God? Forgetfulness open your mouth; let me hurl to you the question. There is a God. I am his favorite. Continued Mill's Political Economy.

New Orleans, February 2, 1851

Continued Mill's *Political Economy*.

Before breakfast: "Ana of an Aspirant,"—as yet preliminarily; after breakfast, French; then to the Office; law especially of Evidence until dinner. Then miscellanies, especially synonyms. In the evening & at the Office 31 Camp Street, Logic. At night, Political Economy, Analyses, & Reflections. Thus, my life. It is princely happy.

I am so poor that I have not without borrowing, money to buy a pair of shoes. Rather than borrow money, I wear a worn-out pair. Feet now not dry. But He who feeds the young ravens will not forget his Eagle. . . . How beautiful on the mountains—

New Orleans, February 9, 1851

Continued Mill's *Political Economy*. Pleased. Mastered the fundamental principles, of Logic. In the doctrine of taxation, creeping nearer perfection. I, on the mountains of knowledge, crawl, like a sloth. I would like a chamois leap, where "Alps on Alps arise." O Knowledge! your base is a wilderness; your middle is with awful groves, girded; your summits are Elysian fields. They would more than honor Jove, of Olympus; Apollo, of Delos; Lemnian Vulcan; or Venus of Paphos. O God! let me not talk; let me work.

New Orleans, February 16, 1851

On Tuesday evening, left, through necessity, the City. Visited during the flight, my home. My mother! brother! my home—yet I will not weep—I— Oh what? "I wish my heart was calm & still To beams that fleet & blasts that chill." Farewell.

New Orleans, February 23, 1851

I grow, a fatalist. Love! Woman! God! Death! Beatrice! Leonore![148] O, God! O, Fate!

To be without God & without hope, in the World! Is my heart broken? Or is [it] but strained! It, it was so wrenched. My heart is turned to stone. I wish it were shattered and the flinders hurled off creation's verge.

New Orleans, March 2, 1851

Finished Scott's *Marmion*.[149] To-day, systematized my aims; adopted rules; I must be to myself yet severer. I must accumulate new knowledge, and refine old. I must yet more vigorously address to my career myself.

I will, I will trust God. Life is such a calm; "No breath of air, to stir the wave."[150]

New Orleans, March 9, 1851

Finished Scott's *Rokeby*;[151] began *The Lay of the Last Minstrel*.[152] Continued Mill's *Political Economy*. Studied the theory of Law, Analyzed; Compared; pondered. Thought of the bearing of Liberia & the American Colonization Society on the abolition of slavery.[153] Through the Report of the Committee of Congress on the establishment of Steamers to Liberia, skated. This week, am to investigate the annexation of Cuba. How shall I accomplish it? Is God present? Is He ever by my side? Does He rule specially the affairs of men? Of All? Or yet of some? Of, one? and through him, the Chosen One, All mankind? Am I not he? Am I not his chosen One, his viceroy, his Pope? My Father, address me; Tell how I may know. . . . The world shall be a Republic, and I its President. Now my God, I feel the impulse; I begin my Active Career. Here commences the political life of Henry Hughes.

What is this life? Why can we not behold it? Jove is in a beastly body disguised. Life stand forth. Give me to look-on, to touch you, though the brightness stun my appalled senses.

"To beams, that fleet; & blasts, that chill, I wish my heart was calm & still."

New Orleans, March 16, 1851

I love; still, still, I love. And she who subjugates my soul, is she fair? Is she constant, "pure & sacred?" Rambling Spirits loving her, would esteem her a burning seraph; and seeing her, an angel. Thoughts of Suicide & fame. O, Time. And I grow weary too. I will learn to labor & to wait. Yet yet, Fate tap the drum, & let the race begin. If to the fleet; I am fleet. If not, the race is not always to the swift.

I will be the Slave of God; He shall look on. I will be the fireman of a flame which shall consume Earth. I gather & heap up the fuel; I do your bidding. See, See, "A God in grandeur—& a world of fire." Oh, woe, woe. "Tis not the river, nor the hill, Nor yet the meadow broad & green Nor mountain wild, nor leaping rill That. . . ."

Woe, woe, Oh—I again invoke you. I will suck from these roses, the dew, I will be a humming-bird and ——. No! I am an eagle. I will fly at the sun. What is Life? Let my soul conceive this. Generate, I shall never here, meet face-to-face, you; by the conception of the Holy Virgin: fill with that divine knowledge, my soul.

Re-perused the *Rime of the Ancient Mariner*.[154] Continued Mill's *Political Economy* & *The Lay of the Last Minstrel*. Thoughts of a method of gradual Socialism.

New Orleans, March 23, 1851

Continued Mill's *Political Economy*. Study while walking, the generation of thought. In eloquence, improved. Every evening—except Sunday—I declaim. Every day, vocalize at length. Every morning study French aloud, too poor to employ a teacher.

My younger Sister Maria Jane Hughes is to [be] married on the first Wednesday of next month to Wm. Thomas Magruder. He is like myself, a native of Claiborne County Mississippi. There is his residence. He is by vocation, a planter. He is young, just emerged from a hereditary debt, by his own struggling. His mind is well educated & by nature of an influential cast. Of its elements, intellect of the practical sort, industry and that quality of the moral principle which implies a consciousness of God's being, balanced strong desires, imagination and Southern inertness. His brother & himself my brother and self, have from earliest boyhood worn each other in our heart of hearts. We were schoolmates & playmates. May the God of Henry Hughes love his sister & her husband. I am to abandon the City next Saturday to attend my Sister's wedding. It will be an absence of a fortnight or less.

I care not much to live! for not for me is "the primrose path of dalliance."[155] My feet are shod; the reins clutched. Off, off, I loiter here. Fate holds his foot in stirrup & hand on the pommel. I paw the air, I smell the battle, Ha ha, ha ha, I smell the battle. You who rode cherubs & the wings of the wind. God, ride me. Let me on this Field be your warhorse! I smell the battle afar off! ha ha.

Steamer Natchez No 2, March 30, 1851

Yesterday left New Orleans. I go to the wedding of my sister. I still pray. I still believe that I am God-guided.

Port Gibson, April 6, 1851

On Wednesday, April 2d 1851, my sister Maria Jane was married to William Thomas Magruder. He is one fitted to change the current of events.

Port Gibson, April 13, 1851

A week of dreams and passion. Earnestly attracted towards the politics of the South. The relation of landlord & tenant is as sinful as that [of] master & slave. Both relations shall be abolished; but not to the hurt of the South.

Steamer Natchez No 2, April 17, 1851

This is my 22d birthday. Alas, Time! I renew my oath of Glory. Last year was one of Fatalism. I esteemed myself, Godguided. If such it is, my delusion was so great that I thought that He had caused a beautiful woman to love me. I parted with her but yesterday and discovered What? I cannot say that she loves me; or that she is indifferent. I know not what! But as to Fatalism: I shall for a while be self-guided only. Day after day, I have communed with God; refered to Him for correction, my judgments, desires, volitions, & actions. For a while this ceases. Carlyle could understand.

New Orleans, April 27, 1851

Last Sabbath-night, omitted this sacred duty.

Returned to New-Orleans from Port Gibson Mississippi, April 18th 1851. Started the previous Monday. Tuesday, April 15th, 1851; witnessed the conflagration of nearly all Grand Gulf. Assisted the citizens. That evening, left on the Steamer "Natchez No 2." Lay several hours at Natchez. Drove through the City, was pleased.

Finished, the first volume of Mill's *Political Economy*. Began the 2d. Began

Lewis' *Restoration of the Jews*[156] &c. Read articles of Reviews on Southern manufactures, studied Politics, wit, & oratory. Health bad; must exercise more freely & think less?

New Orleans, May 4, 1851

Last week studied Oratory; this includes composition & literature. Read or rather skipped through Dickens' *Pickwick Papers*,[157] Dumas' *Fernande*,[158] & Rockingham. Profitted. The week before last was for Politics. This week: law. This is the division of week's work. The dynamics & melody of my voice, which I every day exercise, are improved; but not its distinctness.

I am not averse to death. Action is life. Mine has been of words, not deeds, words & thoughts. But some of my thoughts were deeds.

Law-business punctually regarded. It yields some trifle, pecuniarily. But extorts no action of soul. Shall I be content? If discontent is a devil, let it find in my breast a hell. Leap to me, you subtle power, stir me to something of courage, wisdom or goodness.

Shall I write; but if I did not win the world's ear; if it did not lend—give— press on me, its hearing, I would spurn, insult, spit in the face of once-trusted Destiny, and go to the grave, as a bed. Alas! tear out my tongue; let me have hands only; do, not speak. What here will be my doing? To address a jury; convince a judge. I stand all the day idle, I hold my sickle, I wish that I was in the harvest-field.

New Orleans, May 11, 1851

Continued Mill's *Political Economy*. Investigated Blackstone's Definition of Municipal Law.

After returning from Port Gibson, I wrote to my brother & brother-in-law. Of my writing, the business was [to] request them to procure for me the editorial chair of a Newspaper in Port Gibson. My investigations into physical & metaphysical had been so satisfactory, fruitful indeed, & promissory of success; the prospect of a law-practice here, sufficient to relieve me of pecuniary dependence, so despising; mechanical labor, so rupulsive; that I could not but yearn for some attitude which would secure subsistence, & action in exchange, political opportunities & leisure for philosophy. How would I have loved the Ultimum Organum, How speeded the Universal Republic, How consummated the action, expression, & reasonings of the orator, How pondered the question of slavery, How, lived, loved, How worshipped God? But I submit. It was not. Ere trodden the landscape vanished. I was not wrong. I reasoned rightly! reasoned as if life was God-given.

I was anticipated. The newspaper was purchased. My brother-in-law, whom I so much—so much love—for man can love man—& I will test socially the dear fact! he writes that the possibility of another paper is doubtful. It must be, literature or editing. Ana of an Aspirant: again!

New Orleans, May 18, 1851

Continued Mill's *Political Economy*, 2d volume. Read in the evenings & at the office, twentyfive pages; study in the morning & until twelve o'clk, composition; from then until two, Law.

Of Law, the definition, object, causes, quantity & quality; the classification & interpretation now employ me. At home, during the day & at night, Oratory—persuasion. All this, in pursuance of my aims of life. Of these, one is a perfect reformation of Law. I likewise study invention; this in connexion with another aim of life—perfection of the philosophy of mind. Oratory includes conversation.

Health, bad. Studied desultorily Landscaping as a part of the Beautiful. The element of the Beautiful is in Resemblance; so that of Truth.

I date my writings. These are my mind's best history. I analyze so much, that my memory I think, needs exercise. I also read excessively, perhaps.

I am in love with Rush on the voice. So analytic, perspicuous, earnest, independent, important, I will praise. And my voice is so much better. Studying in Composition, simplicity of Language and rhythmus & metre of prose.

New Orleans, May 25, 1851

Discovered in reading Mill's *Political Economy*, the 2d volume—that the doctrine of Taxation with which I grew enamored is not with me original. The notion but not the reasons of it are contained in the "Graduated-property tax—System." Thus in Politics. And in the philosophy of the mind, Kant has I fear preceded me. Wherefore, fear?

Last week, studied, Oh so profoundly faithfully, victoriously. At the Office; Composition, until Twelve o'clock; Law—its analysis, until two: this of thought. In the evening & at the Office, read about twenty-five pages of *Political Economy*. At home, declaim, vocalize, extemporize, think. I do not talk much.

As to my souls progress: my writings which I date & sign "H H", are the best manifests.

Shall I be melancholy until I distinguish myself?

Blackstone's classification of private relations in his first book of *Commentaries*, is too limited. In Law, all persons are relative.

I have returned to my communion with God. I believe that I am his Favorite, & that He will make me the greatest & best Mortal Man that can be.—

New Orleans, June 6, 1851

Last Sunday this was omitted. Finished Mill's *Principles of Political Economy*. More than instructed. Glanced, with delight, amazement, hope, pity, through *Alton Locke Tailor & Poet*.[159] Skipped through, *Adventures of an Attorney* &c.[160]

A machine which makes visible the rotatory motion of the Earth has in France been invented. This will lead to the discovery of the best method of determining longitude.

One of my soul's friends—Wm. E. T. Griffith is dead. One more is left, and God.

Continuing analyses of Law, Composition, & Mind.

Health, bad. I do not care. For what is life? Commenced, Mill's *Logic*.[161]

"Travel on! O, travel on." What a place is a city?

New Orleans, June 8, 1851

Health, bad. Studying, with a hope. I will woo, & win ——. Power, knowledge, Love: you three divinities; which is fairer? I will be your Paris. Strip to me. Be naked. Let me possess that I may decide your beauties.

Studying the primary principles of Composition, Law, Politics & Invention.

I care not much to live. What as to Politics & Socialism are all the consequences of freedom of mind? What is perfect oratory? How can I subject to volition any given person? What are the doctrines of individual or personal subjugation? Yet all for God & man. And now perfectly control operate myself! Let me fast & pray; then bend to these my powers.

New Orleans, June 15, 1851

Finished Rush's *Philosophy of the Human Voice*. That work I, in gratitude, kissed. Finished Mill's *Principles of Political Economy*. Instructed, not enlightened. Glanced through portions of *St. Ronan's Well*.[162] Studying Politics, Law, Composition & Oratory Commenced an analysis of Bills of Exchange.

New Orleans, June 22, 1851

Continued Mill's *Logic*. Finished a glance through *St. Ronan's Well*.

Arranged the titles of Municipal Law. Studied the science or principles of Influence. Read some Congressional Speeches on the Compromise Measures. Continued study of Composition, practical or physical oratory. Extemporize Declaim, but not industriously, on account of disturbing family & neighbors.

New Orleans, June 29, 1851

Began Brocklesby's *Elements of Meteorology*.[163] Purchased this Logic, Whewell's *Elements of Morality*,[164] *Philosophy of Mathematics*.[165] Began Liebig's *Agricultural Chemistry*.[166]

Health not confirmed. Have the wish to employ in physical labor a few months. This experience & strengthener, I need, so I think. Study & thinking are now all my life. Continue notes on Political Economy.

Have the wish to classify all science art & literature, & arrange them in note-books. I wish then to collect or create all notions useful to the orator, philosopher & statesman.

New Orleans, July 6, 1851

Began Brocklesby's *Elements of Meteorology* & Loomis' *Differential Calculus*.[167]

The courts of the City now close. This is the first season of my practice of Law. It was only a continuance of my course of legal study. It is finished & I must decide the locality of my home. Shall it be here or Port Gibson?

In Mississippi, the election of delegates, to the State Convention occurs in September next. Of this the object is to consider the course of the state. The states-rights party are in Claiborne County in a large minority. As yet they have nominated no candidate. I summer in Mississippi. While there I shall procure my nomination as the candidate of this party. I am of their party, for they are not Disunionists. If I succeed, it would make or break me.

God will guide me.

New Orleans, July 13, 1851

Began *Philosophy of Mathematics*, translated from the French of Compte. Tomorrow, depart for Port Gibson, Mississippi. There I will probably summer. Applied for an editor's chair in one of the City Papers: a vacancy not now disposable. Will I ever work? Ever be independent? O Father pity your son. But God to me is ever good. When I have done all, it is as it should be if unsucceeding.

Finished a glance through *Old Mortality*.[168]

Port Gibson, July 20, 1851

Monday the 14th last, left New Orleans. Arrived at home, Wednesday the 16th. Here, expect to summer.

Plunged through several novels. Read from Borrow's *Bible in Spain*.[169] It occurred to me that in the scheme of a Universal Republic of which I am to be the Godguided means Spain would perhaps be the most suitable European Country to first annex or ally with the United States.

Political discussion here is animated. The parties in leading are the Unionists so called, & States-Rights. To the States Rights party, I shall attach myself. That party alone is compatible with a Universal Republic. Besides its relation to the safe abolition of Slavery & Socialism is more favorable. The party is now a minority. My brother-in-law is a member, not my brother however.

Port Gibson, July 27, 1851

Yesterday, attended a political Barbecue at Rocky Springs in this County. The discussion was between the Candidate for Congress, A. G. Browne; & Wm Sidney Wilson, Candidate for the State Convention, which meets in September, & nominee of the so-called Union party.

Yesterday evening, my brother-in-law Wm. Thomas Magruder, advised me to prepare myself to occupy the rostrum in behalf of ours the Democratic party.

Another barbecue occurs at Grand Gulf next Saturday. I have begun my preparation to appear there. The advise of Thomas was agreeable to my former wishes or designs.

The candidate that opposes Mr Wilson who is a member of the bar a first honor graduate of The College of New Jersey, & advanced in life, is a gentleman who resides in the country. If I make at Grand Gulf, a striking effort; I last night conceived the notion of procuring his withdrawal of candidacy, & my nomination.

These things with earnest prayer. For I have faith that God guides me.

Port Gibson, August 4, 1851

At my Brother-in-law's in the country, I had nearly completed the speech to be delivered at Grand Gulf, when I received my mother's & sister's—elder—most peremptory wishes to abandon it. I honor my mother & forego the effort.

Yet the composition & research has been a reward to itself.

I have friends, but feel friendless; am loved, yet feel loveless. I would not care to quit earth, yet have no wish for Heaven. O God, O God! shall my sighs be constant as trade winds; eyes, tearless as the skies of Egypt. Earthquake my heart, soul.

This forgotten last night.

Port Gibson, August 10, 1851

Skipped—leaped through *Chronicles of the Canongate*,[170] *Red Gauntlet*,[171] & *St. Valentine's Day*.[172] Continued *Philosophy of Mathematics*.

Praying for bodily strength & Memory. Continue political study.

Began an instruction for my brother-in-law Thomas. He has a mind, leisure & a sense of duty. He wishes to be a Speaker. He shall be, & one who will teach & govern men.

Port Gibson, August 17, 1851

Glided through *Legend of Montrose*.[173] Finished "Compte's Philosophy of Mathematics," by "Gillespie."

Praying for love glory & power, both of mind & body.

Wrote for my brother Thomas Magruder a course of exercise for an orator. He will be a governor of Mississippi—so I judge.

Continued Brockleby's *Meteorology*.

Port Gibson, August 24, 1851

Finished Brocklesby's *Elements of Meteorology*. O, Earth, Time, Life, God, Self! Why am I not crazed? why, not dead!

Thoughts of a treatise on our Government & its destiny.

I pray for power, glory & love.

Port Gibson, August 31, 1851

Analyzed, classified, memorized. Studied style & generation of ideas. Prayed; thoughts on religion; Examined the morality of slavery.

Thoughts of becoming a candidate for the Legislature.

Port Gibson, September 7, 1851

Rambled through Scott's *Fortunes of Nigel*.[174] Continued Whewell's *Elements of Morality*.

Began at the suggestion of my dear & respected friend Dr Harper, a legal investigation of the Right of Secession.

Last Monday & Tuesday, was the election of members for the State-Convention on Federal Relations. I voted for the Democratic States Rights Candidate: Dr Irwin. He denied, as I apprehended, that the issue was Union & Disunion; aimed to procure redress for the just if possible, & security for the future; the outlet & absolute control of Slavery nonintervention, & rights of Equality & judgment. But the election throughout the State has established that the issue was Union & Disunion. Such being the case, I would have voted on the other side. Quitman[175] has resigned the canvass & nomination. There will perhaps be a coalition between the two divisions of the Democratic party.

My Father love me, & give me Power & Glory.

Port Gibson, September 14, 1851

Various reading & pleasures.

Trust in God, still greater & greater.

Port Gibson, September 21, 1851

Rambled through *Mordaunt Hall*.[176] Continued *Morality* & review of *Meteorology*. Investigating Wit, oratorically & Philosophically I pray to "Work." This evening at church I thought that this work could be the construction of models of inventions in mechanics & other sciences. Many improvements in cotton-presses, wagons, steam-engines & other contrivances occur to me. I want bodily exercise. And if by some invention I could with its proceeds educate my Uncle Bob's children; I could not; could I my Father do any nobler limited thing?

Read in North British Reviews a paper on "The Recent Extension of Logic."

My Father: Let me be the greatest mortal man that can be; let me be the best mortal man that can be; love me.

Port Gibson, September 28, 1851

Advanced in Whewell's *Elements of Morality*. Continued review of *Elements of Meteorology*. Began Loomis' *Recent Progress of Astronomy*,[177] & Thackeray's *Pendennis*.[178] Read novels continuously; time thus, sincerely seems to me more lucrative than even with the Sciences. Twenty-four hours for a novel & death thirty-six or eighty. How is it my Soul! my body! my God! Oh, Lord?

Pendennis turns towards the Press my thoughts. Of my earthly action, how much will be literary; how much legal; how, philosophic? political! Military? I could die; every day I say "I am ready to die."

This week analyzed, compared, thought. Am I self-deluded? I have studied civil, common & constitutional law; nearly all science & English literature. I want body. Now I am egotistic & affect simplicity. God love me.

Port Gibson, October 3, 1851

Concluded Loomis' *Recent Progress of Astronomy* & 1st volume of *Pendennis*. Instructed. Studied while walking, invention. Invented a cotton-press: a combination of the lever & screw, with a cone instead of cylinder.

Port Gibson, October 12, 1851

Finished *Pendennis*; wiser, abler & I hope, better. Continued review of *Elements of Meteorology*. I wish to get in memory the classifications of all Science. Without this, can the orator be perfect?

Studying by reading & reflection, philosophy, science & oratory.

Thoughts still tending towards literature. I would first win by the beauties & potencies of composition, the attention of the public. Next, instruct & persuade; finally govern them. The physical & metaphysical leader has never been consummated; nor a destructive & constructive reformer. No Statesman has yet been both speculative & practical; theoretical; & actualizing. No idealist has yet been a realizer; the planner, seldom a builder. Of the moderns, Lamartine failed & Richelieu approximated; of the ancients, Caesar approximated, Socrates failed. May I perfect.

Port Gibson, October 19, 1851

Wherefore? Why? Speak! Open your lips: and tell—What?—Fool! child, babe, dreamer. Oh! Eye of God! Oh, Jesus'—bosom, Oh Holy Dove, coo in my ear. These fingers;—I clutch my hands; beat my bosom; tear my scalp;— swell veins & pop. There's blood; that: real. It is pain.——That is in my mind; my mind is myself. Myself,—I, am—am: Planets, the blue deserts, wanderers of the camel's foot, & night-bird's eye: that man god of War & Glory. I am Glory's boy & Destiny's. Farewell: we will meet in ——.

Mississippi River Steamer Magnolia, October 26, 1851

Yesterday morning, left Port Gibson, Mi. I go to New-orleans & to business. Read with an occasional hiatus Garland's *Life of John Randolph*.[179] I love John Randolph. **** Of me, of all, how much is *un*told, unknown. Wherefore should it be? God will take care of me. Traveling, I listen. Sometimes, suggest.

I like working-men. Several improvements of the steam-engine occurred to me; I have been talking to the engineers about them. Engineers are my favorites.

Faith unwavering as to my destiny & God.

New Orleans, November 2, 1851

Arrived in New-orleans, Monday last the 28th of October.

Begun the Reformation of the Law. I am still in the office of Durant & Hornor. I love Mr. Durant, & respect him. Of whom else can I say this?

I can write all my soul's history. The Esoteric is still incommunicable. I despise the practice of Law; this, as it is not as it must be, I will—I will trust in God, I will spike my hand to the ploughhandle. If I must not; He will show me. Will He? If doubt is the raiment of my Hopes; Let them come blushing naked.

New Orleans, November 9, 1851

Continued "Reformation of the Law."

I am a strange man; wicked, religious, egotistical, virtuous, vain, haughty, modest, manly, boyish.

Continued Review of *Meteorology*. Thoughts of teaching in the "Public Night School." This, to make me independent of the assistance of my mother & sister & to enable me to educate two of my Uncle Bob's children. He is poor. I am poor; but I am God's young raven. He will feed me when I cry. He will change me to his eagle.

New Orleans, November 16, 1851

Thus Time passes. All is vanity. Finished review of *Meteorology*. Continued *Elements of Morality*. Begun the practical reformation of the Law Dreamed waking, vice tempts me. My confidence in God wavers. I try Him. Why should He work for me miracles? I am vain, egotistical, wearied. O Sabbath, O Saint's rest. Where will be my bed? Will it be the rosy banks of Paradise, or fiery lake, or "ground burning frore." Gods bosom;—in his arms, beneath his down-bending face; where his eyes will see me close; where his heart will throb to mine; there let me nestle. Let me there close my lids on Heaven & to dream & dream. If but once I could be loved as I would be; I could, I think, press on vice's lips a farewell kiss & sleep in virtue's never-sating & celestial bed.

New Orleans, November 23, 1851

Continued Mill's *Logic* & Whewell's *Elements of Morality*. I feel a peace above all earthly dignities; then, discontent; and despair. But Faith is all-triumphant. Its panoply is Cyclopean. My faith was dipped, drowned in the Styx.

Thoughts of Literature. Skipped through a portion of Kennedy's *Life of Wirt*.[180] Wirt was not a "born able man."

The theory of life; if it wastes in perishable labor my hours, is it true. I abhor the practice of the Law; abhor alike all mechanic toil, all effort, less than world-wide & philanthropic.

Think of commencing directly my labors of life.

New Orleans, November 30, 1851

Continued Mill's *Logic*, Ethics, & Zoology. Tomorrow, begin writing for publication. This, for power, fame, & subsistence. I must get money for both my Uncle & self. To-day, dined at Mr Durant's, Rarely visit, my life is solitary.

New Orleans, December 7, 1851

Continued *Elements of Morality*, & French Exercises.

Invented improvements of the Steam-engine & Cotton-gin.

Think more, read less though diligently.

Investigated Logic & Rhetoric. Logic is a contrivance to economize "distribution."

What am I? Poor; but fifty cents; that's now all my money. But I am loved, respected, admired, wondered at. What would not my friends, for my sake, do? What not, my mother, both my sisters, Willie & Tom? God loves me. I am his darling's boy, his pet-child. Is it that He spoils me? I feel so powerful. But what, Do? How, begin?

I seem to think that there is nothing which I could not actualize. Am I now vain. I do not think so; deceived, perhaps. But I feel like as if I was talking of another & not myself.

Began an oration or dissertation on Public Improvements. This in pursuance of my aims of life.

New Orleans, December 14, 1851

Begun a dissertation of the "Best scheme of Public-Improvements." I must distinguish myself. Made my first speech this season before one of the City Magistrates. He complimented me in passing judgment by saying that it was the "best effort which could be made." This was the first time that I ever appeared before that Court.

Continued investigations, analysis Comparisons & inventions. Applied to steamboats the privileges of the lever, screw male & female, inclined-plane, & improvements of the wheel & axle. I study the mechanics of Locommotion as a means of a "Universal Republic."

Of the virtues, many must be developed. Most Americans seem ashamed of Friendship, many, of piety, many of charity. Let me not squander the hours.

New Orleans, December 21, 1851

Ambition; something nobler; its altar still for me is burning. My vestal thoughts, hopes & memories still watch its sleepless flame; still heap on it fuel of incense, oils & spices. If it expires or flickers, may I be buried in disgraceful clay. Oh, God! Oh Father! Love me, my Papa. Hold me on your bosom. Let our hearts beat against each others'. Oh my love, let me be your pet. Am I not your darling? May I in Heaven, sit on your knee? Oh Jehovah, dandle me. Let me show astonished men that you are God. I am not mad. Am I crazy? Please help me. Push me on. I am half frightened. I am not. It is true. I must be the Greatest mortal man that can be; I must be the best mortal man that can be. I am God's Favorite. Earth, posterity, believe & obey.

Continued review of *Mineralogy*, Continued Sedgwick on *Damages*.[181]

New Orleans, December 28, 1851

Invented an improvement of wagons. By this, the weight is made a power. Invented various cottonpresses.

Law-business, quite limited.

Nobody ever talks to me. In every conversation, I lead or nothing or little is addressed to me. The little-boy in our office talks to me; that is, if we are by ourselves.

Was Washington, the only great man whose mind & nature was what is called, healthy? Were all others, morbid?

I wish to be a happy, healthy greatest man. Continued the dissertation.

New Orleans, January 1, 1852

The oath and Consecration of Henry Hughes. This oath was first taken after he loosed his soul from Emma Caffery. Now my Father, I consecrate to Glory, myself. By our loves, by your omnipotence and omniscience, I swear it.

The year is past. Am I wiser, braver, or better? God: my Love, kiss me, hug me; close, close—so.

New Orleans, January 4, 1852

Looked through the novel *Fernley Manor*.[182] Continued *Logic* & *Elements of Morality*. Exercised in Composition. Now I know soul-idleness, & till now never, perhaps.

What is Love? Did ever I love? I think that I did. Do I now love? I think that, nay, nay; not to think is happiness. This is the first of the year. A Ship sailing out of the harbor. I am an argosy. But breeze, gale or hurricane fills the silks. Come South wind. Blow, North.

New Orleans, January 11, 1852

I pray more; I seem sometimes to pray without ceasing.

This week, I dreamed. They were love-dreams. I "courted the luxury of tender thought." What of marriage? Shall it be for life? What of polygamy? Is it sin? Can many be loved? Yet I studied. Began an analysis of the emotions.

Read aloud every morning except sunday, poetry, Classify, synthesize, compose, Study French.

New Orleans, January 18, 1852

Dreams? Do I dream? Am I still asleep? When shall I awake; when open my eyelids & shake off the fair hallucinations?

Always I am either merry or melancholy. This, being solitary; that social.

This week read but little. God is my dearest, most familiar friend, with Him, I commune almost hourly. To me, life is still a romance. It is full of loves, joys, & ambitions.

New Orleans, January 25, 1852

Kossuth[183] is my fore-runner. He is St John: I am the ———.

How vain the attempt to write my soul.

I take Polka lessons. For dancing is a power.

Miss Martha Parker[184] is now in the City.

To me this week will perhaps be critical. Then I shall be atheist or fatalist, which?

My brother William has sold his store in Port Gibson Mi. As a merchant, he was popular, prudent & successful.

What is life? What love? What God? Still, pray & aspire to peerless human glory.

In the City is an order called the "Lone Star." Its object is so far as published, "The extension of the Area of liberty." Can this to me be useful? For all honest powers must be used.

My sister Mrs. Magruder is the mother of a boy: William Hughes Magruder. Must I pray for him?

New Orleans, February 1, 1852

Finished Whewell's *Elements of Morality*. This week, begin memorizing classifications. This for oratory, Philosophy & Reformation of the Law.

I Still pray, & daily, almost hourly commune with God. Compose every day. I have the wish to be a poet; the God, Apollo is within me.

Take private polka lessons with a class of ladies and some gentlemen.

New Orleans, February 8, 1852

This week my chief emotion has been weariness. I was tired. Yet of what? Was I worked down; or thought down? For some time, I had a pain in the breast. I wish that I had wealth & leisure to educate my body.

To-morrow, My Mother, bless her, comes. She will stay some weeks. God guard me through the coming week & through life.

New Orleans, February 15, 1852

Thoughts of Suicide—Vanity, Vanity, no more. Let me sleep.

The secret of existence is settling on me. What is man? What am I? O life, O Death! O God! Yet live. For I must do the work given.

New Orleans, February 22, 1852

I am about to form a mutual Improvement Club for Oratory, Debate, Composition, & Knowledge.

What is Life? What God?

Preparing for the Presidential Campaign.

Thoughts of Suicide. Gloomy, Oh so gloomy. Then all glee & mockery.

New Orleans, February 29, 1852

Began the *Passions of the Human Soul*,[185] by Charles Fourier. Life grows practical. And such practice. Law—I abhor it. Was I destined to squander precious hours in squeezing from it a scanty & unsatisfactory livelihood? And yet I hope—I think that this is not extravagance or self-delusion. This coming week—He will help me to number my days.

New Orleans, March 7, 1852

Finished Thompson's *Castle of Indolence*.[186] Liked it.

On my suggestion, my friends D. F. Mitchell & E. Halloran, have with myself decided to form a Mutual Improvement club. It must be that God guides me.

I am very poor. I have not money with which to buy books or other necessaries. But God provides for me.

New Orleans, March 14, 1852

Continued Fourier on *The Passions of the Human Soul*. The Social problem: Shall I solve it? Studied Invention; the Steamengine & cotton-press. So many improvements suggest themselves.

This week study Invention, the cotton-press, Oratory, Composition, Philosophy, Politics, Conversation, & Law. Pray, & read. Talk but little; earnestly then, & to ladies, gaily; if to men, gravely. My aversion to spending time in the practice of Law, grows.

But God is my Father; still I am his darling. When will I achieve anything? Oh! no, no:—Achievement! When will I begin to achieve?

New Orleans, March 21, 1852

  Continued Fourier on the *Passions of the Human Soul*.

  Hereafter I shall pray to achieve. How long shall I arm? Let now. God, God, Oh God! Let me achieve, I care not;—let it be to scrawl but an essay or model a cotton-press. Almighty! Let me realize. I am a child. Nurse, where are my toys? Look in the side of the bottom drawer, and bring me the little horses and ships. The wooden soldiers were about the size of a tack. Get me my little box of carpentry tools. And, and I will play. Come to the big oak. There it is shady. I am a boy; I am not a man. There are no men. Suck your chops, gray-beards. With your dotard walking-canes, draw in the sand new stables, cowhouses and kitchens. Plot, eat, sleep. Alas, to die is noble; for after the shroud is ripped-off a robe is put on. Hercules where he had about his shoulders the band and gussets Nessus' shift; what did he do?

New Orleans, March 28, 1852

  This week, studied oratory. Began to write some elements of an ideal Society. Of this the occasion was a request of my two friends of the Mutual Improvement club; a constitution being needed.

  Studied Invention. Apply as I develope them, the principles of it to the cotton-press and Steam-engine. In a perfect contrivance every part, material and quality must have the greatest fitness.

  What is Life; what Death; what God, why am I? Why here & now? What is Fame? "I wish my heart was calm and still To beams that fleet, & blasts that chill." I am desolate. That is, my heart hungers. It is famished. I am tired. What, what is death? Would it be curious to meet and examine it? Ah, Well-a-day: When I am a general, the soldiers shall all love me. Does God really love me? Am I his darling? Heigh ho: No, no, no: before ever I sigh, let groans and agonies nestle in my breast. These coming days: what will I do in them? Read a book! Write words words, pah, always words. Ever the tongue, never the hand.

New Orleans, April 4, 1852

  Continued Fourier's *Passions of the Human Soul*. My twenty-third birthday draws near. Oh God! "To beams that fleet, & blasts that chill, I wish my heart was calm and still."—What shall be done with my body? *Two years before the Mast* [187]—I want that book.

  And marry whom? For what? Study?! And if I die? But a perfect body! Could I yet perfect my body?

I—I—Stars yonder: That is the moon. She is a corpse. For he said that some planets are dead. Death? What is Death? What Life? Love? Earth? Self? Men? Glory? God?

New Orleans, April 11, 1852

Continued Fourier on the *Passions of the Soul*. Studied Oratory, Take lessons in elocution, Mandeville's system:[188] Eveleth professor, my Uncle sends me.

She comes again, and I have seen her.

New Orleans, April 17, 1852

I consecrate to Glory, myself. My Father: by our long loves, by your omnipotence and omniscience, I swear it.

My Father: Let me achieve.

New Orleans, April 18, 1852

Purchased Bourne on the Steam-engine. On yesterday my birthday my elder sister presented me the *History of the Course of Modern Philosophy*,[189] by Cousin.

Mr. Durant my preceptor has directed me to write a brief for the Supreme Court. Began it yesterday. Let it be perfect. I have prayed on account of it.

Let me achieve. Spent a portion of my birthday in meditation, resolution, and prayer.

New Orleans, April 25, 1852

My preceptor Mr Durant wished me to write a brief in one of his appeal-cases: finished it. I will hear to-morrow, perhaps his opinion. Sometimes I am now wild-spirited. Many ask "what is the matter with me?" Some, "am I tipsy"; some "he is crazy!" Strangers say "who is that laughing young gentleman; is he a poet, or artist?"

Alas! My morning dream comes back. Within the gates of this world, I feel myself a stranger; my home seems in another—a far country. When shall I rise & journey thither? There is my Father; there solitude; "To beams that fleet & blasts that chill I wish my heart was calm & still."

New Orleans, May 2, 1852

Finished the first volume of Fourier's *Passions of the Human Soul*. That book's influence on me! May God guide & govern it.

I have a yearning for action. I am weary of thoughts & words only. Let come thoughts & deeds. I would be a Soldier, a pitt-sawyer, a worker-out of my own inventions. Can I love? The moon shines; I have but returned through it, from clasped hands & whispers, sighs, glances, tenderness, devotion. When shall fame begin, and power? Reflection, first; then resolve; then achievement. Let me achieve; that's for God, the Power's ear.

New Orleans, May 9, 1852

Continued Fourier on the *Passions of the Human Soul*.

What, what is life?—Last night a meeting of citizens was held: the object was the establishment of a Navy-yard here; and deepening of the mouths of the Mississippi River. They passed resolutions which urged upon the Federal Government, these enterprises. A committee of Twenty was voted; it was to carry to Washington City these resolutions and there enforce them. The Chairman of the meeting is to appoint the Committee. This morning it occurred to me to procure on this committee, an appointment; this evening I have decided to undertake it. Expense is perhaps the chief objection.

The committee will be composed of prominent citizens. They will be both Whig & Democratic; the Chairman will probably be Whig; the Secretary, Democratic. The Secretary could perhaps secure from the position, both power & fame. I will undertake to be Secretary.

To secure appointments will bring me in contact with some of the Editors & merchants. Succeeding in the appointment my contact with the editors shall produce, correspondence and on return, editorial possibly. Acquaintance with merchants can be profitable professionally.

Being thus appointed I shall endeavor to procure appointment as Delegate, from Mississippi, to the Baltimore Convention of the Democratic Party. This meets next month.

Thus I shall see & study, Congress also; thus get a distinction slight perhaps, but useful matrimonially. My law-practice, will be benefited by the undertaking; this I may, I think safely say. I have prayed; God will help me.

New Orleans, May 16, 1852

The Committee on the Navy Yard resolutions was appointed before I applied. So, this is once.

Continued Fourier on the *Passions of the Human Soul*.

Studied Oratory & Composition; Law not much.

I cannot write my esoteric history. My Soul will have no confidant.

Finished "Lessons on Mandeville's System of Elocution," Eveleth, the master. Profited, but not much.

Health not confirmed. I think that I have laryngitis.

Law-business somewhat improved. Why do I abhor the practice yet like the study of the Law.

How much I want to grapple with something. I would be a soldier, but not in peace; physician, but not in health; sailor but not in port or calm. But I give up all to the good God. He is brave; He loves; He destines me.

New Orleans, May 23, 1852

Continued Fourier on the *Passions*. I do not think that this book will mislead, nor make me visionary. It will generate conceptions; it will supply elements. These I can combine; can accept or reject.

The Mutual Improvement Society meets regularly Monday evenings. Mr Ginder a talented & amiable young gentleman formerly of the U.S. Coast Survey has been admitted as a fourth member. We give & receive reports upon Geography, Trade, General Law, Science, Art, Literature, Politics, Religion. At the last meeting were views of the Lumber Trade; Longitude; East Indian Company & Law. Midnight sometimes hears us enthusiasts.

I have suggested to them, Devoteeism. Let me know & use everything.

Body; body; how shall I get body? Let my soft muscles be sailor's—brawn— "each petty artery hardy as the Nemean lion's nerve."[190]

Let me this week, collect and survey my knowledge; let me arrange and supply. Above all, let my will be inexorable and crushing. Let it too be a will of Decision. So may I be the greatest and best man that can be.

The time draws nigh, and the Devotees' life begins.

The disease of Learning again comes to me. Let it rage, till the eyes wear out & the shameless pulse Slackens.

New Orleans, May 30, 1852

Continued Fourier on the *Passions of the Human Soul*. Began Cousin's *History of the Course of Philosophy*, translated. I wish a thorough course of political history. I wish to study the Career of Caesar & Napoleon. I wish to study the French Revolution also. It had realities.

I rest on God. He will furnish the work.

Oratory is a means. Men must do what I tell them. How can I be most powerful? Oratory is the power of controlling. I wish to study Military Science. This is all study; will I never actualize, never begin life, the hero life; or is, Oh horror! life now begun & I not a hero?

Let Oratory now fix my Soul! then let me wield it. I want body, grace, voice, strength! I want wit, humor, fearlessness, daring, will, judgment, reason, fancy, memories & words. God, I am your Devotee & Aspirant; fasten in me all these, and goodness such you will with a bounding heart, behold.

I am poor, but He will supply me; charitable, He will fill & open, my palm.

Oh Life! and after death, what? Is it now a reality? Marked in my note-book certain reforms in jural rights; these are for consideration.

This week let me, My Father let me be intellectually what shall please you through fastidious[ness].

New Orleans, June 7, 1852

Finished Fourier on the *Passions of the Human Soul*. Began notes on Macintosh's *View of Ethical Philosophy*.[191] The Democrats have nominated for the Presidential offices, Pierce & King. How will that make me more powerful or glorious? How every book makes me wiser.

Bodily Strength is an element of the supreme hero. I must be strong. I wish that wars were. I detest the practice only of the Law. It is too Mechanical. What ruby hours are by it hurled away in handfuls, like cockle-shells?

Of my Father who died when I was old enough only to love but not appreciate him; the more I hear, the more I venerate him. He attempted to reform the dishonesties of cotton factorage; he would have succeed[ed] but death came. He was "of the early breed of Athens."

New Orleans, June 13, 1852

Learned something of the essence and nature of Descriptive Geometry. Saw in a review an article on the *Influence of Authority in matters of Opinion*.[192] It is in criticism of Lewis' work. That will be of use in my political & social plans—works I mean. For if all my life, I am but to plan and dream, had I not now better die? I have but one character; that is Hughes the Aspirant. But in that are Ambition, Love, Friendship, Familism. I like Henry Ginder, and D. F. Mitchell.

I never had an esoteric friend. Can such be, and not woman? Is my wife, my esoteric friend? This week, studied wit. Are the ultimate objects of wit states of mind only; as skill, and knowledge, emotions? or intellectual states only according to Brown's classification? Concluded examination of Macintosh's *View of Ethical Philosophy*.

New Orleans, June 20, 1852

Studied Oratory, Wit, & Invention. Collected general information; classified & adjusted.

Perhaps my letters will be my best history. I write regularly to no one but my elder sister. She is a wise, pure, earnest woman; she is heroic, and knows it not. Her spirit is an angel; an angel is with her and she knows it not. Julia is her elder child, and so worthy of her. Julia, Uncle's darling. I have to Heaven that child commended, and while I prayed embosomed in God, held her for blessing & consecration.

When will the life-work begin? Lord, I stand by the vineyard; command me to enter. Bless my mother bless my sisters; theirs, my brother, & brother-in-law; My Father bless all, all men, and let me be your darling.

New Orleans, June 27, 1852

Read Macaulay's Essay on Bacon.[193] It was good. Particularly, read the two examples of Bacon's style.

I wish my style to be perfect classification. What is perfect style?

Studied Wit, Oratory, Philosophy and general knowledge. I learn of everybody; I think hour after hour, —I must not be [an] egotist.

Wednesday, I go to the Parish of St Mary in this State. I go in fulfillment of a promise to ——. What will follow? Ought I? or ought not? I trust God.

Read from a book concerning murders.

Kissed a young lady—this was gallantry only—on my part. Talked immodestly to another one; she liked it; I was as usual learning; during the talk, reflected what was most immodest, so as to utter it over her chair & in her ear. Was this bad? I have begun to study the politics & sociology of marriage.

Steamer Delia, Bayou Plaquemine, July 4, 1852

Left New Orleans last Thursday. Arrived at the town of Franklin Parish of St Mary, Friday evening and went to John B. Murphy's; he is my Uncle & a sugarplanter. This morning, left there on the route to New-orleans.

Why this has been; whether for power & glory; for wretchedness or bliss, I will not utter. Sometime, but not now, it may be told. It may be told when some are in the grave; it may, I say, be told when violets bloom over what has been beauteous & faithful, fond.

Oh, Angel's heart! Why should it be thus? Tears now are in my eyes; hereafter it will not be so, for the bosom which was flesh to love must be marble to forget! How did she apprehend all! How bowed to the fate.

Oh fondest dream: but when awake, if it before Heaven and Gods rewards to his hero-son; when my lids unclose; rather let them never, or but to look forward and upward, and not into a soul where happiness should have been and misery is.

My Father, you made me—let me talk so—I was your darling & hero; this was so; but if in what is thus done by me and through you, I am beguiled; if Oh my Soul, there is for me no Father, no caressing God; let then all Earth yawn its chops and gorge with men & blood its gut of fire: let all stars suns and comets shoot short into solid coal and flicker into ashy nothing. For a soul is lost, lost; a soul is, is lost! I fear that then my soul is lost.

Port Gibson, July 11, 1852

Monday last, July 5th 1852, returned from Attakapas to New-orleans. Left the next day for Port Gibson. Arrived here Friday last 9th July. What shall here be done, where I shall live, what pursue; these are known alternatively, not absolutely. I may have here my home. Here I may work out by literature, politics, law, philosophy, science, what God has sent me to do.

It may be that I shall go to New-orleans to be a money-catcher. That life & prospect, I abhor. If existence is a conflict, death has there the slow victory. There are all hateful things; Sickness is there; there adulteries, seductions, hypocricies, syncophancies, selfishness; & whatever I have shrunk from, whatever loathed.

Finished Macaulay's review of Bacon. I have Bacon's Works, by Montague.[194] I expect soon to attack them. With him I feel equality & recognition. How little Macaulay knew the esoteric Verulam.[195]

Bought Keble's *Christian Year*.[196]

Port Gibson, July 18, 1852

Read Lord Bacon. There I met a man. He is a peer; with him I feel an intellectual equality. So with Julius Caesar. Yet I feel that Alexander the Great; he was young; Cromwell who was not hightaught; and Napoleon who was not freeminded when young, because his profession was essentially disciplinary, were not my soul-peers. If Aristotle had been in his maturity, a wealthy man, or if by art, circumstance and education Shakspeare's mind had been all disclosed, if all its envelopments had been peeled or shorn-off, there would have been one with whom I could have always dwelt. We would have recognized; we divined each other's every thought & feeling. If it were that Metempsychosis were not a surmise only, then Julius Caesar was myself.

Omniscience is higher than omnipotence; if it could be so, or so to dream and whisper, our two souls were from God the Wisdom and God the Love; the Son and the Holy Ghost. I have perhaps no reverence; yet in my prayers and visions I seek boldly & filially the Father & the Son, but am awed by the Holy Spirit.

Read from Cousin *Course of History of Modern Philosophy*.

Port Gibson, July 25, 1852

Received Tennyson's Poems[197] and read enchanted. Began Fletcher's *Studies on Slavery*.[198] This was from my Brother Thomas Magruder.

Heard to day that Miss E.C. had arrived. Now, now my Soul.

Saw Miss M.P.; the Fate seemed coming. How now it shall is with God. My Faith shook never for a moment, and now I still can smile.

And shall Circumstance push me back? I will not doubt, though there shall be delay; I mean delay may be.

My right hand is in God's palm.

This week has been very happy. Feeling leaves my cheek and squats upon my brow.

Port Gibson, August 1, 1852

Read from Bacon & Tennyson. Continued Fletcher on *Slavery*.

Oh Woman Tennyson, Sweet Tennyson; darling, dearest. My love, you are not a—a man. Are you? Say "no." But you are wild-eyed, tender, tipsy girl. You are half drunk of Apollo, Bacchus never. The lovely God is in you. The sleepy, dreamy, sunny God.

A black & liquid luxury of round ringlets is billowy on your brow. And looks—Pish that's the churchbell. Anon—I come.

She of my thoughts did not come. A mistake of women, to fright me from my stool.

The love-scheme moves well. God loves me, the Fate, the long Bliss comes.

Port Gibson, August 8, 1852

Nearly concluded Fletcher on *Slavery*. My darling, wise brother Tom has brought me in 1. Calhoun on Government.[199]

How very mixed is the cup of life; how sweet & bitter; spice, aloes, and confection of roses. My mother has been quite sick; better now. Is it better not to have a heart? For mine so frightens me.

Began day before yesterday and nearly finished, an obituary of Margaret Newton Lindsay, Sherbourne.[200] This undertaken by request of my uncle Dr Lindsay. I prayed before commencement of it. The very first anectote of myself while I was almost a baby was related to me by a lady; she saw me playing where some little boys were throwing stones, and on asking me whether I was not afraid, I replied seriously, that if my eye was put out, I would get Uncle Aleck who was a teamster, to drive me in his wagon up to Heaven; and God there would fix my eye for me.

And so the coming week; what shall happen? I have prayed, but is prayer enough?

Port Gibson, August 15, 1852

Began Calhoun's Disquisition on Government; able work, pleased. Looked through *Uncle Tom's Cabin*[201] by Mrs. Beecher Stowe. That book is womanish & I am afraid absurdly unprincipled; written by a woman clearly. I feel like I am the man for times coming.

Concluded Fletcher on *Slavery*. It is very weak & very strong, but oftener that than this; a first effort I judge. He seems to say nothing of Whewell.

My mother recovers slowly.

I did not publish the obituary which was almost completed. I read it to Sis—Mrs. Morehead—who objected that it would do well if it was for Mr. Clay. I substituted some scripture texts.

It was written in Saxon idiom chiefly: its predecessor was in the high Latin Style. I shall of course use both, but more, the Saxon, I think. Tennyson drew to it my attention and applause.

Port Gibson, August 22, 1852

I wish that Time had a serpent's coil weighing down his wing. O! Hours, O! Days O! Month, so fast, so mettlesome you swallow up, you hunger and gorge the racing ground.

I have been very happy. Is what they say about the misery of this life, false? What shall I say?

Read Calhoun on Government & the Constitution; Read Webster's Reply to Calhoun[202] on the South Carolina Tariff Matter. The spirit of Commerce pervades Webster; of Agriculture, Calhoun. The heroic element is larger in Calhoun. Calhoun's argument for nullification is strong but ineffectual; for the right of Secession, better than he was conscious, so I think. But let me not prate.

There is a new attempt which I will probably achieve, to complete the Railroad between this place and Grand-Gulf. How can I get most power & glory out of this? So of all things.

Thus of Ambition. How of Love? Never let me speak. God helping, Willed act hastens towards me happy.

I study theoretically & practically popularity. I wish to have this, county, Congressional District & state, wholly under my most welcome government. I am a governor; I know it; I am not vain, thus speaking.

Study oratory the colloquial rather, & Invention, every week, & philosophy every night.

The model of my cotton-press was very clumsy: my handwork all is. After awhile, it will not, I hope, be so.

I am solitary in habit; staying if not reading most with God and myself. Shame on my egotism. Is it because I am happy?

Vicksburg, August 29, 1852

Left Port Gibson, last yesterday. I come here on account of business of my Sister Mary Ann.

In this journey as in everything else, I pray for greatest power and glory. I do not wish to be the greatest mortal man that can [be] for my own sake, but for God; something pushes me! Something is in me, I am God's, I am Destiny's.

I do my Sister's business; when I am away, herself or Willie.

Port Gibson, September 5, 1852

Returned on Wednesday from Vicksburg. While there I had a conference with Major Roach & Mr Crump of the Vicksburg & Jackson Railroad. This was concerning our railroad to Grand Gulf, and resulted in a letter from Major Roach to myself. This letter contained a low estimate of the proposed work, with desirable information. I left it with the leader of our enterprise.

Port Gibson, September 12, 1852

The little child—Willie—of my Sister Mrs Magruder is very sick. They are here with us. I think that this is the first time that ever I felt pity. The eyes of a suffering baby, they stick my heart. I have prayed, I pray that he may get well.

When steam from a pipe strikes the air action & reaction are equal. If the pipe be the radius of a circle and steam escape, at a tangent there is motion from reaction. Action & reaction may be increased by increasing either the force of the steam or the force of the resisting medium. I have invented a steam-engine in which a resisting medium of increased density as hot water or steam of a different temperature is substituted for the atmosphere. This was last week. Yesterday I went to my mercantile friend Henry Merrifield Esq. and explained to him both that and the Cotton-press. I think that he did not apprehend the steam-engine as it now is. I go again.

I love, and am loved. I can not be beguiled—so I dream.

Began Randal on *Sheep-Husbandry* [203] & Bentham on *Legislation* [204]—by Dumont translated by Neal. I wish that I had all Bentham's published works. Was he heroic?

Studied the Cotton-gin. If by invention one could lower the average price of cotton one cent only, how would the world be served? Is to do this better than to frame indictments & petitions?

Mr Mitchell has returned to the city. I like him.

Studied generation of thought. From a given period, what periods & in what order may be generated? What the best periods, & best order?

Suppose that the Senate were divide[d] into Northern & Southern concurrent chambers. Suppose that the Southern States had a federation concurrent with the general federation?

Port Gibson, September 19, 1852

Last Monday, my Sister Maria's child "Willie" died. I loved the child, and at its funeral wept like a woman. They read, I mean Mr Butler, the friend of my heart, who ministered at the funeral, the passage of Holy Writ, which recites Gehazi's journey to the child.

To me, the Hereafter has never before seemed so real. God and Heaven are now substantial as this whirling earth.

Studied Invention, the laws and application.

Invention is either to form or to reform: either to create or to improve. Of Improvement, the first law is Exhaustive-Description. This is an analysis to all the elements of the contrivance whether local, aggregate, or atomic together with an analysis of their properties. Then let their [. . .] be the description, conception or development of all their fitnesses, and the fitnesses required. Then developement of other succedanea and selection. This, crudely.

Continued *Physiolog[y]* & *Sheep-Husbandry*; finished Dumont's Benthams *Principles of Legislation* glanced again through *Pilgrims of the Rhine*.[205]

Port Gibson, September 26, 1852

Went Wednesday to John Routh's Esq.[206] on Lake St Joseph, Tensas Parish, La. Returned same day, late. Went on law-business in which I get a large fee. What an aristocracy or able-class, the slave-states have.

Read—or rather looked through Edinburgh Encyclopedia on Hydrodynamics. Began the article on "Heraldry." Read much miscellaneously, Studied Oratory, Wit, & Invention, Prayed for achievement in these, this every night.

What is the province of Woman? That is the most difficult question in Sociology.

How can the perennial water supply of navigable streams be best affected? Can the power of flowing water be a means to this?

Last night strained my back. Every night—Sunday excepted, I gesticulate, also exercise chest.

Finished Randals *Sheep-Husbandry*. Life now full of ambition, study, & happiness.

Port Gibson, October 3, 1852

To-day my brother returned. He has been North.

Begun Gillespie on *Roads & Railroads*.[207] Read and spoke French. Began a tale of the Catholic Religion. It was "Mary the Star of the Sea." A young lady leant me it. Got some new ideas.

My expression of Philosophy will be the Ultimum Organum. Shall I be the last Philosopher, Statesman, Conqueror, Jurisprudent? And shall I be also a Priest? Shall I be the Last Organ of God? This to me is now new.—Studied with prayer nightly thereto—Oratory, Wit, Invention. Looked through Edinburgh Encyclopaedia's Heraldry.

What am I? New schemes of Theology, Cosmogony. The world is in front.

Port Gibson, October 10, 1852

Received from Mr Durant, reports of two speeches delivered by him in opposition to the New Constitution of Louisiana. What is the best system of Representation & Taxation?

Looked into Mrs. Eastman's *Aunt Phyllis' Cabin*,[208] continued Gillespie's *Roads & Railroads*. Found several ideas of railroads which I originated in myself, also developed, there—as continuous bearings for rails.

Last Tuesday went to St. Joseph Tensas Parish La. Court was in session. I applied for Administration of Estate of Wm Lindsey decd—father of my Uncle in New Orleans—and for guardianship of minor heirs.[209] This by understanding and for a large fee.

Still, the desire for philosophy, politics, sciences, literature, jurisprudence, but, not the practice of law. I still meditate the Ultimum Organum Scientiarum. Study invention to that end. Pshaw, "Wherwithal shall I be clothed?"

Port Gibson, October 17, 1852

Finished Gillespie's *Roads & Railroad*; "Give me to eat." A morbidity to read has me—to study—to think.

Meditated perfect oratory. Invented a screw with a variable thread. Apply same principle to other mechanical powers.

What new motors; what new mechanical powers are there?

Mississippi River Steamer Southern Belle, October 24, 1852

Friday last left Port Gibson. I go to the City.—The world again begins. I will—I am—yes I am—I am ready! I trust in God—My Father—What is life: Time is gone.

Why, why does Carlyle thrust himself into my thoughts? This Winter: death or distinction. Every day, pray for achievement. A Universal Republic, Ultimum Organum, Longitude, Slavery Perfect Society; Myself, the Godbeloved, the human supreme of Earth's Politics, Society, Philosophy, Economics, Religion & Aesthetics; Of these I am the devotee.

New Orleans, October 31, 1852

Continued Cousin's *History of Philosophy*. Studied [. . .]. Began earnestly the mastery of Law.

Arrived here last Tuesday the 26th.

Read with profound benefit, Savage's *Reuben Medlicott*.[210] Esoteric biography cannot be written.

Attended last night the Polymathic Society. Begun the mastery of the Beautiful.

New Orleans, November 7, 1852

Continued Cousin's *History of Philosophy*. Studied Law. Analysed in Mathematics.

Applied for admission into the "Order of the Lone Star." If this Order is honorable, and I trust it, I wish to use it in my life-aim of a Universal Republic.

In all things existence grows more practical.

Calhoun, Clay, Webster, all are dead; I had rather not be than to be no more than they were.

"Perseverence keeps honor bright." Analyze next week bills of Exchange; Study fluency of ideas & words, Study the forcible of expression, Study Invective and Panegyric, Study Fascination, Study Criticism, Study the prospective oratory of Annexation, Quote-Practice self-concentration—presence of mind and decisiveness from reflecting.

My Father in Heaven: Love me.

New Orleans, November 14, 1852

Looked through Randolph's tale about slavery.[211]

Is Savage freedom better than civilized Slavery? Is the American slaves condition better than that of the native African? Let it be that our slaves are exchanged for their value of African Savages; these transported hither; those, to Africa! What would be the ethics, politics, and economics of this?

Study—observing—human passions.

I have patience; life-work will come.

I wish that I could meet a genuine able-man.

Continued Cousin *History of Philosophy & Physiology*.

Body, body wants development. My Father in Heaven; What am I; What is life; What, this scene of things; what the end?

New Orleans, November 21, 1852

Read Hawthorne's *Blithedale Romance*,[212] Continued Cousin's *Hist. of Philosophy*.

Studied this week, To Kalon & To Dikaion. Studied Oratory. Indifferent days. Nothing but the Ultimate—the Extreme in power, fame or pleasure seems to me worthy. Begun French Lessons.

New Orleans, November 28, 1852

Finished 1st volume of Cousin's *History of Modern Philosophy*. Purchased Emerson's Essays,[213] Browning's—Elizabeth Barrett—Poems,[214] and Redfield's *Men of the Times*.[215]

Studied French, Law, figures in Rhetoric, Aesthetics, & Steam-engine. Can the values of a steam-engine be inserted in the piston?

New Orleans, December 5, 1852

Study Law-Reform, Constitutional-Law of Fugitive Slaves, Wit, Figures in Rhetoric & Steam-Engine.

Can steam be condensed—absorbed—by some *chemical* agent, which by process of condensation or change of fluid to solid, shall generate heat, as lime? How can Printing be economized? There are two leading processes, composition & distribution. Can composition be by a digital motion only, and not by brachial & digital motion? Can distribution of types be through electrical or magnetic, or electro-magnetic attraction; or by putting types of certain specific gravities in fluids of certain specific gravities? or by sifting the types? Finished 1. Cousin's *History of Phylosophy*. Began the second volume.

Last Friday, the 3d of December 1852, I was initiated into the order of the Lone Star.

I have the need, the necessity, to act on something; this has made vicious many men.

I want bodily development. I trust in God.

Reviewed portions of Political philosophy, Ethics, Polity, & International Ins. Studied Aesthetics, & French.

New Orleans, December 12, 1852

Finished Cousin's *Course of History of Modern Philosophy*. Studied Fugitive-Slave Law. Why have I such a passion for war? Why does a soldier's life seem my coming destiny?

What of Spiritual-Rapping, and coming-revolution?

What of marriage, civil & religious? What is best?

Power, power, What else? Something to clutch! that is the necessity.

New Orleans, December 19, 1852

Begun again Kant *Critic of Pure Reason*. Continued Mill's *Logic*. Studied Invention & Oratory, Law.

The contents of a steam-boiler are hot water & vapor. Are their temperatures the same? If the temperature of the hot-water is less, ought not it to work against the piston?

The red-corpuscles of blood yield to pressure; is this to prevent lesion or disorganization of the blood under pressure abnormal — in its vessels?

Called this evening on Doctor Bennett Dowler.[216] Had a long conference on matters chiefly scientific. He and my Uncle were at one time neighbors. Doctor Dowler gave me some of his views of Thermometrical observation, and an allowancy for degrees of shade, which with other enumerated causes of error, he suggested.

So, so, what is life? The year is almost gone.

New Orleans, December 26, 1852

Civilization is hateful. Bodily development is needful. Every thing is clothed; nothing, naked. Time passes; what is done? Of, Life, Death, World.

New Orleans, January 2, 1853

The poet is wrong; he mistakes; the years do not "snow," the flash; their sheet lightens between two darknesses, both to me now, black as tempest— midnight, the Eternal & the Everlasting. But it is not so; for it is a black world, and after that, brightness must be everything.

My chest has become so weak as to draw me to some means of strengthening it. Probably I shall go home, and to the Country.

This must be a year of actualization. I must develope memory, the recollective & recognitive; imagination also and reason.

I must master the Artificial. Let me arrange the elements, this year, of all Sciences & Arts. Let me study & master fascination of women, men, & children; with all modes of power. And perfect philosophy, politics, theology, economics, & sociology; towards these, let me advance. And let Time pass; but let it give me power and glory, so that I shall be tried and the grave have rest. God and myself.

New Orleans, January 9, 1853

Have I ever had a pleasure in which woman was not an element? Since my eighteenth year, I have not been unloved. And so again and—still—clasped hands, embracing arms, kissed lips and pillowing bosoms, Ambition and Love, these are my life.—Desire in prospective; power & possession to the full shall come, with wing of speed and beak of strength.

Miss M.R.P. is still ——. It is predestined that she shall be ——. I know it. It shall be, I know it.

Looked through *Wandering Jew* of Sue.[217]

New Orleans, January 16, 1853

Closed Sue's *Wandering Jew*. Health bad; weak chest; weak, all the winter, too-much stooping I suppose.

I go Tuesday-evening, to Vicksburg. This, on account of business of my sister. I will return by Port Gibson.—This for health, for home-duty, and for what hereafter may be at large unfolded.

Thomas S. McCay, my high-minded and talented schoolboy rival has been elected parish Senator from the City.

I want now development of body. To a great man, a great body is as necessary as a great mind.

Are the women of civilization, slaves? Are they dependents? Can they be independents, without the elements of courage? Is one element of courage ability to defend? In this connexion, what of improved weapons, weapons equalized? What is the extent of societary Insincerity? What, of a perfect Orator? How can all wit be generated? & anecdotes? What of second sight, What of fascination?

Port Gibson, January 23, 1853

Left New-orleans last Tuesday & went to Vicksburg & Transacted business and came home. Arrived Friday evening. More experience; life is experience.

I wish to marry, reside here, go next winter to the State-legislature, and afterwards to Congress, or be Secretary of State. We shall see.

Chest weak. Home is blissful.

Port Gibson, January 30, 1853

Concluded *The Wandering Jew* by Eugene Sue. Got from it, much power. "Fireside enjoyments, homeborn happiness," these, these again.

The other day, bought for my mamma a spade; carried it through the streets home; working in the garden. Chest & bronchial, feeble.

Expect to return with my sisters to the City on Friday next.

New Orleans, February 8, 1853

This omitted, Sunday.—Left Port Gibson Friday last with my sisters and niece Julia Morehead. Arrived in the City February 7th. Health better.

What is life? I shall soon be twenty-four years of age.

New Orleans, February 13, 1853

Looked through Faben's *Life on the Isthmus*.[218] Not instructed. Begun Dix's *Winter in Madeira*.[219] My Little Sister presented me with several books of Travel, of my own selection. These now and geography with a view to the life-aim, a Universal Republic, and politics. I begin to study the development of Commerce. For this, Free-Trade and new-markets chiefly. With these Government has a revenue relation. Portugal is in debt; Madeira ought to be negotiated into possession of our Government. In this connexion now adjust the present famine there, and the Armstrong Case.

There is no capillary attraction. Hydrous liquids rise in tubes because the pressure of the atmosphere within is diminished by the walls of the tubes; this on the principle of the *Vena-Contracta*, in Hydraulics. Mercury in Capillary tubes is depressed. This depression is entirely mechanical? Mercury presses upward; the tube, downwards; this downward pressure is greatest in the direction of the tube and diminishes laterally: least therefore in the centre, making a concave.[220]

The principles of the mechanic-powers apply to liquids and gases. The Vena Contracta illustrates the wedge power.

In water, rock is one-half lighter than in air. If then on one end of a lever be suspended a rock weighing four-hundred pounds, and on the other end, a weight of three hundred and fifty pounds, the four-hundred pounds or power, will depress the three hundred and fifty, or weight: if after depression, the rock or power be surrounded by water or other liquid of proper specific gravity its weight while in water will be lessened one-half—generally—and the other end being heavier elevates it. This makes an engine. I conceived it this week. Secondly, the rock may be immersed in a liquid and of this the specific gravity be alternated by chemical additions.

New Orleans, February 20, 1853

Finished *Winter in Madeira and Summer in Spain & Florence* by Dix. Begun *Cuba & the Cubans*.[221]

1. If a cylinder with a piston be immersed in water to a given depth, and alternately admitted to the two sides of a piston in its cylinder-chambers; cannot the force thus produced pump back the water emitted and give a surplus of power for machinery.

2. In an airtight cylinder cannot a vacuum be got and thence reciprocating motion, by burning out the air & alternately admitting it to the piston, in the cylinder-chambers; this an engine on the principle of cupping glasses.

In gin-houses, a large amount of cotton is carried to the second or third floor. By making portions of the floor movable vertically, this weight of cotton may be used as power to move the gin or mill. So of all weighty materials to be modified by machinery.

The Mississippi Association is proposed. I am invited to membership. Sisters & Julia gone home.

New Orleans, February 27, 1853

Continued *Cuba & the Cubans*—stupid. Assisted in organizing the Mississippi Society and drafting its constitution. That part is mine relating to the glory of the State and degrees of honorary membership. Had a conversation with a friend who is a minister of the gospel. It was of professions. He commended "Lecturing." Cited Thackeray. I am making at my profession not a support even. I trust in God. What is life? And if my body fails? Sound mind in a sound body; how much I know of that.

This week: what will it bring forth?

New Orleans, March 6, 1853

This week is the mother of a giant brood. So at least, to me. To-morrow, I will begin *The Aspirant*.[222] Miss M.R.P. and Miss E.C. are both in town. Is there providence; What is this life? Next month is my birthday. I go to the grave.

New Orleans, March 13, 1853

Last Monday begun *The Aspirant*. I do not mean it to be a novel, but an announcement, real, earnest, practical, truthful and in faith.

Begun Macfarlane's *Japan*.[223] Superior.

What of Love? They were here, and one is gone. The coming womb of Time is heavy, and swelling; let it break and disgorge. Come what come may.

Haria H. is gone to Mexico. Lizzie is a widow. Mary H. is "single yet."

New Orleans, March 20, 1853

Continued *Aspirant*. What I write, I usually date and note with my initials.

At Mr. Durant's suggestion, investigated the constitutionality of Railroad tax.

Tomorrow, call on Miss M.R.P. "There is a tide." Read Shakspeare's *Much Ado About Nothing*. Study the wit of Shakspeare.

Begun *Vanity Fair* of Thackeray.[224]

They nominate April 4th in Claiborne County Mi. a candidate for House of Representatives of State. Pike Maxwell Esq., who is one of my oldest & best friends has possibly, consumption.

New Orleans, March 27, 1853

Finished *Twelfth Night* and Macfarlane's *Japan*. Begun Montesquieu's *Spirit of Laws*.[225]

M.R.P. is still here. "Dim Hour, that sleepst on pillowing clouds afar Oh Rise and yoke the turtles to thy car."[226]

How Spring cheers. Yet I am shut in chambers with famished eyelids locked against the free sight of growing grass.

New Orleans, April 3, 1853

Looked through *Villette*[227] and "English Items." Read 1. Montesquieu's *Spirit of Laws*.

Attended meeting of Mississippi Association. Vocalized twice a day. Voice improving. My classmate James Alexander who is on the way to California called to see me.

Enamored more and more of Oratory.

For some years, I have been chaste. I think that I shall be six feet in stature. I am, I believe, still growing. Health good. How time passes. I have been elected a member of the Academy of Arts and Sciences, lately established here.

New Orleans, April 10, 1853

Finished Montesquieu's *Spirit of Laws*.

I have been elected a fellow of the New Orleans Academy of Arts & Sciences. Dr. Bennett Dowler—my friend—is president. Vocalize daily.

Capillary Attraction is Capillary impulsion. Atmospheric pressure in a tube is less than outside of it. The wedge-principle applies to liquids & fluids. In hydraulics the *Vena-Contracta* illustrates the wedge principle. In capillary tubes & others, the atmosphere cannot press equally in all directions. The resultant pressure is therefore less & the fluid liquid rises. Capillary tubes *mechanically* depress mercury.

Investigated Endosmose & Exosmose. Evaporation is one cause of the circulation of the blood. What of the Collocation of the brain, heart & stomach?

Studied oratory. Moral aspirations not to be a practising lawyer. What of the Mormons? Who shall be Christ's forerunner? Lord is it I?

New Orleans, April 17, 1853

I consecrate to Glory, myself. By You, my God, I swear it.[228]

New Orleans, April 17, 1853

This is my birth-day. I am twenty-four years of age. I was borne the seventeenth of April 1829. This week I have been sick I am now in bed.

God helping me, I will pursue my aims of Life. I grow more & more averse to the practice of the Law.

To me, it sometimes seems that I shall never be called.

Port Gibson, April 24, 1853

Left New-orleans, Thursday last. I leave home in a few days to make the tour of Europe. Lawrence Pike Maxwell goes with me. His health is bad. I return in the fall probably. This tour is to complete my education.

So, God love me.

Port Gibson, May 1, 1853

A week of reverie & reflection. If a rock of four pounds weigh-down at one end of a lever a weight of three pounds, this three pounds will weigh down the four pound rock when it is immersed in water; for of rock the specific gravity is two. I tried this experiment this week. I think that it will produce an engine, the limits of whose motion will be the evaporation of water, or other medium. This invention occurred to me in the city.

Could hydraulic pressure be used in medicinal baths?

After leaving the city, flowers and fresh air are to me voluptuousness. This breathing is indulgence.

Do we want a new-Jesus? Mormonism will succeed on account of its social organization. Mormonism is not civilization; Monogamy is the essence of civilization.

The democratic Candidates for the legislature here have both resigned.

John Albert Feaster Coleman

"Oh! When we feel 'tis hard to toil
And sweat the long day through
Remember it is harder still
To have no work to do."

The above poetry should be strongly impressed on the mind of every young man (i.e.—the verasity of it) and on the Aristocratic portion of the community particularly as they are generally taught that labour is a dishonor rather than an honor. The ladies should know it also.

—July 5, 1849

November 1, 1848
Was in Columbia and sold cotton at five and an eighth cents per lb. Sorry price that.

November 3, 1848
Arrived home accompanied by Daddy[1] who went to Columbia with me, not being there before in five years.

November 4, 1848
Very rainy. Packed cotton in morn.

November 5, 1848

Being Sunday and still rainy I wrote to David R. Coleman of Chambers Ala. ie *the married man*.

November 6, 1848

Commenced sowing wheat, ground in fine order for sowing.

November 12, 1848

Very rainy which made a disappointment at the singing.

November 13, 1848

A show at Monticello where was shown animals of various classes—some of them were the Lion & Lioness & Tiger and Leopards, Monkeys, & Bears in abundance. Then came the Raindeer, Wolf, Ocelot and a great many more that I will not mention. The Lion was drove in harness but it was a very short drive. A man and his wife entered his cage and cut some very distressing circumlocutions. We came home unhurt, ie by the *Elfant*.

November 18, 1848

Rainy & cold with snow at night being the first snow this winter.

November 20, 1848

Division of Grand Pa Feaster's estate.

November 24, 1848

Killed eight hogs weighing fifteen hundred pounds nett, "so they did."

November 28, 1848

Amy's leg was amputated by R. W. Coleman assisted by McClurkin, Means, Dupre and Simeton. Nothing of any importance took place in the remaining days of this month except that we finished picking cotton on the last day.

This has not been a marrying month so it ain't, but I guess there was some sparking done in the time and perhaps marrying will be the alternative in after months as time will show. Cotton generally all gathered.

December 1, 1848

Sowed rye and other small grains.

December 2, 1848

Is distinguished highly by the lawsuit between Maj. John Coleman & Matt Weir. Decision in favour of M. Weir by Justice R. Morgan.

December 3, 1848

Being Sunday there was preaching at Red Hill. House crowded. Preaching undigestible.

December 4, 1848

Sale at Grand Pa Feaster's old place.

December 7, 1848

Marriage of Joseph Clowney[2] and Miss Jenette oldest daughter of S. H. Stevenson by the right Rev'd Boyce. Waited on by Miss M. C. Yongue and Misses Clowney on the one part and Miss Juliana Stevenson[3] and Mr. Keenan of Union on the other hand. We had a nice supper and nice fixings every way.

December 10, 1848

Our muster day in Feasterville. A tremendious quarrel between Jim Morgan & Wyat Cohen but not fighting. (Hurra for those that are brave—"Taylor.")

December 19, 1848

Was in Columbia and sold cotton at five & a half which is a little better than formerly. John J. Coleman and Albert arrived here on this date from Goran County Ala. safe & sound.

December 22, 1848

Miss M. S. McConnell came to see Drucy[4] and Isa.[5] We had a dance and enjoyed ourselves finely. Ob ie Albert seemed desperately taken in by Miss Mc and I am afraid he will cut some of the younger Blades out.

December 23, 1848

Miss Martha departed for home and left Ob & myself in a very horrid condition for Ob's eyes watered considerably and his mouth was taken with a much longer protuberance than common.

December 24, 1848

Preaching at cool branch by the Rev'd Mr. Rollins & Newlin. *My piece wer'nt thar.*

December 25, 1848

First of Christmas. Anticipation of much fun throughout the holidays. But had no fun until. . . .

December 27, 1848

at which time we had a judicious dance at Henry J. Lyles' and may him & Lady be blessed forever for giving the dance for it was the only in Christmas. So no more of December, last of 1848.

January 1, 1849

Killed hogs. Fine weather for the business. Came from Uncle Sam's on this morning, left all well. Joy to the New Year.

January 7, 1849

Look sharp. Miss M. D. Mc came home with Drucy & Isa and as good luck would have it to snow therefore it done so and the way we played snowballs was anything but wicked. But every sweet has its sour for she went home on the day following escorted by G. W. Punkins alias D.R.F.[6]

January 9, 1849

John J. started for Virginia. Cold weather.

January 11, 1849

D. R. Feaster was at our house. We went over and mustered with the Buckhead Troopers commanded by Jos. Clowney who is their capt.

January 12, 1849

Came home for Esq Feaster's in company with Trez and John Cockrell. I worked hard all this week until Saturday then went to a quilting at John F. Coleman's. We danced until eleven o'clock PM. and then came home.

January 21, 1849

Preaching at Salem by *Cater.*

January 22, 1849

Started to Columbia in company with W. M. Yongue.[7] Got there safe & sound. Sold cotton at six and twenty some hundredths cents per lb. Purchased the piano on this date from A. C. Squier.

January 29, 1849

I was attacked with a violent cold.

January 30, 1849

Finished working on David's house which we have been at since the last of December.

January 31, 1849

Last day of this month we commenced working on the Brown place.

We will not brag on this month, however some parts of it yealded ample harvests of diversions, for instance the seventh was very *Judiciously* enjoyed. But no marrying at all, although I think some of it is not far off. A fine month for ploughing was January.

February 1, 1849

Begins on Thursday, a cold and wet day. Packed cotton.

February 4, 1849

Preaching at red hill and the day on which Andrew Colvin Sr. was buried at the above church. Died of pheumonia.

February 6, 1849

Miss R. Robertson and Mary Yongue came over and Isa & Drucy gave them some on the piano.

February 9, 1849

David Feaster came and invited us to a party at Jacob F. Feaster's on the tenth. I made plough stocks on this date assisted by Ob.

February 10, 1849

Killed four hogs and commenced ploughing. I went to the frolic late in the evening and found them a dancing like rips, and I was soon in the same game. We danced until eleven o'clock AM and then left. I went home with the Steamer ie D. R. Coleman and stayed all night, and on the eleventh left for church at Cool Branch where was delivered two sermons by the Divines Fowler & Holms to a very large audience. Miss Mostic appeared though as if she was mighty pretty. She is that way and no mistake. I came from church as far as Screws and eat my dinner. Do. Morgan. Thense home and went to bed, had fine dreams, &c. But on rising in the morning it was raining, so we packed cotton until noon at which time it seaced raining. Afternoon we hauled leaves and horrible to relate the mules ran away with the wagon, tore down trees and broke loose from the waggon. No bones broke but lots of timber. On the Thirteenth I warned the seargents & corporals to warn the defaulters to a court martial. John J. arrived safe and sound from Va. on this date not liking the country in any *shape, aspect,* or *form.*

Pappa,[8] Henry and Bob started for Columbia on the Fourteenth in company with Uncle Jonathan.

February 16, 1849

Very cold. Went home with the Esq and smoked segars until evening. From thense I went to S.H.S. and brought Isa home from her school. Dave & John J. swapped horses on this even. And so did I swap Paddy for Rosa May from Jacob Sharp. *A good trade.*

February 17, 1849

We had a fine dance at A. E. Coleman's. The Miss Mcs, P. Feaster, C. Feaster, Sarah & Isa Coleman were the principal ladies of the party. The Mcs came home with Isa and Ob, Bob and A. E. Coleman[9] came with me. After getting home safe from any hurt we danced until ten o'clock. *Punkins some of it.*

February 18, 1849

The coldest kind of weather with snow. The Steamer & Judge came up so upon the whole amount we had a *select* crowd. The Miss Mcs left for home escorted by A.E.C. leaving the remainder of us gallants looking daggers at him as he rode off with them.

February 19, 1849

The day on which John J., Ob and E. S. Cockrell left this country for Green & Pickens counties Ala. They crossed at Lyles' ford intending to go the upper route.

February 22, 1849

This day will be handed down to the last generations as one amonge the illustrious for Elbert Feaster was married by the Rev'd Walker to Caroline Teauge of Laurens Dist. The lamentable death of Colonel David Crosby occurred on this date. He died of [. . .] leaving a vacancy in state legislature and the office of Colonel. A man of rising popularity. Sarah, C. and J. F. Mc stayed all night from school. Had fine music on the forty-string banjo. They left in peace the next morning for Feasterville, Fairfield, S.C. &c., &c. Visited the Esq. on the twenty-fourth and hunted squirrels.

February 26, 1849

Being extremely cold we killed some more hogs averaging one hundred and sixty pounds nett and we surveyed a piece of land for Screw off the Borow Track containing twenty-six acres.

February 27, 1849

Unforgettable by the infare[10] given in honor of the nuptial uniting of E. H. Feaster & Cady, honored by the attendance of Col. Calhoun & daughter Miss Harris, Miss Coleman and many others from Laurens. We danced all day. I left them a dancing and seemed as if they would not stop soon.

February 28, 1849

Last day. So it is.

March 1, 1849

The Laurens guest departed for home having danced nearly a full week in succession, day after day. They went off adancing for they danced a cotillion in the Flat as they were crossing the river and was dancing on from the latest news. Hurra for kin.

Dr. Bybee gave a lecture on Phrenology at Feasterville. Drucy went visiting to A. McConnell's.

March 2, 1849

Set all hands to ploughing, the ground being in fine order for the business &c. Darkey Jake and Charry Bill came up and took dinner. [. . .] played and sang some on the Piano. Widdow Tucker also was present. Lecture again by Pross Bybee. Mrs. [. . .] Davis died last week and Miss [. . .], her daughter, the week before.

March 3, 1849

Beautiful day but very dry for ploughing.

March 4, 1849

I came from Jacob Fry's in the eve accompanied by "Punkins" to Dr. Coleman's where we saw the Miss Mcs who looked very pretty. We left the Steamer there with them and came on to Uncle Jonathan's where we found Dr. Bybee in tet-a-tet with the family. Also the day on which Gen. Taylor seated himself in the Presidential Chair.

March 5, 1849

Disagreeable day being cold and clowdy. Commenced breaking the Esq's yonge mule.

March 8, 1849

A beautiful day, clear and warm. M. D. Mc & S.C.C. came in the evening from school. Sarah played finely on the piano and Martha looked prettier than ever, if possible.

March 10, 1849

Muster at Feasterville and a lecture in the evening on the Telegraphic Principle (etcetera) by Dr. Bybee. Also Mrs. Steve Crosby & Miss Priscilla Nevitt visited us on the same eve. Miss P. is not to be *grinned* by every toothless person &c., &c.

March 11, 1849

Meeting at cool Branch but no preaching as it was a very rainy day. Billy, Siss, Dave & Sarah were over and so on &c., &c.

March 12, 1849

Started to Columbia and got there on the Thirteenth safe after breaking down and turning over several times.

March 14, 1849

Sold cotton to J.B. [. . .] from six and five eighths to seven and a half sents per lb. Got back home on the fifteenth after sundown and found all upp and a doing and in possession of plenty of rain. So on the sixteenth as the ground was too wet for ploughing we spent the day in fencing. Also the seventeenth in the same employment until dinner at which all hands ceased working until Monday morning. After eating dinner I rode over to the Esq. and went fishing and stayed all night. The next morning being Sunday I left for Esq. Feaster & John Q. Arnett's[11] on a visiting spree &c. Came home in the evening accompanied as far as Feaster by A. C. Feaster.

March 19, 1849

I was to be found bursting up cotton stalks for the purpose of planting corn. Some hands droping cotton seed for manuering the corn. Mrs. Morgan and Widdow Tucker was over and took dinner. Mrs. M. gave us a brief narrative of being bit by a mad dog when very yonge. She certainly had a miraculous escape from being killed by the poison, but as she said it was because they doctored her so physically that she didn't die &c. I left the old lady talking.

March 20, 1849

Ploughed until the middle of the afternoon, being stopped by the rain which commenced at the above time and rained very hard til sundown with considerable prospect for more. Uncle Tom come over and began stocking ploughs for us. Mamma went to Dave's & Billy's and had to stay all night on account of the rain.

March 21, 1849

As it was too wet to plough we planted irish potatoes and a big patch at that and we also bedded the sweetpotatoes, patched upp the garden, ginned a little, hauled some manure, &c., &c. The Esq came over with the report that he was ploughing. He ain't smart. I give him some potatoes & [. . .] and told him to go home and Pappa went with him for safeguard. A tremendious storm just at sundown, fences prostrated &c.

March 22, 1849

Very cool in the morning with some frost. Warm at noon. Ground too wet to plough. Went over to the Esq in the afternoon. Killed squirrels and other reptiles and finally stayed all night and played cards until bed time. We arose in due time on

March 23, 1849

to go turkey hunting. Heard lots of gobbling but could not get a shot at them. I came home in the morning and found them working [. . .] Wm. McLane's on the fence, bushes & briars &c. Commenced ploughing after dinner over on the Brown plantation. Ground almost too wet but had to do so it did.

March 24, 1849

A pleasant day, fine for ploughing. At it until dinner at which time all hands ceased from working, being Saturday. Andrew E. Coleman came up in the middle of the afternoon with the report that he was done planting corn. He is Punkins. We anticipate a fine time at Salem on tomorrow as the Miss Gs are expected to be there. Pappa went down to the lower plantation, came back at sundown. A.E.C. & myself were greatly disappointed on the morning of the twentififth for it commenced raining very soon in the morning and rained all day incessantly, consequently we could not go to church but remained home and read some very good book and so on. "Some men grow mad by studying much to know. But who grows mad by studying good to grow." Again. "An egg today is better than a hen tomorrow." "Keep thy shop and thy shop will keep thee." At Daddy's 8 o'clock PM Sunday eve. &c.

March 26, 1849

Clear and cold being windy so we killed three more hogs weighing one hundred and fifty pounds each. Sent one over to the Esq who is wanting lots of meat. A.E. left for home soon in morn. Commenced ploughing again after dinner but the ground was not in good order. I do hope that it may not rain soon for we are considerably behind with our crop. Uncle Tom come again and began stocking more ploughs. Billy Jenkins & Silas Boling came up to rent land. Saw Mr. Willson the Tobacconist. "A ploughman on his legs is higher than a gentleman on his knee."

March 27, 1849

A very cold & windy day. Ploughed over at the Brown plantation. Went patrolling at night with A. C. Feaster, T. D. Feaster,[12] D. R. & J. H. Coleman Jr.

March 28, 1849

Still cold but milder than yesterday. Pappa started to Winnsborough via R. G. Cameron's.[13] Mrs. Tucker & S. C. Coleman were over. "All is not gold that glitters" &c.

March 29, 1849

Very pleasant day. Finished ploughing at the Brown place. Killed a large hawk which was eating a squirrel. Commenced planting corn on yesterday ie on the twentieighth. Saw Screw who was a sheep hunting in our field.

"The discontented man finds no easy chair." "Great talkers, little doers."

March 30, 1849

A pretty day being clear & warm. Finished planting corn in one field of fifty or sixty acres, ground getting hard. Hauled cotton seed for manure to the

Brown field. Received a letter from Ob who had landed safe at home without marrying, but I fear he will be compelled to marry soon judging from his writing.

As good fish in the sea at this time as have ever been caught out of it.[14] So says the old adage. Longum vale.[15]

"Keep the cents and the dollars will keep themselves."

March 31, 1849

is the last day of March. Planted corn in the Brown place until the middle of the afternoon at which time all hands stopped working. The ground is in very fine order for planting. Went turkey hunting in the morn but killed nothing as usual.

"Never make a Doctor thine heir."

So ends March having been a very illustrious month in the way of storms &c. but not in marriages for there has been nothing of the sort and not even any sparking done of any consequence but look sharp & take no notice in April.

"Men are as barrels, the emty ones making the most noise."

I am going to meeting at Red Hill tomorrow. "The master's eyes will do more good than his hands." Franklin.

April 1, 1849

All Fools day being Sunday I went to preaching at Red Hill. E. Fant delivered a sermon that was not fitted for dogs to hear. It is surprising that he is permitted to pretend to preach. I consider his preaching ridiculous. Come home and went patrolling with A. C. & T. D. Feasters, D. R. Coleman and D. K. Feaster, Esq. We [. . .] it on to a good many considering. I got home after night, went to bed, arose in the morning crowing, ie on

April 2, 1849

Commenced planting corn again and will soon finish if it does not rain. Went to Stinson's shop in the eve. Saw Jacob Sharp who is a full team and a horse to spare &c.

April 3, 1849

Finished planting corn for this year having planted over a hundred and fifty acres. Commenced ploughing for cotton in the eve. The Steamer came up and went partridge hunting by the way to Stinson's shop but killed none except some doves &c.

April 4, 1849

Was favored with a beautiful rain which will bring the corn upp very soon. The trees are putting forth rapidly. I went over to the Esq's in the evening and went squirrel hunting with him. He killed one and I killed six, however he still thinks that he can beat me shooting, but that won't do. We got out of the bed on the morning of the Fifth and went a turkey hunting. I saw nor heard an[y]one. The Esq saw several but did not get a shot. I brought Sis over home with me. R. Morgan Esq came over &c.

April 6, 1849

Cool in the morn but pleasant in the afternoon. I made a ditch on upland being the first we ever made. Also received a letter from R. Woolen stating that he and kin were safe & sound &c. Mr. Adams came up to see us and went hence to S. H. Stevensons.

April 7, 1849

Ploughed until noon at which time all stoped from work being Saturday Eve.

I made two more ditches being very good ones. D. R. Feaster came up. We killed several doves and larks &c. Went to Jacob Fry's and stayed all night and in the morning of the Eighth we left for Mr. Mc's where we found Trez. I stayed until three o'clock PM then left for home leaving the Mr. Feasters still at Mr. Mc's. The day on which Esq. Morgan moved to Santuck in Union Dist. "Never make a Doctor thine heir" so said Franklin.

April 9, 1849

A very warm & pleasant day—commenced chopping cotton seed, also hauling seed from Grand Ma's to plant. The ground is in firstrate order for planting. I killed three squirrels in the afternoon, rending all their heads assunder, "some to shoot." "Nothing dries sooner than a tear," nor is there anything more detestable than for Republicans to aspire to the haughty chair of Aristocracy which although is getting very common for we have numerous instances in our immediate neighbourhood of men who have accumulated more of this world's goods than other of their neighbours, and then he is changed from what he formerly was, will scarcely speak to his old friends whom he once esteemed—outwardly—and never associates with them but is trying to push himself into a higher circle than the one he was reared in. And the consequence is that he by extravagance soon falls lower than where he first commenced—if not himself it falls upon his posterity, which is still worse. And as soon as an aristocrat becomes bankrupt, just so soon is he deserted by his once flattering friends.

April 10, 1849

A nice day for planting cottonseed. Drove the cattle down to Grand Ma's as we have a fine pasture there of Egyptian grass &c. The Esq. came over and took dinner, also Aunt Betty, Sol & Sister and Grandma & Ailsey came in the afternoon. I layed off some taters today.

April 11, 1849

The day on which Pappa started to Columbia and arrived there on the twelvth and sold cotton at 6¾ and got home on the Fourteenth safe & sound.

April 14, 1849

A very warm and pleasant day. The corn is coming fourth very nice. All hands ceased from working at noon being Saturday. I went to A. E. Coleman's in the afternoon and stayed all night with him. It commenced getting very cool after dark as if it would frost and continued so on the morning of the Fifteenth only a little worse and lo & behold near eight o'clock it began to snow like rips and continued on until three in the afternoon having snowed more than at any other time in several years, and in April at that, it being so cold as to kill the cotton and corn considerably, also some leaves and all garden plants were injured. It is not always warm in the summer.

April 16, 1849

Still cold but fair, the wind coming from the northwest. We finished planting cotton seed on this date and commenced ploughing corn which looks extremely sorry on account of the snow and judging from appearances it is a bad chance for bread meal or any other vegatibles. "Nothing dries sooner than a tear."

April 17, 1849

Still cool but milder than yesterday but still cold. Ploughed corn today which looks any way but nice. I set some traps for birds that are pulling up the corn. Notice the grammatical construction of the above verse.

April 18, 1849

Very cold in the morn, wind blowing from the west pretty hard and a heavy frost at night on all low places and the Nineteenth was cold too but more moderate than yesterday. Sis & Aunt Polley Jonathan was at our house to day and we had cakes for dinner.

April 20, 1849

A pretty severe frost in the morn but pleasant in the middle of the day. Some prospect of more frost to night. Commenced ploughing corn at the Brown pl. after planting lots of watermelon seed being near an acre of land in one patch besides several surplus patches. I went to the P.O. in the eve, got no letters *as usual*. N.B. Look on the other page for the remainder of April. "Never despair in adversity."

April 21, 1849

Still cool and very dry. Being Saturday I let all hands stop work so as to be in good order by Monday believing that a hand will do more work by giving them half a day every Saturday than to work all the week throughout the whole year.

April 22, 1849

Was visited by A. E. Coleman. We rode over the farm to see the frost bit corn &c. I went home with Billy and Sis and stayed all night. Went turkey hunting on the morning of twenty-third but killed nothing which has become very common with me. Thense to Esq's—rode over his diggins but saw nothing very attractive. Thense home to my own affairs. Receied a wild-cat's skin as present from Mosses W. Coleman of Winston Missi., brought by George Cooper who has just arrived from that county. Mosses sends me word that him & his father killed seven wildcats, twenty wolfs and any number of dear. The laws of that country allow any man three dollars for killing a wolf.

April 25, 1849

Quite warm and very dry, the ground being extremely hard. I rode my colt Rosa May to day being the second time she was ever backed. She cut some tall antics. Had a glorious rain the evening at the home place but scarcely any at Brown's place. Commenced reading *Fortescue*,[16] a very foolish book but quite tempting, &c.

April 26, 1849

Nearly finished ploughing over our corn for the first time. Fanny was blest with a female colt on this date. I received my magazines from Columbia, having had them bound there by Mr. Jonston, price one dollar & a quarter each. They were conveyed to me by the politeness W. Coleman.

April 27, 1849

Finished ploughing over corn for the first time. Went to P.O. in eve accompanied partly by the Steamer vis D.R.C. There came a moderate rain at night which we needed *much*.

April 28, 1849

Clowdy in the morn but clear in the eve. Finished sprouting the Brown place by noon and then to rest until Monday. "Too much is as great an evil as too little."

April 29, 1849

Sunday. Went to Uncle Jacob Feaster's,[17] H. J. Lyle's, and John Q. Arnett's accompanied by the Steamer, who spent the last night with me. We got back home and found the Esq. & lady at our house but after eating supper they individually returned to their respective habitations. I began a letter to R. W. Nolen of Chambers Ala., being one of my first cousins and who was in this county several years ago. He is my senior by a few months. Had my hair cut off today and had great pleasure in hearing Esq. Feaster's conversation and looking at his beautiful corn. Blessed are they that get good rains and work their corn.

April 30, 1849

Began ploughing cotton which looks like a bad chance for it is not half come upp, and what has come out has commenced drying, consequently it is an inferior prospect. I made two very nice ditches near the house, almost a quarter of a mile long. Rode Rosa over to the Brown place to look after the traps and found them statu quo, but Miss May became possessed of the idea of running away which she did in a very prospicious manner—however not with me upon her—and I became convinced that Betty's pigs were rooting upp our corn in an unbecoming way, for which conduct I shall inform against them surely.

Saw Mr. Lewis Roberts going from Mill. He got his meal.

Thus ends April, having been an uncommon cold April, having had snow and frost in an abundance with plenty of cold winds mixed in with it, &c. This has been a dry month in the marrying line, for I have not had the pleasure of recording any hymenial news. But I fancy May will have its share of double-blessedness as reports would make us believe such if we were inclined to be superstitious.

Never eat as much as your appetite craves, but stop in time to prevent yourself from being a glutton, &c. Nor drink alkihol, nor steal, nor lie, nor speak ill of another, but always mind your own business and you will ever be loved and respected.

May 1, 1849

Warm in the morn and until evening when we were blessed with a beautiful rain which was much needed. Cotton begins to show the effect of it, also the grass and other vegetation. Went to Soloman's after my gun. Saw Aunt Rebecca who was there &c.

May 2, 1849

Heard the joyous news of the marriage between James M. Morgan and Miss L. Coleman who were married on last night by Jacob Feaster, Esq., John C. Feaster, and Miss Savilla Coleman officiating as attendants. This union has been anticipated as they were courting several years. After making the match they should have given a generous invitation to the fandango, but no—they had but very few to witness their "junction," the Misses Henderson being the only ladies in attendance. I was not there myself. Edith Lyles[18] and Polly came up to day &c. I went in the eve to the Esq's. He will get done ploughing cotton the first time tomorrow. He is smart, aint he?

May 3, 1849

Made a very long ditch suitable to mind.

May 4, 1849

Went with Drucy and Polly to Uncle Sam's after Isa had fun lots and an ample share of music on the Piano Forte. Major plays admirable for a beginner. We all went to M. S. Yongue's in the after-noon, thense back to Uncle Sam's, from there home with Polly behind me on old Kate, ie a mule.

May 5, 1849

Saturday. Finished ploughing cotton the first time, having went over it in five days with nine plough hands. Went seighning in Broad River at Lyle's Mill with H.J., J.F., Dr., D.A., D.R. Sr., D.R., Jr., H.J. Jr., W.P.C., H. A. Colemans and T. D. & D. R. Feasters and minor other individuals. We caught near three hundred cats with considerable number of scale fish, catching thirty four at one drag.

May 6, 1849

Was visited by Henry Lyles, Tho. Colvin, J. C. Feaster, R. G. Cameron & son. Punkins came home with me last night. We went over the Brown [place] looking at the corn which looks sorry, thense to Esq Dave's. He & wife had just left so went to Billy's and they were in the act of leaving. Finily we left for home via Major John Coleman's.

May 7, 1849

An election for a representative to the legislature to fill the vacancy of David Crosby dec'd. W. S. Lyles[19] being the only candidate, consequently he is elected. Commenced ploughing corn the second time. The earth in judicious order. Edith and Polly departed from our house for Uncle Jonathan's. Pappa & Momma went to Grand Ma's etcetera. I myself attended to my business besides hoeing my watermelons which look extremely promising. The day on which we began choping our cotton, only two pieces of hands at it. Rode Miss May out in the fields. She seems quite bedable.

May 8, 1849

is Tuesday. I went over to the Esq in the evening &c. Daddy informed of the particulars of the death of Andrew Feaster Sr. who was brother to Grandpa Feaster. He was shot by a man by the name of Jacobs after night & who was at that time laying out from the sheriff then in pursuit after him aided by A. Feaster, H. McMakin and E. Wolly. It was the intention of Jacobs to kill Wolly but was deceived by the horse for he rode a white horse, but Uncle Andrew rode of the same color on that fatal night and Jacobs shot him through a mistake for Wolly. Jacobs was arrested and imprisoned but broke out just before his trial came on and was again arrested after fleeing justice for the long lapse of twenty years, having fled to Florida which at that time did not form a part of the United States. He was brought back, tried, condemned, and hung being a very old man. He killed Feaster in eighteen hundred and —— and was executed the year eighteen hundred and ——.

May 9, 1849

Finished ploughing over the corn at home and began at it over at the Brown diggins. The corn does not look like maze but grass. It is infested by worms which are literally destroying it. However I killed a nice yongue squirrel this eve which is some satisfaction. Commenced raining at sunset. Saw Armstrong, also H. J. F. W. Coleman Esq. (some name).

May 10, 1849

Rained all day incesently. Brought a load of fodder from Grand Ma's, also did the Esq's. Transplanted sweet potoatoes, being a fine time, and worked on the Egyptian grass which was progressing rapidly on the Brown place. I found some roots fully two feet deep in the earth and one over three feet in length. It got on that place by sowing oats that grew on Beaver Creek. It was then owned by Uncle Feaster. Was informed of the sad news of G. W. Punkins being taken with chill & fever.

May 11, 1849

Quite cool, being clowdy and every appearance of frost to night. Went to the P.O. in the eve. There I received a letter from H. D. Coleman living in Walton County Ga and who lived in this county last year. Also was my schoolmate. The ground was too wet for ploughing on this date.

May 12, 1849

Saturday. Had all hands hoeing cotton, and they finished their tasks by twelve o'clock. Isa & I went to Uncle J. H. Coleman's in the evening and re-mained all night. On the morning of the Thirteenth the Steamer & I departed for Cool Branch where we found a crowd of homines and some few of the fairer sex—Miss M. D. McConnell in particular. She was escorted homewards by the Right Hon. T. L. Feaster Esq. who by the by is a noted gallanter of the softer ones. I come back to H.J.C.'s and eat my dinner and thence home and lo & fine who would we find there but Miss M. C. Yongue. Consequently I remained statu qua until after the golden rays of Sol had shone a considerable time on the morning of

May 14, 1849

at which time she left for home. I went to ploughing corn and planted an acre for comfort. Aunt Polly Feaster & her daughter Mary Drucilla Rawls and her son Ben were at our house on this eventful Day. *"Glory."*

May 15, 1849

Finished ploughing over corn the second time. Had some rain in the eve. The Esq was over. I feel very bad, having a severe headache and other disor-ders which renders me quite weak and unhappy, but the Sun does not always shine nor is it forever clowdy but every sour has its sweet, visa versa. Near 8 o'clock PM at Daddy's. The mulberry in Daddy's yard was transplanted by Uncle David H. Coleman when he was quite yonge &c.

May 16, 1849

Pappa departed for Columbia with Uncle Jonathan. I commenced hoeing cotton with all hands. Killed an owl. Went to Billy's & Esq's. They came home with me. Had chicken fixens & flower elvings for dinner.

May 17, 1849

Commenced raining last night and continued on incessantly and now slow. Planted potatoe slips &c. Commenced a letter to Henry D. Coleman of Social Circle Ga.

May 18, 1849

Continues to rain having been at constantly for thirtysix hours with no prospect of seasing at this time. My ditches have performed excellently and to a good purpose.

"A goose quill is more dangerous than a lion's claw." — Franklin.

May 19, 1849

Now fair weather, having rained near forty-eight hours in succession. The ground as wet as can be. Hoed cotton to day. Pappa come home from Columbia. He sold cotton from 6¼ to 7 cents per lb. Sold to R. Cathcart. [20]

There was a frost last night which killed Simon Hill's peas, but it was not a general frost, not killing any other [. . .] as yet heard from. Dave & Sarah is with Daddy to night.

May 20, 1849

Sabath. Preaching at Red Hill by E. Fant. Large audience with some very pretty girls of whom were Miss E. Bostic, Julia Parrott, and Miss E. Satterwhite. By the by T. D. Feaster escorted Miss Satterwhite homewards. A. E. Coleman & I went up to Dr. McClurkins from church, thense home. The newly married couples were there ie Colvin & Wright.

May 21, 1849

Still hoeing cotton, being near half done. I ploughed myself to day in the cotton. Pappa carried his surplus stock to the pasture being three in number &c. Prospect of more rain.

May 22, 1849

Quite warm, corn growing finely. Went to the pasture with Pappa & Esq and eat dinner with cousin J. M. Morgan.

May 23, 1849

Very warm. I ploughed to day, the balance were hoeing. On this date we heard the sad news of the death of Mr. Daniel Kitchens who was overseeing for Jon B. Coleman. He came to his end in a very extraordinary manner, having ploughed all day in perfect health. And in ploughing he began eating a root called commonly jelico, which he found in the field. But near night he & his brother found a weed which they imagined to be the above named plant and each of them eat of it and never discovered their fatal mistake until after getting home. Then they began to feel sick after eating their supper. They soon conjectured the cause being poison and immediately sent after Dr. McClurkin. But before he could get to them the elder, Daniel, was dead and his brother near the last stage, but has not expired as yet, from latest news, although there is no hope for his recovery. It was ascertained by examination that they had eaten the root of hemlock, which resembles the jelico very much. This occurance should be a warning to every person in eating things that he is a stranger to &c., &c.

May 24, 1849

I went to the Esq's and Billy's. Killed four partridges on the way. Saw Mrs. Yongue & Widdow Millings.

May 25, 1849

Began ploughing cotton the second time with five hands. Cotton very grassy. I sent to the Post Office in the eve but got no letters, consequently my only comforter was the *Yankee Blade*[21] which paper I take published by Mathews & Co., Boston, price two dollars per annum. G. W. Punkins came over after his broad clothe to weare to the pic-nic on tomorrow at Feasterville. Fine fixens in anticipation. Daddy was eighty-four years old on the nineteenth of this month. He was born in Halifax County N.C. and emigrated to this county when about ten years old.

May 26, 1849

Picnic at Feasterville. Danced & played spark near all day. The Miss Mc's were reighning belles of the day. I did not attend but went down to the pasture escorted by the Steamer.

May 27, 1849

Sunday. Went home with A.E.C., remained there until evening, thense home. Miss Jane Ferguson & Sarah Sterling came home with Pappa & Isa who had been over in Ireland.

May 28, 1849

Finished hoeing cotton over the first time. Aunt Kizanah Feaster[22] and her daughters Lizy, Drucy, and Sally came up to see us from Columbia, also Sarah Coleman visited us on this date.

Received a very severe lecture from Daddy on the impropriety of so much visiting. The conclusion of his lecture was that it would be the ruin of the whole of us, &c., &c.

May 29, 1849

Very warm in the middle of the day. Went to Uncle Sam's in the evening in company with Jane Ferguson, Lizy Feaster and Peggy. After got there had some fine music by Drucy, Lizy & Juliana. After being there a short time Miss Mary Yongue & John Brice riding up though as if they were sparking.

May 30, 1849

Aunt Kizanah left our habitation for Rebecca Coleman's. The Esq commenced planting peas, he being an early bird certainly. Miss Jane & Sarah depart for home on tomorrow if not prevented. I hoed my watermelon vines which look very promising considering the extreme wet seasons and flourishing grass etc.

May 31, 1849

Miss Jane Ferguson & Sarah Sterling departed for home accompanied by Pappa. We commenced harvesting wheat. Very warm day. Billy, Sis, and Mrs. Yongue were over today. Mr. W. B. Pearson with Daddy and I to night. Candidate for clerk of the court. Opposed by J. W. Lahon & Thompson.[23] I am going for the former strongly. So ends May.

June 1, 1849

An election for Colonel of the 24 Regiment S.C. Ed Taylor and Wm. Bell[24] candidates. The former received forty nine votes and the latter fourteen at Feasterville.

June 2, 1849

Went over to the Esq's with G. W. Punkins. Came back and found lots of gals at our house, viz Lizy Feaster and her sister Drucy., S. C. Coleman, Mary Yongue and Miss Jane Simon. We danced a few after dark. Finished ploughing cotton the second time (grass lots).

June 3, 1849

Went to preaching at Red Hill. Sermon by E. Fant. Text 22 ch 3 v of Mathew, however it was not to the point. Rode with Miss J.S. without being kicked to death &c., &c.

June 4, 1849

Began ploughing corn running four furrows to the row. The corn is growing very fast, having a beautiful color. Saw Armstrong Screw and Jon D. passing by the field.

June 5, 1849

The warmest day in this season. Rain in the evening. Carried the wheat to Screw's thrasher. The Esq came by from J. D. Colemans. I killed three squirrels.

June 6, 1849

Very warm with a hard shower of rain in the evening. Went with Lizy and Drucy to Mrs. Yongues and brought Isa home with us. Eat a fine mess of cheeries and other vegatibles. Saw J. L. Cameron ploughing cotton neare knee high. "Hold thy head up & look brave as the d——l."

Watermelons look flourishing, so they do *"hoss fly."*

June 7, 1849

Ground too wet to plough until noon at which time we began and finished the field by night. The Steamer came up and found me cuting sprouts but I did not get ashamed. Lizy, Drucy & Drucy went to S. Crosby remained all day and brought some beautiful flowers home with them and gave me a nice *nose gay*.

My [. . .] or Labour in a farm is considered by some of our would-be-uppertons as a perfect disgrace also not an honorable occupation in any shape or form whatever. And they are useful to our country in proportion as the lunatics are to its citizens or as drones are to bees. More rain at this time being 8 o'clock PM (gone to bed). The Election for Colonel on the first proved after counting the votes an equal number to each candidate.

June 8, 1849

Went over to the Esq's thense to Uncle Sam's with Lizy and the Druceys. Brought Isa home &c. The Esq's Scientific American came on this mail. Fine paper by Mimm & Co., N.Y.

June 9, 1849

My birth day being twenty one years old, alias a man—or a citizen of the United States.

June 10, 1849

Lizy, Drucy and myself went to preaching at Cool Branch. Newlin & Buchanan preachers. Grudge viz. A. C. Feaster & G. W. Punkins came home with us. Rained every night since Tuesday in succession &c.

June 11, 1849

Ploughed corn and lots of it but the ground was too wet. However ploughing must be done immediately else the grass will take the crops and depart (i.e) run away. Saw Wm. McLane ploughing his new ground. "Pretty is as pretty does." Sons of Temperance are increasing.

June 12, 1849

Finished ploughing over corn the third time having gone four furrows in each row leaving a small row in the middle which we will plough out then [. . .] it layed by with the plough. A little rain in the morn.

June 13, 1849

Commenced ploughing cotton the third time running as near to it as possible. Some hands cutting rye. I wrote a letter for Uncle Sol Coleman[25] to his son Wm in Randolph County Ga. A tremendious rain in the evening which has made the ground too wet again, but consider all things as for the better.

June 14, 1849

Finished cutting rye by noon. Then all hands ploughing cotton. The Drucy's and Lizy returned from a visit to Grand Ma's, John F's and Uncle Jonathan's, accompanied by the Steamer who brings intelligence of having very good looking corn. There is no two men alike in this world either in looks or in mind (ie) not an exact semblance.

"Birds of a feather flock together"—old adage.

June 15, 1849

Uncle Jonathan & Lady came up. I looked over our farm with him. Went to the P.O. in the evening. Got a letter for Lizy from her brother John D. Feaster. Saw the Steamer and others. On Miss Anna Bread—while toasts there lovely graces spread—And fops around them flutter—I'll be content with Anna Bread—And won't have any *but her*.

"The most powerful gal-vanic battery we know of is a room of pretty girls"— *Yankee Blade*. Sweethearts are plenty.

June 16, 1849

Miss M.C.Y., J.S., and Widdow Milling visited us, but in the afternoon. William Yongue and Lady came and remained all night, also Dr. L Bybee and H. J. Coleman, Jr. We played Poker until Bed time.

June 17, 1849

We all went to preaching at Red Hill. The preacher said that an infant was as great a sinner in its youth as in the years of discretion and never could enter the Kingdom of Heaven until made anew, no matter if it should die when only a month old—hell would be its portion. His name was Nicholasson. No man would preach such doctrine if he was possessed of a good heart.

June 18, 1849

Nearly finished ploughing cotton the third time. I went to Mrs. Robertson's in the evening to get my coat renovated. I went via Billy's and the Esq's on my return home.

June 19, 1849

Commenced plowing over the cotton again being the fourth time. Went with Drucy & Lizy to J. Q. Arnett's. Stayed all night. Examined A.E.'s farm which is very [page torn] according to my judgement &c. We got home by 10 o'clock PM on the Twentieth. I went to the Esq's in the evening. Saw Miss Mary C. and Mother &c. Drank Lemon Syrup at Arnett's with Liz & D.M.C.

Never drink any intockicating liquors by no means.

June 21, 1849

Has become quite warm after several days of cool weather, the wind coming from the east. Commenced laying corn by i.e. giving it the final ploughing. Also I was exterminating the grass from my melon patch. Began reading John S. Skinner's letter to the Revd's Aiken & Lansing on the principles of their faith—Presbyterianism. He gives it to them most judiciously, especially on Total Depravity.

June 22, 1849

Mrs. Dr. McClurkin, the Esq & Sarah were with us. Esq & myself went to the P.O. in the evening. I received a letter from E. S. Cockrell stating his safe arrival home &c. Daddy also received from Aunt Betty Nolen, all well, good crops, &c. Sad news of the death of her grand daughter, infant of Isabella her oldest and of John G. Coleman Jr. of Green Ala who was in this state in the year '46 purchasing Negroes and on his return home married the said Isabella Nolan.

June 23, 1849

Finished laying by one field of corn. S. Coleman & Henry came by from Mrs. Robertson's. R. H. Coleman remained all night. On the morning of the 24th J. P. Feaster and A. E. Coleman came up also T. D. Feaster. We sat about the house all day except going to the orchard &c.

June 25, 1849

Still ploughing corn. J.P.F. & A.E.C. left this morning for Uncle Jake's and Arnett's. I accompanied Lizzie and the Drucies over to the Morgan place. Found some huckleberrys, shot the gun, etcetera. "Laugh and grow fat and become happy." "Oh Hush!"

June 26, 1849

Beautiful rain in the evening. Went with John P. & the Steamer to the river and had a fine swimming frolic. Eat dinner with Jacob F. Coleman. Saw Dr. I. A. Dupree &c. Took a fine bee gum, ie we extricated the honey from the hive of the bees. J.F.C. shot Lahon's cow in the foot. Finished laying by my corn crop by noon. Nothing now to do but work the cotton. John P. Feaster departed for Columbia on this evening, intending to remain with Aunt Rebecca Coleman to night. Lizy & Drucy accompanied him as far as there. I killed four woodpeckers, one squirrel, and a dove to day. John shot several times but killed nothing. I learnt how to take the figures 12345 and make a square of them and have them to make fifteen in any way, *that's smart.*

June 28, 1849

I went down and brought Lizy and Drucy from Aunt Rebecca to home.

June 29, 1849

Went over to the Esq's, from there down after Isa with Lizie and the Drucys.

June 30, 1849

Saturday, last day of June. Let the hands stop working at noon. I went over to Mr. Mc's, bought a curry comb, price twenty-five cents. Wrote a letter to Mosses W. Coleman, Louisville & Winston, Miss., formerly of this District and sons of Misses Cockrell &c., &c.

Thus ends June having been a very wet month in beginning but dry in the end and if July proves dry until the middle there will be sorry crops of corn made.

"The man who lives with dogs may expect fleas for companions, and visa versa."

"He that would by the plough thrive must either hold himself or drive."

"Contentment is a great blessing." Melons getting ripe.

July 1, 1849

Preaching at Red Hill by Fant. Large audience, &c.

July 2, 1849

Ploughing cotton & corn. I wrote a letter for Lizie to Miss M. B. McCullock of Columbia. She wrote one to Miss A. P. O'Neale. Drucie wrote to Dr. John P. Feaster. Drucies & Lizie went to Becky's.

July 3, 1849

Quit ploughing corn for good or bad. I went over to the Esq's. Very cool nights and mornings, being very dry.

July 4, 1849

Ever memorable day to the American, celebration at every public place of any importance in the Union. I went to the barbecue at Lockard's old field where the troopers and infantry were drilled to their full satisfaction. There was no liquor on the place and consequently no drunkenness. I quit tobacco on the second of this month, believing it to be a very nasty practice.

July 5, 1849

Set six hands hoeing cotton, the remainder finishing the ploughing. Lyle and the Drucies with Henry departed this morning for B. A. Weather's to see Miss E. Meader. They intend staying with her tonight and tomorrow. They will go to Jacob F. Coleman's. Cousin Sarah C. came up just after they had left. She went over and staid with Sis.

Ex-president Polk died at his residence in Tennessee on the seventh of June last.

> "Oh! When we feel 'tis hard to toil
> And sweat the long day through
> Remember it is harder still
> To have no work to do."

The above poetry should be strongly impressed on the mind of every young man (i.e. — the verasity of it) and on the Aristocratic portion of the community particularly as they are generally taught that labour is a dishonor rather than an honor. The ladies should know it also.

John Gladdney died of disintary in the last week of June.

July 6, 1849

Went to the P.O. Letter for Daddy from his niece Sarah Gosey who has a cancer or [. . .] on her breast &c.

July 7, 1849

Sarah C., Lizy and Miss Mary A. Gedding left for Uncle Jonathan's. They remained all night with us. Miss Mary came up with Isa as she came from Winnsborough. I went squirrels to hunt with R. W. Coleman. Killed six or seven.

July 8, 1849

I went down to J. W. Arnett's, Uncle Jake's, and Henry Lyle's. They have fine crops as it has rained abundantly in that settlement. Miss May A.G. came back to our house and remained all night again. Dr. J. Bybee at Uncle H. J. Coleman's from certain information. It is quite presumable of them making a match of double-blessedness ie Bybee and Sarah and not as the sentence reads Bybee and Jonathan.

July 9, 1849

Went down after Lizzie from Grandma's. Miss Mary departed homewards via S. H. Stevenson in lieu with Isa. Had a fine rain in the eve which was needed very much not having had any of importance in several weeks. Corn shows the benefit of a shower &c.

July 10, 1849

A. E. Coleman departed for home early in the morning. The Esq came over before noon. We eat several green water melons out of my patch. He left for Uncle Jonathan's to get his old hat renovated. Lizie, the Drucies, Sally and myself went to Aunt Rebecca's in the after noon, remained until after supper. Drucie Jr. had the toothache and Lizie had the headache. More rain in the eve. My corn appears fine to day. Soon will do to bet on. We have given out all ideas of buying any next year.

July 11, 1849

Raining soon in the morning, continued until nine o'clock. Set out on transplanted potatoe slips. The Esq & wife and Savilla[26] was over, came in the buggy, returned home in the evening. I gave the amount of three dollars and a half to Charles, [. . .] and Mary each in orders to John Q. Arnett's store.

July 12, 1849

I went to Dr. S. B. McClurkin's in company with Lizie and Drucie. Saw Wm. & Garlen Colvins. Had a fine dinner.

July 13, 1849

I went with Pappa to the pasture accompanied by Uncle Jonathan and Steamer. We found all the stock in a prosperous condition. Left the pasture and went through James M. Morgan's farm which looks middling well, thense we were found at J. Q. Arnett's, eat dinner, also several fine watermelons from A.E.C.'s patch. We remained until the mail arrived, ie at 3 o'clock. There was two letters to Lizie, one from John and the other from Miss A. P. O'Neale. All her friends alive &c., &c. I received one from David R. Coleman, Jr. dated June 24th and postmarked the 30th. He states crops to be very inferior in Chambers, corn in particular, also wheat was nearly a total failure in that county. All these calamities were caused by the frost following the snow of 15th of April last.

July 14, 1849

I mustered with the Buckhead Troopers and become a member of that company. David Feaster also joined. I eat dinner at Mrs. Yongue and so did the girls who were at the muster also. John Brice & [. . .] Crosby came over in evening. Lizie gave them some very fine & sweet music &c.

July 15, 1849

Clowdy and cool. Left from home with A.E.C. who stayed all night with me for his residence. After getting there we eat some delicious watermelons with candy-pecans and sugar in abundance. Wrote a letter to S.C.M. Came home in the evening, found all well. Wrote Ike an order to A. F. Thompson to the amount of four dollars on yesterday. Saw Billy & Nancy Majors. Fine connexions are apt to plunge you in a sea of extravagance and then not to throw you a rope to save you from drownding—wrote by the special request of Daddy.

July 16, 1849

Wind blowing from NE consequently very cool which makes the cotton look sick. Eat several melons assisted by the girls, no green ones pulled, &c.

July 17, 1849

Finished hoeing cotton the second time and began hoeing corn on the branches. Carried Lizie and Drucie to Uncle Jonathan's. Lizie divulged a very important secret to me concerning a letter to her from Montgomery Ala. Did Ever. *Du tell.*

The first white person born in N. America was Virginia, daughter of Annanias and Eleanore Dare, and grand daughter of Gov. John White. She was born on the 18th of August 1597 in Roanoke, North Carolina. Her parents were of the expedition sent by Sir Walter Raleigh in that year. There is no record of her history save that of her death.

July 18, 1849

Waggon returned from Lukin's Mill with a load of flour. Daddy rode over our cornfield, thinks it is tolerable good ie as good as his. All hands hoeing corn to day. Eat several delicious watermelons. Gave Martha an order to John Q. Arnett's Store for three dollars only.

July 19, 1849

Started with Isa & Drucy to Winnsboro. Rained very hard in an hour after leaving home. Got as far as Mr. Samuel Gladny's where we remained the night. Lo and behold it was raining when we arose on the morning of the Twentieth and continued raining throughout the entire day so we were compelled by necessity to remain with them another night. I danced and enjoyed myself extremely well in every particular. Mr. Gladny Martin came over and staid all night also. He played the fiddle for the remainder to dance. We started early on the following morn for the Boro. Got there before twelve o'clock. Eat dinner &c. Started back home after leaving Isa there with Mrs. Ladd. Drucy & I came as far as Mrs. Gladny's and stoped for the night. Miss Martha Stett came over by request, enjoyed ourselves finely, left on the morning of the Twentisecond and arrived at Sweet Home by eleven o'clock. Pulled some very fine melons out of my patch. Jonny Major came over in Eve, brought a letter for Lizie from her Pa. Cotton worth 9½ cents per lb. Lizie, A.E.C. and Drucie Jr at Aunt Becky's.

July 23, 1849

Monday. Received a letter on yesterday from Albert Coleman dated the 7th inst. All well, &c. Eat melons throughout the day. Carried cousin Betty two fine ones. Went in the evening after Lyle & Drucie at Becky's. Gave George Armstrong a fill of mellons which is a rare performance. Seven was at Daddy's.

I have been thinking for several weeks of the manner in which the females (of supposed wealth) at the present time are educated, or their own manner of receiving an education. It appears as if their sole desire was to be admired for their external appearance, skin never warmed by the rays of that sun which is the life of all things. They think it a disgrace to one of their own sex to be coloured in the slightest manner whatever by the sun, but if she can keep her hands and face perfect strangers from the source of light, by the aid of gloves, veils, &c., their nerves then are never shocked by the sight of a sunburnt lady. And it is a custom of late among the would-be-uppertins to sleep until half the day has passed and then dress and take a walk of a few rods or perhaps a ride in some vehicle which fatigues them horribly. [They] cannot bear the idea of laboring in any form [and] will not keep company with a person that does. They are not fit to live, being no use to themselves nor to their fellowmen. They are fitted only to be waited on, being too lazzy to dress themselves or to make even their dresses. However they are some at sparking, never tiring, and apparently even in a most judicious humor displaying the best signs of good-natured persons, all smiles of the sweetest mould. My opinion is that all such girls (and they include half of the whole) are a disgrace to our country, our institution, and our name. They should not be noticed, but every one should be valued by their deeds &c. No more of my yarn for the present.

July 24, 1849

Eat a very large watermelon, the largest I ever had. Drucy and Henry went to the Esq's. Lizie & little Drucie remained at home to keep me from the blues.

"Happy is he who does not strive for the root of evil."

"Never place any reliance upon dreams while asleep or awake."

Lizie wrote to her father also to Miss M. B. McLullock. I backed her letters. Mrs. Madison died recently. She was the consort of ex-president Madison.

July 25, 1849

Rained at twelve o'clock. We have had glorious showers for more [than] a week, the first being on the nineteenth, rainy every day since more or less which will make corn abundant for the following year. All vegitation is in a fine growing state. Cotton I think is going too much to weed. Mr. Armstrong came over in the evening—eat some melons. Him & Pappa swapped cows &c. I drove Daddy's hog or swine or sow out of our corn field, which is half kin to shooting.

"A poor man has as much heart as a rich man."

July 26, 1849

Ninth day of rain. Had a nice rain in the evening. Nothing could suit farmers better.

The Misses Sarah & Martha Mc came visiting to night. Mrs. Dr. McClurkin and Mrs. Tucker came down. Eat dinner and then after sitting for some time departing homewards &c. Nearly finished laying by my crop. Get done tomorrow.

Peggy came home from the Esq's. Nathan A. Feaster and John F. Coleman eat dinner with us to day. Nat left via J. Cockrell's, J.F.C. for home.

July 27, 1849

Rode with Miss M. on her return to school. Sighns all right. Report says Bybee is in these diggens. I returned and accompanied Lizie and Drucie to Grand Ma's. There we all eat dinner. I left them there and came by the P.O. but no mail. The way was waterbound and delayed for one day. Mail arrives tomorrow. Saw N.A.Y.

"Contentment is a great blessing" &c.

July 28, 1849

More rain, being the tenth in succession. Preaching to day at Liberty, alms save all by Rev'd Banks. Him and the Rev'd Gillian preach again tomorrow. They are of the Calvinistic creed. Went to the P.O. from church via Uncle Jonathan's where I eat my dinner. Also Mr. Brice & Sloan, Lizie & Drucie came home with me accompanied by A. E. Coleman. D. R. Feaster with me at daddy's tonight. [. . .] to Albert Coleman of Green Ala. John tried to spark the Miss Mc's but couldn't come it quite. I officiated myself per D. R. Feaster.

July 29, 1849

Preaching again at Liberty. A very lengthy sermon in the morning by the Rev'd Gillian, who has fine use of language, speaking very fast. No outward converts. A large audience who were credited for their good cconduct. &c., &c. Tears can at times be forced from the eyes, when not dictated by the heart. Moreover all are not Christian that preach or belong to a church, for there is never any material difference discerned by their becoming outward Christians after the lapse of a few years. But perhaps they become worse as they have a cloak to hide their hipocracy under.

July 30, 1849

Nothing transpired of any importance on this date or on the last. We finished laying by our crop and commenced building houses on the land that came from Grand Pa's estate.

"Come to My Mountain Home" is my favourite song, sung sweetly by cousin Elizabeth M. Feaster. "The Last Link" is another excellent song, with several Temperance songs as sung by Lizie. Cousin Sarah plays "The Rector's Daughter" and "Double Sliding" finely. (*Bad Pen.*)

August 1, 1849

Went from the pasture (i.e. the lower place) to John Q. Arnett's, bought twenty-five pounds of nails, remained all night with Andrew. Eat some most excellent watermelons, also musk melons grown in Arnett's patch. Returned to the pasture. Worked all day and came home on the night of. . . .

August 2, 1849

and found John P. Feaster at our house from Columbia. Cotton on the ascendancy, selling at eleven cents per lb. He came up after Lizie and Drucie.

August 3, 1849

One year since the marriage of David R. and Nancy E. Coleman and the date that I received a letter from them with the sad intelligence of the death of their infant daughter, only five days old. Went to Uncle Jonathan's in company with John P. and the girls, staid all night. Went to Grand Ma's on the fourth and also the pasture accompanied by the above individuals. All returned home with cousin Sarah added to our company.

August 5, 1849

I accompanied the Drucies to Red Hill Church. Sermon by the Rev'd Buckhanan, but to no purpose. Lizie, Sarah, and John P. spent the day with Aunt Becky. All returned to our horses in evening. A horrible deed was done on the first of this month by George L. Dye. Who shot his wife near 10 o'clock PM with a double barrel shot gun, the load entering her right breast and killing her instantly. She was a mother of four or five children. Dye after killing his wife shot himself with another gun by putting the muzzle of the gun under his chin and pulling the trigger with his toe, the contents of the gun came out in the center of his forehead, blowing his brains entirely out, throwing some pieces to the joist of the house. It need not be said that drunkenness was the cause. He had shot several times at her before this.

August 6, 1849

Lizie, Drucie, & Sally accompanied by John P. left our house early this morning for Columbia. The two first having staid with us since the 28th of May last. They will ever remain dear to us because of their agreeableness and other good deeds, &c., &c.

August 7, 1849

Finished two chimneys to the houses at the pasture. Thos. Crowder came to see me. He killed a squirrel with a stone, a second David. I sung all day— my principle "tune" that I sung was—Oh! no, I never mention Her. Quite a sympathetic piece.

August 8, 1849

Carried my gun to the pasture and killed eight squirrels. Have a fine barbacue. Went over to James Morgan's and gave him a mess—his old lady was drying peaches and him smoking, Willis hauling logs for a house with one little mule which he said was a mule before the Revolutionary War. Mamma, Sis, and Uncle Jonathan came down to the pasture in the morning but left forthwith.

August 9, 1849

Set the hands to splitting rails. Killed four squirrels upon one tree. I went from the pasture to Uncle Jacob's via J. Q. Arnett's. No person at home except

John C. I returned by John F. Coleman's new building (or am to be) as he will finish hauling logs on tomorrow &c. Saw J. Morgan raising him a cotton house aided by Willis. Judge & David Feaster have gone to Laurens Dist. sparking.

August 10, 1849

Built a lot fence. Went to the Post Office in the evening. Received for Drucie from Isa, Lizie and Honorah Elkins,[27] all in fine spirits. Isa says she is only tolerable well satisfied in Winnsboro.

August 11, 1849

The hands finished their task splitting rains before noon. I went from the pasture to Uncle Jak's. Eat dinner. Remained there until near sundown. Came home accompanied by John C. Feaster. We saw J. W. Feaster just from Columbia, also Mr. Gigger of Lexington.

August 12, 1849

Went to Cool Branch. Preaching by Rev'd Newlin. Came home, wrote to Lizie and Drucie. Also began one to D. R. Coleman Jr. of Ala.

August 13, 1849

Began pulling fodder. Very hot and dry &c., &c.

August 14, 1849, to August 18, 1849

do. fodder. do. hot and dry
Went to singing school at New Hope. Also did Drucie & Henry, subscribed two scholars to the school. [. . .] teacher.

August 19, 1849

Went home with the Miss Stones who spent last night & yesterday with us. Also went to Church, Red hill sermon by Rev'd Buckhanan. Poor preacher.

August 20, 1849

Finished a letter to D. R. Coleman from whom I received one on Friday last. Also one from E. H. Cockrell of Missi. Pulling fodder to kill, fine time for sawing having had no rain in near three weeks. I'll get done this week.

From the twentieth to twentithird we spent in pulling fodder at which date we finished, being nine days since we commenced. It is remarkable that we finished pulling without having any injured by the [. . .] as it has not rained in a long while. The best fodder that we ever sawed.

August 24, 1849

Sent the Esq some hands to finish his fodder. I went to Mc's store, bought a hat at $2.25, thense I went to Uncle Jonathan's, from there to the P.O., got no letters, but saw Dr. Rawls and Lady, also Dr. R. W. Coleman. The whole a good looking set, &c., &c. Eat some of the Steamer's melons. Was at Widdow Betty's in morning. Her son R. H. Coleman accompanied me in my excursion on to day &c.

August 25, 1849

Went with Drucie to Uncle Jacob Feaster's. Returned home in the evening. Went then with Mamma to the Esq's. I left her there and went to Billy's and stayed all night. R. F. Coleman (my Uncle) was born 6 August 1789.

August 26, 1849

This morning is memorable because of the birth of the Esq's son, a nice boy with blk. eyes.

Went from the Esq's to Cool Branch. Mr. Buckhannan in too delicate health to preach. Prayer by William Crosby Esq whose daughter Mary Ann was married on the twentifirst to Mr. Ensby Colvin by the R. Rev'd Mr. Newlin. Waited on by Miss Emeline Crosby and Miss Sarah balanced by John H. Cockrell and John Colvin. The lamentable part of the wedding is that I was not there &c. A.E.C. was at the infare.

August 27, 1849

Thrashed rye, ploughed the turnip patch, hauled corn & fodder (but not new corn) and had two hands picking cotton in the evening. Not much opened. Cotton generally is not first rate but has improved very much for the last three weeks as we have had no rain that period. The corn in consequence has ripened fast and will be ready for gathering in two weeks. I went to the Esq's. Did not get down. Have not seen my nephew. Came back by Uncle Sol's Mill. Found him and Wagers in fine spirits. I went in his pond and took a *Mud Bath*.

August 28, 1849

Worked down on the lower place, cut willows and made barricades or brush dams. Killed a beef, also two squirrels. I eat no dinner to day. Why? Cause I could not get it.

August 29, 1849

Began picking cotton on yesterday. Opening very fast. Let four hands pull fodder for Daddy. Mary C.Y. and H. E. Coleman stayed at our house on last night. Left after dinner. John F. Coleman came asking aid to build his house. Pappa & Henry went to the Esq's with Miss Mary &c. Daddy alias D. R. Coleman was born the 19th May AD 1765, now in his eighty-fourth year and able to walk any moderate distance say of four or five miles each day.

August 30, 1849
Went from the pasture to Uncle Jacob Feaster's.

August 31, 1849
Went to the P.O. No letters for me. Saw Mr. Davies of Laurens. So ends August.

The family of John C. Calhoun consists of Mrs. Calhoun and seven children. Of these one son is a planter in Ala, the next a Captain in the Army at New Orleans. The eldest daughter is in Europe, wife of charge at Belgium. Of the three sons at home, one is a physician, the others are young men of 20 and 18. Mr. Calhoun has upon his table every thing of Southern production, but is himself a spare eater.

The view from his house commands distant mountain ranges 40 & 60 miles away. His study is twenty feet south of his mansion, has but one room and one door. His library is not large but choice and most of the books relate to the Union and her interests. The key of this building he keeps always under his immediate control when at home. No one enters it but himself unless he is there. His house stands on the Seneca River, 1000 feet above the level of the sea and 200 feet above the river. There are perhaps 70 or 80 negroes on and about the place. The largest part of his Negroes are in Ala., where he owns a large cotton plantation under the management of his eldest son. Mr. Calhoun has a peculiar manner of ditching, drainage and planting, of such utility that his neighbors regards his as a modle farm. His crops are represented as far before those by any other cultivator in that region of country. His farm is known as Fort Hill from a fort that once stood there in the revolutionary war.

Mr. Calhoun's habits are very regular. He rises at 4 or 5 o'clock, exercises on horse back or in a long walk over his farm for an hour, writes until breakfast at 8 o'clock and after breakfast is busy in his library until one or two. On Friday, which is mail day, he rides to the [. . .]. His newspapers of which a large number are sent to him are spread in the hall for the use of his visitors. He is very hospitable, is a great lion even in the neighborhood of his own house and in the relations of private life, is a most estimable, upright and worthy man.
—*Yankee Blade*

September 1, 1849

Day very hot and dry, wanting rain very much. I went over to see my nephew, nice boy considering.

September 2, 1849

Preaching at Red Hill.

September 3, 1849

Went to the singing at New Hope. The company was honored by the presence of Miss Peck & Wade of Columbia. Fashionable stock. Went with A.E.C. to Mr. Lands and remained all night. Wrote some poetry & prose in Lizie's album. Attended singing again on the 4th. Miss Peck gone home joyful. Miss Lucretia Mobley[28] was there, very pretty but not so much so as Martha Brice.[29] A.E.C. rode with Miss Swinton, Jno. [. . .] Lemon & M. C. Yongue &c.

Returned home in the evening and found Miss Honorah & her brother Benj. Elkins at our house. Remained all night until 3 o'clock PM on 5 ult. at which time they departed for home. Mr. Nevitt of Ala. gave us a call this evening. He is a citizen of Pickens and neighbour of E. H. Cockrell, also in favor of Banking Principels. Some had banks in Ala. Picking cotton. No rain as yet being time out of mind since raining. Not sowed turnips yet. Bad time.

September 6, 1849

Went over to Widdow Betty's. Read *The Deserted Wife*,[30] continued in Robt's *Saturday Evening Post*. Returned home and found the Esq there. I went home with him and remained all night. Mrs. Mary Ann [. . .] departed this life on this date at 10 o'clock. Short illness of but a day & a half. Burried at New Hope Church. Daughter of Jos. [. . .]

September 7, 1849

I went from the Esq's to a shooting match at Darling Allen's who with the Esq beat shooting and of course won the beef, the latter winning two choices, being the first time that I ever made a failure. W. M. Yongue, J. L. & James Cameron came out minus beef. Returned via P.O.

Finished picking over the cotton once, being very thin. Saw Mr. Conner to day who is one of the heroes of the battles of [. . .] now living with Mrs. Claudia Means.

September 8, 1849

Muster at Mc's Store. I made my resignation of clerk of company. Negro trial at Soloman's. Sol Parks & Joe, boy of Uncle Soloman, were convicted of several mean charges such as stealing beegums, cutting off calf's tail, using ill language to Willy Coleman. They were consequently chastised.

September 9, 1849

Preaching at Cool Branch by Mr. Newlin. Some very pretty girls attended, Miss M. D. McC especially. Also a large number of hearers to a very appropriate sermon &c. Monday the 10 we began gathering corn. Very dry as there is no rain as yet.

September 11, 1849

I started in a buggy for Columbia after Sallie. Arrived there at sun down, found all well & hearty &c.

September 12, 1849

Walked over town in company with Dr. John P. Feaster. Visited all the principal places of importance such as the tressel work on the railroads some of which are magnificent being near fifty or sixty feet high. Thense to Asylum where I saw a large number of unfortunate lunatics. Also saw some of Lizie & Drucie's pretty beaus.

September 13, 1849

Went down and examined the Colledge precincts where I saw some beautiful buildings including the Episcopal Church which is a very imposing building. Also I visited A. Crawford's house, built by Ex-Gov. Hammond, a beautiful house. I saw Russel's garden, Hampton's and many other interesting places.

September 14, 1849

Sallie & I departed for home sweet home soon in morning and arrived there safe by sun down but tired.

September 15, 1849

Susan McClurkin came down. Isa came from Winnsboro on the 10th Ult.

September 16, 1849

Isa & myself went to Salem Church. Sermon by Mr. Hoyt. Returned via Uncle Jacob's, &c.

September 17, 1849

I went over to the Esq's and Billy's. Willy Coleman also was there. We had a game of drafts. He proved victor. I returned home and found the Misses

Stevensons and Allans also Uncle H.J.C. & Lady at 11 o'clock AM. They all retired home as the sun began desending in the beautiful scarlet horizon of the West. The Esq came, also in Vesper to get couple of mules to have his corn in costoday etc. I did some close shooting near sun down being two shots in half inch of center, beef taken. Dry, dry, dry, dry weather, warm, dusty, &c.

September 18, 1849

Carried Drucie & Isa to Winnsboro. Saw some very pretty girls at Mrs. Ladd's, Miss Jane O'Hare especially. Stayed all night at the Planter's Hotel. Came home on 19th after having a very dusty ride &c. I paid the seventh installment on rail road money for Uncle J. H. Coleman. Also paid Mr. Jordan the residue for buggy &c. Shot my rifle some to day, made some close shots.

September 20, 1849

Quite windy, blowing dust in every direction. Some clouds in the morning, but clear as a whistle in evening with no appearance of rain whatever, though there has been no rain sufficient to allay the dust since the last of July, being rather a longer draught than for common and which has almost ruined the cotton crop in the Dist., also in some of the adjoining Districts. We will not [have] half a crop which is a general estimate. The cotton is measly maturing &c. The cotton crop from general reports are sorry throughout the U.S. However the corn is most excellent in this section.

"Go to strangers for charity, acquaintances advice, and to relatives for nothing and you will always have a supply." (*Scientific American*)

There is a negress on the estate of John C. Calhoun aged one-hundred and twelve years. She was brought from Africa and has been in his family for a century. She has sixty-three descendants, all living on the same plantation.

"Be prudent, be patient and be persevering and you yourself will be *Some of it*."

"Religion is the best armor that any man can have but the very worst of cloaks."

"The Plough. Its one share in the bank of earth is worth ten in the Bank of paper."

September 21, 1849

Went to the post office in the evening, got no letters as ever. John C. Feaster stayed with me to night. He left for home on the morn of 22d. I went to shooting match at Darling Allen's. Got no beef as usual with me. Went with the Esq on the 23d to Mrs. Yongue's. Remained all day after finding all in very good spirits as they received a good rain on yesterday.

September 24, 1849

Went to singing at New Hope. Not a very good turn out though the prettiest girls were there. A.E.C. & Punkins came from R. G. Cameron's to singing. I went home with Andy where he had not been for two weeks. Found every thing straight &c. Returned on the morning of . . .

September 25, 1849

to singing. Had a fine time of it. The girls looked their prettiest appearantly. M. Brice in particular. Andy rode with her from church, thense he came home with me &c., remained until morn when we left for Red Hill to another singing by Boyd. No one there scarcely. Andy went home in eve. Shooting match for Mrs. Mobley's hog. I got none.

September 27, 1849

Esq & Sarah was over accompanied by the nephew. Frosty the cow died by falling in a gully and not being able to get out &c.

September 28, 1849

Dry weather and warm. Picked twelve hundred lbs of cotton having averaged over a thousand per day for two weeks.

September 29, 1849

Went to the post office, received a letter from Drucie & Isa, each in fine spirits. Also one from Albert Coleman Green, Ala. Sickly in that county. The Esq received one from John G. Coleman Jr. who was in this county in 1846. Very sickly in his section. Finished reading *Seclusaval*,[31] a continued tale in the *Yankee Blade*.

September 30, 1849

Shooting match at our house. I got third choice by hard shooting &c. Went home with the Esq, stayed all night. Had a fine rain near daybreak on the morn of 31st. Went down to W. M. Yongue's, thense we all came over to our house where I wrote a letter to Isa & Drucie. A little more rain in the evening. Hope we will have enough in time. All things are for the better than thee believe.

I read an exelent piece in the South Carolinian by Ned called "Mrs. Scruggins Goin a Fishun" of 27 Sept. Some idea of going westward this fall, &c.

October 1, 1849

Very warm. Some rain at noon & evening. Went to Widow Betty's. Read the continued tale of *The Deserted Wife* &c.

Dr. R. W. Coleman was over to see Anton and Ike. The Esq came after a mule. I eat some very good watermelons &c.

October 2, 1849

had a very fine rain which made the cotton too wet. Commenced preparation for ginning. Hung some gates. Went to Soloman's Mill, got Wagers to work on my triggers, etcetra.

From the 2d until the fifth nothing transpired of any note. I shot some at the distances of one hundred yards, formerly shooting at sixty yards only. Had a shooting again on the 6th. I got the fifth choice. All bad shooting.

Aunt Kizanah Feaster and daughters arrived this eve from Columbia not intending to return any more but live in the barn &c. The Esq was taken sick on the second Ult. with the fever which laid him quite low. I stayed with him on the night of the sixth. Came home on the morning of the 7th. Very cool &c.

Andrew E. came up early in the morning. We sat awhile and then we went in the buggy to Red Hill. A very large audience in attendance to a sermon by Rev'd Fant. A. C. Feaster went home with Miss E. M. Bostic.

The Steamer and Punkins came by and et dinner. Lizie Feaster went home with the Steamer to see Sarah.

October 8, 1849

Very cool almost frosted. Pappa came from the Esq's, says he is getting better. Lizie came alone from uncle Jonathan's &c. Brought plank from Brice's saw mill to complete the barn for the reception of our kin &c.

October 9, 1849

Cool in morning. Susan McClurkin came down on her way to J. Q. Arnett's and I went with her by request. I purchased a coat and pair of pants for eleven dollars only. The gins did not do so well on today as Isaac reports. I wrote a letter for Uncle Soloman Coleman to [. . .], his son in Charleston. I wrote one last week to A. Coleman and week before to E. S. Cockrell. Pappa was at Arnett's in the evening &c. Lizie & Drucie grabbing [. . .] in the evening &c., &c.

October 10, 1849

James Morgan commenced working again on the barn or as Lizie & Drucie call it, the cottage, fitting it out for the reception. Loaded the wagon with seven bales cotton for Columbia. Killed a beef, backed cotton &c. L & D went to Becky's.

October 11, 1849

Discovery of America, AD 1492.

October 12, 1849

Pappa left for Columbia. Sent a load of wheat to Meadow's Mill, the remainder of us picking cotton.

October 13, 1849

Began raining early in the morning and continued until near night. Went to the P.O. Got a letter from Isa & Drucie from Winnsboro.

October 14, 1849

Went to preaching at Cool Branch via Mc. Sermon by the Rev'd Brooks, a missionary. Pappa returned from Columbia with a load of J. M. Feaster's furniture, moving to the cottage. Jacob came up with him, &c., &c.

"Laugh and grow fat"—so says the editor of the *Yankee Blade.*

"It is thought by many that man cannot have religion without a long face to accompany it"—J. A. F. Coleman.

"He that believeth shall have everlasting life. But he that believeth not shall be damned." This is a text ever quoted by orthodoxes to establish the doctrine of endless misery.

"Death, the last enemy"—Universalism. All things shall be made anew. Common reason, viz. Deism. Tho's Paine, the framer of the constitution of the United States, and an infidel too.

Poor preach, poor pay. No pay not any preach.

TRUTH

Before thy mystic altar heavenly Truth
I kneel in manhood, as I knelt in youth
Thus let me kneel, till this dull form decay
And life's last shade be brightened by thy ray.
Then shall my soul, not lost in clouds below
Soar without bounds, without consuming glow.
                    —*Sir Wm. Jones*

Professor Samuel B. F. Morse. The inventor and perfector of the magnetic telegraph, also an artist of much taste &c.

October 15, 1849

Warm and appearances of rain as it is a little cloudy. I. & I shot some at a mark and rode over the Brown place, thense to cousin Betty's and then home. Daddy commenced hauling cotton to the machine &c.

Wm. Colvin was married on last week to the Widow Estes.

Troopers mustered on Saturday last. Shooting match at W. M. Yongue's. I won three choices with seven shots &c. James Morgan began putting up ceiling this evening.

October 16, 1849

Packed eight bales cotton. Start to Columbia tomorrow. Jake went to H.J.C. and Grand Ma's. Came back by dinner. Esq came over as he is getting well again. Pappa has the eye & headache. Uncle Jonathan came up in the evening preparing for Columbia &c. Cloudy today. Wind blowing from the southeast. Wrote to Isa & Drucie.

October 17, 1849

Started from home for Columbia in company with Jacob Feaster & Uncle Jonathan. Commenced raining near twelve o'clock and continued all night though we were quite comfortable under cover of a tent.

October 18, 1849

Still raining in the morning and continued perpetually on us until arriving in Columbia at three o'clock. Sold cotton to P. P. Chambers at 10+°/₁₀₀. Slept at Uncle John's. Rained all night. Loaded on the 19th with his furniture. Left for home after four o'clock. Still raining on us. Left the camp on the next morning in the rain. Traveled twenty-six miles on the 20 inst. Camped at Mr. Gladney's. Rained all night. We got up on morning of the 21st with a gloomy time as it was raining harder than ever and continued so to do until arriving at home, having rained every day on us being five in number &c. This trip will be memorable. Uncle John & John P. came up at night on day. . . .

October 22, 1849

too wet for picking cotton. Began sowing rye. Moved darkey to the Brown place. Killed a beef &c., &c.

Battle of Red Bank 1777.

Franklin died Seventeenth of April 1790.

"Use yourself to thinking and you will find you have more in your head than you thought of."

Columbus born 10th July fourteen hundred and forty seven.
"One eye of a master sees more than four eyes of his servant."
"He who eats of one dish never wants a physician."
"Oil and truth will get uppermost at last."
Read the above maxims with care.

October 23, 1849

Got up this morning just before the break of day which is a very uncommon thing with me. The reason we rose so soon was the want of a very necessary article of bed furniture. Went home. Staid about there until ten o'clock. Went to Grandma's for fodder. Whilst coming home the fodder began to fall off. After some trouble we got home, then saddled the horses for Lizzie & Drucie to go to Aunt Becky's. The two Sallys rode them back. We then had a partridge hunt with a net. Drove one about considerable but could not catch him. Think we will fix him tomorrow. Came from hunting saw Samuel Coleman. Think Pa will take his [. . .]. Contentment is the blessing most needed in our country. Wrote by John P. Feaster M.D.

I & A.F.C. went in company with Uncle John & Daddy to the Esq's and Savilla's. The former and myself came home by dinner and then the partridge hunt as given by J.P.F. above &c. James Morgan finished the cottage excepting the door in partition which he will make tomorrow.

October 24, 1849, to October 29, 1849

Passed off without any particular occurrences except the moving of Uncle John's family into the cottage which was performed on the twenty-fifth inst and on the twentieighth A.E.C. & J.P.F. and self went to New Hope Church, sermon by Rev'd Boyce.

October 30, 1849

Isa, the Drucies, John P. Henry and I went to the singing at New Hope, had fine time &c. Came back by Johnnie Brice's

John P. and myself went after Drucies & Isa on twenty-fifth ult. Court week at Winnsboro.

Esq Feaster and Uncle John's to night personally.

October 31, 1849

Last day of October 1849. John & I rather got into the arraignment of partridges today as we before dinner netted sixteen at one drive, though we lost two. Went again in the evening and caught nine. Total per day, twenty-five, which is pretty good haul for the beginning &c.

Mr. Benjamin Revis came up from Columbia to Uncle John's. Cotton rising rapidly. Selling from ten to eleven.

Cupid is a tricky little fellow and makes men feel curious and act more so.

Gold pens are excellent for writing though every gentleman does not own one.

November 1, 1849

A beautiful day, clear and temperate. Revis, John and myself went netting in forenoon and caught only two after riding over near every hill on Beaver Creek. We got home by dinner. After partaking of a prodigious morsel of aliment, we sallied forth again in eager pursuit of partridges and soon after leaving the house we spied a covie. After some preliminaries were performed the net was set and then after a few more preliminaries enacted went eleven into the net. So after the neck-breaking, stringing to saddle, and other preliminaries we sallied forth again and very soon had four more netted. It is needless to say that they were doomed fatally as the former ones. We still continued the hunt and finally entrapped five more which were dealt with like unto their brethren. So upon a correct calculation we found the total massacre to be twenty-one, leaving out the one that slipped through the mesh. Adding yesterday's proceedings with todays, make by addition forty six.

The Esq. and wife were to see us today, &c., &c.

November 2, 1849

Mr. Revis & Esq and myself (i.e. Mr. Coleman) went netting again in the said Esq's enclosure and very soon after entering therein we commenced hostilities against a covie numbering near twenty. After considerable maneuvering we rather forced five into the deceptive threads. Their heads were dislocated from the neck and then attached by a twine to Mr. R's saddle. Pursuing again. Found a very large flock and drove them into the net "but horrible to relate and too bad to tell" I found (after getting my perceptive faculties into operation) a hole in the net and the partridges running out like [. . .] though I curbed three before they got out. So ended our hunt for today. Total eight.

Grand Ma came up yesterday and went home today &c.

John & Jake assisted in hauling corn from Grand Ma's[.]

Went to P.O. Saw Steamer returning from Columbia. Sold cotton at 10⅗, the best at 10¾.

Dug potatoes today. Quality only moderate.

R rode dearest Mae to the P.O.

Look over on page 49 for more news. "Sufficient until the day is the evil thereof."

"Early to bed and early to rise will make a man healthy, wealthy and wise." So says Franklin.

"Far happier are the dead methinks than they
Who look for death and fear it every day."

November 3, 1849

{The weather is beautifully serene and one would readily suppose it to be the ethereal mildness of spring rather than the melancholy season of autumn.} (Well done Miss Isa. Poetical.)[32]

November 4, 1849

Mr. Revis departed for home with a countenance expressive of much happiness and looks forward to the future as one continue walk without a stumble. Why? Because it looks so extremely smooth and soft. Happy is the man who looses his heart but finds a lady's instead &c.

November 5, 1849

Started for Columbia at noon in co. with John & Jake who are on their way to Florida.

November 6, 1849

Uncle John started this morning from the cottage for Fa. He caught us while eating dinner. He took a snack and rode on ahead of the wagons. In the meantime Uncle Sam came up. He done as the former. All camped at Frost's 5 miles from Ca.

November 7, 1849

Went in town early. Sold the cotton to R. Cathcart & Co. at ten & $\frac{6}{10}$. Left Uncle John and sons in town who intend leaving on the ninth inst.

November 8, 1849

Left the camp early which was the same place as last night. Uncle Sam and I left the wagons and came on home. I arrived at seven.

November 9, 1849

The wagons came home by noon, safe & sound. A.E. came up in the morning. We left in the eve for the muster at John L. Yongue's. Only got as far as Uncle Sam Mobley's where we remained all night.

November 10, 1849

Departed again for the muster with Joe Woodward in Co. Had a fine time on parade &c. Became acquainted with Mr. B. Ferguson. Eat dinner at Mr. Sterling's where I was much surprised to see Miss Jane P.F. also Merlisa.

Went to Uncle R. G. Cameron's with A.E.C. & Punkins.

November 11, 1849

Left R.G.C. and commenced our return home. Stoped at Jim Cork's. Found Betty well. Got home in the evening. Found a letter from H. D. Coleman. The girls went to preaching at Cool Branch and rode Dearest Mae.

November 12, 1849

Fine weather for picking cotton as it is warm and pleasant, rather nice weather for Nov. All went to singing except me. John C. Feaster came home with them. Isa had a toothache bad. Sent for Dr. Mc who came and extracted it at twelve o'clock at night. John made fine music on violin.

November 13, 1849

Still warm and cloudy. Went to Esq's and Billy's in evening. Went netting. Got only six. Isa has the toothache again and has gone to Mc's to get it pulled out &c.

November 14, 1849

Finished picking over the cotton third time. Pappa & Isa came home from the Dr.'s late in the eve. without getting the tooth drawn. Wrote a letter to D. R. Coleman. Sent a newspaper to R. W. Nolen. Lizie made a present of an orange to me, and I gave part to Daddy. I have felt different for the last week or two than ever I felt, not in boddy but seem dull and low in spirit. I fear love is the cause, and unreciprocated love at that. It is bad to love an object when your love is not returned &c. John Colvin & Emiline Crosby were married on the 13th ult., infare on to day &c.

November 15, 1849

Began hauling corn again at the Brown place. Hauled two loads. The Esq was over. Daddy came to the field where I was &c. Miss Sarah McClurkin is to be married to night to Mr. Thompson. Cloudy and cool. Prospect of rains &c.

November 16, 1849

Harvested eleven loads of corn to day. Saw R. H. Coleman with his gun &c. Also making preparation for killing his hogs.

Pappa went to Post Office but returned after I had gone to Daddy's, so I do not know as yet as the extent of mine communications &c., though I presume they are rather extensive. I feel better today. Worked pretty hard which is very good medicine to any love sick, low-spirited, no-account, good-for-nothing, trifling scamp. So now I pray you take the above perscription and maladies as used or possessed by myself.

Evil communications corrupt good manners.

November 17, 1849

Received a letter from E. S. Cockrell, also one from M. W. Coleman. The Steamer came up and eat dinner with me and then we left for his home accompanied by Lizie and Drucie. Went patrolling at night &c.

November 18, 1849

Returned from Uncle Jonathan's. Took super with Aunt Kizanah. Went huckleberry hunting with the girls &c.

November 19, 1849

Hauling corn again. Have sixty in all i.e. loads. Get done tomorrow &c.

November 20, 1849

Beautiful weather, being warm, resembling spring more [than] Autumn. Did not finish hauling corn. A. E. Coleman came up asking hands to his cotton picking. We will send three. Soaking wheat to night in bluestone. Stacked fodder &c.

I wrote a hasty letter to Albert Coleman of Green Ala.

November 21, 1849

Began sowing wheat. Ground in fine condition. Very warm. No prospect of rain. Wrote some pieces in E. M. Feaster's album.

November 22, 1849

Warm weather. Too warm for Nov. Probably we have leaped one month. Dancing school at Feasterville. Only two ladys. None of us attends. Mr. Wilson camped near the cottage.

November 23, 1849

A very warm day. Too much so for wearing a coat. Made some fine ditches. Still sowing wheat. Henry went to P.O. No letters. Pappa & Esq went down to the pasture. Got back by super &c. Saw Uncle Jonathan & Steamer hauling boards to cover Jacob F. Coleman's house. Split by Jake Varnadore &c. The Steamer stumbled with his loads of boards.

November 24, 1849

Finished sowing wheat by twelve o'clock at which time I let all hands stop working. Billy & Savilla came in the evening, also A.E.C. and John C. Feaster. We all collected together after super and had a fine dance at our house. J & A gallanted the girls over to the cottage and remained all night &c.

November 25, 1849

Billy, John, Andrew & self left in haste for Salem Church via Mrs. Yongue's where we came in contact with several more persons on the same road. I escorted Miss Micky. Sermon by Hoyt. I came as far as Esq Feaster's and eat dinner, thense home.

November 26, 1849

Raining early in the morning. Ceased after raining until ten o'clock, thense blowing off, clear and cool. Drove Savilla home in the buggy. Pappa went after brick at Wm. Lyle's &c. A.E.C. with him.

November 27, 1849

Began picking cotton again. Went to singing school at New Hope &c. Mrs. E. Coleman of Union Dist. at our house to night &c. Lizie and most any of the rest remained at home to day. Miss B. look Punkins &c. So did Miss Peggy &c. Isa & Drucy did not come home today but stayed at Uncle Sam's and Mrs. Yongue's &c.

November 28, 1849

Went again to the singing. Drucie rode in the buggy with me, had fine fun at the singing. Last day of the school but will have another singing on Friday three weeks hense &c. Miss Brice is pretty to kill. Got home by sun down. Mrs. E. Coleman from Union is sick to night with chills &c. We have the alarming news of killing hogs in the morning. This is not a pen of one of the inspired penman but a turkey quill.

The above is ugly writing which will be readily perceived at a single glance. But I am under the necessity of writing with a turkey quill made into a pen by daddy with a dull knife &c. Look on the other page.

November 29, 1849

The same bad pen. I feel ashamed of the manner in which my book is blotted which I will endeavour to make the last instance &c. Too warm for killing hogs according to Pappa's opinion. Nice weather for picking cotton. Drucy & Lizie stayed all night at Daddy's in my stead &c.

November 30, 1849

Carried little Drucy & Isa to Billy's where was collected the widow Millings, Miss M. C. Yongue and Esq & wife. The Esq and myself went partridge hunting but found none. Left B. for the P.O. where was a letter from Uncle John to his wife, also two for Lizie &c. Hogs i.e. droves and hogs at Feasterville selling at 3¼.

"Tinder—a thin rag such for instance as the dresses of modern females, intended to catch the sparks, raise a flame, and light up a match."

"Pleasure is like cordial: a little is not injurious but too much destroys."

"The grave buries every error, covers every defect, extinguishes every resentment. From its peaceful bosom springs none but fond regrets and tender recollections."

December 1, 1849

Cloudy in the morning and began raining near noon and rained until night. I went with Drucie Sr. and Sarah to McStore. Was detained from coming home until evening by the rain. Eat dinner at D. R. Coleman's where was Miss Martha Mc who report says will marry the 12 of this month &c. Stayed all night at Aunt Kizanah's. Played seven up and whist.

December 2, 1849

Raining in the morning and continued to rain incessantly throughout the entire day. Began a letter to Henry D. Coleman. Saw Ryan Mobley yesterday from Green Ala. A. E. Coleman came up in evening &c. at Daddy's 7 o'clock without candles.

December 3, 1849

Ceased raining early in the morning and became quite cool, so much so that we concluded to kill hogs. We at it hot headed and killed twenty seven though some of them might properly be termed pigs as the total amount was only thirty-five hundred pounds net.

The Esq & Billy came over today looking for ground to sow wheat in. They found it at the Brown place. Also a hog drover came to see if he could sell us any meat. The answer was no. His price was three and a half however some drovers are selling at three and a fourth, which is very cheap according to the price of cotton. Nick the Lyles's mason began the chimney of the cottage. Looking for Ben & Carrie Bell up on Thursday next.

Finished my letter to Henry D. Coleman of eight pages on foolscap. They much like long letters.

December 4, 1849

Very foggy in the morning and cloudy all day but quite cool. Salted meat, hauled and penned shucks, ginned cotton, split boards, work on the ginny &c. I wrote two for Soloman, one to John Lankford and the other to Wm. Coleman, the former of New Orleans and the latter of [. . .] Ga. Backed one to Uncle John. Sent four to the Post office by boy Alexander, &c., &c.

Receiving an invitation to appear personally at Feaster fully equiped and prepared as the law directs in such cases on the 12th inst. At six o'clock PM, I shall be very impatient until that time arrives &c. for it must be something of most importance to require so much caution and precision. Perhaps there is a nigger to kill or a mule to lend. Who knows? I went over to Cousin Betty's and read the continued tale, *The Deserted Wife* in the *Saturday Evening Post*, which will be concluded in next week's paper, having been in twelve or fifteen papers. It is an excellent piece of literature by Mrs. Southworth, author of *Retribution*,[33] &c. Billy Yongue's folks began ploughing for sowing wheat over on the Brown place by plowing up the stalks with two mules to a plow.

"The way of the sinner is hard."

December 5, 1849

Very similar to yesterday as being foggy &c. Went to preaching at Mrs. Yongue's. Sermon by Rev'd Hoyt. Caught thirteen partridges in the net.

December 6, 1849

Went netting with Wm. Yongue. Caught naught. Henry Gladden[34] eat dinner with me. Went in the evening to Mr. McConnell's after Mrs. Ladd who is there making preparation for the fandango. Brought her home with me, also Josephine.

December 7, 1849

I carried Mrs. Ladd to Uncle Jonathan's in the buggy, also Isa, the 2 Drucies, and Little Sarah where we got cousin Sarah Sr. and departed in peace to the party at Monticello leaving Mrs. Ladd at Uncle Feaster's. Got to town at 3 o'clk. Put up at McCrory's. I commenced dancing near 4 o'clock, danced until 2 AM. Slept until morn, danced again, then came home, leaving my heart stolen by Miss A.M.

December 8, 1849

After coming home from Monticello we heard of the coming in of D. R. Coleman and wife Nancy from Chambers, Ala. who have been absent since their marriage on the 3d of August 1848 which is noted in the first of this book. Stayed with Dan at Betty's until morning of the ninth when we came home where we found Benjamin Revis who came up last evening alone, not bringing Miss Connel as anticipated &c. Raining a little all day. The Esq came over in the morning &c.

December 10, 1849

Raining all day and very warm indeed. Plenty of cotton leaves green as yet. A. E. Coleman and D.R. went to James Cork's via Mr. Simeton's. Mr. Revis and myself went netting in evening but caught none. Packed cotton. Likewise ginned, hauled leaves, cut wood, and did various other evolutions too tedious to call &c.

Daddy tells me that going with his horse to the stable he found a stalk of cotton in a fine growing condition which he suffered his horse Dick to eat. This is a rare event to have cotton growing the 10th of December.

December 11, 1849

Cleared off in the morning quite cool. Wind blowing from the northwest. Started the wagon to Columbia in company with Daddy's & Aunt Becky's wagons. I will start tomorrow morning in co. with Mr. Ben Revis. This date is memorable doubly on account of the marriages of Trezavant D. G. Feaster to Miss Martha, third daughter of Andrew McConnell Esq, also Dr. Christopher Simeton to Miss Jane, second daughter of Rob't G. Cameron. The former match was quite unexpected though the ways of youth is as the changing winds. Each of the parties above mentioned are young, the oldest not exceeding twenty-five.

David R. & A. E. Coleman returned from James Cork's by suppertime in a very cold condition. D. went on to Betty's and A.E. remained at daddy's with me. I was at Aunt Becky's this evening where I saw Drucilla K. Feaster. Mamma & Pappa went to see the Esq and Savilla. Returned by super. Drucie Feaster gave me a letter for the Post Office in Columbia to Uncle John.

PAPEROPATHY

Take the Yankee Blade
(Of papers there's no better)
Read it fairly through
To the very letter.

Read the poetry
If you like the muse
Read the foreign items
If you want the news

Read the money matters
If you take to money
Read the paragraphs
Some of them are funny

Read it as you will
Summer time or winter
And you'll happy be
If you've paid the printer.

December 12, 1849

Left home for Columbia in company with Revis. We got to his house at Supper time. Passed the wagons at dinner.

December 13, 1849

We went from Revis's to Columbia where we got by ten o'clock. Sold cotton to N. A. Feaster at $9^7/_8$, $9^5/_8$ & $9^{15}/_{100}$. Stayed all night at Mr. Popes Entertainment.

December 14, 1849

Left soon in morn. Got home by dark.

December 15, 1849

Felt very tired after getting up. Went partridge hunting with D. R. & R. H. Coleman. Caught eight. A.E.C[.], John Feaster and Jack Holly was with us to day. The two last named gentlemen left after taking dinner &c.

December 16, 1849

Raining slowly incessantly throughout the entire day. David & Bob H. left for home in evening. Danced last night some. Stay at Aunt K's. Was at Aunt Becky's who received a letter from Mary Slaughter of Va. All well. Uncle Jonathan gave us a call in the afternoon &c. Ben Revis is [. . .]. So is Bob. Seabrook Gov. of So. Ca.[35]

December 17, 1849

Picking cotton, warm and fair. Went partridge hunting in the evening with D.R.C. and the two Peggy's. Caught nine. Aunt K. got a letter from Uncle John. All well and at home.

December 18, 1849

Savilla, Sarah, Billy and Esq eat dinner with us. Also D.R.C. of Ala. Went to the shop with Billy. Caught four partridges which makes one hundred and three in all my slaughtering. Last day of the dancing school at Feasterville.

December 19, 1849

Raining in the evening. Stayed all night at Aunt K's &c. Had a small retaliation with Charles &c.

December 20, 1849

Cloudy. Killed hogs for daddy and went to the singing at New Hope. Flew around considerable, i.e. around the fair ones of the human race &c., &c. Rode back in the carriage. Got sick &c., &c.

December 22, 1849

A tremendious storm before day break which blew down every fence nearly on the plantation, consequently we were fencing all the day. Stayed all night at Widow Betty's in co. with D. R. & R. H. Colemans.

December 23, 1849

Very cold. Benjamin Revis came up in the evening &c., &c., &c., &c., &c. D.R.C. & myself with daddy to night. Talked on Scripture, Freemasonry & Odd fellows.

December 24, 1849

Christmas eve. Warm and cloudy. Went to Jacob Feaster Esq's with D. R. Coleman Jr where David received six hundred dollars in part of the legacy come from Hiram Coleman's Est to Pancy his wife &c. Edith Lyles very sick, also J. Q. Arnett ailing. J.C.F. played excellently on the violin, gave me a few lessons on dancing &c. Very cold being clear and windy. Put a letter in the P.O. for Mrs. E. Nolen, one for Miss M. B. Holms and E. S. Cockrell Esq. At Daddy's 7 o'clk PM I hear numerous Christmas guns exploding in a westerly direction, suppose the shooters have plenty of ardent spirits around and in them &c.

December 25, 1849

First day of Christmas. Pretty cool. Went partridge hunting, caught several &c. R.H.C. & D.R.C., Mr. Revis, D.R.C. of ala. were at our house at night. Danced some little. Mr. Revis went over after the dance to Aunt K's, &c., &c., &c.

December 26, 1849

Extremely cold. Uncle Jonathan came up soon in morning, going to a hiring at Wm. Brice's dec'd, though he stoped long enough to invite us to a party at his house on tomorrow. The Drucies and myself went to Uncle Jonathan's, Grand Ma's and John F's. Returned home in the eve and found Miss Jane Moore at home. We after super danced considerably. Miss Jane is a very good dancer and the most excellent performer on the piano that I ever heard.

December 27, 1849

Left soon in the morning for the fandango at Uncle H's, leaving Miss Jane and Druce at home. We had a fine dance. Miss Jane Mc appeared though as if she was the belle of the dance. All danced a plenty by sundown having commenced at 9 o'clock AM. Returned home and danced more. Miss J. gave us some more music. Too good.

December 28, 1849

Began hasty preparations quite soon in morning for the cotillion party at Monticello. Miss Jane Moore accompanied us as far as Uncle Jon's where we stopped and she went on to Maj. Lyles'[36] after eating dinner at Jon's. We left in haste with the addition of Sarah in our company. Got to Monticello by 3 o'clk. Began dancing by night and continued until 3 o'clk AM when we went to J. McCrorey's and slept until morning i.e. sun up &c.

December 29, 1849

Went back to the dancing room and danced until [. . .]. Left for home in fine glee. R.H.C. and D.K.F. riding in a buggy together &c. Got home by night.

December 30, 1849

Went in the buggies with D.R.C. and wife. Also R.H.C. and James Corks. Remained all night. Raining at night &c.

December 31, 1849

The last day of 1849. Went partridge hunting with Cork. Caught only five. Came home in evening. Found Mr. Harris and Jas. Coleman from Laurens Dist. Likewise D. R. & H. C. Feaster. Danced some little.

January 1, 1850

Very cold. Began overseeing again for pap. Too cold to work much.

January 2, 1850

Began sowing rye again and making ditches. Also hauling pouplar stocks to the sawmill. Let J. D. Coleman have a piece for shaft for gin wheel. Went to Savilla's who was taken sick on this inst. though not dangerously I hope. I remained all night. Made some very long & fine ditches today &c. Packed cotton, etcetera.

January 3, 1850

I came from Billy's by daybreak. Finished hauling stocks by M. then began hauling rails also splitting the same. Made a few more fine ditches. Mamma & Pappa went to Savilla's late in evening. Dr. Mc, A.E.C. and Wesly Mayfield called this evening &c., &c. D.R.C. and R.H.C. burning a tar kiln.

January 4, 1850

Went partridge hunting with D.R. & R.H.C. Caught twenty-two. Went to P.O. A letter to Aunt Becky from John J.C. with the news of Obs marriage to Miss Mobley. I say hurra for him. No letters from Florida. One to Soloman from N. Orleans.

January 5, 1850

Fencing all day and on returning home from work I found A.E.C. in good health &c. Also heard that B. Revis was up again sparking &c. Hurra for aristocracy and Richland.

January 6, 1850

Sabbath. Went over early in morning to see Revis. Found moderately well. I thank yea. How do yea yourself. Went to preaching at Red Hill in co. with Little Drucie, also A.E.C. and sister Drucie. Sermon by Rev'd Fant. Went from church to Mr. Land's with Isa who was going home with Miss E. Bostic so that she might come home with Isa. Eat dinner at Mr. Lands and then left for home in co. with Strip, Lizie, and Isa. Began raining before getting home. Rained all night. A.E.C. stayed all night with me again.

January 7, 1850

Raining very hard all day. Fenced a little. Mr. Revis left for home. I wrote to [. . .] Coleman a long letter as he has become a benedict &c.

January 8, 1850

Finished fencing. Mules ran away with wagon. Broke it. Miss E. Bostic left for home in company with Drucy and Henry. I wish that I could have went but no, I had not the chance. However I killed one rabit or hare and netted four partridges alone, loaded the wagon for Columbia. Began gining the Esq's cotton which he finished hauling to day.

January 9, 1850

Pappa left for Columbia. Began raining in the evening sowing rye. Splitting boards and ginning &c.

January 10, 1850

Packed five bales of cotton for the Esq. Made several ditches, caught ten partridges in company with D.R.C. & James Cork, also R. H. Coleman &c.

January 11, 1850

Still raining moderately, having rained an immense quantity. Ground very wet. Went to the P.O. in evening. Received a letter from John P. Feaster from Florida. He arrived there safe and sound &c.

January 12, 1850

I mustered in the Buckhead Troopers [to] which company I belong. Eat dinner at Mrs. Yongues. Came home in evening with A.E.C. Pappa got home after night, sold cotton $10^{30}/_{100}$ to R. Cathcart. Brought a double barrel gun from Revis for me.

January 13, 1850

Went over to Billy's. Netted twelve partridges with D.R.C. &c.

January 14, 1850

An election for Clerk Court, Thompson and Lauhon and Pearson candidates. I voted for Thompson. Very cold and windy. Began moving down to the pasture. David & Nancy was at Daddy's &c., &c. Shot my new gun a few times.

February 5, 1850

From the above date until now which is the 5th February I was so very busy that I could not get an opportunity to note any items in my Journal. A great many changes have taken place since the fourteenth of January, viz. Thompson is elected Clerk of Court by a large majority. Henry has gone to Uncle R. G. Cameron's to school. Isa and Sarah Feaster have gone to Winnsborro to Mrs. Ladd. So has M. A. Feaster. David Feaster has gone to Laurens. Nancy and Bob have gone to Alabama. They certainly have had a disagreeable journey for it has rained nearly half the time that they have been gone. And finally I have moved down into the pasture, living alone. I moved on the Fourth of Febr. I have received several letters latterly, one in particular from E. S. Cockrell. I have spent the night generally while working on my house with Grand Ma, Uncle Jonathan, A.E.C. and Uncle Jacob Feaster.

February 4th 1850 I moved into "Printer's Mansion." A.E.C. came down with me and aided in arranging my household furniture, &c. At night I wrote a letter to Isa, gave her a full description of my house, eating, &c. Kill two birds for super, the hands splitting rails and hauling.

Fifth very cold, the coldest weather we have had this winter. The Drucies came down to see me and stayed all day. I do love them. I went over to Jacob F. Coleman's with them. He lives in half a mile of me. The D's will stay with Grand Ma to night. I killed a squirrel late this eve. Get more rails split tomorrow, then I expect to commence plowing.

February 6, 1850

Very cold as yet. Had Alex ploughing also Darkey. After dinner Pappa came down. We laid the worm of the pasture fence.[37] I had squirrel for dinner. Wrote a note to D. R. Coleman requesting him to come down &c.

February 7, 1850

Very pleasant day. Finished fencing and splitting rails. Mamma, Pappa and Bob came down and stayed all day, also A.E.C. The Esq eat dinner with me though left soon after eating. Mamma stayed all night with Grand Ma, also Pappa and Bob. Andy and I slept together. He come after the wagon to go to Columbia. I went to McConnell's store but could not get in as the clerk was not there. I had four hands plowing in the afternoon. Killed a squirrel for breakfast on the eighth.

February 8, 1850

Started seven plows agoing. Went to Esq Feaster's blacksmith shop, also to the P.O. No letter for myself. John C. Feaster come home with me and stayed all night & played the violin.

February 9, 1849

Went back to the shop. Negro trial at Arnett's store. Saw Mrs. Mobley & J. Maberry. Went up home in the evening as being Saturday.

February 10, 1850

Went over to Billy's. Eat dinner. Sis gave me a bottle of molasses. I came back home in the evening.

February 11, 1850

Set all hands ploughing. Went to Mc's store after washpan &c. Billy came down and eat dinner with me.

February 12, 1850

Made a plowstock of ash. Mr. Morgan came over after a drawing knife, auger &c. Killed two birds. Very warm and pleasant weather & ground in fine order for plowing. J. C. Coleman Jr. stayed all night with me on Sunday night.

February 13, 1850

Soon as being aroused from my morning slumbers I was made aware of its raining by the noise of the water falling upon the house top. And after getting up I found it had rained considerably. So much that the ground was rendered too wet for plowing. Consequently I raised me a stable for the accommodation of my nag Pigeon whom I got from J. C. Feaster by the way of exchanging Miss Rosa for her. Sent Alex to the shop also to the store for bridle colors &c. Raining all day and until now which is bed time.

I finished reading one of Waverly Novels viz *Anne of Geirstein*[38] which is an excellent work.

February 14, 1850

Still raining with some snow and hail in the evening. Went over to A.E.C. who had just returned from Columbia last evening. He got eleven and thirty one for his cotton and swapped off Buck and Kate for a couple of fine horses. We hauled corn in the afternoon. Finished my stable &c.

Very lonesome to night so I shall go to bed soon and try to sleep sound until morning. Then I shall go to my work.

February 15, 1850

Wrote several Valentines to several particular ladys &c.

February 20, 1850

A.E.C. came over in the evening and we left the pasture for home. Found the girls ready for the party at Winnsboro on the 21st.

February 21, 1850

We started i.e. Sarah C., Drucy, A.E.C. and myself. Got there safe and sound. Went to the cotillion party at seven o'clock. I escorted Miss J. Mc and A.E.C. escorted Brooks. Danced until two AM. Saw some very pretty girls, Miss Cook, Hall, Chambers &c.

February 22, 1850

Waked up after having some heavenly dreams. Had our dagarratypes taken together and then I had mine taken alone by Mr. Scorbb. Rained so that I could not get off so we sparked around all day. Went to bed and had worse dreams than last night.

February 23, 1850

Fair morning so we left our hearts and Winnsboro and came home.

February 24, 1850

Rained all day without interruption. Came from home to Uncle Jonathan's and stayed all night.

February 25, 1850

Got down to the pasture having been gone for five days. Ground too wet for plowing. Went to shop in co. with Jake Coleman. Saw Misses Feaster, Lyles, Ken Coleman & Arnason all in tet-a-tet. The latter gentleman is agent for Griswould's gins.

February 26, 1850

Began sowing oats. Ground very wet having rained nearly every other day for two weeks.

February 27, 1850

Went to the tax collector &c. Rained again to day.

February 28, 1850

Last of February. Sowed oats to day. Killed a crow, dove and squirrel. Went to the P.O. under the impression that it was Friday. It being Thursday. Also went to Jas. Morgan. "On hearing Miss Jane More singing"

> My soul is an enchanted boat
> Which like a sleeping swan doth float
> Upon the silver waves of thy sweet singing
> And thine doth like an angel sit
> Beside the helm conducting it
> While all the winds with melody are ringing.[39]

March 1, 1850

Friday. Sowing oats in the pasture. Saw a turkey but did not get a shot. Went again to P.O. Received a letter from John P. Feaster of Micanopy Fla. The Steamer stayed all night with me on this date. He was very much pleased with the Mansion, i.e. my log cabin.

March 2, 1850

Saturday. Planted my Irish potatoes and finished sowing oats. Shot at a turkey and wounded it, though I could not get it. Let the hands work in their patches in the afternoon. I went home.

March 3, 1850

Went to Red Hill with the Peggys, also to Dr. McClurkin's where we found A.E.C. The judge came home with us from church and we all took dinner with Aunt Kizanah. I came home with Judge and eat supper with him. Saw the Mrs. Feaster, that is Elbert's and Trez's wives. I got home after night and went to bed and slept until morning.

March 4, 1850

Began beding corn ground again. Finished by noon then commenced laying my cotton ground.

March 5, 1850

Plowing all day. Pappa came down and seemed very well pleased at my work. I made a ditch. A.E.C. came and stayed all night with me. Bob has been with me all the week.

March 6, 1850

Went to the shop. Eat dinner with A.E.C. and aided him to plant his Irish potatoes, then we came to my house. Rained in evening. Put a letter in the P.O. to John P. Feaster.

March 7, 1850

Ground too wet in the morning for plowing so we made a cow pen &c. until noon then began plowing again. I gave Wm. Jenkins some potatoes for planting.

One of my hens hatched three chickens so made a coop to put her in. Just let my old hen stand. Bob is asleep so I believe I will go to bed too.

March 8, 1850

Worked on the road. Uncle J. M. Feaster came home from Fla. on the 6th inst. Sarah & Drucies came down to see me &c. Got four letters by today's mail from H. R. Feaster, E. S. Cockrell, &c.

From the 9th until the 23d I done but little of any thing for it was raining almost continually. Some of the greatest freshets ever known in the creeks. Uncle John and Pappa was down today. I kill three hogs which was penned &c. Went to the river with H. J. Coleman. Came via Maj. Seymor's after my boots mended by Sims. Charged four dollars.

March 24, 1850

Went to New Hope with the Judge. Flew around more than considerable. No body but the Judge and Miss Margaret Jane. Eat dinner at Uncle Sam's. Came from there to Trez. Had happy dreams for the remainder of the night. Received a letter from Isa, all well. She's chosen *May Queen* &c.

March 25, 1850

Began plowing though the ground mostly too wet. Went to Esq Feaster's in the evening. Had my nag shod. Got a double plowstock. Brought my double plowstock home and began planting corn about fifteen minutes before sun set. Wrote to Mr. B Revis.

March 26, 1850

Planting corn fast. Shot at a turkey but did not kill it. The Drucies came down. We went fishing to Bever Creek. John Feaster came to us on the creek looking for sheep. All came to the mansion and eat super then John went home and I carried the D's to Grandma's. Wrote to Isa, Henry and E. S. Cockrell.

March 27, 1850

Very cool, the wind blowing from the north and cloudy. About 8 o'clock it began raining and continued so to do the entire day. Stoped planting corn before noon. Went to see Jake Coleman in the evening who is down with the chills and fever.

March 28, 1850

Hello. Got out of the bed and lo and behold the whole face of the earth was covered with snow. Now aint that some. Made a mammoth ditch to day, a perfect canal. Hauled manure, killed several doves. Had a pie of course. Was compelled by necessity to give Dave a thrashing. Very cold all day.

March 29, 1850

A heavy frost in the morning. Went turkey hunting with Coe Taylor, Wm. Meador and Wm. Smith. No killing done by any of us. Plowed my mellon patch. Too wet for planting corn.

March 30, 1850

Cloudy and cool. Began raining at noon. Read some excellent tales in *Godey's Lady's Book*. Going home to night.

March 31, 1850

Last day of March. Staid up at home all day. Pappa & Lizie returned from Winnsboro in the evening. Uncle John has gone to Columbia.

April 1, 1850

Planted a mellon patch. Raining nearly every day throughout the whole week, only half day suitable for planting corn. Mr. W. A. Lonegan stayed two nights with me this week. He is working on the monument at the Grace Yard.

April 6, 1850

Raised the monument. Uncle John, Pappa, A.E.C., John C. Feaster and Foot all eat dinner with me. I went home with A.E.C. and remained all night.

April 7, 1850

Dressed up and rode down to Winnsboro and stayed until 6 o'clock PM then returned by eleven. Very tired after getting home.

April 8, 1850

Ground too wet for corn planting. A great hail on Friday last. Saw one stalk of corn up to day.

April 9, 1850

Began planting corn again, not having planted any since Tuesday week. At noon John Feaster came after his sheep, eat dinner with them, went with his sheep homewards. Mr. W. Henderson remained all night with me. He is from the West. The excessive rains have extended as far as he traveled.

April 10, 1850

More rain. More rain last night. Rained all day today very hard making the ground as wet as wet can be. Went squirrel hunting with Jake. We killed seven. After getting home I saw a drove of thirteen partridges close by the house so I got my net and set it and netted ten of them. Sent Grand Ma a part, mended some old broke over ditches today, sent and borrowed J. Morgan's shovels for ditching tomorrow. No green leaves out as yet. Very late spring.

April 11, 1850

More rain and very cool, wind blowing from the N.W. Pappa came down to day and took dinner with me &c. Went with Wm. Jenkins to the crow nests. I killed three of them, two on the wing and a hawk upon her nest.

Allan & Henry A. Jr. was with me to night. Rec. letters from E. S. Cockrell and D. R. Feaster.

April 27, 1850

Give the hands to day to plant their crops &c. Went fishing with Alan and Henry. Caught an eel and lots of cats. Came back home and found the Esq, wife and son, also Billy, wife and daughter. Went with them to Jake's and Wm. Jenkins's, then home. Got there and found Uncle John very low though he thought some better. Went home with Esq and stayed all night.

April 28, 1850

Tried Pigeon in buggy. She would not come it. All came back home. Found Uncle John a good deal better. Remained about home all day. Dr. Coleman,

Jesse Gladden,[40] John F. were at Uncle John's. Came down in the evening to the mansion.

April 29, 1850

Plowing corn. Went with Grand Ma fishing, caught many. Saw H. J. Lyles[41] on the creek. Came to Grand Ma's where she gave me some beans. Mr. G. W. Bower & D. R. Feaster came and stayed the night with me. They are citizens of Laurens Dist.

April 30, 1850

Went up home with Mr. Bower and Feaster and got ready for going to Winnsboro. Left in evening. Got there by sun down. Put up at McMasters. Went up to Ladd's and saw four very pretty girls &c. Quince the reformed drunkard lectured on temperance &c. Going to May party in morning.

May 1, 1850

In Winsboro as large as life in company with G. W. Bower and G. W. Punkins. In the evening the Steamer and Judge came down to the lodge at Crawford's. Went to May Party at 7 o'clock. Miss Bell Coleman Queen. Danced until 3 AM. Miss More was in attendance.

May 2, 1850

Left for home in company of May girls and boys. Got home by 3, then came down to the pasture and went to bed very soon.

May 3, 1850

Went to Uncle Jake's and P.O. No letters. D. Feaster with Bower with me tonight again. Eat dinner with A.E.C.

May 4, 1850

Bower & Punkins left for Laurens early. A.E.C. came in morning and stayed until eve. We were reading *The Knights of the Golden Horse Shoe*. We went home in even, found Uncle John slowly recovering and some of our Negroes sick.

May 5, 1850

Had a fine rain. Drucie & Sarah, A.E.C. and Mr. Lyles went to Bower's fork and caught some fish. Came home or to the mansion and finished reading our tale.

May 6, 1850

Began plowing cotton. Bad stand indeed. Went with A.E.C. to his house and eat dinner. Went to A's store, saw Mrs. E. Lyles and Miss M. A. Feaster. I got me a [. . .] in eve &c. Went fishing in eve. Caught some fine ones, enough for my supper & breakfast.

May 7, 1850

Pappa, Drucie & Isa came down. We went fishing, had good luck. I had a severe headache all the evening, feel very bad all over.

May 8, 1850

Still in bad health. Henry was with me last night. He came after a mule to work to Columbia. Uncle Jonathan starts to Georgia to day after Betsy, his daughter. Had a fine rain in evening. Set out collard plants. This rain is glorious to farmer's. I feel better this evening though I still have a bad cough, sore breast and throat.

May 9, 1850

Still feel very bad, fear that I am taking phneumonia. Cough almost incessantly. Ground too wet for plowing or planting corn. Set a hen, got the eggs from Grand Ma. Wind blowing quite cool from west, which was the case the other day which dries the ground fast also makes a lake. Reading to day in *Magnolia*, old magazines of 1841 printed in Savannah Ga. Some most excellent pieces in them, some of which are *The Knights of the Golden Horse Shoe*, *Maj. Cunningham*, *All's in Luck*, &c. Went in the evening to John B. Smith's. [. . .] came by Nevitt's looking for a strayed [. . .] which went off last fall, did not find him but heard of him. Jake gave me some white & drumhead cabbage plants. I still feel very bad, head aching this evening, horrid, coughed all night.

May 10, 1850

Beautiful morning. My head has ceased aching though the cough holds on to me. Wm. Jenkins sent me some N&O and Grand Ma has made me some composition for soreness of throat. Went and stayed at Grand Ma's at night. Pappa came after me.

May 11, 1850

Went home soon in morning and went to bed. Was sick for two weeks with phneumonia.

May 26, 1850

Came down once more to the pasture. Left Mamma very unwell. Rec'd letters from G. W. Bower and D. R. Coleman on the 24 inst. Uncle John is mending save Feaster has quit Laurens &c.

May 27, 1850

All hands hoeing cotton. T. D. Feaster took dinner with me. Michaja B. Pickett and family, also Uncle Jonathan arrived from Ga. Mr. Pickett is a preacher. The Judge stayed all night with me.

May 28, 1850

Began plowing corn the second time. Heavy rain at sun down. Went up home, found Mamma improving slowly, also all the other sick ones. Wrote to J. F. Feaster and E. S. Cockrell.

May 29, 1850

Ground too wet for plowing. Finished hoeing cotton. Plowed some very grassy and bad looking cotton where the ground is almost always too hard though full wet today. Began in evening to prepare a piece of Jake Coleman's land for corn, land that was too rough for him to plant in cotton. Rained on us but not enough to stop us from plowing. William M. Mobley died to day leaving no family except his wife, also one of his little Negroes died near the same time.

May 30, 1850

Finished planting my corn at Jake's. W. M. Mobley was buried at the Mobley graveyard. Raining slowly all day. Pappa came down. One of D. R. Coleman's little Negroes died on this date, himself very sick.

May 31, 1850

Plowing grassy cotton. Went up home, met Uncle John & wife coming to grave. Went from home to the Esq who's sick with cold &c. Came back to Grand Ma's. Eat dinner. Found Mrs. Pickett and Sarah Coleman there. Went with Uncle to D. R. Coleman's who is very sick. Came back by sundown. Raining moderately in evening.

June 1, 1850

Rained all night and on until noon. Went up again to D. R. Coleman's with Uncle John. He remains the same. Drs. Dupree & McClurkin attend him.

Came home by Drucie. Sun shining in evening. Too wet for plowing so I've got the hands hoeing corn.

June 2, 1850
Went to Liberty Church. Sermon by the Rev'd M. B. Pickett. Heavy rain in evening. Came to my mansion in evening.

June 3, 1850
Plowing cotton. The Drucies came down. We had strawberry pie for dinner.

June 4, 1850
I plowed all day myself.

June 5, 1850
Put letters in P.O. to J. D. Feaster, D. R. Coleman & G. W. Bower. Went to shop. Came back and went to plowing.

June 6, 1850
Finished my cotton for the second plowing. Pappa came down.

June 7, 1850
Plowing corn. Very hot weather. Went to P.O. No letters. Saw Mrs. D. Rawls, Miss Bird, Wm. Lonegan &c. Met and stayed with the Esq at night. He is very low.

June 8, 1850
Came by Uncle John's. He came down with me to the mansion, rode over my farm. I went to A.E.C. and eat dinner, thense we went to the Esq's, carried him some lemon syrup, stayed all night. He is some better.

June 9, 1850
My birth day. Uncle and Aunt came to the Esq. We left there and came via home to Aunt Becky's, so Drucie, Mary Pickett also N. A. Feaster and J. C. C. Feaster.

June 10, 1850
Three hands and myself plowing cotton, the remainder at home cutting wheat. Very tired at night.

June 11, 1850

Still plowing. No rain. Ground getting hard. Plowed all day. Sallie, Mary & Sarah Pickett come home, got strawberrys &c., had some done up brown in sugar and cream.

June 12, 1850

Cool and dry. My cotton very grassy. T. D. Feaster come on to see my crop. Didn't get my letter off to P.O. Uncle Jonathan came in evening. I worked until Friday when I went to the P.O. Got a letter from Isa. D. R. Feaster stayed all night with me.

June 15, 1850

Went to David's. He is little better. Went to Mrs. Yongue's in evening, stayed all night at David's.

June 16, 1850

Was at home all day until evening. Came to the mansion, &c.

June 17, 1850

Hoeing cotton, wrote letters to Isa and J. P. Feaster.

June 18, 1850

Went to shop. Eat dinner at Esq Feaster's. John C. came home with me and stayed all night. Serletia Morgan, wife of James Morgan, died in the evening of this date. Miss Irena, daughter of Riggers Mobley died on Sunday last.

June 19, 1850

Hoed cotton, myself in particular. W. Jenkins came to where I was and the lazzy struck me instanter so I quit an hour before PM. Then went after plows at shop, saw D. L. Lyles, D. R. Feaster and Crowder plowing &c. Darkey sick to night.

June 20, 1850

Hot & dry and hot. I hoed cotton until dinner. Pappa, Mamma and Bob was down. Darkey very sick in evening. Pappa went home, leaving Mamma & Bob.

June 21, 1850

James Morgan & John Feaster came to me hoeing. The latter remained until after dinner. I went then with him to Buckhead. No letters. Got the *Brother Jonathan*, *Blade* and *Herald*. Slight shower in evening. Very warm all day. Mamma and Bob stayed all night.

June 22, 1850

Very warm with some sighns of rain. Jake's wife & Nance Jenkins came to see the sick. All hands got done their tasks before dinner. I hoed some corn in the bottoms. Had black berry pie for dinner as usual. Went up home in evening.

June 23, 1850

Passed the day in reading &c.

June 24, 1850

Finished hoeing my cotton second time. Hoed over an acre myself.

June 25, 1850

Plowed my bottoms. Uncle John & Pappa came down. I went to P.O. & shop. D. R. Feaster came home with me. Wrote to Isa & T. D. Feaster.

June 26, 1850

Began plowing cotton with two hands in the corn. Heavy cloud and thunder at noon. No rain from it. Grand Ma came down to see me. Slight shower of rain in evening. Feaster and I went fishing, caught seven.

June 27, 1850

Some prospect of rain, heavy thunder at noon. Rain much needed. Feaster departed for his brother Jake's. Laying by some of my corn. Saw three corn silks today. Sent Alex up home after meat. Went to Jake's in evening to see my late corn. Looks very well considering. Rained again this evening a little. Want more again. Saw Jenkins plowing cotton. He says we'll have plenty of rain soon. My melons look fine.

June 28, 1850

Warm and cloudy. I hoed corn till dinner. Come to house and found Feaster reading. We eat dinner as usual.

Went to Buckhead P.O. in evening in company with David R. Feaster Esq. Received a letter from Benj. T. Revis Esq. He is coming up about the twentieth of July if he can execute his present intentions. In fact he wants to come badly. Mr. D. R. Meador came with me from the P.O. We rode over my farm and then into his plantation. So Alex his brother is hoeing his corn &c.

June 29, 1850

Still plowing both corn and cotton. The ground in bad order. Want rain bad. Hoed my watermelon patch, look flourishing indeed. Gave my hands this evening to rest. Then went home, pick black berrys with Lizie & Drucie.

June 30, 1850

Last of June. Went to preaching at Salem. Sermon by the Rev'd Hoyt. The girls went in carriage. Came in the evening to Esq. Feaster's and eat dinner, played marbles, &c., thense departed homewards. At Uncle Andrew's we separated, I for the Mansion and the girls for their home. Drucie had the headache very bad. Oh, how lousy I am to night. I fear that I am too miserable. My situation is a bad one in every particular. Saw some very pretty girls at Church—Miss Gladdeny, Green, Shields, Beard, Yongue, &c.

This has been an uncommon dry month, not having been a rain of any importance since the 28th of May last. Corn is now suffering very much. The crop will I fear fall short of a third the crop.

July 1, 1850

Plowing corn and cotton both. A fine rain went all around us. Henry stayed all night with me. Turned out some of the cattle from the pasture as it is getting short of grass. Dry, dry weather. Poor farmers need something better than sympathy.

July 2, 1850

Finished my cotton i.e. running around it and commenced plowing out the middles. Went to the shop in evening. Plows sharpened &c. Killed Grand Ma's mutton. Henry come down after his colt.

July 3, 1850

I went to Lyles's Mill. Met Pappa & H. going to Nevett's after the bull. Hot and dry today. Oh, why don't it rain? Began plowing the yongue corn at Jake's. It looks as if it would die. Eat dinner with him, also Mrs. E. Pickett and Sarah. The Esq A. Feaster came to see me. The latter carried off Old Charley, given to him by Uncle John Feaster. Rain away off today. It seems as if it cannot rain about the mansion. A.E.C. stayed with me to night.

July 4, 1850

Hot and dry enough for any zone. Finished my corn at Jake's and began splitting out cotton middles. I will keep diggin' if it don't rain.

July 5, 1850

Finished plowing my crop until it rains. Began hoeing corn. Jake came over and drove the bull into his pasture. Went to P.O. in evening. Received letter from Isa and first No. of Southern Press printed in W.C. A.E.C. came home with me. Stayed all night. Went up home early in the morn of Saturday 6th. After dinner went to Billy's. Drucie went to Becky's. Very warm to day and no rain as usual.

July 7, 1850

We went to Red Hill and Dr. Mc's. Large audience. Sermon by Mr. Newlin. Saw Miss Victoria Wilks besides many other pretty girls. Came home. Eat dinner at Arnett's.

A little rain in evening but of no consequence. A.E.C. came down with me and stayed all night. Prospect of much rain but proved bad for we got scarcely any.

July 8, 1850

Hoeing corn which looks tremendious bad. Went over to Jake's bean patch, picked a mess, gave Becky a squirrel. Killed two today. David Feaster called in and took dinner with me. He is going to Winnsboro tomorrow. Sent a letter by him to Isa. A slight rain again but only enough to lay the dust.

July 9, July 10, and July 11, 1850

Were all of a sameness, only we went seighning on Tuesday. Caught not very many. No rain.

July 12, 1850

Went to H. J. Lyles's. Eat dinner, then went down to P.O. Eating a fine cleance of watermelons in his patch on the way. Received letter from J. P. Feaster. Went to W. M. Yongues at night.

July 13, 1850

Mustered at Mrs. Yongue's. My first debut as lieutenant. Eat dinner at Mrs. Y's. Went from there to H.J.L.'s with D.R.F. and A. C. Feaster. Stayed all night.

July 14, 1850

Came up home with the said D.R.F. Found Uncle John, wife and Lizie, Uncle Jonathan, son John and wife and children. The Peggys and Henry gone to Salem. Came down to pasture by sundown. No rain as yet. What can we do and what will we do are questions not to be answered at present.

July 15, 1850

Dry, dry. Want rain so very bad. Done no good today I know, though I don't know as I started to Columbia in company with Uncle Jonathan.

July 16, 1850

Arrived in Col. Sold cotton to H. R. Cathcart & Co. at 12^{30}/$_{100}$.

July 17, 1850

Left Col. in morning. Got to Bill's Mill before camping.

July 18, 1850

Uncle & I went in washing at the mill. Got home by 12 o'clock.

July 19, 1850

Came down to mansion, thense to A.E.C. Went seighning with him & H. J. Lyles and Mayfield. A. came home with me at night.

July 20, 1850

Went fishing on Bower creek. McGill was with us. Caught 300. I went up home at night.

July 21, 1850

Stayed at home until after dinner then went to Uncle Rob Cameron's. Stayed all night.

July 22, 1850

Went to muster at Yonguesville. Had a fine time for parrading as it rained considerable. Went and stayed again at Uncle Rob't.

July 23, 1850

Muster again Yonguesville. Got turn out, more rain. Rained on us all the time on our return from muster. Got home, had a fine rain, which looks and feels strange. Got to my mansion after night. Saw Mr. Revis at Uncle's.

July 24, 1850

Wrote letter to J. P. Feaster. Went up home. Mr. Revis came down with me before dinner and of course we eat dinner in the mansion. Eat some very good melons. He left in evening for Uncle's.

July 25, 1850

Plowing corn which looks much better since the rain though too late to be of much advantage to old corn.

July 26, 1850

Went up home again. Met Mr. Revis returning home. I got back before noon. Cousin Sarah came down as far as her home with me. Went in evening to P.O. Letter from J. P. Feaster. No *Blade*. The Steamer came by with me.

July 27, 1850

Plowing cotton again and for the last time. Went to pick nic at Lyles's Ford. Had much amusement. Had a fine rain in evening which made the corn look still better.

July 28, 1850

Was at home all day. The Steamer was with me. Got home by sundown.

July 29, 1850

Wrote a letter to J. P. Feaster. Plowing cotton. Killed two squirrels.

July 30, 1850

Very warm. Plowing cotton. Went to the shop in afternoon. Saw Dr. Bybee at Esq Feaster's. D.R.F. went with him to Maybenton. Got a book from Uncle Jake's. Thrilling adventures among the Indians.

July 31, 1850

Daddy, Pappa & Henry came down after the bull. Rode over my crop. Praised a little. Very warm indeed. Eat a mellon. Soon have plenty ripe.

August 1, 1850

Grand Ma, Aunt Kizanah, Drucie and Sarah came down. We had fine cleance watermellons. I went with Drucie & Sarah fishing, caught but few. They all stayed at Grand Ma's.

August 2, 1850

Went up home soon in morn. Went over Pappa's cotton. Looks fine. He came down with me and eat dinner. I went to P.O. No letters. Stayed all night with A.E.C. Got done working my crop to day.

August 3, 1850

A.E. and I came to the mansion in morning. Eat melons, then went up home. Some rain.

I WILL REMEMBER THEE

Remember thee; let Time's decay
And all the waste of earthly care
Upon my heart their pressure lay
Thou wilt be still as fondly dear
As in all my life thou wert to me
I will, I will remember thee.

Remember thee; What tho' apart
Harsh destiny hath doom'd our lives
In day, in night within my heart
The slumbering thought of thee revives
Altho thy face I cannot always see
I yet, I yet remember thee.

Remember thee; let wealth abound
And pave my way with jewels bright
Or let chill want my life surround
With terrors darker than the night
In deepest gloom, in fullest glee
I'll still, I'll still remember thee.

Remember thee; go ask the sun
If it forgets to rise and set
Go ask the stars when day is gone
If they their lasting watch forget

Sure as those truths we ever see
I will, I will remember thee.

Remember thee; it would be well
Could I forever crush the thought
Which chains me like a mystic spell
From some deep spring of poison brought
In vain I struggle to be free
Till death, I will remember thee.

John A. F. Coleman
July 5th, 1850

August 3, 1850

Went home with the Esq. Stayed all night.

August 4, 1850

Came from the Esq and went to church with the Drucies. Sermon by Rev'd Newlin. Large audience. Eat dinner at Uncle John's. Negroes had a fight on the way from church. Got to the mansion by night. Had some rain after going to bed.

August 5, 1850

Began building a cotton house. Killed a mutton for Grand Ma. James Morgan, Wm. Jenkins, D. R. Feaster & John C. Feaster all come to eat melons. The latter two stayed until after dinner. Little more rain about 12 o'clock.

August 6, 1850

Finished raising the cotton house, then began clearing a new ground. Wrote letter to John P. Feaster. Went to Biggers'es watermellon patch. Eat some fine ones.

August 7, 1850

Went to shop in morning with a broke wagon. Came back with Henry Lyles by Mr. McGills. Had some very fine melons. We three then came via the mansion to a sale at Mrs. Chapman's dec'd. I bought a chest. Returned from sale to Maj. Seymore where we eat dinner and some extra fine melons. Considerable rain at the Maj's though found but little at home when I returned. Got two ripe muskmelons this evening. First I've had.

Wm. Sims married to night to Miss Louanne Mobley. They had a long courtship, though proved effectual at last. Married by H. Mayo Esq.

August 8, 1850

Went up home. Eat dinner at Daddy's. So did J. & J. M[.] Feaster, H. H. D. A. Coleman and G. W. Armstrong. Got back in evening &c. Mr. Armstrong was out with a warrant for Negroes that were engaged in the riot of Sunday last.

August 9, 1850

Went to the Negro trial. The court after much and long deliberations decided that three should have one hundred lashes, one seventy-five, and another ten. Got back as far as home and stayed all night.

August 10, 1850

Came down with Pappa as far as Uncle Jonathan's where they went in to his bottoms. Henry and I came on to the mansion. I gave Dave a thrashing. Went to P.O. Got no letters. Came back by dinner. Uncle Jonathan, Pappa, George & Bob was with us in evening. All left for home. Found M.B. & [. . .] Picketts at Uncle Jonathan's. The last went up to Uncle John's. Found F. H. Land and Miss E. Bostwick at our house &c.

August 11, 1850

Went to church at Salem. Miss E. rode in buggy with me. Rained while at church. Left in the rain. Got very muddy. Had a fine season at home. All got home and stayed all night.

August 12, 1850

Got to mansion, sowed turnips, began covering cotton house.

August 13, 1850

Wrote to J. P. Feaster. Was sick today. Grand Ma came down to see me. Eat a muskmelon, finished covering cotton house. All hands clearing. Went to Jake's, &c.

August 14, 1850

Went to P.O. Got a knife and some leads. Got back before dinner. Wm. Jenkins came down. Cut stock to take to sawmill. Went to Grand Ma's. Saw

Esq Feaster. Read an excellent tale in *Graham's Magazine* (1848), "The Cruize of the Gentile." Saw many open bolls of cotton, two on a stalk. Saw A. E. Feaster alias Judge covering his house near P.O., &c.

August 15, 1850

Went to the sawmill after plank. Saw Mr. Wm. Dawkins for the first time. Swaped my gun to Jenkins for a calf and cow. He stayed all night with me.

August 16, 1850

Killed sheep for Grand Ma. Saw Dr. Coleman. Billy & I drove my cow into the pasture. Clearing on in a high style. Went to P.O. in evening. Jenkins wants to see Old Frank i.e. his horse. Got a letter from Isa. Stayed all night at Henry J. Lyles's.

August 17, 1850

Went to barbecue at Hall's old place. Orations by W. S. Lyles, W. Robertson and Dr. Clark, each a candidate for legislature. Went up home.

August 18, 1850

Was about home all day. Aunt Becky sick or mad.

August 19, 1850

Clearing still. Sent up home after basket wood.

August 20, 1850

T. D. Feaster came over. Eat dinner with me &c. Began pulling fodder in evening. Very hot day.

August 21, 1850

All hands pulling. I went to P.O. A letter to Isa. Went up to Esq Feaster's. Saw Polly. She had just returned from wedding at Mr. Herr's, that of A. E. Green and T. H. Crooks, Esq. They left in evening for Philadelphia visiting their relations. Mule ran away with me returning home though didn't throw me off.

Pappa was at mansion when I got home. We eat several melons. Rode over farm.

August 22, 1850

Pulling fodder. Went over to Jake's. Betsy, Pickett, they will leave for their home in Georgia on tomorrow.

August 23, 1850

D. R. Feaster slept with me tonight. Went to Esq Feaster. Stayed all night. Got letter from J. P. Feaster. Heavy rain in eve.

August 24, 1850

Started to Winnsboro in company with Miss M. A. Feaster & D.R.F. Got there by 9 o'clock. Went to pic nic. Much rain in evening. Saw some very pretty girls. A tremendious storm at night. Blowed down many shade trees i.e. 78 and nearly ruined the crops. Got home by 3 PM. Eat at Esq F's. Got home with Judge with me &c.

August 25, 1850

Splitting boards &c. H. J. Lyles, H. J. Coleman Jr. & Dr. John Feaster and Jake Varnadore came over to eat melons &c.

August 27, 1850

Sawing timber and splitting boards. Mr. Wm Lonegan and D. R. Feaster with me today eating melons &c. Grand Ma, Aunt Dolly and Sarah C. came in eve. Eat a few melons then made their exit for Jacob's. W. Jenkins also came for melons. Mr. Lonegan and Feaster left in evening.

August 28, 1850

Pulling fodder again. W. Jenkins & I eat many melons. Allan & Franklin also. The Steamer sent them by after some for him but I wouldn't send him any. Went over and looked at Jake pull fodder a while.

August 30, 1850

Pulling fodder in high style, got nearly done. A.E.C., Mayfield and McGin-nins came over, took dinner, eat melons &c. Fine weather for foddering.

August 31, 1850

Took up fodder until dinner. Rain at noon. Killed beef at Grand Ma's. Went up home in evening &c., &c.

September 1, 1850

I went to preaching at Red Hill with Drucie and Peggy. Sermon by Rev'd Newlin. Rained while at church. Heard that Lucretia and Lizzie Robertson were married last week, also Miss Marg't Simeton.

September 2, 1850

Began picking cotton, finished taking up fodder in evening. D. Feaster assisted me.

September 3, 1850

Picking cotton, sowed some turnips, wrote to J. P. Feaster, went to P.O., eat dinner at A.E.C. Pappa came down to kill beef. We had a terrible time butchering of it as we had no help scarcely. He took a fine mellon home with him. I got some homespun at store to make knapsaks for picking cotton &c., also some super fine tobacco at 50 cts. per lb. Sent Jenkins some beef and in return they sent me some cucumbers. Saw Marcus Pickens at Esq Feaster's (a gun smith). Three hands at home helping pull fodder.

September 4, 1850

Started up home soon with the sighn. Stoped at Uncle John's. Had the girls getting ready. The Drucies rode horse back. Lizie and I rode very composedly in buggy. She was mad. We went on to the Esq. Caught a few fish, went down to Billy's, saw Sam Stevenson and Mrs. Yongue and daughters Rebecca & Isa. Eat some fine melons. Returned home by dark.

September 5, 1850

The Drucies and Sarah left with me for the mansion quite early. Had the Esq's company soon after leaving. Got to mansion safe. We eat melons of the richest flavor, played whist &c. Had much fun. Read some. I began a tale by Elen Wallace, *The Clandestine Marriage*.[42] Most excellent piece. My visitors left in evening.

September 6, 1850

Remainder of my hands came over. Finished hauling crib logs, board &c. Engaged Mr. Morgan to assist me in finishing. D. R. Feaster came as Morgan left. Finished my book. It belongs to Miss M. E. L. Bostwick. Went to P.O. in evening. Took some old axes to shop &c. Got some that are finished &c. Got letter from J. P. Feaster and papers. D. R. Feaster came home with me.

September 7, 1850

Went to muster at Mrs. Yongue's. Had an election for Col., Caldwell and McCullough candidates. The former was elected. Maj. Parr commanded our company.

September 8, 1850

Went to Red Hill church with the Drucies no I stayed home and Drucie went to Salem.

September 9, 1850

Morgan came to work, got plates &c. for cribs. My hands picking cotton.

September 10, 1850

Raised the cribs by noon.

September 11, 1850

Put on the plates, hued the rafters and so on.

September 12, 1850

Put up the rafters and end timbers.

September 13, 1850

Got out lathes &c. Morgan quit after dinner and went home. I made a door for cotton house. Rain at night.

September 14, 1850

Cotton too wet for picking. Got board timber, hauled it up &c. Went up home in evening.

September 15, 1850

Stayed at home all day. Mrs. Arnett, Mayfield, Billy and Esq's families were over. Dave Feaster came home and stayed all night with me.

September 16, 1850

Had to work the road. Tuesday the same and then not done but concluded to stop until a rain. Wrote to Isa. Beautiful weather for picking.

September 18, 1850

Morgan worked for me until 4 o'clock PM. Went home to sick Negro. All hands picking cotton.

September 19, 1850

Morgan split boards all day. I covered crib in evening. Read Military Tactics.

September 20, 1850

Covered on the crib until time to go to P.O. Got no letters. Morgan worked all day. D. R. Feaster came over.

September 21, 1850

Nearly finished the crib, would have if it had not rained just before night. Jenkins, Silas Bowlin & Feaster came in evening. The latter & myself went up home in Feaster's buggy.

September 22, 1850

Went to Salem church via Billy's. Sermon by the Rev'd Montgomery. Came to Esq Feaster's and eat dinner. Brought Feaster's little pup Laura home with me. The Steamer accompanied me to mansion from Esq's. Remained until bed time.

September 23, 1850

Picking cotton. Pappa & the Esq came down, eat dinner with me, bringing the news that J. P. Feaster had arrived from Fla. I went up with them, so did the Steamer. Had all the dogs along as the Esq had a coon treed. Went by Uncle John's, got J.P.F., then went by Billy's, got him, dogs, axes. Cut the tree down and got the coon. We went up to the Esq's and went to bed. Miss M. E. Bostwick and Mrs. Dr. McClurkin departed from this county for Green County Ala.

September 24, 1850

Went out soon in morning i.e. by three AM cooning. Caught a fine fellow. Got back to mansion by noon. Swaped Pigeon for Lollie [. . .] to a horse drover.

September 25, 1850

Went to P.O. with a letter to M. W. Coleman. Saw H. J. Lyles, A.E.C., McGinnis, &c., &c.

September 26, 1850

Mr. Revis & J. P. Feaster came down. The latter stayed all night. The former went after his heart &c.

October 15, 1850

Caught an opossum last night assisted by D.R.F. Went up home, saw Miss Mary. Got up safe &c.

October 16, 1850

Went up again, saw Miss Mary.

October 17, 1850

Went fishing with Jake at Broad River. Jake caught a small redhorse. Got back by sun down. Went hunting with Steamer, Jess Gladden, caught nothing.

October 18, 1850

Waked up and heard it raining, not having rained since 21st Sept. Finished reading *One in a Thousand*.[43] Went to P.O. in evening. Got no letters.

October 19, 1850

Went up home, went chestnut hunting with Isa & the Drucies up at Mr. Lands, got a great many. Got back, then I went to muster ground, making arrangements about the barbecue. Stayed all night at Billy's. Was very unwell at night.

October 20, 1850

Came home and stayed until near night, leaving Uncle's folks with the idea of leaving for Fla in a few days. A.E.C. came down to mansion with me.

October 21, 1850

All hands pulling pea vines over at Jake's. Reading *Ivanhoe* novel. Loaned wagon to Jake to haul corn. Eat a mellon to day.

October 22, 1850

Went fishing to river. Caught a fine fat fish. Began hauling corn. Brought in six loads. I was unwell at night.

October 23, 1850

Loaned Jake the wagon again. Moved little crop &c. Then all hands pulling corn. Feaster came over just from party at Winnsboro. He went to Columbia &c., brought Polly home. Went up home in evening and found that Uncle J. M. Feaster's family had gone via Mr. Pickett's to Fla. Left him, Mary Bell at our house. She looked very pretty indeed. I beat her playing seven up. Came back to pasture. Went patrolling at night.

October 24, 1850

Hauling corn, myself driving the wagon. McGill came by also A.E.C., neither called. Beautiful weather for work. Went home (No I didn't).

October 25, 1850

Went up home. Met R. R. Coleman coming down to see me. He has just returned from Chambers Ala. We went over to muster ground, making arrangement for barbecue for tomorrow, thense we went to P.O. No letters. From P.O. we went to pasture and stayed all night.

October 26, 1850

Went to barbecue. Muster in morn. Had four volunteers to join, had a fine dinner, and an excellent speech from Maj. W. S. Lyles. Mr. Newman came home with us and tuned the piano. Uncle Sam, John Cameron, Billy & the Esq also.

October 27, 1850

All went to church. Miss Mary rode in buggy with me. Came down to mansion with the Steamer who stayed all night with me.

October 28, 1850

Went up home early and left there for Columbia with R. H. Coleman, Drucie, and Miss Mary & myself. We got down to depot in time for the cars and was in Columbia by 6 o'clock. Bob & I roomed with J.P.F. Drucie & Mary put up at Mr. Fram's.

October 29, 1850

Left Columbia by 5 o'clk AM, leaving Miss Mary and my heart behind. Got to Alston by 8 o'clk, then home by noon, thense came to mansion.

October 30, 1850

Picking cotton having finished pulling pea vines. I went to P.O., thense to Uncle Jacob's. Soon after the Steamer and Sarah called. Had some music on the new piano belonging to Polly. Got home by noon. Sarah gave me an invitation to a quilting & dance at Mrs. Dr. Coleman's on tomorrow eve. Eat a fine watermellon to day which I fear will be the last until next year. Wagons gone to Columbia. Uncle John expects to leave there on tomorrow.

October 31, 1850

Last day of October. Covered the pea house, put up fences, went over to Jake's &c. Went to the quilting in evening. Began dancing at 5 o'clock and quit at 8 o'clock. Miss Jane Mc was belle of the fandango. I got home by 9 PM and went to sleep and when awoke it was. . . .

November 1, 1850

Picking cotton. Went to P.O. in even. Got letters from E. S. Cockrell and Sally Goldfoot—the latter is a new correspondant whom I don't know. She hails from Pleasant Ridge, Ala. Feaster came home with me. We went patroling at night. Lashed several.

November 2, 1850

Whiped Ike in morning and lo after breakfast he was missing. Hauled corn and pea vines. Made 21 loads of corn. Made a gate assisted by Morgan. Stayed all night [at] Mansion.

November 3, 1850

Went up home in morning and found Ike. Gave a good one and sent him home. Jess Gladden came down to Mansion and stayed all night.

November 4, 1850

Finished hauling pea vines &c. Jake's Mary very ill today. Went up to Mc's Store with Jenkins after tobacco.

November 5, 1850

Finished hauling fodder and stacking then to picking cotton again. Went over to McGill's [to] see about his living with Pappa next year, thense to Arnett's store. Going to Miss Mary C. Yongue's and John Lemon's wedding tonight. Pappa came down and went to Mrs. Robertson's as she wants to see him concerning living in the Brown house &c., &c.

Left pretty early in evening for the wedding. Got there in proper time. Married by the Rev'd Hoyt and waited on by Dr. Yongue, Andrew Yongue, Isa and Juliana Stevenson. Had a fine supper &c. All retired to rest about midnight.

November 6, 1850

All left Mrs. Yongue's at 11 o'clock, going to the infare. Arrived there by one. Had most and excelent dinner. Left Mr. Lemon's at 5 PM. Had the pleasure of Miss Julian[a's] company coming up. We remained at Mrs. Yongue's all night.

November 7, 1850

Came by home and thense to the mansion. Went then to A. E. Coleman's also to Mr. D. H. Kerr's. Paid him one hundred and ninety dollars for the Esq. A.E.C. came home with me. Jake's oldest daughter died this evening at 1 o'clock PM, also B. Weather's youngest son died same time.

November 8, 1850

Went to graveyard and assisted in digging the grave for little Mary. Maj. Seymore and Foot eat dinner with me. Went to P.O. in the evening, then up to Esq's. Went hunting with Feaster, Boykin, Lyles, and Rob't Means,[44] caught nothing. Came to mansion at night and all four slept in one bed.

November 9, 1850

Feaster after Boykin and Rob't left remained until after dinner when he went as far as Uncle Jonathan's with me on my way home. Stayed all night.

November 10, 1850

Went to Salem via Mrs. Yongue's, found the Esq & wife very sick though mending. Sermon by Rev'd Bowman. Came with A.E.C. to J. Q. Arnett's and eat dinner, thense I traveled to mansion, wrote E. S. Cockrell, who is a submissionist to the wrongs of the South.

November 11, 1850

Rained half the day. Sent to Mill, made a new lot &c. Read Shakspeare till bed time.

November 12, 1850

Picking cotton. Uncle Jonathan and A.E.C. came in, the latter stayed all day. Fed my pigs, five of the prettiest kind. Reading Shakspeare at all leasure moments etcetera.

November 13, 1850

The Steamer picking cotton for Jenkins. He came over in course of the day. Went patrolling at night.

November 14, 1850

Pappa & Uncle Jonathan came to where I was picking cotton. Pappa wants me to aid him in killing hogs tomorrow. Went up home after night, also three of the boys.

November 15, 1850

Killed fourteen hogs. Brought four to pasture, cut them up &c. Very warm at night.

November 16, 1850

Salted meat, then went to picking cotton. I went to A.E.C., eat dinner, also went to G. Feaster Esq. Heard Miss Polly play on piano. Good music. A.E.C. came via mansion with me. Going home found Mr. Duffy & Miller at home, the former is trying to make a school.

November 17, 1850

Very cold. Stayed about home until eve, then came to mansion. Bob accompanied me. Very cold night indeed.

November 18, 1850

Heavy frost in morning. Picking cotton. Wrote to R. W. Nolen of Chambers Ala.

November 19, 1850

Cut down a tree and split it up into gate timber. Hauled it to house and nearly made a gate before night. Feaster came just before sundown looking very bad.

November 20, 1850

Rained moderately nearly all day. Feaster left soon in morning. I went to Esq. Feaster's to get some fixins to hang my gate. Ordered Post Master to have the *Yankee Blade* stoped as it is getting very rank on Abolitionism, Fugitive Slaves, &c. Got back to dinner then hung the gate &c. Read Feaster's new book *Big Bear of Arkansas*[45] plum through. Bob still with me &c. Finished reading one of Shakespeare's dramatic pieces, "Love's Labor" and began reading "Merchant of Venice."

November 21, 1850

Faired off very pretty. Made a cowpen after breakfast. One of my calfs died some time in the night. Began picking cotton in the morning. Bob & I went squirrel hunting. Killed one but it lodged so that we could not get it &c. Pappa came down in evening and carried Bob home. I read Shakespeare at night.

November 22, 1850

Went to A. E. Coleman's, thense to P.O. Got no letters. Read news at night.

November 23, 1850

Went over to Jake's. Feaster and Henry came to see me.

{Monday the 25th. Went netting and caught nothing as yet. This you see and reckolect me nothing more at present.

May auspicious days be thine 1850.

Ego non prose scribe amplus.

—W. B. Lyles}

Mr. Boykin Lyles made bold to do the above. —J.A.F.C.[46]

November 23, 1850

Went up home in evening in company with Feaster, thense to the Esq's where we stayed all night, had a race with dogs after a coon skin.

November 24, 1850

Went to Salem. No preaching. Went from there with Feaster, Congers, Felder, W. B. Lyles, Rob't Means &c. to Rocky Creek church. Got there when Mr. Brooks was in middle of his sermon. Came to A.E.C.'s and eat dinner, thense home. Mr. Congers stayed all night with Feaster &c.

November 25, 1850

Boykin Lyles came over. Went netting as he has stated on opposite page. He stayed all night with me.

November 26, 1850

Lyles and myself went up to his Greenbriar plantation netting but caught none. I then left him and went to the Esq's, got my dogs, being left there since Sunday, came home via Billy's, where I saw Mrs. May Lemon. Pappa killed twelve more hogs today.

November 27, 1850

I picked cotton, read Shakespeare &c. Feaster came at night and remained until morning. Went patrolling, caught Kerr's Jerry.

November 28, 1850

Rob't visited until dinner then went home to see James Cameron from Florida. Him and his father stayed all night &c.

November 29, 1850

Went to Uncle Jake's early in morning. Had Sally's good foot shod. Eat dinner at which time it began raining very hard. Went down to P.O. Got letter from D. R. Coleman. Came home in rain after night in company with the Steamer as far as Grand Ma's &c.

November 30, 1850

Went up home very soon in morning, preparing for going to the muster at Columbia. R. H. Coleman stayed all night with me.

December 1, 1850

Raining near all day. Left home after noon for Columbia via Dave's, Billy's, Cameron's, Mobley's, all of whom are going to muster. I went with the baggage wagon to Cap't Clowney and staid until morning. Miss Juliana was there.

December 2, 1850

Made an early start via Monticello. Had much fun on the way. Camped near [. . .] Creek.

December 3, 1850

Left the camp and rode into Columbia by ten o'clock. Had no rain as was expected. Camped in a cotton yard. Much liquor drank.

December 4, 1850

Had a large military review. Speeches by the Governor, Generals Buckhanan, Martin and Means. Our company escorted the Gov. All stayed in town at night. Saw Calhoun in [. . .] &c.

December 5, 1850

Departed for home by 9 o'clock. Camped at Hendrix's old field.

December 6, 1850

I got as far as Esq Feaster and remained all night. Much rain at night.

December 7, 1850

Came via mansion. Going up home found all things O.K. Went to Billy's and remained statu quo until morning when I came home and stayed until eve, then came to mansion. Very cold. Mrs. Meador died to day about 2 o'clk PM. I kept wake. Morning very cold &c. Helping Grand Ma kill hogs &c.

From the above date until the end of the month I was going and staying at different [places] so much that I could not keep any note of things whatever. Pappa departed for Florida on the 21st inst., also brother Henry. I carried them as far as Alston. The evening before Christmas I left for Columbia on business for J. M. Feaster and to bring Drucie home, who I carried down to Mrs. Bell's two weeks ago. Got home on Friday the 27th, the day on which Susan Cockrell died.

I spent most of Christmas at home as it was very cold &c.

So I've lived to the finis of another year.

January 1, 1851

This year begins on Wednesday. I am attending to all Pappa's business while he is gone to Fla. Was picking cotton and hauling my crop to gin to day, also began ginning. Very cold. No mail this week.

January 2, 1851

Began snowing about noon and continued all night. I was a little sick, had some fever &c., &c.

January 3, 1851

Found a very heavy snow had fallen, the average depth foot and half. Went down to my mansion, eat dinner.

January 4, 1851

Went to Billy's thense to Mrs. Yongue's where we all went hunting but caught nothing. Came home by sundown. Cousin Sarah staid all night with us.

January 5, 1851

The ground still covered with snow. Went to Aunt Becky's in afternoon. Wrote a letter for her to Lizie & Drucie Feaster. The Steamer & Judge called coming from church.

January 6, 1851

Snow began melting a little. Hauled wood until near night when we came down to mansion to haul cotton tomorrow &c.

January 7, 1851

Hauled cotton. Began picking again, beautiful day.

January 8, 1851

Susan McClurkin came home accompanied by D. H. Coleman of Ga.

January 10, 1851

Got letters from E. M. Feaster, Miss Mary Bell &c. D. H. Coleman staid all night with me, also Sarah C.

January 11, 1851

Went to muster, poor turn out. Pappa & Henry got home at night from Fla., having been gone three weeks.

January 12, 1851

Remained at home all day.

January 13, 1851

Picking cotton and ginning.

January 14, 1851

Finished picking cotton. Mrs. Milling & Mrs. Lemon also Esq and wife were at our house today. Came down to mansion at night with all hands and a load of cotton seed. Wrote to J. M. Feaster at night for Pappa.

January 15, 1851

All hands and myself chaping in new ground, cutting rail timber &c. Went up to Grand Ma's and Jenkins's in morning, had [. . .] and pumkins for dinner, also backbones, so I eat a very substantial dinner &c. Cloudy and windy in afternoon. Caught a mouse in my trap last night, but alas in trying to kill it the creature got away and ran off i.e. under the mansion. Sent the letter to J. M. Feaster to the P.O.

January 16, 1851

Larky quite sick with rising in her head. Went to Dr. Coleman's, got a plaster, &c. Grand Ma came down and fixed it on. Sam Feaster at Feasterville as

Mr. Simons moved yesterday. His school will commence immediately. Chaping again to day. Some appearance of rain at noon. Caught a mouse last night and killed it sure. Also went fire hunting at night, killed seven but only got five.

January 17, 1851

Feaster came into new ground before dinner. Caught rabit out of a log. Eat dinner, then went to P.O. Got no letters, though had the honor of being in His Excellency Gov. Means[47] company or presence. Feaster came back home with me and staid all night.

January 18, 1851

Still cuting in new ground. All hands quit after dinner. Went up home in eve where I found Ga. Dave. Very cold indeed.

January 19, 1851

Went over to Sol's with Dave. Staid a few hours then came home, thense came to mansion via Uncle Jon's where I left Dave &c. Drat this pen. I'll quit it.

Having got a new pen I'll proceede and see if I can't get along better. Well on Monday 20th we worked in new ground. Pappa & Uncle Jonathan came down and staid until after supper.

January 21, 1851

Cuting and spliting rail timber on Wensday. Dave Coleman came down in evening, staid all night.

January 23, 1851

We hunted some, went over to Jake's field &c. Dave staid at Jake's.

January 24, 1851

Went to P.O. Got no letters. Gov. Means was present and many other illustrious men. Pappa came to P.O. having came via mansion but I will rest there.

January 25, 1851

Went up home in evening. Drucie and Isa being down to see me to day. Sarah C. went up with us &c.

January 26, 1851

Left home before dinner and went to Uncle Jonathan's from thense went to Uncle Uriah's with Foot, thense to J. Fry's, thense with Morgan to mansion. Wrote letter at night to Drucie and Sarah.

January 27, 1851

I cut all day. Began letter to E. S. Cockrell.

January 28, 1851

Went to P.O. where I saw midshipman Ed Means &c. Mail my letter. Got back by dinner. Very cold weather indeed. Ground frozen all day.

January 29, 1851

Worked in my new ground. Still very cold.

January 30, 1851

Went again to P.O. Got nothing but papers &c.

January 31, 1851

All quit work at dinner. Went up home.

February 1, 1851

Dave's & Billy's families were over. The Steamer also came up. Him & I started to Winnsboro. Staid all night at Uncle Jake's.

February 2, 1851

Got to W. by 11 o'clock. Sheriff's Sale began at 12. Aunt Rebecca Coleman's two Negroes were sold. Uncle Jake buying Bill & the Steamer Ell, the former at $980 and latter at $910. Staid all night at Crawford's Hotel after hearing a most excellent speech by W. S. Lyles.

February 3, 1851

Got home by sun down. Much rain on yesterday.

February 4, 1851

Went to Sol's (slave of Mrs. McAshan) trial for insolent and incerrection conversation to patrolers. Sentenced to two hundred lashes. Pappa came home with me. Brought the bulls. Fencing and hauling rails today.

February 5, 1851

Very windy. Spliting rail, also hauling and fencing &c. Went duck hunting late in eve with Sol S. Crowder and Jenkins. Killed partridge.

February 6 or 7, 1851

Fenced until near night, then went to P.O. Got two letters from D. R. Coleman & Drucie Feaster. Came with Uncle Jonathan as far as Grand Ma's.

February 8 or 9, 1851

(Don't know which as I've no Almanac). Finished one of my pasture fences before dinner. Then began burning brush in new ground. Also finished splitting rails. Worked until dark so I staid at the mansion one Saturday night in 1851 already.

February 9, 1851

Went up home in morning, thense to preaching at Liberty Church. Sermon by Rev'd Simons. Came to Uncle Jona. and eat dinner &c.

February 10, 1851

Went to election for delegates to Southern Convention. Voted the fire-eater's ticket. A great many drunk people. Feaster came home with me.

February 11, 1851

Went to Arnett's, carried two letters to P.O., one to Drucie Feaster & Sarah and one to D. R. Coleman. Came back and went to burning brush &c. Read in *Blade* at night.

February 12, 1851

Day that the votes were counted for delegates of Southern Convention. Didn't hear the decision. Finished one of the pasture's lane fences. Mamma, Aunt Polly, Jona., Louisa Meador and Grand Ma called on me in evening. All very lively. Grand Ma in particular. They left, so did I to my work. After supper I read in *South Carolinian*. Went duck hunting with Jenkins soon in morning. Saw a great many and got two shots but killed none.

February 13, 1851

Finished my other pasture fense of one hundred and fifty panels. Fastened my hogs into it. Worked all day and eat one of the biggest suppers 'prapse. I shall study tonight what I shall do tomorrow. Hope it will terminate well.

February 14, 1851

Raining before noon. Sent to Mill, raking up manure &c. Planted a collard bed. Went to Simm's shoe shop, got many shoes mended &c.

Went to P.O. in evening. Rained very hard throughout the entire evening. Uncle David H. Coleman arrived at P.O. by 3½ o'clock from Green Ala. Came by public conveyance via Winnsboro. I went up to Daddy's with him. He left all in good health &c.

February 15, 1851

Came down to pasture soon. Found all doing finely i.e. working the things up brown &c. Began raining by 11 o'clock with thunder and some of the tallest kind of raining. Read all the news and began on Shakespeare's *King John* having just finished *Macbeth*. Oh how it rains at this present time being thirty-two and half minutes after noon &c. by my time piece. Jenkins came down after dinner and sat all the evening. We had a game of seven up &c. Went up home by night where I found Uncle David H. Rained nearly all night.

February 16, 1851

Very clear in the morning and cold. Went down to Daddy's with Pappa and Uncle D. where came the Esq, Billy and John Cameron and afterwards Uncle Jona. and John F. Coleman. Came down to mansion in company with the two latter as far as Uncle J's. Pretty cold night. Why can't a man do something each day throughout his whole life which would [be] of service to himself or his fellow men or in other words, why may he not do something *good* every day as long as he sourgins [sojourns?] here below?

"Love thy neighbour as thyself—and thy sweetheart better than all."

February 17, 1851

All's well. Finished hauling wood, rails in my little new ground. Repaired couple of plowstocks. Jenkins came down and made plowstocks. Grand Ma also came down in a very ill humor with Jenkins or some one else. Spilt the ink on my book. Sent up home after seed oats per Alex.

February 18, 1851

Rolled logs in little new ground. Finished by 10 o'clock, then began plowing three hands, breaking up the new ground and one plowing in oats. Uncle Jona., David H., Pappa and the Esq came by, going to Jake's before noon. Rabit hunting. I went over after dinner. We went out and caught one after much hunting. Read the *Palmetto State Banner* at night. Went to bed ten minutes after eight. Hope I may rest well, also the whole posse of mankind, also the entire brute creation, insects omited.

{A person would Judge from the manner in which Mr. Coleman writes that he is a very affectionate, thinking & well-read man, however he is quit the reverse. I therefore, Coleman, circumscribe myself your most humble and obedient well-wisher & also hope that you may rest well & also mankind & insects not excepted.

Yours truly

D. R. Feaster}

I can't say how a person would of Mr. Feaster's writing judge, but as for myself I judge he ain't very use'nt to it as any one may see from the above chirography, and see how he spells *quite* &c. He has certainly been taking a little stimulant.[48]

February 19, 1851

Still plowing until near night when we finished breaking up the new ground. I went to Arnett's store, paid in full all my debts to Mr. Arnett. Burned logs after getting back. Feaster came at night on his way to the party at Winnsboro. Went to where Dr. Means had treed a coon. Saw the fight. Hunted until near midnight.

February 20, 1851

Lent Feaster my nag to ride home. A.E.C. & David from Ga. came just before dinner. Lent them a mule to carry their wagon home. Began making corn beds to day. Ground most too wet.

February 21, 1851

Raining when I got up. Wind blowing from south. Killing trees &c. Shucking and shelling corn. Raining incessantly from six AM until 4 PM. Mending shoes. Went to P.O. in eve in company with Jake. Got no letters myself, two for Isa and one for Grand Ma from Lizzie Feaster. *Blade* didn't come. Uncle Jake gave me the *Hornet's Nest*[49] to read, published in Charlotte, N.C.

February 22, 1851

Went to mill. Killed tree. I went up home thense to the Esq thense to Billy's then rabit hunting, caught five. Went coon hunting at night, caught none. Went to Mrs. Yongue's at night with the Esq.

February 23, 1851

Went to Salem Church, sermon by Rev'd Boggs. The Miss Gladdeny's were out looking alarmingly beautiful & exquisite. Came to Esq Feaster's and eat dinner in co. with Judge. Uncle somewhat sick. Got home at night. Saw his Excellency at church.

February 24, 1851

Reset an old fence of 120 pannels. Pappa and Uncle Dave came down in eve but didn't stay long. I feel very tired to night. Read some of *Godey's Magazines* (1840, 42 & 45 &c.)

February 25, 1851

Burned brush in my big new ground all day and ain't done yet. Jenkins came down and told me of the murder of James Gage by Eldridge Land by pistol. He died on last night having lived some two or three days. A beautiful day. Warm enough to plant corn. Mules got out to day and have gone off.

February 26, 1851

Still burning brush and logs. I went up home in morning where I heard that Mr. Gage was not dead but mending and likely to get well. Brought my mules home. Got home by dinner. Pretty day and fine for burning new ground. Sent my watch to Columbia to get the christal put in by mailboy.

February 27, 1851

Beautiful Spring day, had two plows running today, the balance burning and piling logs. I am as smutty as a yongue Sandhillian tonight, feel very nasty, of course look so. Didn't [. . .] food.

February 28, 1851

Still rooling logs and finished my portion for cotton. Two hands plowing. Windy &c. Went to P.O. in evening. No letters. Went thense to Esq Feaster's. Eat supper. Got a few Irish potoatoes. Came home in rain and dark &c.

March 1, 1851

Planted Irish potatoes. Began breaking up my big new ground. Went up home in evening. Slept with Uncle Dave.

March 2, 1851

Went to Red Hill. Sermon by Rev'd Guinn. Came down home with Jake, Jim Morgan and Steamer. The next to latter staid all night with me &c.

March 3, 1851

Plowing again in new ground. Burning brush, logs &c.

March 4, 1851

Finished breaking up my new ground. Went to the sale at Arnett's store where was sold the residue of Aunt Becky's property.

March 5, 1851

Plowed all day myself for corn and eat a very hearty supper &c.

March 6, 1851

Raining so that couldn't plow. Repaired collars. Moved gates. Cut pines &c. John F. came in morning asking help to his log rooling. Read no old magazines. Went to Fax paying at Feasterville in evening. Began plowing late in day.

March 7, 1851

Raining soon in morning. Hauling manure. Sent John F. a hand. Set eleven eggs &c. Rained all day the hardest kind. Jenkins came down and spent the evening with me. Too much rain to go to P.O.

March 8, 1851

Went to P.O., A.E.C. and Esq Feasters. The medium came home with me &c. We went up home after dinner. Our Dave and Daddy's Rosa Etta were married at 8 PM by Esq Feaster's [. . .] George.

March 9, 1851

Stayed at home until evening when A.E.C. and myself came down to mansion, also to Infare. Morgan and Feaster came late in eve. All left me alone by sundown.

March 10, 1851

Uncle Dave departed for home via Alston. Plowed, scattered manure &c.

March 11, 1851

Plowing and cleaning upon creek, ground just getting in good order. Went over to Jake's in afternoon. Changed my mamouth ditch so that the water will [. . .] it.

March 12, 1851

Plowing near Jake's. I went over and looked at some of his farming calculations &c., &c. Changed some more ditches.

March 13, 1851

Still plowing i.e. laping cotton land, also ditching and old Isaac cleaning up the bottoms &c. Jenkins began planting corn on yesterday. Beautiful weather. Some herbs that begin growing but few green leaves; none on the large trees. Burnt of the broomsedge in graveyard pasture after sundown.

March 14, 1851

Went to P.O. Got letter from Drucie, all well &c., corn up in Fla.

March 15, 1851

Finished laping my cotton ground, then began breaking up new ground again. Went up home in evening, found Miss Pollie Feaster there, also Georgia Dave.

March 16, 1851

Strolled about in the woods until dinner. After noon came down to mansion, began letter to Drucie at night.

March 17, 1851

Fenced until dinner, repairing and putting up blown down fences &c. Pappa came down after dinner. Began plowing again in afternoon in new ground. Set out some collard plants.

March 18, 1851

Very cool and cloudy also very windy. Began ditching in my bottoms. Wrote letter at night for Grand Ma to E. M. Feaster.

March 19, 1851

Very cold. Went to shop and P.O. Put letters in P.O. to Lizzie & Drucie Feaster and E. S. Cockrell Esq. Brought Pappa's new gin from Arnett's and went up home after dinner. Saw Wily vis Screw, Mr. Pickens and R. H. Coleman. Came back by sundown.

March 20, 1851

Went duck hunting soon in morning but saw none. Finished breaking up new ground second time. D. H. Kerr Jr. came over and spent the day with me.

{March 21, 1851

Stayed with John. Went turkey hunting in the morning, killed nothing. Came home and killed two doves near the lot and if it had not been for one thing would have killed more. Guess what it was? D. H. Kerr

"Competition is the life of buisness." Franklin (J.H.C.)
"Competition is the life of business." Franklin (D.H.K.)
"Competition is the life of busines." Franklin (L.L.C.)
Competion is a word not to be found in Walker's Dictionary.
"Competition is the life of busnesses." Franklin
Competition is a word not be to
"Competition is the life of business." (Daniel) [50]

On the 20 March is memorable for the accident which happened to John's watch injured by myself breaking the chrytins —Daniel} [51]

March 21, 1851

Went to P.O. in company with D. H. Kerr Jr. where I left him and went to shop and had my nag shod. Got no letters. Came home and found Bro Bob at mansion. He stayed all night.

March 22, 1850

Sallie came down from Grand Ma's. We all went fishing but was hindered for rain. Mrs. Jenkins was stoped by rain at the mansion on her way to her mother-in-law's. She went back home after the rain had somewhat ceased. Hauled cotton seed on my corn land. Carried Bob & Sallie home. Found R. H. Coleman there.

March 23, 1851

Went down to Daddies early in morning. Found him quite well &c. Went back up home, eat dinner. Came to mansion in evening. D. R. Feaster came and stayed all night with me.

March 24, 1851

Feaster left for school. Went to plowing out cotton stacks in forenoon. After dinner made cotton beds in new ground &c. Wrote three Aprils fools to Misses ——, Y——s, and K.

March 25, 1851

Pappa came down in morning and found me planting corn, being my first. I went after dinner to Winnsboro as witness in Mr. Morgan and Screw's lawsuit. Judge Withers presiding. Put up at McMaster's Hotel &c., &c., &c.

March 26, 1851

Was about the C.H. until after dinner, when Esq Feaster and I left for home. Morgan's case didn't come on. Stayed all night at Esq Feaster's.

March 27, 1851

Left the Esq by daybreak and got home at sunup. Found all alive &c. Finished planting my old land corn. Ground in first rate order. Some appearances of rain to day at ten o'clock. Went to P.O. in evening as the mail is changed from Friday to Thursday &c. But lo and take notice, the mail didn't come and won't until tomorrow. Saw W. B. Lyles, J. L. Cameron and Ch. Mobley also Esq Feaster. Came on my return from P.O. with Grand Ma.

March 28, 1851

Burned of the remainder of my new ground. R. H. Coleman came in morning. Him & Mr. Morgan eat dinner with me. Then went to P.O., got no letters, came back to mansion, stayed all night &c.

March 29, 1851

Went turkey hunting soon in morning. Got a shot but killed nothing. Went squirrell hunting after breakfast, killed three &c. Raining slightly at noon, [. . .]. Bob & I went up and stayed all night at home.

March 30, 1851

Went to Salem. Sermon by Rev'd Hoyt. Came to Esq Feaster and eat dinner.

March 31, 1851

Carried load cotton to Winnsboro. Got there by sundown. Stayed at Mc's Hotel. Went up to Mrs. Ladd's after super.

April 1, 1851

Came with Isa home. [. . .] the cotton with Borky & [. . .].

April 2, 1851

Dave down to mansion. Raining half the day. Killing trees and cleaning up on creek &c., &c.

April 3, 1851

Went crow hunting with Jenkins who killed one on nest. Burning logs, cuting bushes and briars on the creek &c. Went to shop & P.O. in evening. My corn is coming finely which was planted only a week ago.

April 4, 1851

Began planting my new ground cotton. Reading *Shannondale*,[52] a novelette by Mrs. Southworth, an excellent tale.

April 5, 1851

Finished planting the new ground. Pappa came down at noon, walked over the farm then went up home as usual.

April 6, 1851

Went to Red Hill. Sermon by Guinn. Came to Daddies and wrote letter for Aunt Becky to Drucie Feaster.

April 7, 1851

Began spliting out cotton middles &c. Pappa came down. Had a terrible rain at night, raising the creek very high indeed &c., &c.

April 8, 1851

T. D. & A. C. Feasters came by look[ing] for stolen game chickens. R. H. Coleman also came. We went hunting in evening, killed five squirrels. Wrote letter for Grand Ma to J. G. Cameron, also wrote more April fools &c.

April 9, 1851

Went to P.O. and A. E. Coleman's. Returned by noon. Killed nothing. Bob, he got shot at turkey but didn't kill it. *No more and he didn't*. Went squirrel hunting after dinner. Bob killed nothing. I *saw* 4 squirrels. Wrote some more April fools at night.

April 10, 1851

Beautiful weather, spliting out my cotton middles or cotton stalks. Went hunting again. Bob killed 7 & I 3, 10 in all. Bob left for home in evening.

Jenkins began plowing his corn to day, fine stand. Much earlier spring than last year. No green leaves this time 1850, the woods green now.

April 11, 1851

Beautiful day. Finished bedding out my cotton ground. Went over to Jake's who I found planting cotton. Becky gave me some seed beans which I planted in afternoon. Also went to P.O. Read military tactics as tomorrow our muster day. A.E.C. came home with me. No mail owing to high water.

April 12, 1851

Went to muster at our regular muster ground. Election for third lieutenant, Cameron & Feaster candidates. The former was elected by a majority of one vote. Went to Mrs. Yongue's and eat dinner, then to the Esq's and stayed all night. Began raining early after supper.

April 13, 1851

Came home where we stayed until after dinner, then came to mansion.

April 14, 1851

Raining in morning, ceased after dinner. Began killing hickrys in new ground. McGinnis came on in evening and eat dinner with me[53] and stayed all night. Began raining again at night and rained until morning.

April 15, 1851

Finished killing trees. Pappa came down and eat dinner. Sent up home after cotton seed.

April 16, 1851

Began planting cotton seed again. Ground very [. . .]. Some frost last night &c., &c.

April 17, 1851

Planting cotton seed. McGill came over, also Pappa who brought Henry's filly down to forage. Henry stayed all night with me. Had the *blues* all day.

April 18, 1851

Went to mill in morning, returned by 9 o'clock. Went to cotton patch &c., &c. Went to P.O. Got letter from Drucie.

April 19, 1851

Planted cotton half hour in morning then began raining. Quit at 10. Began running round corn &c. Went up home and thense to Dr. McClurkin's in company with A.E.C. Stayed all night at the Dr's.

April 20, 1851

Went and spent part of the day with John Simpson. Came down to mansion by night. A.E.C. and myself swaped horses today. I've got Paddy now.

April 21, 1851

Finished planting cotton. Pappa & Dave came down to day.

April 22, 1851

Went to the Esq's fishing, caught none. Finished running round my corn.

April 23, 1851

Began spliting out corn middles. Had Paddy shod at shop. Put letter in office to Drucie Feaster. Plowed Paddy in afternoon.

April 24, 1851

Rained last night, a beautiful shower. Worked on creek until 10 o'clock, then began planting corn & pumpkins in new ground. Had dumplings for dinner. Hen hatching &c., &c.

I am no bigot. I believe that men will be judged by their actions and intentions, not their creed. I am a Christian; and so will Turk, Jew, and Gentile be in heaven if they live well according to the light which was vouched to them. I do not fear that there will be a great gulf between you and me in the world to come, which we both must enter (Southey).

April 25, 1851

Finished planting my new ground corn. Pappa, Mamma came down & I went to P.O. in evening, got an April fool from Winnsboro.

April 26, 1851

Began breaking up my bottoms. Dr. McClurkin sent down two or three cows to the pasture. Pappa came down again. Went up home in eve.

April 27, 1851

Went to Salem in buggy accompanied by Peggy. Sermon by the Rev'd Hoyt.

April 28, 1851

Plowing in my bottoms. Planted some watermellons.

April 29, 1851

Went to fishing at brother David's, saw many pretty girls, too pretty and numerous to mention. Had much fun. Carried [. . .] in buggy.

April 30, 1851

Last day of April! Finished breaking up my bottoms and began planting them. A little rain last night. My cotton coming up finely. Symptoms of rain all day. Thus ends April, having been a very cold month, more so than common though not as much rain as last April.

May 1, 1851

Planting my bottoms, ground in fine order. Went to pic nic at Arnett's. Not a very large concourse. Didn't quite finish planting corn. Saw some corn to day. Plowed the second time. Quite lonely at night.

May 2, 1851

Very cool, there being some frost on the creek. Finished planting bottom corn. Began running around the new ground cotton, looks horrid bad, nearly half has died and is dying. Garden looks first rate. Had a mess of radishes to day. Have had several messes of greens already. Went to P.O. in evening.

May 3, 1851

Still plowing new ground. Went fishing with cousin Sarah, David, Preston, Franklin and sister Isa to the river, caught three in all, had much fun. Sarah & David went up home with us and stayed all night.

May 4, 1851

Made preparations for going to Red Hill. A. C. Feaster, R.H.C. and D. R. Feaster came to see us. Very cool all day. Came down to mansion at night accompanied by H.J.C. Jr. Quite cool at night.

May 5, 1851

Began plowing cotton again. Very cool weather, enough so for frost. Went to shop in evening. Saw Mr. Aromanus Lyles, Henry's father, also Jacob Fry was visable.

May 6, 1851

Still cold. Cotton dying badly, not good stand where I was plowing today. Went up to Daddies and Pappa's. Wrote letter for Aunt Becky. Mrs. Revis alias E. M. Feaster married on 10th ult. by the Rev'd Cooper, all of Fla.

May 7, 1851

Plowed to day myself. Some warmer than yesterday. Ike had a tooth extracted. Uncle Bigger's came to where I was at work, set one hand to boarding off the bottoms in evening. Very tired at night i.e. fatigued.

May 8, 1851

Went to plowing cotton again. Much grass and a bad stand, bad symptoms for a good crop. Pappa, Billy, Savilla, Sarah & the Esq came down at 9 o'clock. Went fishing on Bean Creek with seighn and hooks, caught a fine chance. They departed at 4 o'clock PM, then I went to plowing again, nearly finished my cotton. Had a fine mess of catfish for supper. Eat rather too much to rest well.

May 9, 1851

Finished the cotton, also the bottoms. Then began running around the old corn again. Ground a little crusty, corn looks tolerably well. Went to mill in morning and to P.O. in evening. Warmer to day than any day since March.

May 10, 1851

Very warm and clear being a beautiful day. Uncle Jonathan came down and went seghning with me, caught a fine mess. A.E.C. also came to mansion. Ground geting hard. Went up home &c.

May 11, 1851

Went to Salem Church via Billy's. Came by H. J. Lyles's on my return and eat dinner.

May 12, 1851

Finished plowing my old corn by noon, second time. Then began hoeing cotton in new ground.

May 13, 1851

Hoeing. Went up home in evening and concluded to go [to] Winnsboro in co. with the Esq and Henry. Got there by night. Went up to Mrs. Ladd's, saw several prettie girls.

May 15, 1851

Sold cotton to Woodward & Randolph at 6 & 8 cents per lb. Got home by night. Very warm.

May 16, 1851

Went fishing at Little River. More girls than fish &c. Came from fishing to P.O. in company with John Cameron. No letters.

May 17, 1851

Warm and dry, not rained in two weeks. Fine for hoeing. Tom Rawls and Capt' Feaster gave me a call. Pappa came down and stayed until near night when we went up home after aiding Crowder Jenkins &c. in cuting down a bee tree. No honey in it.

May 18, 1851

Went to Cool Branch. Sermon by the Rev'd Brooks from Revelations. Came to mansion via McConnell's Store. J. M. Morgan stayed all night with me.

May 19, 1851

Still hoeing cotton. Very hot and dry. A.E.C. came after mules and wagon to haul corn from Mr. Stephen Crosby Sr. I hoed my half acre.

May 20, 1851

Went to shop after hoeing my task. Got some smoking tobacco and raisins from Arnett's. A.E.C. finished hauling his corn, brought the wagon home and stayed all night with me. Wanting rain badly.

May 21, 1851

Still hoeing. The ground very hard and dry. I began reading a very interesting novel, *Annie Grey*. Pappa came down after supper and stayed all night with me.

May 22, 1851

Castrated six bulls, quite windy all day. I gathered straw berrys enough for several pies, had one for supper. Eat finely. Finished reading my book and went to bed.

May 23, 1851

Didn't quite finish my task by dinner. Wind blowing very hard and incessantly. Went to Esq Feaster's and P.O. in evening, received letter from Drucie of Fla.

May 24, 1851

Not done hoeing yet. I went pic nic on Little River. Had fine times &c., &c. The Widow Milling was the belle of the fandango. Got home by night. R.H.C. stayed all night with me.

May 25, 1851

Went to Salem. Eat dinner at Esq Feaster's.

May 26, 1851

Still hoeing cotton. Some appearance of rain. Needed very much. Began a letter to Drucie in morning. Finished it at night.

May 27, 1851

Finished hoeing all but a few remnants. Went up home after the mules. Henry came down with me. Had chicken for supper.

May 28, 1851

Began plowing the bottoms, corn looks pretty well. Plowing myself. Very dry.

May 29, 1851

Finished the bottoms by night.

May 30, 1851

Commenced trying to plow the new ground. R. H. Coleman, Feaster and Pappa eat dinner with me. Went fishing in evening, caught a great many. Went to P.O. in evening. Got no letters. The two former gentlemen came home and stayed all night with me.

May 31, 1851

Very dry, not having rain'd but one very small shower in this month. Want rain too bad. We went to Lyles's Mill. Went in washing &c. Went up home in evening.

June 1, 1851

Went to Red Hill. Large audience to Mr. Guinn &c. Saw Miss Irena Feaster, very pretty. No rain since first of May.

June 2, 1851

Plowing cotton and hoeing bottom corn. Plowed myself in evening.

June 3, 1851

Plowed until dinner, then I went to P.O. Sent Drucie & Sarah Feaster each a novel. Morgan stayed all night. Great threats of rain but didn't come. Oh, we want it very bad, according to my wants &c.

June 4, 1851

I plowed Paddy to day. Windy and hot and dry & dusty and so on. Very still and warm at supper. Rained at night a pretty good shower though not enough.

June 5, 1851

Ground plowed finely after the rain. Had a very sick mule and continues so i.e. at dinner time. Hope he won't die. By night the mule was much better. D. R. Feaster stayed the night with me.

June 6, 1851

Had a glorious little rain yesterday evening. I plowed until noon, afterwards went to P.O. Ground in fine order for plowing. {He ain't been to the office a bit now for we are both presnt. Amen. —Dr. Feaster.}[54]

Received letters from Miss Bostwick, E. S. Corckrell and Jas. Cameron. Was appointed one of a committee of arrangements for a barbecue at Arnett's store on 4th July.

June 7, 1851

Pappa came down. Had fine rain [in] afternoon. Went to the Esq at night.

June 8, 1851

Went to Salem, thense to [. . .], thense to Pappa's, and finaly to the mansion.

June 9, 1851

Twenty-three years old. Went to Kerr's plantation after peas, also to shop. Finished plowing over my cotton second time. Then began planting peas &c. Pappa came down after help to cut wheat on Wednesday next.

June 10, 1851

Nearly finished planting my peas. R.H.C. took dinner with me today, then went to the Gov's fishing at Lyles's Ford. Came back to mansion and stayed all night.

June 11, 1851

Sent the hands to Pappa's to cut wheat. I went to Billy's and Dave's after my puppies (three in number). Saw Uncle Sam and Aunt Cinth. Got to mansion by night.

June 12, 1851

The hands still at Pappa's. Fixed gate at pasture &c. Want rain. Plowed in evening.

June 13, 1851

Feaster come early in morn. We went over my bottoms. Look very well. Then went to P.O.

Foot stayed with me on the night of the 21th. Eat a watermelon for the first.

July 5, 1851

Plowing cotton after finishing bottoms. Went up home, thense to the Esq where we remained all night, saw A. Yongue Jr.

July 6, 1851

Went to Red Hill. Sermon by Guinn. Saw many pretty girls. Very warm day.

July 7, 1851

Two hands aiding Pappa in cutting oats. Plowed the new ground cotton, over waist high. Very hot. Rained little in evening.

July 8, 1851

Went up home and Oh who should I find there? Why, Mrs. Milling and Juliana, the prettiest prehaps. Got to the mansion by dark. Happy dream.

July 9, 1851

The hands hoeing cotton. I plowed my melons and cotton. Very warm to day. Hope it will rain.

From the above date to August 21st I was taking a great change in scenes. Left home on 23d July for Chambers County Ala. on a visit to Uncle Isaac Nolen's. Got there on 26 inst. and stayed until 18th August. Got home on 21st. I had a happy and pleasant trip, accompanied by Bob. I never stayed all night at mansion until the night of 28 August. [. . .] around &c., but I am down to [. . .] now.

August 29, 1851

I have domesticated myself at last. A.E.C. stayed with me last night. Very cool. Pulling my bottom fodder to day. Wrote letter to Jack last mail. Went to Bigger's mellon patch—none ripe.

August 30, 1851

Went to shooting match at Feasterville. Mr. Leroy Griffin took dinner with me today. Went home with Judge and staid all night.

August 31, 1851

Went to New Hope Church with Judge. Eat dinner at Uncle Sams, thense to Uncle Andy's where we eat supper, then I came alone to mansion.

September 1, 1851

Still puling fodder in bottoms, spent most of my time reading Kendall's *Santa Fe Expedition*.[55]

September 2, 1851

Finished the bottom fodder. Cotton opening very fast.

September 3, 1851

Wrote letters to J. G. Cameron and B. F. Sawyer. Pappa and Dave came down to see me, stayed all day. Finished puling fodder.

September 4, 1851

Began picking cotton. Went to P.O., to Mean's shop where had my nag shod. Eat dinner at Esq Feaster. Traded my watch to A.E.C. for a mule, yonge heifer and other house hold goods &c. Still reading Kendall's *Expedition*.

September 5, 1851

Went up home in morning, saw the Miss Stevensons & R.H.C. The latter came to P.O. with me, thense to A.E.C. who aided us in driving the cattle over to pasture. All staid at mansion at night.

September 6, 1851

Began raising by 8 o'clock, ceased at 11.

I was so lazzy as to neglect my journal from the 6th until that last day of the month. Monday the 15th the camp muster began. Cap. Clowney, 1 Lieut. D. R. Feaster & myself and 3d J. D. Cameron slept in one tent while the sergeants viz. A. E. Coleman, W. Coban, J. Douglas and J. A. Brice occupied another. Had fine cool weather all the week. Fine and glorious speeches from the Gov. Owens and Aiken. All were dismissed on Saturday 20th.

The following week I went to Columbia, got home on Saturday evening, was at daddies on Sunday. R.H.C. came and stayed all night with me.

September 28, 1851

Began hauling corn after killing the rats. [. . .] and Judge Feaster also W. Saywer, R.H.C., Drucie and Isa did'nt get many. R.H.C. came home with me. Sallie was at the Mansion.

October 22, 1851

Went turkey hunting, nothing. R.H.C. left for home. Bob & Sallie staid with me at mansion. Very cool night, but not rain yet. Bob was quite [. . .]

October 23, 1851

Carried a load of cotton to gin, got done by 2 o'clock. Went to party at Capt Feaster's and dance until 10 PM when most the crowd [went] home while several of us played all night. Didn't sleep any.

October 24, 1851

Went to P.O. No letters. Heavy frost at night, the first frost was on the night of the 22 inst. Grand Ma's little Negro child died last night, buried today.

October 25, 1851

Read the newspapers all day nearly. Went to the Sons [of] Temperance Lodge at night. Remained until near midnight. D.R.F. and I went to [. . .] and staid all night.

October 26, 1851

Rained a little in morning with thunder, cleared off at night and was very cold indeed. Feaster with me at night.

October 27, 1851

Went to H. J. Lyles's, thense to Pappa's, eat dinner, then Drucie and I went to Uncle R. G. Cameron's, stayed all night.

October 28, 1851

Went to Winnsboro attending court in Morgan's and Coleman's case. Lodged with [. . .]

October 29, 1851

Case didn't come on. Sat about C.H. all day. Some very amusing cases were [. . .]

October 30, 1851

The lawsuit was tried before [. . .] Honor J. B. O'Neale, the verdict was not [. . .] until morning. Went up to Ladd's at night.

October 31, 1851

At 10 o'clock AM verdict was [. . .] favour of Morgan. Left for home and [. . .] at the same by 3 o'clock, thense [. . .] Rained several times thus [. . .] Pleasant weather. Fell in love. I [. . .]

November 1, 1851

Walked over to A.E.C. and P.O., thense home. Went to division at night. Rob't Mobley came home with me.

November 2, 1851

Went to Liberty Church. Preaching by Rev'd Jefferson Norris of Ala.

November 3, 1851

Started to Columbia. Arrived there by noon on Tuesday. Sold cotton to R. Catchcart at [. . .] and 5⁵⁵/₁₀₀. Left for home on Wednesday in company with Capt Feaster. Camped at Hendrix Field. Got home on Thursday after evening. Cold.

November 7, 1851

Hauled load cotton in morning. Went to P.O. Got letters from B. F. Sawyer and D. R. Coleman of Ala. Brother Henry with me at night. James M. Morgan departed this life on Thursday 11th of Nov. 1851 after a short illness of but ten days. Was buried beside his wife at Jon. D. Coleman's. Old Mr. Bowlware died on the 21st by falling from his horse, his head striking against a tree and instantly killing him.

Nothing new occurred to me in all this time up to December the 8th. Will pack cotton to day and start to Columbia tomorrow.

Packed fourteen bales by Tuesday ten o'clock, the 9th inst. Sold at 7⁶⁰/[100] and 6⁹⁰/[100]. Brought up goods for Arnett.

December 13, 1851
Our muster day. Didn't attend the division at night.

December 14, 1851
Went to Cool Branch. Eat dinner at J.C.C. F.'s

December 15, 1851
Went to sale of 13 negroes belonging to Jacob Feaster Sr. Sold very high. Very cold day. Killed four hogs to day.

December 17, 1851
Went to the sale of Morgan's Est. and thense to Mrs. Milling's wedding, married to Moses Clowney, had a fine time, eating &c.

December 18, 1851
Went to the Infare at Cap't Clowney's. Danced a little in evening. Very cold indeed.

Nothing new up to the 22d inst. Some parties [. . .] the make up. Not down picking cotton. Began fencing Morgan's [. . .] which Pappa rented. Two days only to Christmas.

December 23, 1851
Went rabbit hunting with Jake, D.R.F., Preston & Wiley Wright. The last three came over to mansion, eat dinner and made some fine music on violin. Went home with Feaster & stayed all night.

December 24, 1851
Went rabbit hunting again. Eat dinner at Esq Feaster's. Polley & D.R.F. came up to [. . .] A.E.C. & myself came via mansion to Pa's.

December 25, 1851

Danced at our house.

December 26, 1851

Went partridge hunting with Pollie, Carrie, Belle, Isa, Drucie, Judge and R.H.C., caught only four.

December 27, 1851

Dance at Feasterville.

December 28, 1851

Stayed all day at home.

December 29, 1851

Danced at Uncle A. Feaster's.

December 30, 1851

Went rabbit hunting with Cap Rudolph, W.F., A.E.C., D.R.F. and W. Lonegan.

December 31, 1851

The last of December 1851. Went partridge hunting with the four last named men. [. . .] at Pappa's. Pollie & D.R.F. went home in eve. [. . .] Nancy, cousin Nancy & Whillis came in from La. last week. R.H.C. staid all night with me. Last night of 1851.

Henry Craft

Will other eyes than mine ever glance through these pages, will others read these lines when the hand which traced them shall have mouldered? It may be so. Then they will find here the record of a heart & mind which were to their possessor the greatest mysteries which he found in all this mysterious home of humanity.

—November 3, 1848

Saturday, April 8, 1848

On this 8th day of April 1848 at Princeton, New Jersey I begin these memoranda which I intend to continue from time to time, if not from day to day. I have for a long time felt the need of a kind of journal and have always intended to open one, but have only now actually undertaken it. I intend it for a brief record of passing events which may concern myself, as also perhaps a record of passing thoughts which those events may suggest. Very often there are moments of sadness, of memory, of indescribable emotion when we like to *muse*, and at such moments it is often a pleasure to commune with ourselves as it were in writing and it may be that it would be pleasant to glance over such communings when written even after the mood which originates them has passed off. What this journal may become I have now no thought whatever. Heretofore my life has been a very wandering one which has rendered it impossible to keep anything like a continuous memorandum of what it fell to my lot to do, to be, & to suffer, and as I look back upon the past, I feel that I would be very glad to have such a memorandum. This feeling applies peculiarly to the last year, which has been by far the most eventful of my life, and as occasionally I remember that the present day is the anniversary of some prominent occurrence, I bitterly regret that I have not a continuous narrative of the whole year. I have little idea should I live even to be an old man (of which I have not the least expectation) that another year will ever combine so much of joy and sorrow. There are epochs in the history of nations, and families of the world & of individuals. 1847 is the epoch in my humble history, an epoch as important and momentous & eventful to me as 1688 to England, 1789 & 1848 to France, 1776 to the U.S. — an epoch too of Revolution, one to which I shall look back every day that I may hereafter live; one from which I will have to date much of what shall be my future history.

This is my *twenty-fifth birthday*. A quarter of a century of my acquaintance with the pleasures & pains, the carelessness & the vast responsibility of life. For many years past I have been accustomed upon the recurrence of this day to jot down some birthday thoughts, some reflections upon the year gone, some surmise as to the year to come. How well can I recollect how time after time I have sat down to write "the 8th of April has come again," how time after time I have looked back upon privileges & opportunities neglected & time wasted, how time after time I have looked into the darkness of the future with yearnings & longings after improvement and resolutions and promises for the time to come. How too, I have always cast a prying glance upon the impervious curtain, and felt a vague desire to pierce its secrets, how time after time I have asked myself, where shall I be when another birthday comes. Shall I be allowed to chronicle it or will its footsteps be upon the hillock over my mouldering dust, and if I live what circumstances will then surround me, what shall I be?

As I look through the past year now, I see myself as I sat at midnight on the 8th of April last in my room at home. I had just returned from a small party at Tuckahoe which succeeded a very large one given there the night before. Very few were there, but they were the gayest of the gay, and the laugh & the dance had reigned unbroken during the evening. She whom I loved was there, whom I loved with all the anxious doubting, fearful hope and anxiety & suspense of one who has not told his love & who has but little reason to suppose that it is returned and as I sat at that table I thought of her, looked forward wondering what should be the end & wrote as now I write of my birthday, and of the circumstances which it found around me. Oh how well for me it was that I could not then look beyond the veil and see what was in store—but why should I now recur to the events which have since transpired which have resulted in placing me here a student at Princeton. I shall never need any record of those events to enable me to *remember* them, and this book when I may be gone cannot fall into the hands of any one for whom such a record would possess interest who is not already well acquainted with what would constitute it. She whom I then loved, of whom I then thought and wrote was wooed and won. I was happy and full of hope, the cup brimful of joy was at my lips. Death came & snatched it away. I followed her, my own, my beloved Lucy,[1] to the grave on the 3rd of November, after being engaged to her six months and the time for our union having been *twice* appointed (July 12th & Oct. 21st). I looked on while her form was lowered into its long resting place and then returned to the loneliness, the desolation of the home whence she had been borne away a corpse in her bridal attire. There with her sister (*my* sister too if there can be such a relationship of heart without the ties of consanguinity) I felt, while her image was reflected by every object, her voice still lingering among the echoes, *felt* that she was gone, that we were bereaved and alone. Darkness, I had almost said despair, came down upon me. I felt as though I had thenceforth nothing to live for, no hope, no object, no happiness. From the associations and memories (no *not* the *memories*) of home I sought refuge here, trusting to find in the emulation and competition of a class not only respite from thoughts, but incentive to study, and discipline of mind, and so now for four months I have been here among students, an old man as it were coming back to the employments of his youth, one whose life is far advanced among those just *preparing* to live, himself needing that preparation too more than any one of them all, and thus, so contrary to all expectation or conjecture, so beyond, as I should have supposed even the pale of possibility, it is by such scenes that this birthday finds me surrounded.

And now as it comes, I turn as heretofore to a retrospect of the past, and also to conjecture of the future. I think of what *has* been and wonder what *will* be. As heretofore I have much to regret of time wasted & opportunities unimproved and many resolutions ready to be formed of a different course for the future, but whatever else may strew the path of these coming months, however [. . .] may mark its course, I will not add the fragments of broken resolves to those ruins. So I go on with an "upward brow" & a callous heart, ready to meet whatever may confront me; ready to be surprised by nothing. My utmost hopes and aspirations for the next year are that it will launch me upon my profession. I will not say that there are no sorrows which it can inflict upon me. I will not say that "Fate has done its worst" and that I defy its power, for such would not be true. My heart has bled indeed—tender, the kindest of all ties, have been severed and I have suffered affliction & bereavement such as few perhaps are called to undergo, yet there are many, many, very tender ties still binding my heart, many, very many blessings still brightening my life. The future *is* future. God has ordained it.

Sunday, April 9, 1848

It is Sunday, one of Spring's loveliest days. The smaller bushes are beginning to be green with leaves, and the fringes are adorning some of the trees. There are many flowers in bloom, and in a short time Nature will look so beautiful in the freshness of her waking from the long sleep of Winter. Spring was ever my favorite season. I don't know why I love it, but I remember that I have been wont to look forward with anxious hope to its coming, and see with regret its exhaustion or development into the garish summer. At home no doubt every thing is green, and the song of the birds & the odor of the flowers & the balminess of the air have become such accustomed things as to be unnoticed.

I have heard Mr. Shields preach today in the college Chapel, an excellent sermon from John 14:1, "Let not your heart be troubled, Ye believe in God, believe also in me." The Sermon began with an allusion to Socrates condemned by his ungrateful countrymen to death by poison, sitting with the fatal cup in his hand, among his friends and pupils and calmly & serenely discoursing to them. This scene has been much dwelt upon by the moralist & philosopher & it was a sublime one as elevating the humanity common to us all, but there was a scene in that small upper chamber in Jerusalem far more grand & impressive in all its characteristics. There followed a comparison of the lives of the Athenian sage & Christ &c. After the introduction, the sermon was explanatory of the manner in which a knowledge or rather belief in Christ also as well as God became "comfort" to the constrained & troubled heart—the evenness which Christ declared to exist between himself & the Father—the horror which must attach to a belief in God without Christ & the beautiful and comfortable completeness of the belief of the Christian in the infinite God, in his own infinite insignificance & in Christ, allied to & equal with the former & also caring for and stooping to the latter. The sermon was beautiful & impressive, but Mr. Shields' composition is too finished to be understood easily in speaking & his manner too languid to command attention, but I anticipate great changes in this respect & do not doubt that he will become a distinguished & useful man. He was one of the [. . .] and I intend appending a sketch of him as he seems to me along with sketches of the other members to the record of that great association, which are in my possession, and which I am anxious to preserve as mementos of some of the most pleasant & profitable hours I have spent in Princeton.

Heard Mr. Greene preach in the afternoon & Mr. [. . .] at night. Took a walk with T. Wall & a long walk with W.B.[2] after church about Maria S., Shields' Sunday School agency, &c. I spend my Sundays very badly. I have got out of the habit of reading on that day. If I stay in my room then I almost irresistibly fall into a reverie & sit & look into the fire and commune with the past all day, and I am only kept from this during the week by the pressure of study. Hence the advantage of being here. I have sadly neglected reading the Bible of late — have made many plans & resolutions about studying it systematically but I still neglect it. I am, but no, I won't write about that now.

Monday, April 10, 1848

Nothing to record for today but mailed a letter to Mrs. Crump,[3] [. . .]ed, attended two lectures by Proff Henry,[4] long walk with Baker (& a talk with him this afternoon about his manner towards me, which I regret & which I fear left a disagreeable impression upon him) & a letter to Matt[5] tonight. How the days go & how little is done, at least by me. Have been forcibly impressed with the importance & the efficiency of perseverance in hearing Henry lecture. He was a silver smith's apprentice. The machinery of a watch excited his curiosity. He was led by it to study mechanics & so on, step by step till now at probably 50 years of age he is the greatest & most eminent philosopher in America, perhaps equal to any in the world. While I listened to him, I asked myself whether it were possible that I should ever be able to master & fully understand *any* even the simplest subject as he seems to have done the whole range of philosophical knowledge. I asked myself, "what do I know *well*?" & was compelled to answer nothing unless it be the roads in North Miss. & how to examine land. I am resolved to be a Lawyer if health & life are spared, and it lies in my power. I aspire to a knowledge of the science, the principles, the philosophy of the profession & if I live I will attain it. I do not expect ever to be eminent, but I can I think be respectable as any man can I am told who has good common sense & will study. I wish I knew what chance there is for me ever to be a *speaker*. I have not an idea in the world, though I am inclined to think that my manner will be very disagreeable. My voice is sharp & monotonous & my action exceedingly forced & ungraceful, yet I think I have an appreciation of eloquence, Nous [. . .].

The moon is shining in its half developed beauty. I could look [at] it for an hour but it is just midnight & bed time. So for now, oblivion of Earth for seven hours.

Tuesday, April 11, 1848

It is 11 o'clock and I have but little to write to night. Heard two lectures from Proff Henry on Magnetism and Galvanism. He gives a singular origin to the latter. Galvana's wife[6] was sick & some *frogs* obtained for her to eat were lying just killed near an electrical machine. (His kitchen & study or laboratory were all one I suppose). A student chanced to draw a spark with his knuckle & he observed that the leg of the frog was twitched. He repeated the operation frequently with the same result & then disclosed it to Galvana,[7] who set himself about investigating the cause & from this slight circumstance has arisen a discovery which has opened a whole new world of phenomena & given man greater power over matter than he ever before possessed. I must try to remember the definition & explanations of magnetism & galvanism. Of the former the "variation," "the dip," &c. [. . . .] & needle points it varies on both sides more and more as distance increases. The Earth is a great magnet. Its N pole is not the magnetic North pole & is strongest at 2 points called the —— pole & the Siberian pole, former is strongest. Needle is only horizontal at the equator, dips both north & south of it owing to magnetism of the Earth. Columbus first observed variation of needle. Galvanic battery—zinc & copper or iron & copper or silver & copper in salt water or sulphuric acid (or nitric acid if silver & copper be used) emitted or otherwise *out* of the fluid. This is a simple battery. This is all new to me now & will be new again in a few months for by that time I shall have forgotten it. Two long walks alone, not much done in the way of study. Have thought tonight what a pleasure it is to be engaged in the pursuit of a profession which one feels that he will master if he lives. I feel so in regard to law. I do not mean by "master" that I can be a great lawyer but that I can understand the practical every day part of it. I feel more anxious now than I ever did before to have life & health to be devoted to study because I think I am beginning to have a clearer idea than I ever had before of something to be accomplished by study. It is cloudy & disagreeable tonight. We'll have rain before morning probably.

Wednesday, April 12, 1848

Nothing to write tonight. Two lectures, two walks, three meals, &c., &c. make up the history of the day. And I'm very sleepy.

Thursday, April 13, 1848

Not much to say except that another day has gone, spent as usual—two recitations (good ones), a hail storm, a walk with D. Baker,[8] a visit from Lundy and W. Baker tonight, and such is the history of the day. Lundy is or was one of the [. . .]. The documents of that body tell something of his character. He is a clever man. When I have time I must devote several of these pages to a sketch of the men & things here as well as of my kind hostesses. It seems that I have the good fortune always to find kind friends among the ladies, or to be thrown among those who treat me well. From my first absence from home till now, whenever I have been in sickness & health I have always met with the attention & kindness almost of Mothers & Sisters. The Ladies in whose home I now am have placed me under many obligations. Lundy, Baker & myself have just dispatched with great gusto a tray of strawberries (preserved) & cream with jelly & cakes which they sent up to me. To us who board at the Refectory such things are peculiarly grateful. So much for Thursday. I am not conscious of having derived much benefit or improvement from it, but I do not feel as I too often do at night that the day has been actually lost. It is something not to be compelled to say, "diem perdide." Sometimes after a day well spent and evident additions made to my small store of knowledge, I feel encouraged, feel that I may yet be able to do something, but then again I sink down, utterly overwhelmed by a sense of the vastness of what I have undertaken & my entire inability. What will the end be?

Friday, April 14, 1848

Heard Mr. Hope[9] lecture this morning on anatomy with a skeleton before him and could not but exclaim how fearfully & wonderfully are we made. How a man can be an infidel who will even give a cursory glance at his own physical organization, I can't image, and then how many, many exhibitions of Divine wisdom & power there are infinitely transcending those of the human mechanism.

Visited at Mr. Field's tonight with E. Wall. Was much pleased with Miss Field with whom I have never conversed before—also much pleased with Wall's bearing & manners—was favorably struck with the truthfulness & earnestness of his character manifested even in ladies' society when men generally affect the greatness, falseness & frivolity—felt much ashamed of my own exceeding levity & rattling flippancy. Ladies may for the time being like the company of a man who laughs & jests & makes them do the same, but such a man does not win their respect or rather *command* it. He goes away & straightaway is forgotten or only remembered as a chattering parrot would be remembered, while such a man as Wall if seen but once, leaves on the memory the shadow of a *man*, if seen frequently is respected, looked up to & loved. I feel more heartily ashamed than I ever did of the harlequin kind of demeanor which I have been accustomed to assume among ladies—and of the low estimate of them which the supposition on my part that such demeanor would please, has implied. I will try hereafter to lay aside the boy, to have principle & character among ladies & to remember that they have both judgment & taste, discrimination & appreciation of worth. In truth I feel much inclined to this change in manner without reference to such consideration of its propriety. I can not *trifle* with the same zest that I once did, cannot throw my whole soul into the laugh & the jest & live entirely within the limits of the hour & the company. Twelve months ago 'twas very different. No human being had a blither or a happier heart. No one could flit to & fro with more sincere sunniness of feeling. It is I think just about 12 months since Mrs. Thomson's party. What a joyous company it was & how joyous among the joys ever I was. I walked home with Lucy. An avowal of my love was trembling on my lips. I had determined to disclose it then but a thunder storm came up. How distinctly I remember it all, but why revert?

At Mr. Field's we met Mr. Lord, the history lecturer.

Saturday, April 15, 1848

Another week gone—they slip off very rapidly. Employment gives a wonderfully accelerated motion to the hours' wings. Beautiful day. Recitation. Afternoon wasted. Evening spent at Mr. Greens—introduced to Miss Green & Miss Solomon. Not much pleased with the latter but with the former very much. I think I shall like her society. Received letter from Mrs. Crump & Cousin Anna, both unexpected. Mrs. C. I supposed I should hear from the middle of next week & Cousin Anna I hardly supposed I should hear from again at all, as my experience has been heretofore that my friends invariably dropped my correspondence as soon as they were married. I hope she may continue to be an exception. How much I should love to see her with her husband. The sight of her writing moves many associations connected with it & with her. She has been a true & tried friend and I prize her regard very highly. I remember when I watched for the coming of her letters oh so eagerly & pored over them and answered them by the very next mail & counted the days & weeks till I could hear from her again. And now though she is married I still like to hear from her, to know that she is happy. And so much for the [. . .]. It seems very short yet I would be glad to have it seem a great deal shorter.

Sunday, April 16, 1848

How sweet the moonlight is. I never saw a more quiet, beautiful night. I do love the moon. Month after month and year after year have I *drank* its beauty with unabated thirst, and a thousand scenes and circumstances are now associated with it, among which at different times I have looked upon it. Sometimes its rays have stolen in upon me through the chinks of the humble log cabin, sometimes have rested upon the silence & solicitude of the forest in which my tent was pitched, sometimes have lighted me on the midnight journey, sometimes on the rapid ride towards Tuckahoe & the lingering but sweet one, homewards from that place. Sometimes have silvered the keen edge of the north wind in winter, sometimes as now floated through the soft still air of Spring. The long stroll, the gay party, the dreaming hour spent in gazing on its sweet face, all then stretch back an interminable line of moonlight memories, and lie before me too in a vista (God only knows whether long or short) which terminates in my grave on which I trust these same bright rays will rest as I have seen them on the graves of those I loved, as I imagine that they are resting now upon *her* grave far, far away. How such a night reminds me of similar ones when I have been in her company, when she has laughed at me about my romance. But enough.

The day has been as sweet as spring time air could make it. Have heard Bishop Dean preach twice. In the morning did not like him at all, but in the afternoon thought his sermon one of the most finished rhetorical compositions, or conceptions rather, I have heard in sometime. He is evidently a poet, yet he must be deficient in taste for in the midst of beautiful, chaste thoughts, he often intrudes a coarse expression which grates upon the ear. For instance, "can you sow common grass seed & expect to have the golden grain in harvest time to *thrash*." "Can you plant an acorn & gather *chesnuts* from the tree." "Can you from the wild vine unpruned, untended &c gather at vintage time the full cluster of *muscat*." He abounds too in rhetorical inaccuracies, as for instance "her *voice* is *severe* as the morning *dew*" &c., &c. Nevertheless I listened to him with much interest. He wears a large & very conspicuous seal ring, the gift I am told of Queen Victoria. I never saw a jewelled finger in the pulpit before & must confess I think it would suit other places better.

Long walk with W.B. this afternoon. Wrote to Mrs. C. nearly a whole letter. The day has passed pleasantly enough, but not very profitably I fear. I do feel more than I ever did before I think a desire to *improve* my time, but somehow the desire vents itself in unperformed intentions.

Monday, April 17, 1848

I must write a line though nevertheless before I go to bed, though I am tired enough. Up soon this morning one or two hours study before breakfast. Good recitation. Letters from Matt Blunt & Matt Fort. Menagerie this afternoon with Green. Thought while I stood among the crowd of a similar scene when I was with *her* about this time last year. Now every thing brings her to my thoughts. I dreamed of her night before last in health & gaiety, but she sleeps on, unconscious of the desolation which her departure has created. Heard a lecture tonight from Mr. Lord on Feudalism & wrote to Sister.

Tuesday, April 18, 1848

Little done today. Couldn't study. Tried to read without much success. Letter from Ma, first since middle of February.

Wednesday, April 19, 1848

Regular snow storm today—ground covered & would have been covered deep but for the rain which preceded the snow. I never saw peach trees adorned with blossoms & icicles at the same time before or hyacinths bowed beneath the weight of snow flakes. 'Tis rather pretty, the contrast. I noticed particularly the peach tress. The snow so much obscured the blossoms that you could not see that they *were* flowers & yet their hue was distinct, thus giving the snow the appearance of being colored. And the poor hyacinths, rather flowers, looked so completely taken aback, so much out of their element in the snow bank, that while one's sympathy was excited, yet he could not escape a sense of the ludicrous in their situation. The supposition is that the peaches at least are all killed. Before night the clouds rolled away, the sun shone out & the snow melted rapidly, though it is not all gone. On the [. . .] tops especially it glistens in the moonlight. I was struck this afternoon in looking from my window with the effect of snow upon the far off hills, mingling with the "azure hue in which the distance robes them." [10]

Heard a lecture from Mr. Lord tonight on the Popes, particularly Gregory VII or Hildebrand. [11] It was interesting. He is one of the most voluble men I ever listened to. His manner is very unique & disagreeable & yet it suits his matter. His lectures are sweeping generalizations based upon very few facts. I do not think they contain much solid information but are entertaining from their peculiar style & the fullness & richness of his language.

I have done very little again today. I am out of sorts entirely. I don't know what can be the matter. Dread the recitations for tomorrow.

Thursday, April 20, 1848

Nothing to record for today. Heard lecture tonight from Mr. Lord on "Schools & Schoolmen of the Middle Ages." Didn't understand it & have forgotten it already.

Friday, April 21, 1848

Diem perdidi. At Whig Hall[12] tonight.

Saturday, April 22, 1848

Spent the morning going over Wentworth's *System of Pleading*,[13] the afternoon in writing letters to send by W.B. Heard lecture to night from Mr. Lord on the Crusades. Good I thought.

Sunday, April 23, 1848

Heard sermon from Dr. Hodge[14] this morning on the office of reason in matters of faith, in college chapel. Walked with William Baker after dinner. Talked of *her* for the first time for some months. He asked me if I thought my character had undergone any change since my coming here. I said yes, I felt that my views of man, my conceptions of the field open for the exercise of his faculties, as also my views of his true dignity had been much elevated. And that I felt more of *purpose*, of earnestness, & of the importance of time. I hope this is all true, but it may be only imaginary for I still am content to waste away my hours & trifle away my thoughts upon nothing. One thing I do know—every day has made me think more meanly of myself. My worst enemy could not despise me more than I do myself when I think what I am.

Monday, April 24, 1848

Recitation as usual. Afternoon spent in writing letters to send by W.B. Heard Dr. Bethune[15] of Phila to night in an address to Soc. of Inquiry in Seminary. The address was extemporaneous & poor. Was much disappointed.

Tuesday, April 25, 1848

William B. left this morning for the Presbytery at Titusville 15 miles distant where he is to be licensed & will go on home without returning. Spent the day in preparing papers for Mr. Field. D. Baker & Ash Green in my room tonight.

Friday, April 28, 1848

Have returned today from Phila. Went down Wednesday night to see William off. Met him at Trenton. Cold, rainy, disagreeable even'g. Stopped at Jones Hotel. Spent the day Thursday very pleasantly. Visited S.S. Union house & was politely shown over it. Had conversation with Mr. Porter's corresponding Secretary. He is a voluble old man, but an interesting one—has much shrewdness & knowledge of me, with great benevolence & no doubt piety. Visited a type & [. . .] type foundry for the first time—was astonished to see that types are mostly moulded by hand one at a time & then pass through a long and tedious process—was much interested in it. Walked on Chesnut Street & stood at the Hotel watching the stream of life which pours along it—men, women & children, black & white, the rich and gay & flaunting & proud & vain—the poor & miserable business men—exquisites—roués—& every other class & quality, occupation, degree & phase of humanity. At night went with William to see Lizzie Mason[16] in Arch Street—was astonished at her improvement in appearance, manners & conversation. Had a long conversation with the principal of the establishment, a fine looking, dignified old lady who is very fond of talking & who talks remarkably well. Evening passed very pleasantly. At 10 returned to the Hotel and at half past 11 went with William to depot & parted with him in the car. I shall miss him very much. He has made an arrangement to act as agent for S.S.U. with which he is much pleased in prospect, but of which I predict that he will grow very weary before the 4 months expire. I don't know whether to think he will succeed or not. The chances are however I should say in favor of it.

Left Phila this morning at 9 o'clock & had a delightful ride back. The road passes through a beautiful country. Found a letter on my return from Brodie Crump[17] telling me that his Mother was very sick when he wrote & containing a message from her that she would not be able to write to me again for a long time, that she was sick much as Lucy was & perhaps would never see me again. In her last letter she wrote of a gloomy presentiment that something would happen to prevent us from again seeing each other. I will not think of her dying, will try to hope that she is already recovered, though it would not be strange if sorrow has been too much for her feeble frame. How we are hemmed in in the world by the little circle of horizon around us. We may be gay & happy in our unconsciousness while those we love at a distance from us are suffering— dying. Now while I write of Mrs. C. she may be well—or she may have been buried. How her loss would increase the desolation of [. . .] for me, but what would be my loss to that of her children. But I will not think of this, will not anticipate, will at least while I may, continue to look forward to many hours of mournful pleasure to be spent in her society.

How full of memories this day, this hour are. Twelve months ago at this time Lucy, Mrs. C. & myself were riding to Tuckahoe. The moon was full & gloriously bright. It was the night of the conversation party. For the first time in my life I was jealous. I thought she loved another & I was miserable, utterly miserable as I had never been before. *She* gave me a bouquet of white roses at Mr. Goodman's that night. I have them yet. At the party she pretended to be much pleased with the attentions of a gentleman from Memphis whom I had never seen before & it seemed suddenly apparent to me that she loved him, had loved him, was perhaps engaged to him, & I, fool that I was, had loved her. It was a wretched sleepless night to me. She too was unhappy, but I did not know it then. She observed what my feelings were & she wished me to be undeceived, but I misinterpreted what she intended to correct my error into aggravations of it. Oh, I shall never forget that night, but it was the dark hour before the dawn, it was the precursor of happiness, such happiness. And now the year has gone & she too, my own loving, noble, Lucy, she too is gone. I am here to trace out the chain of events as day after day brings up new links in the light of memory. I am here to follow on as the train of recollections reaches from week to week till, should I live till then, the joys & disappointments & trials having passed one by one in review, it will end at that sacred spot where she sleeps the long quiet sleep of death. "When man has nothing left to love he falls in love with his very sorrow over the departed." Such is a paragraph in a newspaper which met my eye & which my heart echoed. Almost every hour, often every moment I think of her. The memory of her love is my greatest treasure. I know not whether it be now a sorrow. I am cheerful & hopeful & happy, thoughts of her do not often cause a pang, do not often bring a tear, yet she is dead.

Sunday, April 30, 1848

I was unwell yesterday & had company last night (Burt & Candor). It was the anniversary of one of the most wretched days that I ever spent in my life, a day which at that time I thought the only *miserable day* I had ever known. It was a day rendered so by the pangs of hopeless love. I felt satisfied that *she* loved another, and the hours from noon till night were a continued conflict of emotions, a self upbraiding for my folly in not having seen before what then seemed so clearly revealed. As the evening drew on I resolved to go & see her alone & in conversation upon other matters to discover whether indeed I had loved so utterly in vain. How distinctly is it all now before me. As I rode along masses of clouds swept over the sky, not an unbroken pall, but heavy detached portions between whose black forms the intervals of blue sky were seen. These masses were propelled rapidly along, now obscuring the moon & causing that ominous threatening appearance with which all are familiar & then leaving it for a moment bright & beautiful as though no darkness had never interrupted its rays.

As I reached the Tuckahoe gate, a cloud which had been many minutes making its transit suddenly passed off and as I looked up the moon seemed to smile so sweetly upon me that I felt as though it were an omen, an encouragement.

I had worshipped the moon in her far off home with a passionate worship from my early childhood, and in that hour of anxiety & despair she seemed to acknowledge my devotion, to beam out a look of approbation, a promise of success. With a lighter heart I approached the house and soon sat by her side. Hours had passed when I mounted my horse again, and with a heart still lighter I looked up to the silver orb in grateful acknowledgment of the smile which I felt had not been a delusive one. I had not spoken of love, had not learned from her that I might hope, but I had learned that my fears of another were groundless, and so I passed along the familiar road & laid my head upon a pillow to be visited again by sleep & happy dreams.

Yesterday, the anniversary—if there were mournful thoughts, a sense of des-olation, there were also conflicting hopes to struggle with them. Last night there were clouds in the sky but not moon to shine between them. That day, its pangs, its struggles, its evening, its clouds, its moon, were memories all, and she too alas was a memory. Little did I care for yesterday save it brought up those memories. Little would I have needed its sunshine had the clouds not obstructed it, little would I have cared for its moon had there been one in heaven.

And now it is Sunday night, the clock has struck 11. The day has been a lovely one. A Sabbath day's quiet & brightness have rested upon her nature. I have been very unwell all day and still am so, more unwell than for a long time past. I heard Dr. Hodge this morning in the Sem. chapel—a good sermon as his always are, upon the text "They have Moses & the prophet," &c. While he was at prayer I could not but think how strange the spectacle would seem to any one coming there for the first time into a church who had never heard anything of religion, of God, & how exceedingly solemn we would be compelled to regard were we not so much accustomed and at the same time what a farce it was if there were no God. There stood an intellectual man, with cloud eyes, in the presence of an intellectual audience also standing reverently, while in humble voice he acknowledged the sins which they had all committed, adored the goodness which had spared & so richly blessed them, asked pardon for their transgressions & a continuance of mercies in the name of an incarnate God. And all this addressed to the Creator of the Universe as though he were absolutely present & listening, all proceeding upon the belief & conviction that God was in our midst. If we do believe this, is it not strange that we are so little solemnized? If we do not believe it, is it not equally strange that we are not struck by the ludicrousness of such a farce as uttering solemn words upon the *air*, more of a farce indeed than that of heathen worship addressed to a stone, for *their* God is sensibly present with them? Man in public communion with his maker, an assembly humbly bowing before an invisible but present Divinity. What strange creatures we are that there is nothing so solemn, so impressive, so sublime & fearful that habit does not entirely take away its effect. For years I have heard prayer—thousands & thousands of times before have I stood in the congregation where confessions & petitions were being made to the unseen ruler, but never before do I recollect to have thought, "what is all this?" And even when it occurred to me to think of the real nature of the scene, I was not at all able to *feel* its reality, to realize the sublimity & solemnity of prayer. The mind shrinks away even from the exertion of its powers in an attempt to grasp the thought of God. Immured here in its little shell of sense, in love with the objects around it, it likes not to strive to rise & look beyond its environment. Prone & grovelling in the dust it may mutter mechanically "there is a God," listen to the language of adoration and yield its habitual assent. It runs over the words which represent the attributes of Deity, as does the blinded devotee the beads of his rosary, but it does not strive to grapple with a conception of their meaning. Worship is too often a set of forms & words. Few, very few of those who ostensibly unite in it, have the first idea of its real import.

Have been asleep most of the afternoon. Took a walk with D. Baker since tea. Found E. Wall in my room on my return and have spent the evening in conversation with him. My memory has taken up the thread of last year's events, where it dropped them last night and traced it on through another anniversary. I wrote that 12 mos. ago last night, I had gone home from Tuckahoe not jealous & hopeful. The next morning I arose with the intention of going out & making an avowal of my love, for I knew that *she* would leave in the afternoon to be absent in the country for some days. I was disappointed in my expectation of seeing her for she came to town with Mrs. Crump to Church and I wrote a note telling her what I had intended to say and asking her to leave for me when she left either the note which I sent, in case she meant to answer unfavorably, or, if she would allow me to speak to her upon the subject when she returned, to leave a flower. In the afternoon I rode out with Mr. Keeling.[18] She was gone but had left for me a piece of Arbor Vitae. What a thrill of joy it sent to my heart. It was the beginning of a happiness which none but those who have loved and been loved can appreciate. How all nature seemed bright & happy. How I felt in love with all the world. I have that arbor vitae now. *It* has not mouldered yet. Frail flowers, emblems of what is most fleeting, most ephemeral, have continued to exist, but her hand which plucked them, her heart which blessed them, her love of which they were the first acknowledgment, where are they? No voice may come from the grave at Greenwood,[19] but there is an answer in the silence. Flowers are growing above her now, flowers planted by the hand of bereaved love, watered by the hand of imperishable affection, and can it be that I think and write this unmoved that I have lived to see her dead, to know that the heart is stilled which beat so fondly for me, & am cheerful & happy? But do I forget? When I do may my right hand forget its cunning. And her sister, she who has mourned like Rachel & refused to be comforted,[20] would that I might know tonight how she is. A new grave may have been opened with Spring, opening buds beside that other sacred mound, or in the grave yard in Holly Springs. How little idea I am able to form now of what awaits me in the next intelligence from home. If her disease has taken a favourable turn she may now be nearly well, or at this hour Tuckahoe may again be a scene of anxious watching, a conflict ground of hope & despair, or perhaps once more the home of death.

Monday, May 1, 1848

The day has been chilly and gloomy and very, very unlike what May days generally are in my Southern home, though very similar to the last one there. I have not heard of any May coronations and don't know whether such things are the fashion here, but I should certainly suppose that nature at least does not favor them. I have been sick all day, not able to study—could not attend recitation this morning. Was much disappointed in not hearing from home today. I feel very anxious to receive tidings from Mrs. Crump. A solitary walk this afternoon. Found D. Baker in my room on my return and have talked with him about personal adventures, instances of courage, fisticuffs, shootings, duels, novels & novel reading until 11 o'clock. And now it is nearly 12. I have a violent headache and bad cold and will try to sleep them off. This is the anniversary of one of the happiest days in my whole life, rendered happy by the thought that *she* loved me. It was a cold rainy day. Mrs. Crump spent the day with Ma and Litchfield[21] was with me most of the day in the office. Mrs. C. came out then and sat with us a while in the morning & I had several conversations with her during the day about Lucy. She was reading *Proverbial Philosophy*[22] too & marked many passages in "Beauty." I arranged with Litchfield to go out the next day to the consecration of St. Andrew's Church at Greenwood.

Tuesday, May 2, 1848

It is nearly midnight. The day has been rainy and very disagreeable. I have done no studying at all. Received a letter from my Mother relieving my anxiety about Mrs. Crump in some degree—for the present that is but not affording much ground of hope for the future, but she is going to travel and I trust a change of scene may do her a great deal of good. I am anxious to go home.

Ma's letter made me feel very sad. I have answered it this afternoon & to night written two sheets. Had a letter from Miss Racillia[23] also, the least interesting one I ever received from her. She wrote when she did not feel like it evidently because she knew she had neglected mine too long. What a vast amount of time is wasted (for it is a waste so to write) in writing letters as a rash. When they spring from the heart and the writer feels in the mood, I think it is profitable employment to write.

A walk to Queenstown[24] with D.B. this afternoon. Have felt better than I did yesterday, though my cold is very bad tonight. Hope I shall be able to study tomorrow. Have done nothing for a whole week now. The mind is too clearly linked with the physical organization not to sympathize with its ailings.

Wednesday, May 3, 1848

Too unwell to do anything at all.

Thursday, May 4, 1848

Still very unwell. Finished reading *Wuthering Heights*[25] which I commenced in bed last night. It is the first novel I have read since I have been here. I don't know that I am much pleased with it. It is interesting enough and altogether unique, but too unnatural even for a novel. One of Mrs. Dean's sentiments—a homely housewifery one—is a good piece of practical wisdom—"you shouldn't lie till ten. There's the very prime of the morning gone before that time. A person who has not done one half his day's work by ten o'clock runs a chance of leaving the other half undone." I'll try to remember this. There are some good descriptions in the book & the unity of most of the characters is tolerably well sustained. Heathcliff like Lara, or rather Conrad I believe, is a name "linked with one virtue & a thousand crimes."[26]

Did not attend recitation today. Took a long ride on horseback this afternoon alone, the second since leaving home. It was a delightful afternoon, and I never saw a more beautiful country than this is just now with the orchards in full bloom, the clover lots so fresh and green, the fields newly plowed, and the comfortable dwellings embossomed in roses & shrubbery, just clothed with leaves & the forest trees hung with their long fringes. The air was filled with fragrance. Mr. Voorhees says, "Nature's thank offering for yesterday's rain" and the music of "bees & breeze." The birds flitted busily about, singing the while, and all was so peaceful and at the same time so full of Spring's reviving influence that my ride could not have been more pleasant. It recalled old times to be again on horseback & restored a somewhat unaccustomed life & rigor to feelings. Recalled old times. Yes, I thought of one year ago. There at the same hour I heard Dr. Hawkes preach in the Episcopal Church in H.S. and *she* was there. I had not yet had an opportunity of *speaking* to her since my note of the Friday before, and I longed for the night to come for I was to see her then alone at Tuckahoe and my heart beat rapturously when I thought of hearing from her own lips the sweet confession which her sprig of arbor vitae gave me cause to hope for, and I did see her and I did hear that confession. No, not *hear* it either, though I repeated in words what before I had written—but no, the veil rests upon that interview. We alone knew its history and now that she sleeps where even its memory enters not, in my own heart it will remain written, till the same "effacing fingers" sweep over the lines, and *only* then. They were hours vouchsafed but once to the mortal pilgrim. No shadows of coming events penetrated to that sofa, the cloud was not on the horizon then. Her ring was placed upon my finger that night. I look at it now, on that finger still, and think of that time when it first encircled it, a pledge of her love, and also of that coming time when it shall still encircle it while the flesh is mouldering away in my last narrow home, still too a pledge of her love whose cherished memory will have lived in my heart till its last pulsation. That time may be near or distant, but through whatever scenes I may pass in reaching it, this ring will still be where now it is to mingle thoughts of that 4th of May 1847 with them all. I will wear it so long as I live and if my dying hour be one in which requests may be made, I would with some of my last accents ask that it shall not be removed. It never has been removed since *she* put it on and I know no more earnest desire than this, that it never shall be.

I have written to Mrs. Crump today a short letter. I am hoping to receive at least a few lines from her every day. Saw Miss Hunt since tea & spent an hour at Mr. Green's.

Rec'd a letter from W. Baker written at Pittsburg.

Friday, May 5, 1848

Much better today, have studied an hour or two & read part of [. . .] on Constitutions. Was startled by the novelty (to me) of his arguments & their apparent force, though I could not concur in his sentiments. Must read it again more carefully. Walk with D. this afternoon. At Whig Hall tonight & a walk with Ash Green since returning. It has been a fine day. Spring is fully come & affords already an indication of summer. A strip of a moon tonight—I am glad of that. No letters. It is nearly midnight and I will read myself to sleep hoping to awake entirely restored. My cold is already gone. I have fallen a long way behind the class and I need all the industry which health can give to overtake them.

Saturday, May 6, 1848

Spent most of the day in study. Letter from Bunch[27] which I answered immediately. Walk with D. Spent the evening at Mr. Green's in pleasant conversation with Miss Anna. A storm brought me home in a hurry at 10 o'clock to put down my windows and [an] hour or two more of study & bed closes the day.

Sunday, May 7, 1848

Got up late. Heard Dr. Coleman preach in the college chapel on conscience. Spent the afternoon in reading the [. . .] loaned me by Miss Green—not much pleased with it thus far. E. Wall has been in my room till now (10 o'clock) since tea. We have talked of man, the strange contradictions of his nature—of love, its character & basis—of missionaries, &c., &c. I have been much interested. Am pleased to learn that he has made a most satisfactory arrangement for teaching some young ladies. He is worthy of all that favor & fortune can confer upon him. I have thought frequently tonight of the night 12 months ago. I was at a straw berry party at "the Lodge"[28] with *her*. It seems so lately it is hard to believe that it has been a year since, & *such* a year too. A letter from home this morning, from my Father and Mother.[29] My Father's portion of it wounded my feelings very much and I felt much tempted to reply to it at once in a manner which I would have regretted. It may cause me to go home very soon. And now another sabbath is gone. Another added I fear to this long list of those which I have misspent, misimproved.

Monday, May 8, 1848

Slept late again, studied till 10 o'clock but could not prepare for recitation. Went over to hear the others recite. All except Voorhees *"passed"*. Wrote to Pa this afternoon. May regret hereafter the tone of the letter. Took tea with Misses Briarley in company with Mr. Stebbins, Mr. Baker & Miss Hunt. Walked home with Miss H., shall also probably regret the relation which begins to subsist between us. We are so prone to allow the feeling or impulse of the moment to move us to conduct which the sober second thought condemns that we ought assuredly to be very jealous in observance of the motives by which we submit to be governed. My experience is studded with mementos of this truth & yet how little do I profit by the recollections which retrospects force upon me. The pleadings or reasonings (if that word may be applied so) of passion & impulses are so specious & so deceptive that it is hard to resist them even when we know that they are opposed by judgment & principle & conscience. My intercourse with ladies has been full of illustrations of this—but no more of it now.

Went with D.B. to Whig Hall tonight. We repaired afterwards with Ash Green to No. 22 W. College (Wall's room), where we had an uproarious encounter of wits. Adjourned at ½ past 10 to my room where E.W. & Green on one side of the room with D. for a listener & T.W. & myself on the other side have carried on earnest & interesting conversation till a few minutes since. Now they are all gone. The clock has struck 12 & I close this, the simple record of another of the days of the sons of men so far as it appertains to myself. The evening has been one of the most pleasant I have spent in Princeton, and yet there are compunctuous murmurings of the inward monitor in reference of some of the circumstances which have constituted its pleasure. Have written to Pa that I will start home immediately upon the receipt of a promised remittance. I may regret the resolution, but I must think it formed after due deliberation & full survey of all sides of the subject. I dreamed that I was at home last night, but I have not been impelled to this resolution by a desire to return for really I would rather stay now till the end of the session, but I think it *best to go.*

Tuesday, May 9, 1848

Wakened by Miss Briarley at 8 o'clock. Wrote to Mr. Anderson this morning. Read *To Seem & To Be*[30] this afternoon because Miss Green recommended it to me. It is a trite tale in all its features and not very consistently or naturally told, but it is intended to convey a good moral lesson & perhaps well calculated to do so to female readers for whose benefit it was probably written. The author, a lady, writes like a lady & therefore her own sex can appreciate her. She does not know how to draw *men*, that is evident, nor women either unless my observation of them has much deceived me. A new idea occurred to me on laying down the book as the modus operendi of novel making. It was new to me I mean, and throws much light upon a question which I have been struggling with. It is that novelists in their compositions give themselves up to day dreams or air castles & while in the realizing of them in their heroes & heroines they afford much personal gratification they are also furnished with that *material* which I could never imagine before now they acquired. Under this idea I sat down to indulge a day dream myself by way of experiment. I started my hero upon his path with all the concomitants by which I could wish myself to be surrounded, & I found that as he went on in that path, pursuing the ends which it seemed to me that the character with which I had invested him & the externals which I had gathered about him, would readily suggest as objects of attainments, then a very small exertion of the abstract realizing faculty soon created the minor events, difficulties, adventures, efforts, failures, success, sorrow, joy, personae dramatis, &c. Here is a new clue for me in the labyrinth of romance & one so palpable that I can but wonder it never occurred to me before. This day dreaming or castle building has been one of my besetting temptations & I can now remember many lonely hours beguiled & many long miles cheated of their meanings by indulgence in it. I have often wondered too at the possibility of a rational, practical man giving to such airy nothings for the time being so much of reality, of life, of local habitation.

D.B. has been with me for an hour or two and we have talked of this & several other subjects, among them—great men and slavery. The first in reference to the kind of feelings they experience in seeing their names and as familiar words throughout a whole country, in knowing that they are a part of *history*, and we concluded that they have risen to that position so gradually, have become so much accustomed to it that it scarcely excites a feeling or a thought other than such as we ourselves are wont to bestow upon our own circumstances, circumstances perhaps in which there are others below us in the social scale, who look up to [us] admiringly, wondering what thoughts & feelings they excite in our bosoms. The other subject—slavery—was introduced in connexion with his contemplated agency in N. England & was considered with reference to the manner in which he should encounter the erroneous opinions & prejudices which he will find to exist. He concludes to waive all *argument* upon the subject but to give any *information* in his power, and that as correct a picture as can be drawn of the slave population of the South is one mingling just as the entire population does—all the gradations & phases of existence from the one extreme of kindness, indulgence, care & solicitude on the part of the master & comfort & contentment & affection on that of the slaves, to that other & far more rare extreme of cruelty, brutality, suffering, fear & utter degradation & wretchedness. We think that almost all slaveholders look upon the institution as an evil, a curse to the country & would gladly blot it out could any feasible plan be devised, but in complete destitution of any such plan think that the evil is a necessary one & should be made as tolerable as possible. We think too that the fanatics who are so eloquent in attributing to the slaves the susceptibility to suffering, the feelings & the dignity of humanity ought also to remember that they possess the passions, the weaknesses, & the depravity of humanity & so while on the one hand they are so ready to inveigh against the unfeelingness, the sin of disregarding and trampling upon the former, they might also be prepared to discern & acknowledge the justice & propriety & necessity of restraining & guarding against & punishing the latter. We think that education in a slave county is essential to correct understanding of its condition & our experience is that the most fanatical on both sides are the most ignorant. The best masters as a general rule are those who have been *born* slave holders & the worst those who have acquired such property by their own hard toil or (as is often the case) those who have been born & reared in N. England & removing to the South by marriage or otherwise have become masters. The day has been unpleasantly cool, but bright. The moon half full smiles sweetly. The clock strikes 12 & I'll to bed. Another day is gone. One more step towards the goal. With what strange alacrity & thoughtlessness men run such a race—to win—a grave.

Saturday, June 3, 1848

A long interval this in my journalizing, and I resume it tonight some 2000 miles from the old room in which I wrote last, and now for a short sketch of the why & the how & the where. The 10, 11, 12 May were spent, as well as I now remember, about as usual, and I did not make any record concerning them probably because company or some other kind of engagement engrossed my time. On Friday evening I visited Miss Hunt (went home with her from Briarley's), met T. Wall there &c. On Saturday 13th I received a letter from home containing a proposition from Mr. Mason[31] of a partnership if I would go home at once, which I determined to accept & so went immediately to N.Y. to make arrangements (get money). Stopped at Lovejoy's Sunday, went to Brooklyn, attended church with my Aunt & Cousin, heard a good sermon— dined with them—returned to the city in the afternoon. Heard Dr. Cheever[32] preach in the Church of the Pilgrims—was much disappointed in him. Went back there after tea to hear Mr. King of Dublin—so crowded only remained a short time. Went then to the Tabernacle where the anniversary meeting of the Domestic Missionary Society was being held. Listened to the latter part of a capital address upon the West as a field for Miss. labor. On Monday saw Mr. Fleetwood & Mr. Jeffrey & returned at night to Princeton, packed my trunk partially, saw Miss Hunt to say goodbye & went to bed at 3 o'c. On Tuesday, fixed up all my matters, dined with Mr. Green, visited Mrs. Field, called on Mr. Field & had a long talk with him in which he spoke most flatteringly of the impression I had made upon him. Bid my kind landladies adieu, took a lingering look at the old room in which I had spent so many pleasant & so many gloomy hours & took my seat in the hack with E. Wall & D. Baker who were going with me to the depot & Ash Green who was going to Phila. It rained as we went down. I parted with my kind friends & turned my back, doubtless forever, upon Princeton & reached U.S. Hotel in Phila at 10 o'c thoroughly drenched in a tremendous rain.

On Wednesday 17th walked thro the city with Ash all the morning & dispatched a letter to Miss Racillia. Ash dined with me. We drank a bottle of Sherry & adjourned after 2 hours sitting to a stable where we procured horse & buggy & took a delightful ride of 12 or 14 miles out the ridge road past Laurel Hill & up a small stream through some of the most romantic & lovely scenery I ever looked upon. We talked long & confidentially & I shall remember the ride. Went to Walnut St. Theatre. Saw Collins in Irish Atty[33] &c. & at 12 o'clock Ash bade me farewell in the cars in Market St. where 3 weeks before I had seen William B. off, and I was whisked away to find myself at breakfast time in Harrisburgh. Thence through a pretty country we steamed & rattled to Chambersburg where at 4 o'c we were seated (9 of us) in the stage & bound for Pittsburg. The passengers were a Dr. ———, a Mr. Lanier, two young ladies named King & the rest some quiet nameless ones whose presence we soon forgot. The Dr. & Mr. L. were sociable & rather pleasant & intelligent gentleman. The ladies were placed in the stage by their mother who said, "gentlemen these ladies have no protector," which we all rec'd as an appeal to our gallantry. The Dr. however as a kind of acquaintance took them specially under his charge. The elder one, Miss Mary, was an invalid, not very pretty, probably about 23 years old, well read in poetry & novels & of quiet, lady like manners, good conversational powers. The younger Miss Emma was very pretty, about 20 or 21, not very romantic or well versed in poetry & sentiments, but sociable, accessible & attractive. She was my vis a vis & I doubt not she will remember me as long as she lives, as I shall her. The moon was full, the night was clear & the mountain scenery green & beautiful beyond description. The passengers all slept except the ladies & myself. We did not close our [. . .] but revelled to intoxication almost in the exceeding loveliness of the scene. I have passed few nights more pleasantly. Friday we rattled along all day over the turnpike, the ladies & I keeping each other awake. Once I got out to get some flowers & the stage left me to trudge 4 miles after it under a hot sun. I had got Tennyson from my trunk & we read *Locksley Hall*[34] &c & talked poetry all day. Night came on again as beautiful as before (after a slight thunder storm had cleared away) & still we three with the exceptions of a few short naps talked & gazed & drank in the beauty of heaven & air & earth. That night, Miss Emma, you will scarcely forget.

Shortly after daylight on Saturday we were in Pittsburgh & I parted with my fair friends at the Monongahela House, they to go to the house of an Uncle a few miles in the country, I to get my breakfast & go to the boat. Our party was dissolved & I was alone again. I like stage travelling under such circumstances;

indeed, I prefer it much so far as pleasure & comfort is concerned to the Railroad. I was exceedingly fortunate in having Mrs. & Miss Kennedy's company across these mountains before & not less so in that of the Misses King this time. At 11 o'c on board the Messenger I was on my way to Steubenville. Now that the excitement was passed I was asleep the moment that I sat down & only kept awake by keeping on my feet. At four o'clock I was left at Steubenville. The scenery on the Ohio between this point & Pittsburgh is fully equal to any on this most beautiful of rivers. I met my sister at Col. Collier's & found her *looking better* in every respect than when I was here last, though she is really not so well. I took tea with her then, then went to Paul Collier's, and afterwards left her at the Seminary and sought my pillow at 10 o'c to sleep soundly till 9 the next morning.

Friday, June 16, 1848

Another interval of two weeks. I have been so busy since my return as to be unable to resume the thread of my journey home from Princeton. On Sunday morning the 21st May I woke late from the sound sleep of the night before and breakfasted at 9 o'clock, then went to the Seminary and accompanied Bunch to church. Heard an excellent sermon from Mr. Bruel. He treats his subject in a striking & original manner, is much beloved by his congregation. Heard him again with renewed pleasure in the afternoon. Took tea with Paul Collier. Monday morning spent with Carry.[35] Dined at Col. Collier's. Went to see Martha Wright and walked with her to the Seminary. I like her very much. She is an intelligent, sociable girl & exceedingly ladylike & easy in her manners & pretty when in good health. Hope she will come home with Carry.

Left Steubenville on the Monongahela at 4 o'clock. Found Mr. Ballantine on board, a gentleman from the Seminary at Princeton with whom I had formed a slight acquaintance while there. He was on his way to Arkansas on a missionary to the Creek Indians. I had his company all the way to Memphis & while I was much amused at the effect upon him of travelling & seeing for the first time the "Great West" and making his entree as it were into the world, all of which plainly betrayed the seclusion of his former life. I was also much interested and instructed by his conversation. He seems to me a man of deep & sincere piety, devoted to his profession & anxious to be useful. He is a man of good strong mind, considerably disciplined by sterner studies, but not much polished or refined by literature or general reading and intercourse with society. I was very fortunate in having him for a travelling companion and he professed himself much indebted to my company for a pleasant journey down the River.

Sunday, June 25, 1848

Really I fear the multiplicity of my engagements will prevent me from ever getting these memoranda up again. I find there is a great difference between life here and at Princeton as regards system and uniformity and the call or demands upon one's time and attention. I will hurry on down the Ohio with a general remark as to its beauty and the pleasure of traveling on it. We reached Cin on Wednesday morning 24th May (just a month since). I dined with Mrs. J. C. Wright, and spent the day most pleasantly. I am particularly pleased with Miss [. . .] and [. . .] Wright's wife, though I like them all very much indeed. My visit to them in November last was a delightful one. At six o'clock in the evening still in company with Mr. Ballantine I left Cin on the Western World and we obtained a very fine view of Cin as we moved slowly down the River by standing on the hurricane deck. We kept our position on this deck watching the beautiful river banks till we passed North Bend and darkness gathered around us. We had a distinct view of the home and grave of Harrison.[36] The house is a plain white framed one, two stories high, in the midst of a clump of trees. There is no trace of the log cabin & cider barrel. The grave is on the summit of a considerable mound with shade trees planted over it.

Our boat was new, not at all crowded, with excellent accomodations of all sorts and gentlemanly officers, and our trip to Memphis was entirely pleasant. Except that the weather was not. I spent the time chiefly in novel reading—the only remedy I have been able to discover as yet for the ennui of long days of confinement in a steamboat without female acquaintances or intimate friends. Mr. B. & I spent the cool of the mornings & evenings on the guards supper deck and had many long and interesting conversations.

One night when I had been up till after midnight reading, I went out on the guards and witnessed one of the most beautiful sights that I ever saw. I have loved & watched the moon so many years and under so many circumstances that I thought I knew all that it could do in the way of beautifying, and was familiar with all its effects upon tree & stream & house & flowers & field, but I was mistaken. At the time of which I write, it was not far above the horizon & about half waned. Its position from the boat was exactly in the line of the waves, as in long swells they rolled off from the foaming track we left behind us, the rays falling directly upon these swells at an angle of less than 45 degrees. As they rose & sank breaking into foam at their highest elevation, they had the appearance of a long undulating sheet of silver stretching to the shore with dark shadows every moment thrown upon & removed from different portions of the surface. When the wave parted dazzlingly from it as though it were a brilliancy wrapped in the folds of the water & only disclosed when those folds were for the moment thrown open along the tops of the graceful undulations. I watched in perfect ecstasy until a bend of the River changed our relative position to the moon & the effect was gone.

On the next night I stayed up again on purpose to see it & was not disappointed. It is more than pleasant on a summer night to be out on the deck of a boat alone. The passengers are all asleep. No sound is heard but the regular deep-drawn respirations of the engine, and as the boat glides along now into the ghostly shadows of the trees along the shore, as they stretch far into the current & now along the narrow strip of dark mysterious-looking water which divides their shadows on either side, you feel as though you were surrounded by a kind of supernatural influence. Imagination invests the boat with almost an infernal spirituality & makes you look tremblingly towards the pilot & shrink from approaching him as you see him there defined in exaggerated outline, looking steadily before him into the gloom and guiding the movements of the strange creature which is bearing you along. His gaze seems to penetrate so far into that gloom & is so fixed that you fancy that he is looking at something beyond the realities of this world which that gloom conceals from you and you would scarcely be startled should some unearthly shape come & take its place suddenly by his side or should all those shadows give signs of ghostly life and the gloom before you gradually open into the reality of the spirit world. I know not if others have felt this, but many, many midnight hours have I spent standing or sitting or walking alone on the hurricane deck and these are feelings which those hours have always inspired. There is another thing which I love—it is to watch the stars, shining in the river depths with their light, from out those depths looking as though it were a long bright path stretching down to it, such a path as if it led upwards we might expect angels to travel on when they visit Earth. I believe that I derive as much pleasure from such communings with nature in her quietness & repose & my solitude as from any other source, far more than it ever afforded me to mingle with men, to look upon the artificial world.[37]

On Sunday 28th May at 1 o'clock we reached Memphis & I bade Mr. Ballentine goodbye & stood once more on that old familiar bluff, entered once more the well known Commercial Hotel, saw familiar faces about me & felt that I was drawing near my home. I spent Monday in Memphis. Saw many acquaintances among them Mrs. Craft & Mrs. Wall. On Tuesday took my seat on the driver's box of the stage and after a long hot day's ride was welcomed to the home of which I had been thinking so long. It may be weak & childish, the feeling of homesickness, but nevertheless I acknowledge that I have ever been subject to it. I found all well & everything looking natural, notwithstanding many changes. My room looks less like it did before than any other part of the establishment. My Mother has improved it wonderfully & made it much more comfortable. The town looked old & drearyed & scattered & uncomfortable after coming from the north but this appearance soon wears away. Mrs. Crump had seen me pass Mrs. Lucas's where she had spent the day & came up very soon to see me. She looked better than I had expected to see her though very feeble. Went out to see her the next day & dined with her. It is useless to write of the emotions with which I again approached Tuckahoe, again stood in that house, or of the nature of my first interview with Mrs. C. among those scenes. I had thought many, many times during my absence what they would be.

Saw William Baker next night. He had been absent in the country all day. He has preached here several times & the people are pleased with him. Spent the remainder of the week until Saturday in seeing & talking with acquaintances & friends and getting settled down again. On Thursday morning Maria Shoemaker[38] was married & set off to the North. Would that I could baptize in Lethe's streams one circumstance in which she is concerned. Was at Tuckahoe every day. On Saturday borrowed Carloss from Mrs. Crump & went to Greenwood & stood by *her* grave & saw the flowers & grass & trees growing upon and around it. Would that I might visit it frequently. Went into Mr. Mason's office on Monday and have been there every day since. Formed a partnership with him on 12th June and thus far almost every day has been full of work and I look forward to only a monotonous routine of office duties during the day & lonely, sad evenings. I have not read much as yet, hope to get my license in a few weeks. A week ago on 19th June Mrs. Crump started to the north in company with Mr. Mason. We have not heard from her since she left Memphis & now this record is brought up to this warm, bright Sunday afternoon & I lay it aside.

Monday, June 26, 1848
Very warm this morning & a very hard rain this afternoon. Have been in the office all day but have not done much. Spent a half an hour at Mr. Baker's tonight. Received a letter from Miss Racillia, a very interesting one. I think she is perhaps the best letter writer I ever knew. Received a note from Mrs. Crump today with her daguerreotype. How much I do hope from the effect of this trip upon her health. Considering her peculiar temperament and the tenderness, almost idolatry, of her love for Lucy, it can scarcely be wondered at that the bereavement should have crushed her as it has done when she has been constantly in the midst of associations which brought the subject ever to her thoughts. Since I have returned I find that every single object, the stores,

the streets, the people, are connected with thoughts of *her*. When I walk along the pavement, I think that I walked there once with her. When I go into the store or the Church, the party room or the dwelling houses where she visited, I think of having seen her there. Here I meet the girls with whom she associated, then the gentlemen whom I met in her company, here the Drs who attended her & then the friends who missed her in her illness. Her image is ever rising up before just as I saw her at this or that place, in this or that company & ever rushing down upon that bed of death & changing with that shrouded form & thus it has been every day & every hour with Mrs. Crump, and it is under this ever-present source of her bereavement that she has been prostrated.

It seems to me that I have never yet fully realized my loss, never realized the truth of all that had been. I cannot get rid of the dreamy feeling which seems to have wound itself about my whole being and yet I think & dream of her as dead. My own nature is a mystery to me. I sometimes think that it is the most false, shallow, superficial nature that I have ever known. Such, at least as to its superficial shallowness, is the character of my intellect & it is but reasonable to suppose that my heart is the same. *My heart!* if I have one, it is a hard rock of selfishness encrusted by a thin mould of sentimental sensibility in which mushroom feelings spring up & perish in a day, in which noble true emotion cannot find nourishment for its deep roots because as they strike downwards to take hold upon the strength which lies in the under soil of a genuine heart, instead of that strength they strike upon that strong self within & wither at once away. My worst enemy could not have a meaner opinion of me than I verily believe that I entertain of myself. Self study & self analysis constantly increase my humiliation until loathing, utter contempt, are the only words to express what I feel for everything which I find to be part of my nature. Before grave study & manly exertion, my mind shrinks away in imbecility and I sit or walk about listlessly from hour to hour unable to grapple with a law book. When there is demand for the mechanical motion of my fingers with my pen, I can work as industriously as any other machine, but when I would read anything else than a novel or a wishy washy poem all my faculties cower & shrink into the little corners of my vacant mind.

God knows if annihilation or a future other than that terrible slumber in which dreams may come were before me I would leap joyfully to the embrace of Death. I would sometimes be wretched, oh so wretched, if there were materials enough in my miserable composition, my poor gewgaw of a heart, to constitute wretchedness, if there were earnestness & depth & intensity & strength enough in my inner organization to grasp & contain & realize a sense of what I really am, but I feel a moment and then chatter and laugh an idiot glee &

stumble & roll & chatter & laugh again & hate myself & know that I am a fool & straight away forget it all & for an hour dream another child's dream. Pshaw! My Lucy escaped perhaps a wretched fate, but had she lived might I not have been different?

I have entered upon a profession, a man's profession, a baby at work with carpenter's tools! But I know full well what I can attain in it & shall not be disappointed. I am gratified to be a tolerably good clerk & may, should I live, manage to do Mr. Mason's writing & his dictation for a year or two & then my health will probably have given way, or he become tired of me & I shall die or harry to somebody's concern, my Father's office again perhaps, a kind of daily bread loafer. Such thoughts as these & such anticipations are not the creations of an excited or despondent hour, but they are such as hang ever about my present & upon my future. And the past, the bitter, bitter past, is also mingling every hour with them, and yet I seem happy & cheerful & hopeful. What a liar the *seeming* is. I have never I believe written this before, perhaps never will again, but I have for the once endeavored to make the page a true transcript of my feelings as I write & in all truth & sincerity have written what I have felt. I believe that I know myself thoroughly & entirely. I know well what faculties I possess, how I can most please & how most successfully deceive those around me. I know too then those in whose partial judgments I am capable of much, but I feel that I act the hypocrite when I encourage such opinions. I believe I can talk tolerably good *nonsense*, write a passably readable flimsy letter & beyond that, am fit for nothing but a machine.

I have just read a letter to William Baker from E. Wall. *He* is a noble specimen of humanity, one of those jewels in this drossy mine of mortality which are not often found. I had intended in taking leave of Princeton to make something of a sketch of those with whom I had associated then, write some general remarks of the sojourn which I had made among them & I will try to do it yet when I get the time to spare. Now it is late & I have consumed much more than my daily allowance of pages in my egotism & when I have written a few lines to Mrs. Crump will go to sleep, the thing which I can do better than any other I have ever tried yet.

Tuesday, June 27, 1848

I have only time to write tonight that the night has come and after a busy day I am not sorry to see it. Another thunder storm this afternoon & muddy streets. William Baker is back and I have been down to see him. Nothing in the day's history worth recording. Time's stream flows on with a most smooth & even current for most of our downward journey and each day is like the last, and also the type of the next. Were the individual history of the race [written] twould be a most tame and monotonous recital. We live on unconsciously from month to month & then we all die, passing from childhood to youth, from youth to hoary age, scarcely observing the steps of the transition.

Wednesday, June 28, 1848

It is very strange that I feel dull & restless & unfit for anything during the early part of the day, and at night feel industrious & energetic & am entirely unable to go to sleep till I have lain in bed an hour or two. I have tried hard to reverse the order but unsuccessfully. One consequence of it is that I put Pa out of patience every morning by sleeping late, but really when I can't get to sleep till midnight, I can't get up early. I wonder if I am not all awry, all perverted, any how. It seems so often. We have had another hard rain, with thunder &c. today. I have been out to tea with Mrs. Crump & returned at 10 o'c being very forcibly reminded as I came slowly along the muddy road & looked at the reflections of the stars in the puddles of water of many similar rides on similar nights last year, but what is that does not remind me of last year. The 12th July will soon come—*that* anniversary. Have finished a letter to Mrs. Crump tonight to be directed to her at Phila. Nothing uncommon to record as distinguishing the day. It has gone to mingle with the mass to be lost, a drop in the ocean of the past. I do not know that it has been for me a single step towards anything but my last day. How near may be that!

Sunday, July 2, 1848

No opportunity of scribbling in this book since Wednesday. For two nights past I have been at the Lodge [. . .]. Thursday, Friday & Saturday however were but as other days, the usual mixture of indolence & labor, of sadness & frivolity, of hope & despondency. Last evening I was with Kate Freeman a few moments for the first time since her marriage. She seems little changed and the old parlor in which I have sat so often in happy times gone by retains most of its familiar features. Kate evidently thought much of the past while she talked with me, and I could but notice a certain affectation in her gaiety. Miss Jarratt was there a few moments while I was. I was invited to spend yesterday at William Lumpkin's with a party of young people, but I have no taste whatever for society now. It does not seem to me that there is remaining a single vestige of my old inclination to be with ladies. Conversation with them is exceedingly irksome. My great pleasure, if pleasure it may be called, is in being alone. To ride or walk, to be at Tuckahoe or in my own room. I scarcely feel a prompting of desire towards anything else. It seems as though the predominant & most constant feeling which I experience is one of unrest, of discontent, of vague—not desire, not hope or wish—but sort of undefined notion of change. While at Princeton I wanted to be at home and thought I could be happy here, but now that I have come a sense of disappointment, of disatisfaction, has come over me & I would be willing to be back there again, or almost anywhere else. If I might lie & doze & dream and muse away my life with no one to interest me, no care for the future, no necessity for exertion, I could be more satisfied, it seems to me, than in any other condition, but I have no energy or ambition, feel no enthusiasm or hope in my profession & as soon as the demand from mechanical labor in the office ceases, I relapse into listless, apathetic inanity. The book which I take up does not rivet my attention; while my eye wanders over the page, my mind roves hither & thither in a childish sort of vacancy. I neither think nor study, nor learn, and I don't believe I ever shall again.

Today has been a most uncomfortable one. My Father was so much displeased this morning by my sleeping late that he told me I could not remain in his house unless I changed my habits & I have gone to Mr. Foot's to board, and so the home of which I thought & wrote and dreamed during my absence & to which I so much longed to return, has already cast me out & must henceforth I suppose be the most wretched place to me of all. My father is a strange man and has strange notions. I honor & respect him, and love him too as much as any son ever did a Father, but there are no points of communion in our characters. He has no sympathy whatever with me, no indulgence for my foibles, no pity for my weaknesses; while on the other hand I do not know how to appreciate his firmness & principles, how to yield to the exactions of his character, or how to assume the callous philosophical common places, practical every day-ishness, which he associates with his ideas of a man. The truth is that my own waywardness & fretfulness & selfishness & discontent would make a hell for me of anyplace on Earth. He has been the kindest & best of Fathers and is the kindest & best of men; I never grieve him without regret or go counter to his wishes without self reproach, but to be what he wished I must revolutionize myself & I have not force of will or character enough to do it. He has taken up the idea that I take pleasure in opposing his opinions and notions & thwarting his wishes, that I care nothing for him and am purposely perverse in whatever concerns him, in all of which he is much mistaken, though I am fully conscious that my conduct gives him good reason for thinking so. It is true that I seldom think as he does; there is not the slightest degree of congeniality in our natures. Our education and associations have been altogether unlike and neither of us can enter into or appreciate the other's tastes & feelings, but nevertheless, the least yielding on my part, a little exertion to please him would have prevented this last breach.

I have often resolved that I would act differently, and have many times taken one step towards change, but somehow I have done it always at the wrong time, or else found him so ready to exact another & still another sacrifice of my habits that I have sunk back again into my old routine. For instance, if I get up early, he insists upon my working or doing something else for exercise, or as a next step is ever telling me about giving up the use of Tobacco. God only knows what it will all result, all the little of good that there is within me arrays itself on his side, but that little is so greatly in the minority that its voice is scarcely heard. I know that I am returning ingratitude & disrespect for long years of love & solicitude & paternal love. I know I am setting a bad example before the other children & grieving my mother who I believe loves me as her own son & who also sympathizes with me & sees how it is that Pa does not comprehend my character, but though I know & confess & in some degree feel all this, the enshrined devil of my inner nature will not brook the humiliation of an acknowledgment of it by a change of conduct & will not yield the control of habits which he has guided into such perversity.

It does not seem to me that I can live long. A nature such as mine, so discordant & at the same time so weak & a body so full of listlessness & restlessness do not appear to have a long lease of life. For some time past I have had a kind of presentiment that a few years at most would close my earthly career and if I am ever to remain what I now am, I do not care how soon the end may come. I am as little prepared to die as man ever was, but every day only renders me less so. I am morally as callous & careless as man could be & it does not seem to me that there is a possibility of my being otherwise. I don't know how great a transformation the Spirit of God can make, but really I do not feel as though there were earnestness & depth enough in my feelings, material enough in my character, to make a true Christian of. Heaven can only foresee. What the future may be is in its hands. I look forward utterly without hope of any kind, that is any hope more than the ignis fatuus one which is ever creating need into the belief that *something* will happen before they die to make them fit for death. I have not made up my mind to be eternally lost, or settled down into the belief that there is no possibility of my conversion. So far from it I know I could not look to such a certainty without the greatest agitation & horror & dread, but I am so utterly cold & careless & apathetic, not only upon this but every other subject, that I see no ground for expectation of change. However this may be a few years at most will decide.

What I intended to write when I introduced the subject was that perhaps when I am gone my Father or some one else who may tell him may look over these lines and in that event I would wish him to know that I have not been unconscious of his kindness & affection to me as of my own ingratitude & disrespect & that I have felt all that I have written here. Then perhaps he may pardon what is past. Verily I do believe that no one ever had a better perception of duty, greater sensibility to affectionate treatment, or more persuasions from the [. . .] small voice to walk in the path pointed out by my better nature, though at the same time I know that no one ever exhibited less of such experiences in his conduct, or gave more reason to those who loved him to mourn over his weakness & irresolution & errors & faults. I feel sometimes like sinking down in shame & humiliation & then I resolve—& then—what? Why only this, that another portion of the downward road I travel, paved with good intentions, is broken.

The day has been a rainy, gloomy one. I have not been to Sunday school or church. I did not go to the former because I felt that my conscience would not allow me to sit down as a teacher before children, when perhaps I should have to inculcate upon them duties which I so little regarded myself. A Sunday School Teacher should be pious & conscientious. I did not go to Church because I did not feel like going out where I would see people. I have spent the day in my room in reading some of *her* notes to me & mine to her, in sleeping & in reading "Festus."[39] Another Sabbath like almost if not all I ever spent, sadly misimproved. It is now 10 o'clock and I will try to read a few chapters in the Bible, a very un[. . .] occupation with me nowadays.

Monday, July 3, 1848

An idle & not a pleasant day to me. Nothing has been done in the office. I have listened to some rattling, nonsensical speeches in the Whig Ratification Convention[40] & wondered that men could make so much froth out of words. Much amused tonight to hear Matt & Mr. F. talk over the reminiscences of their early married life. I doubt not that where love is, the days of courtship and the first year after marriage are the most happy of the whole existence. They seem to shed a lustre on after years even down to old age. I can imagine the worthy parents of many sons & daughters sitting down in a quiet home in a pleasant evening & reviewing that far back period & recalling the freshness & *rapturousness* of early love, and the bliss of those warm, gushing emotions, till their hearts seem almost for the time to grow young again, the bloom of youth & beauty & the strength & activity of dawning manhood to come back to their forms and the light of that joy to be momentarily rekindled in their eyes which beamed through them from their full souls ere they had learned what the cares & sorrows of life are, ere they had been pupils in the stern school of the world's experience. The clock strikes 11 & I will court the presence of "tired nature's sweet restorer."[41]

Thursday, July 6, 1848

On 4th heard a fine speech from Mr. Clapp.[42] Sat up all night with Mrs. Bartow's corpse. On Wednesday was busy in Court House & office except when making up for lost sleep. Went at night to hear a lecture at Female Institute from —— on Philosophy of Language & was much interested. Today been in Court House & office all day. Walk with W.B. this afternoon. Very hard rain since sunset, thunder rolls very heartily now & the eaves still drip. I'm sleepy.

Wednesday, July 12, 1848

Nearly a week since I have written anything—the truth is I have nothing to write, nothing in my daily occupations, nothing in my thoughts (for I do not *think*). The past week has been spent in office work and attendance at the Court House where I have been trying to learn something of the machinery of a chancery court. I do not see much to make me in love with the profession, not much that appeals to the natural enthusiasm of a young man. Viewed abstractly as a science, as a structure gradually built up by the successive labors of many generations of great intellects, the Law commands admiration, and awakens in the mind of the young student something of that feeling of reverence which is excited by the sublimity of a noble and venerable edifice which has stood for ages, proof against the strength of time and unaffected by the mutations which have gone on within and around it. In gazing upon such an edifice the thoughts dwell instinctively upon our imagination of the long years which have followed each other in their slow rotation since its foundations were laid, of the forgotten laborers whose work survives them, of the sunshine and storm, the spring flowers & winter snows, and most of all of the generations of inhabitants who have called its shelter their home, who have one after the other, gathered about its hearth stone, lain down to sleep, and risen up to mingle in the scenes of waking life, who have been born, and reared, been married and shrouded and gone away to give their places to others to follow on in the same routine; of the joy & sorrow, the hopes & disappointment, the avocations & cares of the many who have dwelt beneath its roof, who have long since been borne to their family burying ground & mingled with the dust, while the old rooms which they have garlanded, and hung in mourning, the trees which they have planted, the walks they have trod, and the home which they have loved, yet survive them, venerable in their age, melancholy in their imagined associations and almost awful in their unchanged preservation. How jarring to the feelings of one who stood & looked upon the exterior of such an edifice & yielded to the influence of reflections such as these, it would be to pass the threshold, to penetrate to those rooms which his fancy had been peopling with the [. . .] of gone by days, and invested with the sanctity of memorials of the past, and find them occupied, one for instance by the exhibition of a strolling mountebank, another as the arena of pugilistic feats; one as a dram shop with all its appurtenances of degradation and vice, and another as a gamblers hall, while as he strolled on from door to door he encountered the tokens of humbug & trickery and meanness and intrigue at every step.

Somewhat like this old edifice is the Law and something similar is the effect of penetrating within its walls upon the student who has been wrapt in admiration while he contemplated the majestic exterior & thought of the illustrious dead whose labors reared it, or whose lives have been spent under its roof. Within he finds a blazonry of great names and an ostentatious deference to the memory of the departed who have left behind these monuments of their wisdom, but oh how his thoughts sink down into abject grovelling when he learns that his ideal temple of justice is a mart where learning is sold and impunity for villainy purchased, an exhibition room of human depravity & degradation and a prostitution house where for fees, principles are distorted, precedents seduced, and ingenuity and trickery and humbugery made the pimps of the wealth which passes for success, the house of refuge where rascality is hedged about with technicalities and crime protected by a shield of perverted opinions or quibbles and forms.

The profession doubtless has its philosophy & has had & still has its philosophers, those who love it for itself, who find in laborious investigations of its great principles a compensatory pleasure for lives of toil & study, but such I do not hope to be. I only look to it as I fancy that the majority of those do who curse themselves in its school, as a means of subsistence, a field for money-making. It is the Law alone which we find thus made a mere livelihood. Philosophy sees its great principles and revelations sometimes sustaining the jugglers sleight, and almost every other science contributes its aid to the trickster in conjuring pence from the pockets of the gaping crowd. The only difference is that we do not call the *mountebank* a *philosopher* & therefore he is not respectable, but we do call the pettifogger a lawyer (and also the *pill & potion* renders among us doctors) and therefore he is respectable and therefore too I suppose it is that then so many who are willing (as I just professed myself to be) to become circuit jugglers on the science of Law, who would not think for a moment of turning [. . .]ing "five kings" and sleight of hand practitioners. There's much in a name.

Sunday night last I spent at Tuckahoe, slept in the same room and on the same bedstead (I remembered it) where *she* died. I had not been in the room before since I went to take a last look at her living, a short time before she breathed her last. Today is the anniversary of the one so memorable in the history of last year, when her brothers interfered & prevented our marriage which was to take place on the following morning. How I have thought of it all day. I have recollected how I was buried twelve months since in getting ready to travel. How in the afternoon (& I stood this afternoon at the same spot, at the same hour), I went to procure the license & how my trunk was packed and I waited so anxiously for hers to come & how I went to the stage office to look if hers had not gone there & how when I returned to my room at 10 o'c, I found the servant awaiting me with that astounding note from Tuckahoe. And now at this hour how vividly come up before me the stunningness of that note, my ride out there, my conversation in the grove with Mr. C. and her brother and my anxious pacing to and fro over the wet grass while I waited to hear her final decision, and dear departed one, how vividly too are you before me as you afterwards described to me, overwhelmed by conflicting emotions, agonized by the struggles of antagonist affections. "Oh, misery," said her letter that night. And now when twelve months are gone, and she too my own loving true-hearted Lucy is also gone, I am here to think of & remember all that she suffered for me. Yes, "Oh misery that night." This was the expression which the recollection of it wrung from her & how I may echo it now. It was a damp & cloudy night, as tonight is damp, but there was no moon in the heavens as now.

I sent her word to take time to reflect & to write to me at Memphis, and at 10 o'clock came home to start next morning with Litchfield, but I will not anticipate the retrospect. A few hours ago I might have said, one year since I was happy as hope just about to be realized could make me. Now I may say that one year since I was wretched as bitterest disappointment could render me. And she, none but her self ever knew what at that time she endured. God knows whither that hour was not the beginning of her end. Whether those who professed to love her were not then forcing upon her the first bitter draught (no not the first) of the cup whose poison terminated her existence. Day of sad associations your sands are nearly run, and with you may go for the time the memories you have awakened. One other anniversary remains—yes, two— the *other* wedding day, and then the last fatal one which made her the bride of death.

I saw Jane Thomas on Saturday last for the first time since my return & had a long confidential conversation with her. It may be wrong in me to desire to retain her friendship and to keep up our intercourse after the treatment of her relative to me, but Lucy loved her, and she is so linked with Tuckahoe that I cannot give her up. She was there on *that* night & Lucy wrote how she missed her when she went away, and besides I have a most sincere regard for her. She has many faults, glaring ones too, yet I prize her friendship highly & cannot bring myself to forego it. I have always enjoyed her society. She is so different from other young ladies (too much so in many things I think) & so altogether unique that she must interest, but she is heartless & selfish, I am afraid.*43 I have written to Mrs. Crump today by Mr. McEwen. I wonder if she remembers this "noche triste" anniversary. No, I do not wonder, I know she does. How I would like to be with her tonight. I hope to hear from her tomorrow.

Sunday, July 30, 1848

My Journal is sadly in arrears again. When I wrote last it was amid the spectre throng of thick-coming memories, summoned around me by the anniversary of one of the most memorable days of my life. I had intended on the next night to resume the narrative of recollections, and write of my trip to Memphis with Dr. Litchfield, the long weary days which I spent there, of the feelings with which I received Lucy's letter telling me of unchanged & unchangeable love, and her resolution "to throw herself upon me for happiness" come what might, and of the deep rapture of knowing that for me she would willingly endure the frowns & reproaches and even desertion of those whom she fondly loved, who had been to her both brothers and parents; and also this fearful agony of that struggle through which she must have passed when she knew that she must choose between them & me, and the devotion, the true woman's heart, which characterized her conduct under those trying circumstances. Then too would have followed my return from Memphis, my meeting with her, my urgent desire that we should be married at once, Mr. Crump's opposition to it, Lucy's fond faith in his delusive hope of her brother's ultimate reconciliation & consent if the marriage should be delayed & my final though reluctant acquiescence in that fatal postponement until Fall, though I felt convinced as also did Mrs. Crump that so far from doing good it would only make the matter worse.

But now the anniversary is past & it is as well not to dwell upon a theme which only excites unavailing regrets. The thought of it only tends to send my mind off wandering upon the different track which we might have traveled had no delay been then suggested, and in arranging before me the happiness which might have then been ours adds keenness to the pang of the melancholy consummation. It is sufficient to remember that postponement was made & that Death claimed the bride when the marriage day came round, and so the associations of gloom and regret which come with the period when I was writing last May give way to the brighter & sweeter ones of the present, for now, twelve months since, I was again hopeful & happy, seated by her side, talking of the trials she had endured, and the coming joy to which we looked, to compensate us for them all, while the hours flew rapidly by while I was with her & moved laggingly when I was away. Every night I saw her, and none can know but those whom experience has taught, with what pleasure those interviews were fraught. If man ever shakes off the trammels with which intercourse with the world and participation in its vices bind him, and makes temporary approximation to what he should be, surely it is when she who loves him sits beside him and he lives in the atmosphere of woman's purity & woman's devotion.

Last Sunday I was at Tuckahoe, the only time in three weeks. I remarked to Mr. C. as we rode out that it had been long since I was in Holly S. two weeks before, without being out there. Mrs. Crump is at Fredericksburg & has been sick. How I wish she was back again, though I know it is much better for her that she should not be & that I should not see her. The Circuit Court has been in session two weeks & I have been in the Court House all the time till Tuesday last when I started to Commerce and returned last night after a very fatiguing & uncomfortable trip. The road seemed very like an old acquaintance & I remembered many section lines which I had traced in old times, many spots where our camp had been pitched, and many cabins where we had spent the night. I feel frequently a sort of hankering for the old life & impatience under the confinement of my present occupations when I think of the free roving of my woodsman days. How prone we are in retrospect of anything to see only the bright & pleasant & how true it is that the distance lends enchantment to the view. I can for the nonce forget the exposures & privations and hardships & fatigue of land examining & only remember its healthfulness & sunny days & the deer & the birds & the grass of the wildwoods & sigh for them as they are contrasted with the desk & the pen & the long hours of dry work. These half regrets however are only momentary. As long as I can remember I have been anxious to be a lawyer & thought that the profession would furnish a pursuit more congenial to my taste than any other, and I think so still, and now that I have been dubbed "attorney," I am desirous to deserve the name & if life and health be spared, I have no fear as to attaining moderate respectability & competence at the Bar. More I do not aspire to & more I know I cannot reach. This has been a rainy Sunday, no church. I have spent it at home, not profitably, but not asleep. So long a time has elapsed since I wrote before that I forget the circumstances & minutiae of each day, but there has been little worth recording and now perhaps I suspend the memoranda for an equally long interval.

Saturday, August 5, 1848

Another week of attendance at the Court House. The term is now ended, and I have learned a great deal of the practice of Law by observation during the past 5 weeks. There has been nothing I believe in the history of the week worth recording. My old friend Jasper Jones has been with me (being a juror) the past three nights. This is another of those anniversaries of which I have noticed so many in these pages. A year ago I spent the night at Tuckahoe, being prevented by rain from getting home and the next day *she* went to the Country for the last time. She expected to go to the Hardin Springs but was disappointed. I have had no letter yet from Mrs. Crump—have commenced one to her tonight.

Thursday, August 17, 1848

The day after I wrote that I went out to a camp meeting on Cold Water, the first that I have attended for many years. I was introduced to Miss Jackson of Tennessee & gallanted her to the stand, the only gallantry I have done since my return. I came home sick, had a hard chill and high fever after it which continued for four days. I was kept in my bed till the following Friday & dosed & bled &c. Now I am well again and as ingrateful & unmindful of the Power which has raised me up as though I were an insensible stone. Would that it were otherwise.

On Sunday I heard Mr. Baker preach for the first time, was somewhat disappointed in the morning sermon. It lacked method & clearness. The one at night was much better. He writes very beautifully and apparently from the heart. His manner is better than I expected and he has overcome a certain disagreeable drawl which we used to criticize in the [. . .]. I think that there are the elements of a popular and useful preacher in his composition. I do hope he may have seals set to his ministry for I believe that is the great desire of his soul to do something in the vineyard in which he has begun to labor. He is a strange man in many respects, and it seems to me is more destitute of what we call *common* sense than almost any one I ever saw, except perhaps his Father, but he has plenty of uncommon, which is better. He is my most intimate friend, indeed, the only one I have among the young men.

It has rained all day. How dull & gloomy. We moved yesterday to our new office. On Sunday I was at Tuckahoe, that sad, lonely, beautiful place. I lay on that sofa and read her books. Twelve months since today, I started to Hardin

Springs & went by the Lodge and saw her & she was so much surprised and agitated and perplexed at seeing me & I talked so wildly to Mrs. T, and then so much regretted having gone lest I might have embittered her cup the more, but oh it was so sweet to be with her, and I so dwelt in memory upon that short interview. At this hour I was in Ripley engaged in writing to Ma & Mrs. Crump & *her*. Will there ever be other associations with the passing days than these sad ones which meet me ever & anon as I turn back to the past. Have heard nothing from Mrs. Crump yet. Why don't she write? I wish she would come home. Time glides away. Twelve days since I wrote before; how surely & remorselessly the hours do their work, the work of pall bearers (for what else is it?).

We have organized a Law Class & tomorrow is to be the first recitation. It recalls Princeton. I forgot to mention some weeks since that I had read Bulwer's last novel *Harold*[44] and am more pleased with it than any book of his I have ever read. The style is the most polished & elaborate & artistic that I know, and there is more music & rhythm in it than can be found in any other prose, and then (a rather unusual thing for Bulwer) its moral tendency is unexceptionable, not a thought in [it] would stir the colors on the character of the purest girl. The book was sent me by Ash Green. There has been nothing in the days that have intervened since my last writing more than I have written already that is worth writing. I received a letter from Jane Thomas on Sunday, which I am not to answer. And now most probably for another long sleep.

Sunday, August 20, 1848

For 3 days past it has rained almost incessantly. To day has been clear and pleasant. I have heard Wm. Baker preach twice. Was very much pleased with the Sermon in the morning, but the one tonight was extemporaneous & exceedingly scattering & pointless & puerile. I regret that William should have preached such a sermon as his last, but then no doubt many of those who heard him were delighted with it. He goes this week to Arkansas and very probably I shall never see him again. Our friendship has been long & exceedingly intimate & I shall miss him much, more particularly since our Princeton association has created a new bond between us. We shall both look back to the time we spent together there as our farewell experience of the pursuits and pleasures and preparations of youth. We have both entered upon the path which we have chosen through life, and they diverge from that point and must hereafter lead us farther & farther asunder. His is a glorious profession, and he begins its labors with the enthusiasm of one who feels that all his nobler nature under the influence of the great Spirit is enlisted in a work which is the fitting &

highest employment of a rational, moral being & the appropriate beginning of an immortal existence. I have been forcibly impressed with the idea, which embraces all human occupations except that of the minister, that this world & man as we see him living & acting in it is a strange chrysalis state for such an hereafter as stretches out before us. How strange would it seem should men in their preparations for active participation in Life's struggles pass through a course of preparation as strongly contrasted with the duties which they expect to assume & the character of their subsequent occupations. I suppose that a better analogy to this singular contrarity between the beginning & the end may be found in the difference between the helpless infant or prattling child amused with toys & utterly unconscious of its powers & destiny & the strong, active man, pursuing with a stern energy of purpose which disregards all trifles some great object of pursuit or ambition. Though scarcely can we suppose that between even the merest toy which amuses the youngest child & the high purposes & grand obtainments of most exalted intellectual manhood is there such disparity as between the pleasures & employments and interest of men in their every day race after worldly happiness & worldly goods & the almost infinite enlargement of capacity & eternal progress which lies beyond the grave for the immortal soul.

Returning from the digression, most fervently do I trust that the Head of the Church may make William a useful man. I doubt not that he will attain eminence in his profession. Sometimes we have gone forward in imagination through the lapse of years & drawn the picture of a meeting between us, and thought of how we should look back to this time & talk of our young days and their memories. We have thought of my coming up, an advanced, perhaps prematurely old & broken-down man, with languid steps & worn frame to the gate of a neat & quiet parsonage in some flourishing western village; of my approaching the Pastor's study & seeing him through the open door (for it must be on a summer afternoon) seated over his manuscript, with the traces of mature years upon his serious but tranquil face, of sitting down to talk of the history of those lapsed years & of meeting his wife and children perhaps around his board & my curious scrutinizing & analysis of the circumstances of his domestic circle & then of going with him to his church & thinking while I listen to his calm, unagitated voice, of the time when he stood in our basement story pulpit & with voice often faltering & manner often agitated, began his labor of love. Such are the dreams which whisper to us of the Future, the future which exists most frequently only in their deceitful promises. It may be that William will pronounce over my open grave those solemn words, "dust unto dust" & listen to the falling of the first clods which shall mingle with my ashes.

Or it may be—God only knows what may be. It is a fool's errand upon which conjecture goes out into the darkness of the future.

I am disappointed in not yet receiving a letter from Mrs. Crump. Mr. C. heard from her today & she is no better. I would not be surprised should she never reach home. How doubly sad it would be so to lose her, though even were she not so far from those she most loves, perhaps if she must die it were pleasant to feel that her last resting place would be so near the home of her birth & among the scenes of her most happy days, but I will not think of the possibility of her not returning. I have been reading today the memoirs of Aaron Burr[45] for the first time, written however by one who excludes all the details of the moral deformity of his character & except in few general though strong words of condemnation, presents him without trace of his licentiousness, as a kind husband, doting father & indulgent & considerate master; a patriot, a lawyer, a man of unfaltering purpose, unflagging energy & perseverance & lofty talents. Such is the first volume. I have not read the second & it will contain the history of his ambition ungratified, of his revenge, remorse, & punishment. I have stood by his unmarked, almost unknown grave in Princeton & I read his life with interest much increased by my residence in that place. I have been trying to study some during the past week & though I have learned but very little, yet I feel that it is better than the mental blank of some weeks, indeed of almost the whole time since my return.

Sunday, August 27, 1848

Another week has passed away, very like in its features—blank & expressionless features—to the many which preceded. Its first days were rainy, its last ones were hot. Wm. B. has gone, is probably preaching to day in Memphis. On Wednesday afternoon we rode together to Pine Mountain, our farewell ride together. It was the same road that we passed along together one afternoon about six years before, during the Revival in which we both professed conversion, profession how different in results upon our histories. He consecrated himself at once to the work of the ministry, went to Princeton, passed through his course of preparation, and is now a laborer for God. I lived on in the deceitful hope that I was a Christian, for two or three years, but gradually sinking back the while into the same state of worldly prayerless thought and feelings and indulgence from which I had temporarily escaped, until at last I gave up all idea that I had ever known a change of heart, and have since then been callous and careless, wicked and unrepentent, as I feel that I am tonight, but no more of a theme which will be so unprofitable. Our ride on Wednesday afternoon was a very pleasant one, being the last. We looked backward and talked much of what the review presented. And we talked too of the Future, and I rejoiced to see with what buoyancy & enthusiasm Wm. goes out upon his mission, and to hear him say in a kind of burst of feeling that he had a presentiment, an abiding conviction, that there was something for him to do in the world, that he would be called to act a part in some great & stirring scenes. I rejoiced to hear this, not only because I am a believer in presentiments, in the idea that "coming events cast their shadow before," but also because I think that such a presentiment as he speaks of may have a no small influence in working out its own accomplishment. He is gone. May God go with him & keep him & use him.

Yesterday was the Odd Fellows[46] Anniversary & they had quite a grand celebration. I have become acquainted during the past week with Miss Philips, a rather pretty, educated, sensible and talkative young protégé[e] of Mr. Weatherby. Have studied some, read some and worked a good deal in the office & upon the whole have spent the week rather profitably. Heard from Mrs. Crump yesterday through Mr. C. She is not much better, has had the bilious fever. Mr. C. is more & more uneasy about her. I will not allow myself to think of the possibility of her not recovering. I will hope. How I wish she was at home. She will bring Bunch with her. No preaching at the Pres. Church today. Hot tonight.

Sunday, September 10, 1848

I have just returned from the Methodist Church where I have heard from Mr. Neely the most eloquent sermon I ever listened to. Nothing of speaking that I ever heard before so nearly approached my ideal. The mere recollection of having heard it, and the impression it has left upon my mind, I would not part with for a great deal.

Yesterday in company with Mr. Walker, I returned from Ripley where I had spent some days in attendance upon court. It was the beginning of my circuit travelling. I have done nothing publicly as yet in my profession and do not desire to do anything. The people generally feel so little confidence in a young man, and I feel so entirely ignorant of Law that I am very willing to confine myself to the office. Mr. Mason's unavoidable absence on other business was all that caused me to go to Ripley. I am making but very little progress in the profession and have but little cause to hope that I shall ever do better, however, we shall see.

Day before yesterday (the 8th) was a year since I returned from Hardin Spring. Have received a letter from Mrs. Crump during the past week and the fact that she was able to write it encourages hope that she is much better. Dr. Hull[47] has gone for her, and we shall look for her home in a few weeks now.

I have been to Tuckahoe this afternoon and had while there a more vivid, realizing remembrance of the happiness which I once enjoyed there than I have had before for many months.

It is two weeks since I have written before. I have read a good deal, and thought a good deal & wasted a good deal of time, and they are gone, and that word 'gone' comprises their history for I don't know that they have left much trace, not much for good at least, and drops which they may have added to an already overflowing cup of evil can scarcely be much accumulation.

Sunday, October 8, 1848

Little thought had I when I closed this book one month since that when I opened it again it would be to record the death of my best friend, but it is so. Mrs. Crump died two days since (at 8 o'clock PM, Friday, Oct. 6) in the [. . .] House in Memphis, and at this hour her remains are on their way to their last resting place beside Lucy's at Greenwood. Nearly a year have they been separated by the narrow stream of death, but now she too has crossed its floods and while their spirits are together on the Eternal shore, their bodies will lie side by side on this bank of the gloomy Jordan.

Mrs. Crump left Fredricksburgh on 6th of Sept. apparently able to endure the fatigue of the journey. Dr. Hull had not reached there, and she set out accompanied by Brodie alone. Miss Weatherby joined them in Phila and they came on by the canal route to Pittsburgh. Between Pittsburgh & Cin their boat was aground & the trip occupied 6 days. Brodie was taken very ill and the anxiety & fatigue of nursing him rapidly prostrated his mother. On 23 of Sept they left Cin (after remaining there 3 days) on board the Germantown & she was so weak as to be carried on board in the arms of the Capt. She did not rise from her bed again. On the day of her departure, Mr. Wright telegraphed my Father of her condition & informed him that she could scarcely live to get home. In two hours after the dispatch was received, at 11 o'clock on Saturday night, Mr. Crump started to meet her, and at his request I accompanied him. We reached Cairo on the Glencoe on Tuesday morning & after remaining there 24 hours, proceeded up the Ohio on the W. G. Campbell. On Friday morning we met the Germantown on Scuffle Town Bar and found Mrs. Crump on board. We reached Cairo on the 1st of Oct & thence came down to Memphis on the Geo Washington, arriving at Memphis on Thursday 5th inst. When we met her she was exceedingly feeble and emaciated and she sank by degrees almost imperceptibly from day to day. It is almost wonderful that she should have lived to reach Memphis under all the disadvantages of her situation. For two weeks nearly she was on the River confined to a close narrow uncomfortable berth. ⅓ of the time the boat was aground & always crowded and noisy. She had no medical attention and could have none of those articles of diet which were suited to her condition. When I look back to it I almost shudder to think how much she suffered with all these things superadded to her pain & fatigue and for her too who all her life had been accustomed to comfort and tenderness & the gratification of every want. She did not complain, never uttered one word of repining or impatience. She only lay and suffered. Whenever she had strength & opportunity she would talk to me of Lucy. That great abiding sorrow clung to her & occupied her thoughts to the last. She has gone down to her grave broken hearted.

Tomorrow her brothers may look upon her coffin as it is lowered to its cold damp resting place and think that now their work is complete. I had hoped that her grave would be here, where I might visit it often & where her children might gather around it too, but it seems to be otherwise arranged though she expressed a desire to be buried here. For her the change from this world to Heaven is a blessed one—the sufferers are those whom she has left behind. Her children have sustained an irreparable loss. May God be kind to them. For me Tuckahoe will hereafter be doubly desolate. In her own words addressed to me a few days before her death, "how Tuckahoe has been afflicted. I have now lost the two persons who have loved me more than any others ever did & am I not desolate." Mrs. Crump's affection for me was singular. At a time when Lucy was almost the idol of her heart she was taken from her and owing to the peculiar circumstances she seemed in a great degree to have transferred her affections to me. She called me a brother, and I feel assured that she had no brother who was so dear to her. It is a sad pleasure to me that I was with her in her last days, and she is constantly before me now as I saw her in that hard uncomfortable berth so patient & meek & resigned. I cannot yet realize the loss which I have sustained, but I know as days & weeks roll away it will grow continually upon me. She wears in death the ring which I placed upon Lucy's finger as a pledge of our engagement. I requested that it should not be removed. It seems that now I ought to die too.

It was a year yesterday since Lucy was taken sick. Oh God, how Death marks the days in my memory. It does seem to me that if I were not the most callous & insensible wretch in the world, I should be one of the most miserable, but for a year I have scarcely seemed to myself to live in an actual world. Events have overtaken & lived in my memory in the semblance of the charging scenes of a dream. I have lived with an *unreal* sort of feeling, almost constantly upon me & it is still upon me. I often have a kind of presentiment that I cannot live long. Perhaps when these anniversaries which I have recorded in this book come round again there will be no one to note them. Mrs. Crump & I have thought of them & talked of them together & now I am left alone & soon perhaps I too will cease to remember them in Death's "cold obstruction." I wonder if there be a secret, unwritten history of the human heart which would disclose in its annals all the men & women who throng this world as actors & sufferers in scenes such as those which fill this book. Yes, no doubt the dark tide of Death which sweeps every where beneath the sham & parade, the national greatness, the political existence & the intellectual march which constitute the world as it is spread around us & as it lives in history, has ever borne strewed upon its surface the same circle of joys & hopes & happiness which I now see drifting away from my own little spot of life. No doubt all of the untold millions who have gone before me have to a greater or less extent gazed into that gloomy stream, bewildered, stricken, stymied & stupified as I do now. What a record then must be the book which is kept on high by whom who knows all the thoughts of men, all the emotions of their hearts.

Every day of my life strengthens my belief in Providence, Providence which works out its inscrutable designs, making men and things its instruments in all the most minute details. Indeed, the doctrine of Fatalism seems by far the least unreasonable of all the heresies of which I have ever heard. When I look back upon the past 18 months, I find the most striking traces of an infinitely powerful will controlling circumstances to the accomplishment of its own counsel. Why it is that she who is tomorrow to be buried should have been made a victim we may not know, but she was herself always ready to say, "it is God, let him do what seemeth him good" & surely we should try to echo the words. This trip of hers to Va. seems peculiarly to have been overruled in all its details. It has been disastrous from its commencement. Every thing has gone contrary to our expectations & calculations. I was forcibly struck this afternoon by the thought of the utter imbecility of man's mind to counteract the plans of Heaven. Dr. Darcey said to me that he had supposed that Mr. Crump would take Dr. Taylor on with him from Memphis to meet Mrs. Crump. It seems now that he had suggested just the thing that Mr. C. would most naturally [have] done & just the thing which possibly might have enabled [her] to reach her home again, but strange to say Mr. C. did not once think of it in the midst of all his anxious planning for her comfort, nor so far as I know did it occur to the mind of any one else. God had ordained that she should die when & where she did & he withdrew human agency that might counteract his plans, or rather, he worked out his plans by the withholding of human instrumentality which he did not choose to permit man to array against his design.

Yesterday morning I attended Mrs. Crump's burial at Greenwood. Mr. Weatherby was absent from home and no Presbyterian clergyman could be procured to perform the last religious rites over her grave. Mr. Fagg the Episcopal minister read the funeral service of his Church. We could but regret that so devoted a Presbyterian should thus be buried. She lies by Lucy's side. A few of her friends from town were present & a large collection of persons from the neighborhood. The day was a lovely one, wearing that peculiar autumn appearance so appropriate for burials. The sere leaves fell gently from the boughs which [they] had adorned and sunk softly upon the Earth, and all nature was calm & quiet & bright, yet melancholy & telling of the fading year. Twas a fit time for the interment of such a one.

I was one of the pall bearers and as I walked slowly along bearing her body to the tomb, the scene came up to my mind so vividly of the time when she leaned upon my arm as we followed Lucy along the same garden walk & of that other time on the 13th of Nov'r last, when together we went to visit her grave. And then the road which I travelled out there was the same along which we had followed the hearse when Lucy was borne away & along which we went to visit her grave. As I returned I came by Tuckahoe & saw her geranium & verbina sitting faded & neglected on the gallery, while a sad stillness rested upon the whole place. Just so it looked when with her I approached it on our return from Lucy's burial. I have not been out since & don't know whether Mr. Crump has yet returned to his desolate home. Poor man, how he must miss her. And her children! Little idea have they what is the extent of their loss. I don't believe any one could have been taken from the community in whom so many would have felt that they had lost a sister. Indeed, I was not aware that she was so universally beloved. I sat last night & heard my mother & Mr. Weatherby talk about her. Wherever I go, her face is before me, that sweet earnest face, as Mr. Baker calls it. To me the loss is indeed impassable. She is gone, the moon shines tonight so sweetly & beautifully upon her grave. Oh that she were buried where I could go now & after at such an hour as this & sit alone beside the sacred mound & think over what she has been to me & recall her form in the thousand scenes in which it has mingled & hear her voice again & remember her love & her kindness. She is gone. How impossible to realize it, how impossible to feel that I may not still look forward anxiously to her return & hope that she will come back with renewed health & strength. Her spirit will be about me sometimes I know, perhaps it may be now. What a mystery is our life & our death.

Saturday, October 21, 1848

It is the anniversary of the second day appointed for my marriage to Lucy. Twelve months since the bridal robes were again in readiness & wedding preparations made, but there was no smile upon the face of Tuckahoe. No sound of rejoicing in its halls. She who was to have been the bride lay trembling on the verge of death & the suppressed mourning of anxious watchers was about her. Just at this midnight hour I was riding out to hear what tidings they could give. She had not been well since her first attack after leaving town on the evening of the 7th when she had taken cold, but I had seen her in the parlor two or three times between that day until the 12th, when I only saw her for a few moments & she returned to her room, never to leave it again. How little did I think that it was my last parting with her, but it was such nevertheless as I would have wished the last parting to be. She grew slightly worse from day to day, but still on the 16th the Dr. told me I need not fear but she would be well enough for us to be married on [the] 21st. Short sighted mortals. From that time she grew violently sick & when the 21st came, the physicians supposed it to be the crisis of her disease. She passed that crisis. Another cruel disappointment was in store for us. She seemed to be getting well, was pronounced out of danger & we were happy in hope, till on 1st Nov. a relapse came & on the 3rd she died. One more anniversary & the series is closed. I had thought to devote that day to memory in company with Mrs. Crump, but she has not waited to see it. Her death has [. . .]ed the 6th Oct by the side of 3rd Nov in the history of Tuckahoe.

The two weeks which have elapsed since I wrote before have been spent as usual in the office with no external circumstance to vary their monotony. I might write much about them, of their developments of my inner man, of their influence upon my feelings & self knowledge, but not now. It is after midnight.

Sunday, October 29, 1848

A calm, beautiful night after a bright, quiet sabbath. A moon two nights old [has] now gone down and the myriad night-watchers have brightened the sky. We have no minister as yet & Mr. Mason read us one of Melville's sermons[48] in the morning & we have had prayer meeting tonight. En puissant, it has transpired that Mr. Neely, of whom I wrote so rapturously a few Sunday nights since in the journal, is a most arrant plagiarist. One of the sermons he preached here was taken almost entire from Melville & most of the others were identical in texts & often in words with his. I fancy Mr. N. will never come to H.S. again. The language he used from the pulpit in reference to a report which had been circulated concerning [him] went very far to lower him in the estimation of the people & now this plagiarism quite does for him.

After some dull rainy days in the early part of the last week, the weather has become mild & beautiful. I have been at work in the office as usual over writs & declarations, depositions & authorities, but I have seen more of ladies' society during the past week than for a whole year before. Miss Anna Sneed, a beautiful & interesting girl has been at our house & I have passed many hours in her society, besides seeing many other girls visiting her & Carry & also visiting a little myself. I find that the eclipse of sorrow is passing or past from my heart & while I cherish no less tenderly the memory of her whom I loved, while I love her none the less, I can yet feel more interest in society than I had supposed I should ever do again. I begin to feel again the yearnings of the heart after companionship & to be conscious—what I had not supposed— that my susceptibility to affection is still alive. I do not love again, nor have I found any other whom I suppose that I could love, but the feelings which society of ladies awakens, so nearly resemble those, now long unknown, with which I used to meet them in other days, that I can but be aware that I should love again were there some one present calculated to elicit such emotion. Nor do I regret that it is so. For a time my heart has been crushed, stunned as it were, the cords all unstrung, but I rejoice to find that it is not dead, that I may hope yet, should my life be spared, for the happiness of which only a *home* can give. I think no less often of Lucy, turn no less fondly to the remembrance of the hope & the happiness once associated with her name, dwell no less upon the sorrowful anniversaries which are now passing over my head. Indeed, I feel certain that were there another one whom I could love as I loved her, whom love could be dear to me as hers was, I could take that one to stand with me by Lucy's grave & feel the while that Lucy would rejoice could her spirit meet us then, in the hope that another might be to me what she had been, might bring joy & happiness to the bosom which her loss left desolate. I write thus because I wish these pages to be somewhat a record of my inner nature & this is a subject upon which I have been in doubt, at least I have wondered whether I should ever again be able to love & as my heart begins to dictate an affirmative answer to the question, I inscribe it here.

It is most probable perhaps that I shall never marry, for if in all my inter-course with the world Lucy was almost the first (I do not think there was ever but one or perhaps two others whom I ever, ever thought that I would be will-ing to be united to in marriage) whom I met whom I could love, it is hardly probable in the first place that I shall soon find another whom I could love or I would wish to marry & it is still less probable in the second place that should

I find such a one, she would feel in the same way towards me. I know I shall never be rich. I do not hope ever to acquire eminence or fame. I know that my personal appearance is far from attractive & that there is but little about me calculated to win affection & nothing in my character or prospects to induce a woman to marry me from any other motive & so I have but little idea that I shall ever be other than I am, a bachelor. The prospect of lonely, single life is not very attractive, nor is [it] to me very distasteful. While I feel that I could be happy with the right kind of a wife, I also feel that with my books & my business & my love of solitude, I should not be unhappy because unmarried. And then I have been so long & so constantly one of the home family circle & have so much in my parents & sisters & brothers & will have in my married sister's family to give exercise to my affections, so many to love me & feel sympathy for me that I should not be situated as those old bachelors are who are cut off from the world & having no intellectual recourse are left to vegetate in the soil of their own selfishness & to grow tired of life in its solitude & ennui. Of all this however I seldom think. I live emphatically in the past & the present, seldom casting a glance towards the future beyond the termination of the current day or the week, unless it be in some idle, random, conjecture, in some unoccupied moment. My past is a teeming one. My present may be when I choose a busy one & my future will be *what it will be*. I feel not much interest concerning it. At least not much interest of the kind which produces anxiety.

I have been looking at & reading Mrs. Crump's letters today. How often I think of her. This morning Mr. C. came into church attended by all his children with crape on their caps, & she who was wont to come in with them, to take her seat near the pulpit, where was she? Doubtless the question suggested itself to the minds of most of those who noticed their entrance. I have not missed her as much as I expected, doubtless arising to her long absence & to the fact that I have seen her but for a few weeks since I went to Princeton. How consoling it is to think of a dead friend, that departed hence, has entrance into Heaven that Death has not? How it sooths the pain of bereavement & softens the pang of separation.

One year today since I was hunting for a partridge for Lucy to eat. She was pronounced convalescent, out of danger & so buoyantly & joyously after all my anxiety did I tramp with a gun on my shoulder through the long grass, hoping to find a bird which she would like. How the sky seemed to have cleared away after a storm & how brightly & hopefully the sun shone & how happy I felt. I remember it all as though it were yesterday. I almost [. . .]ed in my lightness & joy of heart. I had not seen her, for it was considered imprudent to excite her, but she had talked of me & sent me messages & said she had dreamed about me & loved me more if possible than ever & had appointed a day to ride with me (the very day of her burial) & had arranged all the plan of the buggy being driven to the door & her being lifted into it & my driving slowly through the grove. Mrs. Crump had written & told me of all this & in anticipation I had supported her emaciated form & watched the fresh air playing upon her cheek & the color coming to its sunken wanness & had gazed into her beautiful eyes as the light of health & life [. . .]ed them & had looked forward to telling her of all our fears & tremble & dread & showing her Mrs. Crump's notes (I had dated & arranged them all for the purpose) written during her illness to inform me of her situation. And I had felt—none can know what I had felt but those whose experience can tell them.

On the following night I was at Tuckahoe when the first symptom of relapse was manifested & the Dr. was sent for in hot haste. Our hearts sank within us, but he came & dissipated all apprehensions by saying she only ate too much & there was no danger & this fatal delusion, this mocking security, was unbroken. She did not continue to grow better but scarcely seemed at all to grow worse & in the conviction that it was only the prostration of such long & terrible suffering from which nature was slow to rally, we lived on almost without fear as to the result for three more days. On Tuesday night, 2nd Nov, I left there at a late hour, after hearing from the Dr. that her symptoms were all better than for some days past & that there was no ground for apprehension. Throughout her illness, I had been debarred by the peculiar relation of hostility [. . .] by her friends towards me, from the sad pleasure of seeing her. Indeed in the early part of her sickness, to prevent a meeting between them & me, she had herself requested that I should not even go there to inquire about her. This of course I could not accede to when she had become dangerously ill, even if she had still been able to be conscious of my coming, but I was content with going to inquire. When she grew better I was very anxious to see her, but feared to do so lest she might suffer from it, but she was informed of my coming to the house & some of her brothers & sisters told her that they regretted their opposition to our marriage & would withdraw it entirely & there was every reason to suppose that all of them would do so & so she had appointed the earliest moment when her strength should allow for me to see her & the burden was removed from her mind which the thought of our approaching marriage without the presence or the sanction of those she loved had heaped upon it. She was recovering, opposition was removed, the prospect of a union which it was determined should take place as soon as she should be well again, a prospect too undarkened by those fears of the irreperable displeasure of her brother which had so much distressed her, was before us. So these were my thoughts as I rode home that Tuesday night, these were the thoughts which had occupied her mind during the days of her apparent convalescence & these were our hopes. I slept soundly & hopefully that night, for they said she was sleeping soundly & refreshingly.

At day light the next morning Brodie stood by my bedside & woke me with these words, "Ma says you must come. Aunt Lucy is dying" & he bowed his head upon the bed & burst into tears. Bewildered, stupified, I mounted my horse & was there in a few minutes. The scene I will not describe, the agony of that morning I will not attempt to recall. I saw her. She was insensible, the film of death was gathering in her eyes. The fevered blood was retreating to her heart. An hour afterwards I saw her again, the last agonizing, convulsive gaspings had commenced. I gazed upon her, my own beloved one, as she lay there dying before me, her hand on which my ring lay upon the outside of the bed. I took it for a moment in mine, looked once more into those glazing eyes. Oh God, may I never be called to pass through such a scene again. I had left the room, but that heart rending sound as she gasped away her life echoed every where. For hours it grew more & more feeble. I could not remain where I could not hear it, & yet how terrible it was to listen & realize that it was the last struggle for existence, the last feeble effort of sinking nature. At 2 o'clock she gasped no more.

Once again when the sun was just sinking beneath the horizon I stood beside her. Her form was wrapped in her *bridal* attire & laid upon the sofa where we had sat so often, upon which we sat when I bade her my last farewell before her sickness. I was alone in that parlor with the dead. Many hours had we been there alone before. Her countenance had resumed its natural appearance & was smiling & beautiful in death. She seemed in a pleasant sleep. Unconsciously I called her name. I could not make her dead. That hour that I knelt there beside her as she lay upon that sofa was a sweet, a sacred hour. Grief had exhausted itself, the fountain of my tears was dry. All was calm & quiet & still within me as I held her hand in mine & kissed her cold lips & brow & felt that she was dead & took the last long parting. It was the holiest hour of my life.

As I said, my last parting with her living had been in that room, on that sofa, & had been such as I am glad to remember as the last, such as I could have wished it to be, had I known I should see her no more & my last parting with her dead, in the same room, on the same sofa, was such as I am now glad to recall as the last. The wild storm of sorrow & anguish had exhausted itself. The rebellious accusing struggle against Providence had not commenced. I was calm & was with her who was dead. I might write much of that hour, but suffice it, it was the last. I looked upon her once more the following morning

476 : HENRY CRAFT

before she was placed in the coffin, but the company was gathered. I had *parted* with her before. The ring which I had given her I requested Mrs. Crump to bear & she did wear it & I thought it had been buried with her, but Mr. Crump did not understand my request & so had it removed. My mother wears it now as I hope she will continue to do. I would rather it were on her finger than any other living one.

And now these pages contain a narrative of our love & our disappointment, a narrative brought up to the closing scene. I have purposely written this in order that they should do so. In future years, if I should live to see them, it will be a pleasure to me to read over what I have written, to think over all that found its consumation in that grave at Greenwood.

Friday, November 3, 1848

The last, the fatal day has come, the anniversary of that last day of *her* life & the closing day of this series of memories & introspections. It has rained incessantly almost since early morning, and now torrents are pressing down instead of drops. There could be no more fitting time for gloomy thoughts, or gloomy recollections. Would that I could now recall the feelings of 12 months since, could have her image vividly before me, in her health & in her shroud, as then it was & even surround myself by the desolation which then seemed to have swept over the face of all the world. It may not be so, I can look back through the scenes of the year to that hour when the watchers were talking in tones suppressed, in the house of death & I was alone in my room with my thoughts of the dead, but the vividness of the reality is gone. She with whom I had hoped to consecrate this hour to the memory of that time is also gone.

Here tonight let me take my farewell of Tuckahoe, bury the past & turn toward whatever may be my future. There is a sweet, sacred joy in communing with the dead. There is a holy melancholy pleasure in revisiting the scenes of former happiness & sorrow, and through the year which is now closed, they have been mine in all their various phases. In the busy hours of the day, & the quiet midnight, in solitude & in crowd, far away among strangers & in strange places & at home among friends & among scenes familiar to *her*, has she been in my thoughts, have I dwelt upon her memory. Today I wished to have visited her grave, to have buried there with those two buried ones the memory of what has been. Not that I can cease to remember, oh no. While life lasts this may not be, but I would fain turn my back here upon what is behind as upon a former existence & here summon up energy & hope & strength for new existence which is before. Which is before! God only knows if there be for me a much longer span of days. Another 3rd of November and I too perhaps may have gone to join that buried world of thoughts & memories & hopes & sorrows. I am glad that I have written this book. I here dedicate to the memory of the past year, here inscribe as the tombstone which I rear over the grave of my former life. Will other eyes than mine ever glance through these pages, will others read these lines when the hand which traced them shall have mouldered? It may be so. Then they will find here the record of a heart & mind which were to their possessor the greatest mysteries which he found in all this mysterious home of humanity. This day brings with it no new sadness as I had supposed it would. My first waking thought was, "it is the 3rd of November. One year ago she died." But there is no new pang which memory can inflict, no new echo which can answer those words "she died" in my heart. They have been a year long [. . .] within those hidden recesses & now they are being hushed.

Loved one farewell, once more on the 3rd of Nov, farewell. Death snatched thee to his embrace from the circle of the young & gay & thy form has faded from their sight & thy thought from their minds & there are few now to re-member who it is that fills thy early grave—my sister, *her sister*, whom grief has murdered. Farewell Tuckahoe, desolate Tuckahoe, farewell. The past, the bright, the dark, the joyful, sorrowful past—farewell—farewell.

Sunday, November 19, 1848

Today Mr. Weatherby preached Mrs. Crump's funeral sermon. The congre-gation was good, and all her brothers & sisters & other members of the family were there, as well as her husband & children. It is still very hard for me to realize that she is indeed dead. I have not been to Tuckahoe for several weeks. I feel no desire to go there. I believe I have been in the house but once since her death, and then every thing looked so [. . .] and reminded me so much of the double bereavement that I could scarcely desire to go again. I see Mr. Crump frequently and he looks as he always did. He seems much devoted to his children, and very anxious to train them up as she would have desired. I suppose he will marry again in time (Mrs. [. . .] I think most probably). If he should ever give them another mother their characters will depend much upon hers.

During the past two weeks I have been mostly alone in the office, Mr. Mason being absent. I have been tolerably busy and begin to feel more encouraged as to the possibility of my one day becoming a respectable lawyer. I find that I learn much more of law by seeing it at work, by investigating cases than I had ever done by study & I have no doubt that if I should [live] five or six years and remain connected as I now am with a good business that I shall be able to learn the *machinery* of the profession, and also many of the general principles which bear upon such questions as occur in the usual routine of country practice. I scarcely study at all except for particular cases, and I do not expect to have either inclination or opportunity for doing so. It is perhaps a disadvantage of my connexion with Mr. Mason that my time will be so much occupied in the business details of the office that I shall not have much to devote to reading & that I shall become so much accustomed to depending upon him that I shall not think & investigate for myself, but then on the other hand besides the positive advantage of getting acquaintance with the practical part of the profession (which can only be done by practice) I shall have the additional one of making a living at the same time. I consider myself very fortunate in my situation indeed.

A year since I was on my way to Princeton. I look back now to that year & it seems to have passed very quickly and when I try to estimate what I have gained from it in the way of knowledge, it seems almost lost. So much of it as was spent in Princeton was certainly very pleasant, as far as the society into which I was thrown was concerned, I wish I had such a circle [. . . .] here.

Monday, January 1, 1849

Yes, '49. The clock has just struck and the old year is gone. Perhaps I am the first to register the birth of the infant year. Twelve months since I sat at my table in Princeton at this hour and wrote to Mrs. Crump.

Sunday, January 21, 1849

As the last sand of the old year dropped from the glass I hastened in the above lines to register the advent of '49. I was very busy & had only time to write that the new year had come. And now three weeks of it are gone, and I resume my journal so long discontinued. Two months since I wrote before except the few lines above, and yet as large as the proposition is which they bear to the allotted span of life, they have been to me the mere lapse of days, have brought nothing worthy of record, even in a book of trifles such as this. They have been months of labor too & perhaps have increased my slender store of professional information as much as any other two months have done, and yet they seem, as for all that I have accomplished, all that they have added to my stature as a man, mere gloomy hours, mere increase of age.

In the latter part of November I attended the Circuit Court in Hernando. Early in December I was at Hernando again on business & on 28 December I went to Spring Hill on business. In going there & returning I passed by the Lodge, the first time I have seen the place since I went there to see Lucy in August '47. I might write whole pages of the memories & associations which the sight recalled, of the thoughts, sweet & bitter, pleasant & sad & melancholy which it awaked, but why write more of the past? Why view the past to which I have said farewell however. I did not stop at the Lodge of course, but I could not resist the temptation to ride as near as possible & pause & dwell upon the familiar features of the scene & remember what circumstances had surrounded me then in times gone by. *She* was again before me, her face in the expression which it wore at our last meeting in that parlor, & the thoughts & memories wrung from my heart yet once more the cry, Oh God! Why should all this have been?

I know that He who reigns does not delight in human suffering. I know he does not crush in the arbitrary exercise of his power & I should feel equally convinced that mysterious as are his workings, He had a reason & an end, but yet I cannot repress the desire to look thus far into the counsels of Eternity & repeat the question why should all this have been. The thought has been agony to me, that she may have died for my punishment. For me she suffered while she loved me, suffered as none but the noblest & the finest & the most devoted of women could or would have suffered. For me she endured the frown & the reproach & the malediction of those who called her mother theirs, those whom she loved & who should have loved her as they did not & would have loved her as they should had they been able to estimate & appreciate her character. For me she saw the strong ties severed which bound her to them, for me her heart bled & she uttered no complaint, no repining. And was it for me too that she died? Spirit of my loved & loving one, it may be that now at this midnight hour thou dost hover near me on thy viewless wings. It may be that even now thine impalpable form presses close to the bars of my clay prison, striving to send its spirit whispering through the dull dust & to convey to my caged soul an answer to my question, but of this no more. Anon in that land whither flesh & sense may not go, I too shall dwell & then the broad light of Eternity will be shed upon the mysteries of life.

And now another thought forces itself upon me. I have been subjected to this ordeal & what has been its effect upon me. Have I been purified or elevated or in any whit changed. Conscience reviews its value, & answers, no. The prayer which I uttered beside her shrouded form, beside her new made grave died away in emptiness. I am neither a wiser or a better man. Long years of heaven's benefactions did not awaken my gratitude, the keen agony of Heaven's chastening did not render me repentant. I have lived & live on through all, cold, careless & callow, unfeeling, ingrateful, unchanged. What shall the end of these things be? I record the question here & my immortal spirit shall answer it in the tones of another world, throughout the ages of Eternity.

I was at Tuckahoe a few days since, the first time for months. Once more I stood in that parlor & sat upon that sofa & communed with the thronging recollections of those dead sisters, in that desolate home.

After a long silence, Miss Jane Thomas has written to me again & I answered her letter on New Year's day. She seems to be unchanged in her feelings towards me, as I certainly am unchanged in mine for her. I prize her regard & hope she will continue to write.

On Friday, 5th Jan, I attended a large party at Mr. Mason's, the first I have been at since one at Mr. Niles[49] in the Spring of '47. How changed was the aspect of the company since then, as to the ladies at least. The gentlemen were much the same who were to be met at such places 2 years ago, but scarcely a single one of the ladies. Those who were children then have grown up to be the belles & those who were belles then are mothers now. I enjoyed the party as I believe all did who were present. I have visited the ladies nearly every week for some months past & I find their society just what it used to be. The persons have changed, but the characters are the same.

William Baker is here on a visit from Arkansas. His health has improved. He has preached once. I see but little change in him in the pulpit since I heard him before. He is in a world of trouble which he brought upon himself by his imprudent impulsiveness.

His Father returned from Texas some 5 or 6 weeks since & is now on the point of starting to Galveston where he has consented to become a pastor. It was reported and believed that he had been killed by the Indians in Texas & he enjoys the rare advantage of reading his own obituaries as they go the rounds of the papers. Excellent man. Lot will have gone out of our Sodom when he leaves us. We shall never see his like again.

I have written to Miss Racillia tonight. Since November we have scarcely had a clear day & now for weeks it has rained almost incessantly. I never saw more disagreeable weather. The cholera is raging in New Orleans again & notwithstanding the favorable accounts of its abatement in Memphis, it will reach us here I fear if this weather continues. Almost every one is suffering from a cold.

Our Circuit Court is in session & 2 or 3 days since I made my maiden speech at the bar. It was however but a few remarks on a most meager subject. I was much agitated & trembled tho I was not alarmed or confused.

Sunday, January 28, 1849

This has been a most lovely Spring-like day. Three clear days in succession we have had now, a very unaccustomed occurrence. I have spent the afternoon in riding with Mr. Fort[50] to Tuckahoe where we remained an hour or two and afterward I went to Mr. Clapp's & saw Mr. & Mrs. Donald & Brooks & Litchfield there. Heard a sermon from Chittenden this morning & one from Mr. Jones. Methodist minister to night. William Baker and his Father have both left us. Mr. Mason gave a large party on Friday night last, which I enjoyed more than the one at Mr. [. . .]. Court has been in session all the week & a tedious criminal case closed last night. I have made 3 speeches this week & feel but little embarrassment now. My first case, that is the first one which I have had entirely to my self, was Crisp vs. Hinton. I lost it much to my regret & dissatisfaction, the more so because I think we ought to have had a verdict & I cannot but believe that we would have succeeded if Mr. Mason had managed it before the jury. I suppose I must get accustomed to bearing defeat, but it will be some time before I can do it well. Litchfield has just left me. I feel very little like reading or writing. I have experienced within the last few days more of a kind of listlessness & apathy of mind than for a long time before. The week has been an unprofitable one, and the last 3 days completely thrown away.

Sunday, February 11, 1849

Day before yesterday, I returned from a trip to Yalabusha County, having been absent a week. The weather was exceedingly bad & the waters were very high. I had two chills from the exposure & fatigue while I was gone & have had another since my return & must try hard tomorrow to dodge a fourth. I have suffered much from the fever which followed them & from travelling when I was scarcely able to sit on my horse. I had Mr. Thos. Kirkman of Florence, Ala as a travelling companion in going down & found him an exceedingly pleasant one. He is well informed, full of life & humor & a gentleman in his manners. He is well known as a great horse racer, having won several of the most celebrated races ever run in this county. My trip was rendered entirely useless by the delay occasioned by the water & I most heartily wish I had not made it. I missed a large party at Mr. Taylor's by my absence but don't regret that. All well & nothing new.

Tuesday, March 6, 1849

I scarcely know why it is that my Journal gets so much into arrears. Another proof I suppose of the necessity of method and regularity in all things. I have been sick since Friday last, on which day I had a very hard chill followed by high fever. I am better, almost well tonight. Since writing last nearly a month has slipped away and as I look back upon it now, I see but few prominent points, few things worthy of remembrance. The routine of office duty & office lounging consume the day & morning & night follow each other with such noiseless footfall that one almost loses the consciousness of their progress. Last night after I had gone to bed, the thought flashed across my mind that another day was gone and that life is made up of days, and days easily numbered too, such days as were gliding past me unnoticed, almost unimproved. Oh how bitterly in some occasional moments of reflection, realizing reflection, do I feel the utter vanity of my aspirations & pursuits, and my folly in thinking no more of the great end & aim of existence & in living on without a care for the immortal nature which I bear. I know it is but weak & childish sentimentality occasionally to think of such things & allow the thoughts to pass away in some such record as this on the pages of this book. Alas I know all that I should know too well.

During the past few weeks I have visited occasionally, have attended a concert, a soiree &c., &c. Last week Miss Jane Thomas was in town. I saw her frequently, though never alone & in the way in which I could most enjoy her society. She is looking better than I ever saw her, and her flow of Spirits is unabated. She left yesterday. Her Mother was also in town a week ago & I met her, the first time I believe since Lucy's burial. Dr. Hull has also been here visiting and attending parties, but I have not met him. I have not been to Tuckahoe for a long time, shall go soon. Mr. Crump is absent from home a great deal & I fear the children will suffer from it. I have not seen them recently. A few more years & we all will have gone like them.

I must here record a very pleasant little party of gentlemen which I had in the office on Saturday night, the 24th Feb. It was a bird supper and Jo. Camden, Hackleton,[51] Stearns, Pryor,[52] Wilder, Litchfield & Strickland[53] were present. Ma and Bunch had fixed off the supper & table very nicely for me, and the company were lively & pleasant & intelligent & I don't know that I ever passed an evening more pleasantly. Litchfield & Strickland & I had been out hunting the day before & killed the birds. The weather for 10 days has been delightful. Spring seems suddenly to have come after two or three [days] about the middle of Feb of the coldest weather which we have had during the winter. The flowers are now in bloom, the shrubbery is beginning to put out leaves & the birds to sing. It is much earlier I notice than Spring came in Princeton last year.

Our family are all well. Bunch does not seem to enjoy her life much for some reason or other, and I would be glad to think of some plan by which to liven her from her apathetic, listless, lifeless look & conduct. I feel much solicitude as to her future. Were she different in her disposition or more attached to me, I should derive a great deal of pleasure from trying to amuse & instruct her, but I cannot enter in to her feelings or win her confidence. She seems to have but little in common with any of us in her tastes, and I cannot exert any influence over her. The other children are engaged in their schools & I see but little of them. Helen[54] grows & improves but she is much spoilt. Ma sits in her corner & sews & cuts. I go in very often to talk & laugh with her & admire her unselfish, industrious, cheerful life. Pa figures over his maps & notes & talks to his customers & bustles about his ceaseless changes & improvements on his lot & I have a little conversation with him every day & do not see much of him either. He is the strangest compound I have ever met with yet. Matt has been quite unwell & suffering much with a sore mouth for months, but is better now. She is a model of a wife & busies herself at home & plans & manages with all the care & thought which she could exercise if her sphere were the world & she sole ruler. It affords me much gratification to see her so happily married and so happy in her children & husband & home. Mr. Fort has returned tonight from a ten days trip. He lives on, pursuing the even tenor of his way unexcited, not perhaps undeserving, but apparently contented & happy. How little we thought when as urchins we fished & trapped & went to school together that as men we should stand so nearly related & walk side by side in the world's great thoroughfare.

It grieves me to notice the manifestations of bad feeling towards him & Matt which Ma & Bunch (perhaps I ought not to say Bunch, though I cannot but think that she participates in it) occasionally make. Of course I do not expect, nor could I reasonably do so, that after all that has been, Ma should ever feel for Matt affection or regard, but I would so much like to see the same spirit which Matt exhibits. Ma's greatest fault is the unconquerable character of her prejudices. She & Matt are so diversely constituted that they never could get along together & even more, she cannot overcome old feelings.

My associations now are chiefly Litchfield & Strickland. Litchfield is one of the cleverest men in the world. There are few or no sympathies of taste or pursuit between us, but he is a man of such high principle & correct feeling that I like him. He makes no pretension to literary taste or attainment, but with excellent sense combines great judgment & discretion & with such men one always feels safe. Rumor says he is soon to be married to Miss Brooks Lucas.[55] If it be true, it will be a most excellent match & they will make I think a well assorted & happy couple. I like to see them together. Litchfield looks so happy & his broad beaming face becomes so much more beamy & sunny twould reconcile the veriest misanthrope to his species to look at as he stands beside or watches her movements. There is much of the bond of old association too to bind me to Litchfield. He used to visit with me at Tuckahoe during my courtship & *she* liked him very much. And then he was my confidante and was with me in my troubles & seemed to sympathize in my sorrow. There is about him an equanimity & an imperturbability which I have seldom seen in any one else, never excited unduly & never apparently depressed, he looks the same smiling contented genial-hearted being all the time. In seasons of deep emotion, his presence somewhat grates upon the feelings from this very fact of his stolidity & equanimity, but in all ordinary life he is ever ready to be the companion & friend of the hour & what he was yesterday, you are sure to find him today & my calculated wish certainly that he will be tomorrow. I think he will make a first rate practicing physician, & I hope for him all that success which I feel that his merits as a Dr. and his character as a man richly entitle him to.

Strickland I have only known a few months. He was one of Mr. Mason's students, obtained his license late last year & is now in our office learning the practice & doing some business. He has had few advantages of education or society, but has good, sound natural sense & a heart which does him credit. Though not very polished in his manners, he has the principles & feelings of a gentleman & is one of those in whose discretion & honor I feel perfect confidence. He does not apply himself very closely but learns a good deal by his reading, and his manners are popular among the sovereigns. He will make a safe & a popular, though perhaps never a distinguished, lawyer. His knowledge of the world & men is limited & of books still more so, & there is much less in common between him & me than even between Litchfield & myself, yet I like him very much because he is a high minded, right hearted man. Litchfield has had good advantages of education & position in society, has spent 2 winters in Phila & has seen much of the best of Virginia society. His manners are easy & polished to a certain extent & he is one of our first young men in point of place in Society.

There is one other gentleman whom I like to associate & talk with, though circumstances have never thrown us together a great deal & I cannot say that I am intimate with him. He is much older than I am & has mingled a great deal more with the world. I mean Mr. Jo. Camden. He is emphatically a gentleman. He has read a great deal of almost every thing in the way of general literature, has travelled at the north, has moved in the best society for many years, and is the best informed, that is more generally informed, than perhaps any one in the town. He has more romance & sentiment, genuine sentiment, in his composition than I had supposed it possible for any to carry along with them so far on the journey through a commonplace, rough & terrible life. His taste in books & everything else is refined & cultivated, his sentiments are elevated, his manners very polished, easy & popular & I never heard any one speak ill of him. He is a general favorite with all, without making any other effort to become so than his natural inclination prompts. I enjoy his society more than that of any other gentleman now that William Baker is gone. The circle of ladies whom I visit much is very small. Of them I will write some other time.

Professionally, I have reason to be satisfied. I am learning something, not much, by practice. I do not read or study at all, but I hope to get at it again soon. We have as much business as we can very well attend to. Most of it is small, it is true, but I think the profits of the office will be reasonably satisfactory. At any rate, I shall do so much better pecuniarily than most young lawyers just starting out that I should be well pleased. Mr. Mason I like more & more every day & I would rather be associated with him & make a bare subsistence than with any one else for large pay. He is one of the best of men & then his instruction is invaluable to me. Oh that I had discipline of mind. I feel every day, what I could not heretofore appreciate, the great importance of forming habits of mental training at school. I was always quick at memorizing & I trusted to this for getting through recitations, but what I acquired without labor I forgot at once & now I find it almost impossible to fix & keep my mind upon a subject until I have examined and investigated it & impressed the result upon my memory. I can catch the meaning & immediate bearing of a principle very easily, but it is forgotten, lost at once. Mental discipline is worth all the other acquirements which we can bring from our school days, indeed the greatest benefit of what we call education is to prepare one by this training of the mind & the knowledge of the rudiments of learning to carry on the culture of the intellect in after years. How mistaken the notion of boys, & too often of teachers & parents, that the smattering of school studies to be acquired in "getting an education" *is* an education. If I had my life to go over, I would force myself to study mathematics & would restrain my love of poetry & fiction & my inclination to belles lettres.

After a long spell of fine weather it is raining hard tonight. Twould be moonlight but for the clouds. Took a long rapid walk with Strickland this afternoon & feel better for it. Went to Mr. Clapp's. Tis nearly 12 o'clock & my journal has made progress enough for once.

Sunday, April 1, 1849

Almost another month concerning which I have written nothing. Well let me look back & see if there was anything to write about it. Week before last I was very sick, had five chills on five successive days & was confined to the house nearly all the week. One day I was very sick indeed. I have been out now a week & am quite well again. Two weeks since this afternoon I went with Mrs.

Baker to Waterford & brought Miss Theodora back from there. The trip had much to do no doubt in bringing on the chills again. During the past week I have not been able to do any thing until Thursday. On Friday I went with Mrs. Baker to Memphis on her way to Galveston. I left them on the wharf boat at 10 o'clock on Friday night. It made me feel sad to part with them & think that in all probability I should never meet them again. It will be long before we have another as good a man among us as Mr. Baker. My intimacy with William has brought about a close intimacy in the family, and I felt that I was parting with some of my best friends when I turned away from them. I could not bear to say Good bye & so left them without a word of parting. They took tea at Mr. Coon's & I became acquainted with him & his wife & was much pleased with them.

Yesterday, I came back from Memphis & had a very pleasant journey as the company was as agreeable a one as I ever traveled with. There is a considerable cholera in Memphis now among the poorer & more exposed portion of the population. One of the first sights we saw as the stage was driven through the town was a man carried along on a mattress on the shoulders of some half a dozen others to the Hospital. He had been attacked by cholera in coming up the river & had been just put off the boat. It excited strange feelings, sent a thrill of horror through my system I may say to look upon this first case of disease which I had ever witnessed. There is something very awful in the idea of man's being struck down in his health & strength unwarned by so relentless a foe. Death, comfort us as he may, shakes our nerves & blanches our cheeks, but coming thus in the form of an unbidden & unexpected apparition, rising suddenly in the path of our every day life with no note of warning to prepare us for his approach, he startles us as though he were a messenger from the other world commissioned to reveal the nature of those dread realities which we are so much accustomed to think of as afar off & we start & shrink back as tho we had never seen his terrible form before, nor heard his name breathed or his work of destruction alluded to.

Matt is quite unwell tonight. The other members of the family are in their usual health.

I heard Mr. Chittenden preach this morning a most excellent sermon on religious declension in a church & spiritual sleep among professors of Religion. This sermon was peculiarly appropriate in the present circumstances of our church. Since Mr. Baker left us we have had no pastor, & the people have literally wandered off as sheep without a shepherd. There is now a dancing school in full operation which is called by many the Presbyterian dancing school from the fact that some of the elders & many of the members patronize it. Mr. Chittenden is now preaching for us every sabbath & a most excellent & interesting preacher he is. His style is remarkably chaste & beautiful & his delivery calm & impressive. I don't know any minister whom I would much rather hear.

Tonight Pa & Carry & Stella[56] & I went to hear Mr. Jones at the Methodist Church as we generally do on Sunday night, there being no other preaching in town at night. In the midst of the Sermon tonight an alarm of "fire" was given & the congregation broke up most unceremoniously. It was amusing to see how they rushed for the door. The alarm resulted from a burning chimney. I never saw a meeting broken up in such a manner before. Mr. Jones is the best preacher the Methodists have had here for many years. He is very calm & dignified & generally sensible tho' he is altogether too fond of abstract & metaphysical disquisition & often gets clear out of his depth. He writes poetry for the newspaper, or rhyme at least for it is the veriest stuff generally that can often be found even in newspapers. Tonight when the meeting was broken up he was in the midst of an explanation as to the origin of devils. He argues that they are many, because the common belief or generally received opinion that there is one chief & only power of darkness is erroneous in that it attributes to this being an omnipresence which no creature could possess. I have thought of this before but resolved the difficulty satisfactorily to my own mind by supposing that the Devil might be omnipresent & omniscient too within the limits of this world without possessing what we mean by omnipresence & omniscience as attributes of God. I see nothing impossible in the idea that God has endowed him with these attributes within a certain limited sphere, & I think that the supposition that he has done so is much more consistent with Scripture than Mr. Jones' idea that there are numerous Devils all limited to a certain place tho all acting in concert for the ruin of Man. Upon any explanation or theory, the Devils or Devil must be supposed to possess knowledge of men's thoughts & the secret workings of their inner natures & this knowledge is as much an attribute of God's & as inconsistent with the character of a creature as an omnipresence & omniscience. If I were to incline to any theory upon the subject other than that of the existence of a Prince of the powers of air, I should rather choose that of every man carrying about in his own fallen nature a devil to himself. I do not doubt that there are many spirits, fallen angels who are subjects perhaps of the arch fiend & do his work, yet I must believe in the existence of their Supreme Head and attribute to him powers greater than are possessed by any other creature of whom we have any knowledge.

It is a beautiful moonlight night tho rather cool for Spring. The trees are all green or rapidly becoming so & the flowers & birds & all other accompaniments of Spring are with us, with their fragrance & beauty & music. It is the loveliest season of all the year to me. The vegetation I notice is just about a month more advanced than it was at Princeton last year.

Miss Jane Thomas gave quite a large party at the Lodge on Friday night last. I was in Memphis but of course should not have attended had I been at home. Those who were there give glowing accounts of the enjoyment afforded by the dancing, &c.

Thursday, April 5, 1849

I have been spending the evening at Mr. Mason's. The moon shines gloriously & it is a lovely night. I have passed the time very pleasantly in conversation with Miss Lizzie Mason. She is the most intellectual girl of her age that I have ever known and her society is very different from that of most young ladies. To fine natural abilities she has added considerable information acquired by reading, and she converses with the ease and at the same time with the force & eloquence of a well-educated gentleman. Most unfortunately she is somewhat deaf and the loud tone in which it is necessary to talk with her is somewhat disagreeable, but she is altogether the most interesting young lady in the place, so far as intelligence constitutes interest. About the other girls whom I visit occasionally I will write a word or two.

Miss Brooks Lucas is, after her style, very beautiful. She has large black, moistly lustrous eyes & a striking face & form. Her beauty is of the voluptuous & somewhat languishing kind. Her features are not regular or delicate yet she is one of those girls who attract the first view. In point of mind and attainment she is rather below than above the usual average of girls & yet her conversation is sprightly & engaging. 'Tis said that Litchfield will marry her & they will make a fine match.

Miss Lizzie Mason is another, somewhat younger than Brooks & of her classmates in school days. She has spent a year at a fashionable boarding school in Phila & has brought home the polish without the airs & affectation usually obtained at such places. She has [a] fine complexion & eyes & rather good features, tho her mouth is too large & her other features too prominent for perfect beauty. Her face is a sweet amiable & interesting one, denoting at a glance the simplicity & artlessness & amiability of her character. She is sprightly without being intellectual, and she wins upon rather [than] commands a feeling of interest by her conversation. Her form is not good, yet she is graceful & she sings & plays admirably. She is almost the only lady whom I have ever known who was artless to an extreme.

Miss Emily Roth is another lady whom I like very much to visit. She is much older than either of the others & has much more knowledge of the world. She is intelligent & sociable, quick & fluent in conversation & sings & plays well. She possesses great powers of entertaining & is altogether one of the most pleasant & agreeable ladies in the town. She is pretty & has a great deal of strength of character & firmness & energy of purpose, as well as self reliance & self possession.

Miss Mary Jane Martin is quite handsome, of ordinary intelligence, fine conversational powers & possesses in an eminent degree the faculty of making herself agreeable & her visitors easy & satisfied with themselves. Miss Mary B. Martin is one of the sweetest & most attractive of girls, is very handsome & intelligent & winning in her ways. She converses well & impresses you with an admiration of the ingenuousness & goodness of her nature. She has just left school & I have never visited her tho I have known her since she was a child & know no girl of a more lovely character or possessing more that is calculated to please & win upon those who meet her. There are many other girls whom I visit or meet occasionally, whom I like very much but I do not care to scribble more in the way of description. I doubt if any community can be found whose young ladies would appear better & elicit more admiration than ours. I like ladies' society but feel no inclination to become a ladies man & consequently visit very little. I become wearied of the endless trifling & nonsense which characterize the intercourse of the sexes, & except with a very few find the time to drag heavily when a visit is prolonged. Such ladies as Miss Racillia Anderson, from whom information can be derived & whose society affords rational pleasure & solid entertainment, are not often to be found. Indeed, she is the most superior lady whom I have ever known, I think. She is expected here soon, & I am very anxious to see her once more tho I fear I shall be disappointed by being absent.

Friday, April 6, 1849

I glance over the nonsense of the 2 or 3 preceding pages and think that I must have had very little to do last night and must withal have been in an exceedingly stupid mood.

Today I have been at work most of the day in the office. Tonight Miss Lizzie Mason is with Carry, and I have spent the evening very agreeably in her company, taking a moonlight walk & talking with her in the parlor. Since I came to my room, I have spent half an hour in looking at the moon, another half an hour or more in a kind of reverie, and some time in looking over my letters written to Mrs. Crump from Princeton. I was at Tuckahoe one day last week & requested Nancy to send them in to me & she has done so. They bring up to mind the thought and feelings of my Princeton life, but most vividly the sorrow of the months immediately succeeding Lucy's death. There must be truth in Byron's language, "Man's love is of his life a thing apart,"[57] else how can it be that one year has healed the wounds & rendered me so almost forgetful of the past. Mrs. Crump could not live thro that year. Her grief was more than she could bear, & she died of a broken heart. I often feel & have felt inclined to upbraid & reproach myself for heartlessness. Man's own nature is to himself the greatest of all mysteries. The more I think of Lucy's character (& think of her & her love I do every day) in comparison with that of any other girl I know, the more do I feel that mine was indeed an irreparable loss. There is no other lady in all my acquaintance in whose nature there is one half the strength & nobleness which she evinced, not one who could love as she loved, or who would suffer the tithe of what she suffered for the sake of him whom she loved. Indeed, I doubt very much if it has often fallen to the lot of men to be loved as she loved me, nor do I ever expect again to see such depth & tenderness & devotion. Highly as I estimated her when she was living and as constantly as her worth grew upon me, I now feel conscious that I never was able to appreciate her until I had lost her.

Tuckahoe looks as desolate as heretofore. Nancy keeps the house & every thing about it in excellent order, but she cannot impart a look of life or cheerfulness to a spot upon which such deep shadows rest. She talks of Mrs. Crump & Lucy with all the feeling which she would exhibit had they died by yesterday, and the tears come into her eyes while she dwells upon the recital of what they used to say & do. She is the most affectionate servant I ever saw. She says she can never be happy again. I see the boys but very seldom. Mr. Crump has now been absent more than a month in Alabama & I fear they suffer much from the want of his attention. My Father has been sick in bed all day but not seriously I hope. Matt is up again, the others are well. The Cholera rages once more in New Orleans & on the River. We have heard tonight of the death of little Eliza, though we hope that the report is unfounded. There is no news. The weather is dry & fine & the roads are beginning to get good once more. I went out day before yesterday with Pa to examine a piece of land by way of renewing my acquaintance with old time pursuits. I find that it comes very natural to trace lines &c. My time is passing off very unprofitably now I fear. I am reading nothing & feel every day less & less inclination to do so. My correspondence, formerly so extensive, has dwindled down to almost nothing. I do not write a letter except on business more than once a month. This is well enough I reckon; I have wasted a great deal of time in letter writing & my epistolary composition would make quite a volume if collected.

It is midnight & bed time.

Sunday, April 8, 1849

It is a year since I wrote the first line in this book. I had hoped to finish it with the year and commence a new volume with another birthday, but one thing & another & often nothing at all have kept me from writing in it regularly, until I find the record of a whole twelve months of my life comprised within very meager limits. But is it a record of the time which has elapsed since last 8th of April? My movements & doings have in the main been put down, and my thoughts too. Many such as I would have breathed to no human beings, such, most probably, as no human being would have supposed to have existed in my mind. And yet there have been a thousand nameless & unrecorded trifles which have perhaps influenced the year and gone far to constitute its character to me, which these pages do not show. And there is one subject which has occupied many of my thoughts which no word or line in this book conveys an intimation of. Nor am I going to write it now. Why I cannot explain to myself. I write here what I think & feel as unreservedly as I so think & feel, for no eye ever rests upon the pages but my own, and yet upon this one subject I have shrunk from writing. The subject is *love*, and if I have thought of love, perchance *have* loved, why may I not say so? Is it that my heart whispers to me, even while its affections are turning about a new object, that there was another whom I loved, who loved me, as even woman seldom loves, and that her memory ought to be cherished to the exclusion of all else, that my heart should be dead like hers & with hers buried in that grave at Greenwood? Is it that a reproachful voice comes up from the past, issues from the cells of memory, saying that he who has truly loved never forgets? This may be so, & yet methinks as I have written once before my love for Lucy is strong as when she lived, her memory as cherished as when I returned from her fresh grave & looked for the first time at Tuckahoe in its new made desolation. Methinks if I were now married, I could stand with my wife beside Lucy's grave & feel that her spirit if it hovered over the spot was smiling to see me happy & invoking blessings on the head of her who was what death prevented her from becoming. It is true that my own nature, peculiarly the organization of my feelings, is a mystery from which I cannot myself unravel. Often have I felt in bitter self condemnation that I must be the most heartless of men & it may be so. How little have I mourned Mrs. Crump's death, at least how cheerful & careless I have seemed to be, and yet I know that I felt it and feel it still, but has it taken one smile from my lips? When she was in Memphis dying, on the night of the very day when I had parted with her knowing that I should see her no more, I went to a concert & yet I loved her truly, deeply, I cannot doubt this. Nor do

I doubt for a moment that Lucy was as dear to me as my own life. And I do not forget, cannot, never will, forget, and this is the mystery—but no more.

I said it was *love* that I had thought much but had never written. Yes there is one whom if I do not now love, I know I can love & will love. Yea, I love her already. She is not Lucy's equal, indeed in many qualities which constituted the main elements of Lucy's character she is very deficient. She is entirely different from & still I love her. As yet the feeling is an incipient one, which may be crushed & extinguished by slight circumstances or may be easily cherished & fed till it become intense & enduring. I have not plans in connexion with it. No definite ideas of what I may do. I have little if any reason to hope even (& upon how small a foundation can not a lover build a hope) that she will ever care for me. It may be that I shall never speak of love to her, that in a little while I may be satisfied that she can never be mine & so school myself to think of her no longer, or it may be that I shall tell her what I feel & ask my fate at her own lips. It is one of the subjects over which broods the darkness of the coming year, one of the subjects concerning which now on 8th April, I would send a voice across the abyss of a year & ask another birth-day, what it will say. As I write to night memory runs back along its wire, leaping from post to post, down birthday to birthday. A series of years comes up before me, a series of birthdays whose closing hours have found me thus employed & around each of them still lingers the echo of the cry which I now once more send up, what shall another year bring forth.

Since my last birthday I have left Princeton, have been admitted to the bar, formed a partnership with an eminent lawyer & assumed the position of a man in the world under more propitious circumstance than young men entering professions generally do. I am no longer living along without permanent end or aim but am bound to certain routine of life, have marked out my path & entered upon it. With all this I have abundant reason to be satisfied & for it all would God I could be sufficiently grateful. I have not studied a great deal, nor made such advances as I should have done, yet I feel that my progress has been sensible & if life & health be spared, I feel no fear that I shall not attain a portion of respectability in my profession. How Mr. Mason may be pleased with our connection, I have no means of knowing, but I have no reason to suppose that he will not be perfectly willing that it should continue. What may be my present stand in society here I cannot tell. I have no idea what people think or say about me. I think I have many & warm friends, but at the same time I think that there are many who are inimical to me. Among the young men with some exceptions (the exceptions though are the first young men of the town) I know that I am unpopular. The older men, many of them, dislike me. The married ladies are more generally my friends & the girls look upon [me] as a rattling, scatterbrained character to whom more license is by consent allowed than to many others.

Pecuniarily I am worse off in the world than I have been for 2 years. I have spent all the hard earnings of my woods life & now have absolutely & literally nothing beyond the earnings of the past 9 months which cannot soon be realized. With ordinary prudence & economy I might now have been worth $2000, but I find that 8 or 10 of the best years of my life have been spent in industrious persevering, hard labor—in the endurance of hardship & exposure & toil & now at the age of 26 I am no better off than when I commenced. Yet there are many of my extravagancies which I do not & cannot regret. I would not for instance exchange today the fruits of my traveling & residence at the north for the money which they cost me. And then too my lavish expenditure has afforded me much real enjoyment, has enabled [me] sometimes to be somewhat useful & has given me many pleasant memories from which I would not part. I have lived fast, but I have lived well & I am willing if it must be so, now to start afresh. If Heaven continue its favors, I do not apprehend any difficulty in making a living. I have industry & energy enough for that, though in good truth the thought of being penniless at 26 is anything but comfortable. My health during the past winter has been better than ever before. Now I am suffering the effects of chills, but I hope I shall recover from them soon & be able to work as well as heretofore. I have weighed nearly or quite 150 lbs during the winter, but now weigh only 140. That however is 5 pounds more than I weighed a year since. Oh, for good health, I ask no thing more.

I am comfortably situated in a good room & pleasant office & agreeable companions whenever I want them. I board at my sisters. My Mother has sent me to day a birth day cake which Hackleton & Litchfield & Caswell helped me eat this afternoon. And Sally has just sent me in another fine one. My lot is cast in pleasant places surely, all the members of my father's family seem much attached to me. Ma is a mother to me. Carry loves me. Matt is one of the most devoted of Sisters. Mr. Fort is all that I could desire in a brother in law, with the one exception of lacking energy of character in some degree. Today & for a few days past Pa has been quite sick, but I hope only temporarily & Matt's health is very bad, but I think it results from nursing. With these exceptions all are well & as happy I have no doubt as most families. My Father & Mr. Fort are doing a safe & good business & we all have the comforts & many of the luxuries of life around us. God has been very good to us all. And so I close the brief record of another birthday. Is it my last, or shall I say that I am 27 years old as now I say I am 26.

One year ago tonight I was writing to Mrs. Crump & I asked her, "should we live to see another 8th of April?" She is gone. In taking away from me my best friend, Providence has signalized the year by a misfortune to me only second to that which overshadowed the year before. Outside of the circle of my own relatives, no one could have been taken whose loss I should have felt so much, but I feel sure that tonight she is happy & that if she can revisit those whom she loved, her spirit watches me now as I think & write of her. Oh if I could only know that Lucy too is in Heaven to night, I should be more happy than ought else could possibly make me. This question has been in my thoughts, my heart, oh so often, but it is too painful, too momentous. Whatever it is, to know that she is [. . .]ing the [. . .] of a Saint at this moment would take away all my sorrow for her loss, would reconcile me to that, to anything, but it is thy secret, Eternity.

26 years old!! Youth has gone. Manhood is slipping away, the future, oh the dark imperious future, what does its gloom enshroud? I have heard a Mr. Bard preach twice today, very good sermons. Have spent most of the afternoon in conversation with young men, tho profitably enough. A Mr. Mahon, a citizen of Montgomery Ala, came in this afternoon on business & sat to talk an hour or more after his business was transacted. He knows Bob Johnson & Dav Clopton & Frank McDonald & Peter Williams & Charley & his sisters, has spent much time in Ga. He was in the Mexican war & is a very agreeable man. He is an old bachelor & told me he was not a marrying man unless he could get a large fortune first & then find a girl whom he would know would marry him *only* for his money. I wondered at such a sentiment, but he said that in that event he would know that he was not deceived & added in explanation that if the history of his life were spread before me, I would not wonder at what he had said. Poor fellow, some cruel disappointment has turned his heart to gall.

I have an interesting Sunday School class now composed of 8 or 9 girls who are almost young ladies & I take much pleasure in teaching them. I have had no opportunity to read the Bible today & I am sorry for it. I like to read it every Sunday at least. For many sabbaths past I have been reading Melville's *Sermons*. They are the finest specimens of sermon writing I ever saw & there is no literature I read with more pleasure. His style is exceedingly ornate & imaginative & striking & strong.

And now to one more of my years fancied. Tis a dark record which it has entered against me in the annals of Eternity. I look back to it with much of regret

& repentance, much of sadness & sorrow & much of pleasurable recollection. It has been as happy a year as most persons enjoy & it has had its dark points. It is gone & I turn to the next with hopes & I trust with a sincere prayer to heaven for help to improve it & for gratitude for mercies past.

Wednesday, April 11, 1849

On Monday morning took a ride on horseback before breakfast with Carry and Emily Polk, then worked &c. until 5 in the afternoon when Litchfield & I went by invitation to Mr. Clapp's to Clem's party. It was Mrs. Clapp's[58] birthday. We found Clem[59] & her little cousins seated at the table doing ample justice to a good supper. There was something more sensible & fully as rational in their enjoyment than we usually find in the parties of "children of a larger growth."[60] After their supper was concluded we had ours & and then we spent a very pleasant evening, Litchfield in conversation with Miss Brooks, and I with Mr. & Mrs. Clapp, Mr. & Mrs. Fielding Lucas[61] & Henrietta.[62] I don't know when I have passed a more agreeable evening. Mrs. Clapp is an old friend of his. I knew her when she was the belle of the town & the most beautiful girl I ever saw, except Miss Holcomb. Mr. Clapp too I have known for many years, and while he was an unmarried man, somewhat intimately. He is very intelligent & exceedingly interesting in conversation. He is one of the best speakers I ever heard and while he cannot be regarded as a man of extraordinary *strength* of intellect, he possesses so much of gracefulness & polish of mind & a taste so chaste & cultivated & an imagination so quick that he can pass for all that he should & perhaps a little more. I always liked him very much and feel grateful to him for having taught me one lesson which I shall never forget, viz. that I was in that habit of "giving too much license to my tongue." Mrs. Fielding Lucas is a pleasant & very ladylike woman. Her manners are very easy & she interests by the look of dignity which she always wears. Of her husband I know but little personally, but that little does not prepossess me in his favor.

We came home from Mr. Clapp's at 11 o'clock through the rain. The next day (yesterday) I went to see a man in the edge of Tippah County. On my way I called at the Lodge to deliver a message from Mr. Mason to Mr. Thomas.[63] I had not been to the house before since I went there to see Lucy in August or Sept 1847. I did not go in, but the sight of the grove & the house, all unchanged, recalled the past most vividly. Pursuing my journey I got out of my course & found myself unexpectedly in John Hull's[64] yard. I had never seen the house before & got away as fast as possible when I found out where I was. On my way home in the afternoon I came through the Greenwood plantation (Wm. Hull's)[65] & went through the orchard by a back gate into the garden & stood once more beside the graves of Mrs. Crump & Lucy. I had not been there before since Mrs. Crump was buried. Her grave has been sodded over & a willow tree planted at its head. Side by side the sisters sleep that long sleep & the mother's grave is there too. I like this burying in the garden whose walks have so often been trodden by the feet of the slumberer in life, or would like it, if there was permanency in the possession of property. First the Mother was buried & the daughters wept in anguish while they listened to the falling of the cold damp earth upon her coffin & then came the feet of mourners bearing the youngest of her children, the beautiful darling of her old age & she too was laid in the earth in the bloom & freshness of her beauty & then came the sister leaning upon my arm to weep over that lost one's ashes; and now the sister too has ceased to feel the pangs of a broken heart, and her bed has been made beneath the spot upon which she stood & mourned so bitterly but a few months before. *She* planted a willow over Lucy's grave & a slip of the same willow now weeps over hers.

My visit so far as I know was unobserved. I hoped that it would be so. I never meet any of the brothers now & I am glad of it. There can never be intercourse between us again. This morning I took a ride again with Carry on horseback before breakfast. Have been at work all day in the office. At sundown this after noon walked up to Mr. Mason's & have been to prayer meeting tonight. Tomorrow I expect to start to Phila with Miss Lizzie Mason & Martha Thompson & this journal will be discontinued during my absence. I may never return & if so, in finishing now the record of a day, I am reaching "the last syllable of recorded time" so far as I am concerned, but I am not wont to look upon the dark side & so I look forward to taking up my pen again to say that I have been once more "where men do congregate" in the city's streets.

I received a letter this morning from Miss Jane Thomas & wrote her one in reply & sent her Macaulay's History.[66] I was sorry I could not see her yesterday when I was at her house. I never had a dear friend before under such circumstances.

I was writing the other night about love. Since then I have been in the company of the lady & feel quite certain that if she does not really dislike me, she is utterly indifferent. Indeed, I think my feelings towards her are more fancy than reality. I do not doubt that I am as capable of loving as I ever was, but I cannot love an *ordinary* woman. Lucy's memory, if it has not made my heart dead to all such susceptibility, has given me a knowledge & an appreciation of a true woman's character & of the worth & strength & devotion of a true woman's love such as will render me hereafter perfectly insensible to the attractions of any one who does not, in my imagination of her at least, make a near approach to that ideal which is based upon the memory of her who is gone. From my earliest recollection I have been conscious of the existence in my mind of an ideal of a woman whom I could love & I have never loved or thought of loving except when the object seemed to realize this ideal. Then, I have in one or two instances thought myself in love with girls, and in a few days or months at most felt perfect indifference for them. The reason was that for the time they were identified with my ideal & I only loved them in this identity, and at the moment that a better knowledge of them, a revelation of their true characters by some chance circumstance, disclosed their non-identity with this ideal, that moment I felt that in the proportion in which they were found thus wanting, in that proportion I ceased to care for them & soon they reached the distance of indifference. When I first loved Lucy it was thus I loved her. She was one of those who have a character to wear to the world. She seemed to the casual & even to the old acquaintance, who had not been able to look beyond the outside show, to be a brilliant, careless, gay & rather heartless girl & so for a time I thought her & while I so thought I did not care for her, but I thought that I discovered a certain under-current beneath the surface ice, a hidden & inner & higher & better nature which she did not reveal to all, a nature corresponding in some degree to my ideal & then I began to feel an interest in her, and distinctly do I now remember the painful doubts and dread, the vacillation of feeling which I experienced for a month, as ever & anon the conviction would be almost forced upon me that I had imagined her to be what she was not, that I had supposed her to possess qualities different from those perceptible to the world of Society, had loved my ideal *and* her in a fancied conformity to my ideal, while in truth she did not at all conform to it. And these fears & doubts clung to me, diminishing in their strength until just before we were engaged. Then I knew her real nature and gradually as time wore on & difficulties increased about us & the bitter trials which fell to her lot were pressed upon her, she appeared more & more in her higher & better & hidden character, rose more & more till she transcended my ideal, taught me that women might be what before I had not imagined in my highest picture of her, and so my love for her gathered more & more strength for there was about her that which in its successive developments called for more & more love & dissipating doubts & vacillations, left me to love in confidence that I was not deceived and elevated my love to reach the elevation of its object.

And now there is an ideal which I love—a better than my old ideal, and the question is shall any one ever be identified again with this new standard. The lady of whom I wrote on Sunday night has seemed to me in many things— not all—to rise to the height of this standard, but when I saw her last—last compared her with it—she seemed to fall below it, & I came from her presence cold & careless of her favor. She has changed much of late. I can mark & realize this change & it has not been for the better. Would that I could tonight banish her image altogether from my thoughts & let it find a place there no more. I feel that there is even more probability that in a little while I shall be indifferent to her, than that I shall love her. It will depend not upon what I may think of my chance of winning her [. . .] for if I should be made certain that she is all my fancy has ever painted her, I should only love more intensely as she seemed regardless of me & my love, but it will depend upon the phases which her character shall hereafter assume in my eyes. I must love to be happy, but the dreary prospect of remaining unmarried is now much more palpably before me as my lot than perhaps ever before.

Sunday, June 10, 1849

On Tuesday night last I returned from my trip to the North on which I started on the day after I wrote the last page. On Wednesday I had a very hard chill which was followed by others on Thursday & Friday so that I have been in bed almost ever since I got back and very sick much of the time. Yesterday & today I have missed the chills, and I hope now that I shall get well again. I only open this journal tonight to note the day of my return. When I have time & strength I will write some description of my very pleasant town. There has been a thunderstorm this afternoon & it is quite cool tonight. Heard Mr. Chittenden preach today.

Sunday, July 15, 1849

Three months I have passed without any memoranda, save the short one on this page. I will go back to the 10th April & endeavour briefly to bring up the record. At 5 o'clock we took our seats in the stage & were whirled away towards Ripley. The girls were much overwhelmed by the anguish of parting and they did little but weep for the first few hours. The afternoon was a delightful one. The breath of Spring mingled in the atmosphere & the fragrance of flowers & the smell of the freshly turned ground in the fields & the fresh bright green of the young leaves were combined to make the evening pleasant. As darkness came down upon us & the stage wheels grated along through the sand & the whipporwill uttered its plaintive song, ever repeating its own name as though one of the "voices of the night" were ever asking in its ear, "what of all things is saddest?" & it was ever replying "Whipporwill," "Whipporwill!" & the stillness & quiet settled down on field & forest, I indulged a feeling of delicious reverie—I know not how to describe it—a feeling of the temporary predominance of the spiritual in our natures. We reached Salem to Supper & then after walking up several hills & making many ineffectual attempts to sleep, we reached Ripley before day & went to bed. Spent the 13th in Ripley. I went out to examine some lands & the girls were beginning their experience of the loveliness of strange company. A sudden change in the weather that night & when we got up before day to start on the morning of the 14th it was freezing. Our ride during the day, especially until breakfast time, was exceedingly unpleasant. We reached Tuscumbia about 2 o'clock AM Sunday 15th. When we woke on Sunday morning, the snow was falling & mid-winter seemed suddenly to have supplanted the Spring. On Monday the day was pleasant & to avoid the miserable rail road we procured a comfortable carriage to convey us to Decatur. The road was in fine order & the day's ride was to me perhaps the most pleasant day of traveling during the whole trip. Miss Lizzie conversed with much enthusiasm & animation upon every subject & high as my opinion of her had previously been, I was surprised at the extent of her intellectual superiority over any other girl of her age that I had known.

Reached Decatur 6 o'clock Monday evening & spent the night in comfortable quarters at McCarney's Hotel. Aboard the Boat "News" on the [. . .] River at 2 o'clock PM on Tuesday 17 & had a very delightful trip to Gunter's Landing (or Guntersville as they call it now). Miss Lizzie had never seen a steam boat before, & I took much pleasure in conducting her over it from Hurricane deck to the boilers, from stem to stern & making such explanations as she wished. Martha had travelled on boats before. After the examination was concluded we sat on the guards on the north side of the boat & had a conversation very interesting to me (tho I must confess very egotistical). The girls went to sleep & I remained up to get a glimpse of Paint Rock. This great material curiosity rises perpendicularly from the waters edge to the height I am told of 400 feet & the whole face of it is variegated as though it had been painted different colors. It extends about ½ mile along the river & really presents a grand, gloomy & magnificent appearance at midnight.

We reached Guntersville at midnight & in company with Mr. Collier & his two daughters & Mr. Wood from Tenn who had been our fellow passengers on the boat, took our seats in the stage for Rome about 1 o'clock AM Wednesday 18th. A few miles from the River we got out to walk across a bridge where there is a beautiful cataract & some of the wildest scenery I ever saw & then to clamber up a long steep, rocky mountain. It was dark & gloomy. Breakfasted at Nollie's where we had a good breakfast. We found our fellow travelers very pleasant companions and congratulated ourselves upon having fallen in with them. Reached Rome in Ga that night about 11 o'clock having dined at Blue

Pond which by the way is a curiosity itself, being a small pond, an acre in extent perhaps, of blue, clear water without any outlet & in parts without any bottom so far as has yet been discovered. A good supper & bed at Rome & on the cars next morning before day dashing along by the side of the River to Kingson where we remained in the cars for 2 hours from fear of the small pox & then were rattled off towards Charleston. Had a good view of Stone mountain in passing one of the greatest natural curiosities in the South, being solid rock nearly ½ mile high covering more than 600 acres of ground, with an observatory on the top. One side is perpendicular. I had visited it in '36 when I was at school in Guinnette County, a party of 15 boys made the excursion & met ex-Gov Troup[67] then. He ordered dinner for us all at the Hotel & left while we were on the Mt. In the course of the afternoon we passed through Greensborough, the place where Mr. Collier used to live & where Ma spent the days of her girlhood & was married. I had lived there two years in Mr. Lewis's family in 1831 & 2 I believe. As we travelled through the town I saw a few familiar looking objects, especially I observed that a deep excavation for the rail road had been cut across my old school path & near the house in which Mr. Lewis formerly lived.

Reached Augusta at midnight & slept till 4 o'clock when we were en route for Charleston. We had no opportunity of seeing anything of Augusta, but I have been there before & it is a beautiful place, having one street through the center of the city, Broad St., which is scarcely surpassed in the South. We travelled rapidly on the So. Ca. rail roads sometimes at the rate of 30 miles an hour & reached Charleston to dinner & got a most excellent one at the Charleston Hotel, at least we gentlemen did, the girls wouldn't eat. The girls had never seen any place so citylike as Charleston & noticed the paved narrow streets & the blocks of tall houses & the marks of age about the place with much interest. I went to the Charleston Bank & saw the president Mr. Conner for a few minutes. In the afternoon we went aboard the boat for [. . .] & were soon streaming down the beautiful bay into the Atlantic. Martha soon became sick & went to bed, but Lizzie gaped for hours in rapt enthusiasm from the promenade deck upon the constantly widening blue expanse. She had never seen the ocean before. The afternoon was a mild, bright beautiful one & the water was calm as it could be, and I was delighted to notice the impression made by the first sight of the sublime immensity upon a young, ardent, pure, cultivated & intellectual nature. She seemed perfectly absorbed in her emotions, and her whole soul seemed to have come into her face in the intensity of its feelings. When the sun went down we had been some hours across the bar & were almost out of sight of land. On one side the vision lost itself in the illimitable range of white capped waves with here & there a full fledged bark making its way, homeward or outward bound. On the other, the low line of coast was scarcely distinguishable in the dim distance from a bank of clouds settled upon the horizon. Twas a glorious scene & fully did her nature respond to the call which was made upon it. Few women, I am satisfied, are capable of feeling what she felt then.

We awoke at Wilmington & at 8 o'clock took the cars northward. The journey through N.Ca. is dull & monotonous in the extreme. The road passes over an unbroken tract of flat pine forest, the country in which turpentine is collected. The houses, few and far between, are mostly miserable cabins & the people for the most part are poor, squalid, sallow & dirt eating in their appearance. No farms of any size are to be seen & nothing indeed to vary the aspect of the pine covered country. Sometimes we would cross a swamp in which the cypress & some evergreens were growing with the long moss hanging like gray funeral draping from their branches. In addition to all this, the road is much out of repair & the cars any thing but comfortable. In this country we parted with our fellow travelers, Mr. Wood & the Colliers, & were again alone. We supped at Weldon, a capital supper too, pursued our journey in a miserable car to Petersburg which place we reached about 3 o'clock PM on Sunday morning & sat there in a cold cheerless parlor of a hotel for an hour or two & were then taken to the cars & sat in them two hours longer. The cars however were very fine ones & well warmed by a stove.

Ever since we left Tuscumbia we had noticed on the vegetation the traces of the severe & unusual frost. The trees looked as though they had been scalded & the corn & cotton were entirely cut down. Snow had fallen every where & in Wilmington to the depth of 7 inches. The nights were very cold during the whole trip & shawls & cloaks comfortable most of the time during the day. In an hour or two after leaving Petersburg we reached Richmond & found most comfortable quarters at the American Hotel about 9 o'clock on Sunday morning 22 April. I think it is one of the best hotels I ever saw. The girls spent the morning in their room. I went to church & heard Mr. Stephen Taylor preach a most excellent sermon on the sin of selfishness & the selfishness of sin. I was the more interested in it because the thought & reasoning were in main exactly those which I had planned out for an Odd Fellows speech in case I should ever be called upon to make one. This coincidence I afterwards mentioned to Lizzie. Miss Taylor called & took Lizzie home to dinner with her & Martha would not go down, so I dined alone. At night Martha & I strolled round the City. It is really a beautiful place & is improving rapidly. It is situated upon the side & top of a hill, commanding a very fine view of James River.

We left Richmond at 9 o'clock AM, Monday 23 on the road to Washington. The country over which the road passes is generally old & worn out. There are but few of the old Virginia Mansions to be seen, and no appearance of the wealth & luxury for which the Old Dominion has been famous. Fredricksburg is pretty & quite a large place. As the place of Mrs. Crump's former residence & the scene of Lucy's school girl life, I looked upon with great interest & many sorrowful emotions. At the depot, I thought of Mrs. Crump as she arrived there last year in search of health & as she started away wasted & worn down by sickness & longing once more to see the home which she was destined never again to reach. There was the old bridge, spanning the River, upon which I remembered that she told me she used to stand in the cool of the evening as the termination of her evening walk, & I could almost imagine that I saw her earnest face there again in the midst of a group of friends & heard her voice mingling with theirs. There were many persons at the depot & I wondered if any of them had known her.

At 12 o'clock we embarked on the boat Powhattan on the Potomac at the mouth of Acquia Creek & were streaming up that noble River. We met the Rev W. McClain at Acquia & saw him a moment or two. The dinner on board the boat was one of the most splendid I have ever seen & the trip was a delightful one. We had a fine view of Mt. Vernon as it stands in its solitary consecration on the left Bank of the River & caught a glimpse of Washington's tomb through the trees. The River was covered with schooners & fishing boats & we were much interested in watching their tacking & steerings. The fort (I forget its name) below Washington is a massive structure. When I had travelled on the Potomac before it was night & I had never had a view of it. About 4 o'clock we reached the wharf & found a carriage which deposited us safely at Gadsby's Hotel in the Federal City, Monday 23 April.

END OF VOLUME

I will continue this journal in a large black book labeled "Natural Philosophy" not having been able to get another like this. I began this on my birthday & had hoped to conclude the volume on my last birthday but did not have the time to jot down regularly.

Despite similarities of rank and region, the diarists collected in this volume were very different men. Harry Dixon was vivacious and hot tempered, caught between boyhood's abandon and manhood's bristle. In a single afternoon he could go from throwing dirt clods at his friends to seething with rage because someone hadn't taken him for a gentleman. Henry Craft had little of Dixon's rascality or pride. Caught in a reinforcing cycle of grief and self-loathing, he saw himself as pathetic, forgettable, a sleepwalker, a machine. His diary wasn't a place to capture life, as was Dixon's, but to lament it. Henry Hughes had neither Craft's timidity nor Dixon's joie de vivre. Hughes was a tortured megalomaniac, a dictator-in-training. If he didn't believe he was the Second Coming, he believed something very like it. "Who shall be Christ's forerunner," he asked. "Lord is it I?" John Coleman, of course, would have laughed himself silly at Hughes's pretensions. As a Universalist Coleman believed God had no special place for him that He didn't also have for Hebrews and Hindus and everyone else besides. And anyway, Coleman wouldn't have wanted to rule the world, even if God was offering. His great ambition was to shoot straight, grow fat vegetables, and marry a good-looking woman who didn't mind getting her hands dirty. All four diarists were Southern white gentlemen. This made them elites, but they were not interchangeable. Like most people, then and now, they concentrated most on what made them different from everybody else, not on what made them the same. "I am a fool," said Craft. "I am a strange man," said Hughes. "I am a scamp," said Dixon. (Coleman, of course, never said who he was; his diary wasn't about that.)[1]

Heedless of such differences, the Civil War swept all four men into service and killed one of them. Craft from his law office, Coleman from his farm, Dixon from his college, Hughes from his mother's kitchen (along with a few million others) were each and all sucked into the sectional conflict. The war had the kind of gravity that warped the life trajectories of all who lived through it, and Craft, Coleman, Dixon, and Hughes were no exception. Together they form a sort of collective portrait of the Confederate army, composed as it was of planters' sons and farmers' sons and factors' sons and merchants' sons, all of whose differences suddenly meant very little. Throughout their lives they had all unwittingly been traveling the same road.

Henry Craft joined the Confederate army in 1862 and served creditably as adjutant to Brigadier General James R. Chalmers, commander of the Second Brigade, Second Corps of the Army of the Mississippi. Craft saw little action as an adjutant, though Chalmers praised him publicly for the "order and system" of the brigade. He did not serve long, however, before ill health forced him to return to Union-occupied Memphis. There life served up what he saw as another typical humiliation. "Today I have taken the oath of allegiance," he wrote in August 1863. "[I] looked in every direction for some mode of escape . . . [but] I do not expect to live long enough to suffer much from [the] . . . odium." Of course, it was Craft's peculiar curse to live long enough to suffer. The exact date of his death is unknown, but he survived until at least 1887. To the end he was probably thinking of Lucy and what might have been. Certainly, he was still thinking of her in 1863. "It [was] just such weather as [this]," he noted in November, "when Lucy died. Sixteen years ago! How my life has slipped away. I very often think & feel that it is all down hill before me now, and that I am approaching the bottom rapidly. Such is our life."[2]

In the spring of 1861 Harry Dixon dropped out of the University of Virginia and enlisted as a private in the Eleventh Mississippi Infantry Regiment. There he continued to chafe at indignities, real and imagined, protesting to his accumulating diary that "at home I was, at least, once a gentleman." Dixon survived the war, but, like most, he was changed by it. Indulging too deeply in the iniquities of camp life, he became a cautionary footnote to his own motto, "While we live, let us live." "I am a worse man than I was," he admitted in 1863. "I weep for myself in shame. Oaths now frequently escape my lips. Iron is deeply embedded in my soul. I am alone & I know it." He died of syphilis in 1898.[3]

Henry Hughes enlisted in the Twelfth Mississippi Infantry Regiment and rose to the rank of colonel, serving in Virginia and Port Hudson. Depressed by infighting among Confederate politicians and generals, he repeatedly called for a "New Washington" to unite the South and lead it into a bold new era—but none emerged. In his youth, of course, he had seen himself as such a man. If his health was spared, he had promised his diary in 1848, he would place himself "upon a throne" from which he would "look down on Alexand[er], Caesar, Cicero, Bonaparte, [and] Washington." His health was not spared, however, and, like most who died in the Civil War, he was killed by disease in late 1862.[4]

John Coleman left Feasterville in April 1861 with his brother-in-law Andrew McConnell to enlist in the Buckhead Guards, eventually part of the Seventeenth South Carolina Infantry Regiment. The war made the men, already friends, boon companions. "We both enlisted at the same time," Coleman noted in 1863, "and [we] have been in the same Company, in the same mess, and slept together almost every night [since]." Together the two saw much of the war: they witnessed the bombardment of Sumter and the routing of the Union army at First Manassas; McConnell was wounded at Boonsboro; and Coleman was wounded at Second Manassas. "We have passed over the greater portion of Virginia," boasted Coleman, "from the Potomac to the Roanoke, and along the coast of N.C. from Weldon to Wilmington . . . [and] from Charleston nearly to Savannah."[5]

In late July 1864 Coleman and McConnell's brigade was entrenched along a promontory known as Pegram's salient outside Petersburg. Unknown to them, beneath their feet and while they slept a regiment of Pennsylvania coal miners had dug a five-hundred-foot tunnel and filled it with four tons of gunpowder. The resulting explosion was like nothing the war had ever seen. A vast column of fire and earth shot two hundred feet in the air, bearing men, munitions, and timbers in a fountain of gore that arced out, crested, and then rained heavily back down to the ground. One entire South Carolina regiment was destroyed; another was partially buried. Coleman and McConnell's regiment was just to the left of the blast. As they tried to recover their wits, Federal troops, capitalizing on Confederate confusion, advanced on their position, and McConnell was shot and killed.[6]

John Coleman survived the Battle of the Crater, which ironically proved a Union defeat. Company business prevented his attending McConnell's interment, but he got a pass a couple of days later to visit his friend's grave and collect his effects from the hospital. Returning dejectedly to camp after sundown, Coleman was touched to find that his men had dug him a comfortable hole to sleep in. Lying in his hole, thinking of his bedmate of three years lying far away in a hole of his own, Coleman leafed through McConnell's diary and then took out his pen: "[I] feel very lonely, having to lie by myself," he wrote in the dead man's diary. "My old comrade, dear friend, brother in law, had been with me ever since the war began. We had slept together, eat and fought side beside [each other] till his death, and this night I realized how dear a friend I had lost, and was now as if alone in the world."[7]

Coleman served through Appomattox. He was paroled on April 12, 1865, almost four years to the day from his enlistment. Trading his watch for a horse, he rode directly home and started planting. Hard work, he had always insisted, was the proper "perscription" for any malady. In a last entry in his friend's diary he summed up his feelings for the war: "[We] are completely subdued. . . . I hope the damage may prove beneficial to all." And so it has.[8]

PREFACE

1. Susan Faludi, *Stiffed: The Betrayal of the American Man* (New York: W. Morrow, 1999).

2. Bertram Wyatt-Brown, "Honor, Shame, and Iraq in American Foreign Policy," a note prepared for the Workshop on Humiliation and Violent Conflict, Columbia University, New York, November 18–19, 2004.

3. An important new essay collection appeared while this introduction was being finished: Craig Thompson Friend and Lorri Glover, *Southern Manhood: Perspectives on Masculinity in the Old South* (Athens: University of Georgia Press, 2004). The volume is not a work of synthesis, however. Rather, it laudably seeks to complicate our picture by revealing a "diversity of Southern masculinities" (x).

4. Bertram Wyatt-Brown, *Southern Honor: Ethics and Behavior in the Old South* (New York: Oxford University Press, 1982), and Stephanie McCurry, *Masters of Small Worlds: Yeoman Households, Gender Relations, and the Political Culture of the Antebellum South Carolina Lowcountry* (New York: Oxford University Press, 1995).

5. John Mayfield, "'The Soul of a Man!': William Gilmore Simms and the Myths of Southern Manhood," *Journal of the Early Republic* 15 (1995): 477–500, and "Being Shifty in a New Country: Southern Humor and the Masculine Ideal," in Friend and Glover, *Southern Manhood*, 113–35; and Johanna Shields, "A Sadder Simon Suggs: Freedom and Slavery in the Humor of Johnson Jones Hooper," *Journal of Southern History* 56, no. 4 (1990): 641–64. Other works that nicely complicate reigning paradigms are Anya Jabour, "Male Friendship and Masculinity in the Early National South: William Wirt and His Friends," *Journal of the Early Republic* 20 (2000): 83–111, and Janet Moore Lindman, "Acting the Manly Christian: White Evangelical Masculinity in Revolutionary Virginia," *William and Mary Quarterly* 57 (2000): 393–416. For a seminal work that manages to cover dueling *and* the softer side of antebellum Southern masculinity see Steven Stowe, *Intimacy and Power: Ritual in the Lives of the Planters* (Baltimore: Johns Hopkins University Press, 1987).

6. Scholars interested in the Old South's imperial thought might begin with Robert E. May, *Manifest Destiny's Underworld: Filibustering in Antebellum America* (Chapel Hill: University of North Carolina Press, 2002). Unfortunately, romanticism is a concept out of favor with historians of the Old South. The concept of nostalgia promises to bring it back, though it has yet to find its scholar. Researchers interested in the historicization of nostalgia in a Southern context more generally might begin with the fine notes of David Anderson, "Down Memory Lane: Nostalgia for the Old South in Post–Civil War Plantation Reminiscences," *Journal of Southern History* 71, no. 1 (2005): 105–36. The market's effect on masculinity has been better studied in its Northern context. See, for instance, E. Anthony Rotundo, *American Manhood: Transformations in Masculinity from the Revolution to the Modern Era* (New York: Basic Books, 1993), and Shawn Johansen, *Family Men: Middle-Class Fatherhood in Early Industrializing America*

(New York: Routledge, 2001). On secession as a masculine response see Christopher J. Olsen, *Political Culture and Secession in Mississippi: Masculinity, Honor, and the Antiparty Tradition, 1830–1860* (New York: Oxford University Press, 2002).

7. Much new work seeks, in one way or another, to reduce the sense that masculinity was monolithic or transhistorical. On regional variations of masculinity in the South see Christopher Waldrep, "The Making of a Border State Society: James McGready, the Great Revival, and the Prosecution of Profanity in Kentucky," *American Historical Review* 99, no. 3 (1994): 767–84. On possible discrepancies between yeoman and planter understandings of manhood see Edward E. Baptist, "Accidental Ethnography in an Antebellum Southern Newspaper: Snell's Homecoming Festival," *Journal of American History* 84, no. 4 (1998): 1355–83. On masculinity as a Southern export see Nicole Etcheson, "Manliness and the Political Culture of the Old Northwest, 1790–1860," *Journal of the Early Republic* 15, no. 1 (1995): 59–77. Much of Friend and Glover, *Southern Manhood*, is devoted to the variety of masculine understandings. For a model study on the interconnectedness of market, race, and masculinity in the North see Paul Gilmore, *The Genuine Article: Race, Mass Culture, and American Literary Manhood* (Durham: Duke University Press, 2001). Scott L. Malcomson, *One Drop of Blood: The American Misadventure of Race* (New York: Farrar, Straus and Giroux, 2000), was integral to my thinking about "Indianness" in America.

8. George B. Forgie, *Patricide in the House Divided: A Psychological Interpretation of Lincoln and His Age* (New York: W. W. Norton, 1979); Karen Lystra, *Searching the Heart: Women, Men, and Romantic Love in Nineteenth-Century America* (New York: Oxford University Press, 1989). Anya Jabour perhaps comes closest in *Marriage in the Early Republic: Elizabeth and William Wirt and the Companionate Ideal* (Baltimore: Johns Hopkins University Press, 1989). For a study that examines Northern men's attempt to measure up as fathers see Stephen M. Frank, *Life with Father: Parenthood and Masculinity in the Nineteenth-Century American North* (Baltimore: Johns Hopkins University Press, 1998). The quotation is from Christopher J. Olsen, reviewing *All That Makes a Man* in *American Historical Review* 109, no. 4 (2004): 1233.

9. Catherine Clinton and Nina Silber, eds., *Divided Houses: Gender and the Civil War* (New York: Oxford University Press, 1992); LeeAnn Whites, *Gender Matters: Civil War, Reconstruction, and the Making of the New South* (New York: Palgrave, 2005) and *The Civil War as a Crisis in Gender: Augusta, Georgia, 1860–90* (Athens: University of Georgia Press, 1995). The notion of war as essentially ironic is most thoroughly explored in Paul Fussell, *The Great War and Modern Memory* (New York: Oxford University Press, 1975), and Eric J. Leed, *No Man's Land: Combat and Identity in World War I* (Cambridge: Cambridge University Press, 1979).

10. Michael O'Brien, ed., *An Evening When Alone: Four Journals of Single Women in the South, 1827–1867* (Charlottesville: University Press of Virginia, 1993).

INTRODUCTION

1. Harry St. John Dixon Diary, March 5, May 18, 1860, Harry St. John Dixon Papers, UNC (hereafter Dixon Diary); John Howard Payne, "Home, Sweet Home," from *Clari; or, the Maid of Milan: An Opera* (1823).

2. Steven M. Stowe, ed., *A Southern Practice: The Diary and Autobiography of Charles A. Hentz, M.D.* (Charlottesville: University Press of Virginia, 2000), 57. On Southern sons and coming-of-age see Katharine Du Pre Lumpkin, *The Making of a Southerner* (Athens: University of Georgia Press, 1992), and William Barney, "Patterns of Crisis: Alabama White Families and Social Change, 1850–1870," *Sociology and Social Research* 63 (1979): 524–43.

3. Bliss Perry, ed., *The Heart of Emerson's Journals* (New York: Dover, 1995), 115.

4. Anna King to Thomas King, December 27, 1844, Thomas Butler King Family Papers, UNC; James Henry Hammond to Harry Hammond, July 16, 1859, in *The Hammonds of Redcliffe*, ed. Carol Bleser (New York: Oxford University Press, 1981), 68.

5. William L. Barney, *The Passage of the Republic: An Interdisciplinary History of Nineteenth-Century America* (Lexington: D. C. Heath, 1987), 206; Frederick Law Olmsted, *The Cotton Kingdom: A Traveller's Observations on Cotton and Slavery in the American Slave States* (New York: Alfred A. Knopf, 1953), 475. On sex in the Old South see Catherine Clinton and Michele Gillespie, eds., *The Devil's Lane: Sex and Race in the Early South* (Oxford: Oxford University Press, 1997).

6. Though quoted widely, the letter that bears Lee's quotation is supposed to be a forgery. Whether Lee *ever* said it is now open to question. Apparently, a Northern soldier stationed near Arlington had access to a cache of Lee's letters to his son, and evidence suggests that the soldier forged the infamous letter of April 5, 1852. Whether he borrowed from an earlier letter or merely created a new one from whole cloth has not been definitively proven. See Charles A. Graves, *The Forged Letter of General Robert E. Lee* (Richmond: Richmond Press, 1914) and *Supplemental Paper Read before the Virginia State Bar Ass'n* (Richmond: Richmond Press, 1915). See also Douglas Southall Freeman, *R. E. Lee: A Biography* (New York: Scribner's, 1934).

7. Thomas Roderick Dew, "Baccalaureate Address to the Graduates of William and Mary, 1837," *Southern Literary Messenger*, July 1837, 403, from a speech delivered in Houston by James Hamilton and reprinted in the *Telegraph and Texas Register*, March 27, 1839.

8. I have written more on this subject in *All That Makes a Man: Love and Ambition in the Civil War South* (Oxford: Oxford University Press, 2003).

9. Dixon Diary, May 5, 1860; John Albert Feaster Coleman Diary, March 28, 1850, Coleman, Feaster, and Faucette Family Papers, USC (hereafter Coleman Diary); Henry Craft Diary, May 9, 1848, Craft, Fort, and Thorne Family Papers, UNC (hereafter Craft Diary); Henry Hughes (writing as "St. Henry"), "Re-opening of the African Labor Supply—Number Seven—Wealth Argument," *Semi-Weekly Mississippian* (Jackson), October 4, 1859.

10. No one has yet written a conceptual history of the self. It is everywhere implied and nowhere documented that the self can itself be historicized. Karen Lystra has come the closest in *Searching the Heart*. On the diary as a changing genre in the South see Michael O'Brien, *An Evening When Alone: Four Journals of Single Women in the South, 1827–1867* (Charlottesville: University Press of Virginia, 1993).

11. Obviously, some diarists write specifically for children or spouses. Even in these cases, however, they tend to lose themselves; their intended audience dissolves, and they write unguardedly, occasionally unconsciously. Granting that diaries are not perfect reflections of their keepers, granting that they flirt with a possible audience, they remain

our best entrée into the private thoughts and feelings of the dead. Why should a diary be more suspect than a letter or even a conversation? The self is an ever-shifting construct; wherever we find it, we can be sure only that it is a chameleon. See Thomas Mallon, *A Book of One's Own: People and Their Diaries* (New York: Penguin, 1984), xvii.

12. Dixon Diary, April 3, 1860, June 26, 1860.

13. Ibid., "Family History" (appearing after March 27, 1860, entry).

14. James Charles Cobb, *The Most Southern Place on Earth: The Mississippi Delta and the Roots of Regional Identity* (Oxford: Oxford University Press, 1992).

15. Dixon Diary, August 5, 1860, May 6, 1860.

16. Ibid., March 15, 1860.

17. Ibid., April 8, 1860, March 3, 1860, July 15, 1860.

18. Ibid., March 27, 1860, August 29, 1860, June 9, 1860.

19. Ibid., May 9, 1860.

20. Ibid., April 20, 1860; Harry Dixon to Richard Dixon, March 3, 1860, Harry St. John Dixon Papers, UNC.

21. Douglas Ambrose, *Henry Hughes and Proslavery Thought in the Old South* (Baton Rouge: Louisiana State University Press, 1996), 8–26.

22. Ibid.

23. Henry Hughes Diary, April 16, 1848, Henry Hughes Papers, Mississippi Department of Archives and History (hereafter Hughes Diary).

24. Ibid., October 10, 1852.

25. Ibid., January 2, 1848, January 20, 1850, February 13, 1848, January 9, 1848, February 3, 1850.

26. Ibid., January 18, 1852, October 7, 1848, May 21, 1848, July 2, 1848.

27. Ibid., April 6, 1851, May 11, 1851. On the issue of Hughes's possible homosexuality see Ambrose, *Henry Hughes*, 32–48.

28. Hughes Diary, January 9, 1853, December 21, 1851, March 23, 1851, January 1, 1852. Hughes, like many intellectuals before and since, sought to yoke his sexual energies to his ambition but ended up sexualizing his ambition. See, for instance, February 10, 1850: "She who watches me, believes beloved & rejected. I never where I set my amorous hopes was unsuccessful. But I love Glory, Power, Fame, Energy. What is her name? She is my Soul's idol. To her, I, with a lover's hot devotion, kneel. She is my sweet. Romeo never more truly loved. I am her Antony. In her soft arms, on her fair bosom, beneath her warm eyes and balmy breath, I forget all joys & pains. To me, she is Cleopatra. But for her, I will not lose but gain a world. Come Caesar, Come Lepidus. Glory is mine, or death. Whose bosom, is the softer, I do not care. For soon or late, I will repose me there."

29. Hughes Diary, May 5, 1850, December 21, 1851.

30. Ibid., October 19, 1851. Bertram Wyatt-Brown has compared Hughes to an egomaniacal Whitman and his diary to a pitiable song of himself. See *Yankee Saints and Southern Sinners* (Baton Rouge: Louisiana State University Press, 1990).

31. See Ambrose, *Henry Hughes*; Stanford M. Lyman, *Selected Writings of Henry Hughes, Antebellum Southerner, Slavocrat, Sociologist* (Jackson: University Press of Mississippi, 1985); L. L. Bernard, "Henry Hughes, First American Sociologist," *Social Forces* 15 (1936): 154–74.

32. Coleman Diary, May 5, 1849.

33. Coleman Diary, May 22, 1851, April 30, 1849.

34. Ibid., July 23, 1849, November 14, 1849, November 16, 1849.

35. Ibid., March 21, 1849, February 10, 1849, March 19, 1849, March 21, 1849, December 23, 1849.

36. Ibid., March 26, 1849, September 20, 1849, March 29, 1849, March 31, 1849, June 30, 1849, October 22, 1849, November 30, 1849, February 16, 1851, November 2, 1849, June 30, 1849, July 27, 1849, October 23, 1849.

37. Craft Diary, October 29, 1848.

38. Ibid., April 28, 1848.

39. Ibid., July 30, 1848.

40. Ibid., April 11, 1849, August 12, 1860.

41. Ibid., April 8, 1848; Henry Craft to Martha Craft Fort, February 3, 1848; Craft Diary, April 28, 1848.

42. Craft Diary, June 26, 1848. Hamlet's lines are, of course, "To sleep, perchance to dream—ay, there's the rub, / For in that sleep of death what dreams may come, / When we have shuffled off this mortal coil, / Must give us pause" (William Shakespeare, *Hamlet, Prince of Denmark*, in *The Riverside Shakespeare* [Boston: Houghton Mifflin, 1974], act 3, scene 1, lines 64–67).

43. Craft Diary, October 29, 1848, November 3, 1848.

HARRY ST. JOHN DIXON

1. James Rucks (c. 1790–1862) was born in North Carolina. His first wife, Matilda Hogan (1798–1824), died early, probably while giving birth to their son, Henry Taylor Rucks (1824–67). James remarried in 1827, to Louisa V. Brown (1803–49), in Nashville, Tennessee, where he was a circuit judge. In the 1840s James moved to Jackson, Mississippi, and from there to Deer Creek, becoming one of three plantation owners who cleared the land that would later become the town of Leland. (The others were Richard Lawrence Dixon, Harry's father, owner of Sycamores, and the Percy family, owners of Percy Place.) The Ruckses lived at Three Oaks. The 1850 federal census lists James Rucks as a planter with a real estate valuation of fifteen thousand dollars. The slave schedule for the same year lists him as the owner of 136 slaves. Hereafter information taken from the federal census may be marked simply with "1850C."

2. Probably Eleanor Ryburn Brown (1839–66), James Rucks's niece. Ella's father was John Preston Watts Brown (1815–50), Louisa Rucks's youngest brother.

3. "Hieroglyphics" were a set of symbols that Dixon used to form substitution codes in his diaries. I have playfully named the two symbol sets that he used "Linear A" and "Linear B." Dixon created Linear A in May 1858 at the Deer Creek Select Schoolhouse. For whatever reason (perhaps because he had given his friends a key to Linear A) he later created Linear B. The two codes contain a few of the same symbols, though the letter values for those symbols are not the same.

4. Marian Rucks was the daughter of James Rucks and the older sister of Harry's good friend Taylor Rucks. She was ten in 1850, making her about twenty when Harry was writing (1850C).

5. Probably Harry Yerger, the son of Judge Jacob Schall Yerger. He was eight in 1850, making him about eighteen at the time Harry was writing (1850C).

6. Written in Linear A. Mary Wingate's identity could not be determined with certainty.

7. The 1850 federal census lists a James H. Yerger, twenty-three, as an unmarried deputy sheriff. He must have married between 1850 and 1860, but no federal census records for Washington County could be found for that year. Evidence revealed later in the diary suggests that Mrs. James Yerger was a sister of James Rucks.

8. Possibly Adelaide Stokes Nichol (1841–1926). Dellie's sister, Sarah Jane Nichol (1833–69), had married Henry Taylor Rucks in 1854 and was living at Sherwood Plantation. Whether Dellie was living with her sister or merely visiting her from Nashville is unclear.

9. Probably the Jennie Hunter mentioned elsewhere in the diary. Her identity could not be definitively determined.

10. Probably William H. Lee, the father of Nathaniel Lee, one of Harry's close friends. Wm. H. Lee, thirty-six, was a planter with four children, a real estate valuation of thirty thousand dollars, and seventy-two slaves (1850C).

11. Harry's father, Richard Lawrence Dixon, was born circa 1816 in Abingdon, Virginia. In his late teens he followed his older brother to Jackson, Mississippi, where he became clerk of the Chancery Court. In 1837 he married Julia Rebecca Phillips, Harry's mother. The family lived in Jackson until 1847, when they relocated to their plantation near Greenville. In 1850 Richard owned thirty-six slaves and real estate valued at ten thousand dollars (1850C). After the Civil War Richard moved his family again, to California, to escape Reconstruction. His grandson, Harry's son, was the painter Maynard Dixon (1875–1946).

12. Harry's mother, Julia Rebecca Phillips, was the daughter of James and Sarah Phillips of Jackson, Mississippi. She and Richard had eight children, of whom Harry was the oldest.

13. Jack Phillips was Julia Dixon's younger brother. In 1850 J. Phillips was twenty-three, living with the Dixons as their overseer (1850C).

14. Edward Bulwer-Lytton, *Lady of Lyons; or, Love and Pride* (1838).

15. Louise Yerger was the daughter of William and Malvina Yerger. In 1850 she was six, making her about sixteen at the time Harry was writing (1850C).

16. Possibly Henry Taylor Rucks (1824–67), Judge James Rucks's son from his first marriage. The 1850 federal census lists Henry T. Rucks as an overseer for William and Malvina Yerger. Malvina was Henry's sister. Henry married Sarah Jane Nichol in 1854 and soon after moved to Sherwood Plantation.

17. The 1850 federal census lists two Andrew Carsons, father and son, living in the same household. The first is listed as a fifty-two-year-old planter; the second, his son Andrew B. Carson, is listed as a sixteen-year-old overseer. The context makes it likely that Harry is referring to the son, who would have been twenty-six at the time Harry was writing.

18. Possibly George Yerger, a son of Judge Jacob Schall Yerger and Mary Yerger (1850C). In 1850 George Yerger was fourteen.

19. Probably Catherine S. Lee, the daughter of William H. Lee and the sister of Harry's close friend Nat. In 1850 Catherine was nine, making her nineteen at the time Harry was writing (1850C).

20. William Tappan Thompson, *Major Jones's Courtship* (1840).

21. Dixon has encrypted three lines in Linear A, then inked them over, then blurred some of the ink with water to ensure that they are illegible. Even so, a few of the letters can be made out. The gist of the passage appears to be that either while dancing with Miss Ella or while dreaming of such a dance he became tumescent.

22. There were in fact two Dr. Percys living on Deer Creek, making it impossible to say with certainty which one Harry is referring to. The Percys were a storied family, and their Mississippi wing would go on to produce Senator LeRoy Percy (1860–1930) and the writers William Alexander (1885–1942) and Walker Percy (1916–90). In the antebellum period, however, they were planters and gentlemen of leisure. The Percys' land on Deer Creek was originally owned by Thomas George Percy (1786–1841) of Alabama. When he died three of his sons decided to make Deer Creek their permanent home. The sons were John Walker (1817–64), Leroy Pope (1825–82), and William Alexander (1837–88). At Thomas's insistence all of his boys had learned a profession. John Walker and Leroy Pope became doctors, though they would never really practice medicine. William Alexander went to Princeton and studied law at the University of Virginia, though before the Civil War he would never really practice law. Instead, the boys presided over their Deer Creek estate, known as Percy Place. In 1850 the Thomas G. Percy estate included 114 slaves (1850C). Because Harry is elsewhere careful to specify "Dr. Leroy Percy" it seems possible that he is here referring to Dr. John Walker Percy. John Walker Percy had a wife, Fannie (1823–94), and a daughter, May (1848–76). He did not survive the Civil War. See Bertram Wyatt-Brown, *The House of Percy: Honor, Melancholy, and Imagination in a Southern Family* (New York: Oxford University Press, 1994), and Lewis Baker, *The Percys of Mississippi: Politics and Literature in the New South* (Baton Rouge: Louisiana State University Press, 1983).

23. Nathaniel Lee was the son of William H. Lee and one of Harry's closest friends. In 1850 Nathaniel was seven, making him seventeen when Harry was writing (1850C).

24. William Alexander Percy (1837–88) was the youngest of the three Percy brothers who settled Deer Creek. He was married to Nannie Armstrong, with whom he had five children. After Lincoln was elected, Percy stumped against secession and for the election of Jacob Schall Yerger, also mentioned in the diary, to the Mississippi secession convention. Mississippi was swept out of the Union anyway, and Percy turned his attention to defending the South. As a captain in the Confederate army he saw action at Vicksburg, Wilderness, Spotsylvania, and Cold Harbor. After the war he practiced law in the neighboring town of Greenville and became a politician and railroad promoter. He was known as the "Gray Eagle" for his prematurely gray hair.

25. James P. Dixon was Harry's younger brother. In 1850 James was four, making him about fourteen at the time Harry was writing (1850C).

26. Taylor Rucks was the son of James Rucks and the brother of Marian Rucks, both of whom appear elsewhere in the diary. In 1850 Taylor was eight, making him eighteen when Harry was writing (1850C).

27. Eugène Sue, *The Mysteries of Paris* (1842–43).

28. Possibly A. W. McAllister, a fifty-year-old planter with a real estate valuation of thirty thousand dollars (1850C).

29. Written in Linear A and inked over but still visible.

30. Written in Linear A but inked over and washed out.

31. Written in Linear A and inked over but still visible.

32. Nannie Armstrong (1835–97) was married to William Alexander Percy, the youngest of the Percy brothers on Deer Creek. The couple had five children: Fannie, LeRoy, William Armstrong, Walker, and Lady. LeRoy (1860–1929) later became a senator from Mississippi and the father of William Alexander Percy, the writer. The novelist Walker Percy described Nannie as one of those "lovely little bitty steel-hearted women" who "made everybody do right" (Wyatt-Brown, *The House of Percy*, 174).

33. Wilkie Collins's *The Woman in White* was serialized in *Harper's Weekly* beginning November 26, 1859, and ending September 8, 1860.

34. Victorian custom broke the period of mourning into three stages. Full mourning lasted a year and a day: widows were expected to wear matte black dresses without ornamentation. Second mourning lasted nine months: widows continued to wear matte black, but their dresses could be ornamented with minor ribbons or ruffles, and they could wear mourning jewelry. Half mourning lasted three to six months: widows could wear jewelry and were expected to gradually ease back into wearing color.

35. Translation: "as we have shown above."

36. Leroy Pope Percy (1825–82) was the middle Percy brother. Hypertensive, he never married and lived under his brother's roof most of his life. His nieces and nephews knew him as "Uncle Lee." After the war Leroy suffered periods of paralysis, and in 1882 he took his own life by overdosing on laudanum.

37. Translation: "this is what they were like."

38. Next to this passage a note has been added in the margin: "Connie Dixon, Fresno, Aug. 1874—A happy wife testifies with a full heart that her noble husband fulfills in our daily life the lofty ideal of the boy, as here expressed." Dixon allowed his wife to read all his diaries. Considering the intimate information they contain, this suggests a marriage marked by deep trust and affection.

39. Apparently the birth of Linear B.

40. Written in Linear B. Unfamiliar with the new code, Dixon made a couple of errors, writing "hope of scriggleing her toon" when he clearly meant "soon" and "gratification of an evil pattion" when he clearly meant "passion." I have silently corrected the errors. While the word "scriggleing" may admit of various interpretations (and, indeed, Dixon may have made encoding errors when he wrote it), there can be little doubt that he hoped to receive some sort of sexual recompense for writing Sally's letter. The incident opens a fascinating window on the Old South, one historians need to peer through. There may have been a disturbing version of "doctor" being played on the plantation, a bizarre mixing of adolescent sexuality, curiosity, and attraction, on the one hand, and vast gender and racial inequities, on the other. Young planters' sons, surging with hormones, without access to women, and presupposing the easy virtue of slaves, probably did attempt to leverage sexual favors from neighborhood servant girls. And girls like Sally, probably attractive, possibly sexually active, might have had some bargaining power with their inexperienced, somewhat desperate "masters"—though it would have been a bargaining power bought at the heavy price of ogled bodies and premature sexual awareness. These dramas, played out among the youngest members of the plantation, would have been rehearsals for a later time when everyone was older;

when white men were more sure of their power (sexual and racial) but also distracted by their work and their wives; when black women were more wary and broken but also more aware that sex with whites could bring a complex mix of degradation and privilege, tearing their marriages apart or protecting their children from sale. In short, Dixon's admission implies that the sexual dynamics of life on the plantation were more complex than the histories of such predacious planters as James Henry Hammond, Robert Newsom, and James Norcom might suggest. See Drew Gilpin Faust, *James Henry Hammond and the Old South: A Design for Mastery* (Baton Rouge: Louisiana State University Press, 1985); Melton A. McLaurin, *Celia, a Slave* (New York: Avon, 1993); and Harriet Jacobs, *Incidents in the Life of a Slave Girl* (New York: Dover, 2001).

41. Dixon has clipped an article ("The Pythagorean: A Tale of the First Century," *Harper's Weekly*, February 25, 1860) and pasted it into his diary, where it runs across three pages. The story takes place in Italy. The protagonist is a traveler named Glaucus who falls in love with a milkmaid (Virginia) who is the slave of the local magistrate (Sporus). Glaucus asks Sporus's permission to marry Virginia, but Sporus refuses, wanting her for himself. Virginia refuses to marry Sporus, however, and runs off with Glaucus. The two are caught and thrown into a dungeon, where they are chained together. Glaucus's chains are light (he could escape easily on his own), but Virginia's fetters are heavy and cut her wrists whenever Glaucus moves. This is just one of many tests the couple has to face. In addition to tempting Glaucus with freedom Sporus also tempts him with wine, premarital sex (while Virginia is under the influence), and meat that his religion forbids. Glaucus resists these temptations, but when Virginia dies he is driven mad by grief, starvation, and too much wine, and he eats her corpse. Fortunately, before her death Virginia had convinced him to become a Christian and a preacher, which he does after he is released, so he is ultimately redeemed. The story is derivative of "The Pit and the Pendulum" and "Berenice" by Edgar Allan Poe, *Titus Andronicus* by William Shakespeare, and others, and it uneasily mixes Victorian themes (temperance, sexual restraint, sentimentality, romantic love, Christianity) with gothic ones (especially cannibalism).

42. It may seem ironic that Dixon, a planter's son, would paste a story into his diary that so clearly condemns the institution of slavery (see note above). It is the enslavement of *white* people (especially chaste white virgins) in the first century that has boiled Dixon's blood, however, not the enslavement of black people.

43. A horse that ran a mile in two minutes, forty seconds was considered fast. In "One Horse Open Sleigh," the original title of "Jingle Bells," the bobtailed bay has a speed of two-forty. The song was written in 1857 by James Pierpont and became enormously popular, so Harry may be alluding to it specifically.

44. Jacob Schall Yerger. In 1850 Jacob S. Yerger was a forty-one-year-old planter with a wife, Mary, five children living at home, 101 slaves, and a real estate valuation of twenty thousand dollars (1850C). His son Harry may be the Hal Yerger mentioned so often in Harry's diary. A delegate to the Mississippi secession convention, Jacob Yerger voted against the ordinance of secession.

45. Translation: "we have shown above."

46. E. W. Lane, trans., *The Arabian Nights*, 3 vols. (1840).

47. Augustus Baldwin Longstreet, *Georgia Scenes* (1835).

48. Probably George Bancroft, *A History of the United States* (1834–75).

49. Someone, presumably Harry, has attempted to erase the sentence. "She smiled but it was not the smile of old, only the" was decipherable. The five remaining words in the sentence were not.

50. James Fenimore Cooper, *The Spy* (1821).

51. Fannie Percy (1823–94) was the wife of Dr. John Walker Percy, often referred to as Walker.

52. William Gilmore Simms, *The Life of Nathanael Green* (1849).

53. James Graham, *Life of General Daniel Morgan* (1856).

54. Washington Irving, *The Life of George Washington* (1855–59).

55. In the margin Dixon has written: "* It was his daughter, the mother of Sarah Collins, wife of Jas. Phillips. The commander of the Tories was named Chany, one of whose descendents, Dr. C., lived up Deer Creek in Issaquena Co., Miss."

56. "The Last Arctic Expedition," *Harper's Weekly*, October 29, 1859, 690.

57. At the bottom of the page Dixon has written: "* A mistake, I think; probably it was intended for 1858–59, not 1848–49. For he could not have left England 1857 and have wintered in Ballot Inlet in 1848–49. Likely a typographical error."

58. In the margin Dixon has written: "+ most probably meaning 1859 as the paper from which the quotation is taken was printed in Oct./59."

59. At the bottom of the page Dixon has written: "* his breast was crushed in by falling on a box."

60. Probably Joseph Haven, *Mental Philosophy: Including the Intellect, Sensibilities, and Will* (Boston, 1857).

61. Mary H. R. Yerger, wife of Jacob Schall Yerger, was born Mary Bowen. She was the first daughter of Colonel John Bowen (1780–1822) and Elizabeth Allen. In 1850 she was thirty-three, making her forty-three at the time Harry is writing (1850C).

62. James Fenimore Cooper, *The Prairie* (1827).

63. Joseph E. Worcester, *A Dictionary of the English Language* (1860). Worcester's dictionary preferred British spellings, while Webster's was more permissive of Americanized English.

64. Oliver Goldsmith, *The History of England from the Earliest Times to the Death of James II* (1771).

65. Skim milk.

66. At the end of this entry Dixon has written: "* I have been spelling this word wrong. Hereafter—mantelpiece."

67. At the bottom of the page Dixon has written: "* they say this is their diet."

68. At the bottom of the page Dixon has written: "+ I make notations from my letter here from memory."

69. At the bottom of the page Dixon has written: "* I believe only post mortem."

70. Translation: "we have shown above."

71. Translation: "of what outstanding beauty the woman is."

72. At the bottom of the page Dixon has written: "* or more properly epithets."

73. Possibly John Finlay. The 1850 federal census lists a John Finlay, thirty, as a physician with a wife, Ann, and four children.

74. Translation: "a man of upright example."

75. At the bottom of the page Dixon has written: "* The little soft-eyed woman I so

sincerely spoke of in the closing words of my last entry left today. As I sat in the window at the schoolhouse she drove by in an open carriage about 2 o'clk giving me a queenly bow (much to my gratification) and a lovely smile. Good by!"

76. At the bottom of the page Dixon has written: "* 'How long at length O Cataline will you abuse our patience?'"

77. A note has been added in the margin: "The devil you say! H. 4 June 1862."

78. Translation: "nothing is more beautiful than a woman."

79. David Everett, "Lines Written for a School Declamation" (1791).

80. George Linley, "Ever of Thee" (c. 1830).

81. Stephen Collins Foster, "Gentle Annie" (1856). Foster was antebellum America's most popular songwriter.

82. Harry clearly means "Formerly."

83. Probably James R. Yerger, son of William and Malvina Yerger, older brother of Louise and Bettie Yerger, mentioned elsewhere in the diary. In 1850 he was ten (1850C).

84. Probably William Yerger Jr., son of William and Malvina Yerger, older brother of Louise and Bettie Yerger, mentioned elsewhere in the diary. In 1850 he was eight (1850C).

85. James Thomson, *The Seasons* (1730). Harry is probably referring to the lines "Now swarms the village o'er the jovial mead / The rustic youth, brown with meridian toil / Healthful and strong; full as the summer-rose / Blown by prevailing suns, the ruddy maid / Half-naked, swelling on the sight, and all / Her kindled graces burning o'er her cheek."

86. Probably Mrs. James H. Yerger, mentioned elsewhere in the diary. Because she had recently lost her husband Mrs. Yerger's reaction to her brother's illness is perhaps more understandable.

87. Probably Elizabeth R. Yerger, wife of planter Alexander Yerger. In 1850 Elizabeth was twenty-two, making her thirty-two at the time Harry was writing. Her husband owned eighteen slaves (1850C).

88. Translation: "thus passes the glory of the world."

89. Dr. Leroy Percy was known to be called Lee.

90. Dixon is probably referring to Byron's "The Dream" (1816), which begins, "Our life is twofold; Sleep hath its own world / A boundary between the things misnamed / Death and existence."

91. Written in Linear B.

92. Dixon is borrowing the signature line from Byron's "The Dream" (1816).

93. Written in Linear B.

94. Translation: "for country and women forever."

95. Translation: "to seek refuge in flight."

96. Harry's Latin is just a little off. He probably means "sine oratione blanda" (without flattering entreaty).

97. Anna Jameson, *Characteristic of Women, Moral, Poetical, and Historical* (1833).

98. William Yerger was the husband of Malvina and the father of Louise and Bettie Yerger, mentioned elsewhere in the diary. In 1850 William Yerger, thirty-three, was a lawyer with a wife, Malvina, and five children living at home. He owned sixty-five slaves (1850C).

99. Dixon is referring to a small clipping he pasted near the bottom of the page. It

is titled "A Mother's Love" and reads: "Some of our readers may recollect a thrilling ballad which was written on the death of a woman who perished in the snow drifts of the Green Mountains of Vermont. That mother bore an infant on her bosom and when the storm waxed loud and furious, true to a mother's love, she rent her own garments and wrapt them around her babe. The morning found her a stiffened corpse, but her babe survived. That babe grew to manhood and became the Speaker of the Ohio Senate. How thrilling must be his thoughts of that mother if he be a true, large-hearted man! How deep a mother's love! How many a mother is there who would die for her son, if called in Providence to do so? Let sons, when far away from home, on the land or on the sea, when the eye of no mother is upon them, remember her love, and be restrained by it from entering the path of vice."

100. "Pro patria et feminis semper!" (For country and women forever!)

101. C. Z. Barnett, *The Phantom Bride; or, The Castilian Bandit: A Melo-drama in Two Acts* (1830).

102. Emma Hart Willard, *A System of Universal History in Perspective* (1837).

103. Possibly Socrates Maupin (1808–71), professor of chemistry and chairman of the faculty at the University of Virginia.

104. Harry's Latin is a little off here. He probably meant "temeritas est florens status praecedens senectutis" (ill-considered folly is a vigorous condition that precedes old age).

105. Richard C. McCormick, *A Visit to the Camp Before Sevastopol* (New York, 1855).

106. Translation: "thus is the world."

107. Probably Charles Kingsley, *The Heroes; or, Greek Fairy Tales for My Children*.

108. Joseph G. Baldwin, *Party Leaders* (1855).

109. Jérôme Bonaparte was the youngest brother of Napoleon and renowned for his misadventures with women.

110. Lola Montez, *Anecdotes of Love: Being a True Account of the Most Remarkable Events Connected with the history of Love, in All Ages and Among all Nations* (1858).

111. Theocritus, *The Dictionary of Love, Containing a Definition of all the Terms used in the History of the Tender Passion, with Rare Quotations from the Ancient and Modern Poets of All Nations: Together with Specimens of Curious Model Love Letters* (1858).

112. Alexander von Humboldt (1769–1859) was a German naturalist and explorer. After his death a portion of his correspondence was made public under the title *Letters of Alexander von Humboldt to Varnhagen von Ense* (1860). The book exposed Humboldt's tendency to be publicly flattering but privately caustic.

113. Probably Robert Walpole (1676–1745), first Earl of Oxford and Britain's first prime minister.

114. Alexander von Humboldt, *Kosmos*, 5 vols. (1845–62).

115. Probably Bettie Yerger, sister of Louise Yerger. The 1850 federal census gives Bettie's age as four, making her fourteen at the time Harry is writing.

116. Probably John M. Lee, the younger brother of Harry's friend Nat. The 1850 federal census gives John Lee's age as four, making him fourteen at the time Harry is writing.

117. After Saint Gregory of Nazianzus (c. 330–c. 389), bishop and theologian of the ancient church.

118. Henry Augustus Wise, *Captain Brand of the Schooner "Centipede"* was serialized in *Harper's Weekly* from April 7, 1860, to August 25, 1860.

119. Charles Lever, *A Ride for a Day, the Romance of a Life* was serialized in *Harper's Weekly* from August 11, 1860, to October 26, 1861. By the end of its run its title had changed slightly to *A Day's Ride, a Life's Romance*.

120. George William Curtis, *Trumps* was serialized in *Harper's Weekly* from April 9, 1859, to January 21, 1860.

121. Again, Harry's Latin is just a little off. He likely means "amor patriae vincit omnia" (the love of country conquers all).

122. Laurence Sterne, *A Sentimental Journey through France and Italy*, 2 vols. (1768). The quotation appears in chapter 41.

123. Possibly John M. McCutchen. The 1850 federal census lists a John M. Mc-Cutchen, nine, as living with his sister, Maria, in the house of S. P. Taylor, planter. This would make McCutchen nineteen at the time Harry is writing.

124. Translation: "O Philosophy, the guide of life."

125. Nathaniel Parker Willis, *Pencillings By the Way, written during some years of residence and travel in Europe* (1835).

126. At the bottom of the page Dixon has written: "* a quotation from my letter."

127. Translation: "Justice, the queen of virtues."

128. William Gannaway Brownlow was an outspoken Tennessee newspaperman who would later become famous for his opposition to secession and the Confederacy. Brownlow served as governor of Tennessee (1865–69) and in the U.S. Senate (1869–75).

HENRY HUGHES

1. Henry's father, Benjamin Hughes (1789–1842), was born in Kentucky. He married Nancy Brashear (1797–1875) in 1818. In 1824 the couple moved with their first daughter, Mary Ann, to Claiborne County, Mississippi, where Benjamin worked as a merchant in Port Gibson and Grand Gulf until his death in 1842. Never remarrying, Nancy retained one third of her husband's estate through a law that protected widows from their husbands' creditors. According to the 1850 slave schedule for Claiborne County, Nancy Hughes's property included fourteen slaves ranging in age from two to forty-five. The infrequency with which Henry mentions individual servants suggests that most if not all of these hands were hired out or worked lands remote from the household. Henry's siblings, when he commenced the diary, were all living at home: twenty-six-year-old Mary Ann, who had been widowed in 1844; twenty-two-year-old William, who became a Port Gibson merchant like his father; and fifteen-year-old Maria Jane, who would marry one of Henry's schoolmates, William Thomas Magruder, in 1851. The 1850 federal census also lists Julia and Benjamin Morehead, Mary Ann's twelve-year-old son and ten-year-old daughter, as members of the household. Nancy's real estate valuation is listed as two thousand dollars. See also Douglas Ambrose, *Henry Hughes and Proslavery Thought in the Old South* (Baton Rouge: Louisiana State University Press, 1996), 8–19.

2. William Blackstone, *Commentaries on the Laws of England*, 4 vols. (1765–69).

3. John B. Thrasher was a prominent Port Gibson attorney. In 1850 he had a real estate valuation of twenty-four thousand dollars (1850C).

4. Thomas Jefferson Durant (1817–82) was born in Philadelphia but moved to New Orleans at the age of seventeen. There he studied law, was admitted to the bar, and rose to the top of his profession, serving as U.S. district attorney for Louisiana and attorney general of the state. A Unionist, he was offered the governorship of Louisiana when New Orleans fell in 1862, but he declined. After the war he moved to Washington, D.C., where he continued his legal practice.

5. Henry Hallam, *View of the State of Europe during the Middle Ages* (1847).

6. Henry Hallam, *The Constitutional History of England from the Accession of Henry VII to the Death of George II* (1829).

7. In 1808 Sir David Brewster (1781–1868), inventor of the kaleidoscope, decided to create an encyclopedia that, unlike most existing at the time, was scientifically accurate and up-to-date. He edited the encyclopedia for twenty-two years. The first American edition was released in eighteen volumes in 1832.

8. Edward Gibbon, *The History of the Decline and Fall of the Roman Empire*, 6 vols. (1776–88).

9. William Brashear Lindsay (1806–66) married Henry's mother's younger sister Ruth Caroline Brashear (1807–66) in 1829. Lindsay was a doctor in New Orleans.

10. Oakland College opened as a Presbyterian school in 1830. In 1831 it became the first Mississippi institution to award a degree.

11. William Thomas Magruder (b. 1825) became a planter after college. In 1851 he married Henry's younger sister Maria Jane.

12. Probably Theodore Clapp (1792–1866), the immensely popular New Orleans preacher. Clapp was born in Massachusetts and educated at Yale. In 1822 he accepted an invitation to become the pastor of the Congregational Church in New Orleans. Though Clapp wrestled with the rightness of slavery and often held liberal views, New Orleans loved him and he loved it back. His church became known as the "Strangers' Church" because so many visitors dropped in to hear him.

13. In *De oratore* (55 BC) Cicero concluded that the perfect orator would also be the perfect man. Such a message would certainly have appealed to Hughes.

14. Richard Whately, *Elements of Logic* (1826).

15. George Bancroft, *History of the United States of America* (1846).

16. Edwin Forrest (1806–72) was arguably America's first star of the stage. He was most famous for his interpretations of Othello, Lear, and Coriolanus. See Richard Moody, *Edwin Forrest, First Star of the American Stage* (New York: Knopf, 1960).

17. Hughes is probably referring to John Newland Maffitt (1744–1850), the Methodist minister. Maffitt's son of the same name became famous as a dashing commander of the Confederate navy.

18. Jonathan Elliot, *The Debate in the Several State Conventions on the Adoption of the Federal Constitution* (1836).

19. John Locke (1632–1704) wrote his seminal *Essay Concerning Human Understanding* in 1690. In it he quarreled with Descartes, who had claimed that certain notions, most particularly the notion of God, are innate in the human intellect. Locke believed that man began tabula rasa; anything written on his slate was a result of external experience (sensation) or internal experience (reflection). How then can man know that God exists? "Man knows by an intuitive certainty that bare nothing can no more produce

any real being than it can be equal to two right angles. . . . If, therefore, we know there is some real being [ourselves], and that nonentity cannot produce any real being, it is an evident demonstration that from eternity there has been something; since what was not from eternity had a beginning, and what had a beginning must be produced by something else. . . . Thus from the consideration of ourselves, and what we infallibly find in our own constitutions, our reason leads us to the knowledge of this certain and evident truth, that there is an eternal, most powerful, and most knowing Being" (John Locke, *An Essay Concerning Human Understanding* [New York: Penguin Classics, 1998], IV, x, 3, 6).

20. Demosthenes (384–322 BC) was the legendary Athenian orator who had overcome a speech impediment to become a renowned rhetorician. The deliberateness with which he pursued oratorical greatness surely appealed to Hughes. Demosthenes trained himself to declaim distinctly with pebbles in his mouth, speak steadily while running, and make himself heard over the sound of the ocean.

21. Thomas Brown (1778–1820) was professor of moral philosophy at the University of Edinburgh from 1810 to 1820. He was best known for the posthumous *Lectures on the Philosophy of the Human Mind* (1820), which were influential in the South.

22. Henry Hart Milman, *Fazio: A Tragedy* (1815).

23. James Madison (1751–1836), founding father and fourth president of the United States, kept detailed notes during the Constitutional Convention of 1787. His notes, informally known as the "Madison Papers," were published by the U.S. government in 1840.

24. Joseph Story, *Commentaries on the Constitution of the United States* (1833).

25. Richard Whately, *Elements of Rhetoric* (1828).

26. *Practical Illustrations of Rhetorical Gesture and Action. Adapted to the English drama, from a work on the subject by M. Engel, by Henry Siddons* (1822).

27. James Rush, *The Philosophy of the Human Voice* (1827).

28. James Henry Hackett (1800–1871) was an actor and manager of several theaters, including Astor Place. His correspondents included John Quincy Adams and Abraham Lincoln, both of whom sought his opinion of Shakespeare's characters. Falstaff was his best-known role.

29. Junius Brutus Booth (1796–1852) was a British-born stage actor who came to the United States in 1821. Richard III was his signature role, though he is perhaps more famous as the father of John Wilkes Booth.

30. John Dyer, "Grongar Hill" (1726).

31. James Kent, *Commentaries on American Law* (1826–30).

32. English actor William Macready (1793–1873) arrived in 1849 for a tour of the United States. Though popular in the States, his rivalry with American actor Edwin Forrest touched off the Astor Place Riot of May 10, 1849, in which seventeen people died. See Lawrence W. Levine, *Highbrow/Lowbrow: The Emergence of Cultural Hierarchy in America* (Cambridge, Mass.: Harvard University Press, 1988), 63–68, and Richard Moody, *The Astor Place Riot* (Bloomington: Indiana University Press, 1958).

33. Cicero, *Pro milone* (55 BC).

34. Emmerich de Vattel, *The Law of Nations; or, Principles of the Law of Nature, Applied to the Conduct and Affairs of Nations and Sovereigns* (1759).

35. 1 Corinthians 15:55.

36. Samuel Butler's *Hudibras*, a send-up of Puritanism, appeared in three parts (1663, 1664, 1678).

37. Hughes is borrowing the signature line from Byron's "The Dream" (1816).

38. Alphonse de Lamartine, *Raphael; or, Pages of the Book of Life at Twenty* (1849).

39. Robert-Joseph Pothier, *A Treatise on Obligations, Considered in a Moral and Legal View* (1802).

40. Sir Walter Scott, *The Lady of the Lake: A Poem* (1810).

41. Hughes is borrowing from Byron's *The Corsair* (1814): "Oh, who can tell, save he whose heart hath tried / And danced in triumph o'er the waters wide / The exulting sense — the pulse's maddening play / That thrills the wanderer of that trackless way?"

42. Linus Parker (1829–85) was born in Oneida County, New York. In the 1840s he moved to New Orleans to work in his brother's store. In 1846 he joined the army and served in the Mexican War. When he returned he began the study of law but then switched to theology and joined the Methodist ministry. He served Louisiana Methodist churches in various capacities for the rest of his life. See the Linus Parker Papers, Pitts Theology Library, Emory University.

43. Charles W. Hornor practiced law with Thomas Jefferson Durant.

44. Simon Greenleaf, *A Treatise on the Law of Evidence* (1842).

45. David Page, *Elements of Geology* (1849).

46. John Dryden (1631–1700) was an English poet, dramatist, and critic whose popular translation of Virgil's *Aeneid* (30–19 BC) appeared first in 1697.

47. Psalm 13:1.

48. Shakespeare, *Othello*, act 3, scene 3, lines 358–60.

49. Joseph Story, *Commentaries on the Law of Promissory Notes and Guaranties of Notes* (1845).

50. Hughes is borrowing from Edward Young, *The Complaint or Night Thoughts on Life, Death, and Immortality* (1742). Hughes's own rapturous style often resembles that of Young. Compare, for example, any of Hughes's more ejaculative passages with the Young lines from which he has drawn his quotation: "How poor, how rich, how abject, how august, / How complicate, how wonderful is man! . . . / Distinguished link in being's endless chain! / Midway from nothing to the Deity! / A beam ethereal, sullied and absorbed, / Though sullied and dishonoured, still divine! / Dim miniature of greatness absolute! / An heir of glory! a frail child of dust! / Helpless, immortal! insect infinite! / A worm! a god! I tremble at myself, / And in myself am lost."

51. Joseph Chitty, *A Practical Treatise on Bills of Exchange* (1840).

52. William Cowper, *The Task: A Poem in Six Books* (1785).

53. Joseph Story, *Commentaries on the Law of Partnership* (1841).

54. John William Smith, *A Selection of Leading Cases on Various Branches of the Law* (1848).

55. John Innes Clark Hare, *American Leading Cases: Being Select Decisions of American Courts* (1847–48).

56. William Robertson, *The History of the Reign of the Emperor Charles the Fifth* (1769).

57. Charles Davies, *A Treatise on Shades and Shadows, and Linear Perspective* (1848).

58. Immanuel Kant (1724–1804) was a Prussian philosopher, most famous for his

doctrine of transcendental idealism, which had a profound impact on later romantic thinkers.

59. Joshua Trimmer, *Practical Geology and Mineralogy* (1842).

60. Thomas Babington Macaulay, *History of England from the Accession of James the Second*, 5 vols. (1849–61).

61. Willard Phillips, *A Treatise on the Law of Insurance* (1823).

62. The *Eclectic Magazine of Foreign Literature, Science and Art*.

63. Charles Fourier (1772–1837) was a French utopian socialist who called for laborers to be organized in phalansteries, large planned communities that had varied work and sex routines.

64. Claude Henri de Rouvroy, comte de Saint-Simon (1760–1825), was a French socialist who called on a philosopher elite to lead the world through a peaceful process of industrialization.

65. Byron, *Manfred* (1817), act 2, scene 2.

66. Charles Abbott, Baron Tenterden, *A Treatise on the Law Relative to Merchant Ships and Seamen* (1802).

67. Henry John Stephen, *A Treatise on the Principles of Pleading in Civil Actions* (1824).

68. Alfred Conkling, *A Treatise on the Organization and Jurisdiction of the Supreme, Circuit and District Courts of the United States* (1831).

69. Jonathan Swift, *Cadenus and Vanessa. A Poem* (1713).

70. Matthew Green, *The Spleen* (1737).

71. Probably Charles Rollin (1661–1741), the French historian best known for his histories of the ancient world.

72. Henry Hallam, *Introduction to the Literature of Europe in the Fifteenth, Sixteenth, and Seventeenth Centuries* (1841).

73. Alexander Pope, *Eloisa to Abelard* (1720).

74. Henry Adams Bullard and Thomas Curry, *A New Digest of the Statute Laws of the State of Louisiana, from the Change of Government to the Year 1841, inclusive* (1842).

75. William Benjamin Carpenter, *Principles of Human Physiology* (1843).

76. Jonathan Swift, *On Poetry: A Rhapsody* (1733).

77. William Somerville, *The Chase* (1735).

78. Robert Pollok, *The Course of Time: A Poem* (1827).

79. Edward Young, *The Complaint; or, Night Thoughts on Life, Death, and Immortality* (1742).

80. Joseph Story, *Commentaries on the Law of Agency as a Branch of Commercial and Maritime Jurisprudence* (1839).

81. Charles Barton, *An Historical Treatise of a Suit in Equity, in Which is Attempted a Scientific Deduction of the Proceedings Used on the Equity Sides of the Courts of Chancery and Exchequer* (1796).

82. John Keats, *Endymion. A Poetic Romance* (1818).

83. David Meredith Reese, *Rudiments of Vegetable Physiology* (1846).

84. Henry Jeremy, *The Law of Carriers, Inn-Keepers, Warehousemen, and Other Depositories of Goods for Hire* (1816); Joseph Story, *Commentaries on the Law of Bailments, with Illustrations from the Civil and the Foreign Law* (1832); John Keats, *Hyperion* (1820); John Keats, *The Eve of St. Agnes* (1820); Percy Bysshe Shelley, *Queen Mab: A Philosophical Poem*

(1813); Percy Bysshe Shelley, *Adonais: An Elegy on the Death of John Keats* (1821); Edward Bulwer-Lytton, *Money: A Comedy in Five Acts* (1845); Joseph Story, *Commentaries on the Law of Bills of Exchange* (1843).

85. Shakespeare, *Macbeth*, act 5, scene 5, line 54.

86. Joseph Story, *Commentaries on the Conflict of Laws* (1834).

87. Benjamin Disraeli, *Vivian Grey* (1826).

88. "Mania a potu" can be translated as "madness from drinking" (the delirium tremens) or as an insane passion or unreasonable desire. Henry probably means it in both senses.

89. Alexander Pope, *Dunciad: An Heroic Poem in Three Books* (1728, 1742).

90. George Ticknor Curtis, *A Treatise on the Rights and Duties of Merchant Seamen* (1841).

91. Henry Peter, Lord Brougham, *Dialogues on Instinct; with Analytical View of the Researches on Fossil Osteology* (1845).

92. Joseph K. Angell, *A Treatise on the Law of Private Corporations*, 3rd ed., revised, corrected, and enlarged by Samuel Ames (1846).

93. Hughes has copied excerpts of letters to him into his diary. The letter writer is unknown.

94. Ivan Stepanovich Mazepa (c. 1644–1709) was a Cossack leader of Ukraine. While a young man he was supposedly tied to the back of a wild horse and sent into the steppes by a jealous husband. Byron used the legend as the basis of *Mazeppa* (1819).

95. *Code of Practice of the State of Louisiana, Containing Rules of Procedure in Civil Actions* (1844).

96. Henry Peter, Lord Brougham, *Historical Sketches of Statesmen Who Flourished in the Time of George III* (1842).

97. Thomas Moore, *Lalla Rookh: An Oriental Romance* (1817), third tale, line 279.

98. Shakespeare, *Hamlet*, act 1, scene 2, lines 135–36.

99. Probably James Edward Murdoch (1811–93), the popular Shakespearean actor and lecturer.

100. Hughes is probably paraphrasing Shakespeare's *A Midsummer Night's Dream*: "The lunatic, the lover, and the poet are of imagination all compact. . . . The poet's eye, in a fine frenzy rolling, doth glance from heaven to earth, from earth to heaven, and as imagination bodies forth the forms of things unknown, the poet's pen turns them to shapes, and gives to airy nothing a local habitation and a name."

101. Jean Domat, *Les lois civiles dans leur ordre naturel* (*The Civil Law in Its Natural Order*) (1689–94, translated in 1850).

102. Charlotte Cushman (1816–76) was an enormously successful American stage actress, famous for her portrayals of male characters. See Lisa Merrill, *When Romeo Was a Woman: Charlotte Cushman and Her Circle of Female Spectators* (Ann Arbor: University of Michigan Press, 2001).

103. George Ticknor Curtis, *A Digest of Cases Adjudicated in the Courts of Admiralty of the United States* (1839).

104. Samuel Rossiter Betts, *A Summary of Practice in Instance, Revenue and Prize Causes* (1838).

105. Sir William Oldnall Russell, *A Treatise on Crimes and Misdemeanors* (1824).

106. *Othello*, act 5, scene 2, line 395.

107. Shakespeare, *As You Like It*, act 2, scene 1, lines 13–18: "Sweet are the uses of adversity / Which like the toad, ugly and venomous / Wears yet a precious jewel in his head / And this our life exempt from public haunt / Finds tongues in trees, books in the running brook / Sermons in stones, and good in every thing."

108. The most likely candidates for Hughes's examining committee were Dominique Seghers, Belgian immigrant and New Orleans lawyer; Felix Grima (d. 1887), notary, attorney, and presiding judge of the New Orleans city court; and Alfred Hennen (1786–1870), noted New Orleans attorney. Those who failed to attend included Christian Roselius (1803–73), attorney general for the state of Louisiana (1841–43) and professor of civil law at the University of Louisiana.

109. Roughly translated, "lie in the shade of a leafy beach." Hughes has borrowed the line from Virgil's *Eclogues*, Eclogue 1, line 1.

110. Edward Bulwer-Lytton, *The Caxtons: A Family Picture* (1849).

111. *Macbeth*, act 1, scene 7, line 7.

112. Jenny Lind (1820–87), the soprano singer known throughout Europe as "the Swedish Nightingale," made her American debut in September 1850.

113. Joseph Story, *Commentaries on Equity Jurisprudence as Administered in England and America* (1836).

114. John A. Getty, *Elements of Rhetoric* (1831).

115. Percy Bysshe Shelley was a strong advocate of a vegetarian diet. In addition to lacing his poetry with vegetarian themes he wrote several articles defending the meatless life, including "A Vindication of Natural Diet" (1813).

116. Robert Burns, "Ae Fond Kiss" (1791).

117. Thomas Hartwell Horne, *A Compendious Introduction to the Study of the Bible* (1833).

118. Sir Walter Scott, *Woodstock* (1826).

119. In 1850 Narciso López and several hundred men set off from New Orleans to seize Cuba. After capturing Cardena and burning the governor's mansion López and his men were forced to flee the island. See Tom Chaffin, *Fatal Glory: Narciso López and the First Clandestine U.S. War against Cuba* (Charlottesville: University Press of Virginia, 1996).

120. Sergeant Smith Prentiss died in New Orleans in 1850. That Hughes would have looked up to him was natural. Prentiss was a voracious reader and dynamic speaker, renowned for his ability to extemporize with perfect fluency and grace.

121. Hughes probably means that he had hoped Prentiss would play Hortensius to his Cicero. The two Roman orators were friendly rivals.

122. Benjamin Disraeli, *The Young Duke* (1831).

123. Benjamin Disraeli, *Contarini Fleming: A Romance* (1832).

124. Nancy Hughes's first cousin, Corinna Harrison Brasher (1818–50), married Charles Shreve.

125. Benjamin Disraeli, *Venetia* (1837).

126. Robert Brashear (1769–1858) was Corinna's father and Henry Hughes's grand-uncle.

127. Thomas Carlyle, *Latter-Day Pamphlets* (1850).

128. Archibald Alison, *Essays on the Nature and Principles of Taste* (1790).

129. Sir Walter Scott, *The Monastery: A Romance* (1820).

130. Sir Walter Scott, *The Abbot: Being a Sequel to the Monastery* (1820).

131. Charles Davies, *Elements of Descriptive Geometry* (1826).

132. John Locke, *An Essay Concerning Human Understanding* (1690).

133. Robert Turnbull, *The Genius of Scotland* (1848).

134. Edward Bulwer-Lytton, *The Last Days of Pompeii* (1850).

135. John Stuart Mill, *Principles of Political Economy* (1848).

136. Thomas Carlyle, ed., *Oliver Cromwell's Letters and Speeches* (1849).

137. Frederick W. Thomas, *Clinton Bradshaw; or, The Adventures of a Lawyer* (1835).

138. Hughes is probably referring to Emma Caffery, one of his romantic interests. See also entries for January 1, 1852, July 25, 1852, and March 6, 1853, and Ambrose, *Henry Hughes*, 41–48.

139. William Whewell, *The Elements of Morality, Including Polity* (1847).

140. W. S. W. Ruschenberger, *Elements of Conchology* (1843).

141. Charles Anthon, ed., *The Works of Horace* (1840).

142. Possibly Henry Williams, *The Elements of Drawing, Exemplified in a Variety of Figures and Sketches of Parts of the Human Form* (1814).

143. Philip James Bailey, *Festus, a Poem* (1839).

144. Alphonse de Lamartine, *Genevieve* (1850).

145. Charles Dickens, *The Personal History and Experience of David Copperfield the Younger* (1850).

146. Thomas Carlyle, *On Heroes, Hero-Worship, and the Heroic in History* (1840).

147. In the margin Hughes has written: "On the 17th day of April AD 1855, swore again this oath. God is glory. Henry Hughes."

148. Beatrice is a character in a short story of the same name by Edgar Allan Poe. Lenore is the bereaved narrator's lost wife in Poe's poem "The Raven."

149. Sir Walter Scott, *Marmion: A Tale of Flodden Field* (1808).

150. Hughes has slightly botched his Byron: "no breath of air to break the wave / that rolls below the Athenian's grave" (*The Giaour, a Fragment of a Turkish Tale* [1813], lines 1–2).

151. Sir Walter Scott, *Rokeby: A Poem* (1813).

152. Sir Walter Scott, *The Lay of the Last Minstrel, a Poem* (1805).

153. Between 1817 and 1867 the American Colonization Society helped relocate thirteen thousand freed slaves back to Africa. The colony, known as Liberia, declared itself an independent nation in 1847.

154. Samuel Taylor Coleridge, *The Rime of the Ancient Mariner* (1798).

155. *Hamlet*, act 1, scene 3, line 53.

156. Seth Lewis, *The Restoration of the Jews* (1851).

157. Charles Dickens, *The Posthumous Papers of the Pickwick Club* (1837).

158. Alexandre Dumas père, *Fernande* (1844).

159. Charles Kingsley, *Alton Locke, Tailor and Poet, an Autobiography* (1850).

160. Sir George Stephen, *Adventures of an Attorney in Search of a Practice; or, A Delineation of Professional Life* (1839).

161. John Stuart Mill, *A System of Logic, Ratiocinative and Inductive* (1850).

162. Sir Walter Scott, *St. Ronan's Well* (1824).

163. John Brocklesby, *Elements of Meteorology* (1848).

164. William Whewell, *The Elements of Morality, including Polity* (1845).

165. Auguste Comte, *The Philosophy of Mathematics* (1851).

166. Freiherr Justus von Liebig, *Professor Liebig's Complete Works on Chemistry: Comprising His Agricultural Chemistry* (1850).

167. Elias Loomis, *Elements of Analytical Geometry and of the Differential and Integral Calculus* (1851).

168. Sir Walter Scott, *Old Mortality* (1816).

169. George Henry Borrow, *The Bible in Spain; or, The Journeys, Adventures, and Imprisonments of an Englishman in an Attempt to Circulate the Scriptures in the Peninsula* (1843).

170. Sir Walter Scott, *Chronicles of Canongate* (1828).

171. Sir Walter Scott, *Red Gauntlet: A Tale of the Eighteenth Century* (1824).

172. Sir Walter Scott, *The Fair Maid of Perth; or, Saint Valentine's Day* (1828).

173. Sir Walter Scott, *A Legend of Montrose* (1819).

174. Sir Walter Scott, *The Fortunes of Nigel: A Romance* (1822).

175. John Anthony Quitman (1799–1858) was governor of Mississippi from 1850 to 1851.

176. Anne Marsh-Caldwell, *Mordaunt Hall; or, A September Night* (1849).

177. Elias Loomis, *The Recent Progress of Astronomy: Especially in the United States* (1851).

178. William Makepeace Thackeray, *The History of Pendennis* (1850).

179. Hugh A. Garland, *The Life of John Randolph of Roanoke* (1850).

180. John Pendleton Kennedy, *Memoirs of the Life of William Wirt* (1850).

181. Theodore Sedgwick, *A Treatise on the Measure of Damages* (1847).

182. Mrs. Daniel Mackenzie, *Fernley Manor; or, Edith the Inconstant* (1851).

183. Lajos Kossuth (1802–94) was a Hungarian patriot who led an 1848 revolution against Austria. In 1849 he became the virtual dictator of the new Hungarian Republic, but he was quickly swept from power when Russia interceded on Austria's behalf.

184. Martha Parker was another of Hughes's romantic interests. The exact nature of their relationship is difficult to determine. See also the entries of July 25, 1852, and March 6, 1853, and Ambrose, *Henry Hughes*, 41–48.

185. Charles Fourier, *The Passions of the Human Soul, and Their Influence on Society and Civilization* (1851).

186. James Thompson, *The Castle of Indolence* (1748).

187. Richard Henry Dana Jr., *Two Years Before the Mast: A Personal Narrative of Life at Sea* (1840). Dana was a promising student at Harvard when a case of measles threatened his eyesight. Seeking death or a cure, he enlisted as a sailor on the *Pilgrim*, bound for California. After two years of adventure he returned to Harvard, graduated with distinction, and published *Two Years Before the Mast* while a law student. Dana's youthful brashness would definitely have appealed to Hughes.

188. Henry Mandeville (1804–58) was a professor of moral philosophy and belles lettres at Hamilton College in New York. He later moved to Mobile, Alabama. A renowned instructor of elocution, he published *Elements of Reading and Oratory* in 1845.

189. Victor Cousin, *Course of the History of Modern Philosophy* (1852).

190. *Hamlet*, act 1, scene 4, lines 92–93.

191. Sir James Mackintosh, *A General View of the Progress of Ethical Philosophy, Chiefly during the Seventeenth and Eighteenth Centuries* (1832).

192. James Chesnut, reviewing George Cornwall Lewis's *Influence of Authority in Matters of Opinion* (1849) in the *Southern Quarterly Review*, April 1852, 341–72.

193. Thomas Babington, Lord Macaulay, "Lord Bacon," *Edinburgh Review*, July 1837.

194. Basil Montagu, ed., *The Works of Francis Bacon, Lord Chancellor of England* (1825–34).

195. Sir Francis Bacon was created first Baron Verulam in 1618. Verulamium was a city in Roman Britain near modern-day St. Albans.

196. John Keble, *The Christian Year; Thoughts in Verse for Sundays and Holydays* (1827).

197. Alfred, Lord Tennyson (1809–92) wrote several books with this title: *Poems, Chiefly Lyrical* (1830), *Poems* (1833), and *Poems* (1842), a two-volume collection.

198. John Fletcher, *Studies on Slavery* (1852).

199. John C. Calhoun, *A Disquisition on Government and a Discourse on the Constitution and Government of the United States* (1851). The book was edited after Calhoun's death by his relative and former clerk, Richard K. Crallé.

200. Henry's uncle William Brashear Lindsay had a younger sister, Margaret Newton Lindsay, who married Eugene Amedee Sherburne around 1832. Margaret died on July 25, 1852.

201. Harriet Beecher Stowe, *Uncle Tom's Cabin; or, Life Among the Lowly* (1851).

202. Probably Daniel Webster's "Second Reply to Hayne" (1830). Making the argument for nullification, Calhoun had written "Exposition and Protest," which South Carolina senator Robert Y. Hayne (1791–1839) delivered to the senate on January 19, 1830. In his reply on January 26 Webster delivered one of the most famous speeches in American history, the "Second Reply to Hayne," a spirited argument against nullification and for an indissoluble Union.

203. Henry Stephens Randall, *Sheep Husbandry in the South* (1848).

204. Jeremy Bentham, *Introduction to the Principles and Morals of Legislation* (1789).

205. Edward Bulwer-Lytton, *The Pilgrims of the Rhine* (1843).

206. John K. Routh, thirty-one, was a planter with land valued at $230,000 and personal property at $160,000. This made him one of the richer men in Tensas Parish (1860C).

207. William Mitchell Gillespie, *A Manual of the Principles and Practice of Road-Making* (1852).

208. Mary H. Eastman, *Aunt Phillis's Cabin; or, Southern Life as It Is* (1852) was written in response to Stowe's *Uncle Tom's Cabin* (1852). It was the best-selling of the "anti-Tom" novels.

209. William Lindsay (c. 1769–c. 1817) was the father of William Brashear Lindsay, Henry's uncle.

210. Marmion W. Savage, *Reuben Medlicott; or, The Coming Man* (1852).

211. Charles Jacobs Peterson, *The Cabin and Parlor; or, Slaves and Masters*, published under the pseudonym J. Thorton Randolph (1852).

212. Nathaniel Hawthorne, *Blithedale Romance* (1852).

213. Ralph Waldo Emerson, *Essays* (1841).

214. Elizabeth Barrett Browning (1806–61) did publish a volume titled *Poems* (1844), but Henry is probably referring to her more famous *Sonnets from the Portuguese* (1850).

215. *The Men of the Time; or, Sketches of Living Notables*, an encyclopedia published by Redfield in 1852.

216. Bennet Dowler (1797–1879) was a leading physician in New Orleans. He founded the New Orleans Academy of Sciences and for a time edited the New Orleans *Medical and Surgical Journal*. He was particularly interested in what happened to organisms immediately after death. He authored "A Tableau of the Yellow Fever of 1853" in 1854.

217. Eugène Sue, *Le juif errant* (*The Wandering Jew*) (1845).

218. Joseph W. Fabens, *A Story of Life on the Isthmus* (1852).

219. John A. Dix, *A Winter in Madeira: And A Summer in Spain and Florence* (1850).

220. Capillarity was a subject of intense interest to Hughes. He wrote several lectures on the subject in 1855. His lecture notes survive in the Henry Hughes Papers, MDAH.

221. Richard B. Kimball, *Cuba, and the Cubans* (1850).

222. So far as is known, Hughes never completed writing *The Aspirant*.

223. Charles MacFarlane, *Japan* (1852).

224. William Makepeace Thackeray, *Vanity Fair, a Novel without a Hero* (1847).

225. Charles-Louis de Secondat, baron de Montesquieu, *L'esprit des lois* (*The Spirit of the Laws*) (1748).

226. From Samuel Taylor Coleridge's poem *Darwiniana* (1796).

227. Charlotte Brontë, *Villette* (1852).

228. In the margin Hughes has written: "Sworn-to again: Port Gibson Mississippi, April 17, 1854. Henry Hughes."

JOHN ALBERT FEASTER COLEMAN

1. Coleman's paternal grandfather, David Roe Coleman, was born on May 19, 1765, in Halifax County, North Carolina. He married Edith Beam on September 13, 1787, in Fairfield County, South Carolina. The couple had seven children survive to adulthood, including Coleman's father, Henry Alexander Coleman. David R. Coleman was the owner of thirteen slaves (1850C).

2. Joseph Clowney, thirty-three, was a planter with a wife, Jeanette, a new baby, and a real estate valuation of $2,050 (1850C).

3. Juliana A. Stevenson would later become Coleman's wife. She was born in Fairfield County, South Carolina, on July 14, 1831, married Coleman on October 13, 1853, and died in Feasterville, South Carolina, on December 3, 1913.

4. Margaret Drucilla Coleman was one of Coleman's younger sisters. She was born in Fairfield County, South Carolina, on July 5, 1830, married James LeRoy Hunter on July 18, 1855, and died on January 7, 1900, in Powder Springs, Georgia.

5. Susan Isabella Coleman was another of Coleman's younger sisters. She was born in Fairfield County, South Carolina, on October 3, 1832, married Thomas Manning on August 17, 1852, and died in Marietta, Georgia, on January 29, 1892.

6. Probably David Roe Feaster, Coleman's cousin on his mother's side. Feaster was born on December 25, 1831, and married Victoria Rawls on January 7, 1877, and, after she died, Hattie Porter in December 1878.

7. William Mobley Yongue was married to Coleman's older sister Savilla. In 1850 he was twenty-five. The couple had a young daughter, Sarah (1850C).

8. Coleman's father, Henry Alexander Coleman, was born on September 5, 1797, in Fairfield County, South Carolina. He married Coleman's mother, Chaney Feaster, on December 5, 1822. The couple had eight children who survived to adulthood, of whom Coleman was third oldest. H. A. Coleman was the owner of eighteen slaves (1850C).

9. Andrew Edmond Coleman (b. 1824) was Coleman's cousin on his father's side.

10. An infare is a reception for a newly married couple.

11. John Quirns Arnett (1804–56) was married to Eliza T. Coleman, a cousin of Coleman on his father's side. He was a merchant and planter with four children and a real estate valuation of $8,540 (1850C).

12. T. D. Feaster, twenty-four, was a planter with a wife, Martha (1850C).

13. Robert G. Cameron, fifty-two, was a planter with a wife, Savilla, six children, and a real estate valuation of $21,050 (1850C).

14. Coleman is adapting a nineteenth-century proverb, "There are as good fish in the sea as ever came out of it." The adage gradually evolved into the one we use: "There are plenty of other fish in the sea."

15. Translation: "Farewell for a long time."

16. Probably *Fortescue; or, The Soldier's Reward: A Characteristic Novel* (1789).

17. Jacob Feaster, seventy-five, was a planter with a real estate valuation of eight hundred dollars (1850C).

18. Edith Lyles, twenty-five, was the wife of planter H. J. Lyles and the mother of three children (1850C).

19. William S. Lyles, thirty-seven, was a planter with a wife, Sarah, four children, and a real estate valuation of eleven thousand dollars (1850C).

20. Richard Cathcart, fifty-five, was a planter with a real estate valuation of thirty thousand dollars (1850C).

21. The *Yankee Blade* was a pulp fiction broadsheet newspaper established in Boston in 1841. Like other magazines of the time, most of its column inches were devoted to reprinting short fiction, poetry, and serialized novels.

22. Kisana E. Feaster, thirty-eight, was the wife of John M. Feaster, planter and merchant, and mother of Elizabeth, eighteen, and Drusilla, sixteen (1850C).

23. In 1850 Osmund Thompson, thirty, was a clerk of court (1850C).

24. William Bell, thirty-five, was a planter with a wife, Margaret, three children, and a real estate valuation of sixteen hundred dollars (1850C).

25. Solomon Coleman, sixty-three, was a planter with a wife, Elizabeth, and a real estate valuation of $2,904. He was the owner of fourteen slaves (1850C).

26. Savilla E. Coleman was Coleman's older sister. She was born in Fairfield County, South Carolina, on August 20, 1825, married William Mobley Yongue on March 28, 1844, and died on January 19, 1877.

27. Honorah E. Elkins, nineteen, was the daughter of Elliott Elkins, planter and merchant (1850C).

28. Lucretia Mobley, seventeen, was the daughter of John Mobley, planter (1850C).

29. Martha Brice, sixteen, was the daughter of Robert Brice, planter (1850C).

30. Emma Dorothy Eliza Nevitte Southworth's novel *The Deserted Wife* was serialized in the *Saturday Evening Post* in 1849.

31. Henry Ruffner, *Seclusaval; or, The Sequel to the Tale of Judith Bensaddi* was serialized in the *Yankee Blade* in 1849.

32. The entry is written in a different hand than Coleman's; presumably it is that of his sister Isa. This and other similar incidents suggest that Coleman left his book lying around the house, and, in the communal tradition of Feasterville, people felt comfortable leafing through it and even writing in it. It also suggests that Coleman was proud enough of his diary (and open enough about its contents) to make it available as a public curiosity.

33. Emma Dorothy Eliza Nevitte Southworth, *Retribution, a Tale of Passion; or, The Vale of Shadows* (1849).

34. The 1850 federal census lists a Henry Gladden, eighteen, as the son of Rebecca Gladden.

35. Whitemarsh Benjamin Seabrook (1792–1855) was governor of South Carolina from 1848 to 1850. He was also a lawyer, planter, and author of *History of the Cotton Plant*.

36. The 1850 federal census lists a Major Thomas Lyles, sixty-two, as a planter with a wife, Mary, and a real estate valuation of $14,500.

37. A worm fence, also known as a snake fence or Virginia fence, was a zigzagging series of stacked horizontal rails that joined at the corners like the logs of a log cabin. It was the most prevalent form of fencing in America because it didn't require posts, which were difficult to drive into New England rock or Southern hardpan. To lay the worm of the fence meant to lay out its entire path.

38. Sir Walter Scott's Waverly Novels include *Rob Roy* (1817) and *Anne of Geierstein; or, The Maiden of the Mist* (1829).

39. Percy Bysshe Shelley, *Prometheus Unbound* (1820), canto 2, stanza 5, lines 72–77.

40. Jesse Gladden, twenty-three, was a laborer (1850C).

41. H. J. Lyles, thirty-three, was a planter with a wife, Edith, and three children (1850C).

42. Ellen Wallace, *The Clandestine Marriage* (1840).

43. Probably George Payne Rainsford, *One in a Thousand; or, The Days of Henri Quatre* (1845).

44. The 1850 federal census lists a Robert H. Means, twenty-one, as a physician.

45. William T. Porter, ed., *The Big Bear of Arkansas, and Other Sketches Illustrative of Characters and Incidents in the South and South-West* (1845). Porter was the editor of a sporting magazine, *Spirit of the Times*, that printed humorous stories of frontier characters. The genre is today known as southwestern humor, frontier humor, or the Big Bear school. Thomas Bangs Thorpe wrote the story "The Big Bear of Arkansas," from which the genre gets its name and Porter got his title.

46. See note 32.

47. John Hugh Means (1812–62) was governor of South Carolina from 1850 to 1852.

48. Clearly, Coleman's diary was a source of interest to his (intoxicated) friends. See note 32.

49. When the British army occupied the area around Charlotte, North Carolina,

in 1780 they called Mecklenburg County a "hornet's nest" of rebellious activity. The moniker has been used for area newspapers ever since.

50. It appears that Coleman's friends have been drinking and comparing their handwriting. See note 32.

51. Again, a friend has made an entry in Coleman's diary. See note 32.

52. Emma Dorothy Eliza Nevitte Southworth, *Shannondale* (1851).

53. Coleman has underlined *and eat dinner with me* and written "mistake" underneath.

54. See note 32.

55. George Wilkins Kendall, *Narrative of the Texan Santa Fe Expedition* (1844).

HENRY CRAFT

1. Lucy Minor Hull, Craft's dead fiancée, is a bit of a mystery. After attending school in Fredericksburg, Virginia, she moved with her family to Marshall County, Mississippi. She may have lived at The Lodge or Greenwood Plantation, both Hull family homes. Regardless, she then appears to have moved to neighboring Tuckahoe plantation to live with her older sister and her brother-in-law, William Crump. William Crump, forty-three, was a planter with five children and a real estate valuation of nine thousand dollars (1850C).

2. Probably William Mumford Baker (b. 1825), mentioned elsewhere in the diary. Baker, like Craft, hailed from Holly Springs, Mississippi. He completed his degree at Princeton and was ordained as a Presbyterian minister in 1853. He was the son of the Reverend Daniel Baker (1791–1857) and Elizabeth McRoberts. His older brother Daniel also attended Princeton and was also ordained.

3. Lucy Hull's sister. Her first name is not mentioned in the diary and could not be established definitively. She may have been Elizabeth Hull Crump, mentioned in church records. See R. Milton Winter, *Shadow of a Mighty Rock: A Social and Cultural History of Presbyterianism in Marshall County, Mississippi* (Franklin, Tenn.: Providence House, 1997).

4. Joseph Henry (1797–1878) was professor of natural philosophy at Princeton from 1832 to 1846. While there he built a large electromagnet capable of lifting thirty-five hundred pounds. In 1846 he became the first secretary and director of the new Smithsonian Institution in Washington, D.C. He later served as the second president of the National Academy of Sciences.

5. Martha Craft Fort was Henry's sister. The 1850 federal census lists Martha Fort, twenty-four, as the wife of lawyer James Fort and mother of two young children, Mary and Robert. Henry Craft, lawyer, is listed as living at the same dwelling.

6. Lucia Galeazzi (d. 1790) was the daughter of a senior professor of physics and anatomy at Bologna. Luigi Galvani, see below, attended Galeazzi's lectures on electricity and fell in love with his daughter. Luigi and Lucia were married in 1762.

7. Luigi Galvani (1737–98) was professor of anatomy at the University of Bologna and a pioneer in what would later be called neurology. The story of his first frog experiment is variously told. In some versions his wife is his assistant in a deliberate experiment. In others she is a sick spouse whose dutiful husband was preparing her a frog

broth when he made a startling discovery. Regardless, the Galvanis performed countless experiments together trying to figure out the mechanisms behind the nervous system. Luigi erroneously concluded that the frog's twitch was a result of "animal electricity," a fluidic life force that he claimed was secreted by the brain, flowed through the nerves, and was still present in the dead frog's tissue. Allesandro Volta (1745–1827) rightly concluded that the electricity was in the metals Galvani was using, not the frog itself, and he went on to design the first battery. Despite his errors Galvani's name lives on in "galvanism" (the therapeutic use of electricity, especially popular in the late eighteenth and early nineteenth centuries) and "galvanize" (meaning to stimulate or shock into action).

8. Probably Daniel Sumner Baker (b. 1823). Baker, like Craft, hailed from Holly Springs. He completed his degree at Princeton and was ordained to preach in the Presbyterian Church. He was the son of the Reverend Daniel Baker (1791–1857) and Elizabeth McRoberts. His younger brother William Mumford Baker also attended Princeton and was also ordained.

9. Probably Matthew Boyd Hope (1812–59), Princeton's professor of rhetoric. Hope had graduated from Princeton Seminary in 1834 and University of Pennsylvania Medical School in 1836. He became professor of rhetoric at Princeton in 1846 and chair of political economy in 1854.

10. Craft is borrowing a line from Scottish poet Thomas Campbell (1777–1844): "'Tis distance lends enchantment to the view / And robes the mountain in its azure hue" (*Pleasures of Hope* [1799], part 1, line 7).

11. Gregory VII (c. 1020–85) became pope in 1073. He presided over the church during the Investiture Controversy.

12. Whig Hall housed the American Whig Society, one of the campus's two literary debating societies.

13. John Wentworth, *System of Pleading* (1797).

14. Charles Hodge (1797–1878) taught theology at Princeton for fifty-six years. He is remembered principally for his spirited opposition to Darwinism.

15. Probably George Washington Bethune (1805–62). Bethune had studied theology at Princeton in the 1820s. Though ordained in the Presbyterian Church, he had accepted a pastorate at the Reformed Dutch Church of Philadelphia in 1834. He was still living in that city in 1848.

16. Possibly Elizabeth Mason, daughter of William F. Mason, a Holly Springs merchant. In 1850 she was eighteen (1850C).

17. Brodie Crump, seventeen, was a student and son of William Crump, planter (1850C).

18. Possibly Edward A. Keeling, a member of Craft's church.

19. Greenwood was a plantation owned by the Hull family.

20. Craft is referring to the Bible's Rachel. Her grief is mentioned, for instance, in Matthew 2:18: "In Rama was there a voice heard, lamentation, and weeping, and great mourning, Rachel weeping for her children, and would not be comforted, because they are not" (KJV).

21. Possibly J. D. M. Litchfield, a Holly Springs physician. Litchfield was one of Craft's closest friends.

22. Martin Farquhar Tupper, *Proverbial Philosophy* (1838). Largely forgotten today,

Tupper's moral self-improvement manual was enormously successful, remaining in print for eighty years and selling millions of copies on both sides of the Atlantic.

23. Racillia Anderson appears elsewhere in the diary. Though Andersons were numerous in Marshall County, her name does not appear in the census.

24. The towns around Princeton were named in the eighteenth century after royalty: Kingston, Queenston, Princeton, and finally Princessville. See John Frelinghuysen Hageman, *History of Princeton and Its Institutions* (1879).

25. Emily Brontë, *Wuthering Heights* (1847).

26. Byron, *The Corsair* (1814), canto 3, stanza 24.

27. While the origin of the nickname is unknown, circumstantial evidence strongly suggests that "Bunch" is a member of Craft's immediate family.

28. The Lodge was the first settlement of the Hull family when they moved to Marshall County, Mississippi.

29. Hugh Craft, Henry's father, was born in Maryland in 1799. He later removed to Georgia, where he became a merchant, first in Milledgeville, then in Macon. In 1819 he married Henry's mother, Mary E. Pitts, who died in 1826, three years after Henry was born. Hugh soon married again, to Martha Cheney, a friend of Mary, but she too died. He married a third time in 1830, to Elizabeth R. Collier, who bore him three sons and five daughters. Ruined by the Panic of 1837, he accepted a position as surveyor for the American Land Company. In 1839 he moved his family to Holly Springs, Mississippi, where he set the metes and bounds for lands opened up by the Chickasaw Cession. The 1850 federal census lists Hugh Craft, fifty-one, as a land agent, with a wife, Elizabeth, and five children living at home: Caroline S., Addison, Heber, Stella, and Helen. His real estate valuation at that time was $10,400, and he owned nine slaves. In 1851 Hugh built Fort Daniel Place, still standing and now known as the Hugh Craft House. Paralyzed by stroke in 1860, Hugh Craft died in 1867. Henry Craft is here identifying Elizabeth R. Collier as his mother, though she was technically his stepmother. Collier was born on January 20, 1806, married Hugh Craft in 1830, and died in 1874.

30. Maria J. McIntosh, *Two Lines; or, To Seem and to Be* (1846). McIntosh was born in Sunbury, Georgia, in 1803 and remained pro-Southern during the sectional crisis. She wrote, among other novels, *The Lofty and the Lowly; or, Good in All and None All-Good* (1853), a reaction to Harriet Beecher Stowe's *Uncle Tom's Cabin* (1852). Her brother was Commodore James McKay McIntosh (1792–1860), a hero of the Mexican War.

31. Possibly William F. Mason, one of Holly Spring's leading citizens. In 1850 William F. Mason, fifty, was a merchant with a wife, Matilda, six children living at home, and a real estate valuation of $75,500 (1850C).

32. From 1846 to 1870 George Barrell Cheever (1807–90) was pastor of the Church of the Puritans in New York City.

33. William Bayle Bernard, *The Irish Attorney; or, Galway Practice in 1770: An Original Farce, in Two Acts* (1840).

34. Alfred, Lord Tennyson's poem "Locksley Hall" appeared in *Poems*, 2 vols. (1842).

35. Caroline S. Craft, Henry's sister. In 1850 she was seventeen (1850C).

36. William Henry Harrison (1773–1841) was the ninth president of the United States and the first to die in office. Inaugurated on an extremely cold day, he delivered the longest inaugural address in presidential history, caught a cold that escalated to pneumonia, and died after serving just one month, the shortest term in presidential history.

After being temporarily interred in the Congressional Cemetery, Harrison's body was transferred to its final burial site in North Bend, Ohio.

37. Craft's description of starlight reaching up from the depths sounds much like Poe's "City in the Sea" (1831): "No rays from the holy heaven come down / On the long night-time of that town; / But light from out the lurid sea / Streams up the turrets silently / Gleams up the pinnacles far and free" (*Complete Stories and Poems of Edgar Allan Poe* [New York: Doubleday, 1984], 744, lines 12–16).

38. Maria Shoemaker married William Donoho. The 1850 federal census lists the couple as still living with Maria's parents—merchant Frances Shoemaker, sixty, and his wife, Synthia.

39. Philip James Bailey, *Festus: A Poem* (1839).

40. In June 1848 the Whigs had met in Philadelphia and resoundingly chosen Mexican War hero Zachary Taylor as their candidate for president. After their decision Whigs in various towns around the country held "ratification" meetings to whoop up sentiment for Taylor.

41. Craft is borrowing from English poet Edward Young (1683–1765): "Tired Nature's sweet restorer, balmy sleep!" (*The Complaint; or, Night Thoughts* [1742–45], Night I, line 1).

42. Possibly Jeremiah W. Clapp. In 1850 Jeremiah W. Clapp was a lawyer with a wife, Evelina, four children, six slaves, and a real estate valuation of $9,740 (1850C).

43. Craft has written at the bottom of the page: "* I know Jane better now, and I cannot read this page without recording at its foot a full recantation of a sentiment so disparaging to her. She is *not* heartless & selfish. October 5, 1857."

44. Edward Bulwer-Lytton, *Harold, the Last of the Saxon Kings* (1848).

45. Matthew L. Davis, ed., *Memoirs of Aaron Burr, with Miscellaneous Selections from His Correspondence*, 2 vols. (1836–37).

46. The Independent Order of the Odd Fellows was a philanthropic society formed in Baltimore in 1819.

47. Possibly Isaac Hull. In 1850 Isaac Hull, twenty-seven, was a physician living in the house of William Hull, twenty-five, a planter. William Hull had a daughter, one-year-old Lucy M. Hull, possibly named in honor of Lucy Minor Hull, Craft's dead fiancée (1850C).

48. Henry Melville, *Sermons Preached on Public Occasions* (1847).

49. Possibly Charles Niles, a member of Craft's church.

50. Probably James Fort, Henry's childhood friend and the husband of his sister Martha, known as Matt. Like Henry, James became a lawyer. He owned four slaves (1850C).

51. John H. Hackleton, thirty-five, was a lawyer residing in a hotel owned by Benjamin Williamson (1850C).

52. John P. Pryor, twenty-five, was a lawyer residing in a hotel owned by Benjamin Williamson (1850C).

53. Possibly William Matthew Strickland (c. 1826–1908). In 1850 William M. Strickland, twenty-four, was a lawyer. He rose to the rank of major in the Confederate army. When he married Martha Mildred Thomson he inherited what then became known as William Strickland Place, the first two-story home built in Holly Springs.

54. Helen Craft, Henry's younger sister. In 1850 she was three (1850C).

55. P. Brooks Lucas, eighteen, was the daughter of lawyer Peter W. Lucas and his wife, Clementine. Lucas was the owner of twenty-seven slaves (1850C).

56. Stella Craft, Henry's younger sister. In 1850 she was eleven (1850C).

57. Byron, *Don Juan* (1821), canto 1, stanza 194, line 1.

58. Probably Evelina Clapp, twenty-six. She was the wife of Jeremiah W. Clapp (1850C). The Clapps were members of Craft's church.

59. Probably Clementina Clapp, age six, the daughter of Evelina and Jeremiah Clapp (1850C).

60. John Dryden, *All For Love; or, The World Well Lost* (1677), act 4, scene 1.

61. Fielding Lucas, twenty-nine, was a trader, with a wife, Sarah P. Lucas, twenty-eight. In 1850 he owned four slaves and possessed real estate valued at three thousand dollars (1850C).

62. Henrietta Lucas, fourteen, was the daughter of lawyer Peter W. Lucas and his wife, Clementine (1850C). Henrietta was the sister of Brooks Lucas, mentioned elsewhere in the diary.

63. Possibly Charles Thomas, the owner of the plantation home known as The Lodge.

64. In 1850 John Hull, fifty-two, was a planter with a wife, Ann, and three children (1850C).

65. William Hull, twenty-five, was a planter with a wife, Mary, and two children, including one-year-old Lucy M. Hull (1850C). The family lived on Greenwood Plantation, where Craft's fiancée was buried.

66. Probably Thomas Babington Macaulay, *History of England from the Accession of James the Second*, 5 vols. (1849–61).

67. George M. Troup (1780–1856) was governor of Georgia from 1823 to 1827.

EPILOGUE

1. Hughes Diary, April 10, 1853; Craft Diary, June 26, 1848; Hughes Diary, November 9, 1851; Dixon Diary, March 21, 1860.

2. Craft Diary, August 5, 1863, November 2, 1863.

3. Dixon Diary, December 21, 1863.

4. Hughes Diary, January 9, 1848; Ambrose, *Henry Hughes*, 182.

5. Andrew McConnell married Coleman's youngest sister, Sarah, on April 16, 1857. Sarah (and her baby) died in childbirth in 1858. Andrew J. McConnell Diary, Coleman, Feaster, and Faucette Family Papers, USC, February 14, 1863.

6. McConnell Diary, August 3, 1864.

7. Ibid., August 2, 1864.

8. Coleman Diary, November 16, 1849; McConnell Diary, August 22, 1864.

Montgomery White Sulphur Springs, 48, 204

Moore, Jane, 363

More, Miss, 373

Morehead, B. W., 237

Morehead, Julia, 305

Morehead, Mary Ann (Hughes's sister), 11, 218, 220, 297, 298

Morgan, Miss, 38

Morgan, Mr., 388

Morgan, Mrs., 317

Morgan, J., 342, 372

Morgan, James M., 324, 336, 341, 349, 352, 369, 378, 384, 415; death of, 421–22; husband of Serletia, 377

Morgan, Jim, 311, 405

Morgan, R., Esq., 320

Morgan, Serletia, 377

Mormonism, 308

Morse, Samuel B. F., 350

Morsheimer, Mr., 55, 73, 99

Mosby, Mr., 64

Moses, Uncle, 127

Mostic, Miss, 313

mules, 341

Murdoch, James Edward, 253

Murphy, John B., 294

Natchez, Miss., 275

Natchez Courier, 267

Natchez No. 2 (steamer), 275

Neely, Mr., 472–73

Nevitt, Mr., 345

Nevitt, Priscilla, 316

New Hope Church, 345, 348, 352, 357, 362, 370, 419

New Orleans, La., 212, 307, 481, 491

New Orleans Academy of Arts and Sciences, 307

New Orleans Picayune, 79

Newlin, Rev., 311, 331, 342, 343, 346, 380, 384, 388

Newman, Mr., 392

Niagara Falls, 264

Nichol, Adelaide Stokes (Dellie), 30, 45, 55; courted by Dixon, 56; cousin of, challenges Dixon to duel, 176; description of, 83, 96; riding of, with Dixon, 31; riding or walking of, 47, 48, 49; and sheet music, 115; squeezing of ankle of, by Dixon, 95; visited by Dixon, 32; walks of, with Dixon, 41, 46; and waltzing, 97, 98, 128

Nicholasson, Rev., 332

Nicholson, Mr., 212

Niles, Mr., 481

Nolen, Aunt Betty, 333

Nolen, Mrs. E., 363

Nolen, Isaac (Coleman's uncle), 419

Nolen, Isabella , 333

Nolen, R. W., 323, 355; living in Chambers County, Ala., 395

Norris, Rev. Jefferson, 421

Oakland College (Miss.), 12, 212, 257

Odd Fellows, 362, 467, 502

O'Hare, Jane, 347

O'Neale, Miss A. P., 334, 336

O'Neale, Hon. J. B., 421

oratory, 292

Otis, James, 117

Owens, Governor, 420

Paine, Thomas, 350

Paint Rock, Ala., 500

Palmetto State Banner, 403

Parker, Linus, 238

Parker, Martha, 287, 296, 304, 306, 307

Parks, Sol, 345

Parr, Major, 389

Parrott, Julia, 327

Pearson, W. B., 329, 366

Peck, Miss, 345

Percy, Harry, 35, 120, 191

Percy, Henry, 127

Percy, Joe, 158, 174

Percy, John Walker, 35, 51, 52, 61

Percy, Leroy Pope, 51, 90, 136

Percy, Nannie Armstrong, 41, 50, 94, 101

Percy, Walker, 9
Percy, William Alexander, 36, 71, 131, 156, 167
Philadelphia, Pa., 435, 436, 446–47
Phillips, Emm, 73
Phillips, Jack (Dixon's uncle), 30, 46–47, 53–54, 55, 62, 102, 105, 107–8, 113, 123–24
Phillips, James, 67
Phillips, Sarah, 67
Philson, Mr., 128
phrenology, 315
Pickens, Mr., 407
Pickens, Marcus, 388
Pickett, Mrs., 375
Pickett, Mrs. E., 379
Pickett, Rev. M. B., 376
Pickett, Mary, 376, 377
Pickett, Sarah, 377
Pierce, Franklin, 293
Pine Mountain (Miss.), 466
Pittsburgh, Pa., 447, 448
Polk, Emily, 496
Polk, James K., 335
polygamy, 181
Polymathic Society, 301
Pope, Mr., 361
Port Gibson, Miss., 212, 217, 237, 241, 279
Port Gibson Herald, 212, 245, 266
Porter, Mr., 435
Powhatan (ship), 503
Prentiss, Sgt. Smith, 263
Presbyterian Church (Greenville, Miss.), 50
Presbyterianism, 332–33
Preston, Mr., 103
Preston, Amelia, 103, 207
Princeton: debating societies at, 435, 442, 444; lectures at, 429, 430, 434, 435; sermons delivered at, 428–29, 433, 435, 438, 443; social life at, 440, 443, 479
Printer's Mansion: Coleman's move in to, 366; as log cabin, 369
Pryor, John P., 483

Queenstown, N.J., 441
Quitman, John Anthony, 281

Randolph, John, 283
Randolph County, Ga., 331
Rawls, Dr., 343
Rawls, Mrs. D., 376
Rawls, Mary Drucilla, 326
Red Hill Church (S.C.), 311, 313, 319, 327, 330, 332, 334, 341, 342, 345, 349, 365, 369, 380, 388, 405, 410, 413, 417, 418
Revis, Mr., 382, 391
Revis, Benjamin T., 353, 360, 361, 362, 364, 365, 370
Richmond, Va., 503
Ripley, Miss., 499, 500
Roach, Major, 298
Roberts, Lewis, 323
Robertson, Mrs., 332, 333, 393
Robertson, Lizzie, 388
Robertson, Lucretia, 388
Robertson, W., 386
Rocky Creek Church, 396
Rollins, Rev., 311
Rome, Ga., 500–501
Roth, Emily, 489
Routh, John, 299
Rucks, A., 133
Rucks, Mrs. H., 42
Rucks, James, 32, 45, 86, 128, 142; character of, 46, 75; Dixon's affection for, 139; Dixon's gift to, 160–61; Dixon's visits to house of, 29, 112, 114–15, 155, 177; health of, 131–32
Rucks, Marian, 30, 45, 48, 55, 97, 102; as "Deer Creek belle," 142; description of, 53, 82; Dixon feasts eyes on, 130; Dixon flirts with, 41–42, 46–47, 49, 50, 53, 57, 60–62, 112, 115–16; leaves for Kentucky, 144; quarrels with Dixon, 32; talks to Dixon about poetry, 132
Rucks, Taylor (Dixon's close friend), 38, 42, 107, 127, 128, 148, 158, 161, 176, 188, 189

The Publications of the Southern Texts Society

Printed in the United States
125697LV00002BA/13/A

9 780820 328843